THE IMAGE OF ST FRANCIS

An important new study of the way in which St Francis' image was recorded in literature, documents, architecture and art. St Francis was a man whose personality was deliberately stamped on his Order and Rosalind Brooke explores how the stories told by Francis' companions were at once brilliantly vivid portrayals of the man as well as guides to how the Franciscan way of life ought to be led. She also examines how after St Francis' death a great monument was erected to him in the Basilica at Assisi and how this came to reflect in stone and stained glass and fresco the manner in which some popes and leading friars believed his memory should be fostered. Highly illustrated throughout, including colour and black and white plates, this book will be essential reading for medievalists and art historians as well as anyone interested in St Francis and the Franciscan movement.

ROSALIND B. BROOKE is a Senior Member of Clare Hall, Cambridge. Throughout her academic career she has lectured and taught at various universities including University College London and Cambridge University. Her publications include *The Coming of the Friars* (1975) and *Popular Religion in the Middle Ages* (with C. N. L. Brooke, 1984).

Frontispiece: Cimabue, St Francis, Basilica of St Francis, Lower Church, detail of fresco of Madonna and child with St Francis – see p. 304 (© www.Assisi.de. Photo Stefan Diller).

THE IMAGE OF
ST FRANCIS

RESPONSES TO SAINTHOOD IN THE
THIRTEENTH CENTURY

ROSALIND B. BROOKE

CAMBRIDGE
UNIVERSITY PRESS

CAMBRIDGE UNIVERSITY PRESS
Cambridge, New York, Melbourne, Madrid, Cape Town, Singapore, São Paulo

Cambridge University Press
The Edinburgh Building, Cambridge CB2 2RU, UK

Published in the United States of America by Cambridge University Press, New York

www.cambridge.org
Information on this title: www.cambridge.org/9780521782913

First published 2006

Printed in the United Kingdom at the University Press, Cambridge

A catalogue record for this publication is available from the British Library

ISBN-13 978-0-521-78291-3 hardback
ISBN-10 0-521-78291-0 hardback

CONTENTS

PLATES

FIGURES

PREFACE

This book has been long in the making, and I owe many debts. Professor Paul Binski has given constant help and encouragement, and read all the chapters on art and architecture, which have greatly benefited from his advice and criticism. The Reverend Dr Michael Robson, OFM Conv., also has given constant help and encouragement and been most generous in loan of books, in bibliographical advice and in keeping me in touch with his confrères in Assisi. I have had much valued help from Professor Eamon Duffy, Professor Nigel Morgan, Professor André Vauchez, Professor David d'Avray – and many others.

I owe a special debt to the Cambridge University Press, and especially to William Davies, Simon Whitmore and Michael Watson, my editors, to Alison Powell, Sinead Moloney and Sarah Parker, to my copy-editor Frances Brown, to the designer, Jackie Taylor – and to the anonymous readers of the first draft of this book.

Over the years I have had much help in processing from Mrs Edna Pilmer and my husband, Christopher Brooke – who has himself been aided by the resources of Gonville and Caius College.

For permission to quote extensively from my translation of *The Writings of Leo, Rufino and Angelo, Companions of St Francis* (Oxford Medieval Texts, corr. repr. 1990) I am grateful to Anne Gelling, the Rights Manager and the Delegates of Oxford University Press.

In pursuit of illustrations Dr Michael Robson introduced me to P. Pasquale Magro and P. Gerhard Ruf of the Sacro Convento, Assisi, and Father Ruf introduced me to Herr Stefan Diller of Würzburg. To Stefan Diller I am indebted, as photographer and agent, for the greater part of my illustrations, which include many by Father Ruf. Both of them have generously taken photographs specially for me. Full details of photographers and copyrights are given in the captions, and it is a pleasure to record here the kind and ready help I have had from Stefan Diller, Gerhard Ruf and Pasquale Magro.

Professor Lee Striker provided Plate 23 and Figures 3–9. I have treasured memories of our discussions in the hospitable environment of his home in Philadelphia. Dr Joanna Cannon lent me a print of Plate 75 – and both also generously gave me permission to publish them. Professor Paul Binski lent me the prints for Plates 40–46, and

Dr Grazia Visintainer and the Istituto Germanico di Storia dell'Arte, Florence, gave me generous permission to use them. For other plates I am grateful to the Master and Fellows of Corpus Christi College, Cambridge, and to the Librarian, Dr Christopher de Hammel, and the Sub-Librarian, Mrs Gill Cannell; to the Syndics of the Cambridge University Library, and especially to Mr David Hall and Dr Patrick Zutshi; to the Getty Research Institute, Los Angeles, and Ms Barbara Furbush; to Mme Anne Lesage and her colleagues and the Réunion des Musées Nationaux, Paris; to Mrs G. M. Reynolds, the University of Michigan and the Michigan-Princeton-Alexandria Expedition to Mount Sinai; and to Signore Abbrescia Santinelli and Face2Face Studio, Rome. To all, my very warm thanks.

I acknowledge innumerable debts to my research assistant, secretary, picture researcher, indexer and husband of fifty-four summers and winters, Christopher – whose unstinting help and exemplary impatience have shaped this book. I dedicate it to him.

CAMBRIDGE
5 November 2005

ABBREVIATIONS

Acta Sanctorum: *Acta Sanctorum Bollandiana*, Brussels, etc., 1643–

AF: *Analecta Franciscana*, Quaracchi, 1885–

AFH: *Archivum Franciscanum Historicum*, Quaracchi and Grottaferrata, 1908–

AFP: *Archivum Fratrum Praedicatorum*, 1931–

ALKG: *Archiv für Litteratur- und Kirchengeschichte*, ed. H. Denifle and F. Ehrle, 7 vols., Berlin and Freiburg-im-Breisgau, 1885–1900

AP: *L'Anonyme de Pérouse*, ed. P.-B. Beguin, Paris, 1979

Assisi 1974: *La "Questione Francescana" dal Sabatier ad oggi: Atti del I Convegno Internazionale*, Assisi, 18–20 ottobre 1973, Società Internazionale di Studi Francescani, Assisi, 1974

Assisi 1978: *Assisi al Tempo di San Francesco: Atti del V Convegno Internazionale*, Assisi, 13–16 ottobre 1977, Società Internazionale di Studi Francescani, Assisi, 1978

Assisi 1980: *Il Tesoro della Basilica di San Francesco ad Assisi*, ed. R. B. Fanelli *et al.*, Assisi, 1980

Assisi 1999: *The Treasury of St Francis of Assisi*, ed. G. Morello and L. B. Kanter, Milan, 1999

Bonav.: Bonaventure, *Legenda Maior S. Francisci*, in AF x, 555–652

Bonav., Miracula: in AF, x, 627–52

Bonaventure, *Opera Omnia*, 10 vols., Quaracchi, 1882–1902; and see Bougerol 1994, Delorme 1934

Cat. Générale IV: *Catalogue Générale des Manuscrits des Bibliothèques Publiques de Départements*, IV, Paris, 1872

1, 2, 3 Cel.: Thomas of Celano, *Vita Prima, Vita Secunda* and *Tractatus de Miraculis S. Francisci Assisiensis*, referred to by paragraphs in the Quaracchi editions, AF x (1926–41), 1–331

Chron. 24 Gen.: 'Chronicle of the Twenty-Four Generals' in AF iii (1897)

Clare 1985: Claire d'Assise, *Écrits*, ed. M.-F. Becker, J.-F. Godet and T. Matura, Sources Chrétiennes 325, Paris, 1985

DBI: *Dizionario Biografico degli Italiani*, Rome, 1960–

Eccleston: *Fratris Thomae vulgo dicti de Eccleston Tractatus de adventu fratrum minorum in Angliam*, ed. A. G. Little, 2nd edn, Manchester, 1951

Firmamenta: Firmamenta trium ordinum beatissimi Patris nostri Francisci, Paris, 1511–12: Hugh of Digne's *Expositio Regulae* and *Disputatio* are in this edition in *quarta pars*, 1511

Jordan: *Chronica fratris Jordani*, ed. H. Boehmer, Paris, 1908

Julian, Julian of Speyer: Fr. *Julianus de Spira, Vita S. Francisci*, in AF x, 335–71

Liber Extra, X: 'Decretalium Gregorii pp. IX compilatio', in *Corpus Iuris Canonici*, ed. E. Friedberg, II, Leipzig, 1881

MGH: Monumenta Germaniae Historica

Misc. Fr.: Miscellanea Francescana

MOPH: Monumenta Ordinis Praedicatorum Historica

Narb.: Constitutions of Narbonne, in M. Bihl, 'Statuta Generalia Ordinis, edita in capitulis generalibus celebratis Narbonae an. 1260, Assisii an. 1279, atque Parisiis an. 1292', AFH 34 (1941), 13–94, 284–358

ODCC: The Oxford Dictionary of the Christian Church, 3rd edn, ed. F. L. Cross and E. A. Livingstone, Oxford, 1997

OMT: Oxford Medieval Texts

Ov, Ordinem vestrum: the bull is cited from Eubel 1908, pp. 238–9

PL: Patrologiae Cursus Completus, Series Latina, ed. J. P. Migne, 221 vols., Paris, 1844–64

Potthast: Potthast, A., ed., *Regesta pontificum Romanorum A.D. 1198–1304*, 2 vols., Berlin, 1874–5

Qe, Quo elongati: see H. Grundmann, 'Die Bulle "Quo elongati" Papst Gregors IX', AFH 54 (1961), 3–25

RS: Rolls Series

Salimbene, H and S Salimbene de Adam, *Cronica*, ed. O. Holder-Egger, MGH *Scriptores* XXXII, 1905–13 (H); ed. G. Scalia, 2 vols., Scrittori d'Italia 232–3, Bari, 1966 (S)

Sbaralea: Sbaralea, J. H., ed., *Bullarium Franciscanum*, 4 vols., Rome, 1759–68: referred to by p. and no. – G9 = Gregory IX, I4 = Innocent IV, N3 = Nicholas III, N4 = Nicholas IV, B8 = Boniface VIII; and by no. in Eubel 1908

SL: *Scripta Leonis, Rufini et Angeli sociorum S. Francisci: The Writings of Leo, Rufino and Angelo, Companions of St Francis*, ed. and trans. R. B. Brooke, OMT, Oxford, 1970, corr. repr. 1990

3 Soc.: Legenda Trium Sociorum, ed. T. Desbonnets, AFH 67 (1974), 38–144

Sp S: *Speculum Perfectionis*, ed. P. Sabatier, 2nd edn, British Society of Franciscan Studies, 13, 17, Manchester, 1928–31

Treasury: *see Assisi 1999*

X: *see Liber Extra*

CHAPTER ONE

INTRODUCTION

St Francis 'said: "In pictures of God and the blessed Virgin painted on wood, God and
the blessed Virgin are honoured and God and the blessed Virgin are held in mind, yet
the wood and the painting ascribe nothing to themselves, because they are just wood
and paint; so the servant of God is a kind of painting, that is a creature of God in which
God is honoured for the sake of his benefits. But he ought to ascribe nothing to himself,
just like the wood or the painting, but should render honour and glory to God alone"'
(SL 104).

THE SOFT WAX

In a celebrated scene in Eadmer's *Life of St Anselm*, a fellow abbot described to Anselm
his difficulties with the child monks. 'They are incorrigible ruffians. We never give over
beating them day and night, and they only get worse and worse.' Anselm retorted that
his philosophy of education was radically at fault. 'Are they not human? Are they not
flesh and blood like you? . . . Consider this. You wish to form them in good habits
by blows and chastisement alone. Have you ever seen a goldsmith form his leaves of
gold and silver into a beautiful figure with blows alone? I think not . . . In order to
mould his leaf into a suitable form he now presses it and strikes it gently with his tool,
and now even more gently raises it with careful pressure and gives it shape. So, if you
want your boys to be adorned with good habits, you too, besides the pressure of blows,
must apply the encouragement and help of fatherly sympathy and gentleness.'[1] The
goldsmith created an impression, an image; and elsewhere, we are told that Anselm
'compared the time of youth to a piece of wax of the right consistency for the impress
of a seal . . . If it preserves a mean between . . . extremes of hardness and softness, when
it is stamped with the seal [matrix], it will receive the image clear and whole.'[2] The
goldsmith passed a message to his patrons – and, if his work survived, to posterity; the

[1] Southern 1962/1979, pp. 37–8.
[2] Southern 1962/1979, p. 20. For recent interesting studies on images in history and art see Bolvig and
Lindley 2003, pp. 3–44.

man who makes the impression on the seal creates an image which can be recognised from that day to this as the legal signature of a community or a king – and perhaps too by its beauty it may be an expression of the culture of its day.

This book is about the impression Francis made – intentionally and in spite of himself – on contemporaries and on the early generations after his death, and the ways in which he and they expressed it. But the word impression is too faint for our purpose – it tends to suggest a relatively slight impact. So I talk of his image. Unfortunately 'image' has come to be a cult word, and has had all manner of jargon and mystical meaning attached to it. I have avoided jargon and tried to use it in plain, intelligible senses. When his followers listened to him, reflected on the saint and his message – when buildings rose to commemorate him, when figures in glass and precious metals, and stone, and on wood and plaster were created to record his story – what image of the saint appeared?

The modern, intensive study of hagiography has underlined how superficial it is to set it apart as a historical genre on its own – still more, to downgrade it as a kind of fiction, as has often been consciously or semi-consciously done. Eadmer's *Life of St Anselm* is an outstanding work of biography; but many, indeed most, of the numerous saints' lives written in England in the late eleventh and early twelfth centuries were houses built on sand – collections of stories and wonders rarely credible or revealing of the identity and character of the saint. Eadmer was an exceptionally gifted biographer who lived for years on terms of intimacy with his hero Anselm. At the other end of the spectrum were the hagiographers who had little or no material of a historical nature to provide even a plausible core to their narratives; the author of the *Life of St Rumwold*, who reputedly died when only three days old, had the most extreme shortage of material.[3]

One fundamental and obvious feature of Eadmer's *Life* is that he was writing about a living saint: Anselm was alive when most of it was written, though it was completed after his death. There has been much discussion in recent years about the kind of saintly life which attracted a cult while the individual lived. Sir Richard Southern drew attention, a generation ago, to the tradition of intimate biography of which Eadmer's was an outstanding early example.[4] It was to be followed by the *First Life of St Bernard*, which was already well under way while Bernard lived. The biographies of St Francis were written after his death, but vivid stories about him soon began to be recorded by people who knew him well.[5] The developing interest in contemporary saints combined with the exigencies of the canonisation process to make a clear and determined emphasis on the need for eyewitness accounts the essence of many narratives of the thirteenth century and later.[6]

This was not new: it can be clearly traced in the Gospel and Epistles of St John – 'That which was from the beginning, which we have heard, which we have seen with

---

[3] Southern 1962/1979 and Southern 1963; Love 1996, pp. cxl–clxiv, 91–115.
[4] Southern 1963, pp. 329–36; cf. Brooke 1967, pp. 179–81. For the tradition of intimate biography in the thirteenth century, see Kleinberg 1992; Blumenfeld-Kosinski and Szell 1991.
[5] See pp. 41–2 and ch. 6.
[6] From Innocent III's time on, the popes were insistent on eyewitness evidence: see below, pp. 36–8, 167, 274.

our eyes, which we have looked upon, and our hands have handled, of the Word of life . . . declare we unto you' (1 John 1. 1–3) – words which echoed down the centuries, constantly reappearing in historical narratives and the testimony of witnesses in and out of canonisation processes. While it is the case that the love of truth was a feeble thing in the minds of many who used these phrases, in many more it was not – and it would be quite false to make general statements about the truthfulness of thirteenth-century historical writers based on a few examples of forgers and liars. Eadmer's words – 'it is a shocking thing for anyone knowingly to write what is false in sacred histories. For the soul of the writer is slain every time they are read or listened to, since in the things which he has falsely written he tells abominable lies to all his readers'[7] – would have found echoes in the minds of many of the authors quoted in this book. In every age for which we have sufficient testimony, including the present, the standards of truthfulness have been infinitely various – but some or many have been faithful witnesses to what they have heard and seen.[8]

THE IMAGE

A saint who was also the founder of an Order had traditionally been remembered in three ways: in a pious biography or a series of them; in the rule and way of life of his Order; and in his relics. Yet it was curiously rare for a founder to be equally honoured in all three ways. St Robert of Molesme, the founder of the Cistercians, had much less impact on the Order and the Church than St Bernard; and Bernard himself was rather an inspiration than a role model, for some of his characteristic activities – his frequent travels, his political involvement, his preaching of the Second Crusade – were at variance with the spirit of the *Carta Caritatis*. Bernard was recorded in his biographies and above all in his own writings; much less in his relics.[9] St Norbert, founder of the Premonstratensians, was a missionary as much as a canon regular; and his Order was effectively taken out of his hands after his translation to the see of Magdeburg. St Gilbert of Sempringham had an excellent Life written about him; his Order followed closely the prescriptions anyway of his later years; and his relics made Sempringham a centre for pilgrimages and miracles.[10] But it was a modest Order and a modest centre: Gilbert and the Gilbertines were no match for Francis and the friars. Francis's own contemporary, St Dominic, seems deliberately to have avoided the personality cult: though a remarkable and sometimes impulsive religious leader, he sank his personality in the Order, which became, not a way of life consciously imitating Dominic, but an Order following the

---

[7] Southern 1962/1979, p. 149. But even Eadmer, sadly, had his lapses. Later on, in his *Historia Novorum*, he added copies of the Canterbury forgeries, and it is very unlikely that he believed in their innocence (C. Brooke 1971, pp. 113–14; Southern 1958, pp. 225–6). Kleinberg 1992 discusses the realistic accounts of living saints in late thirteenth- and fourteenth-century lives which emphasise what was especially striking or eccentric about them; most compelling is his account of Peter of Dacia's Life of Christina of Stommeln, in which these effects seem to have been enhanced by invention (see esp. ibid. pp. 50–3, 64–70, 96–8).

[8] The most faithful, needless to say, can be misled or can misremember. The categories in the text must inevitably be over-simple.

[9] See C. Brooke 2006, chs. 9, 13 and Postscript.

[10] For Norbert, see Brooke 1975, pp. 58–9 and refs.; for Gilbert, Foreville and Keir 1987; Golding 1995.

Rule of St Augustine and the Constitutions devised by the various committees called General Chapters.[11]

Francis was remembered in ways both conventional and unconventional. His own writings were copied and circulated, his life was written several times over, his Rule was studied by all his followers and interpreted in their actions and constitutions and in several remarkable commentaries. Although there was minimal relic cult in the conventional sense, the place of his burial was a very grand pilgrimage centre – as it still is.

There are many and varied visible and tangible links with Francis, which can help in providing insights and stimulating the imagination. Assisi is still evocative. He will have been baptised in the cathedral of San Rufino[12] (Plate 11). The font is still there. Outside its west door two Romanesque lions crouch, each with a man's body between his front paws, the head in his mouth (Plate 1). One day, while we were contemplating them, a girl on her way in paused to pat one of the lions and murmured 'buon appetito'. Perhaps Francis as a boy did the same. The actual wooden crucifix painted by an anonymous Umbrian artist in the late twelfth century, which Francis saw and venerated and which spoke to him in the semi-derelict church of San Damiano, situated outside the city walls a little way further down the slopes of Monte Subasio, has survived all vicisitudes (Plate 3). Entrusted to St Clare and her tiny community by St Francis when he installed them in San Damiano, it can be seen today in Santa Chiara. This fragile cross is a remarkable symbol of continuity, immediately linking the world in which Francis grew up with our own day. The Carceri, higher up the mountain slopes, still manages to retain something of the atmosphere of remoteness which drew Francis and his companions to retire there for periods of solitary prayer (Plate 2).

Two specimens of Francis' own handwriting survive, both preserved by his close companion, brother Leo. The first is a small piece of parchment, 10 × 13.5 cm, with Francis' *Laudes* – his *Praises* of God – on one side, and his blessing of brother Leo with the Tau cross inscribed on the other. Brother Leo kept this treasured blessing carefully folded inside his tunic. The folds are still there to see, for before he died Leo annotated (and so authenticated) his blessing, explaining that the *Praises* were written at La Verna after Francis had received the stigmata – that is, in 1224[13] (Plate 12). It seems likely that Leo himself gave it to the Basilica, among whose treasures it is preserved, encased in a reliquary, the most authentic visible relic of the saint before his body was rediscovered in the nineteenth century.[14] Francis's brief letter to Leo, now in the Cappella delle Reliquie in Spoleto Cathedral, was formerly in the possession of the Franciscan house of San Simone in Spoleto, where it is recorded in the early seventeenth century: after the suppression of the house in the early nineteenth century it came into the possession of the archbishop of Spoleto, who deposited it in the cathedral in 1902.[15] The breviary St Francis used for daily worship carries a rubric telling us that brothers Angelo and

---

[11] Brooke 1975, pp. 100–5; C. Brooke 1971, ch. 11.
[12] Sabatier 1893/4, p. 3, pointed out that all the children of Assisi were baptised in the cathedral. This was the custom in Italian cities (C. Brooke 1999, pp. 31–2, 77, 93–4).
[13] Langeli 2000, pp. 30–41; SL Frontispiece; cf. pp. 109, 403.
[14] See p. 356; Langeli 2000, pp. 17–19. It was certainly there in 1338.
[15] Langeli 2000, pp. 19–21.

Plate 1 Assisi, Cathedral of San Rufino, one of the lions outside the west door
(Photo C. N. L. Brooke).

Leo gave it to St Clare's successor, the abbess Benedetta, after the community moved
to Santa Chiara; and there it remained till 1997, when – following the earthquake – the
community and its treasure sought a safer home in the convent of Monteripido di
Perugia.[16] The breviary is largely in Leo's hand and is the most substantial surviving relic
of one of Francis' closest friends. But that is not all. A manuscript at Messina contains
the earliest surviving text of the Testament of St Clare and a copy of the Rule of St Clare
of 1253 – in both of which the scribe seems to have used a certain freedom. In 2000
Bartoli Langeli, in a brilliant detective exercise, showed that its binding incorporated
a draft written by a notary active in Assisi in the 1270s and 1280s – and he argued that

[16] Langeli 2000, p. 83; cf. pp. 8–9. It must have been deposited well after 1253, but before Leo's death
   c.1271.

Plate 2   The Carceri above Assisi: the cell traditionally ascribed to brother Leo
(Photo R. B. Brooke).

the manuscript itself was written by Leo.[17] It forms a further, intriguing and impressive
link between Leo and St Clare.

DAWN?

When I first began to study St Francis I was under the impression that he appeared,
not out of a clear sky, since storm clouds were lowering, but as the dawn of a new day,
bringing a change in the weather, a burst of sunshine. The likening of Francis to the
sun, and to associated images of light, found public expression less than two years
after his death, which occurred during the night of 3–4 October 1226. His friend and

[17] Langeli 2000, pp. 104–29.

Plate 3 The crucifix from San Damiano, now in Santa Chiara, Assisi (© www.Assisi.de. Photo Gerhard Ruf).

patron Pope Gregory IX took as the text for his sermon on the solemn occasion of his official canonisation ceremony, held at Assisi on 16 July 1228:

like the morning star among the clouds,
like the moon at the full,
like the sun shining on the Temple of the Most High.[18]

St Bonaventure elaborated the theme in the preface to his official *Life* of the saint, written between 1260 and 1263. 'By the glorious splendour of his life and teaching, Francis shone like the day-star amid the clouds, and by the brilliance which radiated from him he guided those who live in darkness . . . to the light. Like the rainbow that lights up the clouds with sudden glory, he bore in his own body the pledge of God's covenant [that is, the marks of Christ's wounds on the Cross, the stigmata], bringing the good news of peace and salvation to men, like a true Angel of peace.'[19]

Some of these images were taken up by Dante in a famous passage in the *Paradiso*, in which St Thomas Aquinas honours Francis:

From a mountain slope [facing Perugia]
was born into the world a sun,
even as our sun rises from the Ganges.
Therefore let no-one, speaking of that place,
say 'Ascesi' [Assisi] – the word falls short –
but 'Oriente', if he would correctly speak.

'Ascesi' was the Tuscan form of Assisi in Dante's day; and 'ascesi' was also Tuscan for 'I have risen, ascended.' The Orient – the east of the world – signifies the sunrise. The word is also reminiscent of Luke 1. 78, where Zacharias speaks of 'the tender mercy of our God, whereby the dayspring from on high ('oriens ex alto') hath visited us'.[20]

'Nacque al mondo un sole' – the image of the sun, and of the dawn, was fostered by his own Order, the Friars Minor, and taken up by poets and artists.

But was St Francis so original? He certainly claimed to be doing something new, directly inspired by God and the literal reading of the Gospel. In his Testament, which is in effect his autobiography, he asserted boldly and simply: 'no one showed me what I ought to do, but the Most High himself revealed to me that I ought to live according to the pattern of the holy Gospel'.[21] Again, in a collection of stories about him attributed to one of his close companions, brother Leo, Francis is reported as saying emphatically and publicly to Cardinal Hugolino, later Pope Gregory IX, and the friars assembled in General Chapter: 'My brothers! My brothers! God has called me by the way of simplicity

---

[18] 1 *Cel.* 125. The text is taken from Ecclesiasticus 50. 6–7 (Jerusalem Bible).

[19] Bonav., Prologue, 1, in AF X, 557–8 (trans. by B. Fahy in Habig 1979, pp. 631–2). Cf. Ecclesiasticus 50. 8: 'Like the rainbow gleaming against brilliant clouds'; and for the image of the Angel, Revelation 7. 12. Cf. the opening of the Prologue (c. 1) of *3 Soc.*: 'Resplendent as the dawn and as the morning star, or even as the rising sun, setting the world alight . . . Francis was seen to rise as a new kind of star' (trans. N. de Robeck in Habig 1979, p. 889).

[20] Dante, *Paradiso*, canto XI, 49–54. For the text and interpretation, see Petrocchi 1994, p. 179 and note to line 53: 'Non v'ha dubbio che si debba leggere Ascesi, come hanno i codici; la forma Asisi appartiene a manoscritti dell'area settentrionale.' See also Sinclair 1958, p. 170 n. 5; Singleton 1975, p. 198.

[21] Esser 1976, p. 439; cf. Brooke 1975, pp. 24–5, 117–19, esp. 117.

and shown me the way of simplicity. I do not want you to name any Rule to me, not St Augustine's, nor St Bernard's, nor St Benedict's. The Lord said to me that he wished that I should be a new-born simpleton in the world.'[22] But what was new about his message and his way of life? If we turn the cold eye of analysis on to the ideas and principles and activities which made up the new dawn, cannot we find them, one and all, among his predecessors and contemporaries? Has not the charm of his personality, and the brilliant propaganda of his disciples, bemused us into converting a colourful patchwork quilt of old pieces into a newly woven cloak of many colours?

The very heart of his message and his way of life lies in a quotation from the Gospel – 'If you would be perfect'. The pursuit of perfection – formidable as the challenge seems to ordinary mortals – has always been a central theme of the religious life. The most fundamental of the Conferences of John Cassian, in which the ethos of eastern monasticism was interpreted to the west in the early fifth century, was on perfection.[23] As for the Gospel, it is true that the Latin of the Vulgate prevented the illiterate from actually reading it and vernacular versions were liable to be investigated as potentially heretical. But Italian lay folk, like Francis, were often literate, and the Bible was the medieval school book *par excellence*. The child learnt his letters from the Psalter, and the Bible was used in the teaching of the liberal arts, being studied as part of the syllabus in schools and universities. In the twelfth century a professor of theology was called a 'master of the sacred page' and could take an exalted view of his vocation. A revival and enlargement of biblical study was one of the main features of the twelfth-century Renaissance, and its most remarkable element was a renewed interest in the literal meaning of Scripture – whose effect we see passing into popular consciousness very clearly in Francis' own life and teaching.[24]

He looked in the Gospel for evidence of the life of the apostles; and this, so far from being original, was the most predictable thing a pious man born in the twelfth century could do. The eleventh and twelfth centuries had seen a great blossoming of forms of the religious life, both old and new; some of them to our mind, somewhat bizarre, like the Orders of Knights. In the fervour of discussion and argument these movements raised, certain points formed the constant themes, the clichés of twelfth-century religion.

First, the attempt to pursue the apostolic life. This could involve the effort to discover what the life of the apostles had been like, and imitate it; or (perhaps more commonly), it meant choosing a congenial mode of the contemporary ascetic, religious scene, and claiming for it apostolic authority. In searching the New Testament for evidence of the life of the apostles Francis did what numerous religious leaders of the previous century had done before him. The second point of discussion and argument was the nature of religious and apostolic poverty. Monks had always been sworn to personal poverty, and it had long caused unease among some of them, and even more among their critics, that monks who were individually poor could be members of exceedingly rich monasteries. This came to be seen as a really unhappy paradox by many reformers of the eleventh and twelfth centuries; and poverty lay at the heart of many religious

[22] SL 114; cf. ibid. pp. 57–66.   [23] Pichery 1955–8, 11, no. XI, pp. 100–20.
[24] Smalley 1952, pp. xiv–xviii, 196–263.

movements, orthodox and heretical. Waldo, the founder of the Waldensians, was a rich merchant of Lyon, who abandoned his wealth for a life of poverty and preaching. In many ways his movement in its origin was extraordinarily similar to Francis', himself a merchant's son, reacting against the materialistic values and questionable ethics of his environment. Waldo eventually became a 'heretic', that is to say he left the Catholic church, and his followers now constitute by far the oldest surviving Protestant communion.[25] But many of his like remained orthodox, or returned to orthodoxy, in the late twelfth and early thirteenth centuries, and more than one of these groups won patronage from Pope Innocent III. In embracing poverty Francis was following a very well worn path. There was indeed a special emphasis, an uncompromising rigour, not previously corporately sustained. He had appreciated something of the ambiguities in other religious orders, and insisted that in his Order poverty was to be absolute, corporate as well as individual. The buildings in which the friars lodged, and the sites on which those buildings stood, were not in any circumstances to belong to them, to be their property. They were to own nothing. Money they were not even allowed to handle. There was a new edge to Francis' poverty – but the basic idea was conventional, and the notion that the apostles had been proto-Franciscans in their attitude to money owed more to twelfth-century tradition than to the New Testament.

Then there was heresy. Francis reiterated his obedience to the pope, and firmly excluded all taint of heresy from his Order. But he did not explicitly confront the problem in the way that St Dominic did at first. One of the surprising features of his own writings and the numerous stories and biographies is that heretics very rarely figure in them; little is said of heresy or its dangers. Yet his insistence in his Testament on submission to priests, and his constant awareness from the earliest days of the vital importance of papal approval, underline his own attitude. What makes the silence of the sources so odd is that he lived in an area riddled with heretics: a Cathar bishop presided in the valley of Spoleto in his youth, and Innocent III thought a podestà, or mayor, of Assisi was a Cathar.[26] This silence must mean that Francis was not enamoured of apologetic propaganda; that he believed that the way to counter heresy was to preach, and behave, the opposite. And he was by conviction and temperament as far removed from the Cathars as a man could be. They taught that the material world is wholly evil. Francis called on the birds, and in his Canticle of brother Sun, on the whole of Creation, to bear witness that the visible world is good, that it is God's world and should worship its Creator. He also believed in sin and hell and the need for repentance – his Third Order, aimed to cater for those who remained at home, comprised the brothers and sisters of penitence – but his fervent preaching that the world was God's world may have been as powerful as the Inquisition in undermining the Cathar churches in the thirteenth century.

In his relations with women Francis faced a problem very familiar to the religious leaders of the previous century. Robert of Arbrissel had resolved the many-sided religious inspiration of the late eleventh century by remaining himself part-time popular

---

[25] On Waldo, see Selge 1967; Brooke 1975, pp. 71–4, 148–52; Lambert 1992, ch. 5.
[26] C. Brooke 1970, pp. 62–3; Esser 1958, esp. p. 239; Borst 1953, pp. 231ff.

preacher, part-time recluse, and enclosing the many women who flocked to him in the conventional abbey of Fontevrault. Contrariwise, St Gilbert of Sempringham founded a double Order for men and women; and St Norbert, founder of the Premonstratensians, is said by his biographer to have gathered 10,000 women into his Order in early days. But Gilbert decided (or was made) to segregate his men and women so that they could not even see one another; and Norbert, a born missionary like Francis who hated organisation and committees, was by-passed by his followers, who presently stopped the recruitment of women almost entirely. In thirteenth- and fourteenth-century Germany and the Low Countries, for the first time in the recorded history of the medieval church, women were to become as numerous as men in the religious orders – by the spread of the *Beguines*, and the infiltration of the Cistercians by women.[27] But in Umbria Francis was still caught in the old dilemma. It was always his instinct that God meant his message and his way of life to be for all – particularly for all the poor and humble, outcast and neglected, Christian and non-Christian. It could not be God's will that women be excluded; and when he encountered Clare he evidently saw in her a possible pathfinder among the young women of Assisi with a call to the ascetic life. It seems clear that Francis soon found that his original undefined aspirations for her would incur suspicion, criticism and censure; and he firmly abandoned them – without ever quite admitting to himself or to her or to posterity (if the sources are to be believed) that he had changed his mind.[28]

We could pursue the elements of Francis' inspiration and for every element find some striking anticipation in the previous century. We can never be sure in individual cases how much he knew of his predecessors; but there is no doubt he knew something. Though very much a local man, deeply aware that Assisi was his native city, he had a wider vision, and his father was not a merchant travelling into France for nothing. The pursuit of poverty and the apostolic life was in the air he breathed. Of other marks of his life let one suffice: his half-hearted abdication of the role of Minister General. There is an earlier parallel in St Gilbert of Sempringham, who handed over the office of Master a number of years before his death, at the ripe age of a hundred, to his right-hand man, Roger; but Gilbert was somehow regarded as the real head of the Order till his death, when Roger had to be re-elected.[29] It is most unlikely that Francis knew in detail the recent history of this distant island Order; but the situations, the problems, the divergent needs of leader and administrator were similar; and in the twelfth and thirteenth centuries they could lead founders to withdraw from day to day administration.

How about St Dominic?[30] To the disciples of St Francis it has seemed obvious that Dominic imitated Francis; to students of Dominic the hypothesis has seemed without

---

[27] There is a vast literature on the *Frauenfrage*, the role of women in the religious movements of the twelfth and thirteenth centuries. On Robert of Arbrissel, see e.g. Smith 1978; Dalarun 1985; for the relation of nuns to the Cistercians, see Thompson 1978; C. Brooke 2003, pp. 17–18, 213–14, 275; for the Premonstratensians, Thompson 1991, pp. 134–45; for some of the more independent women religious of the turn of the twelfth and thirteenth centuries, Bolton 1978.

[28] See Brooke and Brooke 1978, esp. pp. 280–3.

[29] Foreville and Keir 1987, pp. xxiii–xxiv, 68–9, 86–9, 130–3.

[30] On the relations between Dominic and Francis, see Brooke 1975, pp. 89–90, 97–100, 103; Brooke 1971, pp. 223–31. For Dominican influence on the Franciscans, see Brooke 1959, pp. 234, 240, 293–6.

foundation. The one meeting that is well recorded may have marked a turning point in Dominic's life. It helped him to see his way to converting his Order (a tiny group still at the time), from a group of preachers among the heretics in Languedoc into a world-wide Order of friars. But if that is so, the compliment was presently returned. Leading Franciscans studied the organisation of the Dominicans and grafted some of it on to their own Order. Francis envisaged that the rank and file of his Order would be uneducated lay brothers who lived the Christian life and taught by example, earning their bread when they could, begging when they could not. Dominic's Order from the first comprised trained, instructed preachers, intended to fulfil the role the parish clergy of the thirteenth century could least effectively perform. And trained, effective preachers is what the Franciscans soon became – so much so that by the late thirteenth century the role of the lay brothers had been forgotten. 'They are useless folk', said the friar Salimbene of the laymen who, in his youth, still represented the Franciscan ideal in its original form, 'they cannot hear confessions, they do nothing but eat and sleep'.[31] So if we look at Francis' most characteristic creation, the friar, we find that as he developed in the course of the century, he owed as much to Dominic as to Francis, and as much to their predecessors too.

In 1228–9 Thomas of Celano wrote that Francis was a 'new evangelist', that 'in him and through him . . . a holy newness was created . . . A new spirit was given . . . when the servant and saint of Christ, like one of the lights of heaven, illumined the world with a new observance and new signs from above. The miracles of old were renewed through him . . . when a fruitful vine was planted in a new Order.'[32] Was this mere rhetoric? Can it really be claimed that Francis 'was born into the world a sun'? Is it not simply that his image has bewitched successive generations, as it bewitched contemporaries, into thinking that he brought a new revelation with him?

---

[31] Salimbene, H, pp. 101–2; S, 1, 145–6.   [32] 1 *Cel.* 89 (my own translation).

CHAPTER TWO

THE IMAGE IN LIFE

THE IMAGE FRANCIS SOUGHT TO PRESENT

Francis was no self-effacing saint. He had a message he thought it vital to put across. He was highly motivated, articulate, self-conscious, and he explored a whole range of possible channels of communication: the spoken word and the written word, but also song, mime, anything that might enhance the impact of his teaching and render it vivid and memorable to his audience. He was preacher, actor, poet, a brilliant teacher. From the evidence of his own statements, writings, actions and the witness of his companions and early biographers we can perceive the images that Francis presented as teaching aids; images drawn from his own experience of conversion.

Francis was born c.1181 in the modest Umbrian hill town of Assisi, which was always to be his home, and where his spirit still presides. His father was a cloth merchant, a man of the counting-house, engaged in a lucrative trade. Because of his family's wealth Francis was able to mix as a young man with contemporaries of higher social status, and when, in the course of one of the local skirmishes which all too frequently took place between Assisi and neighbouring Perugia, he was captured along with many of his fellow citizens, he was incarcerated among the nobles. After his release, presumably for an appropriate ransom, he entertained the not unnatural ambition to exploit his opportunities for social climbing. The disturbed political situation in southern Italy during the minority of Frederick II invited intervention by the adventurous in search of advancement and among those who sought to profit was a noble citizen of Assisi. He planned to lead a band into Apulia to join the forces of Walter de Brienne, a condottiere campaigning under papal auspices, the young Frederick II being a ward of Innocent III. This was c.1205 when Francis was twenty-three or twenty-four. Francis joined the noble's retinue with the object of obtaining a knighthood. His father, who was very generous to Francis and clearly wished to further his son's prospects, allowed him to equip himself lavishly. Francis, excited and eager, indulged in expensive preparations by day and at night he dreamed. He dreamed that his home, instead of containing bales of cloth for sale, was filled with military armour, saddles, shields, lances and so forth, intended for him and his soldiers. Interpreting this as a very favourable omen and imagining he was destined to become a great prince he set out for Apulia; but he got no further than Spoleto. Here, in a second dream, a voice challenged his assumptions. 'Who can do better for you, the servant or the lord?' 'The Lord.' 'Why then do you seek the servant rather than the lord? . . .' 'What do you wish me to do, Lord?' 'Return home, [to perform what the Lord will reveal to you].'[1]

His first biographer, Thomas of Celano, called Francis a 'new soldier of Christ' (1 Cel. 9). The military metaphor was an ancient topos, a cliché of religious language, in spite of its apparent discord with the Christian message of peace and goodwill. In the Benedictine tradition 'militans' meant 'serving' without any bellicose connotation at all; and just as the erotic language of the Song of Songs was used by St Bernard of Clairvaux and others in a purely metaphorical sense, without any hesitation about its carnal, physical meaning, so the military metaphor could always be used in a quite neutral sense. But between the tenth and the twelfth centuries this military language took on a new meaning. The Church had adopted a notion of the 'just war' from its early days; and in the tenth and eleventh centuries there was a more widespread and concerted effort to find a vocation for the Christian knight, so that he could pursue the life he led and to which he was suited and yet feel himself fully a Christian. It was but a step from this to harness the warlike proclivities and qualities of the western nobility and knightly society at large in causes supposed to be Christian and in the wars we call crusades. In the second quarter of the twelfth century St Bernard had inspired the new religious Orders of Knights through a tract on the 'nova militia' of Christ; and in 1146, at the pope's command, he preached the Second Crusade in Burgundy and the Rhineland. Deep and wide as was the popularity of the crusades there had always been doubters; and the ambivalence of the crusades – the many failures, the disgraceful behaviour of crusading armies, their use against heretics and the political enemies of the papacy – devalued them. We have been taught in recent years to take the later crusades much more seriously than in the past;[2] but we have two most vivid witnesses from the early thirteenth century of the doubt and disillusion which could afflict would-be crusaders.

Wolfram von Eschenbach wrote a long epic in the 1210s called *Willehalm*, whose central theme is a plea for tolerance towards the enemy and the infidel – 'spare God's handiwork' – which must undermine the original crusading inspiration.[3] Francis turned his back on his initial knightly aspirations. The type of expedition on which he set out in 1205 was questionable and he seems to have perceived this on reflection. He played a part in the Fifth Crusade, but as a man of peace. He joined the crusading army besieging Damietta in 1219 and proceeded to denounce the basic assumptions of war and to try to prevent battle being joined. Greeted with ridicule, as he anticipated he would be, he crossed the enemy lines and succeeded in reaching the Sultan's camp, where for some

[1] AP 6b; 3 Soc. 6.
[2] For a general account, see Brooke and Brooke 1984, pp. 56–61; St Bernard's *De laude novae militiae* is in Leclercq and Rochais 1963, pp. 205–39. For the later crusades, see Housley 1982, 1992.
[3] C. Brooke 1989a, p. 207. For *Willehalm*, see edn of K. Lachmann, 6th edn by E. Hartl (Berlin, 1926); trans. in Gibbs and Johnson 1984; for its interpretation, see C. Brooke 1989a, pp. 202–10.

days he preached the Gospel to the Saracens, motivated both by missionary zeal and by his longing for martyrdom.[4]

He was still prepared to use military imagery to emphasise a point. He replied to a novice who wanted to have a psalter: 'The Emperor Charles, Roland and Oliver, and all the paladins and strong men mighty in battle, pursuing the infidel with much sweat and toil even unto death, had over them a great and memorable victory: and in the end they were made martyrs, dying in battle for the faith of Christ. There are many who only for recounting what these did wish to receive honour and praise of men' (SL 72). This was a characteristic utterance. It was said that he was named Francis because his father was in France on business when he was born. It was probably his father who first instilled in him a love of French literary and musical culture. He publicly renounced his father, but he did not repudiate his delight in French courtly romances and chansons. He celebrated his freedom from all material possessions by setting out on his way singing praises to the Lord in French. Confronted in the woods by robbers who asked who he was, he replied: 'I am the herald of the great king'; on which they struck him and flung him into a ditch filled with snow, crying: 'Lie there, foolish herald of God!' (1 Cel. 16) But this did not dampen his spirits; it was all part of the adventure on which he had embarked. In later years he felt, and wanted his followers to feel, that the task they were undertaking was as exciting and arduous as any facing a hero of epic or romance. The language of chivalry, the exploits of Charlemagne and of Arthur, coloured his conversation. His brothers could be knights of the Round Table. Men were proud and eager to serve a temporal ruler; how much more gladly and readily should they seek to serve God, the king of kings. He liked to juxtapose stark contrasts and challenge the values of society. The justification of mendicancy in these terms was a favourite topic. The poor religious should not feel shame at begging his bread from door to door. On the contrary, Francis insisted, he should regard the begging of alms for the love of God as a noble and courtly activity, of the highest regal dignity. He compared him to a man who, out of courtesy and generosity, sought to buy a pennyworth of goods and in return offered a hundred marks of silver, only the beggar offered a thousand times more, as the love of God is beyond price.[5]

After he abandoned the military adventure into Apulia and returned home, Francis' behaviour altered. His friends thought he must be in love and began to tease him: 'Are you wanting to get married?' To which he replied: 'I will marry a wife nobler and more beautiful than any you have seen, who will surpass others in beauty and excel in wisdom.'[6] Who was she? Did he mean true religion? Or poverty perhaps? His ideal of voluntary absolute poverty could be presented as a quest. Dante was to pick up this most striking image in the *Paradiso* when he celebrated the theme of Francis and Poverty as lovers. Poverty, so dear to Christ, so close to him, that while Mary was forced to grieve at the foot of the Cross, poverty still clung to him upon the Cross itself.[7]

When Francis exulted in spirit he would often burst into song. Singing was a way of expressing his own joy in God's goodness, and a way of communicating that joy to

---

[4] 1 Cel. 57; 2 Cel. 30; Jacques de Vitry, postscript to Epistola VI, in Huygens 1960, pp. 131–3, quoted in Brooke 1975, p. 204; Jordan, c. 10.
[5] SL 71, 60–1.   [6] 1 Cel. 7; cf. 2 Cel. 55.   [7] Paradiso, Canto XI, 70–2.

others. Once when he was ill he asked a brother to borrow a guitar and improvise a song of praise. He was in pain and wanted through music to turn his physical suffering into spiritual joy and consolation. But the friar was unwilling. 'Father, I would feel ashamed to get one, especially as the men of this city know that I used to play the guitar when I was in the world. I am afraid they might suspect me of being tempted to play the guitar' (SL 24). The brother refused, because he was concerned about what the neighbours might think. Francis' approach was more robust. He was prepared to scandalise, as that could jolt the conventional into rethinking their attitudes. Music could be sanctified. He himself composed a number of holy songs with tunes. His song of praise to the Creator – a version of the Benedicite – beginning: 'Most high, omnipotent, good Lord' has survived. He called it 'The Canticle of brother Sun' because the sun can come nearest to God and because it lights our eyes by day. It is a joyful song, composed, characteristically, in the midst of suffering and darkness, not long before his death, while he lay blind and ill, in a tiny cell infested with mice. He sang it, and taught it to his companions, so that concentrating on God's praise, and on the glory and goodness of God's Creation, he might forget his actual circumstances.[8]

The songs of praise that Francis sang were in the vernacular, so that they could be readily understood and easily memorised. He planned to overcome the reluctance of those among his followers who had been troubadours and to use their talents. He sent for brother Pacifico, who while in the world had been nicknamed the 'king of verses', and told him to organise a preaching tour. He proposed that, first, a good preacher should deliver a sermon, and then Pacifico should sing the Canticle of brother Sun. They were then to say to the people: 'We are the Lord's minstrels, and as our recompense for our performance we want you to live in true penitence.'[9]

So St Francis did not banish as frivolities the romances and courtly songs he had enjoyed in his youth, but made use of them. Sometimes he played the troubadour himself. In a rare personal reminiscence Thomas of Celano records that he had seen Francis pick up a stick from the ground, put it over his left arm and with his right draw across it a little bow bent with a thread, as if he were playing a viol, singing as he did so in French about the Lord.[10] For Francis acted instinctively, as part of his preaching technique. The best known of his dramatic representations was his realistic staging of the Nativity scene one Christmas at Greccio.[11] At night the crib was filled with hay, an ox and an ass were led in, so the whole congregation could see the scene with their own eyes and call to mind the boy born so uncomfortably in Bethlehem. His aim – to stimulate the imagination.

Francis had a vivid imagination. After he had abandoned his knightly ambitions and returned home, uncertain of what he should do, he spent an increasing amount of time in prayer, in remote solitudes and in churches. One church he entered, situated on the slopes a little below Assisi's eastern gate, was dedicated to St Damian. There, as he prayed before the crucifix, it seemed the painted image spoke to him: 'Francis, go, repair my house, which as you see is entirely ruined' (Plate 3). Francis, amazed

[8] SL 43; for the text of the Canticle, Sp S (2nd edn), II, pp. 217–36; Branca 1949.
[9] SL 43, slightly adapted.　[10] 2 Cel. 127; see p. 143.　[11] 1 Cel. 84–6.

and obedient, understood the words quite literally. The church, he could see, was in a very dilapidated state. His first impulsive response was conditioned by his mercantile upbringing. He needed money. Money would pay for the necessary repairs. He took some fine cloth from his father's stock, mounted his horse and rode to Foligno, where he successfully sold all the merchandise and the horse. Making his way back to San Damiano, he offered the money to its poor priest, but the priest refused to accept it, doubting the young man's intentions and fearing the reactions of his parents. So Francis threw the coins on to a window sill. The incident led directly to his breach with his father, who, when threats and ill-treatment failed to deflect his son from behaviour he thought mad and disgraceful, sued him for the money. The case came before the bishop and Francis handed over the money, which had been retrieved from the window sill. He also stripped himself completely naked and returned all his clothes to his father for good measure, exclaiming: 'Henceforth I may freely say: "Our Father who is in heaven", not father Peter Bernardone, to whom, look, I not only give back the money but resign my entire clothing. Therefore I may proceed naked to the Lord.'[12] It is a fine example – and one not lost on later artists – of Francis' fervour and of his sense and use of the dramatic; the action created a memorable impression. But Francis too learned a lesson, which he never forgot. Money had failed him. It had proved not the easy solution he had anticipated but a positive hindrance and embarrassment. His father had not grudged him money to further worldly ambition or to entertain his friends but had flown into a violent passion when he wanted some to repair a church, and accused him, in effect, of theft. The bishop advised him that money that might have been unlawfully acquired could not properly be used for religious purposes. The bishop may have been thinking of the immediate question of ownership. The money belonged to Francis' father, however much the son had been accustomed or felt entitled to spend it. He may have had in mind the more general point of the Church's economic teaching on usury, which presupposed that money acquired commercially was suspect. Francis, impulsive and temperamentally disinclined to do anything by halves, concluded that money was a menace. To him, its complete rejection was a logical step.[13] Meantime San Damiano awaited repair. Although he had been delicately reared, Francis set to work to restore it himself, labouring with his own hands, begging for stones through the streets of Assisi and bearing them on his shoulders.

He spent some two years thus, in solitary prayer, in caring for lepers, and in repairing San Damiano and other churches, including a tiny church in the plain below Assisi, St Mary of the Angels or the Portiuncula (St Mary of the little portion), to which he became very much attached and which he was to make the headquarters of his Order. Here, early in 1209, on the feast of St Matthias, 24 February, a further and fuller understanding of his calling was vouchsafed to him. He listened to the reading of the Gospel appointed for the day: Christ's instructions to his disciples when he sent them out to preach the kingdom of God and penance. 'As you go proclaim the message: "The kingdom of heaven is upon you". Heal the sick, raise the dead, cleanse lepers, cast out devils. You received without cost; give without charge. Provide no gold, silver or copper to fill your

[12] 2 Cel. 10, 12.   [13] On wealth and poverty, see Lambert 1961; Little 1978.

purse, no pack for the road, no second coat, no shoes, no stick; the worker earns his keep' (Matt. 10. 5ff). To make quite sure, he asked the priest to explain the passage to him. Satisfied, he said: 'This is what I want, this is what I seek, this is what I long with my innermost heart to do.' Wasting no time, he signalled his literal obedience to the Gospel commands by taking off his shoes, discarding his stick, and hastening to set out to preach, dressed only in the simple grey tunic tied with a cord that became the habit of the Friars Minor.[14]

He soon attracted followers. Brother Giles was received on 23 April, and he was the third recruit. The first was Bernard of Quintavalle, a wealthy citizen. His admission was in accord with the simple adherence to Christ's teachings which Francis had undertaken. The two went together to a church, where they opened the Gospel book for guidance. The first words they read were: 'If you wish to go the whole way, go, sell your possessions and give to the poor, and then you will have riches in heaven; and come, follow me' (Matt. 19. 21).[15] So Bernard promptly sold everything and distributed the proceeds among the poor. When they were eight in number Francis sent them out two by two to preach peace and repentance. When they were twelve, he wrote a short, simple Rule, using in the main the words of the Gospels, and took the little group to Rome to petition the pope for his approval, an approval which Innocent III was persuaded to give conditionally and verbally.[16]

Francis summed up his experience of conversion in his Testament, which is in essence a brief autobiography, a 'record, admonition and exhortation' as he himself described it, intended to guide his followers.[17] He wrote: 'After the Lord gave me brothers, no one showed me what I ought to do, but the Most High himself revealed to me that I ought to live according to the pattern of the holy Gospel. And I had it written down simply, in few words; and the lord Pope confirmed it for me.' 'I ought to live according to the pattern of the holy Gospel.' Francis took this as a charge and conceived it was his role to give an example to others. I have said that he had a marked sense of the dramatic and used acting as part of his preaching technique. But he was not just acting a part. He was totally involved in what he was doing; he acted on a much deeper level. He lived as he wanted others to live, striving to lead the Christian life as he understood it, literally, without compromise and without sham, in small things as in great. One wintry day his companion obtained a fox skin and urged him to allow it to be sewn inside his thin tunic because he was suffering from illnesses of the spleen and stomach. Francis would only agree to a piece being sewn inside if a corresponding piece was sewn on outside.[18] Even when staying in hermitages he did not relax. One of his friends had a little cell made in a secluded spot, thinking Francis might care to use it for prayer. When he showed it to him, Francis said: '"This cell seems to me too attractive. But if you would like me to stay in it for a few days, have it given some covering of stones

---

[14] 1 Cel. 21–2. 1 Celano 22 contains a pastiche from the three Synoptic Gospels of the charge to the disciples: see AF X, 19 nn. But the version in Matt. 10. 7–19 was the Gospel for St Matthias' day, and it has long been thought most probable that this was the gospel that he heard: cf. Cuthbert 1913, pp. 56–7 and 57 n.1, and now Duffy 1997, pp. 221–2.
[15] 1 Cel. 24; 2 Cel. 15.   [16] 1 Cel. 29, 32.
[17] Esser 1976, pp. 438–44; trans. Brooke 1975, pp. 117–19, and cf. ibid. pp. 24ff.
[18] SL 40; cf. 2 Cel. 130.

and tree branches inside and out." For that little cell was . . . made of wood; but as the wood was planed, prepared with axe and adze, it seemed to Francis too attractive. The friar at once made it more suitable in the way . . . indicated . . . After he had stayed and prayed in it for a few days, he was standing . . . near the friary, when one of the friars came up to him. St Francis asked: "Where have you come from, brother?" He replied: "I come from your cell." St Francis said to him: "As you have said it is mine, another will stay there from now on, and not I"' – an ungracious speech, one of those which show how difficult a man he could be to live with. But the story illustrates also, not only his insistence on visible signs of poverty but his determination never himself to give an example of the relaxation of his own principles.[19] On this he was pedantic. When his friends remonstrated with him that he was too hard on himself he would reply that he had been given to the Order as an example, that as an eagle he might encourage his young ones to fly (2 *Cel.* 173).

THE IMPRESSION FRANCIS MADE ON CONTEMPORARIES

In a seminal paper, 'The rise and function of the Holy Man in Late Antiquity', Peter Brown discussed the question of why the holy man came to play such an important role in society in the fifth and sixth centuries.[20] He sees him as a figure who, by heroic asceticism and the strange acts of power which we call miracles, was set apart from the traditional social hierarchy. In a society which was prosperous and yet often lacked natural or traditional leaders, the holy man could provide a much needed focus of authority. Pilgrims flocked to visit an eminent hermit, to seek his advice and his prayers, to ask for his help in curing sickness and his arbitration in disputes. Peter Brown's comments were directed particularly to the light the activities of the professional holy man could throw on the values and functioning of late Roman society in Syria and in Byzantium at large, but they have a wider application. The circumstances of Italian society in the early thirteenth century, and the ways in which Francis' ministry catered for its needs and expectations, show some interesting parallels. It was a time of rising prosperity. The population was increasing, trade was flourishing, towns were expanding; there were greater opportunities for profit and success. But there was a reverse side to all this expansion. Growth involved exploitation and social dislocation, and there were casualties. The numbers of the poor, the disadvantaged, the victims of violence and greed, increased disproportionately. People then as earlier needed and responded to a man of power who was objective, who demonstrably stood outside the ties of family and economic interest, and so could act as arbiter and mediator, reconciling the violent tensions in communities, and as healer of many ills of mind and body. Peter Brown has drawn attention to the deep social significance of asceticism as a long drawn out solemn ritual of dissociation. The holy man acquired his power by histrionic feats of self-mortification and prayer. He was an athlete who succeeded in conquering the body and winning his way to intimacy with God. His occasional dramatic interventions illustrated a prestige already gained. His reputation was built up by hard, unobtrusive

[19] SL 13; cf. 2 *Cel.* 59.   [20] Brown 1971, esp. pp. 80–1, 91, 94.

work among those who needed constant, unspectacular ministrations; it was earned by living his life twenty-four hours a day. The relevance of considerations such as these to Francis' case is clear.

Francis' rejection of his father was a public act of ritual dissociation. In one dramatic gesture he cut his ties with his family and disowned his mercantile inheritance. He carried his abhorrence of money so far that he would not allow his friars to accept or even to touch it. In the Rule he stated categorically: 'I firmly order all the brothers not to accept coins or money in any form, either themselves or through an intermediary.'[21] When he first changed his way of life and prayed and wept and fasted, the significance of his austerities was not understood. Like the hermits of old, he encountered initial hostility and suspicion. At the sight of his gaunt features, dirty clothes and unkempt hair the immediate reaction of the people of Assisi was that he had gone mad, and they shouted abuse at him and pelted him with mud and stones.[22] But in response to his steadfast perseverance in prayer, self-mortification and good works this soon gave place to acceptance, to admiration, veneration and local pride. The changed Francis made a point of spending time in visiting leper houses and tending the sores of those afflicted outcasts of society, whom he himself had previously shunned. Before his conversion, he recalled, he had so shared in the prevailing loathing and disgust that if he but caught sight of a leper house two miles away he would ostentatiously close his nostrils with his hands.[23] After it, he identified with the poor, respecting them and sharing their privations. The only sign of envy he ever showed was if he found someone poorer than himself. He took unfailing satisfaction in giving away the clothes off his back to any poor person he met, causing constant problems to those who were trying to look after him when he was ill.[24] The keynotes of his preaching were peace and penance. Repentance involves not only sorrow for sin and misdoing but positive acts of reparation and benevolence so that penance, besides its value for the individual, has a social dimension. It can promote the giving of alms to the poor, provision for the sick, the righting of injustice, the fulfilling of obligations. The importance of peace was impressed upon Francis by the inclusion of the instruction 'When you enter into a house let your peace come upon it', in the Gospel passage which inspired the form of life he embraced. He recalled this in the Testament: 'The Lord revealed to me the greeting which we should say: "The Lord give you peace".'[25] It was also driven home to him by the conditions prevailing in the Italy of his day, reinforced by personal experience.

Francis, like Peter Brown's 'holy men', spent a proportion of his life as a hermit, in sites like the Carceri in a wooded fold of Monte Subasio above Assisi, where his cell on the cliff face could be regarded as the Italian equivalent of St Simeon's pillar. It was at another of these remote hermitages, at La Verna near Arezzo, that he received a special sign of his intimacy with God, the mysterious imprint of the stigmata.[26] He had gone to La Verna in 1224, two years before his death, to fast in honour of St Michael the forty days between the feast of the Assumption of the Virgin Mary and Michaelmas, and in

[21] *Regula bullata*, c. 4, Esser 1976, p. 368.   [22] 1 Cel. 10–11.
[23] 1 Cel. 17; Testament, Esser 1976, p. 438.   [24] 1 Cel. 76; SL 52–4; 2 Cel. 83–90.
[25] Matt. 10. 12–13; Testament, Esser 1976, p. 440.
[26] 1 Cel. 94; SL 93; cf. SL Appendix, c. 2, and see pp. 166–8 and n. 13.

Plate 4 Assisi from the south-east (Photo C. N. L. Brooke).

his lonely mountain fastness he meditated so constantly and deeply on the sufferings and passion of Christ that he had a vision of the Seraph, which left him marked with Jesus' wounds. Whatever the true interpretation of the stigmata, it is a phenomenon well recorded by contemporaries. It has happened to others, usually only temporarily. Francis bore the marks until his death. The stigmata added to his pain and made him more of a recluse, but even in his last years he still travelled about when he could. The major part of his time was spent as a wandering preacher. It was in the hill cities of central Italy that he met the people of his day; Assisi and its like were his true context.

Assisi is situated on a hill, as are many other Italian cities which have enjoyed continuous occupation of ancient sites. Hill sites were favoured partly because they were healthier – the plains were marshy where drainage was difficult or neglected – but chiefly probably because they were defensible. Assisi still has something of the characteristic appearance of a medieval city with walls around it, massive gateways and the ruins of a castle, the Rocca, at a high point (Plate 4). Conflict was endemic. The great conflict between Empire and Papacy, which went on intermittently throughout the eleventh, twelfth and thirteenth centuries, was largely fought out in Italy. The German Holy Roman Emperors inherited lands in northern Italy from the breakup of Charlemagne's Empire. When they came to Italy to be crowned, and to put the pope in his place, the valley of Spoleto, on which Assisi lies, was an artery along which their armies marched. In Francis' youth the duke of Spoleto maintained an imperial garrison in the Rocca. But after the early death of Henry VI in 1197 the citizens rose, destroyed the Rocca and established a commune. Pope Innocent III became overlord of Assisi, taking advantage of his position as the young Frederick's guardian, and from the early thirteenth century Assisi was on the papal side in the struggle. When Frederick II grew up he twice attacked her with Saracen troops. One marauding Saracen band was fortunately if rather surprisingly repulsed by St Clare.[27]

There were local conflicts too. There was an ancient enmity between the men of Assisi and the men of Perugia. Perugia was Etruscan, Assisi Umbrian in origin, and the two cities stand in sight of each other on their hill tops. Francis had fought in one engagement, been captured and spent a year in a Perugian prison. Later, he preached in the piazza at Perugia, urging these powerful neighbours not to ignore his warnings because he came from Assisi but to make satisfaction to those they had offended or face the consequences and suffer the self-inflicted calamities of civil war. Here Francis was performing a further function incumbent on the holy man, successful prophecy. The knights of Perugia, bearing their arms, interrupted his sermon by riding their horses through the piazza. Presently a quarrel did break out between them and the townspeople. The knights were driven from the city and proceeded to do all the harm they could, laying waste the people's fields and vineyards and trees. The townspeople similarly laid waste the knights' fields and vineyards and trees.[28] Vines and olive trees, from which come the staple commodities of wine and oil, take time to establish and become productive and the destruction of these plantations would impoverish the city for years to come.

This incident illustrates another category of conflicts by no means peculiar to Perugia, characteristic indeed of Italian city life – internal conflicts, bitter, violent, diverse – quarrels between various classes of society, quarrels between groups holding opposing political or religious opinions. There was conflict between nobles and townspeople – as in this case – conflict between citizens and their bishop, feuds between families, such as that between the Montagues and Capulets in Verona immortalised by Shakespeare. Any or all of these could erupt in sporadic fighting, and those who could afford to defend their homes did so. Nobles built higher and higher towers. That Assisi had towers is evident from a fresco in the little church of San Damiano, painted at the very beginning of the fourteenth century by a follower of Giotto. It depicts a view of the city from the south-east, tightly confined within its walls, a cluster of churches, roofs and towers, in which it is possible to identify a number of buildings which still survive.[29]

The young Emperor Henry VI went hunting in Sicily one afternoon in the late summer of 1197. It was chilly; the ground was swampy; he fell sick and died. With his death imperial authority in Umbria disintegrated. In Assisi the citizens besieged the garrison in the Rocca and, when they captured it, destroyed this symbol of foreign domination.[30] In the difficult and disturbed years which followed they rapidly developed political

---

[27] Waley 1978; *Legenda S. Clarae*, cc. 14–15 (also cc. 21–2 in *Acta Sanctorum, Aug.*, I, 759).
[28] 2 *Cel.* 4; SL 35.
[29] Scarpellini 1978, pp. 114–15 and pls. XXXIII (erroneously placed in Santa Chiara) and XXXV.
[30] For what follows, see Waley 1978, esp. pp. 57–65. The agreement of 1210 is in Langeli 1978, pp. 321–8.

Plate 5 Assisi, the Piazza del Comune with the Temple of Minerva (Photo C. N. L. Brooke).

institutions, and established a commune. To survive, the commune had to govern and
to fight, and a modicum of internal unity was essential. Two treaties of peace were
drawn up in 1203 and 1210, between the 'boni homines' and the 'homines populi',
the 'maiores' and 'minores'. The nobility had favoured the imperial cause and when
the people stormed the Rocca many left the city for their properties and castles in the
surrounding countryside, and some temporarily allied themselves with Assisi's rival
Perugia. But Assisi needed her nobility, who provided the bulk of her cavalry. Those
whose town houses and towers had been damaged were compensated. The two parties
promised not to make separate agreements with pope or emperor or with any city or
lord, not to injure each other or foment discord, but to act in common, for the common
good. Detailed clauses enabled the people to secure freedom from feudal obligations
and services for money payments. Communal officials, after a year's tenure, were to be
ineligible for the next three years. A hearth tax could be levied for military expenses.
The 1210 agreement ends with the words: 'It pleased all, since no-one objected.' The
first evidence of money being spent in the public interest comes from the same year,
when land was acquired for a laundry. The provision of adequate water supplies –
fountains and laundries – and of improved hygienic arrangements generally was often
rendered imperative by the rapidly increasing populations of the towns. Two years later,
in 1212, the commune rented from the Benedictine monastery on the slopes of Monte
Subasio above Assisi a plot of land in the market place on which to build a palace, a
town hall, the Palazzo del Comune, which still stands beside the Temple of Minerva
(Plate 5). An indication of the seeming precariousness of the new civic government is
found in a clause providing that the land was to revert to the monks if the commune
ceased to exist. In the event it prospered. Francis grew up in this world. 1210, the year
of the second peace agreement, was probably also the year in which his Rule was first
approved by Innocent III. He would have been about sixteen or seventeen when the
Rocca was taken and the imperial power in Assisi overthrown. Perhaps his optimism,
his belief that men could be changed and could change their world, was in part the

result of his witnessing and sharing in his city's efforts to achieve a measure of political independence and self-government.

Perhaps the most striking similarity between Francis and the ancient 'holy men' lay in his self-presentation. He developed a mode, a character, an image of himself which he sought to project among his followers and before all who met him. Francis preached *extempore*, in simple words, sometimes in churches, often in the open air. He did not have an imposing presence. On one occasion he preached a sermon in Terni, in the piazza in front of the bishop's palace. When he had finished, the bishop, who had attended the sermon, himself addressed the people: 'From the first the Lord who planted and built his Church has always adorned her with saintly men who have enriched her by word and example; but now in this last time he has adorned her with this poor, little, contemptible, ignorant man' – indicating St Francis with his finger to the whole people – 'on which account you are bound to love and honour God and keep yourselves from sins.' Francis warmly thanked the bishop for his unflattering words. 'For other men say: "This is a holy man", attributing glory and sanctity to the creature and not to the Creator. But you separated the precious from the worthless, like a wise man' (SL 103). But poor, little, contemptible, ignorant as he appeared, and chose to appear, his words had power to move. Jacques de Vitry, bishop of Acre, who came in contact with him at Damietta, in a letter written in the spring of 1220, described him as 'afire with the zeal of faith'.[31]

Francis, in his own conduct and in his writings, showed his respect for bishops and priests. He wrote in his Testament: 'The Lord gave and gives me such faith in priests, who live according to the model of the holy Roman Church, on account of their orders, that even if they should persecute me I wish to run back to them. And if I had as much wisdom as Solomon, and found poor and humble secular priests in the parishes in which they lived, I would not wish to preach against their will . . . In this world I see nothing of the son of God most high in a tangible sense, except his most holy body and blood, which priests receive and priests alone administer to others.'[32] Thus he emphasised his reverence for the poorest priests. None the less he took it upon himself to lecture them on the proper upkeep of their churches and the proper housing of the sacraments, though he considerately did this in private so as not to embarrass them in front of their parishioners.[33] When he came to Imola he presented himself to the bishop, asking his permission to preach. The bishop responded: 'It is sufficient, brother, that I preach to my people.' Francis bowed his head and humbly withdrew, but in a little while he returned. 'What do you want, brother?' said the bishop, 'What are you after this time?' 'My lord', said Francis 'if a father drives a son out of one door he must re-enter by another.' Won over by his humility, the bishop cordially embraced him, declaring: 'You, and all your brothers, have from now on my general licence to preach in my diocese, since such holy humility has deserved it' (2 *Cel.* 147). It was an object lesson in the virtue, and efficacy, of humility. Humble persistence worked. It was genuine humble persistence, but it was something else too. It also derived from

[31] Huygens 1960, pp. 131–3; Brooke 1975, p. 204.
[32] Esser 1976, pp. 438–9; Brooke 1975, p. 117.   [33] SL 18: 'he carried a broom to sweep the churches'.

Francis' supreme self-confidence in the rightness of his undertaking. The bishop was bound to be convinced sooner or later by his importunity. This held true even for the bishop of Rome. If he needed the pope's help he went to him. An obscure penitent with only eleven followers, he went to the top, to Innocent III, in 1210, for approval for his Rule. When some of his followers tried behind his back to alter his arrangements in 1219–20 he went straight to Honorius III. He waited outside the door of the pope's chamber. He did not presume to knock, but he stayed there until the pope came out, and then petitioned him. He asked if he might have the cardinal bishop of Ostia, Hugolino, who was a nephew of Innocent III, as Protector for his Order, because, as he explained, he realised the pope was a busy man.[34]

He had already obtained the friendly interest of some leading churchmen, through the good offices of the bishop of Assisi, Guido, who supported him from the time he renounced his father. When Francis went to Rome in 1210 it was Bishop Guido who introduced him to John of St Paul, cardinal bishop of Sabina. This cardinal agreed to speak for Francis in the Curia and was instrumental in securing a favourable response from the pope. Bonaventure records that he intervened at the critical moment to point out: 'If we refuse the request of this poor man as something new and too difficult, when what he seeks is that a form of evangelical life be confirmed for him, we must beware lest we offend against Christ's Gospel. For if anyone says that evangelical perfection and the vow to observe it contain anything that is new or unreasonable or impossible to observe, he is convicted of blasphemy against Christ, the author of the Gospel.'[35] Cardinal Hugolino became his chief patron and Francis used to stay with him in his house from time to time; he also stayed more than once with Leo Brancaleo, cardinal priest of Santa Croce in Gerusalemme.[36] By a characteristic Franciscan paradox, he who had dramatically renounced every vestige of his father's inheritance found himself honoured in places his father could never have entered. Hugolino was edified by Francis and one reason for this was precisely that, for all his humility, Francis did not modify his behaviour out of deference for the great. For example, when visiting the cardinal he slipped out to beg just as if he were staying with the poor. He returned late for the meal – the cardinal and his other guests had already begun – and proceeded to distribute among them the scraps of food he had begged. Hugolino felt extremely embarrassed, though in fact the broken crusts of stale bread were accepted devoutly. Afterwards, in the privacy of his chamber, he remonstrated with Francis. But Francis justified his conduct. 'I . . . hold it as a very regal dignity and honour of the great king, who, although he is lord of all, wished for our sake to become the servant of all, and although he might be rich and glorious in his majesty, came to us poor and despised in our humanity. Therefore I want the friars . . . to know that I hold it a greater consolation of mind and body when I sit at the friars' poor board and see before me the poor alms which they have acquired from door to door for the love of the Lord God, than when I sit at your board . . . abundantly provided with food. For the bread of alms is holy bread, which the praise and love of God sanctifies.' Hugolino could only reply: 'My son, do what is good in your eyes, since God is with you, and you with him' (SL 61).

---

[34] Jordan, c. 14. [35] Bonav. III, 9; 1 Cel. 32–3; 3 Soc. 35, 47–9. [36] SL 61, 92, 95.

There was always a tension between the humility of the disciple and the self-assurance of the holy man. So the question of authority posed a dilemma for Francis. He could describe the true Friar Minor thus: 'It does not seem to me that I am a Friar Minor unless I am in the state which I am going to describe to you. Imagine that the brothers come to me . . . and invite me to the chapter . . . When they are gathered together they ask me to announce to them the word of God, and I rise and preach to them as the Holy Spirit teaches me. At the end of the sermon it is put to them, what do you think of it? And they say against me: "We do not want you to rule over us for you are not eloquent and are too simple and we are too ashamed to have so simple and despicable a superior over us; so from now on do not presume to call yourself our superior!" Thus they cast me out with insults. It does not seem to me that I am a Friar Minor if I do not rejoice' (SL 83). He resigned control of the Order, possibly as early as 1217. At a chapter meeting he announced to all the brothers: 'From now on I am dead to you. But here is brother Peter Catanii, whom let me and all of you obey.'[37] When Peter died, on 10 March 1221, his place was taken by brother Elias. Francis also relinquished control over the day to day ordering of his personal life, asking to be made subject to a guardian of the Minister's choice.[38] But where the principles of his foundation were at issue he was determined to have his own way; he spoke and wrote and acted with the authority of his divine commission. The difficulties this seeming contradiction were to impose on himself and his Order are well illustrated in the short compass of the Testament. 'It is my firm wish that all the brothers work . . . I firmly order all the brothers on obedience . . . I firmly wish to obey the Minister General of this brotherhood and any guardian whom it may please him to give me. And I wish to be as a captive in his hands, that I may neither go nor act without his will and command, because he is my master.' 'A captive in his hands' – a powerful image and sincere, but only possible on one plane. In the conclusion the holy man soon takes over again. 'The brothers are not to say: "This is another Rule": because this is a record, admonition and exhortation, and my testament' – which could mean that Francis intended only to plead and not to bind, but no, his exhortations are to be heeded; he continued: 'The Minister General and all the other ministers and custodians shall be bound by obedience not to add or subtract from these words. And they shall always have this document with them, next to the Rule. And in all the chapter meetings they hold, when they read the Rule they shall read this too. And I absolutely order all my brothers, clerics and laymen, on obedience, that they shall not put glosses on the Rule or on these words' – they are not to be emasculated or explained away, but as they were written clearly and straightforwardly 'so they shall be understood and put into practice'.[39]

Nor did he undertake responsibility only for the guidance of his own Order. His mission was addressed in principle to every individual without distinction, men and women, rich and poor, Christian, Jew, Muslim, pagan. As he could not possibly hope to reach everyone he wrote letters, some of which have survived. One is addressed to all

---

[37] 2 Cel. 143; cf. Brooke 1959, pp. 76–83. For Peter Catanii's death, see ibid. p. 77 n. 2; Von Matt and Hauser 1956, pl. 177: the date in the inscription carved in the stone of the chapel of the Portiuncula reads: 'Anno Domini MCXXI. VI ID. MARTII'.

[38] 2 Cel. 151; cf. Brooke 1959, pp. 83 ff.

[39] Esser 1976, pp. 440–4; Brooke 1975, pp. 117–19 – and cf. ibid. pp. 24–9.

Christians, members of religious Orders, clergy, laity, men, women, to all people living throughout the whole world, from brother Francis, their servant and subject.[40] It begins: 'As I am the servant of all I am bound to serve all and to dispense the fragrant words of my Lord. Bearing in mind that I am not able personally to visit you individually because of my illness and bodily frailty I have decided to send you a letter.' It is an encyclical letter, and the opening words, 'Cum sim servus omnium', are not so unlike the formula used in papal letters: 'servus servorum Dei', servant of the servants of God. In announcing the word of God to all and calling on all to love, praise and serve God, Francis is assuming the role of the professional holy man, and a number of the specific issues he raises in this letter are identical with the ones Peter Brown distinguished as forming an important part of the holy man's contribution to society. Francis tells his readers that we should do good to our neighbours, and not harm them at all. We must be charitable and give alms, which wash away sin, for we only take our deeds with us, to be rewarded. Judges should judge mercifully and indeed all those in authority should do as they would be done by. Those who serve others humbly are the brides, brothers and mothers of Christ. Such language is calculated to arrest the reader; it is an example of how Francis sought to emphasise Jesus' humanity, to remind us that Jesus was and is a member of a family. He passes on to another, favourite topic, that all creatures of sky and earth and sea are bound to praise, glorify, honour and bless God, a theme he most notably popularised by composing the Canticle of brother Sun. There follows a little sermon on the vital importance of penance – a rare glimpse of what Francis' sermons may have been like – a vivid evocation of a deathbed scene, the sick man, the weeping family and friends. Moved by their protestations he makes over to them all his property before the priest arrives, so he is unable to make restitution for fraud and dishonesty and dies unabsolved. His heirs divide his estate, and far from being grateful that he has forfeited forgiveness for their sakes, start to grumble and curse that he did not leave them more.

In conclusion, he urges the recipients of his letter to take its message to heart and put it into practice. And because effective distribution will obviously be a problem he ends with a special blessing to those men and women who make copies of his letter to send to others.

Another letter is addressed to all those in authority – to podestàs, consuls, judges and rulers.[41] He warns them, with all due respect, not to allow the cares and responsibilities of office to cause them to forget God. They should receive the sacrament devoutly themselves, and be mindful that they will also be answerable for the spiritual well-being of their subjects. They should see to it that every evening a signal is sounded in some way to summon the people to praise God. He ends: Those who keep this letter by them and attend to it may be sure they have God's blessing.

Some of his concern may be characterised as wishful thinking. His companions Leo, Rufino and Angelo noted among their reminiscences: 'We who were with St Francis . . . bear witness that many times we have heard him say: "If I speak with the emperor, I will implore him for the love of God and the intervention of my prayer to make a constitution and decree that no man should trap sister larks or do them any harm whatever; likewise

---

[40] Esser 1976, pp. 207–13 (and p. 213 n. 104). [41] Esser 1976, pp. 274–5.

that all podestàs of cities and lords of towns and villages should be bound each year on Christmas Day to compel men to scatter corn and other grain on the roads outside cities and towns for the birds to have something to eat . . . Every man ought also that night to give a good meal to our brothers the oxen and asses. Similarly on Christmas Day all the poor ought to be sated by the rich"' (SL 110).

But we have one splendid example of his effective intervention when things went wrong. About two years before his death, while he was lying very ill in a little cell at San Damiano, a quarrel arose between the bishop and the podestà of Assisi. The podestà issued a proclamation ordering the citizens to boycott the bishop – no one was to sell him anything, buy anything from him or make any contract with him. The bishop retaliated by excommunicating the podestà. As no one seemed to be making any effort to bring about a reconciliation Francis felt it was his responsibility to restore peace and harmony. He added a topical verse to the Canticle of brother Sun, which he had composed during this same illness.

Be praised my Lord
For those who pardon for thy love
And bear infirmity and tribulation.
Blessed are they who uphold peace
For by thee, O most High, they shall be crowned.

'Afterwards he called one of his companions and said to him: "Go and say to the podestà from me that he is to come to the bishops's palace with the leading men of the city and any others he can bring with him." When he had gone he said to two other of his companions: "Go, and in the presence of the bishop and podestà and the others who are with them, sing the Canticle of brother Sun, and I trust in the Lord that he will humble their hearts, and they will make peace with each other . . ." When all were gathered in the square in the bishop's quarter those two friars rose up and one of them said: "The blessed Francis in his illness has composed Praises of the Lord for his creatures, for the praise of God and to edify his neighbour. He asks you to listen to them very devoutly." So they began to sing and recite them. At once the podestà stood up and listened intently even with tears as if to the Gospel of the Lord with his arms and hands joined. For he had great love for and faith in St Francis. When the Praises of the Lord were ended, the podestà said in front of them all: "In truth I say to you that I would not only give way to my lord bishop, whom I ought to acknowledge as my lord, but if anyone were to kill my brother or my son, I would forgive him." He threw himself down at the bishop's feet, saying: "See, I am ready to make satisfaction to you in everything, just as you please, for the love of our Lord Jesus Christ, and his servant blessed Francis." The bishop took him in his hands, raised him, and said to him: "My office requires me to be humble, but as I am by nature quick-tempered, you must make allowances for me." They embraced and kissed each other with much graciousness and affection.' Friars and laity alike were impressed by the way the reconciliation was effected so quickly and without any bargaining or recriminations regarding what had been at issue between them, and attributed it to the merits of St Francis.[42]

[42] SL 44. SL 42–3 give the context and establish the time.

Popular devotion to the living holy man presented him with problems. He had to guard against the adulation going to his head and corrupting him; at the same time he had to fulfil, to their satisfaction and his own, the expectations he aroused. It could be in some ways easier for the saint who was not recognised as such until after his death. Francis often had to explain the reasons for his actions. He managed to cope with some of the hazards of his profession by withdrawing into himself. He cultivated the ability to become so absorbed in prayer that he was unaware of what was going on around him. On one occasion, when he was going to stay at a leper house, he had to pass through Borgo San Sepolcro. He was riding on an ass, so it was probably towards the end of his life, after he had received the stigmata, as the wounds in his feet made it impossible for him to walk far. The people were expecting him, and crowds thronged and jostled him; many pressed to touch him and some even cut or tore off bits of his tunic to keep, but he remained quite oblivious to it all. As they were approaching their destination he suddenly woke up as it were and enquired whether they were near Borgo yet.[43] He was also protected and aided by those around him, who doubled the roles of nurse and receptionist. While he was staying at the hermitage at Fonte Colombo a cattle disease spread to the oxen of a neighbouring village. A man from the village came to his companions and explained to them that he had been told in a dream to obtain water in which Francis' hands and feet had been washed. So at mealtime they poured the water in which Francis washed his hands into a vessel and in the evening they asked him to let them wash his feet, without divulging their ulterior motive. The man sprinkled the water, as if it were holy water, over the oxen and they recovered. This too occurred after Francis' hands and feet were scarred. He tried hard to conceal the stigmata, but rumours clearly circulated.[44]

Francis was well aware of his reputation and the chief effect this had on him was to make him more than ever concerned to live up to it. He was troubled in conscience when keeping the fast of St Martin, which lasted from All Saints' Day till Christmas, one year at a hermitage, which was probably that at Poggio Bustone. The observance of this fast was obligatory, but the friars cooked the food they prepared for Francis in lard, because he was ill and oil violently disagreed with him. At Christmas, when the fast was over and he preached to a crowd nearby, the first words of his sermon were: 'You have come to me with great devotion, and believe me to be a holy man, but I confess to God and to you that in this time of fasting . . . I have eaten food cooked with lard.'[45]

Francis was very much a man of Assisi, *Asisinatus*, born and bred in the city; and he never tore up his roots. Assisi was always the centre, the hub of his activities. He made the little church of St Mary of the Portiuncula, situated down in the plain, near where the railway station now is, the headquarters of his Order.[46] Missions were sent out from Assisi, and regularly at Whitsun, and on a smaller scale at Michaelmas, the friars returned to Assisi to nourish their fellowship, to discuss, to report and to pray together at their Chapter meetings at the Portiuncula. In the early days the only accommodation there was a poor little cottage thatched with straw, its walls made of

---

43 2 Cel. 98.   44 SL 57.
45 SL 40; 2 Cel. 131; cf. *Regula non bullata*, c. III (Esser 1976, p. 380); *Regula bullata*, c. III (ibid., p. 368).
46 SL 35: 'Asisinatus'; for the Portiuncula see esp. SL 8–12.

withies and mud, which the friars had made when they first went to live there. As their numbers increased it was totally inadequate. So one year, as the date when the Chapter was due to be held approached, the people of Assisi held a general meeting and agreed to provide an assembly hall themselves. In a few days they hastily built at the Portiuncula with great devotion a large house of stone with limed walls, while St Francis was away. Now St Francis was particularly anxious that the Portiuncula should be preserved as an abiding monument to the conditions of the early days, as a witness and model of poverty and simplicity. So he was disturbed when he saw the new house and feared it would set a bad example, encouraging the friars to build large houses elsewhere. Before the Chapter ended he climbed up on to the roof and began to throw down the tiles, intending to demolish the building. He was prevented by some knights of Assisi and others representing the city commune who were there to guard the house, because of the crowds who had gathered outside to watch the friars' Chapter. These expostulated: 'Brother, this house belongs to the commune of Assisi, and we are here on behalf of the commune. We tell you that you are not to destroy our house.' Francis replied: 'If the house is yours I have no wish to touch it' and came down. On account of this the citizens of Assisi for a long time decreed each year that their podestà should be responsible for having it roofed and repaired when necessary.[47] Francis had become their holy man. The success of his movement was a source of local pride and satisfaction and they were prepared to put themselves to some expense to promote its welfare.

In Francis himself they came to take a proprietary interest, and as his death approached they took precautions. While he was staying at the friary at Bagnara above the city of Nocera Umbra, some 37 km north-east of Assisi, his feet and legs swelled with the dropsy and he fell seriously ill. When the men of Assisi heard this 'they feared that he might die there and others have his most holy body' and soldiers were quickly sent to escort him home. Once back in Assisi, he was lodged in the bishop's palace but the people were still uneasy. They feared he might die during the night without their knowing and that perhaps the friars might remove the body secretly, so they decreed that each night he should be diligently guarded by men all round the walls of the palace. When Francis had effected the reconciliation between the bishop and the podestà he had not envisaged this particular bit of co-operation. But there was an individual touch to his performance of his role to the last. Often during the day, and also at night, he caused his companions to sing to him the Canticle of brother Sun. Elias disapproved. 'Dearest brother', he said, 'I am greatly consoled and edified by all the gladness you show . . . But the men of this city venerate you in life and death as a saint. As they firmly believe that because of your great and incurable illness you will very shortly die, hearing these Praises sung, they may think or say among themselves: "How can he show so much joy when he is near death? Ought he not to be thinking on death?"' But Francis felt so united and joined to God through the grace of the Holy Spirit that he could rejoice in the midst of his infirmities, confident of his salvation. He added another verse to the Canticle: 'Be praised my Lord for our sister the death of the body, which no man living can escape', for, he said, 'she is welcome, my sister death'.[48]

[47] SL 11; Eccleston, p. 32.   [48] SL 59, 64–5, 100. The final clause is from SL 64.

CHAPTER THREE

THE IMAGE AFTER DEATH

While he was alive Francis made valiant efforts to maintain the consistency of his position, the purity of his ideals, the rigour and uncompromising commitment of his way of life, in the face of changing circumstances affecting both himself and his Order. For himself, increasing recognition and reputation, and increasingly severe ill health, imposed constraints; for his Order, despite some setbacks and mistakes, increasingly rapid expansion both numerically and geographically brought problems of regulation and administration. Francis tried, in his Testament, to bind his successors, but the growth of the institution led inexorably to change and development. He died during the night of 3–4 October 1226. Death immediately transformed and diversified his image in ways which he was powerless to control.

One day while Francis was lying terminally ill at the bishop's palace at Assisi, one of the friars said to him as if joking and teasing: 'For how much will you sell all your sackcloth to the Lord? Many rich brocades and silken cloths will be put on to cover this little body of yours which is now dressed in sackcloth.' Francis replied, with great fervour and gladness: 'You say true, for so it will be' (SL 98). It may well be, Francis' vision was of heaven; the friar's was of earth as well. And the irony of the story is deepened if we reflect that, for all his passionate love of humility and simplicity and poverty, Francis accepted that it was his role to be a model of the Christian life.

THE EARLY OFFICIAL IMAGE IN WRITING

Detailed information about St Francis' last days, his death, and the rites performed in honour of his corpse, are provided in sources very close to the events they describe. Brother Elias' official letter to the Provincial Ministers announcing Francis' death and making public the hitherto unheard of miracle of the stigmata was written within twenty-four hours. Thomas of Celano was commissioned by Pope Gregory IX to write a biography in the summer of 1228 as part of the canonisation process and his *First Life* was approved on 25 February 1229.[1] His account was therefore written only some two years after these events, while they were still fresh in the minds of those he consulted. The *Scripta Leonis*, though not written down until 1246, represents the memories of his close companions, those who were with him in his later years and nursed him in his illnesses, memories kept vivid through constant retelling to pious pilgrims and devoted disciples.[2]

Death offers its own opportunities for dramatic presentation. The devotion of the citizens of Assisi, their jealous concern to possess the relics of their holy man, threatened to spoil this final scene. Francis was determined to set an example to the last. It was not his intention to die in a palace surrounded by guards. It is a measure of the strength of his will that he succeeded in getting his own way. The bishop, still the same Guido who had befriended him when he stripped himself naked at the outset of his religious journey, was away on a pilgrimage to San Michele at Monte Gargano in Apulia but the communal authorities had to be persuaded to relax the security precautions. When death was imminent he was allowed to return to his beloved Portiuncula, in whose tiny church he had heard the Gospel passage which first revealed to him his way of life. The friars carried him down the hill in his bed as he was too grievously ill to travel on horseback. At one point on the way he asked them to stop and to turn the bed round so that he faced the city. Raising himself a little, he blessed Assisi. At the Portiuncula he lingered only a few days.[3] During this time he performed a number of symbolic acts, including another disrobing, harking back to his initial act of ritual dissociation. In the presence of his companions he got out of bed with difficulty, because of his dropsy and other ailments, undressed and sat completely naked on the bare ground, holding his left hand over the scar in his side to prevent them seeing it. One of them, who was his guardian, understood that he wished to dispossess himself even of his clothes. He picked up the tunic and breeches and the little sackcloth cap which Francis wore to cover the wounds made when the doctor cauterised his cheek as a treatment for his eye infection, and told Francis he was only going to lend him these garments and that a condition of the loan was that he had no power to give them away. Satisfied that he had thus established his total poverty, Francis later told his companions that, as soon as he was dead, they were to repeat the performance; they were to undress him, put him on the bare ground and leave him there for as long as it would take a man to walk a mile.[4]

One act of friendship, unexpected and uncharacteristic, brightened these last days. Francis had kept women at bay most of his life. Jesus had mingled freely with the women of Bethany and Magdala and elsewhere; Francis found he could not, except for a short time at the beginning of his religious life, and at the end. Clare joined him in 1212 and all the evidence, including her own testimony, is that she came at Francis' urging and invitation. But it is only too evident that, once she was established among the friars, she wished to lead their way of life, serving the poor and the sick of Assisi and other cities,

---

[1] Elias' letter is in AF x, 525–8 and Lempp 1901, pp. 70–1, see below, note 8; 1 Cel. is in AF x, 1–126; for its date, ibid. p. iv.
[2] SL, ed. R. B. Brooke, OMT (Oxford, 1970; corr. repr. 1990). See ch. 6.
[3] 2 Cel. 220; 1 Cel. 108–9; SL 99; 2 Cel. 214–15. [4] SL 46–8, Appendix c. 3; 2 Cel. 214–15, 217.

and that this threatened scandal.⁵ Within a few years she was enclosed at San Damiano, following a way of life almost indistinguishable from that of a Benedictine nun. And Francis hardly ever saw her in later years. Clare was herself very ill when Francis was dying and was bitterly unhappy because she could not see him; and Francis wrote her a letter of comfort.⁶ He also dictated a letter to another lady, Jacoba of Settesoli, the wealthy widow of Graziano Frangipani, alerting her to his condition and asked for two presents, one cloth the colour of ashes, the other some marzipan. But before the letter could be sent the sounds of horses heralded her arrival from Rome with her son and retinue. Francis with joy ordered 'our brother' to be admitted at once. 'Open the door and bring her in, for in the case of brother Jacoba the rule concerning women is not to be observed.' At her coming he seemed to rally. She had brought everything he wanted, and more. She prepared for him the honey and sugared almond marzipan, which she had made for him many times in earlier days in Rome, and Francis managed to eat a little and was reminded of his first disciple, Bernard of Quintavalle, and invited him to share the treat. Lady Jacoba also brought a quantity of wax and had many candles made, ready to burn before his body after his passing. The friars made the tunic in which he was to be buried from the ashen grey cloth, and Francis instructed them to sew sackcloth on to it in token of humility and poverty.⁷

On the evening of Saturday, 3 October 1226, after Vespers, many larks gathered in the twilight – a time when they are normally at rest – and circled low over the Portiuncula, singing. The friars were unsure whether their song signified their joy or sadness. Francis was especially fond of larks and loved to see them. He said of the lark: 'Sister lark has a hood like a religious and is a humble bird . . . As she flies she praises God, like a good religious despising earthly things, for her life is always in the heavens. Moreover her clothing is made like the earth, her feathers that is, giving an example to religious that they ought not to have coloured and fancy clothing but as if dead, looking like soil.' He would have interpreted the larks' evensong over his deathbed as a sign of God's blessing, just as he understood the dawn chorus two years before at La Verna as a sign that it was God's will he should remain there in prayer. Shortly after darkness fell, he died.⁸

Elias' letter

For all his faults brother Elias had an instinctive sympathy and understanding for the grief of those who loved Francis but could have been at a disadvantage because of their sex. It is said that he placed the dead body into the arms of the weeping Lady Jacoba, saying: 'Here, he whom you loved in life, hold in death.' Through her tears she saw the wounds in hands and feet and side and marvelled at the hitherto unheard

⁵ Brooke and Brooke 1978; Jacques de Vitry in Huygens 1960, pp. 75–6.
⁶ SL 109.   ⁷ SL 101, 107; 3 Cel. 37–8.
⁸ SL 110, 93; 3 Cel. 32. Elias' letter describing Francis' death is strictly contemporary evidence for the date of his death: 'quarto nonas Octobris die Dominica [i.e. 4 October], prima hora noctis praecedentis [3 October], pater et frater noster Franciscus migravit ad Christum' (AF X, 527; Lempp 1901, p. 71). That is, he actually died on the 3rd, but as the religious day could be reckoned to start with Vespers on the preceding evening, his feast day is kept on 4 October.

of miracle and drew comfort from it. 'Her instant advice was that this unprecedentd miracle should not be denied or in any way hidden, but that it would be wiser to reveal it to all, eye to eye.'[9] Brother Elias, whom Francis had appointed Minister General on Peter Catanii's death, wrote to inform the friars throughout the Order. His words are crucial evidence, the strictly contemporary, eyewitness account of a responsible official. The letter addressed to Gregory of Naples, the Provincial Minister of France, and all his friars, has survived. 'I announce to you a great joy and a novelty among miracles. Throughout the ages such a sign has not been heard of, except in the Son of God, who is Christ the Lord. Not long before death our brother and father appeared crucified, bearing in his body the five wounds which are in truth the stigmata of Christ: for his hands and feet had as it were the punctures of nails pierced through on either side, retaining the scars and showing the blackness of nails; his side appeared to have been lanced and often oozed blood.'[10]

Francis had hidden the stigmata as carefully as he could while he was alive. He kept his hands withdrawn into his sleeves; he covered his feet with woollen socks. When washing, he dipped his fingers in water rather than the whole of his hands, and only rarely and secretly washed his feet. When one of his companions happened to catch sight of the marks in his feet and asked: 'What's that?' Francis told him to mind his own business. But it was inevitable that his close companions, who nursed him, should become aware, and one of them, Rufino, touched the wound in his side once when he was rubbing him. Brother Elias was the only person credited with having seen the side wound while Francis was alive.[11] But after he was dead his body was washed in preparation for burial and the wounds were revealed. It was not felt appropriate to conceal them now. On the contrary, publication of the wonder helped to comfort the friars in their grief. Through the night that he died and during the next day the wounds were displayed for veneration. The friars who had gathered around the deathbed of their founder viewed them, Lady Jacoba and her son John also, and as the news spread, crowds converged from Assisi and the surrounding countryside and villages. The fact that so many people were able to see the stigmata for themselves corroborates the evidence of Elias' letter. Furthermore, because the appearance of stigmata was unprecedented, many doubted its existence. Medieval people were not so credulous as is sometimes thought. Some, like the apostle Thomas, would not believe unless they saw and touched. Some of these were later prepared to testify both to their doubts and to their personal verification of the fact. Celano recorded in his *Treatise* on Francis' miracles, written at the instigation of John of Parma while he was Minister General and probably between 1250 and 1252, that John Frangipani, Lady Jacoba's son, who grew up to become a proconsul of the Romans and a count of the papal palace, freely swore to what he

---

[9] *3 Cel.* 39, where Elias is called 'vicar' of St Francis: see Brooke 1959, pp. 106–22.

[10] AF x, 525–8; Lempp 1901, pp. 70–1; cf. Jordan, c. 50. Frugoni 1993, esp. chs. II–IV, attempts to show that Elias and the friars invented the stigmata. The Franciscans believed the miracle unheard of. Vauchez (1968, pp. 598–9) showed that all the surviving evidence of other cases in the early thirteenth century suggests that they were probably either spurious or self-inflicted. This evidence bears witness to the way in which growing devotion to the human Jesus could lead to a desire for such wounds; but the hierarchy was doubtful of their genuineness and orthodoxy.

[11] *1 Cel.* 95; *2 Cel.* 135–9; but see p. 143. Rufino as well as Leo was with St Francis at La Verna when he received the stigmata (Eccleston, p. 75).

had seen with his eyes and touched with his hands on that occasion, confessing all his doubts.[12] Bonaventure noted that a number of citizens of Assisi were admitted to contemplate and to kiss the stigmata and that among them was a knight named Jerome, who was educated and prudent, and a man of high reputation. He was sceptical of what he saw, and, in the presence of the friars and other citizens, he boldly used his hands to move the excrescences resembling nails in Francis' hands and feet and to feel the side wound. Physical contact convinced him of the truth of the stigmata, and the sight of his enquiring fingers probing the flesh dispelled the doubts of other onlookers.[13]

So the stigmata were seen and kissed and handled in the hours immediately after his death, and access to them was not restricted to members of the Order. None the less the opportunity for personal verification was necessarily limited to those who were actually in or near Assisi at the crucial time. Those who were able to avail themselves of that opportunity were in effect a privileged few. In other regions of Italy, and beyond, and as time passed, many did doubt, and doubt was not confined to outsiders but was shared by some members of the Order. In an attempt to counter this, the Minister General John of Parma, during a full session of the General Chapter held at Genoa, probably in 1251, called upon brother Bonizo, who had been one of Francis' companions, 'to tell the friars the truth about his stigmata, because many throughout the world were in doubt about this'. He replied with tears: 'These sinful eyes saw them, and these sinful hands touched them.'[14]

It has been necessary to discuss the evidence for the stigmata at length because they played such an essential part in determining the way Francis' image was to be projected from their discovery and publication onwards.

More and more people gathered into the friars' small enclosure at the Portiuncula as the night advanced, with mourning balanced by a great sense of occasion. The friars solemnly sang God's praises and the whole place was ablaze with candles.

The music and the bright lights created an atmosphere of exultation; it seemed to be a wake of angels.[15] When morning dawned the whole of Assisi turned out, clergy and people. The body was placed in a coffin and borne in procession back to the city with great honour: branches of olive and other trees were carried, hymns and praises sung, and trumpets sounded. For the second time in those few fraught hours brother Elias was mindful of one in particular of Francis' grieving friends. The cortège was stopped at San Damiano. The coffin was carried into the church. The little window through which the Poor Ladies received communion was opened. The coffin too was opened, and Clare and her community were able to gaze on Francis for the last time and to kiss his stigmatised hands. Then the procession resumed its way up the hill.

The coffin was lodged for the time being in the church of San Giorgio. This church was closely associated with Francis' early life and ministry. As a small boy he had learnt

[12] *3 Cel.* 39. Celano does not refer to John Frangipani as dead; but his two children, who outlived him, were dead by 9 January 1254, when Innocent IV refers to his widow and to the fact that his two young children Peter and Philippa had not long outlived their father. See AF x, pp. xxxvi–xxxix.
[13] Bonav. xv, 4. Jerome was subsequently prepared to swear on the Gospels to the truth of the stigmata.
[14] Eccleston, p. 74. For the date of the chapter at Genoa, cf. Brooke 1959, p. 257 and n. 2. For early discussions on the authenticity of the stigmata, see pp. 166–8 and note 13, 299.
[15] *1 Cel.* 116 – and 116–17 for what follows.

his lessons there, and it was there that he preached his first sermon. It was in the piazza of San Giorgio that Bernard of Quintavalle, Francis' first permanent disciple, distributed all his possessions to the poor, and it was to San Giorgio, on St George's day, 23 April 1209, that brother Giles came seeking Francis, as he wanted to be with him for the love of God.[16] We do not know the exact position of this church, as in the 1260s the site of which it formed part was redeveloped to become the church and monastery of Santa Chiara. Jordan of Giano says that Francis wished to be buried at the Portiuncula, but that the people of the district and the citizens of Assisi feared the Perugians might seize his body by force, and so they carried him to San Giorgio 'near the walls of Assisi'. This could mean that the church was just outside the city walls, but more likely it was situated just inside. Excavations of the ancient walls have so far proved inconclusive. When the whole complex of Santa Chiara was built, the enclosed area was enlarged and a new stretch of wall constructed.[17]

The papal bull of canonisation

On 19 March 1227 Francis' friend and patron Cardinal Hugolino was elected pope, taking the name of Gregory IX. A year later he was driven from Rome by the partisans of the emperor, Frederick II, on whom, as a result of problems inherent in imperial–papal relations, he considered himself obliged to exert pressure. The Curia travelled northwards through the Papal States, stopping at Rieti, and Spoleto, and then at Assisi. During his stay there, from 26 May to 10 June 1228, the pope visited Francis' tomb and held several discussions with the cardinals concerning his canonisation.[18] Information about the many miracles that were being performed by the dead founder was collected, checked and approved.

The process by which a holy man was enrolled among the saints officially venerated by the Church had been redefined and reformulated in the early thirteenth century by Innocent III. Whereas it had been customary in Western Christendom for local bishops to give recognition to popular 'canonisations' having local effect at particular churches or shrines, in the course of the twelfth century episcopal prerogatives in this regard as in others came increasingly to be assumed by the popes. When Thomas Becket was murdered in Canterbury Cathedral in 1170 his supporters applied to Rome. Alexander III canonised him in March 1173, with the approval of the cardinals, and made his cult universal. Innocent III's bull of canonisation for Gilbert of Sempringham, dated 30 January 1202, marked the logical culmination of the trend and laid down the canonical models that were subsequently followed.[19] Before he would proceed to canonise Gilbert, Innocent had insisted on two elaborate inquiries: the first embassy

---

[16] Bonav. XV, 5; cf. 1 Cel. 23; Jordan, c. 50; *The Life of Brother Giles* in SL 318–21.

[17] Gatti 1983, pp. 20–35. Sites adjacent to or overlapping city walls were characteristic of Franciscan convents (and those of other Orders of friars) in many parts of Europe: they helped municipal or other authorities to keep the walls clear of satellite housing and obstructions. See C. Brooke 1985, p. 61; Stüdeli 1969.

[18] Potthast, I, 706–7; 1 Cel. 122–3.

[19] Foreville and Keir 1987, pp. xc–cviii and *passim*; and for the development of canonisation, see esp. Vauchez 1997.

from England with written testimony and witnesses was deemed insufficient. Further detailed investigations had to be made of witnesses in England – searching inquiry, for instance, was made on oath whether individuals who it was claimed could now see had really been blind before; more written testimony, more witnesses were summoned to the papal Curia. To this the proceedings for Francis' canonisation seem to have formed a marked contrast, for the facts in his case were well known in the Curia; Pope Gregory IX had been his friend for many years. In the course of the pope's visit to Assisi in the summer of 1228, 'the friars asked Pope Gregory and the cardinals at Assisi to canonise St Francis' (SL 30); but we have very few details of the evidence that was produced. We know that there was a written list of miracles, for it was read out in the final ceremony; we know that the pope himself and others gave testimony. The *Scripta Leonis* contains a story of a nobly born friar who thought to himself when Francis, 'weak and ill', was riding on a donkey and he was walking, 'His parents were not the equal of mine, and now, see! – he rides, and I go behind him urging the beast on, and worn out!' With prophetic insight Francis read his thoughts and got down from the ass, saying 'Brother, it is not right or suitable that I ride and you go on foot, as you were more noble and powerful than I in the world' – which produced tears of repentance from the friar, who reported the incident to pope and cardinals when they were discussing Francis' canonisation.[20] Clearly discussion took place, but we have no evidence of long and detailed depositions like those on the miracles of Gilbert or – a few years after Francis' canonisation – on the life and miracles of St Dominic.

Other urgent business caused Gregory IX to transfer to Perugia for a month but he returned to Assisi in the middle of July. The canonisation ceremony was performed on 16 July, the ninth Sunday after Pentecost. Thomas of Celano has given us such a vivid and detailed account of the whole proceedings that it is probable he was himself present on the occasion.[21] The pope, attended by cardinals, bishops, abbots and lay magnates, of whom the most distinguished was John of Brienne, who had joined the papal forces after being ousted as king of Jerusalem by Frederick II, was escorted into the city with great pomp. A special place had been prepared, it would seem in the Piazza San Giorgio as, at the close of the ceremony, Gregory IX descended from his high throne and entered the sanctuary by the lower steps to offer vows and oblations, to kiss the new saint's tomb and to celebrate mass. A great crowd had gathered, clergy, monks and friars, nuns also and laymen and women. The weather was beautifully fine. Everyone wore their holiday best and green branches of olive and other trees decked the scene. The pope was resplendent in pontifical robes laden with jewels. Around him the cardinals and bishops wore jewelled collars and snow-white vestments. First of all, the pope preached, taking his text from Ecclesiasticus: 'like the morning star among the clouds, like the moon at the full, like the sun shining on the Temple of the Most High'. Next, Octavian Ubaldini de Mugello, one of his subdeacons, read out the dossier of miracles 'at the top of his voice'. Then a cardinal deacon, Rainerio Capocci

---

[20] SL 30.
[21] see 1 *Cel.* 123–6 and notes (AF X, 98–103), and for what follows; for the date AF X, 103 and n. 8. The pope's text was Eccles 50. 6–7. For Octavian and Rainerio, 1 *Cel.* 125, AF X, 100–1 and n. 13. For Rainerio see also Jordan, c. 16.

de Viterbo, a Cistercian who had shown his keen interest in Francis and his movement by attending the General Chapter of 1221, discoursed on the miracles. As he spoke, he wept. The pope burst into floods of tears; the prelates followed suit, such expressions of feeling in public being regarded as natural and acceptable. The splendid vestments became wet with tears. Finally the people were likewise moved to tears, and as a result of the long drawn out excitement grew mightily tired. In Celano's words, 'vehementius fatigatur', we may perhaps detect a feeling comment on his own reactions at this stage. Raising his hands to heaven, the pope proclaimed: 'to the praise and glory of Almighty God, Father, Son and Holy Spirit, the glorious Virgin Mary, the blessed apostles Peter and Paul, and to the honour of the glorious Roman Church, we pronounce, having taken counsel with the cardinals and other prelates, that blessed Francis, whom God has glorified in heaven, shall be venerated on earth and enrolled in the catalogue of the saints and that his feast shall be celebrated on the day of his death'. The *Te Deum* was sung, led by the pope and cardinals. Organs played and everyone joined in hymn singing, including some new hymns specially composed in Francis' honour.[22]

The papal bull, *Mira circa nos*, in which the canonisation was announced to the archbishops, bishops, abbots and lesser clergy throughout the Church, reflects the formal requirements of the canonisation process as established by Innocent III and continued by his successors Honorius III and Gregory IX. It publicises a papal decision, taken with the advice and consent of the cardinals. It quotes the text of Gregory's sermon on the actual occasion, and may indeed reflect the gist of that sermon, which Celano described as a 'most noble eulogy'. The bull is a rhetorical document, an impressive example of the educated style of the time, packed with a wide-ranging assortment of mixed biblical metaphors and allusions. The flavour of it is as follows. Behold, it begins, at the eleventh hour, the Lord, who when the flood waters destroyed the earth steered the just man by means of a contemptible wooden plank (a reference to Noah and the ark), has raised up his servant Francis, a man after his own heart, sending him into his vineyard. Francis tirelessly broke the chains of the alluring world, like another Samson, snatching up the jawbone of an ass, which signifies preaching. For he did not use the persuasive words of human wisdom adorned with rhetorical colours – in marked contrast to Gregory's own effusion – but strengthened with the power of God, who chooses the weak of the world to confound the strong, he touched the mountains and they smoked, and brought back into the spirit of service not just a thousand but many thousands of Philistines. Like Jacob he ascended the ladder by the fifteen steps of virtue which are mystically contained in the psalms. But lest he alone should make progress on the mountain by embracing Rachel, who signifies contemplation, beautiful but barren, he descended to the forbidden bed of Leah, driving the flock, fertile with twins in the womb into the inner desert to seek diligently for the pastures of life and sowing his seed with tears, so that set apart from the clamour of the world he might joyfully bear the sheaves to the eternal granaries. To us, such language evokes disconcerting images. The recipients of the bull, hopefully, were trained to understand that Gregory was informing them that Francis divided his time between the active and

[22] For antiphons and hymns attributed to Gregory IX and some of the cardinals, see AF x, 375–88.

contemplative life and converted many to enter religion and to follow Christ. A few, a very few, facts about Francis' life can be discerned lurking in biblical guise. He left his father's house, like Abraham. He renounced his worldly possessions, so that he might more easily enter by the narrow way, conforming himself to Christ, who when he was rich made himself poor for us. It is the fact of Francis' sanctity that is important and that is extolled. His qualifications can be summed up in a concise statement at the end. The distinguishing marks of his life are well known to Gregory, as while he was a cardinal he was personally acquainted with him, and his miracles have been vouched for by reliable witnesses.[23]

Thomas of Celano's First Life of St Francis

The bull of canonisation was followed by a further bull, *Sicut phialae aureae*, urging all the archbishops, bishops, abbots, priors, archdeacons and so forth to encourage their people to venerate St Francis.[24] But as yet they were provided with little subject matter for their sermons on his feast day, though they might perhaps be able to elicit some supplementary information from Friars Minor in their districts. But the situation was about to be remedied. Only four days later, on 25 February, according to one manuscript, Gregory IX received and approved the *First Life of St Francis*.[25] He had ordered brother Thomas of Celano to write this, most probably while he was staying in Assisi, 26 May to 10 June 1228, and holding discussions with the cardinals concerning Francis' canonisation.[26] The more usual practice was for a *Life* to be written before canonisation, for use as evidence, but in this case the pope knew the candidate well. 'Yet, though not a working brief, the *Life* was written with a definite purpose, and this determined its tone, scope, and who was chosen to write it. It catered for readers whose interests and expectations were different from ours and answers to questions we might like to ask may not be given simply because they were not considered relevant. Francis' acts were thought worthy to be recorded to the praise and glory of Almighty God, and those who read about them and him might hope to be edified and moved to thanksgiving. He had a circle of close friends who knew him intimately and loved him, but it was not one of them the pope asked to write the official life.'[27]

Not much is known about Thomas. He was Italian. Celano is a town in the Abruzzi, in the diocese of Marsica.[28] It was not considered good form to include details about oneself in a work of hagiography, unless they were relevant. He implies that he was among the group of noblemen and educated men who joined the Order at the Portiuncula

---

[23] Sbaralea, I, 42–4, G9 no. 25; Eubel 1908, p. 8 n. 48; Potthast 8242.

[24] Sbaralea, I, 49, G9 no. 34; Eubel 1908, p. 8 n. 47. It is dated 7 id. Iulii in Gregory IX's Register (thus Sbaralea, Eubel, Auvray 1896, col. 120, no. 204), which would be earlier than the canonisation itself. Eubel (ibid. n. 2) suggested that it might be that the date of the canonisation in 1 *Cel.* 126 was mistaken; but his alternative, 7 July, is impossible: Gregory was at Perugia that day. *Sicut phialae* was registered among bulls of July 1228: it seems probable that 'Iulii' was written in error for 'Augusti', and that it should be dated 7 August 1228. Sbaralea printed it from an original at Assisi, now lost, which was dated 21 February 1229: thus it seems likely that it was reissued a few months after its first promulgation in August 1228.

[25] See AF X, p. iv; 1 *Cel.* 115 n., AF X, 115.   [26] Cf. 1 *Cel.* Prologue, 123 and nn.

[27] Brooke 1967, p. 182.   [28] AF X, p. iii and n.

shortly after Francis was compelled by illness to abandon a missionary journey. This would have been c.1215. He notes with evident satisfaction that Francis treated these particular recruits honourably and worthily, 'giving to each his due'.[29] At the General Chapter that Francis held at the Portiuncula at Whitsun 1221, Thomas was among about ninety friars who volunteered to take part in a mission to Germany, which was considered dangerous. He is named among the twelve clerics who, along with fifteen laymen, were selected by the Provincial Minister, Caesar of Speyer, to accompany him. In 1223 Caesar made him custodian of Mainz, Worms, Cologne and Speyer – the only custodian he appointed – and later in the same year, when Caesar returned to Italy 'because he yearned to see St Francis and the brothers in the valley of Spoleto', he entrusted the administration of the province to Thomas, leaving him as his vicar. On 8 September a new Provincial Minister held a Chapter at Speyer at which Germany was divided into four custodies, which were put into the charge of other men. Thomas seems to have been relieved of his responsibilities and may have returned to Italy before the end of the year.[30]

Thomas of Celano, then, was in Francis' company occasionally, but he did not know him well.[31] His qualifications were those of a writer. His style and his presentation of his material were inspired by the literary models that were the normal equipment of learned men of his generation. His knowledge of the Bible was extensive and he quotes from it on every page. He makes frequent use of the two standard models, Gregory the Great's *Dialogues* and the *Life of St Martin* by Sulpicius Severus, and of the more recent *First Life of St Bernard*.[32] In citing these authorities Celano was following a normal convention, but his reliance on them inevitably raises doubts as to his accuracy and reliability. He did not incorporate stories about other saints that took his fancy and attach them heedlessly to his hero, as was often done, but this does not settle the issue. Any biographer must select. Were his criteria governed by a desire to portray Francis' essential characteristics or did literary authorities dominate his selection? His description of Francis' physical appearance may be taken as an illustration of this problem. Celano had actually seen St Francis and could describe him from personal knowledge and observation. A pen portrait from him could be illuminating and the inclusion of a pen portrait of any sort in a medieval saint's life can by no means be taken for granted; all too often any attempt at personal description was omitted as irrelevant. But when we examine Celano's attempt it is clear that he shared the difficulty, noted by Southern, that medieval hagiographers apparently had in achieving a physical description without a model.[33] He has used a model: the *First Life* of St Bernard. But is his description therefore invalid? In secular biography the descriptions of Suetonius and Sidonius Apollinaris were used as models, and when Einhard described Charlemagne's appearance he used Suetonius' framework and borrowed all he could, but altered and adapted where his model was inapplicable, so that the finished product, though mostly couched in borrowed language, was yet a vivid and revealing portrait of Charles and not a literary reconstruction of a composite

---

[29] 1 Cel. 56–7.   [30] Jordan, cc. 16–19, 30–1, 33; and see pp. 49–50.
[31] These next three paragraphs resume and adapt Brooke 1967, pp. 182–3.   [32] AF x, p. ix.
[33] Southern 1963, pp. 326–7. The earliest painting of Francis is a fresco at Subiaco, dated 1228–9, but it does not purport to be a portrait drawn from the life. See pp. 162–3.

Caesar.[34] It would seem that Celano has done likewise. He adapted the detail from St Bernard's *Life* to fit St Francis and added further details so that what he says is probably true as far as it goes. This is not to deny that he might have given us a more lifelike impression had he trusted his own inspiration. The display of erudition, though it probably did not result in actual falsification, could impede and inhibit revelation of the truth.

This conventional approach makes it all the more important to ascertain and assess what other sources he used. He assures us in his preface of the high value he attaches to historical accuracy and that he has therefore supplemented his own knowledge with information gained from 'faithful and approved witnesses'; but such statements were common form in prefaces and need to be checked. The book was completed within nine months of being commissioned. It is unlikely that he could have spared much time for collecting material. A few informants could be quickly consulted, and he had access to some who could tell him so much and were of such standing that it would have been unnecessary for him to prolong his inquiries.[35] The pope himself talked of St Francis and of his own relations with him when he commissioned Celano to write, and his testimony which can be discerned in several passages is at one point specifically acknowledged.[36] The bishop of Assisi is likely to have been another. Bishop Guido had played a significant role from the start. It was he who had sat in judgement when Francis had been arraigned before the ecclesiastical court by his father, and he had befriended him then, covering his naked body with his cloak, and on many occasions later, most notably in Rome when Francis sought confirmation of his Rule from Innocent III. Celano describes the negotiations, including Francis' interview with John of St Paul, cardinal bishop of Sabina, in some detail; and it was Bishop Guido who introduced Francis to the cardinal and who was probably the source of this material.[37] Brother Elias, to whom Francis had entrusted administrative control of the Order during the last five years of his life, was at Assisi, and eager to put at Celano's disposal all that he knew about the close friend he was actively engaged in glorifying. Elias' reputation was tarnished later, but his subsequent disgrace and notoriety do not alter the fact that St Francis loved and trusted him. As a witness to the saint's life and character the only criticism that could be levelled against Elias would be that he was partial, that he admired him so much that he would be unable to say anything to his discredit.[38] And that indeed could be said of all Celano's informants, the pope included. A number of Francis' first disciples were still alive. Celano names a few – Bernard, Giles, Philip – and from them, and from others not named, he could have derived his account of the years before he himself joined the Order.[39] A handful of anecdotes can be attributed to other individuals. For example, two incidents illustrating Francis' concern for lambs Celano learnt from a brother Paul, whom Francis had appointed Minister in the March of Ancona.[40] Towards the end of his life Francis had gathered round him a small group of

---

[34] Cf. Townend 1967, pp. 101–4.
[35] Moorman 1940, pp. 67–8, favoured a later date, allowing more time for the collection and arrangement of material. This seems unnecessary and improbable, as has been argued by Bihl 1946–8, pp. 21–3.
[36] 1 *Cel.* 101; cf. also cc. 73–4, 99–101, 121–6.   [37] 1 *Cel.* 15, 32–3; 3 *Soc.* 47 ff.; cf. Robson 1997, ch. 2.
[38] Brooke 1959, esp. pp. 97–105.   [39] 1 *Cel.* 24–5, 30.   [40] 1 *Cel.* 77–9; cf. also cc. 48–50.

companions who tended him in his sickness and were in continual close contact with him. They formed the habit of authenticating their reminiscences with the hall-mark 'we who were with him'. Celano renders this 'those brothers who dwelt with him', and he gathered much information from them, particularly for his account of Francis' last two years.[41] These few faithful and approved witnesses could have provided the bulk if not the whole of what Celano needed to discover orally.

He also used a few written sources which the Order already possessed or had access to. His account of Francis' death is partly based on Elias' letter, written immediately after that event, and the final section on his miracles is condensed from the actual list of miracles read out by Octavian, one of the pope's subdeacons, at the ceremony of canonisation. The papal bull *Mira circa nos* assisted his own recollections of that ceremony.[42] Finally, he recognised and used what was after all the most important source: the saint's own writings. The references to and quotations from the two redactions of the Rule, the *Regula prima* and the *Regula bullata*, Francis' letters, admonitions, prayers and praises, and his Testament occur even more frequently than do literary sources.[43] Celano used the Testament just before it became a controversial document. A little over a year later, on 28 September 1230, Gregory IX was to decide, in the bull *Quo elongati*, that it was not legally binding on the friars;[44] but it provided Celano with a framework and a touchstone he welcomed. It was largely autobiographical and it emphasised what Francis himself considered most vital and significant in his experience. His use of the Testament and his quotations from the Rule, letters and admonitions enable us to affirm that Celano faithfully recorded the saint's own priorities, and the sense and intention of his teaching.

This is important. Sabatier accused Celano of distorting his account of Francis in the interests of the papacy; and it has been widely held that the hierarchy was intent on manipulating Francis' inspiration and using his Order for its own ends – and that Celano was its tool.[45] It is true that Celano wrote at the pope's command, and spoke positively of Gregory IX's role as Cardinal Protector and of Francis' devotion and obedience to the Church, to the pope and to the hierarchy from bishops to humble parish priests. He would have spoken falsely if he had done otherwise, for Francis' own writings testify abundantly to all of this. Celano spoke in glowing terms of the bishop of Assisi, and it would indeed have been impolitic to criticise him as he was still in office, but the praise was in fact deserved. Francis and the early friars were indebted to Bishop Guido for much friendly interest, good advice and practical help. Celano has been accused too of bias in favour of brother Elias. If this were true, it would reflect on his reliability in general. I have demonstrated elsewhere that the charge is unfounded.[46] Elias' conduct while he was Minister General, 1232–9, his deposition and excommunication, ruined his reputation. The friars were ashamed of him, and shame and indignation combined to distort the record of the part he had played. But when the *Vita Prima* was written in

[41] 1 *Cel.* 88–118, esp. 115: 'qui cum illo conversati sunt fratres'. For 'nos qui cum eo fuimus' see ch. 6; SL Index, p. 352 s.v. Companions; Manselli 1980.
[42] See pp. 38–9.   [43] For all these see Esser 1976.
[44] Sbaralea, I, 68–70, G9 no. 56; Eubel 1908, no. IV.   [45] Sabatier 1893–4, esp. pp. liv–lv.
[46] Brooke 1959, pp. 8–20, refuting in particular Lempp 1901.

1228–9 all this was in the future. Its early date enhances its value as evidence on two distinct counts. Celano could and did consult many people who had known St Francis well, and who, moreover, were representative of a wide range of viewpoints, so that the account is balanced. It was written before Elias disgraced himself, before the status of the Testament was called in question, before serious rifts developed between those who wanted to adapt to changing conditions and to promote efficiency and those who clung to the past and wanted to retain unaltered the uncompromising standards of the early days. The *Vita Prima* presented an official image but not a polemical one.

The book is divided into three unequal parts. Part 1 opens with a diatribe on the way children are brought up, to underline the contrast brought about by Francis' conversion, when he was approaching twenty-five, from a spoilt, rich young man to a saint in the making. Key moments in this process are interpreted as stages of a spiritual education, so that Francis' personal journey is set in the wider context of Christian experience. The work has jarred on some readers because of the polished, rhetorical Latin in which it is written. When he first mentions St Clare, Celano cannot resist a word-play on her name, which means bright – bright in name, brighter in life, brightest in conduct.[47] But he can succeed in conveying a sense of immediacy which reflects the quality of his information. He gives a vivid account of the day the twelve set out on their return journey from Rome, so excited and uplifted by their experiences that they talked together ceaselessly about what the pope had said to them, how graciously he had received them, how they should fulfil his instructions and observe the Rule they had undertaken, how they might benefit their neighbours; and that they were so absorbed in these discussions that it was evening before they noticed how tired and hungry they were and that they were in a remote place with nowhere in sight where they might seek food and shelter.[48]

Celano stated in the Prologue that he intended to follow the historical order, and his account of the early years is narrative in form. He gives a lyrical description of the bearing of the first friars, these obedient knights as he calls them, emphasising their total obedience, their poverty, their humble service, and also the joy they experienced and the mutual affection that grew out of their shared privations.[49] But having launched the Order, by describing the initial gathering of disciples, the writing of the first Rule, the visit to the pope, the return to the neighbourhood of Assisi, and Francis' decision, inspired by words in the Rule, to call them the Friars Minor, Celano tells us little about its further development. The contrast with Jordan of Saxony's account of Francis' contemporary, Dominic, is very striking. Jordan's *Libellus* is in form a life of the saint, in content a history of the foundation of his Order of Friars Preachers.[50] Celano was concerned, first and foremost, with the personality and attributes of Francis. Events in the world at large hardly feature at all; and those that do, only as they impinge on

---

[47] *1 Cel.* 18. On Celano's style, see also Brooke 1967, p. 186. Celano has been credited with authorship of the great Requiem Hymn, the *Dies irae*, which if correct would reveal him as a poet of exceptional spiritual insight and depth. See J. Szövérffy in *New Catholic Encyclopaedia*, iv, 863–4, with bibliography. It is usually held that the earliest MS is late twelfth century, and so too early for Celano. But some have doubted this: see Savage 1957, p. 443 n. 3.

[48] *1 Cel.* 34, echoing Luke 24. 17; Matt. 14. 15.   [49] *1 Cel.* 38ff.

[50] Ed. Scheeben 1935: on it see C. Brooke 1971, ch. 11; cf. Brooke 1967, p. 185.

him – the ostentatious cavalcade of the Emperor Otto IV on his way to Rome for his coronation, because he ignored it; and the Fifth Crusade, because he tried, between the battles, to convert the Sultan peacefully by preaching.[51] Only occasional incidents can be dated, and these not precisely, since Celano took as his point of reference St Francis' conversion, which was not a sudden, shattering, single call such as St Paul experienced on the road to Damascus, but a process with more than one significant stage. So he tells us that in the sixth year of his conversion Francis embarked for Syria, intending to preach the Christian faith and penance to the Saracens, but was prevented by contrary winds. Not long afterwards he set out again on a similar enterprise, heading for Morocco. For at this stage in his career Francis was motivated by an ardent desire for martyrdom, and succeeded in instilling a like desire in some of his followers. But he had got no further than Spain when he was overtaken by a prolonged illness and was obliged to abandon his mission and retrace his steps.[52] Not long after Francis returned to the Portiuncula it seems that Celano joined him.[53] But here, just when he could begin to fill out the account from his own experience, Celano abandons his hitherto basically chronological narrative. Instead, he continues the theme of Francis' attempts to preach to the infidel, and jumps straightaway to the thirteenth year of his conversion, when Francis finally succeeded, reaching the Sultan and preaching to him and his court, which can be dated to 1219, as it happened during the Fifth Crusade.[54]

Meanwhile, Celano then tells us (that is, between his joining the Order c.1215 and 1219), Francis, in the course of a journey along the valley of Spoleto, noticed, near Bevagna, that large flocks of birds had congregated. He approached them and greeted them in his usual way: 'The Lord give you peace.' As they did not fly away he preached to them. Celano quotes some of his words and adds that Francis himself used to say, and those who were with him, that the birds responded by lifting their necks, stretching their wings, opening their beaks and gazing at him.[55] This, then, is one of the stories Celano had from Francis' own mouth. It was to capture the imagination of contemporaries and succeeding generations and become the story most intimately associated with the saint.

The incident evidently impressed Francis, and he made use of it as a teaching aid. Although it has sometimes been sentimentalised, it does represent a genuine aspect of Francis' mission, and proved a formative influence. From then on he took care to urge all birds, animals, reptiles and even inanimate objects – flowers, cornfields, vineyards, stones and forests and mountains – to praise and love their Creator.[56] A causal inspiration links his preaching to the birds and his Canticle of brother Sun.

---

[51] For Otto IV, 1 Cel. 43 and nn. 4–5: Celano states that Otto IV passed by on the road close to Rivotorto on his way to his imperial coronation, which took place in Rome on 4 October 1209; but his itinerary suggests it was actually on his return in late 1209 or early 1210, when he visited Assisi. For the Fifth Crusade, 1 Cel. 57; cf. Jordan, c. 10.

[52] 1 Cel. 55–6. The abortive journey to Syria was probably in the second half of 1212 and to Morocco probably in 1213; the voyage to Egypt in 1219. For Brother Giles' reflections on martyrdom with their perhaps implied criticism of Francis, see *Life of Brother Giles* in SL, pp. 346–7.

[53] See pp. 39–40.   [54] 1 Cel. 57.

[55] 1 Cel. 58; for the greeting cf. Francis' Testament (Esser 1976, p. 440); and for stories received from Francis' own mouth, 1 Cel. Prologue.

[56] Cf. 1 Cel. 81.

He befriended creatures. He put fish that had been caught and offered to him for supper back into the water, telling them to be more careful.[57] The fish is a Christian symbol, and anything that he could specifically associate with Christ – and he could think of a great many such – he especially reverenced, lambs in particular, and the poor, because Christ made himself poor for our sakes.[58] This cast of thought and behaviour leads Celano to introduce another strand of potent imagery. He suggests that Francis strove so intensely and successfully to follow the Gospel and to model his life on that of Christ that incidents of Christ's life on earth found echoes and repetitions in his. A subtle transition is made from the response of a wild creature to kindness – the tameness of a hare or rabbit released from a trap, for example – not actually very remarkable, to a claim for a general obedience of Creation to him that strains credulity. Water was turned into wine for him when he was seriously ill at a hermitage. When he entered any city clergy and people rejoiced, children clapped their hands; and often, taking branches in their hands, people went out to meet him, singing.[59] He is being groomed for a role not claimed for any saint before, that of another Christ.

Celano tells us that the very name of God so moved him that he treated the written word with reverence, and that 'a certain brother' once asked him why he diligently picked up every scrap of paper, since some of them contained no reference to God. Francis replied: 'Son, because the letters are there from which the most glorious name of the Lord could be constructed. Everything worthwhile they contain relates not to their pagan or other authors but to God alone, to whom all that is good belongs' (1 Cel. 82). Maybe it was Celano himself who asked him this. Francis carried his respect for every letter written down so far that if a mistake, in grammar or spelling, was made in any letter he was sending he would not allow it to be crossed out. The truth of Celano's testimony on this point is nicely illustrated in a letter Francis wrote to brother Leo with his own hand, which begins: 'f leo f francissco tuo salutem et pacem'. He has spelt his own name with an additional 's' and the greeting should begin: 'f leoni f franciscus tuus'.[60]

Celano then offers a description of Francis' qualities and personal appearance, and returns to the saint's chief desire – to observe the holy Gospel in all things – and to the events in Christ's life which chiefly occupied his meditations, the passion and the incarnation. This brings him to describe the manner in which Francis decided to celebrate Christmas at Greccio, in the third year before he died. This would make it the Christmas of 1223. Celano could have returned to Italy, from Germany, in the autumn of 1223, and his lengthy, detailed, vivid account of this celebration, which occurs nowhere else in the early literature, reads like the testimony of an eyewitness. Celano was good at creating word pictures, and the scene inspired him. Francis had alerted a local nobleman, called John, to make the necessary preparations a fortnight in advance, and on the night of Christmas Eve the manger had been made ready, the hay brought, the ox and ass led in, and Greccio represented a new Bethlehem. The people of the neighbourhood came with lighted candles and torches. The night was as light

[57] 1 Cel. 61.   [58] 1 Cel. 76–80.   [59] 1 Cel. 59–62.
[60] 1 Cel. 82 and n. 9; Esser 1976, p. 218; and see p. 4. Francis' eccentricity in this regard was also noted by Eccleston (p. 32), who says he sent a letter to the schools of Bologna which contained bad grammar.

as the day (Psalm 139. 12), the woods rang with their voices and the rocks re-echoed their jubilation. Mass was celebrated on the manger. Francis wore the vestments of a deacon – he refused out of humility to proceed to priest's orders – and sang the Gospel with a sonorous voice; for his voice was an ardent voice, a sweet voice, a clear voice and a sonorous. Then he preached to the people, his whole being filled to overflowing with love and joy. When he uttered the word 'Bethlehem' his voice resembled the bleating of a sheep, and when he spoke the name 'child of Bethlehem' or 'Jesus' his tongue licked his lips as if he were savouring the sweetness of the word.[61]

Part I ends fittingly here with this moving experience that Francis had impressed upon his memory, and that Celano's record has preserved.

Whereas Part I covered eighteen years of Francis' conduct and activities, Part II concentrated on the last two years of his life. In his introduction to this (1 *Cel.* 88) Celano strikes a more provisional note than he did in the prologue to the whole work. He intends to be brief, and for the present will deal only with the more important matters, as he hopes that those who wish to say more may be able to find things to add. Can one detect a feeling of dissatisfaction, a feeling that he is not succeeding in doing justice to his subject, even a suppressed undercurrent of exasperation? One has a sense that Francis' close companions were breathing down his neck. We know some criticism was voiced. Such is an author's lot. Brother Leo told brother Peter of Tewkesbury who told brother Thomas of Eccleston that the vision of the seraph came to St Francis in a rapture of contemplation, and more distinctly than was described in his *Life*.[62] He will have told others as well. And yet Part II of the *Vita Prima*, which includes the account of the stigmata, is Celano's *tour de force*. Before resuming his narrative he launches into a panegyric of Francis, offering his readers an imaginative appraisal of his achievement and assessment of his significance. Some of the imagery he uses has already been quoted. 'The new evangelist, like one of the rivers of Paradise, by his pious irrigation spread the waters of the Gospel over the whole earth . . . so that in and through him there arose an unhoped for rejoicing and holy renewal of the whole world . . . A new spirit was given . . . when the servant and saint of Christ, like one of the lights of heaven, glittered from on high with a new observance and new wonders. The miracles of old were renewed through him, now that in the desert of this world a fruitful vine was planted . . . extending everywhere the branches of holy religion. For though he was a man subject to like passions as ourselves he was not content to observe the ordinary rules but overflowing with the most fervent charity tackled the way of utter perfection and gained the summit of perfect holiness . . . Therefore everyone, whatever their status, sex or time of life, has, through his means, clear lessons in the doctrines of salvation and excellent examples of holy works. If any should propose to set their hand to the hard tasks . . . let them look in the mirror of his life and learn every perfection . . . His glorious life sheds a brighter light on the perfection of earlier saints: the passion of Jesus Christ proves this and his cross shows it most clearly. In actual fact the venerable father was marked in the five parts of the body with the signs of the passion and the

---

[61] 1 *Cel.* 84–7. Moorman 1940, p. 62 n. 7, suggested that Celano's account of the crib at Greccio was based on his own reminiscences: for Celano's movements, see pp. 39–40.
[62] Eccleston, p. 75.

cross, as if he had hung on the cross, with the Son of God. This is a great sacrament [cf. Ephesians 5. 32], and shows the majesty of special love, but in him lies hid a secret counsel and is woven a reverend mystery known only to God, so we believe, and revealed in part through the saint himself to one man.'[63] It is remarkable the extent to which the images developed by later writers are already explicit here. *The Mirror of Perfection* was the title given to a popular collection of stories compiled in 1318. The resemblance to Christ of Francis, another Christ, was depicted in art and pursued to extraordinary lengths in literature. It is a splendid passage and a seminal one, designed to highlight the renewal in the Church achieved by the friars and the totally exceptional nature of Francis' holiness, at once sublime and mysterious.

Francis devoted part of his time to work for the good of his neighbours, but he also found it essential to reserve time for solitary contemplation. For this, he might retire to a remote hermitage, but, wherever he was, he relied on a few close companions to protect him from interruption. He had a favourite quotation from the Psalms which was a private signal to them courteously to dismiss unwanted visitors.[64] Two years before his death he retired to the hermitage on the summit of La Verna. While he was there he saw a vision, of a man standing above him, his hands stretched out, his feet joined, fixed to a cross; he was like a seraph, having six wings, two raised above his head, two stretched out for flight and two covering the whole body. While Francis pondered the significance of the vision, the marks of nails began to appear in his hands and feet. Celano gives a more detailed description of the stigmata than Elias had done in his letter. 'His hands and feet seemed to have been transfixed through the middle with nails, with the heads of the nails showing on the inner sides of the hands and the upper sides of the feet, and their points emerging on the opposite sides. These marks were round in the palms of the hands, but oblong on their backs, and little pieces of flesh protruded, like the tops of nails bent back and hammered down. Likewise in the feet the marks of nails were impressed, and raised above the rest of the flesh. His right side also was as if pierced by a lance; a scab formed which often oozed blood, so that his tunic and breeches were many times spattered with holy blood. Oh, how few were worthy to see the sacred side wound while the crucified servant of the crucified Lord was alive! But lucky Elias, who by some means deserved to see it while the saint lived; but no less fortunate, Rufino, who touched it with his own hands. For once, when brother Rufino put his hand on the saint's chest, to massage him, his hand slipped, as can often happen, to his right side and he chanced to touch his precious scar.' Francis reacted sharply, not simply to the pain but to the discovery; for he concealed it so carefully that even those closest to him did not know of it for some time.[65]

After the imprint of the stigmata Francis grew increasingly ill. He had worn out his body with constant travelling and preaching. Often in one day he would make the round of four or five villages or even larger centres of population, preaching the Gospel; and he edified his hearers as much by his example as by his words – he made a tongue of his

---

[63] 1 Cel. 88–90.   [64] 1 Cel. 91, 96.
[65] 1 Cel. 94–5; and for the seraph cf. Isaiah 6. 2; Ezekiel 1. 5–14, 22–5. For Elias' letter, see Lempp 1901, pp. 70–1 and above, pp. 33–4.

whole body.[66] Now, since he could no longer walk, he travelled about the country on an ass. He developed a very severe eye infection, which was aggravated by lack of care, and brother Elias and Cardinal Hugolino eventually persuaded him to seek treatment, but the remedies – cauterisation, blood-letting, plasters and salves – were harsh and ineffective.[67]

The account of the final months shows signs of hasty composition, which is not surprising. Celano must have worked fast and hard to complete his task so quickly. In the sixth month before Francis' death, while he was undergoing treatment for his eyes at Siena, a longstanding stomach illness flared up, he developed hepatitis and vomited a lot of blood. Brother Elias rushed to his side, he rallied and Elias moved him to Celle de Cortona. Here his abdomen, legs and feet became swollen, his stomach ailment grew worse so that he could hardly retain any food, and at his request Elias brought him to Assisi. He died at the Portiuncula, a place which he believed especially holy.[68]

But at this point Celano must have realised he had dispatched him too precipitately. He proceeds to recount in detail a selection of deathbed scenes calculated to edify and encourage the friars. Francis had blessed his brothers, just as the patriarch Jacob had blessed his sons and as Moses had blessed the children of Israel. He summoned to him the brothers he wanted, and they sat around him, brother Elias being on his left. By now he was blind. He crossed his hands, so that he laid his right hand upon Elias' head, and asked to make sure on whom his right hand rested. Told it was Elias, he said: 'That is what I wish' and he bestowed on him a special blessing. This happened while Francis was still in Assisi, staying at the bishop's palace. After it he made his urgent request to be taken to the Portiuncula.[69]

When death was imminent, he ordered two of his close companions to welcome death by singing to him the Canticle of brother Sun, and himself attempted to sing Psalm 142. Elias prompted him to forgive and to bless all his friars, and Francis, now very weak, charged him to announce his forgiveness and absolution, and to bless them all on his behalf. He then asked for a particular passage from St John's Gospel to be read to him, and told them to put a hair shirt upon him and to sprinkle him with ashes.[70]

Celano's description of the jubilation in Assisi at the news that Francis had died on his home ground – which meant that they would possess his relics – and of the joy that tempered the grief even of the friars on the revelation of the stigmata, suggests that his own personal affections were not involved. He describes the appearance of the body again, and comments that the signs of martyrdom did not arouse horror in the beholder but gave beauty and grace 'just as little black stones do set in a white pavement'.[71] The stigmata were of supreme importance in Celano's estimation. 'Oh singular gift and proof of especial love', he exclaimed, 'that the soldier is adorned

---

[66] 1 Cel. 97.   [67] 1 Cel. 98–101.   [68] 1 Cel. 105–6.

[69] 1 Cel. 108. In his *Vita Secunda*, which he wrote when Elias was excommunicate and deprived of the habit of his Order, Celano tried to minimise the significance of this blessing, but he did not attempt to deny that it had occurred: 2 Cel. 216–17. For Celano's reliability on what concerns Elias, see my discussion in Brooke 1959, pp. 8–20; and for this blessing, esp. ibid. pp. 17–19.

[70] 1 Cel. 109–10. Celano does not name him, but it is clear from the context that it is Elias. The Gospel passage was John 13. 1. Celano in error quotes the first verse of ch. 12. He gives the correct verse in 2 Cel. 217.

[71] 1 Cel. 112–13, 115.

with the very same glorious arms that befitted the only king . . .!' (1 *Cel.* 114) It leads naturally into the opening words of Part III, which completes the story with an account of Francis' canonisation and an appendix of miracles. The dead Francis, he asserts, now stands before the throne of God, and applies himself to dealing effectively with the concerns of those he has left on earth. What, he asks, can be denied to him, seeing that the stigmata give him the appearance of Christ himself, who is co-equal with the Father and sits at the right hand of the majesty on high? Surely he will be heard who, conforming to the death of Christ in the fellowship of his passion, exhibits in hands and feet and side the sacred wounds? In other words, the saints are powerful, and can be very useful; and Francis is pre-eminent. He is unique. He excels them all.[72]

How did members of the Order react to the fame of their founder? We have a comment, humorous and unaffected, from one, brother Jordan of Giano. He is a good touchstone, both because he had seen Francis and heard him preach, but did not know him well, and because he and Thomas of Celano were friends. He was a native of Umbria – Giano is in the valley of Spoleto. At the General Chapter of 1221 he was assigned to the group which succeeded in establishing a province in Germany, where he remained.[73] In his chronicle he noted under 1226 the death of Francis, and the concern of the citizens of Assisi lest he should be snatched from them by the Perugians because of the miracles God had worked through him, so that they buried him – not at the Portiuncula as he wished – but in the church of St George, close to the city walls. He also noted the letter they received from brother Elias, containing the news of the stigmata and announcing to all his blessing and absolution on St Francis' behalf.[74] Under 1228 he recorded Francis' canonisation.[75] In 1230, at the General Chapter which took place immediately after the translation, the administration of Germany was divided into two, and new Provincial Ministers were appointed, but brother Simon, an Englishman and a distinguished theologian, chosen for Saxony, died before he could assume office. Brother Jordan, who was custodian of Thuringia, was sent to Italy to request the Minister General to appoint another. His business concluded, he called on Thomas of Celano, who had also been a member of the mission to Germany, and with whom he had worked closely in Worms and Mainz and Speyer. Thomas gave him some relics of St Francis.[76] Can we tell what these relics may have been? How did Thomas come to have them in the first place? They were not very large; nor were they heavy; for Jordan slipped them into the bosom of his tunic, and forgot about them, as we shall see.

In his *Second Life of St Francis* Thomas of Celano included the following little story. While Francis was lying ill at the bishop's palace at Rieti undergoing treatment for his eye infection, a brother of the custody of Marsica was troubled with grievous temptations. He said to himself: 'Oh, if only I had something belonging to St Francis by me, even if it were no more than parings from his nails, I do believe the tumult of all these temptations would be put to flight.' He obtained leave to go to Rieti and explained his object to one of the saint's companions. He replied: 'I do not think it

---

[72] 1 *Cel.* 119. For his account of Francis' last days and canonisation see also pp. 34–8. For medieval attitudes to the saints, see Brooke and Brooke 1984, pp. 14–45, and bibliographies, ibid. pp. 158–60; Vauchez 1997.

[73] Jordan, cc. 16–19, esp. c. 18.   [74] Jordan, c. 50.   [75] Jordan, c. 54.   [76] Jordan, cc. 19, 30, 57–9.

will be possible to give you any of his nails, because, although we do clip them for him sometimes, he orders that they be thrown away, forbidding us to preserve them.' At that moment the companion was summoned to the saint, who asked him to find the scissors and cut his nails. He did so, and handed over the clippings to the brother who sought them. He kept them devoutly and was relieved from all temptation (2 *Cel.* 42). It is in its way a typical miracle story, but not particularly impressive, or memorable, except to the brother concerned. Why did Thomas of Celano think it worth including? The place, Celano, from which he sprang, is situated in the diocese of Marsica, and Thomas may have gone back to his native region after his return to Italy from Germany. It is at least possible that this story represents a personal experience. It is a record of how one friar acquired relics of St Francis; and not many friars succeeded in doing this. Perhaps Thomas gave Jordan a share of his little hoard of nail parings – as an act of friendship, and an indication of how pleased he was to see him again.

When Jordan arrived back at Eisenach, the brothers, to his astonishment, instructed the porter not to admit him through the convent door but to direct him to the church. There they formed a procession, carrying crosses, a censer, palm branches and lighted candles, and welcomed him joyously, singing: 'This is he who loves his brethren.' Jordan, disconcerted, signalled with his hand for them to desist, but they exultantly continued singing the antiphon through to the end. This gave him opportunity to reflect, to recollect the little parcel, and so to respond with an appropriate climax. 'Rejoice brothers', he said, 'for I know that you have been praising not me as myself, but our father St Francis in me . . . who, while I remained silent, excited your spirits by his presence.' And he placed the relics on the altar. Jordan enjoyed telling stories against himself. He ended this one with the comment that, having seen Francis while he was alive, he had entertained a rather human opinion of him. From now on he held him in greater reverence and honour.[77]

---

[77] Jordan, c. 59. For another story told against himself, see Jordan, c. 18. Extracts from Jordan of Giano's *Chronica* are printed in translation in the Documents section of Brooke 1975, pp. 205–13.

CHAPTER FOUR

THE OFFICIAL IMAGE IN STONE: THE BASILICA OF ST FRANCIS AT ASSISI

THE CREATION OF THE BASILICA

THE ACHIEVEMENT OF BROTHER ELIAS

The supreme expression of the place of St Francis in the affections of the friars and the people of Assisi – and, above all, of brother Elias – is the Basilica of St Francis at the western end of the city (Plates 6, 7). Here the apostle of poverty is enshrined in a spectacular church, richly adorned with frescoes purporting to show the poor, simple, humble life he led. Not far away are some of the churches of Francis' own choice – the modest San Damiano, 'nestling like a lark under the heather' on the hillside below the city, and the tiny chapel of the Portiuncula, now encased in a later church down in the valley. The contrast aroused the wrath of the great liberal Protestant romantic Paul Sabatier. 'Go and look upon it, proud, rich, powerful, then go down to the Portiuncula, pass over to San Damiano, hasten to the Carceri, and you will understand the abyss that separates the ideal of St Francis from that of the pontiff who canonized him'[1] (Plate 2).

Legend has it that the contrast also shocked some of his most intimate companions: that Leo was punished for breaking the handsome vase put up by brother Elias to collect funds for the Basilica; that Giles, after inspecting the Sacro Convento, observed: 'Now you have need of nothing except wives.'[2] But both stories come from late sources of doubtful veracity; the implicit comments in the stories told by the companions themselves are ambivalent. Some acknowlegement that Francis' relics could not be clothed in a ragged habit after his death is clear from the story of a friar who asked him in jest, as he lay ill, 'for how much will you sell all your sackcloth to the Lord? Many rich brocades and silken cloths will be put on to cover this little body of yours which is now dressed in sackcloth.' To which Francis replied 'with great fervour of spirit and

---

[1] Sabatier 1893/4, p. 345; cf. ibid. p. xxxiii.
[2] Chron. 24 Gen., AF III, 33–4, 72 (Leo), 90 (Giles); Speculum Vitae in Lempp 1901, p. 163 (Leo); cf. Brooke 1959, pp. 149–50.

Plate 6 The Basilica of St Francis at Assisi: the Lower and Upper Churches from the south-east (Photo C. N. L. Brooke).

Plate 7 The Basilica of St Francis: the Upper Church from the east (Photo C. N. L. Brooke).

gladness: "you say true, for so it will be".[3] The vision may have been of heaven, but few imaginative readers could avoid picturing an earthly shrine. The paradox does not lie simply in the contrast between Francis' personal tastes and those of Pope Gregory, or brother Elias, but in the difference between what was fitting for the *poverello's* earthly habitation, and what would best reflect God's blessing on a great saint and his

[3] SL 98; see p. 31.

work – and provide a home for a great community and throngs of pilgrims. But there can be no escaping the implications of passages in the writings of the companions which emphasise poverty in churches and dwellings. They include Francis' commendation of the Portiuncula, and his clearly expressed wish that this tiny church should remain 'a mirror and good example to the whole Order'; and his description of how a new convent and its church should be designed. 'Let them have poor hovels prepared, made of loam and wood, and some other small cells where the brothers can sometimes pray and may be free to work . . . Let them also have small churches built. The brothers ought not to have large churches made for preaching to the people, or for any other reason, since it is more humble and gives a better example when the brothers go to other churches to preach; so they may observe holy poverty and their own humility and probity. And if at any time any prelates and clergy, regular or secular, should turn aside to their friary, their poor houses and little cells and their churches will be sermons to them and they will be edified.'[4]

However we regard it, the Basilica was an amazing achievement. An Order vowed to poverty acquired the land and collected the resources in money, men and stone to build a very original and exciting building with great rapidity. This was unthinkable without the support of the pope, who initiated the project to build this special church in St Francis' honour, and granted indulgences to all who contributed to it, an incentive to which many near and far responded (Plate 8); equally unthinkable without the organising ability of brother Elias – whom the documents clearly show us as the master and director of the building.[5]

The documents show us brother Elias (who at the Whitsun Chapter of 1227, a few months after Francis' death, was relieved of his duties as Minister General), receiving land on behalf of Pope Gregory on which to build the convent and the church in which the most blessed body of St Francis was to be laid. The main site was given by Simon Puzarelli, citizen of Assisi, on 30 March 1228 and an additional plot by another citizen, Monaldus Leonardi, in July 1229.[6] The gifts were perhaps not quite as generous as they seem: the region was a slum area known as the Collis Inferni, Hell's Hill, before the advent of the Basilica turned it into the Collis Paradisi; but there is no doubt of the generous fervour with which the people of Assisi supported the cause. The church and other buildings erected on the site were to be the property of the Holy See and subject only to papal jurisdiction.[7]

The work of clearing, levelling and preparing the site must have begun at once for already on 17 July 1228, the day after the canonisation ceremony, Pope Gregory IX laid the foundation stone of the church. In April 1230 he named the Basilica 'caput et mater', 'head and mother' of the whole Order, and granted it numerous privileges. This bull, *Is qui ecclesiam*, was addressed to the Minister General and the friars staying

[4] SL 8–10, 16.
[5] Elias is 'dominus et custos ecclesiae Sancti Francisci Assisinatis' in a document of 1239 (Lempp 1901, pp. 173–4). Cf. Salimbene, H, p. 157; S, 1, 231; Brooke 1959, esp. p. 145. For the privileges and indulgences, see Sbaralea, 1, 60–2, 64–5, G9, nn. 47, 50.
[6] Langeli 1997, pp. 10–14, nos. 6, 8; Lempp 1901, pp. 170–1; Thode 1885, pp. 201, 539–40. Cf. Brooke 1959, pp. 137–8.
[7] Brooke 1959, pp. 137–8 and refs.

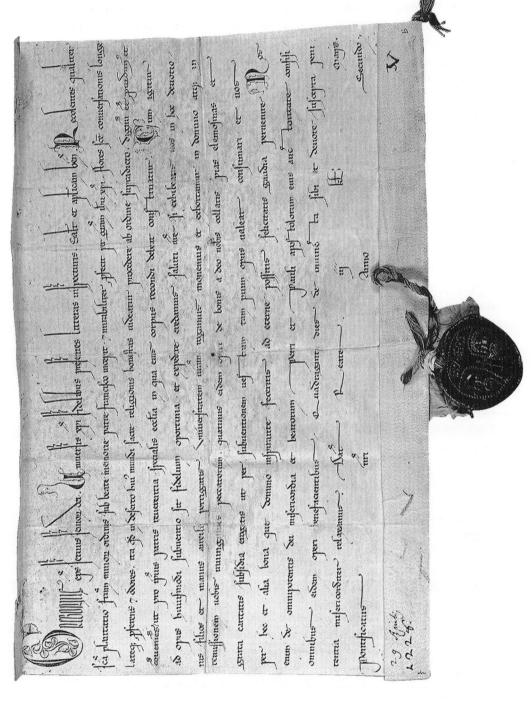

Plate 8 Bull of Pope Gregory IX dated 29 April 1228 granting an indulgence to those subscribing to the Basilica: Assisi, Archivio del Sacro Convento (© www.Assisi.de. Photo Gerhard Ruf).

at the Church of St Francis in the place which is called *Collis Paradisi*.[8] So work on the conventual buildings of the Sacro Convento must have been proceeding in conjunction with the work on the church. By May 1230 the church was sufficiently advanced to be the setting for a formal translation. The translation was the occasion for an extraordinary drama. It had been planned for 25 May, and Gregory IX – himself tied to Rome by negotiations with the Emperor Frederick II – was duly represented by cardinal legates. Some late sources describe a splendid procession, in which, to the sound of trumpets and other instruments, the wooden coffin containing the holy body made its way through the crowds on a wagon, richly adorned, drawn by oxen draped in purple.[9] No doubt this celebration took place on the proper day; but it was not strictly speaking the translation. For we have unimpeachable evidence that the body of St Francis had actually been secretly moved to the Basilica three days earlier. Just over a fortnight after the official event, the pope issued an angry letter excommunicating the podestà and people of Assisi for usurping the function of the Minister General by seizing the body and moving it without authority. No blame is attached to brother Elias by the pope; yet it was implied by the well-informed brother Thomas of Eccleston that it was Elias who masterminded the premature translation.[10] It is likely that Elias himself had succeeded in giving the pope an abbreviated version of the event. For it seems virtually certain that Elias and the citizens were in league; and the combined evidence of this secret translation and the extreme security with which the body was interred make it clear that Elias and the citizens feared for its safety. Whether they were anxious to avoid relic hunters who might dismember it, or a raid by the citizens of Perugia who might carry it away altogether, we cannot be sure: but everything points to the perceived need to keep the body safe from pious and impious hands alike. The pope in his anger rescinded all the privileges of the Basilica, subjected it to episcopal jurisdiction, and laid the convent under an interdict: no brothers were to live there and no General Chapter might be held there. But not long after he relented.[11]

On 25 May Elias had also been implicated in an attempted coup. At the General Chapter meeting held after the festivities a group of the rank and file of the friars, who were excluded from the formal sessions, vociferously carried Elias to the chapter-house door, which they broke through, and tried to substitute him as Minister General in place of John Parenti in defiance of the Provincial Ministers. John Parenti succeeded in quelling the tumult by disrobing. Elias retired to a hermitage to do penance.[12]

---

[8] Sbaralea, I, 60–2, G47; cf. Brooke 1959, p. 138.

[9] Bonav. XV, 8 (AF X, 626) states that the translation took place on 25 May, but gives no relevant details. Later citations giving their source as 'ex Regesto' of Gregory IX all go back to Wadding 1731–1933, II, 233–4, who gives the above account, including the splendid procession, followed by the text of the bull *Speravimus hactenus* (note 10 below), with reference to the register: see Brooke 1959, p. 140 n. 2 and refs.

[10] Sbaralea, I, 66–7, G9 no. 54 (72); Eccleston, p. 65.

[11] Sbaralea, ibid.; Brooke 1959, pp. 138–40. In fact no general chapter was held in Assisi after 1230 until 1269. Jordan (c. 50) is an independent witness to the danger from Perugia (see p. 49).

[12] Brooke 1959, pp. 143–5.

Plate 9 A view of the Basilica from above (Photo R. B. Brooke).

PROGRESS OF THE BUILDING AND ITS DATE

The site which Elias secured was on the modest summit of a foothill on the lower slopes of Monte Subasio at the western end of the city, just outside the walls (Plate 9). The church was built on the same axis as Assisi, west to east. It was laid out in the reverse of the normal orientation: the east end faced the city and, when the Upper Church was complete, it provided the natural main entrance. The west end, facing the world, formed the choir and apse. As the modern traveller passes along the valley of Spoleto and looks up at Assisi, the Basilica dominates the skyline at its western end: the site was evidently chosen to make the Basilica a splendid and conspicuous monument, marking the special character of the city of St Francis.

What stage had been reached by May 1230? How much was regarded as appropriate, or indeed necessary, before the translation could take place? We must speak with some caution of the architectural history of a complex building 750 years old which has been subjected many times to alteration and restoration. The message of the stones must in some measure be obscured. Yet some conclusions may be drawn. It seems that there were stages in the evolution of the building. There is a break in the structure and design between the third and fourth bays of the nave of the Lower Church, which suggests that initially it consisted of three bays only.[13] What can we deduce from this? It could well be that this relatively small church – by normal standards – was designed to provide temporary shelter for the saint; for Elias faced a challenge in 1228. He was evidently a man in a hurry. If security was his aim, it is at first surprising that the translation could take place so soon, for he needed a reasonably secure building. Security at St George's presumably depended on an armed guard mounted by the citizens of Assisi, and so was precarious.[14] But burial in a shell of a building with only temporary doors or walls would have been worse. So, it seems, the first priority was to erect a relic church that could be completed quickly; but, if so, it can only have been as part of a grander design. Building started, as was usual with medieval churches, with the choir – in this case, therefore, furthest from the city, at the west end. Examination of the stonework suggests that the component parts of the entire western face – apse, staircase-turrets and transepts – were all part of a single design, and built under the direction of a single architect or by a single group of masons. The staircase-turrets are bonded into the original walls of the apse, and were clearly intended to lead from the Lower Church to some structure above; and the way the courses of ashlar are laid has been thought a strong argument for the view that the whole of the west (liturgical east), end was built in a single campaign[15] (Plate 10). There is little doubt that Lower and Upper Church form part of a single design. Many analogies have been cited, a variety of functions for the two churches have been suggested,[16] but the clearest logical ground for the plan seems to follow naturally from the urgent need for a first, relic church to be completed in two years. The Lower Church as originally planned could form such a first church. But a Lower Church consisting of choir, a crossing, a nave of three bays, and a narthex, can never have been the goal of Elias' ambitions. It is a relatively low – almost crypt-like – structure, a tomb-church. It is clear that it was designed to have another church laid over it – as a church on its own it would be unbelievably squat and unworthy of its site; and it always had the strength to support a much loftier structure.[17] The double

---

[13] See esp. Hertlein 1964, pp. 22–7; Schenkluhn 1991, pp. 80–3. Rocchi Coopmans de Yoldi 2002 came into my hands too late for me to do full justice to his arguments. See below, notes 16, 21. For a general view of construction planning, see A. Erlande-Brandenburg 1994.

[14] This is a reasonable assumption because the citizens mounted a guard on him in his last weeks. The church is mentioned in 1 *Cel.* 118, but not named: for the name, see Bonav. xv, 5 (AF x, 625). See pp. 30, 35–6.

[15] Schenkluhn 1991, p. 24 and fig. 16, p. 60 and fig. 45.

[16] For the single design, see esp. Hertlein 1964, pp. 13–16 on the *torrioni*; Schenkluhn 1991, pp. 99–100. For a recent assessment, see Rocchi Coopmans de Yoldi 2002. On analogies, Hertlein 1964, pp. 71–99, 116–225 and Schenkluhn 1991, pp. 125–72, both ranging widely over Italian and French parallels in design – Tau-shaped churches, double churches, Gothic aisleless churches, and so forth – and style. Hertlein 1964, pp. 71–99, discusses at length the parallels with Angers. They are indeed close, but both writers (and many others) have shown that there were other sources of inspiration in France and Italy. And see pp. 68–9.

[17] For the early structure, see esp. Schenkluhn 1991, fig. 90. On the thickness of the walls, see ibid. ch. 11, esp. pp. 19–24; Hertlein 1964, p. 62, fig. 20.

Plate 10 The apse of the Basilica, seen from the fifteenth-century cloister (Photo Wim Swaan
Photographic Collection (96.P.21), Research Library, The Getty Research Institute, Los Angeles).

church must already have been conceived by July 1228, when the foundations of the Lower Church were sufficiently advanced for a formal foundation stone to be laid by the pope. A double church, such as was soon to be built, must have been in the mind of brother Elias and his architect as the Lower Church was begun.

If there is force in these arguments, the church was – from the outset – intended to be completed in two stages: first, the Lower Church with only a three-bay nave; subsequently a loftier church could be built above it. It may well be that some or much of the western wall of the Upper Church was built before the translation; there is no way in which we can tell. What precautions were taken to protect the body of St Francis inside the Lower Church became clear only when the exact location of the tomb was discovered by excavations early in the nineteenth century.[18]

Elias' penitence – he retired to a hermitage near Cortona and allowed the hair of his head and beard to grow – was taken at face value. Two years later, in 1232, he was back in favour and, with papal approval, he became once more Minister General.[19] What happened at the Basilica during his absence is not entirely clear – there may perhaps have been a short intermission in the building programme; but there is evidence from a document now lost that the Minister General, John Parenti, acting in the pope's name, put Piccardus Morico in charge of the funds for the building works, with instructions to collaborate with Philippus Campellus, and to render account to the Cardinal Protector. This suggests that Philippus Campellus may have been the master of works employed at this period.[20] As General, Elias spent almost all his time in Assisi, where he could concentrate on directing the building of the Basilica once more. With such zeal and efficiency did he forward the work that the whole complex, Lower and Upper Church, was virtually complete by 1239, when he fell from power.[21]

If the experts who have studied the structure are correct, it would seem that, in the original plan, the church was to consist of a double choir and a double three-bay nave approached through a single-storey narthex; no campanile was envisaged, and seemingly no semicircular buttresses along the nave.[22] The structure was strongly supported at both the western and eastern ends; the lofty walls of the Upper Church nave would have been comparatively flimsy in construction. When building work recommenced after the translation (either fairly promptly or after Elias became Minister General in 1232), this plan underwent successive modifications. It was decided the Upper Church should have a longer nave. This involved altering the narthex so as to extend in its place the Lower Church nave to four bays – on which a four-bay Upper Church nave could rise – and laying the foundations for a new façade. The first buttressing was at the corners where the nave joined the crossing and against the sides of the façade, but presently semicircular buttresses were added, buttresses which Vasari christened

---

[18] See pp. 464–71.   [19] Eccleston, pp. 66–7; Jordan, c. 61; Brooke 1959, pp. 143–5.
[20] Thode 1885, p. 202; and see pp. 66–7, 69.
[21] See p. 140; for Elias' residence in Assisi, see esp. Salimbene, H, pp. 157–8; S, I, 231–2. I wrote in Brooke 1959, p. 145, that 'the Church . . . was practically completed in 1239'; Schenkluhn supports my date, though arriving at it by a different route. Hertlein believes that there was a major interruption in the building programme when Elias fell, and that the Upper Church was largely French in inspiration, and later (Hertlein 1964, pp. 235–41). A date in the 1260s for the completion of the Upper Church is argued in Rocchi Coopmans de Yoldi 2002, esp. p. 73.
[22] See esp. Schenkluhn 1991, pp. 119–20 and fig. 90; cf. now Rocchi Coopmans de Yoldi 2002, p. 59.

'torrioni'. These torrioni echoed the staircase-turrets of the apse, knitted the superimposed naves together, and enhanced the appearance of the whole with their vertical lines and contrasting coloured stone, as well as strengthening the walls.[23] For the Lower Church and the torrioni were built of reddish limestone, while the Upper Church and the campanile were built of a pale yellowish-grey limestone.[24]

It is quite clear that the bell-tower, the campanile, was not originally catered for, at least in the position where it is. It is sited in the angle between the south transept and the nave, and obstructs and interferes with earlier features. It is built right up against the first torrione of the nave, so close that the string-course near the base of the torrione had to be cut away where they met.[25] Inside the campanile, on the first floor, a secure treasury was provided, that could only be reached from the sacristy in the south transept of the Lower Church. The building of the stairway from the sacristy to it involved the breaching of the south transept wall and its adjacent corner tower, the blocking up of the window of the first bay in the Lower Church nave, and the winding of the stairs round the outside of the first torrione to reach its destination – a remarkably strange and inconvenient route – and convincing evidence that the torrione was already built at least up to the level of the Upper Church.[26] Furthermore, the second floor of the campanile ends at the height of the cornice of the Upper Church, and its bulk greatly obscures the windows in the first and second bays – indicating that the nave wall must have been in place before the campanile was added. Finally its third-floor level is at a height such that the roof of the church can be reached through a door.[27] If we can date the completion of the campanile, we can date the completion of the Upper Church itself.

In 1237 Elias sent out visitors to the provinces, whose unpopular activities began the process which led to his downfall in 1239. One of their tasks was to collect yet more money for the Basilica. Salimbene tells us that the Provincial Ministers responded by paying the costs of casting a bell at Assisi. Salimbene saw this bell, which he describes as 'great and beautiful and sonorous', together with five others like it, and notes that they filled the whole valley with their delightful harmonies.[28] We cannot prove when he heard them ringing out, but the inscriptions on two of these original bells have been preserved. One reads: 'AD 1239 brother Elias had me made. Bartholomaeus Pisanus, with Loteringio his son made me. Blessed Francis, pray for us. Hail Mary full of grace. Alleluia.' The other inscription is longer. There are oddities in the Latin as recorded by seventeenth-century antiquaries. But it is again dated 1239. It names Pope Gregory IX and the Emperor Frederick, as well as brother Elias and St Francis, and records that Bartholomaeus Pisanus with Lotharingio (sic) his son made the bell, which is called 'Italiana'.[29] It is likely that this great bell was the very one paid for by

[23] Schenkluhn 1991, pp. 119–23 and figs. 91–2.

[24] Gatti 1983, p. 69; Hertlein 1964, p. 40, citing F. Rodolico, *Le pietre delle città d'Italia* (Florence, 1952), p. 300.

[25] Schenkluhn 1991, pp. 88–91, 123, figs. 70–1, 93; cf. now Bonsanti 2002a, I, 60–1, pls. 29–30.

[26] Schenkluhn 1991, pp. 88–90, figs. 7, 56, 53–4, 72.   [27] Schenkluhn 1991, pp. 90, 123 and fig. 93.

[28] Eccleston, pp. 38–9, 67–8 (cf. Brooke 1959, pp. 162–3); Salimbene, H, p. 107; S, I, 151.

[29] Thode 1885, p. 203, partly based on Petrus Rodulphus, *Historiarum Seraphicae religionis libri tres* (Venice, 1586), printed by Thode, pp. 541–2, partly, it seems, on F. M. Angeli, *Collis Paradisi amoenitas seu sacri*

the Provincial Ministers. The rest of the bells seem to have been cast by a bell-founder from Perugia betwen 1239 and 1243.[30] The campanile would presumably have been under construction if not finished or nearly so before the costs of casting them were incurred; and the Upper Church south wall and the first torrione on the south side (at the very least) preceded the campanile. [31] Perhaps the bells rang out to celebrate the completion of the great church just at the moment that Elias fell from power and was exiled from the scene of his triumph.

Salimbene also tells us that Gregory IX had a great palace made within the precincts of the Sacro Convento, both to do honour to St Francis and to provide him with some-where to stay when he came to Assisi. It contained many rooms and passages, and Elias accommodated a number of friars there – presumably when the pope was not in residence – some of whom were reputed to have acquired skills in alchemy before they joined the Order.[32] The nucleus of the convent was already in place by 1230.[33] These original buildings were reopened and excavated in the 1960s and 1970s. I was privileged to be shown them by Father Palumbo. They were large and commodious, but very plain and simple. The size of the chapter-house and dormitory, which survive virtually intact, presupposes a community which might grow to 120 or 150 or so – that is to say, they were designed to accommodate the friars who came to the General Chapter. The whole complex bears witness to the very careful thought which Elias gave to the function of the buildings, and his determination to provide adequately for foreseeable needs.[34] Surviving documents indicate that Elias had a private room which he used as an office. A notary called Bonaventura drew up a document there on 29 May 1237.[35] Another document, dated 27 May 1239, was drawn up and witnessed in a 'certain room' at the Basilica in the presence of brother Elias, who is described as 'dominus et custos' of the church of St Francis at Assisi and of brother James of Mevania, 'sindicus et procurator' of the church and convent.[36]

conventus Assisiensis Historiae libri II, tit. xvii, p. 30 (Montefalisco, 1704: cf. Thode 1885, pp. 192 n. 1, 203 and n. 3). Angeli has not been accessible to me. The inscriptions are also (from Thode) in Lempp 1901, pp. 89–90; Bonsanti 2002a, II, 1166, pl. 2298; IV, 633.

[30] They were ordered by Albert of Pisa as Minister General (1239–40), and cost 100 lire for four (Langeli 1997, pp. 30–2, esp. p. 31 n. 3; cf. Thode 1885, p. 203).

[31] Rocchi Coopmans de Yoldi (2002, pp. 78–9) suggests the bells could have been for a different campanile, later replaced by the present one; but this is entirely hypothetical.

[32] Salimbene, H, p. 160; S, I, 235.   [33] See pp. 53–5.

[34] Elias' chapel is illustrated in Bonsanti 2002a, II, 1200–1, pls. 2335–7; see note in IV, 639, dating it to 1232–9; for plans of the Sacro Convento, see ibid. II, pp. 1168–9. There should have been thirteen provinces and about sixty-five friars coming to the General Chapter in 1227, though not all may have attended; in 1230 the number was restricted to two per province – the Provincial Minister plus one custos. But in the 1230s Elias' aim was to raise the number of provinces to seventy-two, and if only two had come from each, that would have made a total of 144. The number was reduced to ninety-six in 1242 (Brooke 1959, pp. 129–31, 236–7). As it turned out, Assisi was not to host a General Chapter until 1269, but Elias was not to know this. One contributing factor was John of Parma's decree that General Chapters should be held alternately north and south of the Alps (Eccleston, p. 74). This constitution was passed either at Lyon in 1247 or at Genoa in ?1251 (Brooke 1959, pp. 269–70).

[35] Lempp 1901, p. 172.

[36] Langeli 1997, no. 16, pp. 23–5; Lempp 1901, pp. 173–4. Whitsun in 1239 fell on 15 May, so that the General Chapter in Rome in the presence of Gregory IX at which Elias was deposed cannot have been held at Whitsun, but must have been later in the year (cf. Brooke 1959, pp. 163–6). A document of 15 October 1238 refers to Elias as 'rector ac administrator' of the Order (Lempp 1901, p. 173).

FURNISHING THE BASILICA

Some furnishing of the Upper Church took place while Elias was Minister General. Eccleston gives details of an account he received from an eyewitness present when Gregory IX celebrated mass and preached at Assisi on the occasion of St Francis' feast day, 4 October. This must have been in 1235, the only year the pope was in Assisi at the appropriate time. He celebrated outside the church on a table under the open sky (*sub divo*). The reason given is that he could not celebrate inside the church because of the multitude of people.[37] But I think it is safe to say that there was not as yet a high altar in the church, for, if there had been, surely the pope would have consecrated it then? But, about this time, Elias commissioned a great crucifix, dated 1236, which was painted by Giunta Pisano. Most unfortunately it was taken down, in 1623, from its position surmounting the screen which separated the sanctuary of the Upper Church from the nave, cast aside and lost. It bore an inscription: 'Brother Elias had me made. Blessed Jesus Christ have mercy on the praying Elias. Giunta Pisano painted me. A.D. 1236. Indiction 9.' Elias was painted kneeling at the foot of the crucifix, and an eighteenth-century engraving based on a copy of this survives.[38] Father Palumbo suggested that this crucifix would not have been commissioned until the high altar was in place or nearly so. He argued further that the ceramic tiles of varied geometric design which decorated the original three steps of the high altar should be dated shortly after October 1235.[39] A wax seal, bearing the legend 'sigillum administrationis S. Francisci', built into the altar, which was discovered when the altar was moved, in 1898, from its original position in the centre of the crossing, could have belonged to Elias, and, if this attribution is correct, would be a further proof that the altar was in place before Elias fell in 1239.[40] Another crucifix painted by Giunta Pisano, which is now at the Portiuncula, was probably commissioned for the Lower Church, perhaps at the same time. Elias employed a range of Pisan craftsmen – the bell-founder and his son also hailed from Pisa.[41]

The high altar of the Lower Church consists of a central rectangle made of four blocks of the reddish limestone of Monte Subasio surrounded by an arcade of colonnettes, some plain, some twisted, joined by cusped Gothic arches whose spandrels are inlaid with cosmati work. Rectangle and arcade together support a massive monolithic 'mensa', or altar table. Little oil lamps hang within the arches[42] (Plate 16). Its design marked a new development in Italy, and was imitated within the Order and in

---

[37] Eccleston, pp. 89–91. Eccleston gives no date, save that Gregory celebrated on the feast of St Francis, i.e. 4 October. From the details given in Potthast, this can only have been in 1235. Eccleston characteristically names his witness: brother Augustine, brother of William of Nottingham (Provincial Minister of England, 1241–54: Little in Eccleston, pp. 86 n. 2i, 100–1 and n. 3a), later in the household of Innocent IV and bishop of Laodicea. Augustine told the story 'publice' in the convent at London (Eccleston, pp. 89–90).

[38] Wadding 1731–1933, II, 397; Brooke 1959, frontispiece and p. ix; Lempp 1901, pp. 89 and n. 1, 139–40 and n. 4; Palumbo 1972, p. 9 and n. 11.

[39] Palumbo 1972, pp. 7–10 and nn.; Bonsanti 2002a, II, 1162–3, pl. 2288–95; IV, 633.

[40] Palumbo 1972, p. 10. Elias is referred to as 'rector ac administrator' in a document dated 15 October 1238 (Lempp 1901, p. 173; cf. note 36 above).

[41] See p. 60; Palumbo 1972, p. 9.

[42] Gatti 1983, p. 278; Gardner 1981, pp. 30–1 and pls. 3.1 and 3.2; Bonsanti 2002a, I, 94–5, pl. 70; I, 414–15, pls. 722–9.

the Second Order of Poor Clares.[43] It was also an early representative of a new trend, possibly stimulated by developments in liturgical fashion, for altars to become much wider. The altar table is 3.72 m wide, 1.80 m deep and 20 cm thick.[44] It is very heavy – it has been reckoned to be 3500 kg – and has been identified with the huge stone transported from Constantinople to the Basilica, which in transit fell on top of one of its hauliers. By the intervention of St Francis he arose unscathed.[45]

Was Elias responsible for this beautiful altar? We cannot be sure. But he would certainly have intended a magnificent high altar on this site, which later excavation proved to be directly over St Francis' coffin.[46] The high altars of both the Lower and the Upper Church are notably elaborate. Both have mosaic decoration – the mosaic inlaid slabs of the sides of the Upper Church altar are original.[47] It would seem that the two high altars were constructed at the same time; the mosaicists could have worked on both during one visit. To send for an altar table all the way from Constantinople was feasible between 1209 and 1259, during the Latin occupation of Constantinople, as at no other time during the Middle Ages. It was not till 1253 that the pope, now Innocent IV, consecrated the Basilica; but it is well known that papal consecrations had more to do with the papal itinerary than the state of the buildings: when the papal Curia went on tour, local churches old and new were consecrated, or reconsecrated, however recently or long finished – just as a conscientious medieval bishop gave the sacrament of confirmation to the young and not-so-young he encountered when he visited his diocese.[48]

It has often been supposed that it took a generation at least to build a major medieval church; and to some it may seem incredible that the Basilica of St Francis was effectively completed in eleven years. But speed of construction depended on the concentration of resources, on good planning, on the energy and determination of those directing it – then as now; and the work reflected a quite unusual enthusiasm in which very many from near and far co-operated. It has equally been doubted whether it could be true that Canterbury Cathedral was almost wholly rebuilt by Archbishop Lanfranc in seven years in the 1070s. But the monk Eadmer was there when it happened, and he tells us so – 'almost finished,' 'ferme', which can only mean that the bulk of the work had been done.[49] If that was possible, the more advanced technology and economy of central Italy in the early thirteenth century could have achieved it too. The documents seem clearly to say so, and the logic of Elias' actions and the evidence of the structure fit together with surprising neatness.

43 Gardner 1981, pp. 30–1 and pls. 3.4, 3.5 and 3.6.

44 Gatti 1983, pp. 278–9 and n. 176. Gatti notes that the measurements were differently calculated by the various authorities he cites: those above are quoted by him from Scarpellini 1982a, p. 257.

45 Gardner 1981, pp. 30, 35 n. 14. The miracle is described in Bonav., *Miracula*, iii. 7. The story may have been based on the similar miracle recorded in c. 6, itself based on 3 Cel. 57; but it seems likely to reflect early tradition that the *mensa* came from Constantinople, whose treasures were extensively looted while the Latin emperors ruled there between 1204 and 1261. Gregory IX gave a cross adorned with precious stones containing a relic of the true cross in 1230 (3 *Soc*. 72).

46 See pp. 455–64.   47 Gardner 1981, p. 30.

48 R. Brooke and C. Brooke 1984, pp. 105–7, 164, and see note 63.

49 Eadmer, *Historia Novorum* in Rule 1884, p. 13: 'ferme totam perfectam'; cf. C. Brooke 1971, p. 173 and n. 25.

THE INSPIRATION OF THE BASILICA

But what of the building itself? It is an extraordinary concept: a noble and lofty, though aisleless, French Gothic church sits on the vaults of a relatively low Romanesque church, which has led some commentators to assume that the Upper Church was the work of a different architect from the Lower[50] (Plates 6, 7, Colour Plate 5). We have grown so used to think of Romanesque and Gothic as contrasting styles – and of Gothic as superseding Romanesque in fashion and popularity – that we tend to forget for how long, in many parts of Europe, they coexisted. An architect of international experience could easily design churches in both styles: like Classical and Gothic in eighteenth-century England, they coexisted – the patron chose which he wanted, or what combination suited him, and the same masons could do the work.[51] The Basilica is a highly eclectic building, but there is nothing implausible in finding a building so original at the heart of the Order – for already in Francis' lifetime it had become cosmopolitan; and the Order of Friars Minor, with provinces stretching from Ireland to Syria, and from Scandinavia to Sicily and Spain, was one of the most international elements in an exceptionally cosmopolitan age. There are few things more striking about twelfth- and thirteenth-century Christendom than the speed and distance men and ideas travelled. Art and architecture – like learning and the art of war – could travel hundreds of miles with surprisingly little difficulty; and the friars were in some ways the most surprising examples of it, since they travelled on foot.[52] So we might well expect the Basilica to combine elements of central Italy with features from elsewhere.

The influence and inspiration of architectural features from France, Italy and Jerusalem – to name just the most pervasive – have been found in this remarkable building. It has been seen as the expression of the piety and ambition of Pope Gregory IX, as a papal church with a papal palace attached: it has been seen as the expression of the personal devotion and ambition of brother Elias, the agent of pope and friars in its creation. It is unthinkable that so original and substantial a building could have been created in the circumstances of central Italy in the 1230s without the favour and patronage of the pope: we need not doubt that he was consulted in its planning, just as he was appealed to for incentives, indulgences, to provide the funds. But the pope was an exceedingly busy man, and had many other things on his mind.[53] And it remains impossible to imagine that so remarkable a building campaign could have been completed without constant and energetic measures in Assisi itself. These we may attribute

---

[50] See, for example, plates in Poeschke 1985 and Bonsanti 2002a, I and II.

[51] This point was first made clear to me in conversation with Neil Stratford. In Italy and Germany Romanesque and Gothic coexisted throughout the thirteenth century; in late twelfth-century England Wells Cathedral and the church of Glastonbury Abbey were being rebuilt within 6 miles of one another, Wells essentially Gothic, Glastonbury Romanesque. Even in France, where Gothic triumphed earlier and more completely than elsewhere, there are cases of Romanesque churches born out of time.

[52] For travel in early medieval Europe, see C. Brooke 2000, ch. 9 and p. 430. For some of the travels of the leading early Franciscans, Albert of Pisa and Haymo of Faversham, see Brooke 1959, chs. 7 and 8; for Elias in Syria, ibid. pp. 11, 23, 104–5, 146.

[53] For a brief survey of Gregory IX's immensely varied activities, see C. Brooke 1971, ch. 9; for his relations with Frederick II, see Abulafia 1988, esp. chs. 5, 9–11. The argument in Schenkluhn 1991, ch. 4, esp. pp. 190–9, that the Basilica reflected above all the aspirations of Gregory IX himself has to be seen in the context of his other activities.

in large part to Elias. Not for nothing was he accused as Minister General of refusing to travel.[54] He had to oversee every phase of the building programme.

GREGORY IX

Papal involvement was crucial. Gregory IX initiated the project and evinced a keen and active interest in its success. He took the whole complex of church and convent under papal protection, and bestowed on the Basilica the title of 'caput et mater' of the Order. No other religious Order's centre has been given this title; it is shared only with St John Lateran – the mother church of Christendom and seat of the papacy – which boasts the title 'caput et mater omnium ecclesiarum'.[55] Site and layout are redolent of Rome. The Basilica is oriented west/east – like the Roman basilicas St Peter's in the Vatican and St John Lateran. While it is true that the configuration of the site made this orientation the most convenient, this may be a reason why it, rather than any other, was chosen. It would have been possible to acquire a site within the city walls.[56] 'The ground plan of the Lower Church, with its salient, originally flat-ended transepts and round western apse, is strongly reminiscent of the early Christian basilica of St Peter's, like Assisi itself a tomb church.'[57] Set in the centre of the choir of the Upper Church is a papal throne, with the inscription 'Thou shalt go upon the asp and the basilisk: the lion and the dragon shalt thou tread under thy feet' – the same inscription as on the papal cathedra in the choir of St John Lateran[58] (Plate 51). The high altar, originally in the centre of the crossing, is a papal altar, and the high altar of the Lower Church is likewise a papal altar. The Roman basilicas, St Peter's and St John Lateran, had double altars, one at the west end, the other at the east end; only at Assisi the double altars are one above the other. In the Lower Church a basilisk lurks in the foliage on the capital of one of the altar columns, echoing the inscription on the papal throne above.[59] It is possible indeed that Gregory IX played a major role in the provision of both altars, that he discussed their installation and decoration with brother Elias when he was in Assisi in 1235 to celebrate St Francis' feast day. He had already given a number of vessels for the service of the altar and many beautiful vestments at the time of the translation.[60] And the mosaicists presumably came from Rome. When the pope resided at the Sacro Convento the Basilica became a papal chapel. The papal palace was erected to the west of the apse in Assisi as at the Lateran.[61] Two eagles, which may be his family emblem,

---

[54] Salimbene, H, pp. 96, 104, 157–8; S, I, 136, 147, 231–2.

[55] Sbaralea I, 60–2, G47; cf. Hertlein 1964, pp. 112–14; Schenkluhn 1991, ch. 4, esp. pp. 190–257.

[56] E.g. on the site of the Rocca? On the orientation of the Roman basilicas, several of which had their high altars towards the west, see Krautheimer 1975, esp. pp. 46–9, 55–60, 179; Krautheimer 1977, p. 14.

[57] Gardner 1981, p. 30.

[58] Psalm 90 (91). 13; Belting 1977, p. 27; Hertlein 1964, pp. 111–12 and n. 4. For the basilisk in the foliage on a capital in the altar of the Lower Church, see Gardner 1981, p. 30. The base of the throne is of Umbrian craftsmanship, made of local stone from Subasio. The lions are considered the work of a sculptor active in Rome in the middle of the thirteenth century. This central throne may have been constructed for the consecration ceremony in 1253, but parts of it may be earlier. The steps used to be decorated with majolica, which is now in the sacristy. The baldachin is later, possibly c. 1270 but probably c. 1280–90. Bonsanti 2002a, II, 1000–1, pls. 1915–19; IV, 574–5.

[59] Gardner 1981, p. 30; Hertlein 1964, pp. 111–12.

[60] 3 Soc. 72.   [61] Hertlein 1964, pp. 111, 114.

are carved to either side of the façade, just above the string-course; if so, they present a proud and conspicuous statement of Gregory IX's personal involvement, endorsement and protection.[62]

INNOCENT IV

Papal involvement continued with Innocent IV. He and his retinue resided in the papal apartments at Assisi for the best part of six months, from 27 April to 6 October, in 1253. On the anniversary of the official translation, 25 May, he dedicated the Basilica, consecrating both high altars: that of the Upper Church to the Virgin Mary, that of the Lower Church to St John the Baptist. To the high altar of the Lower Church he donated a relic of St John the Baptist, which is encased in a column inserted under the mensa. This column is quite different in style from the colonnettes which ring the central block of the altar, and would appear to be a later addition – confirming that the altar was in place, and functioning, before its official consecration[63] (Plate 16).

On 10 July 1253 Innocent IV issued the bull *Decet et expedit*, concerning the Basilica.[64] It is worth quoting, because although it is couched in the language of the papal bureaucracy, it genuinely reflects the attitudes which prompted and promoted the enterprise. Philippus Campellus, to whom it is addressed, was named in a document of John Parenti's generalate, so he probably continued as master of works throughout, though while Elias was Minister General (1232–9), Elias will have been in overall control.[65] At some point Philip had joined the Order, and had also taken on the responsibilty for the finances.[66]

'To his dear son Philip de Campello OFM, Master and *Praepositus* of the works of the church of St Francis at Assisi, greeting and apostolic blessing. It is fitting and expedient to build splendid basilicas for those who have – glorious in their merits – attained the loftiest habitation of the heavenly palace. Thus those who have been held worthy of the honour of being lifted up in the world above, should be in every way revered on earth by Christ's faithful people with a worthy devotion; and famous churches may be made for them by the faithful, in which the Almighty may be fittingly

[62] Assisi 1999, p. 32; Bonsanti 2002a, II, 653–7, pls. 1344, 1353 and esp. II, 658–9, pls. 1354–5; IV, 450: the eagles may be the family emblem of the Conti dei Segni or symbols of regeneration and resurrection.

[63] Innocent IV set out from Perugia for Assisi on 27 April 1253, and left Assisi for Narni and Rome on 6 October 1253 (Potthast, II, 1231–47); he left Rome c. 27 × 28 April 1254, and was in Assisi by 2 May. He left Assisi after celebrating Pentecost there, 31 May, and was in Anagni by 2 June (Potthast, II, 1278, 1283). He consecrated the basilica on 25 May 1253, according to the *Vita Innocentii* of Nicholas de Curbio (Potthast, II, 1234). On the altar and the relic, see Plate 16; Hertlein 1964, p. 114; Gardner 1981, p. 31 and pl. 3.2; Scarpellini 1978, pl. IX, pp. 87–8 and n. 24. According to Bonsanti 2002a, IV, 393–4 the monolithic altar table could have been in use in 1230. The reliquary can be seen behind and between the two central colonnettes in Bonsanti 2002a, I, 414–15, pls. 724, 728. This column, with its different style of capital, is all that remains of decoration undertaken in 1253. The existing decorative arcades are datable to c. 1270, but as they are so similar to those depicted in the Assisi altar panel (see p. 174 and Colour Plates 3, 4), they probably reflect an earlier similar scheme. Cf. Lusanna 2002, pp. 215–16. Gardner, Palumbo (Palumbo 1972, p. 10) and Scarpellini all date the altar earlier than 1253.

[64] Sbaralea I, 666, 14 no. 489.   [65] See p. 59 and note 20; and cf. Langeli 1997, pp. 30–2.

[66] Similarly two Florentine architects joined the Dominican Order in the mid-1250s. To brothers Sisto and Ristoro we owe the final form of the church of Santa Maria Novella designed in 1279 (Meersseman 1946, pp. 179, 185–6; plan, p. 154). As Philip is addressed as 'Master and Praepositus' it is possible that he was architect as well as administrator.

worshipped, and the memory of [the saints] be publicly honoured – so that while thus the beauty of God's house is loved, and the tabernacle of his praise carefully set forth, his mercy may be more readily and fruitfully obtained by the intercessions of the saints themselves. Hence – because the venerable church of St Francis at Assisi is not yet completed with fitting workmanship, as is proper – we, desiring for the reverence of the same saint, a sedulous supporter of the Christian people before God, that the said church be completed with a noble structure and decorated with the peak of splendid workmanship, grant [indulgemus] by apostolic authority that you, and other *Praepositi* of the works of the same church who may be from time to time, may receive offerings in money at the altars of the same church and elsewhere also, for the same works, to be wholly and faithfully spent for the same works, as our venerable brother the bishop of Ostia and Velletri, or another Cardinal of the Roman Church, who may be Protector of the Order of Friars Minor, shall think fit to ordain and dispose – any statutes of the same Order or prohibitions of the General or Provincial Ministers or the custos or the guardian of the house or any other brothers of the same Order not at all withstanding . . . These present instructions will cease to be valid after the twenty-fifth year.'

This bull has been taken as evidence that the church was still unfinished,[67] but I would interpret the wording to refer to the need for improvement and embellishment, for decoration not substance. The church is described as 'venerable', which would hardly be appropriate if it still lacked a roof. For the first time in an official document the word 'basilica' is used with reference to it, and in Innocent IV's view, as a basilica it clearly is not splendid enough. We cannot be sure whether brother Elias intended to decorate, but it is probable that he did. His campanile is decorated with ceramic half-plates, or bowls, very likely made in Assisi or its immediate vicinity, and certainly inserted in the course of its construction. They are slightly concave, the colour of verdigris and measure 25 cm in diameter. They are set as lunettes under the ornamental arches of the cornice below the bell-chamber, and though only about half survive of the original sixty – there were fifteen on each of the four sides of the tower – these are still visible today.[68] The steps of the high altar of the Upper Church were originally decorated with ceramic tiles, and mosaic inlay adorns its sides; the colonnettes and arches of the Lower Church high altar are decorated with sculpture and cosmati work. Both altars are worthy of a basilica, and Elias was probably responsible for both.[69] He commissioned the great crucifix painted by Giunta Pisano in 1236. It is possible that he planned to have walls and ceilings covered with frescoes – as they later were. Alternatively, there is an indication that he intended rich mosaic decoration.[70] But his fall in 1239 prevented the realisation of any plans he had.

To Innocent IV the Basilica, and in particular the Upper Church, with its large expanses of plain wall, and windows of plain glass, must have looked bare, and there-fore unacceptable and incomplete. But St Francis had been wedded to poverty. 'Let the brothers take care that churches, humble lodgings and all other things that will

---

[67] E.g. Hertlein 1964, p. 239; Rocchi Coopmans de Yoldi 2002, esp. pp. 73, 96.
[68] Palumbo 1972, p. 11.   [69] See pp. 62–3, 66.
[70] Belting 1977, pp. 31 ff; cf. Gardner 1978/9; White 1984, ch. VI, p. 153.

be built for them are never accepted unless they are in harmony with holy poverty, which we have promised in the Rule, always living there as strangers and pilgrims', he had written in his Testament.[71] The pope anticipated objections from members of the Order, from the highest to the lowest, and overruled them in advance. The Minister General at this time was John of Parma. He was known not to be in favour of relaxation of standards with regard to buildings. When he visited England in May 1248 he had 'ratified provincial constitutions dealing with poverty in buildings and the need for economy, and he may have passed some statutes himself against extravagance in the dimensions and decoration of buildings'.[72] At the General Chapter at Genoa, probably held in 1251, at which he presided, brother William of Nottingham, Provincial Minister of England, and brother Gregory of Bosellis, presumably a custos, persuaded the friars to agree to suspend the provisions of Innocent IV's bull, *Ordinem vestrum* of 14 November 1245, which were laxer than those of *Quo elongati* – a decision reaffirmed at the General Chapter of Metz in 1254 and again at Narbonne in 1260 – and also to abstain from utilising a privilege Innocent IV had granted in August 1247 which threatened to render Franciscan poverty and renunciation of property little more than illusory.[73] Innocent IV, indeed, was extraordinarily cavalier in his treatment of the Franciscan conscience. In the winter of 1243–4 he had deposited the papal treasure for safe-keeping in the secure treasury brother Elias had incorporated in the campanile at the Basilica![74] Now, determined to ensure his orders were implemented, the pope put the Cardinal Protector in charge of the embellishment programme. A month later he allowed the use of precious metals and fabrics for liturgical equipment for the altars and for those who serve them, and for other adornment of the church, decreeing that the Basilica may have 'books, chalices, thuribles, crosses, basins, either of gold or of silver, tunicles, dalmatics, chasubles, copes, copes for wet weather (*pluvialia*), and other clothing and apparel, either of silk or such like . . . bells, large and small, and other ornaments and ecclesiastical vessels'; concluding with the injunction that no friar or General Chapter was to remove them.[75]

SOURCES OF INSPIRATION

The Roman basilicas were not the only models that seem to have inspired the pope, Elias and their architect in designing the building. In Italy, other analogies can be found here and there – two-storied buildings, for example, at Montecassino, and at San Nicola Pellegrino at Trani.[76] The Church of the Holy Sepulchre in Jerusalem – itself a two-storied structure – is an obvious possible source. It stands on a hill, where the Cross was believed to have stood. The tomb is carved into the rock, and the rotunda

---

[71] Esser 1976, pp. 440–1; translation from Brooke 1975, p. 118.
[72] Brooke 1959, p. 261 and nn. 4–5, esp. Eccleston, p. 98.
[73] For the general chapters, see esp. Brooke 1959, p. 257 and nn. 2–3; Eccleston p. 42 and n.; for the decision not to use *Ordinem vestrum* and *Quanto studiosius*, see Brooke 1959, p. 264 and n. 3. Under the terms of *Quo elongati*, one custodian was to come with the Provincial Minister as the representative of a province to General Chapter (Brooke 1959, p. 130).
[74] Brooke 1959, p. 265 and n. 2.
[75] *Dignum existimamus*, 16 July 1253, Sbaralea I, 666–7, 14 no. 490.
[76] Schenkluhn 1991, pp. 136–41, and pls. 99–102.

above it lies west of the church. There is an atrium between the rotunda and the church, which was called 'the garden of Paradise', 'hortus Paradisi', owing to a legend that Adam too was buried on the site.[77] Elias was Provincial Minister of Syria 1217–20, and St Francis joined him after his intervention at Damietta during the Fifth Crusade. They returned to Italy together in 1220.[78] It would be tempting to imagine them visiting the holy places in Jerusalem together, but alas, from the battle of Hattin, in 1187, when the crusader army was virtually annihilated and Jerusalem fell, until 1228–9, when the Emperor Frederick II succeeded in regaining access for westerners by negotiation – an achievement for which he was excommunicated by Gregory IX – Jerusalem was inaccessible to pilgrims.[79] But it is very likely that the Church of the Holy Sepulchre was described to them, and Elias may have seen fortress sepulchres carved out of the rock in Syria. His sojourn there may well have given him the idea of placing the coffin of the saint in a rock-hewn tomb in Assisi.[80]

But the main inspiration of the Basilica seems to be French. There are close analogies in Rheims: in Rheims cathedral there is sculpture on capitals similar to sculpture on capitals in the Basilica.[81] But closest of all is the analogy between the aisleless nave of Angers cathedral – early Gothic of the late twelfth century – and the aisleless nave of the Upper Church. It is unlikely that Gregory IX had been to Angers, though not impossible, since he was a student in Paris in early life.[82] Elias never set foot in France, so far as we know. In any case the analogy between Angers and the Upper Church is one that must have been thought out by an architect or professional mason. The Upper Church is not wholly French in inspiration, as has often been emphasised; but the French element is highly sophisticated, and fundamental. In Angers the bare nave walls are partly filled with large windows and arcading: the walls of the Upper Church nave leave far more wall plain; the windows start higher up; there is no arcading.[83] It must be a matter of speculation whether or not Philippus Campellus was French: Champeaux or some such place name could easily lurk under his surname – but he may have been an Italian 'de Campello'.[84]

Granted that it was a highly cosmopolitan building in conception from the start, and that the rapidity of its construction presupposes an admirably clear plan – modified certainly, but in essentials adhered to – we may reasonably suppose that the whole Basilica was the fruit of collaboration between Gregory IX as patron, brother Elias and an architect experienced in a variety of idioms, who may have worked at Rheims, with some knowledge at least of Angers cathedral, achieved with the help of local masons.

[77] Hertlein 1964, pp. 104–5; Schenkluhn 1991, pp. 145–7 and pls. 105, 115–17.
[78] Jordan, cc. 7, 9–14; Brooke 1959, pp. 23, 64–5 and 65 nn. 1, 2.
[79] For Frederick II's (temporary) recovery of Jerusalem, see Abulafia 1988, pp. 182–5. Cf. Basetti-Sani 1972.
[80] Brooke 1959, p. 145.
[81] Schenkluhn 1991, pp. 13–14; Hertlein 1964, pp. 167–72 and plates, esp. 25, 28–35.
[82] Brem 1911, p. 4 n. 4.
[83] Hertlein 1964, pp. 71–99 and pl. 21. Paul Binski has pointed out to me that the window tracery of the Upper Church is very self-consciously French: the tracery type originated in Picardy or Paris. The design of the transept windows consisting of four lights surmounted by foils stems from the nave clerestory of Amiens Cathedral designed in 1220: see Wilson 1990, figs. 69–70.
[84] Sbaralea, 1, 666 n. a, observed that there is a Campello near Spello. The rest of his note, suggesting that Philip had been a disciple of James the German, the first architect of the Basilica, is based on Vasari, and of no authority: see Thode 1885, pp. 202–9.

THE FUNCTIONS OF THE DOUBLE CHURCH

There are features about the Basilica which reveal an extraordinarily imaginative and far-sighted concept of its function. In the early days the Orders of friars did not need churches of their own for preaching purposes. They preached by invitation in cathedrals and parish churches, and in the open air – certainly to heretics, who would not enter a church. In St Francis' time the majority of his friars were laymen, but some, and as time passed an increasing number of them, were priests; the Dominicans were from the start an Order of priests – and priests were required to celebrate the Divine Office in a church. This needed only to be large enough to house the community – space for the public was not necessary.[85] In many places the friars were offered existing churches. These could vary very much. They could be small and humble; they could be semi-derelict and in need of restoration; they could be very grand, like Santa Sabina in Rome, the exquisite fifth-century basilica granted to the Dominicans by Honorius III. The first church St Francis received was tiny, and had been for a long time almost in ruins. It was known as St Mary of the Portiuncula, St Mary of the little portion – a name that greatly delighted St Francis. He and his brothers repaired it with their own hands, and he sent every year to the abbot of the Benedictine monastery on Monte Subasio, who granted it to him, a small wicker basket full of little fish in token that the friars did not own it.[86] The first Franciscan chapel in Cambridge was so very poor that a single carpenter erected the wooden framework in one day using fifteen split tree trunks.[87] There was a honeymoon period when many bishops welcomed the friars as badly needed helpers in the work of evangelisation, and the parish clergy had accepted their ministry, by and large. But sources of friction soon developed. The townspeople flocked to the friars' sermons and neglected their former pastors. The secular clergy saw their free will offerings, legacies, burial dues, diverted to these new and fashionable beggars, and as their revenues diminished their hostility grew. They invited the friars to preach in their churches less and less frequently, or even forbade them altogether.

Both Orders were affected by this changed climate, and felt it necessary to build larger naves to accommodate lay congregations in their own churches. At the same time their own needs were changing, requiring a new strategy. They were very successful and their numbers were growing rapidly. The Dominicans were an Order of priests by definition, and the Franciscans virtually ended the recruitment of laymen in 1242, and became likewise an Order of clerics.[88] This meant there were more priests needing facilities to celebrate Mass. So, from the 1240s on, the churches of both Orders tended to develop in a somewhat similar fashion, as large and commodious two-celled buildings, with an ample open space for the faithful to hear the friars' sermons and attend their masses, and a more modest, but still sufficient, space for the private worship of a religious community. Sometimes – perhaps most commonly – the two churches were put end to end: the people's church forming a large nave, the friars' church the choir of a single building. This was what was done, for example, at Bologna, in the church where

[85] Meersseman 1946, pp. 139–40.
[86] For Santa Sabina, see Von Matt and Vicaire 1957, pls. 149–50; for the Portiuncula, SL 8.
[87] Eccleston, p. 22.
[88] Brooke 1959, pp. 243–5. For the need to build larger churches, see Meersseman 1946, pp. 158–60.

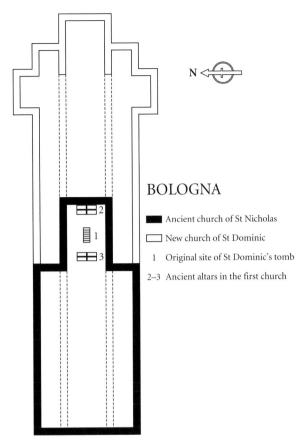

BOLOGNA

■ Ancient church of St Nicholas

□ New church of St Dominic

1 Original site of St Dominic's tomb

2–3 Ancient altars in the first church

Figure 1 Bologna, Plan of the Dominican Church, based on Meersseman 1946, p. 154

St Dominic was buried (Figure 1). Sometimes, where the site was too constricted for lengthening at either end, a different solution could be adopted, as at the Dominican church of Santa Maria Novella in Florence, where, in 1246, a second church was built alongside the first[89] (Figure 2).

The Basilica of St Francis, begun in 1228 and completed in 1239, precedes most of these developments. It anticipates the fully developed friars' churches of the next generation. Its architect clearly had the brief, when designing the Upper Church, to provide an aisleless hall, a large open space in which crowds of townspeople and pilgrims could gather to hear the friars' sermons. The intention to provide an efficient work environment for preaching created an opportunity to introduce into Italy an example of the new Gothic style with its ribbed groin vaults and tall lancet windows. It was filled with light, in contrast to the dark, meditative Lower Church. Lay people were not wholly excluded from the Lower Church. They were presumably admitted to the nave at certain times to worship before the shrine. When the blessed Angela of Foligno came to the Basilica on pilgrimage with a group of men and women companions in

[89] Meersseman 1946, pp. 157, 160–1.

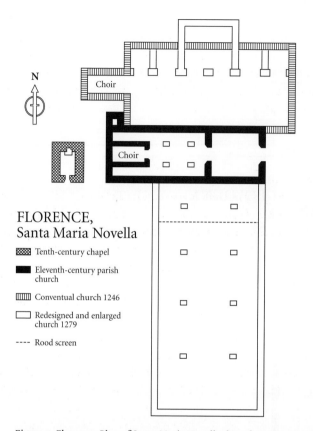

N

Choir

Choir

FLORENCE,
Santa Maria Novella

▨ Tenth-century chapel

■ Eleventh-century parish
church

▥ Conventual church 1246

▢ Redesigned and enlarged
church 1279

---- Rood screen

Figure 2 Florence, Plan of Santa Maria Novella, based on Meersseman 1946, p. 154

1291, around the time of St Francis' feast day, they probably all spent some time first in the Lower Church. Later in the day, after a meal, they went back to the church, but on this second visit entered the Upper Church. In 1300, the Jubilee year, Angela was again in Assisi for the Portiuncula indulgence. She attended masses, along with crowds of other pilgrims, in the Upper Church and in the Portiuncula. On the eve of the Feast of the Indulgence, 31 July, which that year was a Sunday, she describes how a vision was vouchsafed to her while Mass was being sung at the high altar of the Upper Church, 'about the elevation of the Host, during the singing of the angelic hymn "Sanctus, sanctus, sanctus"'. On the Monday, 1 August, which was also the Feast of St Peter ad Vincula, she went to communion at an altar on the right side of the Upper Church – very probably the altar of St Peter in the right transept. After it there was a procession from the Basilica down to the Portiuncula.[90] Such details afford us glimpses of the worship to which the laity had access.

Elias' vision found spaces for the friars, for the pope, and for the laity and pilgrims in both the Upper and the Lower Church: they amounted to two double churches. Yet

[90] Thier and Calufetti 1985, pp. 182–4, 496–8 and n. 14, 614–18. Thier and Calufetti are mistaken in saying that Mass on 1 August was at the altar of St Michael (p. 497, n. 14), which is in the left transept: see ibid. p. 624.

there was a difference. The Lower Church was pre-eminently the home of the saint and the church of the friars: an oratory suitable for prayer, meditation, the offices, the mass – but also for occasional visits from the wider world. In the Upper Church friars, pilgrims and devotees of the saint could more freely meet and mingle. In creating this all-embracing, spectacular and unique 'fourfold church' he showed the way forward more generally, by indicating what a friars' church needed to provide.

CONCLUSION – THE IMAGE

What image, then, did the Basilica present? It was, first and foremost, an expression of faith, a witness to the glory of God. It also epitomised the devotion to St Francis of brother Elias and the Order of Friars Minor, the citizens of Assisi, and the papacy, who had collaborated to achieve it. It is a brilliant evocation of the international fashions of the day, a monument to the cosmopolitan adventures of the friars. Its site, and the extra height inherent in its design, afforded it maximum prominence. The local provenance of the stone used in its construction, its two contrasting colours and the quality of the workmanship rendered it in harmony with its surroundings and beautiful to look upon. The sound of its bells filled the valley, summoning its inhabitants to prayer and preaching. Its symbolism was richly varied. The ground plan of the Lower Church is in the form of a Tau cross. This Tau form – a Latin T – was the favourite of St Francis. Celano noted that: 'He took it for a special token, which he preferred to other tokens, by which alone he signed his letters, and inscribed where he would the walls of cells.'[91] In the blessing he wrote for brother Leo: 'he made this Tau sign with a head with his own hand'.[92] At the base of this Tau sign on Leo's blessing St Francis drew something not now easy to make out, but Leo called it a head, and it has been interpreted as Adam's head. 'Francis' little drawing is a somewhat eccentric adaptation of a . . . crucifixion, with Christ's cross rising above the grave of Adam on Golgotha.' The words of the blessing itself contain the words the Lord delivered to Moses to be spoken to the people by Aaron. Elias, in a letter to the brethren announcing Francis' death, had likened him to Moses and Aaron. 'Francis . . . has thoughtfully and deliberately collated the words of Aaron with the mark of Aaron in a unified document that speaks of penance and salvation in the Age of Grace.'[93]

In marking out the shape of St Francis' burial church as a Tau cross – though not in the scale of the building he erected upon it – Elias was true to St Francis. The Tau cross also marked the ground plan of the Lateran and Vatican basilicas. It may be that St Francis also had a special devotion to this sign of the cross because of his devotion to the papacy. So in imitating the orientation and the ground plan of these Roman basilicas, Elias may again be said to be faithful, in his own way, to St Francis. There is an intriguing paradox here. Affinities with the Church of the Holy Sepulchre in Jerusalem increase the resonances. Already in Thomas of Celano's *First Life* of St Francis, composed and

---

[91] *3 Cel.* 3; Fleming 1982, p. 112 and n. 22. For a fascinating discussion of its iconographic significance, see Fleming 1982, pp. 99–128, esp. pp. 102–14.

[92] See pp. 109–11 and Plate 12; SL, Frontispiece and pp. 7–8; Fleming 1982, pp. 105–7 and n. 13.

[93] Fleming 1982, pp. 107–9, 121. For Elias' letter, see p. 34.

completed while the Lower Church was a-building, St Francis is at times portrayed in the role of another Christ.[94]

Brother Leo is buried in the Basilica, and so are some other of the early friars and St Francis' companions, including brothers Bernard of Quintavalle, Sylvester and William the Englishman, whose drawing of the Christ of the Apocalypse was treasured by Matthew Paris.[95] These three, with two others, were buried in the right-hand transept of the Lower Church, in one tomb under Cimabue's Maestà (Plate 32). Brothers Leo, Masseo, Rufino and Angelo were buried in a balancing tomb in the left transept. So it looks rather as though his companions were not implacably opposed to the Basilica. After St Francis' body was discovered and the crypt was built, these four companions were moved, in separate caskets, into four niches set into the walls of the octagonal centre of the crypt, near to St Francis, on the eve of his feast day, 3 October 1932.[96]

To understand the impression the new Basilica must have made upon contemporaries it is worth contrasting it with the other churches of Assisi, and particularly with the recently rebuilt cathedral, San Rufino. This cathedral was the tangible expression of the victory of the commune over the bishop and was the pride of the townspeople. It contained the relics of the martyr Rufinus. Early in the eleventh century the bishop had wanted to transfer these to his cathedral, Santa Maria. In one of his sermons, St Peter Damian alleged that, in a trial of strength, about sixty men pulled and tugged for the bishop till they were exhausted. The sarcophagus would not budge. Then, a mere seven, for the people, lifted it and carried it into their church. As a result, c.1029, the cathedral was transferred to San Rufino. The rebuilding was perhaps begun c.1140, but was still not quite complete in 1210.[97] It has been conjectured that the altar of San Rufino was consecrated by Gregory IX in 1228, when he was in Assisi for the canonisation of St Francis.[98] San Rufino, much larger than Santa Maria, is well placed and looks especially impressive from above; it has a fine façade, with lions and other animals, birds and flowers, and a lovely rose window[99] (Plates 11 and 1). But the building as a whole is not comparable to the Basilica: the site is less dramatic, the building smaller, the design less original.

It is instructive, too, to compare the burial church of St Francis, founder of the Order of Friars Minor, at Assisi, with the burial church of St Dominic, founder of the Order of Preachers, at Bologna. St Dominic died at Bologna in 1221, when he was about fifty years old. He was buried in the church of St Nicholas of the Vines, which had been given to the Dominicans by its priest in charge, the bishop having granted permission at the instance of none other than Hugolino, cardinal bishop of Ostia – later Pope Gregory IX – who was the personal friend of both Francis and Dominic. Hugolino arrived at

---

[94] 1 Cel. 61–3, 89–90, 114, 119; and see p. 189.

[95] Gatti 1983, pp. 397–8; Schenkluhn 1991, fig. 28. For William the Englishman and his drawing, see Little 1914a and pls. I, II; Little 1937, ch. IV, pl. I.

[96] Gatti 1983, pp. 397–406 and nn. Their tomb had been opened in 1607 when a new altar was constructed for their relics. They were placed in a wooden coffin divided into four compartments. The head of Rufino was placed separately in a silver reliquary, and was shown to the people annually on the fifth Sunday after Easter, when the feast of the dedication of the Basilica was celebrated (Gatti 1983, p. 398).

[97] Nicolini 1978, pp. 256, 264–5.

[98] Thus Von Matt and Hauser 1956, p. 4, but without citing evidence.

[99] Von Matt and Hauser 1956, pls. 5–8.

Plate 11 Assisi, Cathedral of San Rufino, west front (Photo C. N. L. Brooke).

the convent with his retinue just after Dominic's death, and officiated at his burial himself.[100] Bologna was the Italian headquarters of the Order, and a university city. So many students and teachers joined the Order that both convent and church soon had to be enlarged. St Dominic was buried in the presbytery of the original church. His tomb became a place of pilgrimage, but the friars, at first, rather surprisingly, were indifferent to his relics and found the pilgrims rather tiresome. The prior admitted that Dominic had performed many miracles of healing, but he seems to have kept no record

[100] Tugwell 1982, pp. 59, 68–9, 76, 78

of them. Men and women had brought candles and wax images to the tomb, and some had wanted to cover it with silks, but he and his colleagues had vetoed the suggestion. They thought that it would look as if they were encouraging the cult from motives of greed or pride.[101]

About 1223 they decided to prolong the church to the east, so as to provide themselves with a new choir, more spacious and more private. They began by demolishing the presbytery, so for a time Dominic's tomb lay exposed to the elements, till the walls were extended and reroofed. They kept to the same width, but about doubled the length (Figure 1). The new choir was probably finished in time for the General Chapter which was held in Bologna in 1228.[102] In July of the same year, 1228, Gregory IX canonised St Francis and the Basilica in his honour was begun in Assisi. The pope, who had admired both men, urged the Dominicans to show more honour to their founder. So they began to restore the old part of the church; and they also acquired a more fitting sarcophagus, made of marble, and performed a ceremony of translation on 24 May 1233. Gregory IX canonised him on 3 July 1234. The building works were completed, and the church consecrated, in 1251.[103]

The differences between the two churches are striking. The Franciscans built a new church; the Dominicans enlarged an existing church, and theirs is therefore much inferior architecturally. At Assisi two churches are built one above the other. At Bologna a new church was added on to the end of the old, making the whole disproportionately long. This underlines the imaginative quality of brother Elias' conception, and the rich and inspiring originality of the monument he raised to the apostle of poverty.

---

[101] Meersseman 1946, p. 153; Tugwell 1982, pp. 66, 69; cf. also ibid. pp. 59, 70–1.
[102] Meersseman 1946, pp. 153–7 and plan, p. 154; Vicaire 1964, p. 381.
[103] Meersseman 1946, pp. 155–6; Tugwell 1982, pp. 69, 71, 78, 81; Vicaire 1964, pp. 381–8, 528–9.

CHAPTER FIVE

THE AUTHORITY OF ST FRANCIS: EXPOSITIONS OF THE RULE

No one questioned that Francis was the founder of the Order of Friars Minor. But a vital part of his image in his lifetime and in the years following his death – and for many generations after that – concerned his authority over the Order. Was he just a revered founder and one-time Minister General, whose authority died with him? Or was he uniquely their legislator, whose Rule reflected divine inspiration, whose lightest word must be sought out and followed by the brethren of the Order? Did the authority of his Rule depend on Francis' authorship, or, as he claimed, on God's direct call to him, or on the papal bull in which it was enshrined in 1223, which gave it formal authority in canon law?

The first Exposition of the Rule, though it has not generally been considered as such, is St Francis' Testament.[1] In this moving document he assured them that these his last requests did not constitute a new Rule, but rather a testimony and an exhortation to help them the better and more faithfully to keep what they had already promised to observe. He believed that between them the Rule and the Testament made all that was needful abundantly clear. They were to be learnt and obeyed as they stood, simply and literally. No one, not even a Minister General, was to presume to alter a word of either, or to put any learned construction on them. He, their founder, was in fact to remain for all time the sole and final exponent of his own teaching.

At the General Chapter of 1230 both the Rule and the Testament were subjected to criticism and so insistent were some of the speakers that John Parenti reluctantly agreed to countenance an appeal to Gregory IX. His reaction to their representations was not quite as encouraging as they had hoped. His affection and reverence for Francis were sufficiently strong to prevent his wholehearted acceptance of a programme he knew to be directly opposed to Francis' wishes. His official reply, contained in the bull *Quo elongati* of 28 September 1230,[2] is a strange medley of conflicting good intentions. The brethren it addressed were also the prey of conflicting emotions and aspirations, which

[1] Esser 1976, pp. 438–44. For the Rule, the *Regula bullata*, see ibid. pp. 366–71.
[2] Grundmann 1961, pp. 20–5.

is perhaps one reason why a solution that was neither consistent nor in much of its detail acceptable was made the foundation of what was to be an abiding compromise, and found greater favour than later more coherent answers to the same problem. The main essentials of the friars' case are noted in the bull. Gregory was informed that there were certain perplexing and obscure passages in the Rule that called for explanation, an explanation that they were precluded from attempting by the absolute veto of the Testament on all glosses; the Testament in addition imposed other injunctions, for instance that which forbade them to ask for papal letters of any kind, compliance with which was bound to involve the Order in serious difficulties. In the same vein was their somewhat startling announcement of the hope that the Rule did not oblige them to a literal observance of the Gospel in its entirety, for that was more than they had ever intended to undertake. Both these were unashamed frontal attacks on what St Francis held most dear. Gregory admitted that according to Roman and Canon Law the Testament could not be held to be binding, as neither the Order nor even the Ministers had been consulted and as no one had the power to bind those who succeeded to his authority. As to the counsels of the Gospel that were not quoted in the Rule, they were not bound by them unless of their own goodness they offered them as a rich sacrifice to the Lord. The implications of the remaining queries were less serious. Might they, with a clear conscience, let faithful friends do their business transactions for them, provided these did not act as their accredited agents? Who owned the few utensils, articles of furniture and such like that they had to have? For they were hearing it said that these in effect belonged to the Order, and this insidious and plausible argument was occasioning them much distress. Gregory quieted their scruples over money and property with a reassurance that was masterly in its tact and sanity. If the brethren needed to make a purchase or to settle an account they could introduce to the vendor anyone wishing to make them an offering, or his representative. This person, albeit introduced by them, was to act as the vendor's or the donor's agent, not as theirs, and he was to complete the transaction on the spot and in such a way that no money intended for the friars' support remained unspent. Benefactors, and their agents, might deposit contributions to meet the brethren's imminent necessities with friends of the Order, who might then disburse such sums as need arose. As to property, they were to possess nothing, either individually or in common. Necessary utensils, books, furniture they were allowed the use of only.

So, in effect, on the plane of Francis' sanctity, Gregory IX extolled and exalted him, but with regard to the Order the pope treated Francis as a past Minister General, now dead – though he knew very well both that Francis had refused to undertake the office of Minister General himself, and that he had strained every nerve to continue to influence his Order from beyond the grave.

THE *EXPOSITION OF THE FOUR MASTERS*

Once Gregory IX had decided that the Testament had no sanction in law there was nothing to prevent the brethren from undertaking the work of exegesis themselves and contributing a literature of their own on the sense and syntax of the Rule. The first decisive move was made by the Chapter of 'diffinitors' which met at Montpellier in 1241. The provinces were ordered to elect committees from among their learned men to study the Rule carefully and report back to the Minister General.[3] Only one such report has survived. It was delivered by the province of France and is now generally known – somewhat incorrectly – as the *Exposition of the Four Masters*.[4] It was commissioned by the French Provincial Chapter of 1241, in accordance with the instructions just received from the Chapter of diffinitors, and was addressed to Haymo of Faversham at the next General Chapter, which was held in Bologna at Whitsun 1242. It was written by Alexander of Hales and John of La Rochelle, both celebrated Masters of Theology, with the assistance of Robert of La Bassée and Eudes Rigaud, later archbishop of Rouen, who at this time were still Bachelors.[5] Although it was perfectly legitimate for them to expound the Rule, the Four Masters took care to state explicitly in their Prologue that they were not going, as some had gloomily predicted, to do anything so scandalous, so contrary to the Rule, as to produce a new exposition or gloss. Rather, they would seek to draw out the full meaning of the Rule 'simpliciter et pure', not in accordance with their own views but as its own words required.[6] 'The intention of the Rule' is a phrase that runs right through the *Exposition*[7] – countering the taunt flung at the Minors by contemporary and by modern observers that all but a few faithful disciples flouted the intention of the Rule and did what they could to get round its letter. When discussing the extent of the brothers' obligation to obey the Gospel their touch is less felicitous. They quote Gregory's ruling, and by a cunning use of sophistry bolster it up, instancing the Testament to prove that St Francis only meant them to be bound by those passages which 'he in few words and simply caused to be written down'.[8] However their better nature soon reasserted itself. Because the Ministers were charged with the care of the brethren some were apparently arguing that they could lay in supplies. To this their reply is confident and unequivocal. The Gospel enjoins us to take no thought for the morrow, and the Rule of the Friars Minor is to observe the Gospel. The passage from St Matthew that they cite is not found in the Rule.[9] Throughout they favoured a strict interpretation of duty. It is wrong for them to enjoy fixed or perpetual alms or to cultivate fields sufficient to provide their sustenance, for there are two degrees of evangelical poverty, the one imperfect, when nothing superfluous is retained, the other perfect, when neither superfluities nor necessaries are reserved, and it is this absolute, mendicant poverty that the Minors offer to God.[10] When it came to money the learned Masters out-Francised Francis. As distinct from objects which the brethren might use but not own, money was something which they might neither use nor own, and by the term money should be understood not only actual coin but anything whatever accepted not to be used by the brethren but to be given again as the price of something else.[11]

---

[3] Eccleston, pp. 70–1. The 'diffinitors' comprised a chapter of representatives of the rank and file of the friars (Eccleston, pp. 70–1 and n. 2b; Brooke 1959, p. 233).
[4] Oliger 1950.   [5] Oliger 1950, pp. 17–24, 123–4.   [6] Oliger 1950, p. 124.
[7] Oliger 1950, pp. 130, 132, 133, 136, 160, 163.   [8] Oliger 1950, pp. 125–6.
[9] Oliger 1950, p. 147.   [10] Oliger 1950, pp. 157–8.   [11] Oliger 1950, pp. 142–3.

The method adopted in tackling many of the difficulties raised is markedly juridical.[12] The definitions and principles of Roman Law are appealed to as offering acceptable solutions on a variety of issues: the necessity of understanding the Rule properly; the precise meaning of money; the nature of such negotiations as buying, selling, borrowing, lending, etc.; the validity of majority decisions; and so forth.[13]

The commonsense of the Four Masters is particularly evident in their handling of 'necessitas'. Necessity, they assert, cannot be simply defined, because it can take many forms. A man may be excused from fasting because of physical weakness or exhausting toil or because he has in any case insufficient food.[14] Their *Exposition* upholds the Rule – the direction to wear sorry clothing means that in each district the brethren's clothing should be such as is esteemed cheap there, both in price and in colour, for the value put upon certain cloths is not a constant, but varies from place to place.[15] It also transcends it. The requirements of the Rule with regard to fasting were in some respects different from those of the Church as a whole and some friars took up the attitude that they need only keep those particular fasts enjoined in the Rule. To which the Four Masters replied: 'The religion of the Friars Minor does not absolve me from Christianity; nor does it relieve me from the Christian fast.'[16]

Their policy of frequently incorporating a representative cross-section of opinion on disputed topics into their discussion lends vividness and added interest to their *Exposition*. There was much serious and informed consideration of the Rule and its implications, at least within their circle. Nor did they only preserve for us the responsible or scholarly comment that they approved or that they thought might advance understanding. They also quoted a few downright vicious and specious opinions they thought it necessary to refute. There were friars who contrived to find loopholes in the wording of the Rule, who said that as they could eat what was set before them they could 'fast' on a meat diet, and who defended their laziness by protesting that the spirit of prayer would be extinguished in them every time they were told to do anything by their superiors.[17]

The Four Masters succeeded in producing an *Exposition* that did little violence to the Rule. Their attitude to individual vexed questions, like privileges, money and property, and to the spirit of the Rule as a whole shows genuine piety and genuine respect and loyalty to Francis. There is however one significant omission. That portion of the Rule which deals with learning is passed over without comment.

Their comments on the powers of the Minister General reflect the immediate past history of the Order, the circumstances of Elias' deposition and the statutes to rectify matters drawn up, mostly, by the leading academics of the Order in 1239. Alexander

---

[12] For a discussion of the use made of Roman Law by the Four Masters see Oliger 1950, pp. 28–30. I think however that he goes too far in saying that they proceeded 'iuridice et non ascetice'.

[13] Oliger 1950, pp. 124 and n. 3, 142–3, 152–5, 161; and cf. Lambert 1961, p. 40 and n. 5.

[14] Oliger 1950, pp. 134–6, 139.

[15] Oliger 1950, p. 136. Local variations caused a certain amount of difficulty. Some friars opposed St Francis' wish that all their houses should be made of wood and clay, saying that in some provinces wood was dearer than stone (SL 77). In England William of Nottingham had the stone walls of the dormitory at Salisbury removed and replaced with mud, with great devotion and at very great expense (Eccleston, p. 23).

[16] Oliger 1950, p. 139.   [17] Oliger 1950, pp. 138–9, 149.

of Hales and John of La Rochelle, two of the authors of the *Exposition*, had played a leading role throughout these events.[18] The Four Masters raise the question of whether statutes limiting the power of the Minister General and regulating the procedures of chapters and elections which had been passed by the friars, the Minister General and the other Ministers in General Chapter can be subsequently changed to the contrary by order of the Minister General – hypothetically a serious possibility in 1241–2.[19] 'As it is the intention of the Rule that the General Chapter is held, it is the business of the Chapter to make ordinances by which the purity and perfection of the religious life can be safeguarded, in such a way that no-one be he superior or inferior can by any means violate them. Therefore if the Chapter, in order to prevent danger to the religious life, restricts the power of the General or Provincial Ministers and ordains some other wholesome measures to be observed by the friars in general on the authority of the Rule, which underpins the authority of the General Chapter, these cannot be repealed by the Minister General.'

The Four Masters stress the paramount importance of the Rule. The Rule cannot be changed, but its meaning, its intention must be made clear. For them, writing in 1241–2, the intention of the Rule is safeguarded and implemented by means of supplementary legislation enacted by common consent in General Chapter and approved by the papacy. St Francis is receding into the background. Gregory IX had declared in *Quo elongati* that the friars are not bound by St Francis' Testament because 'without the consent of the brothers and most of all the Ministers, all of whom it touched, it could not bind them'; nor 'did he bind his successor in any way at all, since equal has no power of command over equal'.[20]

Thus in 1241–2 the Four Masters developed a constitutional doctrine of consent, of a kind which was becoming fashionable in the chapters and parliaments of the day throughout western Europe.

HUGH OF DIGNE

Although some later Expositions of the Rule had wider circulation – such as those by John Pecham[21] and Peter John Olivi[22] – outstandingly the most significant is that of Hugh of Digne, for Hugh deeply influenced both Innocent IV and St Bonaventure and was himself a friar of exceptional zeal.[23] Had he lived a generation or two later, he would undoubtedly have been reckoned among the Spirituals. If we did not know of this from other sources, his *Exposition* would not have told us. The groups of Spirituals suffered much in their lifetime but benefited posthumously from an exaggerated and misleading reputation for fidelity to primitive Franciscan observance, whereas in fact

[18] Jordan, c. 61; cf. Eccleston, p. 67; Brooke 1959, pp. 161–7.
[19] Oliger 1950, pp. 160–1; Brooke 1959, pp. 210–46. [20] Grundmann 1961, p. 21.
[21] This commentary was attributed from the fifteenth century on to St Bonaventure, and is printed among his works in *Opera Omnia*, VIII (1898), 391–437. Harkins 1969 convincingly argued that it can be ascribed with some confidence to John Pecham.
[22] Flood 1972; cf. esp. Burr 1989.
[23] I quote Hugh of Digne's *Expositio* from the very helpful edition of David Flood, OFM: Flood 1979. There is an admirable account of Hugh in Poulenc 1969, and a balanced view of his place in Franciscan history in Burr 1989, pp. 18–24.

they differed as essentially from St Francis and his first companions as they did from the main body of the Conventuals. They claimed Hugh as one of their early protagonists and so his *Exposition of the Rule* and other writings provide a wholesome corrective to former views of the Spiritual movement.

A few facts about his home and parentage are given in a biography of his sister, St Douceline, who was born c.1214–15 and who died in 1274. He was a native of Provence, where he passed most of his life. His father, Berengar of Digne, was a merchant.[24] More vivid if perhaps less reliable are the accounts of him by Salimbene. Hugh was dark and of medium height, with a voice that thundered. He was quite an important person in the Order. He had been a Provincial Minister, but at the time Salimbene knew him he was of his own choice a subject friar, living in the small convent the Minors had established at Hyères.[25] Something of his worth can be judged from the quality of his friends, John of Parma, Robert Grosseteste, Adam Marsh.[26] He made a great name for himself as a preacher – and here the testimony of Joinville corroborates Salimbene's. When St Louis returned from the Crusade in July 1254 he landed at Hyères and sent for Hugh. Hugh came, followed by great crowds of men and women on foot, and delivered a sermon appropriate to the occasion. Its burden was an attack on the number of religious who frequented the royal court. The Scriptures 'say a monk cannot live outside his cloister without mortal sin any more than a fish can live without water' – a commonplace medieval proverb utilised also by Chaucer. And he proved by example that he meant every word of his tirade for he angrily refused the pleadings of both Joinville and St Louis to remain with the king during his stay in Provence.[27] Innocent IV also liked to hear him and the papal court fared no better than the royal. Both at Rome and after it had moved to Lyon he attended the Curia and lashed the cardinals with his tongue as if they were schoolboys.[28] He was able to rate cardinals and courtiers with impunity because he had the favour of pope and king: he employed other techniques to draw the common people in crowds to hear him. To them he was prepared to utter prophecies and they listened to him as readily as they would to John the Baptist. For them he painted the ineffable glories of Paradise, the hideous torments of Hell. His words were honeyed, wonderful, edifying, telling, salutary – Salimbene cannot praise them enough.[29]

Hugh was an ardent Joachite and possessed copies of all Joachim's works. He never tired of talking of Joachim, or Salimbene of listening.[30] In being thus absorbed they were by no means indulging an unusual taste. Joachim's doctrines and prophecies were exciting great interest at this time, especially among the Franciscans, many of whom

---

[24] The *Life* of Ste Douceline, ed. in Albanés 1879; see esp. pp. xl–xli; English translation in Garay and Jeay 2001: see esp. pp. 7, 11. The *Life* was written in French in 1297, and revised c.1315 (Albanés 1879, pp. xxi–xxv; Garay and Jeay 2001, p. 16).

[25] Salimbene, S, I, 324, 365–6, H, pp. 226, 253–4.   [26] Salimbene, S, I, 334–5, H, pp. 232–4.

[27] Joinville, *Histoire de saint Louis*, ed. N. de Wailly (Paris, 1874), pp. 360–3; cf. Runciman 1954, p. 280 and n. 3.

[28] Salimbene, S, I, 324–34, H, pp. 226–32.

[29] Salimbene, S, I, 324, 336–7, H, pp. 226, 234–5. Hugh's preaching is described in the *Life* of Ste Douceline as 'luzens e escalfons aissi con le solels' (shedding light and warmth like the sun: Albanés 1879, pp. 4–5).

[30] Salimbene, S, I, 455–6, H, p. 313; for Joachism, see esp. Reeves 1969.

believed that they were the barefoot Order of contemplatives Joachim had foretold would herald the third era of the world. Even John of Parma, the Minister General, was a convinced Joachite. It was on his behalf that Salimbene borrowed Hugh's manuscript of Joachim's *Exposition of the Four Gospels* and took it to Aix, where he and his companion copied it out.[31] Unfortunately speculation provoked by Joachim's works, and by spurious works attributed to him, all too easily crossed the borderline into heresy. In 1254 Gerard of Borgo San Donnino, a young friar from Sicily who had been appointed to the key post of lector to the Franciscan convent at Paris, published, on his own initiative, a sensational book, *The Introduction to the Eternal Gospel*, in which he rashly asserted that Joachim's writings would replace the New Testament in the age that was just beginning. It was taken to the pope by William of St Amour, a regent master at Paris, who was hostile to the friars and glad of the opportunity to injure them, and condemned.[32] The seer's doctrines were further discredited when Frederick II inconsiderately anticipated the span of life allotted to him in his role as Antichrist and died in 1250, ten years too soon. When in addition the fateful year 1260 passed quietly by, Salimbene, who had never been more than a passive, fair-weather adherent, gave up his Joachism and declared that henceforward he would believe only what he could see.[33] He had evidently taken this question of the date seriously for he saw fit to record in full a very lengthy disputation between Hugh of Digne and Peter of Apulia, the lector of the Dominican convent at Naples, on this very subject. Hugh defended the thesis that Frederick II must live to be seventy and must die a natural death and marshalled such a galaxy of arguments and quotations from the Old and New Testaments, the works of Aristotle and the 'Prophecies of Merlin' to his support that his opponent had to admit himself defeated. Salimbene headed his concluding remarks 'How brother Hugh gave the laity a good example' and, unconscious of the irony, recorded that the bystanders were much edified and consoled, and departed saying: 'We have heard wonderful things today. But on the next holy day we should like to hear something of the doctrine of our Lord Jesus Christ.'[34]

Hugh, then, would seem to have been an influential and popular figure in the land of his birth. His sister, St Douceline, a mystic who had ecstatic visions, gathered round her at Hyères a group of devoted women. He took a great interest in her career and achievement and wrote a Rule for her. She regarded him as her spiritual director and spoke of him as 'the author of our Order'.[35]

Hugh died at Marseille and was buried in the church of the friars' convent there. In the *Life* of St Douceline it is stated that the bereaved sister was visited and consoled by John of Parma while he was still Minister General.[36] Hugh was alive and full of vigour in July 1254 when Joinville heard him preach before St Louis, so his death must have occurred between then and early 1257, when John of Parma resigned.

---

[31] Salimbene, S, 1, 428, H, p. 294.
[32] Gratien 1928, pp. 210–18; Reeves 1969.   [33] Salimbene, S, 1, 441–2, H, pp. 302–3.
[34] Salimbene, S, 1, 344–65, esp. 364–5; H, pp. 239–53, esp. p. 253.   [35] Albanés 1879, pp. 150–1.
[36] Albanés 1879, pp. xlviii and n., l–lii, 134–7; Garay and Jeay 2001, p. 71. A will has been preserved dated 31 August 1260, bequeathing a legacy to Douceline, sister of the late brother Hugh of Digne, OFM (Poulenc 1969, col. 317).

The Spirituals regarded Hugh as one of themselves. Ubertino da Casale called him 'a man of outstanding holiness and wisdom', 'a zealot for poverty and a professor of this Rule and a truly impressive cleric'.[37] A zealot for poverty – the hallmark of the Spiritual. Hugh wrote two treatises on poverty: the *Disputation between a zealot for poverty and a colleague hostile to poverty* and *On the aims of poverty*,[38] and many of his arguments were utilised and quoted with approval by the Spirituals' leaders, Olivi, Clareno, Casale. He was like them in his learning and his Joachism. Like them he studied the Rule closely and in his *Exposition* he made great use of the *Regula non bullata*.[39] The tract in which he comes closest to them is the earliest of these works, his imaginary disputation between a zealot and a relaxed friar. The zealot heaped reproaches on his brother for alleviating the proper hardships of poverty and his slippery opponent wriggled from one plausible excuse to another. 'I marvel', he would say, 'that you get so worked up. After all, poverty consists not in this external show, but in the heart . . . Besides, for everything that I have and use I can show you a reasonable cause and the authority of my superior . . .' Good tunics are cheaper in the end than ragged ones. 'In a nice thick tunic I feel the cold less and so I can sing the Office better and pass the night in prayer. More money is needed too to keep us in rags, for one good tunic will last a long time while an inferior one is soon worn out . . . How you do go on. I repeat, it is the intention that counts . . . Very well, if you see an excess go to your superior about it, and let that satisfy you. You, perhaps, will set the Order to rights.' This final ironic and derisive thrust provoked a passionate, bitter reply strongly reminiscent of the later Spirituals. 'It would profit me nothing to have recourse to [the superiors] as many not only disdain to hear but cruelly persecute those who dare to open their mouths.' You taunt me with my powerlessness, but I firmly believe that those you try to destroy will at last purify the Order – we are not dismayed by your pettifogging and your threats.[40]

Hugh was a scholastic and this is most clearly evident in *The aims of poverty*, in which his argument is developed in successive syllogisms according to the strict rules of technical logic. His style seems to us pretentious and singularly lacks grace of rhythm or vocabulary.[41] In this work Hugh uses *Quo elongati*, so was writing after 1230; he also quotes from the *Liber Extra* – the *Decretals* of Pope Gregory IX promulgated on 5 September 1234 – and some lapse of time after that date must be allowed for the *Liber Extra* to have circulated. The *Aims of poverty* cannot be as late as 1242, since it shows no

[37] Ubertino da Casale in ALKG III, 58; *Arbor Vitae* (Venice, 1485), v. 5, fo. E III rb.
[38] *Firmamenta* IV, fos. 105ra–108 vb; Florovsky 1912, pp. 277–90.
[39] See esp. 'Prologus', Flood 1979, p. 92.
[40] *Firmamenta* IV, fos. 106r–108v. The attack on superiors suggests either a youthful work by a man who had not yet assumed high office, or the disillusioned utterance of an old, retired, ex-Minister. But between Hugh's retirement and death, John of Parma was Minister General, and the tone of the *Disputation* accords ill with the reign of Hugh's friend, the zealous John of Parma; there is a hint on fo. 105v that the 'zelator' is young. Thus I accept Poulenc's view that it is an early work, though it cannot be at all precisely dated. There is, however, a passage (fo. 107) in which Hugh tells how St Francis had assured someone suggesting that something be set aside for future necessities that the Blessed Virgin would rather her altar was denuded than that anything be done contrary to her Son's instruction (*consilium*); and the same story is told – with specific reference to Peter Catanii and the altar of St Mary of the Portiuncula – in 2 Cel. 67. It is striking that Hugh tells the story with the minimum of verbal resemblance to Celano's version, so it is improbable that he received it from Celano, and it cannot be argued from this parallel that Hugh was writing after 1247.
[41] See Florovsky 1912, e.g. p. 287.

knowledge of the *Exposition of the Four Masters*. It can thus be dated 1234–42, and seems likely to belong to the mid or late 1230s.[42]

Hugh's *Exposition of the Rule* was written later than mid-1242.[43] He speaks of Gregory IX 'of happy memory',[44] and the pope died on 22 August 1241; and he makes constant use of the *Exposition of the Four Masters*, which was composed 1241–2 and sent in to the General Chapter held at Whitsun 1242. But the most significant indication of the date at which Hugh was writing is provided by his sole comment on that passage of the Rule which affirms the brethren's obedience to the pope and the Roman Church. It runs: 'that is to say, to the College of the Cardinals with whom authority chiefly resides while the Apostolic See is vacant'.[45] The point is not made in either the earlier *Exposition* of the Four Masters or the later one of John Pecham. Usually the interval between the death of one pope and the election of his successor was sufficiently short for the allegiance of the Order to the College of Cardinals during the interregnum to be a matter of slight practical consequence. But once, and only once, during the period in which Hugh might have written his *Exposition*, there was a prolonged vacancy which lasted (apart from the three weeks' pontificate of Celestine IV) from the death of Gregory IX in August 1241 to the election of Innocent IV in June 1243.[46] It was evidently this unusual state of affairs that prompted Hugh's comment. If Hugh had been writing after the vacancy had been filled, he would surely have phrased this passage differently, adding it maybe as a corollary. There was no reason to make this specific point alone – and no other points – if it was not of actual concern and relevance. It seems highly probable therefore that Hugh began to write his *Exposition* while the papacy was vacant. We know from Salimbene that Hugh was in Rome for some time during the vacancy so he would have had some awareness at close hand of its impact and application.[47] This means that he must have begun work as soon as was practicable after he had received a copy of the *Exposition of the Four Masters* at or soon after the General Chapter held at Whitsun 1242. But he did not finish in a matter of months. The passage on the correct temporary arrangements during a papal vacancy occurs near the beginning, in his commentary on chapter 1 of the Rule. It was not finalised until the summer or autumn of 1245.

Among the questions the Four Masters thought needed to be referred to the pope for settlement was a doubt as to whether the Order was permitted to expel perverse religious.[48] In his discussion of this problem Hugh, while quoting from the Four Masters, takes the line, as he does occasionally elsewhere, that this is a matter of

---

[42] Florovsky 1912, pp. 283–4, 287.
[43] In Brooke 1959, p. 221 and n. 2 Hugh's *Exposition* was dated 1242–3, but without detailed evidence. The date was accepted by Poulenc in *Dictionnaire de Spiritualité*, VII, 1 (1969), col. 877; but rejected by J. Paul (1975a and b) and Flood (1979, pp. 50–71), who both argue for the early 1250s, Flood for 1252, Paul for 1253. As will be seen, I have modified my earlier view, but still believe it was composed between Whitsun 1242 and November 1245.
[44] Flood 1979, p. 193. Although such a phrase may occasionally have been used of the living, it is reasonable to assume that Gregory was dead (cf. Knowles, Brooke and London 2001, pp. 10 and n. 3, 240).
[45] Flood 1979, p. 97, in Hugh's commentary on c. 1 of the Rule.
[46] The other vacancies in Hugh's lifetime were exceedingly brief – two days in 1216, one day in 1227, five days in 1254. It was not until 1268 that there occurred one of comparable length to that of 1241–3.
[47] Hugh preached a sermon in the convent at Siena on his return from Rome, according to Salimbene – who resided in Siena c.1241–3: Salimbene, S, I, 336, cf. p. 60; H, pp. 234–5, cf. p. 44.
[48] Oliger 1950, pp. 133–4; Flood 1979, pp. 108–9.

commonsense – by implication, there is no need to trouble the pope with it. It is obvious, he says, that incorrigibles have to be expelled, just as putrid limbs have to be cut off for the sake of the health of the body. He agrees with the Four Masters that the provisions of the Rule prevent the granting of letters of dismissal to those thrown out. A final sentence, however, states briefly that now letters of dismissal have been conceded by a privilege. This refers to a bull, *Paci et tranquillitati*, issued to the Order on 16 August 1245, stating: 'Those expelled from your Order or departed from it – except to Augustinians, Templars, Hospitallers or any arms-bearing Order – you can give them licence *cum vestris testimonialibus litteris*.' There are three originals of this bull at Assisi.[49] Hugh's final sentence reads like an addition, an editing of the passage to bring it up to date. I conclude that Hugh's commentary was begun soon after Whitsun 1242 and finished soon after 16 August 1245, at precisely the period when the friars and the pope were entering the discussions which issued in *Ordinem vestrum* on 14 November 1245. It seems probable that he finished, or revised, it as a contribution to these discussions, and that the verbal links between the commentary and the bull are due to the use the draftsmen made of Hugh's subtle arguments. Thus a good starting point for further investigation is provided by the Papal bull *Ordinem vestrum* of 14 November 1245.

THE BULL *ORDINEM VESTRUM*

Ordinem vestrum was based primarily on *Quo elongati*.[50] It was not a fully fledged commentary; it did not consider all the chapters of the Rule or take them in order, but followed much the same plan as the earlier bull. All the topics treated by Gregory, with the exception of the Testament, are re-examined. The pope answered, in the affirmative, two of the questions the Four Masters had specifically said should be put to him. The competence of the 'nuntius' was extended: he might transfer funds destined for the friars to another person, who did not have to be nominated by them, or to another place. The brethren might enter nunneries not only to preach or to beg but for any other honest and reasonable cause. Three replies seem to show an awareness of observations made by them, and perhaps by others also. The Order's moveables as well as immoveables are expressly declared to be the property of the Holy See. The Ministers might delegate their duty of acting as confessors for reserved offences to responsible subordinates. Not only the Ministers and custodians but anyone entrusted by them with these tasks should show proper solicitude for the needs of the sick and for the clothing of the brethren.[51] *Ordinem vestrum* refines Gregory IX's definition of who might be admitted to the Order – now restricted to those who on the evidence specifically 'of their literacy and other praiseworthy circumstances' can be useful, and

---

[49] Sbaralea I, 371–2, 14, no. 87; Eubel 1908, p. 36, no. 370 and p. 36 n., correcting the date to 16 August 1245 (of the three originals at Assisi, two are so dated, one – evidently by a slip – dated 17 July). Flood p. 109 n. 2 identifies the privilege with a later reissue.

[50] *Ordinem vestrum* (henceforth *Ov*) is quoted from Eubel 1908, pp. 238–9.

[51] *Ov*, pp. 238–9; cf. Oliger 1950, pp. 152, 157; 159; 146. Cf. Hugh of Digne in Flood 1979, pp. 132–4.

profit others by their example.[52] Gregory's mild suggestion that they might want to offer compliance with Gospel counsels not quoted in the Rule as a free sacrifice to God is left out. Useful as well as necessary things are brought within the scope of legitimate marketing through others' agents. Such an agent is no longer required to spend the entire sum entrusted to him on the spot but may keep the change for a future occasion. The permission of the Cardinal Protector or of a Minister need not be sought before giving away or otherwise disposing of articles of little value.

One cannot help wondering how far the bull really met the views of its promoters inside the Order, and who among the friars had any hand in framing it. Certainly it did not hold the field for long. Yet it is significant that the successful attack upon it was made not because it was too conservative but because it was not conservative enough. At the General Chapter held at Genoa, most probably in 1251, William of Nottingham, the English Provincial Minister, and Gregory of Bosellis persuaded the assembly, in the teeth of strong opposition, to repudiate the papal privilege enabling money to be received through procurators and to suspend *Ordinem vestrum* in so far as its interpretations were laxer than those of *Quo elongati*.[53] Comment on the Rule was no easy task and required great delicacy and tact. Innocent IV's modifications of Gregory's wording, slight enough in a way, suggested comfortable worldly wisdom; and although he did not go much beyond Gregory he none the less went further than the common conscience of the brethren would allow.

The crucial question whether or not Hugh of Digne used *Ordinem vestrum* when composing his *Exposition of the Rule* is complicated by the fact that this bull of Innocent IV's is modelled very closely on Gregory IX's *Quo elongati* of 28 September 1230 both as regards subject matter and in vocabulary and sentence construction.[54] Had he both bulls in front of him when he wrote, or only one, and if so which? It may be relevant that he refers, in the singular, to the 'expositio apostolica', or the 'responsum apostolicum';[55] he never once uses the plural.

Until it was repudiated by the Order at the Chapter at Genoa, probably held in 1251 – a repudiation confirmed at the Chapter at Metz in 1254[56] – *Ordinem vestrum* as the more recent pronouncement replaced and superseded *Quo elongati*. After that *Quo elongati* was once again effective. If he were writing between 1245 and 1251 it would have been quite in order, indeed proper, for Hugh to have ignored *Quo elongati* as out-of-date. But in fact it is quite certain that he used it, and used it in preference to *Ordinem vestrum*. On the question of how much of the Gospel was binding on them the statement in *Ordinem vestrum* is succinct: they are only bound to observe those Gospel precepts or prohibitions explicitly quoted in the Rule. *Quo elongati* had established this point, but had also recorded why the friars had asked the question and had expressed the hope that

[52] *Ov*, p. 238. The bull *Gloriantibus vobis* of 19 June 1241 (Sbaralea, I, 298, G9 no. 344; Eubel 1908, n. 311). On the constitution restricting the recruitment to literate applicants, see Brooke 1959, pp. 243–4, where it is argued that it can probably be dated 1242.

[53] Eccleston, p. 42 and n. The privilege enabling money to be received through procurators was *Quanto studiosius* of 19 August 1247. Sbaralea, I, 487–8, 14, no. 235; Eubel 1908, n. 478.

[54] For *Quo elongati* (henceforth *Qe*), see Grundmann 1961; for *Ov*, Eubel 1908, pp. 238–9. Flood discusses the relationship in Flood 1979, pp. 50–1, and most helpfully italicises words in common in his text.

[55] Flood 1979, pp. 99, 97, 174. [56] Brooke 1959, pp. 257 and nn. 2, 3, 264 and n. 3.

of their own good will they would go beyond what was obligatory. Hugh's treatment includes the additional material in *Quo elongati* and follows its wording quite closely. He could have taken the element of pious hope indirectly, as this passage from *Quo elongati* is quoted in the *Exposition of the Four Masters*, but there is no mention there of the friars' unwillingness to be bound to observe everything in the Gospel. It is clear therefore that Hugh was quoting from *Quo elongati* itself.[57] Hugh also quotes Gregory IX's decision that St Francis' Testament is not binding 'cum non habeat imperium par in parem' – 'since equal has no power of command over equal' – and the problem of the Testament is totally omitted from *Ordinem vestrum*.[58] These examples establish beyond doubt that Hugh had access to a text of *Quo elongati* itself.

On some points *Ordinem vestrum* goes further than *Quo elongati*, along lines suggested by the Four Masters, and on these Hugh's attitude is distinct and exceedingly interesting. Gregory IX's restrictions on entering nunneries appeared over-strict. The Four Masters had commented there was doubt whether 'they can go to inner apartments, to cloister, to chapter house, when they go together in general processions with the people, or preach with bishops in chapter houses. And so a papal exposition on this issue would be required.' The explicit authorisation they desired was duly provided by *Ordinem vestrum*: 'those friars who have permission from their superiors on the ground of their age or suitability can go to other convents of nuns [but not to houses of Poor Clares], just as other religious, and can enter to preach or seek alms, or for other honest and reasonable purposes'. Hugh draws on *Quo elongati* and the *Exposition of the Four Masters* in his discussion of the problem but makes no reference to Innocent IV's settlement of it. 'We are bound – not to the intentions of St Francis of which we are ignorant – but to the common and reasonable understanding of the Rule to which we are vowed . . . It tends to the scandal of the Order when brethren do not enter the inner apartments,

---

[57] Compare the following passages:

    Ov, p. 238: 'dicimus, quod per eamdem regulam quoad observationem evangelii, quam iniungit, non nisi ad ea dumtaxat evangelii consilia tenemini, quae in ipsa regula praeceptorie vel inhibitorie sunt expressa'.

    Qe, p. 21: 'Unde scire desiderant, an ad alia evangelii teneantur consilia quam ad ea, que in ipsa regula preceptorie vel inhibitorie sunt expressa, presertim cum ipsi ad alia non se obligare intenderint et vix vel numquam omnia possint ad litteram observari. Nos autem breviter respondemus vos ad alia consilia evangelii non teneri per regulam nisi ad ea, ad que vos obligastis in ipsa. Ad cetera vero tenemini sicut reliqui christiani, et eo magis de bono et equo, quo vos obtulistis holocaustum domino medullatum per contemptum omnium mundanorum.'

    Hugh of Digne (Flood 1979, p. 95): 'Cum autem dicitur quod regula . . . fratrum minorum est . . . sanctum evangelium observare, evangelii nomine iuxta responsum apostolicum ea tantum evangelii consilia designantur quae in ipsa regula praeceptorie vel inhibitorie sunt expressa, praesertim cum fratres ad alia non se obligare intenderant et vix aut numquam omnia possint ad litteram observari. Quod sanctus confirmasse videtur quando, ut praedictum est, ait: Ipse altissimus revelavit mihi quod ego secundum formam sancti evangelii deberem vivere. Et ego, inquit, paucis verbis et simpliciter feci scribi. Dixit ergo evangelium fratribus observandum quantum ad ea quae simpliciter fecit scribi. Ad alia vero tenentur sicut reliqui christiani, et eo magis de bono et aequo quo se obtulerunt holocaustum Domino medullatum per contemptum omnium mundanorum.'

    The Four Masters (Oliger 1950, p. 125): 'Et breviter respondetur: nisi ad ea, ad quae in ipsa regula se obligaverunt, ad consilia alia evangelii non teneri. Ad cetera vero teneri sicut ceteri christiani et eo magis de bono et aequo se obtulerunt holocaustum Domino medullatum.'

    Hugh's quotation from the Testament (Flood 1979, p. 95) is also in the Four Masters (Oliger 1950, pp. 125–6). Where *Ov* has 'dicimus' and *Qe* 'respondemus', Hugh cites the 'responsum apostolicum'.

[58] *Qe*, pp. 20–1. The Four Masters quote from the Testament and refer to it, but omit all mention of Gregory IX's ruling on it.

the cloister [or else 'claustrum' in the original sense, the enclosure, the 'clausura'] in general processions in common with the people and with bishops to preach in the chapter house or for other grave necessity, confession or special counsel at the instance of anyone gravely ill . . . It is not structures but persons who make a "monastery" – and it is they who are for us the whole occasion of the prohibition. On this account wise brethren willingly avoid a house of nuns.'[59] It seems hard to believe that Hugh would have written as he did after the publication of *Ordinem vestrum*.

The question of who owned the moveable property used by the friars should also have presented no difficulty after Innocent IV's definite statement that the Order's moveable and immoveable goods belonged to the Holy See. Papal ownership had been implicitly recognised in *Quo elongati* in that Gregory IX had there said that the friars might not dispose of anything without licence, but many felt that it would be advisable for the presumption thus created to be reinforced by a more open acknowledgement, and their concern was given voice by the Four Masters. Hugh argues from the presumption and not from the fact. People can still, it seems, ask the question: 'To whom do the buildings and things the friars use belong?' To such Hugh replies: 'I can say that whoever it may be it is not us or the Order, and that suffices us for the purity of conscience.'[60]

When however he comes to the subject of money Hugh sets the textual critic a stiffer problem. At this point *Ordinem vestrum* is longer than *Quo elongati*. In the first section, where the two bulls run parallel, Hugh agrees with *Quo elongati* against *Ordinem vestrum*.[61] But then Hugh's *Exposition* contains, in closely similar wording, the additional, second section in *Ordinem vestrum*, which is not in *Quo elongati*: that is, Hugh seems initially to follow *Quo elongati* and then to switch to *Ordinem vestrum*.[62] These verbal agreements can only be explained in one of two ways. Either Hugh had copies of *Quo elongati* and *Ordinem vestrum* in front of him and drew upon both, or *Ordinem vestrum* is in some way based upon Hugh. Let us suppose first that Hugh used *Ordinem vestrum*. In that case it is inconceivable that he wrote his *Exposition* between 1245 and 1251, during which time the problems concerning ownership of property and entry into nunneries (which Hugh treats as unsolved) were solved officially for the Order by that bull. If he wrote after 1251 he might treat *Ordinem vestrum* as a source but not an authoritative one, and this would explain the reopening of questions that that bull had settled. But to postulate such a date we must suppose that a friar was prepared to use the words of a bull which his Order had rejected while ignoring its provisions – a bull moreover which had been issued by a pope still living (or very recently dead),[63] and which had never been repudiated by him. The Order had no authority to rescind the bull – it could only abstain from taking advantage of its clauses and choose to live by a stricter standard. A date after 1251 is thus as objectionable as any date after 1245.

---

[59] Flood 1979, pp. 189–90. Cf. *Qe*, pp. 24–5; Four Masters, Oliger 1950, pp. 167–8; *Ov*, p. 239.

[60] *Ov*, pp. 238–9; *Qe*, pp. 22–3; Four Masters, Oliger 1950, p. 152; Flood 1979, pp. 145–8, esp. 146.

[61] *Qe*, p. 22, and Hugh (p. 126): 'negligens fuerit vel necessitates ignoraverit eorundem'; *Ov*, p. 238: 'negligentes fuerint vel necessitates aut incommoda ignoraverint eorundem'.

[62] The common wording of Hugh and *Ov* (but not always of Hugh and *Qe*) is italicised in Flood 1979, pp. 126–7. Hugh continues in the singular, *Ov* in the plural; and *Ov* inserts 'vel commodo', a phrase not to be found in Hugh.

[63] Innocent IV died on 7 December 1254.

These general objections to a date after 1245 are reinforced by an analysis of Hugh's text on the subject of money. He begins with a ringing endorsement of the papal declaration – in the singular – adding that in any case reason and truth support the argument that the friars can present an intermediary and have recourse to him for the purchase of goods and the settlement of debts without infringing the Rule, 'as a fuller explanation below will make clear'.[64] He proceeds (prefaced by the words: 'You may therefore observe') to quote from *Quo elongati*, interspersed with his own comments. Where *Quo elongati* ends the text runs on smoothly, still dealing with the same person nominated or presented by the friars, the 'nuntius' under discussion.[65] If Hugh was at this point switching to another bull, it is odd to say the least that he does not mention this, and contrary to his practice of specifying his source. Furthermore if he was here using *Ordinem vestrum* he would have found the words 'or convenience' after 'necessity'. This was a modification, a relaxation, which caused the friars great heart-searching. The Chapter where it was agreed to suspend the provisions of *Ordinem vestrum* in so far as they were laxer than those of *Quo elongati* was probably held in 1251, but in any case its decision was confirmed at the General Chapter at Metz in 1254. Yet it is suggested that Hugh wrote his *Exposition* precisely within this period, in 1252 or 1253, when awareness within the Order of the implications of this crucial issue was heightened and articulate.[66] It is surely inconceivable that Hugh not only would not have commented on this loosening of rigour, but would have suppressed the words themselves. The conclusion must surely be that he was not commenting on *Ordinem vestrum*, but continuing his commentary on *Quo elongati*. The text reads like that, and continues: 'For then, as has been said'. Indeed the passage is pivotal to his argument, a necessary link between the provisions of *Quo elongati* and the lengthy unfolding of his thoughts.[67]

We do not know sufficient about the working of the papal Chancery to be able to prove it, but the probability is that the drafting of *Ordinem vestrum* was left to the Chancery clerks, perhaps under the direction of the Cardinal Protector, particularly as it was in the main a reissue and presented no major difficulties. To guide them in drawing up the new bull they had *Quo elongati* which they took as their model but the Order must have been in some way consulted in a matter that so closely concerned it. Possibly the friars sent in some notes or a rough draft of what was desired. It is conceivable that Hugh himself provided just such a draft. We know that he was frequently at the Curia both at Rome and afterwards at Lyon and that Innocent IV respected him.[68] This would explain the verbal agreements. But there was input from at least one other source. It was not Hugh who caused the insertion of 'and/or useful things' every time bar one the word 'necessities' cropped up.[69]

The evidence that Hugh's *Exposition* was written between Whitsun 1242 and November 1245 is in harmony with other indications. When giving his opinion as to whether

---

[64] Flood 1979, p. 126.   [65] *Qe* and Hugh use the singular, *Ov* the plural: see above, nn. 61–2.
[66] Flood suggested 1252, Paul 1253 (see note 43); Oliger also placed it after *Ov*, dating it 1245–*c*.1255 (Oliger 1950, p. 78). For the chapters at Genoa and Metz, see Eccleston, p. 42 and n.; Brooke 1959, pp. 257 and nn. 2, 3; 264 and n. 3.
[67] Flood 1979, pp. 126–30.
[68] Salimbene, S, I, 324–34, esp. pp. 324, 331, 333; H, pp. 226–34, esp. 226, 231–2.   [69] *Ov*, p. 238.

or not the brethren ought to study and to lecture, he writes 'What person in his right mind would say that Master and brother Alexander of Hales ought to have preached and taught, "blessed are the poor in spirit" when he was rich, and after he had made himself poor for God's sake ought to have held his peace?'[70] The absence of any such pious phrase as 'of holy memory' does not prove that Alexander is still alive, but it comes at the climax of his argument and it is unlikely that he would have chosen to mention Alexander – the only contemporary example given – if he were not still an important figure in the Order. Alexander died between 15 and 22 August 1245.[71]

We do not know where Hugh received his higher education, but it is possible, even likely, that it was at Paris. The Order sent many of its brightest recruits there and Hugh acquired a very high reputation as a scholar. He could have been in Paris in the mid-1230s. We know that after he had finished his university studies he was Provincial Minister of Provence, and that by 1248 he had resigned from office.[72] If he was already a Provincial Minister in 1238–9 he would have been involved in the constitutional discussions and decisions surrounding brother Elias' fall.[73] He was certainly by then keenly interested in such matters. Again, if he was a Provincial Minister in 1241 he would have been among those who tried to gain entry to the Chapter meeting of diffinitors at Montpellier at which Expositions of the Rule were called for. The sentence in the Prologue which reads 'The discussion that has taken place in the Order bears witness that the Rule is especially profound, concise and full of meaning, and on this account is in some places obscure' surely refers to these consultations of 1241–2.[74]

THE SOURCES AND CHARACTERISTICS OF HUGH'S
EXPOSITION OF THE RULE

Hugh states at the outset of his Prologue that he is writing because he has been ordered to do so on obedience, and he makes extensive use of the *Exposition of the Four Masters*. In the course of his own *Exposition* he quotes almost the whole of this work, sometimes with acknowledgement, sometimes without. For the most part he cites the appropriate sections literally and in full; occasionally he reproduces their substance in his own words.[75] The likelihood is that he was commissioned promptly in 1242 by the then Minister General Haymo of Faversham to take an ongoing process of experiment and commentary a stage further. Hugh is considering the latest thinking, on observance of the Rule and the balance to be struck now, in the early 1240s, with St Francis dead,

---

[70] Flood 1979, pp. 186–7.
[71] Brooke 1959, p. 162 n. 1; cf. Doucet 1952, pp. 69*–70*. For the life of Alexander of Hales, see Doucet 1951, esp. p. 75*. For Alexander as canon of St Paul's and prebendary of Holbourn, see Greenway 1968, p. 54: he had been succeeded by 14 December 1237. Flood 1979, pp. 53–4 argues that the mention of Alexander of Hales could suitably refer to the quarrel between the friars and the University of Paris in 1252–3; but the Franciscan Master involved at that date was not Alexander of Hales but St Bonaventure, who was finally given his master's degree by the university in 1258 (Gratien 1928, pp. 205–14). Bonaventure himself incorporated this passage in his *Epistola de Tribus Quaestionibus* (*Opera Omnia*, VIII, 335; composed 1253–7: see p. 248).
[72] Poulenc 1969, cols. 875–6; Salimbene, S, I, 366; H, p. 254.
[73] Brooke 1959, pp. 163–6.   [74] Flood 1979, p. 91.
[75] Flood 1979, pp. 97, 173. Hugh shows his respect for the Four Masters as 'celebres . . . doctores', 'magni et doctissimi . . . viri' (Flood 1979, pp. 98, 103).

between the saint's intention and commands, and regulations passed subsequent to his death by properly constituted authority within the Order. Hugh wrote his *Exposition* at the Sacro Convento at Assisi, working in the convent library. He studied the Rule in a scholarly way, writing with the actual text of the Rule, enshrined in Honorius III's bull *Solet annuere* of 29 November 1223, in front of him. He quotes the original of Gregory IX's bull *Quo elongati*, which was also available to him in the Sacro Convento, as were texts of other papal bulls to which he refers.[76] When Hugh describes his sources in his Prologue, he states that he had received instruction 'by words and writings both from the close companions of St Francis and others pre-eminent in sanctity and learning'.[77] But he seldom gives specific stories about the saint or his companions or from the early biographies. Hugh presupposes a knowledge of Francis. He nowhere refers specifically to *The First Life of St Francis* by Thomas of Celano; but his statement that the early friars were content with one tunic patched within and without echoes both 1 *Celano* and the Testament of St Francis.[78] From this and a handful of other passages it is clear that 1 *Celano* was a part of the mental furniture of a learned and fervent friar of Hugh's generation[79] – as were the writings of St Francis. What is remarkable is that there are no traces whatsoever of the written testimony St Francis' close companions did in fact produce; testimony which Hugh could have and surely would have used if he had been writing in the 1250s.[80] What we are given is a general picture, laced with a very few examples of oral witness.

The early days of the movement, at once more heroic, more spiritual and more carefree than the present, appealed to Hugh, as they did to the later Spirituals, as a standard that could be put alongside the Rule to illustrate and to confirm it. 'Since the holy life of the fathers who are our predecessors is our pattern, while talking about the Rule I think it right to insert something of the manner of their life, lived in accordance with the Rule.'[81] His explanation of the Order's failure to maintain the early rigorous standards was that modifications that had occasionally been allowed

---

[76] For Hugh's reference to the original of *Solet annuere*, see Flood 1979, pp. 158–9. He also had access to what he referred to as 'the original Rule': 'in originali regula, in regula originali' (Flood 1979, pp. 162, 172). This was a version significantly different from the well-known *Regula non bullata* of 1220–1 (on which see Esser 1976, pp. 373–404). Two of the three surviving fragments of the version presumably earlier than 1220 are in Hugh's *Exposition* and 2 *Celano* – the third, intriguingly, in a MS in Worcester Cathedral Library. Since it impinged very little on the later literature and never got into general circulation like the *Regula bullata* and *Regula non bullata*, it seems likely that Hugh had privileged access to a single copy; and this is most likely to have been at Assisi. On the fragments, see Esser 1976 ch. 17, esp. (for Hugh) pp. 307–11, and (for Celano) pp. 311–12; cf. Esser 1973, pp. 59–77; Flood 1967. As well as *Solet annuere* (the *Regula bullata*) and *Quo elongati*, Hugh quotes *Pio vestro collegio* and *Paci et tranquillitati*; cf. Flood 1979, p. 114.

[77] Flood 1979, p. 92.

[78] 1 *Cel.* 39–40; Flood 1979, p. 110; cf. also Flood 1979, pp. 76, 96–7; the Testament, Esser 1976, pp. 439–40.

[79] E.g. 1 *Cel.* 29; Flood 1979, pp. 118, 183. In both places Hugh refers to Francis sending the brothers out 'binos et binos'; among surviving sources widely circulated this is most likely to echo 1 *Celano*. Cf. also 1 *Cel.* 22; Flood 1979, p. 110.

[80] Hugh worked off documents and literature at the Sacro Convento (note 76). Leo, Angelo and Rufino sent in their material to Assisi, where it seems to have remained (see pp. 103–7). A copy of 2 *Celano*, written in 1246–7, was almost certainly kept at Assisi, and after that date Hugh could have consulted this too (see p. 107).

[81] Prologue, Flood 1979, p. 92.

by the brethren, because of their urgent necessity or evident utility, had insidiously ensconced themselves as customs which became increasingly hard to eradicate. 'Even the stoutest spirits can be deflected little by little by custom. Thus many things that are today taken for granted would have seemed intolerable in the past.'[82] As a result the novices entering the Order are now set an example less high than heretofore and accept the imperfections they find as right and proper.

Hugh was a learned man and proud of his learning. He had no intention of trying, in St Francis' words, 'in a measure to resign his learning, so that stripped of such a possession he might offer himself naked to the arms of the Crucified'.[83] 'Ignorance does not excuse a professor of the Rule. If he does not know he is bound to enquire diligently. He is not a whit less dead who dies with his eyes shut . . . He does not walk in simplicity who walks imprudently.'[84] The section in chapter 10 of the Rule, 'Let not the uneducated seek to learn letters', provoked him into a frank and open defence of learning. 'The saint in this passage does not command within the Order primary education or "old men learning the alphabet".[85] To many, study of letters leads to negligence in the study of prayer, devotion and charity towards the brethren. Religion calls us to the virtues rather than to letters. If you wish to be a good student study to put goodness and discipline before knowledge. But since the Rule says: "Let not the uneducated seek to learn letters", and the Lord says in the Gospel: "Do not wish to be called Rabbi" – does this mean that the brethren cannot take up the study of letters and especially the Master's chair? They can do both. The holy founder of the Rule did not forbid study to the literate but to the laity and the illiterate, that, according to the apostle each one might remain in the vocation to which he was called. He did not wish the illiterate to learn: but he did not forbid the literate to progress in letters. Otherwise he himself would be acting contrary to the Rule who having a little learning when he joined the Order later perfected himself not only in prayer but in study. St Francis wished the other brothers to study Scripture and commanded that doctors of the Sacred Page should be held in the greatest reverence as those from whom they receive the words of life.[86] Whence since he understood that the name of "doctor" might be venerated, he understood that the Gospel had not forbidden it . . . I say therefore that according to the Gospel the ambition and vanity of this name are to be condemned and in no wise sought, but the office can be assumed. Whom does it not beseem to teach the Gospel, or to have the authority to teach it which is conferred by the master's degree, more than

---

[82] Flood 1979, p. 135.

[83] 2 Cel. 194; for the history of 'nudus nudum Christum sequi' see AF X, 241 n. 6; Constable 1979.

[84] Flood 1979, p. 91, quoting Proverbs 14. 16. In the preface to his De finibus paupertatis, the earliest of his works, Hugh denied that his thesis comprised a 'gloss'. His reasoning is subtle. There are some who contrive to find roughness in what is smooth, curvature in the straight, ambiguity in what is certain – and if against these he builds an argument taken from the words of the Rule itself, then he is not glossing the Rule but defending it (Florovsky 1912, p. 280).

[85] Cf. Seneca, Ep. 36, 4: 'turpis et ridicula res est elementarius senex'. The whole passage is from Flood 1979, pp. 186–7; the biblical quotations are from Matt. 23. 8 and 1 Cor. 7. 24.

[86] Hugh is quoting St Francis' Testament here (Esser 1976, p. 439, sec. 13), but not in the way we might have expected: he quotes it not to restore but actually to distort St Francis' intention. The quotation from the Apostle is 2 Tim. 1. 11.

the Friars Minor who profess and serve the Gospel? . . . The pomp of mastership is condemned but the office and the study approved.'[87]

Poverty is the theme of two of Hugh's works, and he evidently attached great importance to the principle of extreme poverty, defined as the renunciation, without exception, of all proprietary rights. Yet his attitude to the actual working of this principle in practice is extremely reasonable and moderate. He is by no means rigid or inflexible, and shows himself both an idealist and a realist. He can on the one hand see the fallacy behind seemingly laudable exceptions, and on the other allow full weight to what he regards as genuine human needs. He denounces as false and treacherous the plea that churches should be magnificent, worthy of the Lord they honour. 'The oratory [in early days] was humble but honest, not expensive or painted with diverse colours, but having been most purely and most brightly adorned it shone forth, representing by its beauty the grace of the angels and the glory of the resurrection.'[88] Even on this issue, however, his standards were not uncompromisingly puritanical. In the *Dialogue*, when his opponent asks whether he includes the beautifying of churches in his condemnation of fine building in the Order, the zealot replies: 'I do not altogether exclude superfluities in length, breadth and decoration of churches, which take the form of varied materials curiously fashioned, grouped and coloured. But I do make an exception of certain honourable ornaments, as images of the Crucified, and his virgin mother and the blessed John the Baptist and John the Evangelist, and the like.'[89]

Hugh's defence of the friars' use, as opposed to their ownership, of goods is the only argument that he reproduces in all three works and is characteristic of his style.[90] Everyone is indispensably bound by the precept of Natural Law to preserve life. 'Therefore the Order of Minors neither individually nor in common can renounce those things without which being cannot be preserved . . . Besides, as the use of things which pertain to the conservation of natural being is necessary, so also is the use of things necessary to the fulfilment of vows . . . As it is necessary to use foods and coverings for the preservation of life, so it is necessary to use the books and other things required for the Divine Office for the fulfilment of the vow . . . I understand the same with regard to books necessary for the office of preaching or lecturing, as teaching and the office of preaching are imposed by the Rule. Since the brethren ought to preach not fables but the divine word, which they cannot know unless they read or read unless they can have books, it is agreed that they can have both books and preach in accordance with the perfection of the Rule.'[91] However while he defends what he regards as coming within the bounds of legitimate use he insists that the greatest care must be taken to prevent superfluities from entering under the cover of the plea of necessity. Superfluities and

---

[87] Flood 1979, pp. 186–7. This passage in Hugh was quoted by Bonaventure, *Epistola de Tribus Quaestionibus*, *Opera Omnia*, XIII, 334–5: see Flood 1979, pp. 45–7.

[88] Flood 1979, p. 137.

[89] *Firmamenta* 1511–12, fo. 106vb. The inclusion of St John is symptomatic of his interests. *Narb.* permitted representation of the Crucified, the Virgin, St John, St Francis and St Anthony in the east windows of Franciscan churches (*Narb.* iii.18 in Bihl 1941, p. 48).

[90] Flood 1979, pp. 153–5; Florovsky 1912, pp. 288–9; *Firmamenta* 1511–12, fo. 108ra.

[91] Flood 1979, pp. 153–5.

extreme poverty are incompatible. Whatever can be taken away leaving a remainder that suffices is superfluous.[92]

His attitude to money is realistic, and is essentially the same as that of the Four Masters. He is in wholehearted agreement with Gregory IX's pronouncement on the subject in *Quo elongati*. For him the pope had an undeniable and overriding power to regulate and to interpret. He writes: 'In what manner the brethren are to conduct themselves with regard to money offered or entrusted to them the papal declaration, which ought to suffice the faithful for the removal of doubts, makes it clear that they can present a "nuntius" and have recourse to him.' A little later he makes the same point more emphatically: 'as the Lord Pope teaches, whose office it is to elucidate doubts and to establish the laws themselves; to impugn whose decision is the height of madness, which blinds even men of letters, even religious'.[93] He proceeds to paraphrase the bull and to elaborate its argument further along the same lines. It is both rational and opportune for the friars to procure the help of benefactions and to transact business through a 'nuntius', who albeit introduced by them is not their representative but rather his on whose authority payment is made, or else the vendor's. In every case the agent and the money sent through him belong to the sender. Similarly a man entrusted with sums to meet their future needs is not their banker but the depositor's. The friars may have recourse to him if he is negligent, or ignorant of their requirements, and they can hardly expect him to divine their needs if they do not tell him anything. By taking advantage of the services of such agents the brethren are not receiving money themselves or through interposed persons for it is not their *wish* or *intention* that money should be held for them in this way although they know it is committed to the agents for their necessities. Furthermore in certain cases the brethren may justifiably break St Francis' command. 'Necessity knows no law' and in real necessity, as may arise for instance in time of persecution, they may receive money. The use of the metal itself is not automatically included in the prohibition. Thus gold and gems can be worked up into chalices and ornaments for the altar and into fit repositories for Our Lord's body.[94]

Hugh did not oppose all change. He allowed that the Order possessed the power to regulate itself and that decisions reached by common counsel of its leading members in General Chapter were binding upon all. The brethren had therefore a perfect right through their elected representatives to enact a constitution restricting the free exercise of the permission contained in the Rule to eat all that was set before them.[95] He was not always prepared to treat the Rule as uncomplicated and straightforward and was at times unquestionably guilty of over-subtlety and equivocation. The rule against riding strictly meant that the brethren were not allowed to travel on horseback. Whether they were equally forbidden to sit on the backs of other animals or journey in horse-drawn

---

[92] Flood 1979, pp. 155, 159–60.
[93] Flood 1979, pp. 126, 129–30. Hugh accepts Gregory IX's decision on the Testament, closely following the argument of the Four Masters: 'While blessed Francis was alive obedience was owed to him . . . But without the consent of the brethren, and especially of the Ministers, he could not oblige them to new statutes in perpetuity. Whence according to the apostolic reply we are not held to the Testament' (Flood 1979, p. 97).
[94] Flood 1979, p. 124.   [95] Flood 1979, pp. 121–2.

vehicles was not clear, though it was safer and more meritorious for them to fatigue themselves on foot. 'Some put their trust in chariots and some in horses; but we will call upon the name of the Lord our God.'[96] But it was on the subject of work that he produced his finest piece of prevarication. The clause in the Rule ran: 'Those brethren to whom God has given the grace to work, are to labour faithfully and devoutly, in such a way that while they exclude idleness, the enemy of the soul, they do not extinguish the spirit of holy prayer and devotion.' This, said Hugh, was clearly not in the nature of a command, for suppose St Francis were to say in similar fashion that the brothers to whom God had given the gift of tears were to cry in moderation, in such a way that they did not destroy their eyes, he would not be ordering them to weep. Furthermore the manual labour that St Francis had recommended for his first followers, whilst admirably suited to men unlearned but willing and apt for toil, was not appropriate to the present complement of clerics and men of education. The preachers, procurators and ministers also 'worked' and their work, being of the spirit and of the mind, was superior to bodily toil and excused them from it. Like the two feet and two hands in the body, action and prayer should work together. One can scarcely run home on one foot. Worldly occupations are on a lowly plane and must on no account be allowed to detract from the Divine Service. The prudent and faithful servant ministers to God now as Martha, now as Mary.[97]

St Francis asked his brethren to keep their sermons short in imitation of our Lord. Hugh endorsed this sentiment, remarking that 'prolixity is the mother of tedium and makes even the best discourses wearisome'.[98] He does not however seem to have been fully alive to the pertinence of his own maxim. The accounts of his sermons and debates that Salimbene inserted into his chronicle are sufficient evidence that brevity of speech was not his forte. Nor was his written style more concise. The brief settlement of doubtful points in *Quo elongati* had developed into the full-scale commentary. Hugh outdid not only his predecessors but his successors also. His *Exposition* takes up nearly twenty folios in the sixteenth-century printed collection *Firmamenta Trium Ordinum*. The Four Masters' occupies less than three and a half folios, John Pecham's thirteen and a half folios in the same edition.

THE BULL *EXIIT QUI SEMINAT*

In the 1260s and 70s a series of new commentaries on the Rule were produced – by David of Augsburg (probably in the 1260s), John of Wales (late 1270s) and John Pecham (c.1274–9) – culminating in Nicholas III's bull *Exiit qui seminat* of 14 August 1279, the most elaborate of all the papal interpretations of the thirteenth century. 'David of Augsburg, close to pastoral work and marked by his experience as novice-master, wrote his commentary as a ghostly father.'[99] It was clearly not intended as a

---

[96] Flood 1979, p. 120.
[97] Esser 1976, p. 368; Flood 1979, pp. 139–42 (partly quoted by Bonaventure, *Opera Omnia*, VIII, 334; cf. Flood 1979, pp. 43–4). On Mary and Martha see now esp. Constable 1995.
[98] Flood 1979, p. 177.
[99] Flood 1972, p. 101; Harkins 1969, p. 189 and n. 81; for excerpts see Lempp 1899b, pp. 345–59.

work of controversy nor to reopen the subtle issues of poverty so carefully aired by Hugh of Digne and the major papal settlements.[100] John of Wales was a man of quite exceptional learning, with an encyclopaedic knowledge of the literature of the past, which he succeeded in making relevant to the study of the Rule. It is an academic friar's commentary, for young, intelligent, intellectual friars.[101] An *Exposition of the Rule* which, from the fifteenth century on, came to be attributed to St Bonaventure is now ascribed to John Pecham.[102] It provides a lucid synthesis of Bonaventuran doctrine expressed in very similar language and imagery. St Bonaventure's doctrine is also enshrined in the bull *Exiit qui seminat* which draws on his *Apologia* and *Epistola de tribus quaestionibus*,[103] and endorses the Bonaventuran virtues of simplicity and austerity united with wisdom.

Gian Gaetano Orsini, Cardinal Protector of the Friars Minor, was elected Pope Nicholas III in November 1277. In 1278 he made Jerome of Ascoli, the Minister General, a cardinal. In May 1279 he attended the General Chapter at Assisi, which elected Jerome's friend and companion Bonagrazia to succeed him, and asked the new Minister General and the members of the Chapter if there was anything he could do to help the Order. Shortly afterwards Bonagrazia, accompanied by Provincial Ministers, waited on the pope at his summer residence at Soriano to request that he would appoint a Cardinal Protector to succeed himself, and that he would provide them with a new, authoritative interpretation of difficult issues arising from the Rule. A commission was appointed which included two Franciscan cardinals, Nicholas III's confessor Bentivenga Bentivengi and Jerome of Ascoli, the Minister General Bonagrazia, the Provincial Ministers of France and Ireland, and Benedict Gaetano, the future Pope Boniface VIII. Peter John Olivi, who was in Rome at the time, also contributed a position paper at the request of his Provincial Minister.[104] But the pope took a keen personal interest. Philip of Perugia, Provincial Minister of Tuscany and a member of the deputation, who had been in Nicholas III's service while he was Cardinal Protector and was treated by him as a personal friend, has left an account of the manner in which Nicholas appointed one of his nephews, Matteo Rosso Orsini, Cardinal Protector, after studying a secret ballot, and of what happened next. 'From that day forward the pope bent his mind to his declaration on the Rule, so that for almost two months he entirely set aside all other business, to the amazement of the whole Curia. What he was actually engaged in was unknown to all outside the circle of his immediate helpers.'[105]

The bull begins with a beautiful cadence: 'Exiit qui seminat' 'The sower went forth to sow' (Matt. 13. 3).[106] The seed – the word of God, the Gospel teaching – falls on all alike, some on stony hearts, some on the good soil of meek and obedient hearts, so

[100] On *Ordinem vestrum* see pp. 86–90.
[101] 'Declaratio super Regulam' in *Speculum Minorum* (Venice, 1513), 3a pars, fos. 98v–106r; cf. Flood 1972, pp. 100–1 and refs., esp. to Balduinus ab Amsterdam 1970; for a general account of John of Wales, see esp. Swanson 1989 (and p. 230 for his *Expositio Regulae*).
[102] Harkins 1969.
[103] Harkins 1969, pp. 185–7. On the relation of *Exiit* to Bonaventure, see Maggioni 1912; Moorman 1968, p. 180; Flood 1972, pp. 101–2. On the differences, see Flood 1972, pp. 106–7.
[104] Gratien 1928, p. 328; Moorman 1968, p. 179; Burr 2001, p. 50. The pope's presence at the General Chapter is specifically referred to in the text of *Exiit*, Eubel 1908, p. 291.
[105] Philip of Perugia in Salimbene, H, pp. 683–4; and see p. 288.
[106] The bull is in Sbaralea, III, 404–16, N3, no. 127; Eubel 1908, pp. 290–300.

especially on the poor and humble Friars Minor. 'This is a religious way of life (*religio*) pure and immaculate in the eyes of God the Father; it comes down from the Father of lights through his Son; it has been handed by his Son by example and word to the Apostles, and finally to St Francis through the Holy Spirit – and as it has inspired those who follow Francis, contains within itself as it were the witness of the whole Trinity. This it is which no one (as Paul bears witness) should harm henceforth, which Christ has confirmed by the stigmata of his passion, Christ who willed that its founder should be visibly inscribed with the signs of his own passion.'[107] But the cunning of the devil has sown tares among the wheat; motivated by jealousy, barking dogs are biting the brothers and tearing at their Rule as if it were illicit, impossible to observe and hazardous. The ringing endorsement of the evangelical credentials of the Order, with its markedly Bonaventuran tone, was the papal response to potentially devastating attacks on the Franciscan way of life mounted chiefly by secular masters.[108] As he had only recently emphasised to his nephew when appointing him Cardinal Protector, Nicholas III considered protection of the Order from external criticism and enemies of prime importance. But the metaphor of the dogs suggests that the pope was also aiming at the Dominicans, 'Domini canes', the dogs of the Lord. He declared in the bull that 'the renunciation of ownership of all things both individually and in common for God's sake is meritorious and holy; which also Christ, by showing the life of perfection, taught by word and confirmed by example', thus setting the seal of papal approval on the theoretical basis of Franciscan poverty. The suggestion that because of the nature of their poverty the Franciscans attained a higher degree of perfection than other religious was naturally obnoxious to the Dominicans, especially as in practice the manner of life of both Minors and Preachers was very similar.[109] To ensure that everyone took notice, this bull, unlike previous papal pronouncements on the Rule, was addressed, not to the friars, but to the Church universal.

After the firm, even fierce, rejection of diabolic assaults, the pope emphasised that his work was based on Gregory IX – that is, on *Quo elongati* – as confirmed in the Council of Lyon (1245), and was the outcome of the affection in which he had held the Order from his earliest years. On many points he was content to reiterate Gregory's pronouncements. But two crucial issues are given extensive reconsideration in the light of contemporary concerns. The first is the extent of the obligation incurred by the vow to observe the Rule, which requires the friar to obey the Gospel. Gregory IX had ruled that the friars were not bound to Gospel counsels not quoted in the Rule, though it would be good if they chose to observe them. Nicholas III refined the distinction. The wording of the Rule shows that it was St Francis' intention to distinguish between Gospel precepts, expressed as commands or prohibitions, and counsels, indicated by words of admonition, exhortation and advice. His ruling: the friars are bound by vow only to those Gospel passages expressed by words of command, prohibition or their equivalent. His intention in adding 'or equivalent words' to Gregory IX's pronouncement on the issue was to expand the category of Gospel precepts, but

---

[107] Eubel 1908, p. 291; quoted Flood 1972, p. 107, n. 144.
[108] Discussion of later thirteenth-century commentaries has had to be curtailed for lack of space.
[109] Eubel 1908, p. 293; Harkins 1969, pp. 177–8; Burr 1989, p. 154 and nn. 50, 52, and p. 161.

the phrase was imprecise and susceptible to different interpretations. Paradoxically it created ambiguity, inviting gloss.[110]

On the second issue, theoretical and practical concerns relating to poverty, the basic point, that the friars must be allowed the use of necessities, is repeated. Innocent IV's extension of the permission, in *Ordinem vestrum*, to include useful as well as necessary things, which had aroused strong objections within the Order, is omitted. On one point only is Innocent IV specifically mentioned, and that is to confirm that everything given to the Order for its use becomes the property of the Holy See.[111] Nicholas III was most concerned to clarify the legal aspects. He seems to have taken it for granted that restricted use, 'usus pauper', and lack of ownership form essential components of Franciscan poverty – and that they were therefore binding on the friars through their vow – but he does not spell this out, only implies it.[112] He distinguished five possible relationships to temporal goods: ownership (*proprietas*), possession (*possessio*), the use and enjoyment of property belonging to another with some implication of a right to do so (*ususfructus*), the right of use (*ius utendi*), and simple use of fact (*simplex ius facti*). The friar who freely vows poverty for Christ renounces all power – *dominium* – and has no right of use; only the last, simple *de facto* use of necessary things, is allowed him.[113] This is stringent, but the accompanying definition of necessities is elastic. The pope assures them that, according to the Rule, moderate use of fact both of things necessary to sustain life and of those needed for the performance of their office, money excepted, is conceded to the friars. As well as food, clothing and shelter adapted to the region and the time of year, and everything required for the celebration of divine service, they need the books and libraries prerequisite for preaching. The ministers can arrange with their procurators, who act for the Holy See, not only for the provision of all these, but also for imminent necessities. They can therefore legitimately, for example, make plans and arrangements with the Order's friends for acquiring books and constructing buildings. On the possible ramifications of their relations with agents and potential donors much casuistry is expended, as it is earlier on Christ's and the apostles' involvement with a purse.

Exiit reflected the perceived situation in the late 1270s and embodied the philosophy which justified and shaped it. The Order had changed spectacularly since its beginnings, accumulating a large membership, a range of new responsiblities and a remarkable growth in influence. St Bonaventure and Nicholas III were far from alone in regarding these developments as progress. A wide consensus on the positive merits of their evolution for the Church and for society stretched back to the 1240s. Hugh of Digne considered the Order to be legitimately in a different situation in his day than it had been when St Francis founded it. St Bonaventure, in his *Epistola de tribus quaestionibus* quoted key passages from Hugh without acknowledgement.[114] Hugh's argument on 'necessity' and on the importance and propriety of study find echoes in

[110] Grundmann 1961, p. 21; Burr 2001, pp. 56, 133–4.
[111] Eubel 1908, pp. 293–4; and see p. 86.   [112] Burr 2001, pp. 57–8, 133–4.
[113] Eubel 1908, p. 293; see the very lucid exposition of 'dominium' and use in Brett 1997, pp. 16–20.
[114] Burr 1989, pp. 19–20; Flood 1979, pp. 45–7; and see pp. 93–4, 147, 247–8.

Exiit.[115] Olivi claimed that his own views on 'usus pauper' were in harmony with those decreed in Exiit and contained in the writings of St Bonaventure, Pecham and Hugh of Digne.[116]

A thread runs through the bull emphasising continuity with the past and adherence to observance of the Rule according to its intention. There is a moving attempt to reach out, to be as inclusive as possible. In his brief autobiographical excursus setting out his credentials, his qualifications for the task of interpreter, Nicholas III goes out of his way to remind the Order how, even in the years before he became Cardinal Protector, 'we held frequent discussions with some of the saint's companions, to whom his life and conversation were well known, concerning the Rule and St Francis' own intention'.[117]

Towards the end of the bull St Francis' Testament is quoted. The words of the Rule are not to be glossed; and the friars are in no way to seek any letters from the Apostolic See. Nicholas III must have had a mischievous streak in him, and a sense of humour. He proceeds to employ some of St Francis' own words from the Testament to endorse his own apostolic letter containing his own and some of his predecessors' interpretations of dubious points in the Rule. He strictly enjoins on obedience that his bull, along with other constitutions and decretals, is to be learned in the schools. He commands, on pain of excommunication, that when his bull is thus being studied, it is to be faithfully expounded to the letter, 'ad litteram'; it is not to be glossed. Nicholas III intends his decisions to be final; the friars are to observe them precisely and inviolably in perpetuity. And there is to be no further discussion. They are not to be criticised in writing, or in sermons; there is to be no debate in public or in private.[118] Yet he should have realised that his attempt to dictate, to stop the clock, was doomed, just as Francis' attempt had been doomed. He quoted the Roman Law maxim that 'equal has no power of command over equal' that Gregory had employed in *Quo elongati* to justify his decision that the Testament was not binding on the friars.[119] It could only be a matter of time before one of his successors acted on this maxim. In the last two decades of the thirteenth century and the first two of the fourteenth, tensions over the practice of poverty escalated beyond the sphere of discipline. Increasingly sharp and bitter argument developed between parties, now being labelled Spirituals and Conventuals, about the direction the Order should take.

Eventually an exasperated Pope John XXII demolished the whole edifice. First, in March 1322, he ended the ban on discussion; then, in the bull *Ad conditorem* of December 1322, he refused to accept 'dominium' over the Order's goods in future or to appoint

---

[115] Eubel 1908, pp. 293–4.

[116] Burr 1989, pp. 92, 110; Burr 2001, pp. 50–61. On Olivi, see Burr 2001; also Flood 1972, pp. 1–23, who lays out in helpful detail the shifting spectrum of scholarly opinion and judgement on Olivi, separating him from the parties of the fourteenth century. Olivi's commentary on the Rule is dated 1288–92 in Flood 1972, p. 69. Although some of his theological ideas were challenged and condemned, he remained a faithful son of the Holy Roman Church; nor did he use his commentary, as had John of Wales, to parade his learning. As his editor and interpeter David Flood wrote of the work: 'Olivi gave simple friars some concrete help in living a rule which corresponded to his ideal of Christian perfection. He constructed an understanding of the Rule to help his fellow friars stride towards their high destiny' (Flood 1972, p. 103).

[117] Eubel 1908, p. 291; for conversatio see p. 112 and note 24.   [118] Eubel 1908, pp. 299–300.

[119] Eubel 1908, p. 299; Grundmann 1961, pp. 4 and nn. 1–2, 21; and see pp. 78, 88.

any more procurators. It was ridiculous to pretend that every egg and piece of bread given to and eaten by the Friars Minor belonged to the pope. Finally, in November 1323, in *Cum inter nonnullos*, belief in the total poverty of Christ was declared heretical.[120] The intellectual structure underpinning a cherished fictitious idealisation of Franciscan poverty, devised by Gregory IX and carefully reinforced by Nicholas III, lay in ruins.

[120] Burr 2001, pp. 275–7. On the background to John XXII's decisions, see now Nold 2003.

CHAPTER SIX

REMINISCENCES: THE CONVERGENCE OF UNOFFICIAL AND OFFICIAL IMAGES IN WRITING

Information relating to St Francis that was written down in the middle years of the thirteenth century was to be of crucial importance in focusing an image of the saint that was projected, successfully, in the early fourteenth century, and has endured to this day. In 1244 the newly elected Minister General, Crescentius of Jesi, with the approval of the General Chapter, ordered the friars to send to him such signs and miracles of St Francis as they knew or could discover. This tapped a vein of reminiscence far richer than can have been anticipated. The new material did not immediately result in any wide dissemination of a radically altered image. It was made use of: in the first instance by Thomas of Celano, who was officially commissioned to write it up into a supplementary biography, his *Second Life of St Francis* (2 Celano). Somewhat later, some parts of it were used by someone, whose name we do not know, when he was compiling a biography of his own – the work known as the *Legend of the Three Companions*. He seems to have had no official backing, but his labours must have been sanctioned by the custos or guardian of the Sacro Convento – he was permitted to work there.[1] We do not have the original manuscript, but it was not destroyed in 1266 and was later copied. The original material sent in to Crescentius has not survived either, but some of it at least was believed to be still in Assisi at the beginning of the fourteenth century.[2] Material based on it re-emerged and was given a new lease of life early in the fourteenth century. But because we do not have the originals it has been necessary to try to identify the core contribution of the mid-1240s and to disentangle it from all the later accretions, embellishments and fabrications it acquired over time. The problem posed has proved to be exceedingly complex and controversial, earning for itself the title: 'la questione francescana'.[3] It has to be tackled here because, although in a written form the new image did not command a wide circulation in the thirteenth century, its launch dates from the mid-1240s; it was kept alive and circulated in oral

[1] See pp. 156–7.
[2] Ubertino da Casale's testimony is quoted in SL p. 55, from ALKG III, 168, 177–8, and see p. 125.
[3] Its historiography was the theme of the first Convegno of the Società Internazionale di Studi Francescani, *La 'Questione Francescana' dal Sabatier ad oggi*, Assisi, 1974.

form; and its intrinsic qualities were such that in succeeding centuries it was able to compete with, and eventually to a significant degree supplant, the official version by St Bonaventure. The best of the Franciscan sources of the mid-thirteenth century are among the supreme records of Christian sanctity.

In the prologue to his *First Life of St Francis*, Thomas of Celano speaks in the first person singular: 'on the orders of the glorious lord Pope Gregory I . . . have taken pains to expound the deeds and manner of life of our most blessed father Francis'. In the *Second*, Celano writes in the first person plural: 'The holy community of the general chapter and you yourself, most reverend father [Crescentius, Minister General], were pleased to enjoin *our* little selves that *we* should describe in writing the deeds and sayings of our glorious father Francis – we who knew them more than any others from constant intercourse and intimate friendship with him . . . First of all this little work contains some wonderful facts relating to the conversion of St Francis, which were not included in the legends compiled about him long ago, since they were not known to the author.'[4] Celano writes on behalf of companions more intimate with Francis than himself; and his words echo the letter prefacing the manuscripts of the *Legend of the Three Companions*.

'To their reverend father in Christ, brother Crescentius by God's grace minister general, brother Leo, brother Rufino and brother Angelo, formerly companions, though unworthy, of the most blessed father Francis, offer due reverence and devotion in the Lord. By command of the last general chapter and of yourself, the brothers are bound to send to you, father, such signs and miracles of our most blessed father Francis as they know or can discover. We who, though unworthy, lived long in his company, thought it right to send in to your holiness – with strict attention to truth – a few accounts of his many acts, which we ourselves have seen, or could discover from other holy friars' (whom they name). 'We do not write in the manner of a *Legenda*, since *Legende* have been composed long since . . . But we have picked as it were from a field of flowers those we thought the most fair: we have not followed a continuous narrative, but have carefully omitted many events elegantly and accurately told in the *Legende*; and if in your wisdom you think it right, you can have our little collection, which we have written, placed in its context in the *Legende*. For we believe that if they had been known to the venerable men who composed the *Legende*, they would not have passed them by, but would have adorned them with their polished style . . . and left them for posterity to recall . . . Given in the convent at Greccio, 11 August 1246.'[5]

A 'legenda' was a book to be read, a collection of lections, 'lectiones'; in the twelfth and thirteenth centuries the word came to compete with 'vita' as the description of a saint's life – usually without any of the sceptical overtones of our modern use of 'legend'. In early Franciscan manuscripts, *vita* was at first more commonly used for the writings of Celano and Bonaventure; but 'legenda' was an acceptable synonym,[6]

---

[4] *1 Cel.*, prologue; *2 Cel.*, prologue 1–2: my italics. There seems to be some confusion here betweem the plural *legendis* and the singular *auctoris*. Presumably Celano had *1 Celano* and the *Legenda Chori* also composed by him in mind. But it is also clear from the companions' letter that he was grappling with a source which referred to more than one author.

[5] SL, Introductory Letter, pp. 86–9.

[6] As in the fourteenth-century MS F of Bonaventure's *Legenda Maior*, Assisi, Bibl. Comunale MS 346 (AF X, pp. lxxv, 557n.).

and the companions and Celano himself were referring to Celano's *First Life* and some other early legend or legends, probably Celano's *Legenda Chori* and the *Vita S. Francisci* of Julian of Speyer. It later came to be applied to the *Speculum Perfectionis* – 'this work was compiled in the manner of a legend' – which in its context indicates the systematic arrangement of stories taken from a diversity of sources.[7]

The contrast intended in the companions' letter is not in doubt – they were sending in, not a biography, but a collection of reminiscences which could be incorporated into one. Nor is the authenticity of the letter itself in doubt. It is virtually inconceivable that a later forger could have produced so convincing a list of witnesses as the letter provides, and the prologue of *2 Celano* – so markedly different from the prologue to his *First Life* – is unintelligible without just such a source to explain it.

Yet it is also apparent that the letter is not an appropriate introduction to the *Legend of the Three Companions*.[8] The contrast it draws between the 'field of flowers' it says it offers and the more formal life or legend is very emphatic; but the *Legend of the Three Companions* (henceforth *3 Soc.*) is no such field: it is a complete biography, even though its coverage is uneven. It gives a very full and attractive presentation of Francis' early life and of the early days of the Order, closely parallel to *1 Celano* and the *Anonymous of Perugia*, with a rather perfunctory epilogue carrying the story to Francis' death and canonisation.

THE WRITINGS OF LEO, RUFINO AND ANGELO

Francis is most intimately recalled in the stories written down by his companions Leo, Rufino and Angelo, and sent to the Minister General Crescentius from the house of the friars at Greccio on 11 August 1246, twenty years after Francis' death. They are of outstanding quality, fresh, loving, vivid, personal: they show us the saint in speech and action. The *Scripta Leonis* (SL) are of the highest quality as spiritual literature and religious biography.

Yet how can this be? Many scholars still doubt that the stories as we have them truly represent what the companions wrote. Some think a few of the stories wholly authentic; some hold that we have to reckon them, with all comparable stories about Francis, as fourteenth-century documents, as none survives in any manuscripts earlier than 1300. Since Paul Sabatier made the inspired discovery of a similar group of stories over a hundred years ago, they have come to be known – very roughly – in three forms: in the version I edited as SL, and in the two forms discovered by Sabatier: the *Mirror of Perfection* (*Speculum Perfectionis*, Sp S) of 1318 and the later *Speculum Vitae*.[9]

---

[7] Sp S. 1 (1928), pp. xxii–xxiii for the rubrics in the two families of MSS, both of which say 'istud opus compilatum est per modum legendae'.

[8] See pp. 108, 147–8.

[9] See SL, Introduction, esp. pp. 5–7. For the earlier literature, see note 11 below. In the 1980s and 1990s Dr Maurice Causse revived Sabatier's view that the texts in the *Speculum Perfectionis* represented the earliest stratum of the stories, going back in essence to the 1220s. I regret that the note I had prepared, explaining why I remain convinced that the texts in SL (with possibly an occasional exception) are more primitive than those in Sp S, has had to be omitted for lack of space. He accepted, as have all recent scholars, that Sp S in its present form is dated 1318.

The attribution to Leo, Rufino and Angelo depends on the Introductory Letter in which the three friars claim to be sending a group of stories: 'a few accounts of his many acts . . . not . . . in the manner of *Legende*' – not a 'Life' to compete with 1 *Celano* – 'but we have picked as it were from a field of flowers those we thought the more fair: we have not followed a continuous narrative, but have carefully omitted many events elegantly and accurately told in the *Legende*'. This fits the stories in SL like a glove. But the letter has not survived in company with the stories – it is only found in manuscripts of the so-called *Legend of the Three Companions*, whose contents it does not accurately describe.[10] It would seem to belong properly to some other collection; and when I published SL in 1970, I followed F. C. Burkitt and John Moorman in attaching it to the collection of stories which most obviously answers its description. But many scholars still doubt if I was right, and the highly technical case I presented needs rearguing in plainer language.[11]

The stories survive, in a text clearly distinct from the *Mirror of Perfection*, in six manuscripts of the fourteenth and fifteenth centuries, of which one, the Perugia MS 1046 (**P**) – now in the Biblioteca Augusta of Perugia – is the earliest, the most complete, and outstandingly the most important. Such has become its prestige that it is treated almost as an icon by some scholars, and four editions have been made of the stories in it which pay little attention to each other: my own edition is the only text based on all the known manuscripts: but I omitted stories clearly derived from Celano's *Second Life*, and I added the Introductory Letter – and some other stories, from another source. It is necessary to emphasise that **P** is not an isolated text: its message can only be understood as one of a group.[12]

None the less, it is of the first importance to establish its date and origin. Recent discussions of its date have produced a consensus in favour of 1310–11. The most important evidence lies in the papal bulls the manuscript contains, an ample collection of major and minor bulls from 1220 to 1310. In the margins are some notes which refer to variant readings 'in the original': the compilers of the manuscript evidently had access to a substantial collection of original papal bulls and worked systematically on them. It is most unlikely that this could have been accomplished anywhere else than in the Order's headquarters in Assisi. In 1312 Pope Clement V issued a major bull on the government of the Order, *Exivi de Paradiso*: of this lengthy text there is no trace in **P**. Yet the codicological evidence is cogent that we have virtually the whole of this part of the original manuscript; *Exivi de Paradiso* could not be fitted into the known *lacunae*.

---

[10] See pp. 147–8.

[11] Burkitt 1926, pp. 40–2; Moorman 1940, pp. 89–109. When I edited the *Scripta Leonis* I took it for granted that scholarly opinion – in the main – accepted that the deposit of stories which can be recovered by critical sifting of Perugia, Biblioteca Augusta Comunale MS 1046, and half a dozen related manuscripts, were the work of Leo and his colleagues in the years 1244–6. This view had been argued by Père Delorme in the 1920s, and developed and sophisticated by Professor F. C. Burkitt and Bishop John Moorman and others in the second quarter of the twentieth century (Burkitt 1926; Moorman 1940, ch. 5). I had much to add to their findings; but, working on their foundations, I assumed that the majority of scholars were of this opinion. This is no longer the case. A catena of studies from the late 1960s on has revealed that there is no consensus among scholars (e.g. Clasen 1967; Assisi 1974, *passim* (esp. E. Pasztor, pp. 199–212); Manselli 1980; Stanislao da Campagnola 1977).

[12] The four editions are Delorme 1922, Brooke in SL 1970/1990, Cambell 1966 and Bigaroni 1975. For comment, see Gattucci 1979; Brooke 1981. For the MSS, see SL pp. 26–42.

The most cogent – and the least understood – of my own arguments on this point was that **P** also contains a fourteenth-century index to the bulls, which firmly establishes that *Exivi* was not there. The collection is otherwise remarkably comprehensive, and we can be reasonably certain that it was completed in 1310 or 1311.[13] The manuscript contains a variety of items – the bulls, the stories (SL), and St Bonaventure's *Legenda Maior* are the most significant – but there are good reasons to suppose that it was written in a single campaign. Contemporary quire numbers and a fourteenth-century foliation seem to guarantee its unity. We may therefore assume that the book as a whole was composed about 1310, very likely in preparation for the vital discussions on the Order at the Council of Vienne in 1312. This is important, because it establishes that the collection of stories in **P** is earlier than the very popular attempt to put them in a more systematic frame or 'legenda' in the *Speculum Perfectionis* of 1318.

Thus the earliest and most complete of the manuscripts of these stories probably comes from the heart of the Franciscan establishment in Assisi. But is there not a paradox here? The tradition they represent – whether in SL or Sp S or *Speculum Vitae* – has commonly been seen as the tradition of the Spiritual Franciscans – of those who reacted against the ways of the Order as a whole, against the Conventuals, and sought to preserve, or revive, the poverty and simplicity of Francis himself: hence the emphasis on Francis' intentions in many spheres of the friars' life which the stories contain. This judgement is doubtless too simplified. The *Mirror of Perfection* circulated in the Order at large, and not just in those communities which strove to revive the fervour of the Order – nor only in those regions in which the Spirituals' ideals were cultivated, or in those communities from which the later Observants were to spring.[14] The stories in Sp S were incorporated into the *Speculum Vitae*, which was influential among the Observants, and blossomed when disinterred from there by Sabatier to become a major ingredient in all the good modern biographies of St Francis.

At about the time that **P** was compiled, and precisely in the year 1311, the Spiritual leader Ubertino da Casale described 'a book, which is preserved in the friars' library [or book-cupboard: *in armario fratrum*] in Assisi' in brother Leo's hand, and some leaflets, also in Leo's hand, which he had by him when he wrote. He goes on to quote a little group of stories commonly called the *Intentio Regule*.

[13] See SL pp. 27–8: the original collection of bulls ended in 1304, but was later continued to 1310; the index conforms to the collection. Some bulls seem to have been added in lost quires at the end; but the surviving clues suggest they were not later than 1310: see SL p. 31 n.1. Since this chapter was completed I have been able to study Langeli 1999, which has advanced our knowledge of **P** by brilliant codicological analysis. He argues that the main hand of **P** is also that of Assisi 342 (Angela of Foligno: see p. 486 note 54) and Assisi 572 (the Greek ascetic Isaac of Nineveh); and he confirms that **P** was written in the scriptorium of the Sacro Convento, and by 1381 at least kept there in the 'libraria publica' (ibid. pp. 16–21). He dates Assisi 342 to the end of Angela's life, i.e. *c.* 4 January 1309, which fits well with the date 1310–11 or 12 for **P**, which he accepts (citing references to support this date on pp. 26–7, but not including SL or Brooke 1981).

[14] For the MSS of Sp S and their provenance, see Sp S I, pp. ix–x, 11, 1–73, supplemented in Clasen 1967, pp. 47–158. Rusconi (1999, p. 386) points out that the fact that three MSS – Angela of Foligno in Assisi 342, **P**, Perugia 1046, and Isaac of Nineveh, in Assisi 572 (a tract well known to the Spirituals) – were all copied by a friar working in the scriptorium of the Sacro Convento in the opening decades of the fourteenth century underlines the complexity of the orientations among the Friars Minor at the turn of the century, 'non riconducibili, in sostanza, alla dialettica semplificata di una contrapposizione fra *Communitas* e *Spirituali*'. See note 13.

The six manuscripts in which SL survives fall into two main groups: one group, of which **P** is the principal member, clearly derive from a book which contained all the stories in SL, with possibly a very few exceptions. In the other group, now represented by a small but stout book in the library of the Collegio Sant'Isidoro in Rome of the late fourteenth century (**I**), and an ampler book now in Oxford (**L**), the stories are arranged in quite a different order, and some in distinct groups, including the *Intentio Regule* quoted by Ubertino in 1311. In general terms, it is now clear that **P** is a copy of the book in the brothers' library at Assisi, and that **I** and **L** derive from the 'leaflets' which Ubertino had by him. There is also ample fourteenth-century evidence that some or all of these stories were attributed to brother Leo.

We can go further, and explain the relation between 'leaflets' and book. It is likely enough that the stories were originally gathered in little groups on single leaves, bifolia and the like – as we know to have been the case with medieval letter collections. These could readily be rearranged; and **I** and **L** represent one arrangement, or perhaps more likely a series of disarrangements; **P** and its fellows a serious attempt to arrange the whole collection in order. If Ubertino was correct that both book and leaflets were in Leo's own hand, we could attribute both stages to brother Leo. Leo died in or about 1271; but substantial pieces of his handwriting, and others attributed to him, undoubtedly survived;[15] it is not impossible that Ubertino was correct – but it is unwise to lay much weight on such hearsay evidence.

What was the book doing in the friars' library? For the General Chapter of the Order, in 1266, had decreed that all *legende* save Bonaventure's should be destroyed. Now this decree was in one sense very effective. Whereas 1 *Celano* had evidently circulated widely before 1266 and is represented by many surviving manuscripts, 2 *Celano*, of the late 1240s, only survives in two manuscripts;[16] and although some early legends survive in more, there is little evidence of effective dissemination in the thirteenth century: apart from 1 *Celano*, the early *legende* seem to have escaped oblivion quite narrowly. On the other hand, very little seems to have been totally lost: SL, 1 and 2 *Celano*, Julian of Speyer's legend, the two versions of the *Legend of the Three Companions*, all these miraculously escaped the general destruction. And SL survived 'in the friars' library' in Assisi itself. The natural explanation is that the officials in Assisi – or a prudent librarian – locked away safely in a cupboard the forbidden materials. Strange as it may seem, there can be little doubt that SL survived at the very heart of the Order.

This would be easier to understand if the book and leaflets were indeed thought to be – perhaps in the hand of brother Leo – at least the work of Leo and his colleagues. The fourteenth-century tradition is very strong that these stories were written by Leo. The only thirteenth-century evidence lies in the Introductory Letter. It is most unlikely that the later tradition derived directly or solely from the letter, for two reasons. First

[15] SL pp. 7–9, 53–6. For MSS in Leo's hand, see Langeli 2000; for Leo's death, a contemporary entry in the breviary of St Francis, fo. 11r, Langeli 2000, pp. 92–3, gives the date of Leo's death as 13 November in the early 1270s (the final digit or digits of the year are missing) (see note 20). Later tradition had it that Leo died on 14 or 15 November 1271 (Wadding 1731–1933, IV, p. 334, citing Marianus of Florence, ii. 20 and cf. i. 5).
[16] The Assisi MS is complete save for 2 *Celano* 220a; the Marseille MS only lacks cc. 221–4: see AF X, pp. xxx–xxxi. For the decree of 1266, see p. 244.

of all, in all manuscripts – that is in a tradition going back to the mid, probably to the early fourteenth century – the letter is attached not to SL but to the *Legend of the Three Companions*. Secondly, it ascribes the stories not solely to Leo, but to all three companions, Leo, Rufino and Angelo.

The more deeply one studies the stories in **P**, **I** and **L** the more clear it becomes that they began life in 'leaflets', in single sheets and bifolia comprising small groups. The more one studies the *Legend of the Three Companions* the clearer it becomes that its Introductory Letter began life likewise on a single sheet. I suggested in my edition that the introduction to the stories in **P**, **I** and **L** was on a loose leaf and became detached by accident.[17] I hazard a further suggestion now. The letter was originally written as a covering letter after the brothers at Greccio had finished collecting their materials. It was written on a separate sheet. It is easy to imagine that it could in time become detached from the materials it was sent in with. I suggest that the compiler of *3 Soc.* simply put it, attached it – the original letter itself – at the head of his biography, instead of going to the trouble of copying it out. This would explain why the letter occurs in all the MSS of *3 Soc.*, why it does not occur in any of the other MSS collections, such as **P** and Sp S, compiled later than *3 Soc.*, but why it was available earlier, in the period before *3 Soc.* was compiled, and was made use of by Thomas of Celano, when he was writing his *Second Life* in 1247.

But how strong is the evidence that it truly originated as a 'leaflet' with the stories?

In around twenty places in SL the claim is made that the story was written – not specifically by Leo – but by one or more companions: 'we who were with him' is the common phrase: but in one case it is: 'he who wrote this saw it and bore witness' (SL 22); in another: 'he who wrote saw this many times and gave testimony' (SL 60). These are not idle or naive words; they deliberately echo the claim in St John's Gospel and in St John's First Epistle, that the authority of the text or the writer depends on eyewitnesses – 'that which we have seen and have heard, we declare unto you'; 'This is that disciple who giveth testimony of these things, and hath written these things; and we know that his testimony is true' (1 John 1. 3; John 21. 24 – Douai-Rheims version).

Raoul Manselli wrote a deeply interesting book on the stories which contain these phrases, called *Nos qui cum eo fuimus*. Employing the techniques familiar to students of the New Testament as form criticism, he went intensively into the place of the stories, as they appear in SL, among early Franciscan texts; and he found abundant confirmation that they were indeed – in this form – the work of companions of the saint. But he omitted the Introductory Letter – technically because it is not in **P**, but perhaps also because he wished to establish some consensus among scholars, and avoid controversy. Nevertheless the more elaborate phrase of the letter echoes 'We who were with him': 'brother Leo, brother Rufino and brother Angelo, formerly companions, though unworthy, of the most blessed father Francis . . . We who, though unworthy, lived long in his company, thought it right to send in to your holiness . . . a few accounts of his many acts, which we ourselves have seen, or could discover from other holy friars: and especially from brother Philip, visitor of the poor Clares, brother Illuminato de

[17] SL p. 48; and see pp. 147–8 and note 136.

Arce, brother Masseo de Marignano, brother John, companion of the venerable father, brother Giles, who received much of his information from the holy brother Giles, and brother Bernard of holy memory, St Francis' first companion.'[18]

Can we connect the named authors of the Introductory Letter with the stories in SL? Can we identify the anonymous brothers who, in the stories, describe themselves as 'we who were with him'? I believe we can.

In a reliquary in the Sacro Convento at Assisi is a scrap of parchment. It bears the autograph of St Francis himself and of the man who, more than any other, kept his memory alive and human, his companion and confessor, brother Leo (Plate 12). On one side St Francis had written an ecstatic prayer of praise to God, and on the reverse of the leaf the blessing the Lord delivered to Moses [Numbers 6. 24–6] and the words, 'May the Lord bless you, brother Leo.' Before bequeathing this precious fragment to the Sacro Convento Leo annotated his blessing, in red ink, in a schooled hand: 'Two years before his death St Francis kept a Lent in the friary on La Verna in honour of the blessed Virgin Mary, the mother of God, and of the Archangel Michael, from the feast of the Assumption of the Blessed Virgin Mary until the feast of St Michael in September. And the hand of God was upon him. After the vision and speech of the seraphim and the impression of Christ's stigmata on his body he composed these praises that are written on the other side of the leaf, and wrote them with his own hand, giving thanks to God for the benefit conferred on him. St Francis wrote this blessing with his own hand for me, brother Leo. Likewise he made this Tau with a head with his own hand.'[19]

The breviary used by St Francis in his last years has also been annotated and authenticated by brother Leo. On the back of the first folio he penned this note: 'St Francis acquired this breviary for his companions brother Angelo and brother Leo because when he was well he wished always to say the office as required in the Rule, and when he was ill and could not say it he wished to hear it, and he continued to do this as long as he lived. He also had this Gospel Book[20] transcribed so that on a day when he could not hear mass because of illness or some other insuperable obstacle he had the Gospel for that day's mass read to him; and he continued to do this until his death. For he used to say: "When I cannot hear mass I adore the body of Christ in my mind's eye in prayer in just the same way as I adore it when I see it at the mass." When he had heard or read the Gospel St Francis always kissed the book because of his very great reverence for the Lord. For this reason brother Angelo and brother Leo urgently beseech the lady Benedetta, abbess of the Poor Ladies in the monastery of St Clare and all the abbesses of that monastery who shall come after her, that in memory of and in reverence for the holy father they preserve this book, from which he read so many times, for ever in the monastery of St Clare.'

---

[18] SL pp. 86–7.

[19] Esser 1976, pp. 142–3; Brooke in SL p. 8. On the Tau cross, see Fleming 1982, ch. 4, esp. pp. 105–7 and n. 13, 109.

[20] The breviary of St Francis comprises three books bound together: the breviary, the gospel book (i.e. gospels arranged for liturgical reading) and a later psalter (Van Dijk 1949, esp. pp. 24–5; Van Dijk and Walker 1960, pp. 129–30; Langeli 2000, pp. 79–103). Since the earthquake of 1997 it has been deposited for security at Monteripido di Perugia.

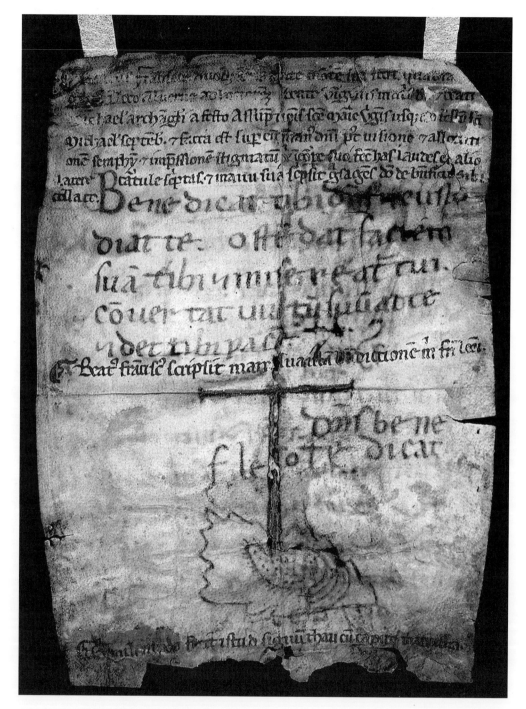

Plate 12 The blessing of brother Leo by St Francis: Assisi, Basilica, Cappella delle reliquie
(© www.Assisi.de. Photo Gerhard Ruf).

The annotations brother Leo wrote on his blessing and on the breviary are too brief to reveal much about his style. But in spite of this, something of his style, and of his attitude towards Francis and his way of telling things about him, does emerge. He gave the details about where and when Francis gave him the blessing at length, stressing that Francis wrote the words on both sides of the sheet and the sign of the Tau cross and the head all with his own hand. His note on the breviary is even more revealing. He emphasised that Francis was in some ways a man of routine – he did this every day and went on doing it right up to his death – and this carried the implication that he, brother Leo, was constantly with him and knew his daily habits. He could not refrain from calling attention to Francis' poor health – those who nurse those they love are painfully aware of the realities of illness and find the details of their ministrations hard to forget. He quotes Francis' actual words. Words and phrases in his note on the breviary that may be useful as indications of style include: 'tempore infirmitatis sue . . . et hoc continuavit dum vixit'; 'occasione infirmitatis . . . et hoc continuavit usque ad obitum suum'; 'fecit etiam scribi'; 'multotiens legit'; 'osculabatur semper'.[21] His attitude to Francis is illuminated, too, by the breviary. He treasured the book because Francis had used it daily, and made arrangements for its safe-keeping. But he did not regard it as a relic. He continued to use it. After Haymo of Faversham's Ordinal was published during the period 1245–51, he went through the book and made several corrections, erasing what Francis had read in order to keep it up to date and usable.[22] He wished for, and obtained from Francis, a tunic he was wearing shortly before he died, and kept it for a time. Perhaps later he feared he might be regarding it as a possession, for he gave it away.[23] He was so close to Francis that he did not idealise his portrait. He venerated and loved him, but Francis remained in his memory as a man, an inspiring and saintly teacher, but unpredictable, racked with pain and ill-health, human.

Could the stories in SL have been written by brother Leo and his friends? Perhaps the most revealing for our purpose is SL 50. This story is in **P** and the best of the other parallel manuscripts, that at Uppsala, and it was repeated in the *Speculum Perfectionis*, but was ignored by Celano and occurs nowhere else. It is short, about the same length as Leo's note on Francis' breviary, with which it is most interesting to compare it. The story is about a fire; one of a little group illustrating Francis' love and respect for all created things. In telling it, the simple daily routine is revealed in the context of a dramatic incident.

'Another time, when he was keeping "Lent" [that is, a period of fasting – on this occasion from 15 August to 29 September] on Monte La Verna, his companion one day, when it was time for the meal, was lighting the fire in the cell where they ate; when it was lit he came to St Francis in the cell where he prayed and slept, as it was his custom to read to him the portion of the Gospel which was recited at mass that day. When St Francis could not hear mass, he always wanted to hear the Gospel for the day before

---

[21] This passage resumes Brooke in SL pp. 8–9, 19–21. For examples, see SL 4, 26, 40–1, 43–5, 69, 77; (multoties) 13, 93, 106; (semper) 95; etc.

[22] Van Dijk 1949, pp. 17–18, 24. The Ordinal was completed in 1243, and published, after Haymo's death, in 1245–51 (Van Dijk and Walker 1960, pp. 292 and ch. 11, esp. pp. 321–2).

[23] 2 Cel. 50; cf. 2 Cel. 49, and AF X 161 and n. 15, which enable us to identify him as Leo. Cf. also SL pp. 294–5, Appendix c. 1 and n. 1.

he ate. When he came to eat in the cell where the fire had been lit, the flames of the fire had reached the gable of the cell and were burning it. His companion began to put it out as best he could but he could not manage alone. St Francis did not want to help him, but picked up a skin, with which he covered himself at night, and went out into the wood. The brothers of the friary, although they lived far away from the cell, as the cell was a long way from the friary, when they sensed that the cell was on fire, came and put the fire out. St Francis afterwards returned to eat. After the meal he said to his companion: "I do not want to have this skin over me any more, since through my avarice I did not want brother fire to eat it"' (SL 50).

We may see the actual Gospel Book from which the readings were taken, still guarded by the Poor Clares. The companion who read to him, and so who lit the fire, was either Leo or Angelo. The procedure described in Leo's note is portrayed in action in the story. In both there is emphasis on the regularity of Francis' habits. In both, a saying of his is reported in direct speech. To Thomas of Celano the story of the burning cell was not obviously edifying: he omitted it, while retaining most of the other tales in its context. This is hardly surprising: at first sight it only tells us how tiresome Francis could be and how difficult he was to live with – his final comment is characteristically whimsical; the story seems to reveal only his perversity, not any notable principle of the Franciscan way of life. Why did Leo, or Angelo, tell it? In the Introductory Letter the companions state: 'we wished to make known striking examples of his discourse (conversationis) . . . for the instruction of those who wish to follow in his footsteps'.[24] Francis' reaction to the fire was highly characteristic. His unwillingness to extinguish it was part and parcel of his normal teaching method. He taught by example and by acted parables, and often their very unexpectedness and exaggeration served to impress their lesson on his audience. This instance shows him going further and making capital even out of his mistakes. He regretted his behaviour on this occasion and admitted as much, thus disconcerting everyone again. For his regret was not that he had been uncooperative, but that he had been surprised into reacting as men of property do when fire threatens – he had removed something he valued to save it from the burning. Yet it remains essentially a story designed to reveal what Francis was like, warts and all. Only total absorption in Francis as he was vividly remembered can explain why it was recorded.

This story has the best credentials of any in the collection in **P**. It was surely penned by either Leo or Angelo – perhaps most probably by Leo, as we have his own autograph testimony that he was with St Francis on La Verna that 'Lent'.[25]

There is another story, too, culled from that same fast on La Verna.

'At one time St Francis went to the hermitage on La Verna and because it was so very remote he liked it so much that he wanted to keep a fast there in honour of St Michael. He had gone there before the feast of the Assumption of the glorious Virgin Mary; he reckoned the days from the feast of St Mary to the feast of St Michael and they were forty days. So he said: "To the honour of God and the blessed Virgin Mary his mother and St Michael the chief of all angels and souls, I want to fast here forty days." When he

---

[24] 'Conversatio' normally means 'manner of life'; but it also has the narrower meaning 'conversation, discourse', and sometimes (as perhaps in this context) carries both meanings.
[25] See p. 109.

entered the cell in which he was to remain continuously he asked God that first night to give him a sign that he might know whether it was his will that he should stay there. For St Francis was always careful when he stayed in any place continuously for prayer, or when he went through the world preaching, to know the will of God as to which was more pleasing to him. Because he sometimes feared that on the pretext of staying in a remote place to pray his body wished to rest, refusing the labour of going through the world to preach, for which Christ descended from heaven to this world. He always made those who seemed to be dear to God ask Him to show them his will, whether he ought to go through the world preaching or whether he should stay a while in a remote place to pray. The next morning at dawn as he stood in prayer many different kinds of birds came over the cell where he was – not in a group, but first one came and sang his song sweetly and flew away, and another came and sang and flew away, and thus did they all. St Francis wondered greatly at this and received very great comfort from it. He began to meditate on what it might mean and it was told to him in spirit by God: "This is a sign that the Lord will benefit you in this cell and will give you many consolations." Which was true. For among many other consolations both secret and open which God gave him, the vision of the Seraphim was shown him by God, from which he received much comfort in his soul in communion with God for the whole of his life. When his companion brought him food that day he told him all that had happened. Although he had many consolations in that cell, at night demons greatly tormented him, as he told this same companion. He once said: "If the friars knew how much suffering demons inflict on me there is not one of them that would not have great pity and sympathy for me." Therefore, as he many times told his companions, he could not satisfy the friars himself or sometimes show them the friendliness they desired.'[26]

The precise way in which the dates of the fast and its intention are defined at the beginning is very similar to that of Leo's note on his blessing. Francis' words are given in direct speech and again are put into the context that it was his custom to act in this way – he was always careful to ascertain the will of God before undertaking any major project of preaching or of prayer. The detail is meticulous. The birds did not sing altogether, but first one came and sang and flew away, and then another.

We know from Eccleston that Rufino as well as Leo was with St Francis on La Verna. The saint 'told brother Rufino his companion that, when he saw the angel from afar, he was exceedingly frightened; that the angel treated him harshly', and revealed four prophecies about the Order. 'St Francis told Rufino to wash the stone on which the angel had stood, and anoint it with oil; and this he did.' This information comes, not directly from Rufino, but from Leo, who told Warin of Sedenefeld, who wrote it down. As Leo's duty was to read the Gospel to Francis, it may be that the brother who brought him food that day was Rufino.[27]

In any case it is clear that this story is told by Leo or Rufino, or jointly – that is, by one, or two, of the companions named in the Introductory Letter.

The story about the fire occurs in **P** in the midst of a long series of stories mainly concerned with Francis' illnesses, especially his eye illness. An earlier story (SL 43) tells

---

[26] SL 93; cf. SL p. 21.   [27] Eccleston, p. 75.

how, two years before his death, while he was very ill and suffering particularly from pain in his eyes, he spent fifty days in a lean-to made of rushes at San Damiano, waiting for the weather to improve sufficiently for him to be taken to a doctor for treatment. He 'could no longer see in daytime the light of day, nor at night the light of the fire'. Unable to sleep for pain and the scuttling of mice around and over him, he suddenly felt himself assured of salvation, and determined not to feel sorry for himself, but to rejoice and to give thanks to God. 'I want, for his praise and my consolation, and the edification of our neighbours, to make a new song.' The fruit of his meditation was his own version of the Benedicite, the Canticle of brother Sun. The likelihood of this story, with its intimate detail, being reliable, and deriving in truth from companions close to the saint especially in his later years, is supported by the survival of the Canticle of brother Sun among St Francis' writings.[28] In the story Francis is recorded as saying: 'In the morning when the sun rises, every man ought to praise God who created it, because through it the eyes are lighted by day. In the evening when it grows night, every man ought to praise God for his other creature, brother fire, because by it our eyes are lighted at night.' He said: 'We are all as it were blind, and the Lord through these two creatures lights our eyes.' In the Canticle he sang:

Laudato si, mi signore, per frate focu,
    per lo quale enn'allumini la nocte,
      ed ello è bello e jocundo e robustoso et forte.

Be praised, My Lord, through brother fire,
    Through whom you make light the night-time,
      And he is fair and joyful and robust and strong!

When the weather eased, Francis was moved to the hermitage at Fonte Colombo near Rieti, as there was a doctor at Rieti experienced in treating eye infections. He proposed to cauterise the 'cheek up to the eyebrow of the eye which was the worse of the two' (SL 46). So, 'one day the doctor came, bringing the iron . . . He had a fire made to heat the iron and when it was lit put the iron in it. To comfort his spirit so that it should not be too greatly afraid, St Francis said to the fire: "My brother fire, noble and useful among all the other creatures which the Most High has created, be courteous to me in this hour, because I loved you formerly and still love you for the love of the Lord who created you. I beseech our Creator who made you to temper your heat so that I may be able to bear it." His prayer finished, he made the sign of the cross over the fire. As for us who were with him, we all fled out of love and pity for him and only the doctor remained with him. When the cauterisation was over we returned to him. He said to us: "You cowards and men of little faith, why did you flee? I tell you in truth that I felt no pain nor the heat of the fire"' (SL 48).

The searing memory of the cauterisation reminds the companions of another story and leads naturally into a digression. 'It is not surprising that fire and other creatures at times showed their respect for him, since, as we who were with him have seen, he loved and respected them with such charity and affection, took so much joy in them,

---

[28] Esser 1976, pp. 123, 126; the text quoted here is on p. 129.

and was moved to such concern and pity over them, that if anyone did not treat them properly he was upset. He chatted to them with inward and outward joy (a favourite phrase of the companions), just as if they felt, understood, and could talk about God, so that many times in this way he was wrapt in contemplation of God.' They had just written a most vivid instance of Francis talking to a fire as if it could understand and respond when he besought it to be courteous to him, and bearable. They now tell of an incident when St Francis was sitting so close to the fire that his habit caught alight and his guardian had to be sent for to extinguish it. 'For St Francis did not want to put out a candle or a lamp or a fire, as is usually done when it is necessary, so moved was he with piety and love towards it. He even did not wish a friar to throw out a fire or smoking wood . . . but wanted it to be laid flat on the ground out of reverence for Him whose light it is.' It is notable that for Francis fire is a manifestation of light even more than of heat. For him it is part of the first phase of creation, a symbol of the divine light; it is purity, brightness, clarity – 'claritas'.[29]

In *Nos qui eo fuimus* Manselli proposed to set aside traditional methods of historical criticism and look afresh at a particular group of stories which specifically claimed to have been written by eyewitnesses, using the methods of New Testament form criticism. However, a serious flaw in the arguments of the early form critics, such as Bultmann, was precisely their shunning of all other historical techniques, in order to see their stories in isolation from the literary texts in which they were preserved. They treated them as isolated pericopes, items of oral tradition, reflecting the human setting in which they were written down – the *Sitz im Leben*, the historical context of the authors – rather than as the words or acts of Jesus himself. So abstract did their work sometimes become that the supposed *Sitz im Leben* itself was an arbitrary construction little related to the actual world of late Antiquity or early Christendom. Even more abstract was their approach to the central figure: for in the effort to free themselves from presuppositions about the life and personality of Jesus, they tended to forget that it was the personality of Jesus himself which coloured the form of these stories as deeply as the tradition in which they were preserved and passed down. Here the parallel with Francis is particularly close, for it is evident to any imaginative reader of **P**, as with many Franciscan sources, that the powerful and original figure of Francis lies at the root of the forms in which the story was recorded.[30] Form criticism, if used too abstractly, can be very misleading. For study to advance, account must be taken of every appropriate technique of historical inquiry. The tendency of Manselli's method is to isolate certain stories from the rest of **P** as being peculiarly significant. Certainly his analysis of these stories builds up a compelling picture of the authenticity of his selected group. But does this validation really only apply to these few? My own view is that the links between these and the rest of the stories in SL are numerous and crucial.[31] Let me take an example. By concentrating exclusively in his survey on stories which contain the phrase 'we who

[29] SL 49. The reading 'claritas' in the Uppsala MS is clearly preferable to 'creatura' in **P**, which Manselli accepted, owing to his use of the edition of Bigaroni.

[30] This passage resumes Brooke 1982, pp. 666–7.

[31] Cf. Brooke 1982, p. 667 n. 51. For links among the stories, see especially the evidence cited in SL pp. 20–5, 79–85; Moorman 1940, pp. 99–104.

were with him' and the like, Manselli at one point highlights an almost continuous run of narrative, which he groups into three consecutive pericopes.[32] He begins – in pericope VII – with Francis' removal to Fonte Colombo for his eye treatment (SL 46), and his expression of his appreciation for the broken nights and taxing duties of the companions who nursed him (SL 47); the treatment – the cauterisation – he underwent (SL 48), and the digression on his extreme unwillingness to have fire extinguished, even when his habit was smouldering ((SL 49). Pericope VIII continues the digression with more details of Francis' reverence for God's creatures, mentioning water, rock, wood, vegetables, flowers and herbs, and how he had composed the Canticle of brother Sun 'so that God might be praised by all through his creatures' (SL 51). Pericope IX returns to the subject of eye illness, telling how St Francis, rather misguidedly as it turned out, sought to relieve the poverty of a poor woman needing treatment from the same doctor but unable to afford it, though he was in fact prepared to treat her for the love of God (SL 52). These pericopes thus comprise SL 46–9 and SL 51–2; SL 50 is omitted. Manselli suggested – and I would agree with him, because I argued for this and more in 1970 – that these stories epitomise authentic recollections told by companions who knew Francis well, particularly in his later years, companions who can be identified with the very friars who, according to Celano in his *First Life*, St Francis chose to look after him in his last two years of illness, 'friars who deserved to be dearly loved by him' (1 Cel. 102).[33] Manselli removed from its context and omitted from his pericopes VII–IX, the story of the cell on fire (SL 50), on the grounds that it does not contain the authenticating phrase. Yet SL 50 is an integral part of the collection and has been shown to have the best credentials of all.[34] Because he created pericopes using the artificial and inadequate criteria of form criticism, Manselli was also led to separate the story of the composition of an additional verse in praise of the virtue of forgiveness to the Canticle of brother Sun (SL 44) – his pericope XIII – from its context, the story of the circumstances in which the Canticle was composed (SL 43), and the story of how Francis 'similarly composed some holy words with a tune for the greater consolation of the poor ladies of the house of San Damiano' (SL 45). The Canticle, the additional verse and the song for the Poor Clares were all composed during the fifty days spent lying, very ill and unable to see, in the lean-to made of rushes at San Damiano. It was his own awareness of illness and of the burdens that this necessarily imposed on others that led him, in his message to the Poor Clares, to urge them most of all to 'see that those who were well should be patient in the labours they bore for their sick sisters, and the sick patient in their sickness and in the unavoidable suffering they had to bear' (SL 45). Pericope XIII properly belongs with, and prefaces (together with its own associated stories) pericopes VII–IX. Furthermore, these pericopes, indeed all Manselli's pericopes, form part and parcel of a much greater collection of stories which do not consist simply of clearly separable pericopes; there

---

[32] Manselli 1980, pp. 45–6, gives a list of the formulas. He accepts pericope VII, pp. 119–33 (= SL 46–9), pericope VIII, pp. 133–7 (= SL 51), pericope IX, pp. 137–43 (= SL 52).

[33] Manselli 1980, pp. 54–7 and cf. pp. 242–4. For my earlier argument, see SL (edn of 1970), esp. pp. 10–11.

[34] SL (edn of 1970), pp. 17–25, esp. pp. 20–1; and see pp. 111–12.

are themes that are sustained, and, although there are numerous digressions, links which join together its loose construction.[35]

There is indeed a remarkable unity in the collection: a vivid scene is set, a tale told; it comes to a climax in a pregnant saying – sometimes a little homily – by Francis, or a general point made by the authors. By such means we are given a sharply focused insight into his way of life, the principles which mattered to him – most memorably portrayed in deed and word and acted parable – and of many of the less dramatic, but none the less revealing, moments of his life, especially of his later days. The stories are also bound together, not only by themes but by recurring phrases indicating familiarity – besides 'we who were with him' and 'we saw with our eyes' or 'we saw and heard', there are 'he often said', 'he said many times', 'it was his habit' or 'it was his custom'; there are many references to 'inward and outward joy'.[36] Some of these are commonplace; but they recur with sufficient frequency to give a strong impression of the fundamental unity of the collection, which is confirmed by the literary form of the stories and the range of interest and the outlook they reflect.

The image of St Francis as presented by Leo, Rufino and Angelo

An impression of the quality of the stories in the *Scripta Leonis* will have emerged from the examples already given in the course of this discussion of its provenance and credentials, and elsewhere in this book. The companions 'wished to make known striking examples of his discourse and his holy will and pleasure, to the praise and glory of God and of our holy father Francis, and for the instruction of those who wish to follow in his footsteps'.[37] Though pre-eminently concerned to record incidents they had witnessed – 'we saw' occurs more frequently than 'we heard' – some characteristic remarks found a place. 'Go your way, brother fly', he said to one of his early converts, a friar 'who prayed little, and did not work and did not want to go for alms because he was ashamed: but he ate well' (SL 62). Though on principle showing reverence to all God's creatures, Francis does not seem to have had a high opinion of flies. He used the same phrase when rejecting a postulant who gave his property to his relations instead of to the poor (SL 20). He dismissed money in the same fashion. The soldiers of Assisi who were escorting him back to die in their city stopped on the way for a meal but could find nothing to buy. They said jokingly to Francis that he would have to give them some of his alms, to which he replied 'with great fervour of spirit: "You have not found anything because you trust in your flies, that is in pennies, and not in God. Return to the houses in which you sought to buy, do not be ashamed and seek alms of them for the love of God, and the Holy Spirit will inspire them and you shall find abundance"' (SL 59). Which they did. When they arrived at Assisi Francis was lodged at the bishop's palace. He was presently visited by a doctor from Arezzo who was a close friend. This doctor's name was Good John (*Bonus Johannes*), and Francis had given him a nickname,

---

[35] For a brief list of contents and summary, indicating the links between individual stories and groups of stories, see SL pp. 79–85; cf. ibid. pp. 47–9.

[36] SL pp. 24–5; Moorman 1940, pp. 99 ff.   [37] SL pp. 86–7, from the Introductory Letter.

'Finiatu', 'For St Francis did not want to call anyone "Good" when it was his name, out of reverence for the Lord who said: "No one is good save God alone".'[38]

One of Francis' great strengths was his ability to respond to the whole range of his experiences with joy. 'This was St Francis' chief and principal concern: he was always anxious to preserve spiritual joy in himself internally and externally, although from the beginning of his conversion until the day of his death he severely afflicted his body. He always used to say: "If God's servant always strives to have and to hold inward and outward joy, which comes from a clean heart, demons can hurt him in nothing, saying: 'Since the servant of God has joy in tribulation and prosperity we shall not be able to find any means of access to go in to him, or to hurt him'."' According to this passage, the phrase 'inward and outward joy' was central to Francis' spirituality; the companions derived their fondness for it from him. They were echoing Francis' own words when they used the phrase, as they did quite frequently, in the stories they told about him.[39] 'Once he [Francis] rebuked one of his companions because it seemed to him that he was sad and looked sad. He said to him: "Why are you sad and miserable about your sins? Set them between yourself and God, and pray him of his mercy to restore to you joy in his salvation, and always strive in the presence of me and others to be happy, because it is not suitable for the servant of God to show himself spiritually dull in the presence of his brother or any other and have a troubled face . . . If ever I feel tempted and spiritually dull, when I think about the happiness of my companion, through that joy I return from temptation and dullness to inward and outward gladness"' (SL 97).

'When St Francis chose from among the friars those whom he wanted to take with him, he said to them: "In God's name go on your way two by two and behave as you should, especially by keeping silence from daybreak until after Terce, always praying to God in your hearts. Let not idle or unprofitable words be uttered among you. For although you are walking, let your behaviour and life be as righteous as if you were in some hermitage or remaining in your cell, since wherever we are or wherever we walk we have our cell with us. Brother body is our cell and our soul is the hermit, which remains inside its cell, praying to God and meditating. Thus, if the soul does not remain in quietness and solitude within its cell, of little good to the religious is a cell made with hands"' (SL 80). St Francis himself prayed standing upright and bare-headed, or on his knees. If he was travelling he always stopped and stood still. 'Once . . . on the day he left Rome it rained the whole day, and as he was then very ill, he went on horseback. But to say his prayers he dismounted, standing beside the road, although it was raining and he was completely soaked. He said: "If the body likes to eat its food in peace and quiet, when the food and the body itself will be food for worms, with how much peace and quiet ought the soul to receive its food, which is God himself"' (SL 95).

[38] SL 65. Several names incorporating 'Bonus' occur in Assisi and its environs in this period. Brother Elias had a servant called Boniohannes in 1253; a woman, Boniovanna, is mentioned in 1246; Bonusaccursus, a smith, in 1236; two men called Bonuscangnus, one a notary, are mentioned in 1219, and another, also a notary, in 1233; Bonus and Bona also occur on their own. Cf. Langeli 1997, pp. 9, 18, 21, 36, 56 and Index, pp. 400, 402.

[39] SL 97; cf. SL p. 25. The phrase, in the form 'letitia interior et exterior' or 'letitia interius et exterius', occurs in cc. 49, 51–2, 91, 97; cf. 37, 92, 100, 108; a similar phrase, 'letitia utriusque hominis', occurs in cc. 19, 31, 36, 65, 100; cf. 84, 109. In c. 108 Francis is recorded as using both the words 'interiori et exteriori' and 'consolatione utriusque hominis' when speaking of brother Bernard.

These spoken illustrations of Francis' piety lead on naturally to a consideration of stories exemplifying the wider meaning of his 'conversatio', his manner of life. He was acutely conscious that his vocation was to lead and to convert by example first and foremost. Preaching and exhortation were adjuncts to living, round-the-clock witness. 'As he often said to the friars, because it was essential for him to be the model and example for all the brothers, he did not like to use either medicines or even necessary food in his illnesses' (SL 38). Again, 'one day he said to his companions: "I want to live before God in hermitages and other places in the same way that men know and see me in public"' (SL 40). He should surely be the patron saint of perfectionists.

Another story most vividly illustrates the veneration in which Francis was held while he was still alive. He was the guest of Hugolino, cardinal bishop of Ostia, and had slipped out to beg, so he was late for dinner, but his place – the cardinal always wanted him to sit next to him at meals – had been kept for him. He presently handed out a portion of the alms he had brought to table – scraps of stale, coarse bread – to each of the assembled guests, who were knights, relatives of the cardinal and the cardinal's chaplains. 'All alike received it with great devotion, some eating, some preserving it out of devotion to him; moreover, they took off their insignia out of devotion to St Francis when they received the alms' (SL 61). It evokes a wonderful mental picture: a formal dinner party, the guests wearing 'black tie' and 'gongs', with, in a place of honour on high table, a beggar in a torn patched habit distributing gifts on God's behalf.

Francis himself put sanctity, and image, into perspective. 'He said: "In pictures of God and the blessed Virgin painted on wood, God and the blessed Virgin are honoured and God and the Blessed Virgin are held in mind, yet the wood and the painting ascribe nothing to themselves, because they are just wood and paint; so the servant of God is a kind of painting, that is a creature of God in which God is honoured for the sake of his benefits. But he ought to ascribe nothing to himself, just like the wood or the painting, but should render honour and glory to God alone"' (SL 104).

One day, when he had still as yet few followers, but had already acquired a reputation, Francis went to a church in a village belonging to Assisi; 'he began to sweep it, and news of him at once got round the village, as the people were keen to see and hear him' (SL 19). A peasant called John left his ploughing, came, took the broom from him, finished the sweeping and expressed his wish to serve God. Francis explained the conditions for joining the brothers: he must give all his belongings to the poor. John immediately went and unyoked one of the oxen and offered it. His parents and younger brothers and sisters began a great wailing, and Francis was moved to pity 'especially because it was a large family and helpless'. He exercised a founder's licence, showing himself at once compassionate and cavalier, and modified the Gospel precept central to the Rule. He told John to expropriate himself of the ox by giving it back to his family. 'All were consoled at St Francis' words, and they were especially glad that the ox was returned to them, because they were poor.'[40] John was a simple man. Francis took him for his companion, and John studied to emulate the saint in all things. He copied all his

---

[40] Contrast Francis' treatment of a postulant who chose to give away his property to his relations in the next story, SL 20; cf. p. 143.

gestures. 'If St Francis bent his knees or clasped his hands to heaven or spat or coughed he did the same.' Francis was disarmed by such holy simplicity, and, after John's early death, he took delight in talking to his friars about John's manner of life, and used to call him 'St John'.

One of the interesting features of this story is the argument Francis used to reconcile this peasant family to the loss of their son (at the time less cogent, perhaps, than the practical inducement of the restored ox, but striking, considering that the Order was still in its early days). 'St Francis said to them: "Your son wants to serve God, at which you ought to be glad, not sorry: and not only in the sight of God but also in the eyes of the world this will be considered to your honour and to the profit of your souls and bodies, since God does honour to your flesh and blood, and all our brothers will be your sons and brothers."' In the eleventh and twelfth centuries a peasant who became a monk, even if only a humble lay brother, improved his standard of living as well as his standing in the eyes of God. The poor peasant of this story would not have improved his standard of living – Francis intended the friars to be as poor, even poorer than the poor (SL 88); but Francis already takes it for granted that a peasant's standing in the world would be enhanced by becoming a friar.

It is also important to remember that this story was written down about four years after the recruitment of laymen to the Order was formally prohibited in a general chapter presided over by Haymo of Faversham, the Minister General most responsible for making the Order a more clerical institution.[41] To reach a balanced understanding, sensitivity to the historical context is essential; but, as with the Gospel stories it is necessary to emphasise also the vital imprint of the exceptional and powerful personality of Jesus upon them, the same is equally if not even more true of these Franciscan stories. For if we read them with care and imagination, it becomes abundantly clear that the authors combined two aims not always in harmony in historical writing – or rather, often regarded by historians as incompatible: a passionate desire to portray Francis as they, his companions, vividly recalled him, and an equally passionate desire to keep the friars and the Order in strict accord with his views and principles, as expressed in his Rule and Testament and in his acts and sayings.

The same dichotomy is highlighted by another story characteristic of the companions' art.[42]

'One day, when St Francis returned to the church of St Mary of the Portiuncula, he found James there, a simple brother who had come that day with a leper with ulcerous sores. The holy father had strongly recommended this leper and all other lepers who

---

[41] The constitution effectively prohibiting the recruitment of laymen, Narb. 1 c. 3, was probably first enacted in 1242: cf. Brooke 1959, pp. 243–5.

[42] This story is discussed in Manselli 1980, pp. 214–21, as pericope XVIII. He observes that the formula 'nos qui cum eo fuimus' etc. occurs only in stories about the last two years of Francis' life, which were the work of companions of that period. He suggests (p. 221) that this story was not the work of one of these companions, since it has a different formula of witness, and is earlier in date: Francis appointed Peter Catanii Minister General in 1217 or 1218, and he died in March 1221 (Brooke 1959, pp. xv, 76–83). But Angelo was probably one of the earliest friars, and it is not at all likely that Francis took as his close companions in his last years friars whom he did not already know intimately (cf. SL pp. 11–14, and on Angelo, Schmucki 1971, p. 144). As explained above, I believe that the whole collection comprises stories told by the companions and their informants covering a wide range of time; and this particular story is very characteristic of their common style, e.g. in the use of 'inward and outward'.

were badly afflicted to him. For in those days the brothers used to stay in leper hospitals and this brother James was, as it were, the doctor of those who were most afflicted, and willingly touched, dressed and healed their wounds. St Francis said to brother James as though criticising him: "You ought not to bring Christian brothers here, as it is not seemly either for you or for them." St Francis called lepers "Christian brothers". The holy father said this because, although it pleased him that James should help and serve them, he did not want him to take those who were badly afflicted outside the hospital, particularly as this brother James was very simple and often went to the church of St Mary with some leper; and people were in the habit of shrinking from lepers who were badly afflicted. As soon as he had said it St Francis blamed himself and confessed his fault to brother Peter Catanii, who was then Minister General, because he believed that by rebuking brother James he had shamed the leper. So he admitted his fault, to make satisfaction to God and to the leper; and St Francis said to brother Peter: "I am going to tell you the penance that I wish to do for it so that you can confirm it for me, and not contradict me at all." Brother Peter said to him, "Do as you please, brother." For brother Peter was so respectful and afraid of St Francis and so obedient to him that he did not presume to change his orders even though on that occasion and on many others he was distressed inwardly and outwardly. St Francis said: "May this be my penance that I eat from the same dish with the Christian brother." This was done, and when St Francis sat at the table with the leper and the other friars, a dish was put between the two. The leper had sores and ulcers all over him and in particular his fingers, with which he ate, were contorted and bleeding, so that always, when he put them in the dish, blood flowed into it. Seeing this, brother Peter and the other friars were much upset, but they did not dare to say anything for fear of the holy father. He who wrote this saw it and bore witness' (SL 22).

This story illustrates Francis' deep concern for lepers and was doubtless meant to serve as a reminder. Brother James is revealed as the kind of brother Francis warmly approved of – even if he did not care for all his actions: a simple lay brother, who could help other poor folk and the afflicted and set them an example of Christian living. It also exemplifies the paradox of authority within the Order.

One is reminded, as often in the *Scripta Leonis*, of St Francis' Testament, in which he bore witness to how, in his own experience, contact with lepers played a crucial part in his conversion and transformed his understanding of values. The Testament makes it strikingly clear that Francis was obedient to the Minister General and to any of the brothers set over him – so long as they were obedient to him and his divinely ordained instructions.[43]

We can understand from this the special point of his exchange with Peter Catanii, the Minister General: it distils with humour and insight the relations between them. Peter was the Minister General, but Francis was still in command. In later sources Peter and his better-known successor, brother Elias, were called vicars – Francis' representatives, as it were – and the papacy treated Francis as head of the Order until his death; but this was not Francis' own usage or intention.[44] The companions were determined

---

[43] Esser 1976, pp. 442–3; trans. Brooke 1975, pp. 118–19; cf. ibid. pp. 26–9.   [44] Brooke 1959, pp. 106–18.

to emphasise where authority lay, for in 1230, after Francis' death, Pope Gregory IX had been cornered by the Order's officials into saying that the Testament was not binding on Francis' successors.[45] There are many undertones here, echoing Francis' own definition of obedience. Obedience is crucial to the Franciscan Rule, but ideally it is an attitude, a spontaneous subjection of mind and will to others' needs and wishes, fundamental to his notion of religious community.[46]

The story culminates in an acted parable. The memory of Francis eating with the leper from the same dish would never fade. It was highly characteristic of the way in which he put his lessons across, in a visible, physical form. The two stories of the simple lay brothers John and James vividly illustrate Francis' manner of life, but they also by implication reveal something of 'his holy will and pleasure'. When the companions come to deal with their opposites, the learned clerics, they enliven the message with a little drama. In Act 1 we meet a novice, 'who knew how to read the psalter, though not well. Because he enjoyed reading it he petitioned the Minister General for leave to have a psalter, and the Minister allowed it. But he was unwilling to have it unless he first secured a licence from St Francis, more especially as he had heard that St Francis did not want his friars to be eager for learning or for books, but wanted and preached to the friars that they should study to have pure and holy simplicity, holy prayer, and lady poverty.' The companions at this point are scrupulous to record that St Francis did not condemn or despise 'holy knowledge: on the contrary, he venerated most warmly those who were wise in religion and wise men in general', and they quote the Testament: 'We ought to honour all theologians and the ministers of the divine word and to revere them as the dispensers to us of spirit and life' (SL 70). Act 2 takes place in a hermitage. Francis arrives there and the novice explains his longing and his qualms. Francis' reaction, surely tuned to the individual, is histrionic. 'The Emperor Charles, Roland and Oliver, and all the paladins and strong men mighty in battle, pursuing the infidel with much sweat and toil even unto death, had over them a great and memorable victory: and in the end they were made martyrs, dying in battle for the faith of Christ. There are many who only for recounting what these did wish to receive honour and praise of men' (SL 72). In Act 3, a little later, Francis is sitting warming himself by the fire when the novice approaches and petitions him again. 'St Francis said to him: "After you have a psalter you will want and hanker for a breviary; after you have a breviary you will sit in an armchair like a great prelate, saying to your brother: 'bring me the breviary'." Thus saying, with great fervour of spirit he took some ashes in his hand and put them on his head, drawing the hand round his head as you do when you wash it, saying to himself as he did so: "I a breviary! I a breviary!" He continued to reiterate this saying many times, "I a breviary," drawing his hand over his head. The friar was dumbfounded and ashamed' (SL 73). The final act takes place at the Portiuncula, 'by the cell past the house on the road'. Importuned yet again, Francis gives way, and the satisfied novice starts to retrace his steps; but Francis has second thoughts 'and at once called after him: "Wait, brother, wait." He came up to him and said: "Come back with

---

[45] See p. 78. St Francis' Testament is specifically referred to in SL 9–10, 14, and quoted in SL 70 and 77.
[46] Cf. Brooke 1975, pp. 24–9.

me, brother, and show me the place where I said to you as to the psalter that you might do as the Minister told you." When they came to the spot where he had spoken these words to him, St Francis bowed down before the brother and said on bended knee: "I was wrong, brother, I was wrong, since whoever wishes to be a Friar Minor ought not have anything except a tunic, as the Rule allows him, and a cord and breeches, and those who are forced to by necessity or illness may have shoes"' (SL 74).

The historical context that favoured the writing down of such a drama in the mid-1240s was the change that took place in the composition of the Order. This began early on, and accelerated rapidly once the Order expanded beyond Italy. The friars who established a province in northern France arrived in Paris in 1218 or 1219 and were building a house there by 1223. The Channel was crossed in September 1224 by a group of nine, four clerks and five laymen – already the balance is shifting – who quickly split up so as to establish footholds in the key cities of Canterbury, London and Oxford by the end of the year.[47] It was not for the likes of brother James the simple that Francis' followers targeted such centres as Paris and Oxford. St Dominic deliberately made the leading university cities of Paris and Bologna the centres of his recruitment drive, and his successor Jordan of Saxony wrote from England in a letter to the Dominican nuns in Bologna that he had visited the schools at Oxford, where he had hopes of a 'good catch'.[48] St Francis considered learning a stumbling block, a possession peculiarly difficult to renounce. Yet paradoxically the Friars Minor were quite as successful as the Friars Preachers in attracting able and idealistic students and their masters. 'The development was not effected without injury to the Rule. Books, and the expenses and requirements incidental to their keeping, brought with them as an inevitable corollary a mitigation in poverty, an increase in stability, and a distaste for other forms of service. In the interests of study the learned wanted libraries and leisure, and, if they were to read with a good conscience, they had first to alter the obligations of their profession.'[49]

Opposition to brother Elias, a layman who, while Minister General from 1232 to 1239, made no distinction between laymen and clergy in his admissions and appointments policies, and was averse to travelling any distance from his favoured Umbrian residences at Assisi and Celle de Cortona, was initiated by learned ultramontane friars, Alexander of Hales, John of La Rochelle and Haymo of Faversham, all Paris masters. On Elias' deposition in 1239 an élite drawn from the learned and clerical element in the Order assumed control. Albert of Pisa, Provincial Minister of England, was elected Minister General, a man of very wide administrative experience and the first priest to hold that office, but a man too who had known St Francis, and upheld essential and distinguishing Franciscan values – bare feet, shabby clothing and rejection of money. He did, however, favour education and appointed lectors to convents.[50] The Order was reorganised and reformed; the General Chapter passed a number of new constitutions to supplement the Rule, which had been discussed and drafted in advance by a committee of friars elected for the purpose.[51] Albert died on 23 January 1240 and was succeeded in November by

---

[47] Moorman 1968, pp. 65–6, 72–3; Eccleston, pp. 3–9.   [48] Brooke 1975, pp. 187–8 and refs.
[49] Brooke 1959, p. 86.   [50] Brooke 1959, pp. 161–2, 183–94, 202; Eccleston, pp. 49, 67–9, 78–85.
[51] Eccleston, pp. 34–5, 67, 69–70. For a discussion and reconstruction of the 1239 constitutions, see Brooke 1959, pp. 210–35.

Haymo of Faversham. He had been the ringleader of the opposition to brother Elias and their spokesman in 1239, and as Minister General he consolidated and refined the legislative achievements of that year. Not all the arrangements introduced then were proving satisfactory. It was Haymo who was the man mainly responsible for making secure the constitutional foundations of the reformed Order and for setting the course it was to follow. He has a claim to be considered the second founder. He established a balance in the mechanisms of government, restoring to the ministers and custodians wide powers in appointing officials and in decision making, while at the same time explicitly subordinating all the officials, including the Minister General, to the authority of the General Chapter. He drastically restricted recruitment. In future only clerks already competently instructed in grammar and logic were to be admitted; exceptions could only be made in the case of someone, be he cleric or layman, whose admission would be 'mightily edifying'. This constitution involved so fundamental a change in the Order's composition – the recruitment of laymen virtually ceased – that it can hardly be explained simply as a reprisal, due to jealousy at the favour shown to laymen by brother Elias. It sprang rather from Haymo's conception of what the Order should be like, which he was now in a position to implement.[52]

The amalgam of enthusiasm for learning and for strict observance of the Rule is well illustrated in the English province. While a committee of learned friars headed by Adam Marsh were examining doubtful points in the Rule, in response to an order issued in 1241, a brother called John Banastre had a dream, in which St Francis appeared to him and showed him a deep well. John said: ' "Father, see, the brothers want to expound the Rule, but it would be better if you expounded it to us." The saint replied: "Son, go to the lay brothers and they will expound your Rule to you."' As a result the committee contented themselves 'with commenting on a few passages which they sent in an unsealed letter to the Minister General, begging, by the sprinkling of the blood of Jesus Christ, that the Rule be allowed to remain as it had been passed to St Francis at the dictation of the Holy Spirit'.[53] We might almost be listening to Leo, Rufino and Angelo – yet this evidence of Eccleston's is independent of theirs.

Leo, Rufino and Angelo collected and wrote down their contribution to the record in 1244–6, very much in this context. It is scarcely surprising then that among the themes they chose to illustrate Francis' 'holy will and pleasure' were some which, while they encapsulated genuine reminiscence, were also highly topical – for example, the fervour of the early days compared with the present, poverty, simplicity, humility, learning, the Rule, the Testament, disagreements between St Francis and the ministers. The name 'Friars Minor' was revealed to Francis to indicate 'a new and humble people, differing in humility and in poverty from all those who have gone before, and content to have [Christ] alone'; therefore he wrote it thus in his first Rule, which he took to Innocent III, who approved it.[54] Again, he 'caused much to be written in the Rule, which he sought from the Lord with diligent prayer and meditation for the benefit of the Order, affirming it to be utterly God's will. But when he showed it to them, it seemed to the

---

[52] Brooke 1959, pp. 195–209, 235–46.
[53] Eccleston, pp. 70–1; for all this see Brooke 1959, pp. 225–31, 233–7 and nn.; and see pp. 259–61.
[54] SL 67. The name Friars Minor also occurs at the beginning of the *Regula bullata*.

brothers severe and insupportable, and they did not know then what was to happen in the Order after his death' (SL 68).

The dramatised story of the novice and the psalter, SL 70–4, comes from a coherent group – SL 66–77 – that was considered so relevant that it was extracted from the *Scripta Leonis* and circulated as a separate pamphlet in the early fourteenth century. It was quoted at length, though with some abbreviation, by Ubertino da Casale in 1305 in his *Arbor Vitae Crucifixae Jesu*, and he again quoted from it extensively in his last *Declaratio* of about August 1311. Ubertino believed that the *rotuli* he had by him in 1311 were in brother Leo's own handwriting. He could have made himself familiar with Leo's hand by studying his annotation to the blessing St Francis had given him, which he had bequeathed to the Sacro Convento, and it is possible that Leo made the original extract himself, but by no means certain.[55] The title of the pamphlet – *Intentio Regule* – derives from the opening enquiry by a noble and saintly friar who visited Francis in the bishop's palace at Assisi as he lay dying, and talked with him of the achievements of the Order and the observance of the Rule, and questioned him as to his intention and will regarding the numerous books that he and the other clerical friars had. Is it all right, providing they say that their books belong to the Order? He received the uncompromising reply that Francis decided always to adopt after his decisive encounter with the novice: 'I tell you . . . this was and is my original and my final intention and will . . . that none of the brothers ought to have anything except a habit, as our Rule allows us, with a cord and breeches.'[56]

The pamphlet ends with a section on St Francis' wish for poverty in buildings – they should be constructed of loam and wood, especially at the Portiuncula – and quotes the Testament: 'Let the brothers be careful that churches and dwellings and everything else which is built for them are not accepted at all unless they are in accord with holy poverty, which we have promised in the Rule, always lodging there as strangers and pilgrims.'[57] The size and the quality of the buildings occupied by the friars was an issue that was entering a new phase by the 1240s, driven by two distinct but related developments. Their numbers were growing rapidly. Particularly if they had originally settled in humble restricted sites to uphold poverty, the old accommodation became obviously inadequate and they needed to enlarge their buildings or to move to more spacious sites – or both. Major construction works were in progress throughout the Order in these years, much of it in stone. At the same time their very success was arousing the jealousy of the secular clergy, and created a need for them to provide for lay congregations in their own churches. This could often be met most efficiently by the construction of new, purpose-built churches.[58] The companions continue: 'We who were with him when he wrote the Rule and almost all his other writings, bear witness that he wrote much in the Rule and in his other writings concerning which some, and especially the superiors, disagreed with him. Thus it happened that, among the issues on which the brothers were opposed to St Francis in his lifetime, there were points which would have been of real value to the whole Order, now after his death.' It is clear

---

[55] SL pp. 51–7 and nn. Cf. Plate 12.   [56] SL 66, 74; cf. also SL 69.
[57] SL 77; cf. SL 8–16.   [58] See p. 70.

that they were fully aware that they were recording the past with an eye to the present. But this does not invalidate their evidence. All reporting is selective, and their viewpoint is not concealed. There is no deliberate intention to mislead; they are concerned rather 'to put the record straight'. The *Scripta Leonis*, like the Gospels, can be interpreted to provide two layers of information.

Among those close to St Francis were individuals who venerated him deeply. Brother Pacifico, who had a singing voice so beautiful that St Francis wanted him to lead a group on a preaching tour on which the Canticle of Brother Sun was to be sung after the sermon as an encouragement to penitence (SL 43), once had a vision while attending St Francis at prayer in a deserted church. He saw many thrones in heaven, among them 'one higher than the rest, glorious and shining and decorated with every kind of precious stone' and a voice told him: 'This throne was Lucifer's and in his place St Francis shall sit in it.' When he came to himself he threw himself at Francis' feet in the form of a cross and spoke to him as if he were already reigning in heaven (SL 23).

Awareness of his sanctity increased as death approached. After he had been moved to the Portiuncula the lady Jacoba of Settesoli arrived from Rome bringing instinctively the gifts Francis desired, cloth the colour of ashes, and the ingredients for making marzipan; she also brought wax for candles and incense, to honour him after his demise. The companions comment: 'He who inspired kings to go with gifts to venerate and honour the boy, his dear Son, in the days of his birth and poverty, wished to inspire that noble lady from distant parts to go with gifts to honour and venerate the glorious and holy body of his holy servant, who with such love and fervour in life and in death loved and followed the poverty of his dear Son' (SL 101). It is a remarkable analogy – a rare compliment in this period for a woman to be accorded a comparable footing to the Magi. They are also offering their own contribution to the list of comparisons of St Francis to Christ – though theirs relates not to the stigmata but to his devotion to poverty.

On the day the lady Jacoba made marzipan for him, Francis recollected that the very first friar to join him, brother Bernard of Quintavalle, would enjoy this, and sent for him. Bernard came, and sat by his bed, and asked for his blessing. Francis, by now quite blind, stretched out his right hand, but it rested on the head of brother Giles, the third to join, who was sitting next to Bernard. Francis felt his error, and Bernard moved closer and received his special blessing (SL 107). Another day he called for all the friars in the house to gather, and blessed them all in turn, laying his right hand on the head of each, and through them blessed all his friars, including those to come. Then he blessed bread and distributed it, in memory of the Last Supper. The symbolism of the act before his death was fully understood by the friars, as Francis said he thought that day was a Thursday, although in fact it was not.[59]

---

[59] SL 117. This account of the blessing in the *Scripta Leonis* seems to be correcting 1 *Celano* 108, and Celano in his *Second Life* seems to apologise: 2 *Cel.* 216. But Francis blessed his brothers, or individual brothers, on a number of different occasions and SL is not necessarily the better source. For a discussion of how the blessing stories were modified over time see Brooke 1959, pp. 95–100.

The image of St Francis presented by Leo, Rufino and Angelo is pre-eminently that of a man who 'observed the holy Gospel in the letter from the beginning, when he began to have brothers, until the day of his death' (SL 69). He did his utmost to bind the friars to the same observance of Gospel perfection, through the Rule and through his own example. The original short Rule was added to haphazardly through the early years and grew into an unwieldy, rambling document, inflated with quotations. The companions affirm that the ministers caused the deletion of the instruction 'Take nothing on the way' from the final official version of the Rule, the *Regula bullata*, but that St Francis circumvented their purpose by ordering 'it to be written at the beginning and end of the Rule that the brothers are bound to observe the Gospel of our Lord Jesus Christ'.[60] The ministers were concerned with practicalities and with what they considered should and should not be made legally enforceable. St Francis understood the Gospel intuitively, and set out to follow Jesus' words literally as a way of life, not mechanically or stupidly, but in a deeply imaginative way, based on profound meditation on their message. Let us take the text: 'Take no thought for the morrow.' In the days before freezers, peas and beans could only be preserved for the winter by drying – and to make dried pulses palatable they need to be soaked overnight. Francis 'ordered the friar who did the cooking . . . not to put them in hot water in the evening ready for the following day, as is usually done, so that they might obey that saying of the holy Gospel: "Take no thought for the morrow." So that friar put them to soak after the brothers had said Mattins.'[61] Absurd perhaps – but in harmony with the Pauline paradox that the foolishness of God is wiser than men. In his imaginative exaggeration Francis came near to the deepest insights of Jesus himself.

THE *ANONYMOUS OF PERUGIA*

The author of the *Anonymous of Perugia* (AP) – so-called because it survived in a single fifteenth-century manuscript in that city – claims to have known St Francis and some of his earliest followers personally.[62] It is closely linked in word as well as form with 3 *Soc.* – so much so that one must be the principal source of the other. It is not dated and there has been much discussion over their relationship, but all the indications seem to be that AP is the source, 3 *Soc.* the derivative.[63] To incorporate the simple narratives of AP into the much more developed and nuanced account of Francis' early life in 3 *Soc.* is an intelligible task; the reverse – to extract AP at a later date – is difficult to conceive as a sensible enterprise. In one of the most sustained parallel narratives, that of the visit of the brothers to Innocent III in 1210 and the pope's acceptance of the Order, the chief difference between the two comprises some passages in 3 *Soc.* which are closely paralleled in 1 *Celano*, but are missing from AP. There are two possibilities: either that AP used 3 *Soc.* and carefully deleted the passages from 1 *Celano* from it; or that 3 *Soc.*

[60] SL 69. A comparison of the *Regula non bullata* with the *Regula bullata* shows that a great many gospel instructions and other quotations were omitted (cf. Esser 1976, pp. 377–402 with ibid. pp. 366–71).

[61] SL 4, quoting Matt. 6. 34. This text is not specifically quoted in either version of the Rule.

[62] AP 2. The best edition of AP is in Di Fonzo 1972, reproduced in Beguin 1979.

[63] See Brooke 1982, pp. 656–65. For the reasons indicated below, and from closer study of AP, I am more fully convinced than in my former article of the priority of AP.

combined material from *AP* with material from 1 *Celano*. The latter is the only solution which makes sense.[64]

Leo, Rufino and Angelo, as well as sending in their own contribution, forwarded along with it 'a few accounts' which they 'could discover from other holy friars', especially from (among others) 'brother John, companion of the venerable father, brother Giles, who received much of his information from the holy brother Giles, and brother Bernard of holy memory, St Francis' first companion'. It is possible – indeed I would argue that it is likely – that the original of *AP* was one of the pieces which the companions submitted to Crescentius in 1246. It was certainly written later than 1240, since it refers to the death of brother Sylvester; it was probably used as a source for 2 *Celano*, and so is earlier than 1247. It clearly fits into the context of the materials available in the mid-1240s. If this hypothesis is correct, then the writer of 3 *Soc.* did have at his disposal, in addition to the Introductory Letter, a substantial piece that came with it, but a piece written not by the 'three companions' but by a friar who moved in the circle of brother Giles and brother Bernard, brother John, a companion not of St Francis but of brother Giles.[65]

The *Anonymous of Perugia* is unlike other early literature on St Francis. It has a wider perspective. Its most convincing rubric reads: 'On the beginning or foundation of the Order, and of the deeds of those Friars Minor who were the first in that religious way of life and companions of St Francis.'[66] It thus gives prominence not just to 'our most blessed father Francis', but to a small group of holy men he inspired and led, in the belief that a knowledge of their life and doctrine may serve to lead Francis' later followers to God. It is addressed primarily to the friars.[67]

The Minister General Crescentius of Jesi was evidently much interested in the early friars as well as in Francis and inspired a *Dialogue* on the virtues of some of them.[68] It may be that in 1244 he asked the friars to send in not only 'signs and miracles of St Francis' but also edifying material about other members of the Order that 'they knew or could discover'; and that this prompted brother John, companion of brother Giles, to write down information he had received, particularly 'from the holy brother Giles, and brother Bernard of holy memory, St Francis' first companion', and to entrust his manuscript to brothers Leo, Rufino and Angelo for forwarding.[69] Brother Giles and brother Bernard are leading players in *AP*.

---

[64] The parallel passages from 1 *Cel.* 33, *AP* 34–6 and 3 *Soc.* 49–52 are conveniently laid out in Beguin 1979, pp. 258 ff. The comparison is complicated by a substantial passage in 2 *Cel.* 16–17, which may be partly based on *AP* and was clearly used by the author of 3 *Soc.* But the essential point made in the text is clearly indicated in Beguin 1979, pp. 258–9. Cf. also Desbonnets 1972, pp. 91–2.

[65] SL pp. 86–7. The suggestion that brother John wrote *AP* was first made in Di Fonzo 1972, pp. 396–409, and Beguin 1979, pp. 15–17. My own further reflection since my review of 1982 has convinced me too that he was the author.

[66] Di Fonzo 1972, p. 435; Beguin 1979, p. 26.

[67] *AP* 2, Prologue: 'Since the servants of God [i.e. members of a religious order] ought not to be ignorant of the way of life and doctrine of holy men'. See also 48, the Epilogue, quoted p. 138.

[68] Thomas de Papia (Pavia), *Dialogus de gestis sanctorum fratrum minorum*, ed. in Delorme 1923; cf. Brooke 1959, pp. 251–2n. The holy brothers – Anthony of Padua, Benvenuto, Ambrose, Gratian, Roger and others – were not those recorded in *AP*.

[69] See pp. 108–9.

Members of a recently established innovative religious Order – such as were the two main Orders of friars in the first quarter of the thirteenth century, the Friars Minor and the Friars Preachers – might reasonably be expected to wish to know about three separate categories of fact relating to the institution they had joined, while such facts were still within recall. These were: information about their saintly founder, recently deceased; about the foundation of their Order; and about fellow friars, whose lives, while exemplary, might feel more akin to the experiences of the rank and file, and encourage them the more. Jordan of Saxony, Master General of the Friars Preachers, was the first to recognise and address this need. His *Libellus de principiis*, written 1232–3, aimed to provide precisely this service for his friars. 'It seemed good to me, who, though I was not among the first, none the less have conversed with the first brothers and saw the blessed Dominic himself both when I was outside the Order and after I had joined it, and knew him well; I made confession to him and took the order of deacon at his wish, and put on the habit four years after the Order was first founded; it seemed good to me, I say, to put in writing everything in order, which I saw myself and heard, and knew from the description of the first brothers, of the beginnings of the Order, of the life and miracles of our blessed father Dominic, and of some other brothers, as they came to my mind, so that his sons who will be born and arise in the future, shall not be ignorant of the first beginnings of this Order, and wish to know in vain, since passage of time may make it impossible to discover anything sure about those beginnings.'[70] The mixed purpose produced a 'curate's egg' of a book, part hagiography, part history of the Order, in which indeed the personal initiative and influence of Dominic are rather under- than over-stated. AP, written perhaps a little more than a decade later, is an attempt to do something similar for Francis and the Franciscans. AP is more hagiographical, and much less sophisticated in style; but it enshrines a similar purpose; and its prologue echoes the same phrases, in both cases reminiscent, as so often in such literature, of the opening of the First Epistle of St John. 'I who have seen their deeds and heard their words, whose disciple I was, have narrated and compiled some of the acts of our most blessed father Francis and of some of the brothers who came at the Order's beginning.' The parallel is suggestive but there is too much commonplace here to prove a direct link.[71] The writer of AP may well not have known Jordan of Saxony's work but his purpose was the same.

AP begins with the conversion of the adult Francis, described as a merchant by trade and a lavish spender. Its account is noticeably different from that in 1 *Celano*, which it implicitly corrects and supplements. 1 *Celano*, having noted the long illness with its first hint of a change in values, gives a relatively small number of stories, from Francis' decision to join a nobleman to seek wealth and fame in Apulia to his decision to remain with the poor priest at San Damiano. The links between the stories are unconvincing. For example, on waking, Francis considered his dream of his home full of arms an omen of great success, but he nonetheless changed his mind about going to Apulia (1 *Cel.* 3–9). Thomas of Celano knew nothing of this early period at first hand. His

[70] C. Brooke 1971, p. 217 and n. 8.   [71] AP 2; cf. 1 John 1. 1; Brooke 1982, pp. 656–65, esp. 664.

material came to him in the form of individual stories, which in the nature of the case were difficult to fit together. It is to his credit that he has not forced them into a strictly coherent mould. In real life the train of motivation is frequently as disjointed and inconsequent.

AP starts with an incident more particularly applicable to a merchant than the common experience of illness. Francis, preoccupied with the business of selling cloth, refused alms to a beggar, then felt ashamed, and resolved in future always to give when asked for the love of God. The next experience thought to be worth telling was Francis' dream, in which he was led to a palace of indescribable splendour and delight, full of military equipment, the shields hanging on the walls resplendent with the sign of the cross.[72] This dream prompted his decision to seek knighthood at the hands of count Gentile. He prepared expensive attire, engaged an esquire, mounted his horse and set off for Apulia. But during the night, at Spoleto, a voice questioning why he relinquished the lord for the slave caused him to return. On his way back, at Foligno, he sold his rich clothes and his horse. As he neared Assisi he met Peter, the poor priest of San Damiano, and asked him to mind the proceeds of the sale for him. The priest refused, saying he had nowhere to keep it safely and Francis threw the money on to a window ledge of the chapel. The dilapidated condition of the chapel then catching his eye he decided to devote the money to its repair and to live there himself. His angry father heaped reproaches on him and demanded the money back. Francis returned it to him, and the clothes he was wearing, in the presence of the bishop of Assisi, who covered his naked body with his cloak. The Lord now led him by the straight and narrow way, since he wished to possess neither gold nor silver nor money nor anything else, but to follow the Lord in humility, poverty and simplicity of heart. He walked barefoot, wearing a contemptible habit girded with the cheapest cord. Almost everyone thought him mad. His father cursed him whenever they met. So Francis took a poor old man called Albert about with him, asking a blessing from him (AP 3b–9c).

This account, though short, has many precisions of detail and shows a good knowledge of local topography. It also binds the individual episodes into a rational and coherent story. Perhaps too coherent – I think we see here an attempt to impose an ordered explanation on the facts. It represents a later stage, and we know that AP was not written before 1240, as it refers to the death of brother Sylvester, which occurred at Assisi on 4 March 1240.[73] The setting of Francis' dream in a splendid palace, and the crosses on the shields, are clearly embroidery supplied by an imaginative oral tradition. In contrast, the dream, as told in 1 *Celano* 5, has the ring of truth: the arms filled his home, and Francis wondered at it, because he was not used to see such things in the house, but rather cloth stacked for sale. AP's account so far relates to the time before Francis acquired permanent companions and is not attributable to known eyewitnesses: some of its precise details are probably reliable, some not. But from this point on it is on surer ground.

---

[72] AP 5a–d.

[73] AP 13c. Sylvester is said to have died on 4 March 1240: Di Fonzo 1972, p. 441 n. 2, citing Arturi a Monasterio 1939, p. 83 n. 5. I owe this reference to the kindness of Father Michael Robson OFM Conv. Cf. Brooke 1982, pp. 657–8 and references; 2 *Cel* c. 109 confirms that he was dead by 1247.

AP is notably brief on the interval between the breach with his father and the arrival of his first followers (8c–9c), the time during which the fundamental core of Francis' future way of life was determined. Even his earliest followers did not know about this crucial period at first hand, and it enhances the likelihood of the reliability of AP that it becomes more detailed exactly at the point when the two friars named as the informants of brother John – its likely author – enter stage.[74]

AP is slightly different, more detailed, simpler and more direct than 1 *Celano*. Two men of Assisi, one rich, Bernard, one poor, Peter, approached Francis, who rejoicing led them into a church to pray.[75] They asked its priest to show them the Gospel, and it was he who opened the book for them, because they did not as yet know how to read well. Eight days later Giles, who was also from Assisi, joined them, and Francis took him as his companion into the Marches of Ancona, leaving the other two at the Portiuncula. Francis, full of enthusiasm, loudly sang God's praises in French. On one occasion he said to Giles: 'Our Order will be like to a fisherman who puts his net in the water, catching a copious multitude of fish . . . He chooses the big ones, leaving the small ones in the water.' Giles was extremely astonished at this prophecy from the saint's mouth, as he knew the number of brothers to be small (four in all!) (15a–c). Shortly after they returned to the Portiuncula three more men of Assisi joined them – Sabbatino, John and Morico the Little. They now went through a particularly difficult time. Local public opinion was against them. Hardly anyone was prepared to give to them: they were seen as feckless scroungers who had abandoned their own goods and wanted to eat the bread of others (16c–17b).

One day Francis called his followers to him in the wood near the Portiuncula, where they frequently went to pray, with a purpose. 'Consider, my dearest brothers, that our vocation, to which God in his mercy has called us, is for the profit and salvation of many, not simply our own. Let us go, therefore, through the world, exhorting and teaching men and women, by word and example, to do penance for their sins and bear in mind the commandments of God.' His instructions were laced with Gospel quotations: '"Fear not, little flock" [Luke 12. 32]. Do not murmur that you are foolish and uneducated. Remember Christ's words to his disciples: "For it is not you that speak but the Spirit of your Father which speaketh in you"' [Matt. 10. 20]. He warned that while some would receive them gladly, others would reject them and their words, and they must be prepared to bear everything patiently and humbly. As they looked alarmed he ended with a prophecy: '"Be not affrighted" [Mark 16. 6]. Know that before long many wise, prudent and noble men will come to us and be with us. They will preach to the nations and peoples, kings and princes, and many will be converted to God. And God will multiply and increase his family throughout the whole world.' He blessed them and sent them off in pairs (18a–d).

There follows a long section on how they fared on their own (19a–24b). They obeyed Francis' teaching scrupulously. When, on their way, they came to any church, in use or derelict, or to a cross, they knelt and prayed devoutly, saying: 'We adore you, Christ, and bless you, and in all your churches which are in all the world, because by your holy

---

[74] AP 10a–14c.   [75] AP 10a–11a; 1 *Cel.* 24–5.

Cross you redeemed the world.'[76] Despite the Gospel's and Francis' assurance, they did find it tough going answering the many and varied questions thrown at them. But to the basic question: '"Where are you from? . . . What Order are you from?" they replied simply: "We are penitents, and we were born in the city of Assisi." For as yet the way of life of the brothers was not called an Order' (19c). Many reckoned they were either fools or knaves, and concluded: 'I do not want to receive them into my house, lest perhaps they pinch my things.' So very often they lodged in the porches of churches or houses (20a).

One such occasion is described in great detail – a personal reminiscence of brother Bernard. He and his companion arrived at Florence and traipsed through the city seeking shelter in vain. At the entrance to one house they noticed an oven in the porch and said to each other: 'Here we might stay.' They asked the lady of the house if she would be kind enough to take them in, and when she at once refused, they begged she would allow them to spend the night near the oven: which she did. When her husband came home and saw them there, he asked: 'Why have you granted hospitality to those rascals?' She replied: 'I did not want to let them in to the house, but I permitted them to lie outside in the porch; they cannot steal anything from us there, unless perhaps wood.' Because of their suspicions they were not prepared to offer the brothers any covering, though the weather was extremely cold. While it was still night the two rose to go to Matins at the nearest church. When it was day the woman went to the church to hear Mass, and noticed them devoutly and humbly praying, and thought to herself: 'If these men were criminals like my husband said they would not persist so reverently in prayer.' While she was thinking this, a man named Guido went about the church distributing alms to the poor that he found there. When he reached the brothers and wanted to give them each a penny like the rest, they refused. He asked them: 'Why do you not accept money like the other poor, since you appear to be in want and destitute?' One of them, brother Bernard, replied: 'It is true that we are poor, but our poverty is not burdensome, as with other poor, because through God's grace and by fulfilling his counsel we are made poor.' He asked in wonder if they had owned anything in the world, to which they replied that they had, but had distributed it to the poor for the love of God. The woman, mindful of the brothers' refusal of the money, came up and said: 'Christians, if you would like to come back as my guests, I will willingly receive you inside the house.' They answered humbly: 'The Lord reward you.' But perceiving that they had not been able to find lodging, the man took hold of them, led them to his house, and said: 'Here is the lodging the Lord has prepared for you. Stay here as long as you please.' They gave thanks to God, who had mercy on them and heard the cry of the poor. They stayed with him several days. As a result of their words, which he listened to and their good example which he saw, he was afterwards much more generous to the poor (20b–22b).

I have retold this passage at length in order to give a flavour of the author's style and method. Two things that are striking are its frequent use of direct speech, and

---

[76] AP 19a, from St Francis' Testament, Esser 1976, p. 438; translated Brooke 1975, 117; quoted in 1 *Cel.* 45.

the heroic simplicity and virtue of the tiny group of converts in the earliest days of the movement. It says in the prologue that the work is written 'for the edification of readers and hearers', and it seems to me that it was composed with a listening audience very much in mind. Incidents are told dramatically and with pace, as for example the sequel to Bernard and Peter's conversion. Bernard sold all his possessions, and because he was rich they fetched a lot of money. Peter sold his few belongings. The poor of the city were gathered and the two distributed the proceeds of sale among them, while Francis stood by. A priest named Sylvester, from whom Francis had bought stones for the repair of San Damiano, came on the scene, and seeing all this money flowing, coveted some for himself. 'Francis, you did not pay me enough for the stones you bought from me.' Francis, who had renounced all avarice, hearing this unjustified complaint, went to brother Bernard, and putting his hand in his cloak, where the money was, drew it out full of coins and gave them to the priest. Again putting his hand in the cloak, he extracted coins and again gave them to the priest, saying: 'Are you yet fully reimbursed?' 'Fully.' The priest returned home happy. After a few days, inspired by God, he began to reflect on what St Francis had done. 'Am I not', he said to himself, 'a wretched man, who, although I am old, covet and seek after these temporal things, and this young man for the love of God despises and abhors them?' The next night he saw in a dream a truly enormous Cross, whose top touched the skies, but its foot stood in St Francis' mouth. The arms of the Cross stretched from one side of the world to the other. On waking, that priest believed St Francis to be a true friend of God, and that the Order which he had begun would spread throughout the whole world. And so he began then to fear God and to do penance in his own home. A little while later he entered the Order of Friars Minor and lived well and died gloriously (11b–13c). It is a gem of a sermon in miniature.

Francis decided to take the group to Rome to seek papal approval. On the way he said: 'Let us make one of us our leader, and we will regard him as the vicar of Jesus Christ. Wherever it pleases him to turn aside, we will turn aside, and when he wants to take shelter, we will take shelter.' They chose his first recruit, brother Bernard (31a–b). In Rome Francis was recommended to the pope by Cardinal John of St Paul. Innocent III's reaction was brisk and to the point: 'Bring him to me.' Considering his intention to live without possessions hard to sustain, the pope advised him to pray for guidance. The Lord put into Francis' heart a parable, which went like this: there was an exceedingly poor woman in the realm, whose beauty pleased the eyes of the king, and he fathered many sons by her. She became distressed, wondering how, without possessions, her sons were to live. The king reassured her: 'Do not be afraid because of your exceeding poverty, nor for the sons born to you, and the many who will be born, since, as for the numerous hirelings (*mercenarii*) in my house bread abounds, I do not wish that my sons perish from hunger, but I wish them to have an abundance greater than the others' (32b–35a). The same parable is found in 2 *Celano* and 3 *Soc.*, but with an important difference. In 2 *Celano* the king married the poor woman with joy – a likely story! 3 *Soc.* is even more circumstantial. The king, admiring the poor woman's beauty, desired her for his wife. After the marriage was contracted and consummated, many sons were born.[77] This sequence reinforces the argument for the priority of AP. The on-going affair is the source of the other two accounts with their veneer of respectability.[78]

The portrayal, in AP, of the leading churchmen with whom Francis had dealings is very interesting, and may surprise some. The bishop of Assisi is singled out from the very early days of the Order. When their number rose to eight, public opinion in the city hardened. Even their families and relatives could not understand why anyone should give up everything and go begging from door to door, and together with the rest of its inhabitants, small and great, male and female, despised and derided them as out of their minds and stupid. The sole exception was the bishop, to whom Francis frequently went for advice (17a–c). When they went to Rome they found the bishop there; he was delighted to see them, and it was he who introduced them to Cardinal John of St Paul. He lodged them for a few days, formed the highest opinion of them and their way of life, and offered to speak for Francis at the Curia. He told Innocent III: 'I have found the most perfect man, who wants to live according to the pattern of the holy Gospel and to observe evangelical perfection. I believe that through him God wishes to renew his whole Church through all the world.' AP's account differs in several details from that in 1 Celano, which presumably it aimed to amend.[79] It was due to Cardinal John of St Paul that all twelve friars were given the clerical tonsure (36f). He also recommended Francis and his friars to his fellow cardinals, so that they each wanted to have a member of the Order in their household, and Francis graciously conceded to their requests (42a–b).

The institutional structure of the Order began to take shape at this stage. Francis ordered that Chapter meetings be held twice a year, at Whitsun and Michaelmas. On these occasions he admonished, reprimanded and regulated the friars, but he always took care to practise first in his conduct what he preached to them in words. He especially emphasised reverence for ecclesiastical authorities and ordinances, devout attendance at Mass, and respect for priests because they consecrated the sacrament. They were to bow before them and kiss their hands. If priests were riding, they were not only to kiss their hands, but their horses' hooves! They were to judge no one, nor despise any, even those who indulged themselves in fancy food and drink and clothes – perhaps in memory of what he had been like in his youth. They were to announce peace and carry peace in their hearts and be gentle towards all, as they were called to tend the wounded, bind up the broken, and recall the strayed. At the same time he reproved them for inflicting too many hardships and austerities on their bodies; for overdoing fasts and vigils and penances. The friars for their part did not venture to discuss worldly matters, but talked to each other of the Lives of the Fathers, or the perfection of some brother, or how they could better attain grace. If any felt tempted or troubled, listening to Francis' fervent discourse, even seeing him present among them, was enough: temptations ceased. For he spoke to them compassionately, not like a judge, but like a father to his sons, or a doctor to the sick.[80] It is a marvellous evocation

[77] 2 Cel. 16; 3 Soc. 50.
[78] This seems a clear indication that AP is earlier than 2 Cel., i.e. than 1247: see p. 146 and note 128.
[79] AP 32a–36b; 1 Cel. 32–3.
[80] AP 36g–39c. The phrase used of Francis, 'pater filiis et infirmo medicus', is an interesting variant of the theme of Francis as father and *mother* common in other sources: cf. Brooke 1982, p. 657 n. 13.

of Francis' style of leadership and control; a marvellous evocation too of the Order's springtime. And it is not exceptional. Lyrical descriptions of the early days abound. Of course it was never consistently like that. The remembered past is not looked at in the same way as the experienced present. In every generation some older people will tend to look back to the exploits of their youth with a somewhat uncritical or indulgent eye, and to claim behaviour was better then than now. The memories, even of the most truthful people, are sifted and modified over time.[81] The collective memories of religious communities are not immune.

After the death of Cardinal John of St Paul in 1215, according to AP, Hugolino, cardinal bishop of Ostia, who already regarded Francis and his friars with fatherly affection, offered them his advice, help and protection and asked for their prayers. Francis invited him to attend the Whitsun Chapter meeting at the Portiuncula, and he came to it every year. 'When he came, all the friars gathered for the Chapter went out to meet him in procession. He, when the friars came, dismounted from his horse and went with them on foot to the church, on account of the devotion he felt for them. Later he preached to them and celebrated Mass, and St Francis sang the Gospel.'[82]

Eleven years after the birth of the Order – which AP dates precisely to 16 April 1208 – ministers were chosen and missions sent out to almost all regions of Christendom.[83] In some provinces they were received but were not allowed to build places of residence – they were not allowed to establish themselves on a permanent footing: from others they were expelled, because they were suspected of not being orthodox Catholics. AP tells us the reason why: it is 'because up to that time the friars had not had the Rule confirmed by the pope, but only conceded' (44b). AP is the earliest Franciscan source to make this link explicitly. There is not the slightest hint in 1 Celano – nor for that matter in Bonaventure – that the informal nature of Innocent III's approval of Francis' Rule was responsible for the Order's initial lack of success outside Italy.[84] But according to AP it was on that account that the friars, especially those who had gone to Hungary and Germany, suffered many tribulations at the hands of clerics and laity, were stripped by robbers, and returned to St Francis greatly upset and afflicted. They proceeded to tell Cardinal Hugolino all about it. Hugolino then called Francis to him and took him to Pope Honorius III; and he made Francis write another Rule and have it confirmed, and the pope ratified it with his seal. Francis asked the pope for one of the cardinals to be made 'governor, protector and corrector' of the Order, 'as is contained in the same Rule', and he was granted Hugolino (44a–45a). AP's summary of the history of the Order during these formative years (and it is very summary) seems to contain chronological inaccuracies – for example, the appointment of Hugolino as

---

[81] My mother-in-law, a most veridical witness, once assured me that, as children, 'all her sons were little angels'.

[82] AP 43a–c. The last phrase indicates that Francis was already in deacon's orders. For Francis as deacon, see C. Brooke 1999, pp. 233–4, 249–53. Hugolino may not have gone to the chapter of 1221: see Jordan, c. 16; Brooke 1959, pp. 286–91.

[83] AP 44a; cf. 3a – 'impleti sunt anni 1207', presumably (not certainly) meaning we are in 1208. The chapter in which the missions were sent out is dated 1219 by Jordan (c. 3) – but he calls this (if the text is reliable) the tenth year of Francis' conversion.

[84] 1 Cel. 32–3; Bonav. III, 8–10; IV, 11.

Cardinal Protector occurred earlier than the confirmation of the *Regula bullata*[85] – but in its essentials it is corroborated by the independent evidence of Jordan of Giano's Chronicle, dictated in Halberstadt in 1262. Jordan described how the first brothers who went to France were mistaken for Albigensian heretics; how in Germany they were also taken for heretics, beaten, imprisoned, stripped naked and mocked; while in Hungary the shepherds set their dogs on them, beat them and stripped them naked. But Jordan attributed the difficulties encountered by these first missions to the friars' ignorance of the languages of the countries to which they were sent.[86] Jordan also provides independent confirmation that Francis asked Pope Honorius III for Hugolino as Cardinal Protector.[87]

AP next details how Hugolino, once he had the papal mandate, exercised his office. He wrote letters to the many prelates at whose hands the friars had suffered, telling them they should not put difficulties in the friars' way, since they were 'good and religious men approved by the Church, but rather should give them help and advice in preaching and settling in their provinces'. And many other cardinals sent similar letters (45b). AP emphasised, then, that Cardinal Hugolino played a key role – it was he who caused Francis to rewrite his Rule; he wrote letters of introduction and recommendation for the friars; as Cardinal Protector of the Order he was in a position to exercise great influence on its management and direction. The author seems to be casting the cardinal in the role assigned to him by Sabatier. But the conclusion drawn by each was dramatically different. To Sabatier, Hugolino was 'the inspirer of the group who compromised the Franciscan ideal'.[88] It might be assumed that the author of AP would take the same view. For St Francis, in his Testament, had made his attitude to papal privileges crystal clear: 'I firmly order all the brothers on obedience that . . . they are not to dare to ask for any letter from the Roman Curia . . . not for a church or for any convent, not on the pretext of preaching or on account of physical persecution; but if they are not received anywhere they are to flee to another territory to do penance with God's blessing.'[89] But no – AP commends Hugolino's efforts to help the friars in strange lands by giving them privileges: 'In another Chapter meeting, Francis gave the Ministers licence to receive postulants, and the friars were sent back to those provinces, carrying [copies of the Regula bullata] and letters of the Cardinal, as we have said. And so the prelates, seeing the Rule confirmed by the lord Pope and the good testimony concerning the friars provided by the bishop of Ostia and the other cardinals, allowed them to build and live and preach in their provinces. Once the friars were living and preaching there, many, seeing their humble conversation, honest behaviour and most sweet words, came to the friars and assumed the habit of the Holy Order. St Francis, seeing the faith and affection the bishop of Ostia had for the friars, loved him wholeheartedly, and, whenever he wrote letters to him, he addressed them: "To the venerable father in Christ, bishop of the whole world". These prophetic words of the saint were fulfilled soon after when the

---

[85] Brooke 1959, pp. 64–9. But in truth, AP simply anticipates a little in quoting from the *Regula bullata* that Hugolino's office was to be 'gubernator, protector et corrector istius fraternitatis' (c. 12, Esser 1976, p. 371; cf. also the Testament, ibid. p. 443).

[86] Jordan, Prologue and cc. 3–6.   [87] Jordan, c. 14; cf. 1 *Cel.* 99.

[88] Sabatier 1893/4, F, p. 277.   [89] Esser 1976, p. 441; translated Brooke 1975, p. 118.

bishop of Ostia was elected to the Apostolic See and took the name of Gregory IX.'[90] Such a statement, coming from brother Giles' and brother Bernard's circle, seems at first sight astonishing. It is safe to assume that Francis' early followers accepted and shared without question their leader's reverence for priests and prelates, and so themselves would have felt reverence for the bishop of Assisi, and the two cardinals and the popes; but as for papal privileges it seems we may have an ironic contrast here. When Francis was alive, brother Jordan of Giano tells us, he had entertained a rather human opinion of him. But after his canonisation, his friend Thomas of Celano had given him relics of the saint, and presently Jordan came to hold him in greater reverence and honour.[91] Brother Giles' experience was the reverse. He had been initially in awe of Francis, had thought as he did, and had emulated his example: when in Ancona on his way to visit the Holy Land, he worked with his hands, as St Francis taught, carrying water in a jug from a fountain at a distance, and offering it in exchange for bread for the love of God. But in his later years his attitude to St Francis became more detached, even critical.[92] 'When a brother once mentioned to him that St Francis had said that a servant of God ought always to desire to die, and to die a martyr's death, he [brother Giles] replied: "For myself, I do not wish to die a better death than one of contemplation." At one time indeed he had gone to the Saracens, desiring martyrdom for the love of Christ, but after he returned and was found worthy to ascend to the height of contemplation, he said: "I should not have wished then for a martyr's death."'[93] Could it be that men like Giles and Bernard, while they retold to their companions anecdotes from their own experience that vividly re-created privations and abuse unquestioningly and gladly borne, yet also let fall comments critical of some of the consequences of going on a mission ill-prepared? Readiness to accept, and to defend the acceptance of privileges is often reckoned characteristic of the 'conventual' tendency among the friars. It offers us yet another qualification to the traditional notion that parties formed early among the friars. The Four Masters, learned friars who might be expected to appreciate Gregory IX's aims and policies, expressly criticised him for issuing privileges, as the acceptance of any privilege, however useful to the friars, might pave the way for relaxation, and laid them open to criticism. The *Exposition of the Four Masters* was written precisely in this period, in 1241–2.[94]

AP ends with a brief recapitulation of Francis' virtues, and of how God rewarded him with the stigmata and a place of glory in heaven. After his death he performed many miracles, which induced many formerly hard of heart to change their minds, saying: 'We were foolish to esteem his life a madness and his end without honour. Now however he is counted among the children of God, and his lot is among the saints!' (46a–c). When Gregory IX, accompanied by the cardinals, performed the ceremony of canonisation, 'many great men and nobles left everything and were converted to God with their wives and sons and daughters and their whole households. Their wives and daughters were enclosed in nunneries. But the men and their sons assumed the habit of the Friars Minor. And so was accomplished that word which he [Francis] had earlier

[90] AP 45c–f; cf. 1 Cel. 100.   [91] Jordan, c. 59; translated Brooke 1975, p. 212; cf. pp. 49–50.
[92] Leo's *Life of Brother Giles*, cc. 2, 5, 18, SL pp. 322–7, 346–7; cf. SL p. 311.
[93] Leo, *Life of Brother Giles*, c. 18, SL pp. 346–7.   [94] See pp. 79–80.

predicted to the friars: "Before long many wise, prudent and noble men will come to us and abide with us'" (47a–c). A neat and stylish ending, referring back to Francis' exhortation to his little band of six followers when he first sent them out in pairs to preach.[95]

AP's Francis is valued for what he did for others. It is an image that Francis would have appreciated. In parts of the book he is *primus inter pares*: in the Epilogue – addressed to the author's fellow friars – he is not even named. 'I beg you, dearest brothers, that these things which we have written about our most esteemed fathers and brothers, you will diligently meditate upon, rightly understand, and study to implement in deed, that with them we may deserve to be participators in celestial glory.'[96] Every friar is a potential major contributor, a potential saint.

THOMAS OF CELANO'S *SECOND LIFE OF ST FRANCIS*

When Thomas of Celano was commissioned to write his *First Life of St Francis* it was up to him to seek out his material and to approach those individuals he considered most qualified to provide him with the information he needed. When commissioned the second time, he was to write up the material sent in in response to an official appeal to the friars for personal testimony. His role was rather that of editor. It was his responsibility to do justice to the contributions presented to him. That Celano was conscious of the difference is evident from his Prologues to the two works. In 1 *Celano* he writes in the first person singular, in 2 *Celano* in the first person plural. He appears to content himself with being no more than the mouthpiece of the saint's companions, writing in their name and on their behalf. It is they who give his work authority: we who knew him 'from constant intercourse and mutual intimacy' offer new material not to be found in the earlier legends.[97] Here Celano is clearly using Leo, Rufino and Angelo's Introductory Letter, but he recasts it into conformity with his own recognisable style. It must have given him much satisfaction to be able to conclude the Prologue with a characteristic play on words. 'We pray you, kindest father [the Minister General, Crescentius], that you will consecrate with your blessing this offering – modest but not to be disdained – which we have sought out with no little toil, correcting what is false and pruning what is superfluous, so that all that has been well said may be approved by your learned judgement – and may multiply in Christ – growing everywhere with your so fitting name Crescentius [cum nomine vestro vere Crescentio crescant]. Amen.'[98]

Similarly, in the moving dedication to St Francis with which he finishes the book, Celano makes the saint's companions the authors of his *Second Life*, and himself their scribe. 'We beg you with the full affection of our hearts, most kindly father, for your son, who now as once before has devotedly composed your praises. He offers and dedicates this little work to you . . . as do we with him' (2 *Cel.* 223).

---

[95] AP 18a–d; cf. p. 131.

[96] AP 48: reading 'de patribus et fratribus nostris' – de is needed to make sense.

[97] See p. 103; Brooke 1967, p. 187. His authorship of both Lives is noted by Jordan, c. 19; Salimbene, H, p. 176 (includes also 3 *Cel.*); and the *Chron.* 24 *Gen.*, AF III, 262–3 (Thomas 'de Ceperano').

[98] 2 *Cel.* 2 (AF X, 130). 1 *Cel.* 18 contains a similar play on the name Clare: see p. 43.

2 *Celano* is in two parts. The first book (3–25) sets out to supplement the story of Francis' early career as told in 1 *Celano*, based largely on information provided by AP, but also on other material, including some stories from SL.[99] The result cannot be said to be wholly satisfactory.

In order to arrive at the more complete picture now offered by Celano the reader needs to consult the two Lives in tandem, to have both volumes to hand, since Celano does not, in the main, repeat in the *Second Life* what he had already dealt with in the *First*. The need to integrate the still fragmented material into a coherent biography was probably what motivated the compiler of the *Legend of the Three Companions*.[100]

Does 2 *Celano*, Book I, achieve an improved image of St Francis? How does it compare with the image Celano presented originally? His sources were good. Although not entering the public domain until some twenty years after the saint's death, reminiscences came from friars who had known St Francis personally; some had been with him in the early days, some had been close to him in his final years. There was a wealth of additional testimony that had the value of genuine first-hand evidence. Use of it certainly results in a fuller picture. But a variety of pressures led Celano, on occasion, to modify statements. For example, in AP, St Francis tells Innocent III a parable: a king was attracted by the beauty of a very poor woman, and fathered many sons by her. In 2 *Celano* the king loved her, and gladly married her before begetting sons. The tale has been altered to make it moral. In this instance the source is more authentic than the rewrite.[101] 1 *Celano*, AP and 2 *Celano* all give an account of St Francis' dream of arms destined for himself and his knights. In 1 *Celano* accoutrements of war – saddles, shields, lances and so forth – filled the family home, which delighted but also surprised him, as he was not used to see such things in his home, but rather cloth stacked for sale. In AP, Francis is led in his dream to a most splendid palace, full of military equipment, the shields on the walls bearing the sign of the cross. In 2 *Celano* he is shown a splendid palace in which he could see a variety of military equipment, and a most beautiful bride. He is called by name, and allured by the promise of all these treasures. The earliest account, in 1 *Celano*, has the ring of truth. The palace and the crusader shields described in AP clearly derive from embroidery supplied by an active oral tradition. Celano ostensibly 'corrects' his earlier story and contributes the further embellishment of a waiting bride. In so doing he does not 'add value', but diminishes his credibility.[102]

Indeed, 2 *Celano* in general betrays its *Sitz im Leben*. I have shown elsewhere that Celano in his *Second Life* conveys a markedly different impression of brother Elias from that accorded him in his *First*.[103] In 1 *Celano* Elias is, rightly, portrayed as a close and trusted friend of St Francis. He refers to him as 'brother Elias, whom he [St Francis] had chosen to act as a mother to himself and a father to all the other brothers' (1 *Cel.* 98). It was Elias who prevailed upon Francis to accept medical treatment for his eye illness.[104] Later, when at Siena, illnesses of the stomach and liver bore down on him

---

99 2 *Cel.* 11 is partly based on SL 37; 2 *Cel.* 18–19, 21–2 resume SL 8–10, 1–2.
100 See pp. 150–7.   101 AP 32b–35a; 2 *Cel.* 16; and see pp. 133–4.
102 1 *Cel.* 5; AP 5a; 2 *Cel.* 6; and see p. 130.   103 Brooke 1959, pp. 13–20.
104 1 *Cel.* 98. This is corroborated by SL 46.

as well, and he seemed near death; Elias hastened to him from a distance, and at his coming Francis rallied so much that Elias was able to take him with him to one of his favoured retreats, Celle de Cortona (1 *Cel.* 105). In 2 *Celano* his name is suppressed and the few references to him are guarded, hostile and evasive. The reason for this altered tone – which amounts to an implicit recantation of his earlier portrayal – is provided by brother Elias who lost his good name. He succeeded in becoming Minister General in 1232, but provoked criticism both by his personal conduct and by his methods of government. He did not set an example of observance of the Rule, eating specially prepared food and travelling on horseback. He also behaved arrogantly, antagonising the Provincial Ministers, especially by the favour he showed to lay brothers; it was the clerical, learned, official element in the Order that organised effective opposition to him. He was deposed in 1239, and promptly joined the Emperor Frederick II – with whom Gregory IX was at war – incurring excommunication. When Celano was writing his *Second Life* Elias was disgraced and excommunicate and had been deprived of the habit of his religion. It is not surprising that shame, indignation and prudence induced him to alter and omit, but it does detract from the value of his evidence. In so far as it concerns brother Elias, 1 and 2 *Celano* are of wholly disproportionate value: 1 *Celano* of great worth and significance, 2 *Celano* almost worthless.[105]

Celano was a cleric and a learned man; for a short time, in 1223, he was sole custodian in Germany, and administered the province as vicar in the absence of its Provincial Minister.[106] He himself belonged, therefore, to the category of learned clerical friars, office-holders, whose viewpoint gained ascendancy with the overthrow of brother Elias and who reorganised and refashioned the Order in 1239 and the years that followed. His material came overwhelmingly from St Francis' companions and from popular oral tradition. It is to Celano's credit that he endeavoured to satisfy the expectations and assumptions of these two very diverse constituencies. He was aware of the difficulties. 'For who – in such a diversity of words and deeds – is able to weigh everything on the balance of a fine assay, so that all his hearers may be of one mind?' (2 *Cel.* 1).

2 *Celano* has some of the attributes of a biography. It begins with the infant's baptism with the name of John – though it does not explain how he came to be called Francis – and ends with his death and canonisation.[107] Book 1 is narrative in form, focusing on Francis as a young adult, on his conversion, on the early days of the Order, his gaining of papal approval and his securing, later, the appointment of Hugolino as Cardinal Protector. Its chronological framework was provided by its principal source, AP.[108] The material Celano needed to write up into Book 2 was much more inchoate. It consisted of a mass of stories; Leo, Rufino and Angelo characterised their contribution as a bunch of assorted wild flowers, which they did not attempt to arrange in any historical sequence.[109] In the form in which their 'fair flowers' have come down to us in the Perugia MS 1046, very many are linked, more or less loosely, to a connecting thread of

---

[105] For Elias' generalate and subsequent career, see Brooke 1959, pp. 137–77; and see pp. 33–4, 51–67.
[106] Jordan, cc. 30–1.
[107] 2 *Cel.* 3, 217, 220a. 3 *Soc.* 2 is the only early source to explain the name change: see p. 150. 2 *Cel.* 220a is incomplete and probably originally also included the translation.
[108] See table in AP pp. 253–6. [109] Introductory Letter, SL pp. 86–9.

the progressive deterioration of St Francis' health.[110] Celano may or may not have been handed them in approximately this form, but in any case he decided to plan this Book, the major part of his *Second Life*, quite differently. He grouped the stories under themes intended to inspire the friars to remember and honour their founder and to strive to emulate him. The headings begin with Francis' spirit of prophecy, continue with poverty, arranged under subheadings – buildings, furniture, money, clothes, begging and so forth – Francis' zeal in prayer, his understanding of Scripture, various temptations, beginning with what Celano calls 'poisonous sweetness', that is familiarity with women. Also included are virtues – spiritual joy, humility, obedience, charity, holy simplicity – and warnings against vices – foolish joy (vainglory and hypocrisy), idleness, detraction. There are sections on Francis' contemplation of the Creator in his creatures, his special devotions, and on the Ministers and the Rule, and a few others. The work of sorting and marshalling his sources thus must have been laborious and exacting, and was Celano's own personal effort and achievement. This perhaps explains why he prefaced Book 2 with words that, unexpectedly in view of the language of collaboration present in the opening Prologue and the closing Prayer, emphasise his individual contribution: 'I consider . . . I say . . . I think'.

'I consider that the blessed Francis was a kind of very holy mirror and an image of His perfection [cf. Wisdom 7. 26: Wisdom 'is the brightness of eternal light, and the unspotted mirror of God's majesty, and the image of his goodness']. All Francis' words and deeds, I say, divinely offer a certain fragrance of divinity; and if a reader and a humble disciple would study them and learn from them, they speedily imbue him with saving instruction and prepare him for the highest wisdom. After setting down some account of him, though in a modest style and as it were in passing, I think it worth while to attach a few stories selected from very many of those in which the saint is commended to us and our sleeping disposition awakened' (2 *Cel*. 26).

The opening Prologue and the closing Prayer prepare us not to be surprised to discover that material selected from Leo, Rufino and Angelo's contribution formed the core of Celano's sources. Statistics are misleading, since a section in Celano can represent more than one in SL, and vice versa; and many sections in Celano comprise comment and the like, not stories. But we can reasonably boil down the 200 sections in the second part of 2 *Celano* – omitting comments and prayers – to 135 stories, of which seventy-five are from SL, sixty from other sources. The question immediately arises whether SL is complete, or whether some of the sixty may not come from lost sections of SL. There is a group of seven stories which seem clearly to have come from the original dossier of Leo and his friends, but only occur in one late MS of SL; all seven have parallels in 2 *Celano*.[111] It is possible that there were others in the same dossier not now recorded in the MSS of SL. But it is also reasonably certain that Celano had other material. He derived some stories from one of St Francis' companions, one of the 'holy friars' who helped but is not specifically named in the Introductory Letter – brother Pacifico. Celano must have known him personally and taken oral testimony from him,

---

[110] SL pp. 79–85, List of Contents, showing the links between the various stories and groups of stories.
[111] They are printed as an Appendix in SL pp. 294–303; for their relation to SL, see ibid. pp. 292–3. The parallels in 2 *Cel*. are 2 *Cel*. 50, 49, 214–15 and 217, 51, 39, 110–11.

for his detailed and vivid account of Pacifico's standing in the world and the suddenness of his conversion bear all the hallmarks of first-hand evidence (2 *Cel*.106). He was a highly acclaimed singer in the March of Ancona, with a large personal following – the thirteenth-century equivalent of a pop star. He composed worldly songs and was the leading performer of lewd songs. He was called the King of Verses because on one occasion he excelled himself at festivities in the presence of the emperor, who bestowed a crown on him with the utmost ceremony (*pomposissime*).[112] On a day when he and his boon-companions were together visiting a relative of his in San Salvatore de Colpersito, a convent of Poor Clares near San Severino, it chanced that St Francis was visiting the sisters.[113] In the eyes of the singer Francis appeared to have two flashing crossed swords, one running from head to feet, the other stretching from hand to hand across his chest, creating the sign of the cross; astonished, he began to think of leading a better life at some time in the future. But when St Francis had preached to them all, he targeted him: he turned the sword of God's word (Hebrews 4. 12) upon him, first speaking softly of earthly vanity and of contempt for the world, and then lacerating his heart, threatening divine judgement. The singer promptly responded: 'What need is there to sow more words?' – surely an echo of the parable of the sower, Mark 4. 14 and Luke 8. 11: 'The seed is the word of God' – 'Let us come to deeds. Take me away from men and restore me to the Great Emperor.' The impulsiveness and chivalric overtones of this response conjure up a mental picture of the encounter between these two kindred spirits, with their shared love of music and song. One can imagine how Francis might have fired with enthusiasm this 'noble and courtly doctor of song' (SL 23) with talk of his friars as 'knights of the round table' (SL 71). Francis clothed him the next day and gave him the name Pacifico, as he had returned to the peace of the Lord.[114] The two valued each other's company, and Pacifico experienced further visions. He saw on Francis' forehead the great mark Tau (Ezek. 9. 4), with multi-coloured circles which displayed a peacock's beauty.[115]

Pacifico developed profound spiritual insights as a result of his long association with St Francis, including the gift of interpreting visions. One night Francis dreamed of a woman who had a gold head, silver chest and arms, a crystal stomach and iron lower limbs. She was tall and well proportioned, but was covered in a filthy mantle. In the morning he described her to Pacifico, but without comment (2 *Cel*. 82). Celano notes that many, 'having the spirit of God', interpret this woman as Francis' bride, and therefore as poverty, while others apply it to the Order as a prophecy, following the succession of periods according to Daniel.[116] He gives pride of place, however, to Pacifico's own interpretation. 'This woman of comely form is the beautiful soul of

[112] This incident must have occurred during one of Otto IV's incursions south into Italy, in 1209, 1210 or 1211. Placid Herman OFM (Habig 1979, p. 597 n. 154) is incorrect in suggesting that the emperor was Frederick II, who was not crowned until 1220.

[113] AF x, 193 n. 4; cf. 1 *Cel*. 78, AF x, 58 and n. 11.

[114] It was not normal custom then to change name on entering religion. Francis did more than once bestow a new name on a friend. He called Good John, a doctor from Arezzo, Finiatu (SL 65; see pp. 117–18).

[115] 2 *Cel*. 106. For the importance of the Tau form of the cross to Francis, see pp. 73, 335 and note 169; also Plate 12. The peacock is a symbol of Paradise.

[116] 2 *Cel*. 82; cf. Daniel 2. 31–45, which relates Nebuchadnezzar's dream of an image composed of gold, silver, brass and iron, signifying the progressive decline and breakdown of the kingdom.

St Francis . . . the filthy mantle . . . the despised little body in which the precious soul is encased.' This story is evidence of the high respect Celano had for Pacifico, but it also illustrates St Francis' trust in him. Pacifico was among the select few privileged to see the stigmata while St Francis was alive, and on one occasion he took advantage of his closeness to the saint – whom he addressed as 'dearest mother' (mater carissima . . . carissima mater) – asking him to extend one hand and then the other for him to kiss, a ruse to enable a visiting friar to glimpse the wounds in the hands (2 Cel. 137).

It would seem that Celano unobtrusively contributed a few anecdotes himself. There is one story, and one only, where he uses the personal pronoun 'I', as he does in the brief preface to Book 2. When spiritual joy welled up in him, Francis would not infrequently pick up a stick from the ground, 'as I saw with my own eyes', and putting it over his left arm, he would hold a little bow bent with a string in his right hand, drawing it over the stick as if it were a viol, and with this makeshift accompaniment he would sing to the Lord in French. These dances often ended in tears, joy dissolving into pity over Christ's passion (2 Cel. 127). Celano here conjures up a remarkable evocation of a performance that typifies the tension ever present in Francis, the feelings of joy in salvation and praise of God the Creator checked by grief and remorse at Christ's suffering.

In a story illustrating Francis' abhorrence of even the hint of ownership of property, the saint orders the friars to leave a house recently built for them in Bologna – a university centre – 'with haste because he heard it publicly referred to as "the friars' house"' (2 Cel. 58). As it ends 'he who bears witness and writes this [echoing John 21. 24] was at that time ejected from the house though he was ill', it is likely that Celano, a learned friar, was at Bologna, and is recounting a personal experience, though the identification is doubted by some.[117]

In his careful and helpful comparison of 2 Celano with the Scripta Leonis, Moorman noted many cases in which Celano followed his source closely, and many more in which he abbreviated more or less stringently.[118] He also noted some which he had altered, others where he had added detail – for example a place or personal name. In such cases it is likely that Celano had access to more than one version, written or oral. Oral tradition reveals itself most clearly in some of the sayings attributed to the saint. In SL 20 a postulant is told to give all his goods to the poor, and when he gives them to his family, he is sent packing. Francis' blunt challenge at the outset of the story is pithier in Celano. 'If you wish to be joined to God's poor, first give all you have to the world's poor' (2 Cel. 81). Celano then adds that Francis laughed as he dismissed this 'brother fly' – who promptly demanded his property back from his relations – and comments that 'many today' are guilty in this matter, enriching members of their families and defrauding the poor in the distribution of their goods. In his own version of God's words of comfort, loosely based on SL 86, Celano opens: 'Why little man (homuncio) are you so upset?' (2 Cel. 158). The word 'homuncio', an affectionate diminutive Francis may well have used, may have been preserved in popular memory.

Celano adds to the stories on Francis and prayer. Francis considered he had gravely offended if his mind was distracted by idle thoughts when at prayer. He confessed and

[117] E.g. by Bihl, AF x, 166 n. 9; Manselli 1980, pp. 229–31.
[118] For what follows, see Moorman 1940, pp. 113–20.

atoned so promptly and fully that he was rarely troubled by 'flies' of this kind. One Lent he had fashioned a little vase in his spare moments, and while he was devoutly saying Terce one day it happened to catch his eye. As soon as the office was over he threw it into the fire, explaining to the friars that he was sacrificing it to the Lord whose sacrifice it had impeded. 'It should shame us to be seized by wandering, empty thoughts, when at the time of prayer we are addressing the Great King' – a wholly characteristic enacted sermon in a nutshell, with its evocation of courtly romance and royal courts, while based at the same time on a quotation from the Psalms.[119]

Another story of which Celano is the first witness concerns Francis' characteristic way of handling bishops, designed to demonstrate how, using the right tactics, success could be achieved without the need of privileges, through humility and persistence.[120] 2 Cel. 152 has a striking group of sayings on obedience, including Francis' likening of the obedient man to a corpse, totally without feeling or will of his own. 2 Cel. 191–3 reflect Francis' deep conviction that all his friars were of equal worth. They start with a parable of a truly general chapter of all the religious in the world, to which all can come (as indeed the friars had come in the early days); and they go on to describe how Francis insisted on a small tonsure so as not to be set apart from his simple brothers. 'With God there is no respect of persons', he said, echoing St Paul (Romans 2. 11).

On some points, such as poverty and Francis' rejection of the use and handling of money, Celano supplements SL in a very effective way. He resorts to poetry when describing Francis' attachment to poverty. 'He regarded poverty as especially close to the Son of God, and he strove to wed her, whom the world has now rejected, in perpetual love. And so "I became a lover of her beauty and desired to make her my wife" [Wisdom 8. 2] – in the closest bond so that the two should be one in spirit. He not only "left his father and mother" [Mark 10. 7], but set everything aside. Therefore he clasped her in chaste embraces . . . No one has coveted gold as he coveted poverty, nor has anyone been more careful to guard his treasure than this man guarded the pearl of the Gospel . . . From the beginning of his religious life, indeed, till his death, he was rich in the possession of tunic, cord and breeches – and had nothing else.'[121] Celano adds that: 'Psalms which sang of poverty Francis used to chant with especially fervent affection and joyful delight, for example such verses as: "The patience of the poor shall not perish for ever" [Ps. 9. 18], and "Let the poor see and be glad"' (Ps. 68(69). 33(32)).[122] He also records that Francis once rebuked a friar who disparaged a poor, frail little man with the words: 'When you see a poor man, brother, you are shown the Lord and his poor Mother in a mirror' (2 Cel. 85).

A cluster of cautionary tales featuring money gives vivid expression to Francis' distinctive and emphatic teaching. To a friar, money must be abhorrent, filthy, not even touched. He imposed an exemplary penance on a friar who when tidying the altar in the church of St Mary of the Portiuncula merely threw an offering left by the crucifix

---

[119] 2 Cel. 97; cf. Psalm 94 (95). 3. For a discussion of Francis' wide-ranging use of 'flies' as a metaphor, see p. 117.

[120] 2 Cel. 147; see p. 24.   [121] 2 Cel. 55. Cf. the Testament, Esser 1976, pp. 439–40 and pp. 122–3.

[122] 2 Cel. 70. St Francis quoted fifteen verses of Psalm 68 (69) in his *Office of the Passion*, including v. 33 (32). He also used three verses from Psalm 9: Esser 1976, pp. 338–51, 465, esp. pp. 339–40, 342–3, 347–9.

onto a window sill. He had to pick up the money with his teeth and deposit it outside by mouth on to ass's dung (2 *Cel.* 65). So when a couple of friars found a coin lying in their path they argued as to what should be done with the dung. One wanted to give it to the lepers, who were always in need – they were near a leper hospital. The other rejected such false piety and quoted words of the Rule which made it quite clear that found coin ought to be trodden underfoot like dust. The rash brother laughed, stooped to pick up the coin, and promptly lost the power of speech (2 *Cel.* 66). In the final story, St Francis comes upon a large purse in the road. His companion urges him to take it and give to the poor – they would really benefit as it was bulging with money. Francis refuses, explaining that this is a temptation of the devil, and that anyway this money does not belong to them, and to take it, even with a good motive, would be theft. His companion is unconvinced, so Francis contrives a salutary lesson for him. He collects a witness, prays, then orders the friar to pick up the purse – and a sizeable snake emerges from it. Francis says, whether severely or smugly we cannot be sure: 'to the servants of God, brother, money is nothing other than the devil and the poisonous snake' (2 *Cel.* 68). It is worth noting here that the passage from the Rule from which Celano quotes, and which provides the firm foundation on which these stories rest, is taken not from the *Regula bullata* but from a version of the Rule that was in force in the earlier years of the Order, before 1223; a passage therefore that would have been familiar to and appreciated by friars who had joined in the early days and had nostalgic memories. It reads: 'Not one of the brothers, wherever he may be or wherever he goes, may in any way pick up or receive or cause to be received, money or coins, neither for clothes nor books nor as payment for any work: in short, not on any account, except for the manifest need of sick brothers; because we ought not to hold and assume greater utility in money or coins than in stones. The devil wishes to blind those who seek it or value it more than stones. Let us take care, therefore, we who have given up everything, lest for such a paltry thing we lose the kingdom of heaven. If we happen to find coins anywhere let us take no more notice of them than of dust which we trample with our feet, since it is "vanity of vanities, and all is vanity" [Eccles. 1. 2]. If by chance – which heaven forbid – it should happen that any friar collects or has money or coin, save only for the necessity of the sick, let all the brothers hold him for a false friar and an apostate and a thief and a robber and a purse-holder, unless he truly repents.'[123]

Another story, which reads strangely to us today, tells how Francis combatted a temptation to lust one winter night by going out into the snow and making seven snowmen. He identified these as his wife, sons and daughters and servants, and told himself to make haste and clothe them all since they were dying of cold, concluding: but 'if care for their multiple needs burdens you, let your care be to serve only one Lord'.[124]

[123] *Regula non bullata*, c. 8, Esser 1976, pp. 384–5. 'Purse-holder' is a reference to Judas: cf. John 12. 6. For a discussion of St Francis' attitude to poverty and money and its impact on society, see Little 1978, esp. pp. 146–69, 197–217.

[124] 2 *Cel.* 116–17. For the origins of this story, see Burkitt 1926, pp. 57–9. It was told of one of the Desert Fathers who, when similarly tempted, fashioned clay figures of a wife and daughter (PL 73, col. 747).

If we ask what Celano achieved in his *Second Life*, one answer must be, not a great deal. To contemporaries it provided at best a supplement to the *First Life*. It provided a source, and in some respects a model, for Bonaventure, who similarly presents in the *Legenda Maior* a narrative of Francis' early life followed by a thematic study of Francis' qualities and principles, illustrated by numerous episodes. But in the 1240s and 1250s 2 *Celano* had relatively little impact. Only two manuscripts survive, neither complete, and a sheaf of extracts.[125] Even though it was suppressed in the early 1260s, after the completion and promulgation of Bonaventure's *Life*, this is a poor harvest for what set out to be a major contribution to Franciscan hagiography. It compares unfavourably, for example, with the fortune of SL – of which there are substantial remnants in five manuscripts – and which was reproduced, not greatly altered, in the *Speculum Perfectionis* of 1318, of which there are over twenty copies surviving.[126] It is clear that – among all the other reasons for the composition of Bonaventure's *Legenda Maior* – there was a demand for a single, straightforward, unified version of 1, 2 and 3 *Celano*, and this Bonaventure was to provide.[127]

The interest of 2 *Celano* today lies partly in its important contribution in the field of source criticism. Securely dated in the mid-1240s,[128] it provides vital evidence which can help us to determine the complex relationship between a whole group of early sources, as it casts light on the history of AP, SL and 3 Soc. But now that we have these sources available, it must be confessed that in the eyes of modern readers 2 *Celano* suffers from the comparison; simpler, less rhetorical versions of stories are more to our taste.[129]

2 *Celano* also articulates an image of St Francis that enjoyed a wide currency at the time it was written. A major part of the material at Celano's disposal had been sent in by the saint's companions. He edited it, and this editing was conditioned by his education, but there seems little doubt that he tried honestly to represent what they had laid before him. He omitted some of the passages which showed Francis at his most eccentric, such as SL 49–50, in which Francis refused to interfere with brother Fire, and he much abbreviated their account of the Portiuncula, though he faithfully reproduced the essence of those very eloquent chapters; he omitted the story of the mice running over the saint as he lay ill, and a few other details which he presumably thought superfluous.[130] But, as has been shown, he attempted to discharge his role as the companions' mouthpiece with reasonable, if not perfect, fidelity. In the process, by providing Bonaventure with much of his best material, he made a large contribution to the official image of St Francis as it was to flourish in the late thirteenth century and later.

---

[125] AF X, xxx–xxxvi; and see p. 107.

[126] SL pp. 26–40 – I have not included in the count the Florence MS which only contains a fragment of SL (ibid. p. 34); Sp S II, pp. 1–73.

[127] See pp. 245–6.

[128] Bihl in AF X, xxvi, lays out the evidence that it was commissioned in 1244, the main material was supplied in 1246 and it was accepted by Crescentius about two months before 13 July 1247, when he left office.

[129] Cf. Brooke 1967, p. 187.

[130] See list of omissions in Moorman 1940, pp. 118–19. Most of these served brevity rather than edification.

But, a point which has not been sufficiently appreciated, Celano was not simply the mouthpiece of the saint's companions and the friars they represented; he was voicing his own opinions too. And his opinions were representative of another wide constituency, that of the learned friars who had taken over the direction of the Order in 1239. These educated professionals who supplanted the amateurs of the early days were fervent men. They genuinely thought their training and priestly functions were assets which could be grafted on to Francis' inspiration without undermining it. They revered those of his companions who were still living. 2 *Celano* is to be read in the same context as the *Exposition of the Four Masters*, written in the same climate, in 1241–2. The Four Masters had likewise quoted the Testament, stressed the paramount importance of the Rule and upheld a rigorist and uncompromising prohibition of money, which they defined not just as coin but as anything acquired not for use but as a means of exchange.[131] There was much more common ground in the mid-thirteenth century than is sometimes assumed.[132]

THE *LEGEND OF THE THREE COMPANIONS*

The sources of the Legend of the Three Companions *and its date*

It is striking that *3 Soc.* has been very variously appraised by leading Franciscan scholars. The Bollandist Van Ortroy argued that it was a pastiche from known sources and therefore of little value. John Moorman and others have seen it as the most refreshing and vivid of all the sources for Francis' early life.[133] Both views are right in a sense. How can we resolve this paradox?

The sources used by the writer of *3 Soc.* have been subjected to close analysis by Van Ortroy in 1900, and more recently by Desbonnets.[134] They comprise: the Introductory Letter; then *1 Celano* and the *Anonymous of Perugia* (AP), his two main sources; plus Julian of Speyer, Celano's *Legenda Chori* and *2 Celano*, the *Scripta Leonis* (SL) and Bonaventure's *Legenda Maior*, all of which he uses once or occasionally. At one point he shows awareness of the Testament of St Clare.[135] He also himself possessed, or had access to, a fund of local knowledge.

There is no doubt at all that the Introductory Letter forms an integral part of the *Legend of the Three Companions*. It occurs consistently in the MSS of *3 Soc.* and it does not preface, in the MSS, any other collection of stories. The only question is: was the writer of *3 Soc.* one of the authors of the letter, or did he find it already in existence, and use it as a ready-made introduction to his own work? Scholars have disagreed fundamentally in their answers to this. Desbonnets was the leading champion of those who hold that the letter is coherent with *3 Soc.* Van Ortroy, Burkitt, Moorman and I myself are among those who have argued that the letter does not fit *3 Soc.*; that it has been detached from

---

[131] See pp. 79–80; cf. 2 *Cel.* 161, 208, 65–8.   [132] As was already argued in Brooke 1959, esp. pp. 282–5.
[133] Van Ortroy 1900; Moorman 1940, pp. 68–76.   [134] Van Ortroy 1900; Desbonnets 1974, pp. 77–85.
[135] Rejected by Desbonnets 1974, p. 81: see p. 156 and note 176.

its proper context and that it originally belonged to a different body of material.[136] Leo, Rufino and Angelo were among Francis' close companions in his later years; they were with him when he wrote the Rule, with him in his increasingly severe illnesses.[137] We would expect their reminiscences to relate mainly to the closing years of his life; whereas *3 Soc.* concentrates precisely on his early life and those of his early followers. Also in their Introductory Letter they state that they 'have carefully omitted many events elegantly and accurately told in the *Legende*'. But the opening chapters of *3 Soc.* contain a number of passages closely parallel to *1 Celano*: indeed most of chapter VI is taken from *1 Celano*, and nearly half of chapter VIII comes from Julian of Speyer.[138] Near the end of chapter VIII the writer switches to a quite different source, which he has used in conjunction with *1 Celano* in chapters I and II, but which from now on becomes the basis of his narrative, the *Anonymous of Perugia* (AP).[139]

The *Legend of the Three Companions* was written after 1246. It starts with the Introductory Letter which is dated 11 August 1246. It makes occasional use of *2 Celano*, completed in the course of 1247,[140] and seems to quote a few words from the Testament of St Clare, probably written not long before her death in 1253. In the penultimate chapter, chapter XVII, it incorporates a section from St Bonaventure's *Legenda Maior*, chapter XIII. Desbonnets questions whether 'this lone parallel' is enough to overthrow his conclusion – that *3 Soc.* was written (up to and including chapter XVI) in 1246; and suggests that it was completed later by a different writer, that chapters XVII–XVIII were 'a subsequent appendix'.[141] But he adduces no solid evidence in support of this hypothesis, and it simply will not do to dismiss a clear case of literary borrowing just because it is inconvenient. After an unbroken run of no less than eight chapters (IX–XVI, *3 Soc.* 30–67), closely based on AP, *3 Soc.* continues to follow this source, and, like AP, jumps from a chapter (XVI, AP 44–5), on the election of Ministers, the establishment of provinces and the appointment of Hugolino as Cardinal Protector, straight on to St Francis' death (chapter XVII, AP 46). In this chapter, however, he supplements what AP has to offer with material from other sources, from *1* and *2 Celano* and from Bonaventure. This is consistent with his method of working, and establishes that *3 Soc.* was written as a coherent whole.[142] The passage derived from Bonaventure seems to guarantee that the book was not written, or anyway not finished, before 1263. But if so, it is surprising that it was ever written at all: for in 1266 the Order passed a constitution insisting that all the legends save Bonaventure's were to be collected and destroyed.[143]

It is possible that it was precisely in this period, between 1263 and 1266, that *3 Soc.* was written. For the author knew not only the texts he utilised – still available in these years – but also the active oral tradition in Assisi itself. Many New Testament critics in

---

[136] Desbonnets 1974; Van Ortroy 1900; Beguin 1979; Brooke 1982, pp. 656–65; and see pp. 104–8.

[137] SL p. 10.   [138] See tables in Desbonnets 1974, pp. 82–5, esp. pp. 82–3.   [139] See pp. 127–38.

[140] See p. 146 and note 128. For some reason, with the exception of one isolated incident (*3 Soc.* 14, SL 37), he did not make use of the 'little collection' contributed by brothers Leo, Rufino and Angelo.

[141] Desbonnets in Habig 1979, pp. 886–9, 878, and Desbonnets 1974, pp. 80–1, 86.

[142] The parallels are listed in Desbonnets 1974, pp. 83–5. Van Ortroy 1900, p. 124, showed that the MSS supported the integrity of *3 Soc.* as a book.

[143] Moorman 1940, p. 148 n. 7 and refs., esp. to Little 1898, p. 705; and see p. 244.

the past fell into the trap of thinking, when they found parallel texts in the Synoptic Gospels in very different forms, that one or other evangelist had deliberately rewritten the text. Thus half the story of the Syrophoenician woman in Matthew follows Mark very closely; the other half is very different.[144] It is reasonable to suppose that Matthew had two versions – the second either written or oral – and tried to fit them together. This is but one of numerous indications that there was great and widespread interest in the details of Jesus' life and teaching in the early Church – contrary to the view encouraged by a school of critics who believe that there was relatively little interest in such details in the early decades after the crucifixion.[145] This interest explains why there are so many variant versions of his sayings and of some stories told about him.

By the same token, it is apparent that there was much interest in the details of Francis' life and teaching, especially in Assisi; and that as late as the 1260s there were still some alive who had known him personally; many more who had heard tell from eyewitnesses of this or that episode in his life. This is the milieu in which the *Legenda Maior* of St Bonaventure was written – and, as seems likely, *3 Soc.* too. Both are at once exceedingly well informed, and essentially derivative.

The image of St Francis presented by the Legend of the Three Companions

The account of Francis' youth and upbringing and the initial stages of his conversion, in *3 Soc.*, though mainly based on *1 Celano*, is fuller and markedly different in tone. The opening chapter of *1 Celano* is an uncompromising denunciation of the way children are brought up in a supposedly Christian household and community. Francis' parents are depicted as worldly, and their son, by imitating them, as vain and arrogant. In his youth and early twenties Francis is criticised for wasting his time, for surpassing his contemporaries in all manner of extravagances and frivolities. They, his companions, are collectively characterised as wicked, and Assisi is likened to Babylon.[146] In starting in this way Thomas of Celano is deliberately tailoring his material on Francis into conformity with a standard pattern of hagiographical writing, according to which a misspent youth is highlighted in order to provide a fitting contrast to the subsequent conversion and exemplary later conduct. Such a contrast is intended to edify the reader and bears little necessary relation to fact. When, as had been usual, the Lives of saints came to be written long after their deaths, the living were not personally implicated in the details of their spiritual progress, and so these might be luridly recounted with impunity. When the saint was a contemporary, however, the traditional hagiographical method had its drawbacks.[147] Francis died in his forties. Some at any rate of those who had enjoyed his company in their teens were now middle-aged respectable citizens; members of his family were alive and around. It would be surprising if Celano's opening chapter did not cause offence. He began his *Second Life* more circumspectly, in particular going out of his way to rehabilitate Francis' mother, whom he now compared to Elizabeth, the

---

[144] Matthew 15. 21–8; Mark 7. 24–30.   [145] Especially Bultmann and his disciples.   [146] *1 Cel.* 1–2.
[147] For a discussion of attitudes to living saints, especially in the thirteenth and later centuries, see Kleinberg 1992.

mother of John the Baptist, an opening which enabled him to draw alternative moral conclusions.[148]

The first part of 2 *Celano* – Book I – was conceived as a supplement to 1 *Celano*, to be consulted in conjunction with it.[149] The picture of Francis' early life and conversion remained fragmented. The compiler of the *Legend of the Three Companions* aimed to provide a proper biography. In parts, his narrative closely follows his chosen source for stretches at a time, in others he weaves together the various strands of information available to him from several sources into a cohesive pattern. He begins with carefully selected material from 1 and 2 *Celano* and AP.[150] Francis was born in Assisi while his father was away and his mother called him John. His father after his return from France named him Francis. When he grew up he exercised his father's trade as a merchant, but he was unlike him in temperament, being more lively and liberal, fond of games and singing, passing days and nights in the streets of the city with like-minded friends, spending so lavishly on food and entertainment that he might have been taken for the son of a great prince. His parents, because they were rich and loved him dearly, indulged him in all this, not wishing to upset him. His mother, when her neighbours commented on his extravagance, replied: 'What do you think of my son? He yet will be a son of God through grace' (3 *Soc.* 2). He was similarly extravagant in dress, wearing clothes of richer fabrics than were warranted by his position, and was so vain that he would sometimes indulge in whimsy, choosing to have very expensive and the very cheapest materials juxtaposed in one garment. But he was by nature courteous in manners and speech, and was prompted by reflection to extend to the poor the same generosity and courtesy that he automatically accorded to those about him. So although he was a merchant he became a disburser of worldly goods. One day when he was in the shop busy selling cloth, a poor man came to him begging alms for the love of God. Because he was at that moment preoccupied with business affairs and profit making, he refused. But pricked by conscience he presently accused himself of being guilty of great boorishness – 'If that poor man had asked something of you in the name of a great count or baron, certainly you would have given him what he asked for. How much more ought you to have done it for the King of kings and Lord of all!' – and resolved in his heart never again to refuse such an appeal.

The next stage in the widening of Francis' horizons – the subject matter of chapter II – concerns knightly enterprise. Perugia and Assisi being in a state of war, Francis was captured along with many of his fellow citizens. Because of his nobility of bearing he was held with the knights. The other prisoners became dejected, but Francis, naturally happy and light-hearted, did not mope but continued cheerful. One of them muttered he must be mad to rejoice in prison, but Francis replied out loud: 'What do you think will become of me? In time I shall be reverenced (*adorabor*), throughout the world!' At the end of a year peace was restored and Francis and his fellow captives returned to Assisi. A few years later, when a noble citizen of Assisi was raising troops for an

[148] 2 Cel. 3–4. [149] 2 Cel. 2; cf. Brooke 1967, p. 187; and p. 139.
[150] The following résumé is based on Desbonnets' text, not on the translation in Habig 1979, which contains some interpolations, apparently from Vatican Lat. MS 7339 (cf. Habig 1979, p. 856, and below, note 154). References are to sections (1–73); but also, in the text, to the larger chapters (I–XVIII).

expedition into Apulia in search of wealth and honour, Francis decided to join him, aspiring thereby to achieve knighthood. He threw himself into his preparations. Then one night he dreamed he was taken to a splendid and delightful palace, full of weapons of war. He asked whose all this was and was told that everything, including the palace, was for him and his knights. He was thrilled, interpreting the dream at face value, as presaging he would become a magnificent prince and enjoy great prosperity, and was keener than ever to set out on the road to knighthood. Thus far the narrative has proceeded smoothly, but at this point the biographer realised that he had left out Francis' charity to a poor knight, to whom he had given all the expensive trappings and clothes he had newly purchased. Rather than rewrite, he fitted it in here, noting that it had occurred the day before, and adding that in his opinion Francis' chivalrous act may well have occasioned the dream. When he reached Spoleto Francis felt unwell and retired to bed. As he lay half asleep he heard a voice questioning him about his loyalties. 'Why are you abandoning the lord for the slave, the prince for the client?. . . . Go back home, and you will be told what you must do.' After a sleepless night Francis returned to Assisi chastened in mind to await a fuller understanding of God's will for him. He abandoned all thought of military prowess.

The next stage in Francis' 'further education' – according to 3 Soc.'s analysis, chapter III – hinged on his increasing recourse to prayer and his increasing sensitivity to the problem posed by poverty. In Assisi his erstwhile companions welcomed him back and made him lord of their entertainment; and he laid on a sumptuous repast, such as he had done many times before. After their meal they spilled out into the city, singing. Francis brought up the rear, carrying in his hand the rod of office. But he did not sing; he was thoughtful. Suddenly his heart was overwhelmed with such sweetness that he could neither speak nor move. He later said that he was so deprived of bodily sensation that if he had been at that time cut up piecemeal he could not have moved from the spot.[151] When the revellers looked back and saw him so far behind they returned and noticed the change in him. '"What are you thinking about that you do not come after us? Perhaps you are thinking of taking a wife?" He replied viva voce: "You have spoken truly, for I thought of taking a bride more noble, richer and more beautiful than you have ever seen." They laughed at him, but what he said was inspired by God, for this bride was the true religious life he embraced, nobler, richer and lovelier than the rest through poverty.' From that hour he began to despise himself, and to disprize what he had previously valued, but not yet completely, for he was not wholly disengaged from the vanity of the world. Often, almost every day, he withdrew privately to pray in secret, drawn by that sweetness which more frequently visited him. At the same time his almsgiving increased. If he was petitioned when he was out, he gave money; if he had no money on him he gave his scarf or belt,[152] rather than send a poor man empty away. Lacking even such he would seek a secluded spot to take off his shirt to give. He

[151] The information in this section (3 Soc. 7) is based on 2 Cel. 7 (not noted by Desbonnets in his tables, p. 82, as he does not accept that there are borrowings unless the wording is very close: Desbonnets 1974, pp. 80–5).
[152] 3 Soc. 8: 'infula' literally means a bandage or fillet on the brow or the head – but in this context presumably a head-scarf of some kind; 'corrigia' could mean a belt or a purse.

also purchased church vessels and sent them secretly to poor priests. If he was at home when his father was away, and he and his mother were dining alone, he would load the table with bread as if for the whole family. When she asked him why he provided so many loaves he replied he did so in order to distribute alms to the poor, since he proposed to give to all who begged alms for the love of God. His mother, because she loved him above all her other children, bore with him in such things, taking note of what he did and greatly wondering at his deeds in her heart.[153]

Already changed by divine grace, Francis still wore clothes that identified him as a member of secular society (and a wealthy one at that), and he felt an urge to go somewhere where he was not known, where he might exchange clothes with a beggar and experience for himself the other's need and beg alms for the love of God. About that time he went to Rome on pilgrimage. When he entered the basilica of St Peter's he noticed that the offerings of some were meagre and said within himself: '"As the greatest honour is due to the prince of the apostles, why do these people leave such small alms in the church where his body rests?" With great fervour he plunged his hand into his purse, filled it with coins and threw them through the grille of the altar, making such a clatter that all the bystanders were much amazed at the munificence of his offering!' Outside, he took advantage of the many beggars gathered there and surreptitiously swopped garments with one. Then he stood on the steps of the basilica with the other poor, begging for alms in French, because he loved to speak that language, even though he did not know how to speak it correctly. Afterwards he took off the beggar's rags and resumed his own clothing. On his return to Assisi he started to pray God to direct his life. Other than from God he sought advice from no one, except sometimes from the bishop of Assisi (3 Soc. 10).

Even in these first three short chapters several features are already noteworthy: among them, the drawing of Gospel parallels, the sympathetic references to both parents, the filling out of the local Assisi background, and the detailed unfolding of the processes of spiritual conversion.

The story is embellished and interpreted with clear Gospel overtones. Right at the beginning his mother is implicitly likened to Elizabeth, the mother of John the Baptist.[154] Two chapters on she is compared, again implicitly, to the Virgin Mary. The description of her as 'taking note of what he did and greatly wondering . . . in her heart', contains clear overtones of the way the Virgin Mary reacted to the visit of the shepherds.[155] Somewhat later, after describing how Francis found his vocation, and the Lord revealed to him the greeting: 'The Lord give you peace', the writer adds a remarkable rider. Before Francis' conversion he had had a forerunner, a man who frequently went through Assisi calling out the greeting: 'Peace and good! Peace and good!' He continues: 'It is firmly believed that just as John, the forerunner of Christ, ceased

---

[153] 3 Soc. 9: cf. Luke 2. 19.

[154] 3 Soc. 2: cf. Luke 1. 60. 2 Celano 3 had made the point explicitly. The incident of the pilgrim who came to the house, and took the baby in his arms, as Simeon had taken the baby Jesus – which is included in the translation of 3 Soc. printed in Habig 1979, pp. 890–1 – is an interpolation found only in one MS (see above, note 150). I follow throughout, not Habig's version which seems to include all the interpolations, but Desbonnets' more critical edition.

[155] 3 Soc. 9; Luke 2. 18–19.

from preaching when Christ began, so this man as another John preceded the blessed Francis in announcing peace, but after his coming did not appear as before.'[156] In this way the *Legend of the Three Companions* adds an early brick to the edifice raised to glorify Francis as another Christ, whose foundation stone had been laid by Celano in his *First Life*.[157]

Celano in his *Second Life* had sought to make amends to Francis' mother. The writer of *3 Soc.* managed to convey a sympathetic impression of both his parents. He did this quite unobtrusively, through the occasional brief comment. 'His parents, because they were rich and loved him dearly, indulged him' (*3 Soc.* 2); Francis' habit of leaving the table abruptly, without finishing his food, if his friends happened to call for him at mealtime, left 'his parents troubled by his disorderly departure' (*3 Soc.* 9). Even after Francis renounced his father, who, overwhelmed with grief and fury, had gathered up the coins and all the clothes and taken them home, to the indignation of the spectators, who thought he might at least have left his son with something to cover him (*3 Soc.* 20), the writer can still find a good word for him. Francis had gone to live with the poor priest at San Damiano, and was malnourished, ill-clad in a hermit's habit, and exhausted with the hard physical labour of repairing that church. When his father saw him thus gaunt and haggard he was filled with grief and shame and, 'because he had greatly loved him', he cursed him whenever he encountered him (*3 Soc.* 23).

The position of at least one member of Francis' immediate family in Assisi in the middle years of the century, in particular in relation to the Basilica and the Friars Minor of the Sacro Convento, may well have some bearing on the emergence of this kindlier treatment of Francis' parents. The archives of the Sacro Convento contain a wealth of thirteenth-century documents. The earliest mention of Picardo as proctor of the church of St Francis occurs in a legal document dated 27 March 1256, recording his instruction, through a notary, to the judge of the commune to pursue the executor of a deceased citizen over the non-payment of a legacy to the friars.[158] His name recurs many times, usually his full name, Picardo Angeli (i.e. Picardo, son of Angelo). The scope of his office is variously defined as proctor, proctor and syndic, or even proctor, syndic and treasurer (*yconomus*).[159] The need for proctors, laymen willing to act as agents, indeed before long in effect as bankers, for the Order, was recognised early on by those responsible for running its affairs, as the friars were forbidden, by St Francis, and by their Rule, from accepting or handling money themselves. Some of their agonising over this, and the papal bulls issued in successive attempts to square this particular circle, have been discussed earlier.[160] In the pages of the archives we meet one notable proctor in the flesh, as it were. For more than twenty years Picardo seems to have exercised sole financial responsibility for the church and convent at Assisi. But in a letter dated 20 June 1280 the then bishop of Assisi, brother Illuminato, OFM, in virtue of a faculty conferred on him by the Cardinal Protector of the Order, Cardinal Matteo Rosso Orsini, appointed four proctors with powers to receive and disburse sums of

---

[156] *3 Soc.* 26.   [157] See pp. 45–7.   [158] Langeli 1997, no. 37.
[159] Langeli 1997, e.g. nos. 37, 50, 51, 59, 81, 100.   [160] See chapter 5.

money on behalf of the Friars Minor of the Sacro Convento. One of them was Picardo, and this letter provides further evidence of who he was. He is addressed as Picardo, nephew of St Francis.[161] With the help of this clue it is possible from the documents to gain more information about the family. On 27 November 1253 two brothers, heirs of Angelo Pice, agreed a division of their inheritance. Picardo is mentioned first so he was presumably the elder.[162] He received a house near San Rufino with its contents, some specified plots of land, and all that they owned in the mountains. Johannetto got the rest. So Angelo Pice was St Francis' brother. It seems remarkable to us that none of the early lives give their mother's name.[163] It was usual for people to use the patronymic, but the matronymic was also used; and after a father's death the mother's name might be substituted. It may well be that Peter Bernardone predeceased his wife. Picardo is not a common name, and it has been suggested that, as Peter Bernardone was minded to name a son Francesco as the result of a trading trip – which presumably went well – in France, so his son Angelo in his turn may have traded in Picardy, and followed his father's example in the choice of a name inspired by business associations for his own son.[164] On 4 August 1261 Johannetto, who was ill, made his will.[165] His wife's name was Bonagratia and he had a daughter Johannola and a son Franciscolo. This – a diminutive of Francesco – was abbreviated in practice; the son answered to Cicolo.[166] This will – the will of a merchant – is interesting. He left all his property to his children, and to his wife. If the daughter died without heir, the son was to inherit her portion. If he died without heir, she was to receive the sum of £40 (libre), from the estate, and the rest was to be spent for the benefit of the souls of himself and his ancestors, and for forgiveness of ill-gotten gains, at the discretion of Picardo and the custos of the Sacro Convento. It was normal practice to leave bequests to several local religious houses, often also to leper and other hospitals, and some left alms as well to each prisoner in gaol in Assisi and to the deserving poor.[167] In spite of being St Francis' nephew and christening his son after him, Johannetto's only charitable bequests were a derisory 20 shillings (solidi) to the friars and 20 shillings to the church of St Francis. But the next day, 5 August, he added a codicil to the effect that 'whether my children live or die, I want my brother Picardo to give and restore from my goods, according as he sees fit, any goods wrongfully or illegally received, or taken on usury, if ever I may have received

[161] Langeli 1997, no. 110.
[162] Langeli 1997, no. 32; for the form 'Angelo de Pica' see ibid. no. 60. Trexler's conjecture (1989, pp. 16–21), that Picardo was some twenty years younger than his brother, is not supported by firm evidence.
[163] Pica is not in the index of AF x. The opening of 3 Soc., ch. 1, as printed in Habig 1979, p. 890, is an interpolation of the fifteenth century.
[164] Abate 1966, pp. 79–82 and p. 102 n. 14, cites Fortini for this suggestion and attempts to refute it, on slender grounds. Trexler 1989, pp. 8–11, discusses this and other suggestions.
[165] Langeli 1997, no. 60.
[166] Or Ceccolo (Cekole in the vernacular). He appears variously in the documents: as Cicolo Iovanecti in 1281 or 1282, Cecolo domine Bonagratie nepote Picardi in 1284, Cicolo nepote Picardi in 1288, Cecolum Picardi in 1289, C. Iohannecti in 1295 etc.: cf. Langeli 1997, nos. 122, 132, 148, 150 and p. 244 n. 1. For another example of the use of the matronymic, cf. Langeli 1997, nos. 134, 135. In July 1284 'domina Savia, uxor olim Tomassi, infirma corpore' made her will. She died soon after, for in September 1284 her son, when he made his will, described himself as 'Andreolus condam domine Savie'.
[167] Langeli 1997, eg. nos. 100, 102, 104, 116. The Assisi gaol in the Piazza del Comune is pictured in the first fresco of the St Francis Cycle in the Upper Church. This shows the little barred window between the slender columns of what had been in Roman times the Temple of Minerva. See Plate 53.

any such.' This afterthought may have been prompted by Picardo's pious scruples and concern for his more worldly brother's soul.[168]

Picardo was clearly a prominent citizen; probably a lawyer and man of affairs. Many of his fellow citizens appointed him their executor, or as one of their executors.[169] He served the Franciscans in Assisi devotedly as their lay proctor for some twenty-five years.[170] He seems to have been particularly active early on in his service. In 1259 he negotiated the acquisition, from a variety of owners, of a number of individual plots of land adjacent to the Basilica and down the slopes of the Collis Paradisi, either by purchase or exchange, so as to consolidate the Order's property on the hill.[171] The friars were greatly beholden to him, and one of them at least may have sought to show an awareness of the debt they were under, in the middle years of the century, to a member of the next generation of Francis' family by softening the image of Picardo's paternal grandparents.

Another noteworthy feature of the *Legend of the Three Companions* is related to this: it is the care taken to anchor the presentation of St Francis' life and achievement firmly in its native setting. *3 Soc.*'s image of Francis emphasises that he is a local man made good, a citizen of Assisi. Francis was born and bred in Assisi; the crucial stages of his conversion took place in Assisi and its environs; his first followers were men of Assisi. He needed to go to Rome to gain papal approval for their way of life, but promptly returned to the neighbourhood of Assisi; and he and his friars were soon based at the Portiuncula. His Order grew from there. Chapters were held there twice a year, where the friars gathered to discuss observance of the Rule, organise provinces and preaching, assign manpower and elect ministers. After his death, the ceremony of his canonisation took place in Assisi, and the pope himself laid the foundation stone of the church to be built in his honour, to which, two years later, his sanctified body was translated. Manselli concluded that *3 Soc.* should be regarded as an account, not only of a founder of an Order, but of a local saint: 'It would seem to have been composed in Assisi, to celebrate a fellow citizen, to exalt the city in which he had been converted and where in the end he was buried. In other words the *Legenda trium Sociorum* should be considered as the Assisan legend of St Francis.'[172]

The account contributes some reminiscences, and recollections of Francis' own words and of his characteristic way of speaking when uplifted, which probably survived through oral tradition.[173] These included, for example: 'when he ate with the brothers he often put ash upon the foods he ate, saying to the brothers, as a veil to his abstinence, that brother ash was chaste' (*3 Soc.* 15); 'he spoke later' of his first experience of a

[168] Langeli 1997, no. 60 and p. 111 n. 1.
[169] Langeli 1997, eg. nos. 46, 63, 75, 84, 93, 99, 101, 116.
[170] The first mention of him as proctor is in 1256 (no. 37), the last mention as proctor in April 1281 (no. 116). In September 1284 a small legacy – 100 solidi – was left to a brother Picardo ('fratri Picardo'), 'if he should be alive after the death of the testator' (no. 135 and p. 267 n. 4), so it is possible that Picardo joined the Order near the end of his life and died a friar.
[171] Langeli 1997, nos. 47–53, 55–7; and see p. 257.   [172] Manselli 1980, pp. 26–7.
[173] A few precise details credited to *3 Soc.* by those who date it to 1246 or earlier, are contributed by other sources. E.g.: the name of the count Francis hoped would confer knighthood on him, Gentile (*3 Soc.* 5), is taken from AP 5c; that the church to which Francis, Bernard and Peter went to consult the Gospel book was St Nicholas' is first recorded in Bonav. III, 3.

spiritual sweetness which transfixed his senses (3 Soc. 7); when he assumed the role of a beggar on the steps of St Peter's, he begged for alms in French, 'because he loved to speak that language even though he did not know how to speak it correctly' (3 Soc. 10).

In these instances, and in others, where 3 Soc. is using either 1 or 2 Celano as the basis of his account, but adds specific details, alters or omits others, or incorporates notable variations in the telling of a story or in the sequence of events, the most likely explanation is that these vivid stories were circulating orally. They were part of a living tradition and therefore subject to modification and change, as those still alive who had known St Francis, or those who knew those who had and felt qualified to speak for them, retold and retold their memories, some seeking to correct what they considered inaccurate in others' versions, some confusing or softening or hardening with the passage of time.[174] The same applies where 3 Soc. is using AP as his source and the two vary in their detail – as for example in Francis' dream of armour destined for himself and his followers.[175]

Francis also broke into French when he overcame his diffidence in approaching a house where a group of gamblers had gathered, and in fervour of spirit begged oil for the lamps of the church of San Damiano. On another occasion, when he and others were labouring to repair that church, he called out in a loud voice, in gladness of spirit and in French, to everyone, including passers-by: 'Come and help me in the building work of the church of San Damiano which in future will be a monastery of ladies, by whose fame and way of life our Father in heaven will be glorified in the universal church' (3 Soc. 24). This account fairly closely follows 2 Celano 13. But the words Francis utters are almost identical with those quoted by St Clare in her independent account of the same incident: a close comparison leaves little doubt that 3 Soc. is based on St Clare's Testament. This suggests that the author had access to that document.[176]

There is another important document he referred to specifically. At the end of the book he noted Gregory IX's rich gifts to the Basilica, and the status the pope accorded to it. The church was exempted from all inferior jurisdiction and, by apostolic authority, it was made 'caput et mater' of the whole Order of Friars Minor, 'as is clear in the public privilege and bull which the cardinals signed as a body'. The bull is Is qui ecclesiam issued on 22 April 1230. It is an original document and was kept at the Sacro Convento.[177] The listing of Gregory IX's gifts, which included a relic of the true Cross encased in a gold cross ornamented with precious stones and many costly vessels and vestments, comes from Thomas of Celano's Legenda Chori, probably compiled in 1230.[178] But the papal bull is not mentioned there, nor in 1 or 2 Celano, or AP or Bonaventure. It is peculiar

---

[174] Cf. the very interesting discussions of oral history in Transactions of the Royal Historical Society, 6th series, 9 (1999), esp. Geary 1999 and Foot 1999.

[175] For the dream of armour see 3 Soc. 5, 1 Cel. 5, 2 Cel. 5–6, AP 5; on these passages cf. Beguin 1979, pp. 201–3; Desbonnets 1972, pp. 82–94. Desbonnets accepts that AP is here the source of 3 Soc. (ibid., pp. 91–2); and see pp. 130, 151.

[176] Clare 1985, p. 168, nos. 12–14. Cf. C. Brooke 1999, pp. 277–9.

[177] Sbaralea, I, 60–2, G9 no. 49; Eubel 1908, n. 68. Exemption from all inferior jurisdiction was first granted in Recolentes qualiter of 29 April 1228 (Sbaralea, I, 40–1, G9 no. 21; Eubel 1908, n. 43), also kept in the Sacro Convento: see Assisi 1999, p. 16. See Plate 8.

[178] Legenda Chori 17, AF X, 126 and cf. xiii.

to *3 Soc.* The author has clearly seen the document himself, and may well have been a member of the community. That would best explain how he had access to it; indeed how he had access to all the materials he consulted and studied.

The skill and sensitivity displayed by the author in his handling of his subject is apparent even from a reading of the opening chapters, with their detailed unfolding of the processes of spiritual conversion. And by selecting and combining together a whole variety of different elements, he has succeeded in presenting a richer, more comprehensive and more comprehensible account than can be found elsewhere among the early sources. The intrinsic value of *3 Soc.* has been eloquently extolled by Philippart, who, from an analysis of the early chapters, concluded that the work possessed remarkable literary qualities and originality compared to other ancient and medieval biographical and hagiographical productions. 'It is not so much the absence of marvels, which had rejoiced Paul Sabatier, because one could cite other hagiographical texts which are without these and yet lack literary qualities worthy of mention. It is rather the attention of the author to the evolution of his hero, to his progressive "conversion". One knows that ancient biographies are traditionally static. Here one is manifestly in the presence of a new narrative art: this observation leads us to pose the question whether the *Legend of the Three Companions* is not an important witness to the evolution of the biography and of the psychological analysis of heroes in the western world.'[179] A spur to this achievement was surely the circumstance that the author was writing about a charismatic individual who had died sufficiently recently that recollections of him were still vivid, and he was still remembered as having been a real person. While the author may have reworked, in the mid-1260s, images of the saint that were either already written down or circulating orally, *3 Soc.* is not to be dismissed simply as a pastiche. It is a genuine and valid image of the mid-thirteenth century. It was not the author's fault that the Order's decree of 1266 nearly caused his brainchild to be stillborn. It did manage to survive, and it proved congenial to a later audience, an audience that also appreciated the *Mirror of Perfection*. They tended to hunt together in a number of fourteenth- and fifteenth-century MSS.[180]

THE *SACRUM COMMERCIUM*

The *Sacrum Commercium* – 'St Francis' holy commerce with the lady Poverty' – is a delightful allegory of exceptional literary skill which must find a place in any discussion of the image of Francis in the thirteenth century. But where? In the late fourteenth and fifteenth centuries a date of 1227 was attached to some of the surviving manuscripts.[181] Most of the best manuscripts are undated and 1227 has not found favour in recent scholarship.

---

[179] Philippart 1974, pp. 196–7 (my translation).
[180] Eleven of the twenty-two MSS of *3 Soc.* listed by Desbonnets 1974, pp. 39–41, also contain *Speculum Perfectionis*; and eleven out of the fourteen MSS of *Speculum Perfectionis* in Latin listed in Clasen 1967, pp. 47–158 also contain *3 Soc.* (Clasen 1967, p. 163, adds one MS to those listed by Sabatier, *Sp S* I, pp. ix–x, II, 1–73.)
[181] Brufani 1990, pp. 19, 177n. Cf. ibid. pp. 61–2: one of the MSS with the date 1227 is late fourteeth century; the rest are fifteenth century or later. What follows owes much to the excellent edition in Brufani 1990.

Father Cusato argues for a date in the 1230s, relating it to the protests against brother Elias. Desbonnets suggested a date in the second quarter of the thirteenth century. Its most recent editor, Stefano Brufani, prefers a date in the 1250s and 1260s, linking it to the arguments about poverty of that epoch.[182] It cannot be later than about 1300, the date of the earliest surviving manuscripts, and it was cited by Ubertino da Casale c.1305.[183] Within the wider span, however, it seems unwise to seek too precise a date. Cusato and Brufani endeavour to link it to politics and polemic. But it has the timeless quality of imaginative literature; and the critical element, which is severe, seems aimed at the traditional monastic orders, which claim to follow poverty but in fact are rich, rather than at any group among the friars.[184] Lady Poverty seems to expect the friars to be like monks.[185]

It seems to be the work of a highly educated friar of sophisticated mind and remarkable talent, deeply imbued with the text of the Bible. The Franciscan texts with which it has the closest affinity are 1 and 2 *Celano*. 1 *Celano* 35 describes the way of life of the friars before they had any settled home or cloister. 'They began . . . to have commerce (*commercium*) with holy poverty.' Father Bihl noted that this sentence echoes the Pseudo-Senecan *De paupertate*: 'Incipe cum paupertate habere contubernium';[186] and this suggests that the use of *commercium* in this context may well have been of Celano's coining. 'Domina sancta paupertas' was addressed in St Francis' own *Salutatio virtutum* and 'Domina paupertas' occurs at least nine times in Celano.[187] Most significant is 2 *Celano* 70, in which Francis is quoted as saying: 'if the brothers have embraced my Lady Poverty the world will nourish them . . . There is commerce between the world and the brothers: they owe the world a good example, the world owes them necessary provisions.' St Bonaventure contented himself with the briefest of summaries of 1 *Celano* 35 (Bonav. IV, 1). He only refers to Poverty as 'domina' twice: 'he used to call her now mother, now bride, now lady' (Bonav. VII, 6); and 'he rejoiced . . . since he had kept faith with Lady Poverty to the end' (Bonav. XIV, 4 from 2 *Cel.* 215). There is perhaps enough evidence here to suggest that the *Sacrum Commercium* was in part directly inspired by these passages in 1 and 2 *Celano*; and that in its turn may indicate a date between 1247 and 1266, when both were accessible.[188] A date close to 2 *Celano* would fit very well the nostalgia for the life of the first companions evident in the *Sacrum Commercium*. But this is speculation: it is in essence a charming allegory, woven from a rich texture of biblical and poetic imagery.

A brief extract will illustrate its quality. Francis is portrayed as seeking holy poverty from the beginning of his conversion 'with all zeal, all desire, with all determination,

---

[182] Cusato 2000, pp. 42–53; Brufani 1990, pp. 18 (citing Desbonnets), 36–42. Two MSS attribute it to St Anthony of Padua, two – and the *Chronicle of the Twenty-Four Generals* – to John of Parma (Brufani 1990, p. 10 and nn. 22–3); but if the author should ever be detected it would rather be through his literary qualities than these stray attributions.

[183] Brufani 1990, pp. 10 n. 23, 59–60: MSS Assisi, Biblioteca storico-francescano di Chiesa Nuova 2 and Sarnano, Biblioteca Comunale E. 60, are dated by Brufani to the turn of the thirteenth and fourteenth centuries.

[184] Brufani 1990, p. 163, c. 24; cf. the many sections on Avarice, pp. 154–61.

[185] Brufani 1990, pp. 170, 173, c. 30, 2, 25.   [186] AF X, 29 n. 9.

[187] Esser 1976, p. 427; 1 Cel. 35, 51; 2 Cel. 55, 70, 72, 82, 84, 93, 215. For 2 Cel. 55, see p. 144. The phrase occurs three times in SL: 60, 88 (= 2 Cel. 72, 84) and 70.

[188] See p. 244.

fearing nothing, shunning no labour, refusing no bodily suffering, enquiring for her of all he encountered . . . "Direct me, I pray you, to where Lady Poverty lives, where she feeds, where she rests at noonday, for I languish for love of her."' Two wise old men direct him. 'She lives high up in the holy mountains . . . Giants have not been able to reach her footprints and eagles have not soared as far as her neck . . . Lay aside every weight and sin . . . for unless you are naked, you cannot ascend to her.' So Francis chose some faithful companions and encouraged them to climb the mountain of the Lord with him, saying: '"Narrow is the way and strait is the gate which leads to life" (Matt. 7. 14) . . . gird yourselves as men of might . . . Being married to Poverty is wonderful; we can easily enjoy her embraces . . . Lady Poverty marvelled greatly to see them climbing stoutly or rather flying . . . like clouds or like doves to their windows . . . Reclining on the throne of her nakedness she sweetly blessed them.'[189]

Their address to her is a climax of poetic imagination. 'We have heard you are the queen of the virtues and in some measure have learnt this by experience . . . We humbly beg you to condescend to be with us and to be the way for us to come to the King of Glory, as you were the way for Him' our Saviour. 'For the King of Kings and creator of heaven and earth has desired your form and your beauty.' He left his throne and sought you; he adorned you with a crown as a bride. You prepared a fitting place for him. 'When he was born you ran to meet him, that in you and not in earthly delights he might find a pleasing home. He was laid, says the evangelist, in a manger because there was no room for him in the inn [Luke 2. 7]. And you were always his inseparable companion throughout his life on earth . . . Foxes had holes and the fowls of the air had nests, he himself had not anywhere to lay his head [Matt. 8. 20; Luke 9. 58] . . .'[190] You, most faithful wife, sweetest lover, never for a moment left him. . . . You were with him when he was despised . . . cursed . . . spat on . . . scourged . . . [John 18–19; etc.]. You did not leave him in the hour of death, even the death of the cross. On the cross itself, with body bared, arms extended, hands and feet transfixed, you suffered with him, so that nothing appeared more glorious in him than you.'[191] Lady Poverty replies joyfully to the friars, echoing the psalmist: their words to her are 'more to be desired than gold, sweeter than honey and the honeycomb' (Ps. 18. 11 (19. 10)), because they are inspired by the Holy Spirit.[192]

The work ends with a lyrical description of the refreshment they offered her. She asked for cooked food and wine. 'Show me', she said, 'your chapel, your chapter house, your cloister, your refectory, your kitchen, your dormitory and stable, your fine seats, polished tables and immense buildings.' But they brought her hard crusts of coarse bread and cold water laid out on the grass. For her pillow they brought her a stone on which she slept most peacefully and soberly. When she awoke they led her up a hill and showed her the whole world as far as she could see, saying: 'This is our cloister, Lady.'[193]

---

[189] Brufani 1990, pp. 131, 134–8, Prologue 11–12 and c. 2, 1–3, 6–7, 9–10; c. 4, 1–3, 8.
[190] Quoted also in 2 *Cel.* 56.   [191] Brufani 1990, pp. 139–41, c. 5, 2–3; c. 6, 3–5, 9–13.
[192] Brufani 1990, pp. 143–4, c. 7, 3.   [193] Brufani 1990, pp. 170–3, c. 30.

CHAPTER SEVEN

VISUAL IMAGES

Images contributed significantly to Francis' own spiritual development.[1] The painted crucifix at San Damiano spoke to him, giving him direction at a crucial moment. A comparable role played by images in the formation of a saint was unusual in the thirteenth century. In England only St Edmund of Abingdon is recorded as displaying a similar sensitivity. Matthew Paris' *Life* of him provides anecdotal evidence. For example, when he was praying before a statue he was told to study the three concentric circles – signifying the Trinity – instead of the shapes of simple geometry, that is, to turn his mind to the pursuit of spiritual knowledge. Aged about twelve he betrothed himself to an image of the Virgin, placing a ring on her hand as a pledge of virginity. He frequently crossed himself, and circles developed on his hand; this marking of the body is perhaps related to the phenomenon of the stigmata. St Edmund died in 1240 and was canonised in 1246.[2]

No 'portrait' was painted of Francis during his lifetime. This is not surprising. The genre in our sense scarcely existed; and by the time he had grown famous he would hardly have been regarded as a fit subject for a painter, as he looked unkempt, emaciated, unprepossessing. Thomas of Spalato, an archdeacon, who heard him preach in 1222 or 1223, has given us a description of him, contrasting his physical presence with the power of his words. It is especially valuable in being an unsolicited, contemporary assessment made by a member of the secular clergy, not by a friar.[3] 'When I was studying in Bologna, I saw St Francis preaching in the piazza in front of the Palazzo Pubblico, where almost all the citizens had gathered . . . He did not deliver his sermon in the usual way, but in a rousing fashion . . . His habit was dirty, his appearance contemptible and his face ill-favoured, but God gave the man's words such effect that many noble clans, whose violence and long-standing feuds had raged with much blood-letting,

---

[1] This chapter is based on lectures I gave in Cambridge in the late 1970s and 1980s, and also in Philadelphia in 1983.
[2] Matthew Paris, *Vita S. Edmundi Cantuariensis*, in Lawrence 1960, pp. 224–5, 250–2. I am very grateful to Dr Paul Binski for drawing my attention to this analogy.
[3] For Thomas of Spalato see *MGH Scriptores*, XXIX, 580, translated in Brooke 1975, p. 136.

were induced to agree to peace. So great were the reverence and devotion of the people for him that men and women pressed on him in throngs in their eagerness either to touch the hem of his garment or to carry off a scrap of his clothing.'

At the time when St Francis died interest in the personal appearance of individuals was still not fully awakened. Artists attempting to represent great men were more concerned with their rank and status than their physiognomy. A king would be represented wearing his crown and holding orb and sceptre, a bishop wearing his mitre and holding his pastoral staff. Individuals could be further identified by having their name inscribed at their feet or at their head, or by some distinctive emblem. St Peter is shown carrying the keys, for example, St Lawrence his gridiron, St Catherine her wheel, St Bartholomew his flayed skin. In the second half of the thirteenth century and the early decades of the fourteenth significant advances in personal portraiture were made.[4] But this was in the future. Francis is portrayed as the founder of his Order, and as a saint. Not immediately, but quite soon, his own individual identification mark became the stigmata.

The earliest representation of Francis of which there is a record is in a rather unexpected place. It is in the cloister of the Benedictine abbey of Mont Saint-Michel, spectacularly situated on the top of the rocky hillock which juts out into the sea where Brittany and Normandy meet. Early in the thirteenth century the king of France, Philip Augustus, built La Merveille, new quarters for the monks, as a thank offering for his success in driving King John of England out of Normandy. The new cloister, on the third and uppermost storey of La Merveille and one of the most delightful products of Gothic architecture in Normandy, has a double arcade which gives a shifting vista of arches (Plate 13). On its western walk, as well as rich foliage decoration, there is a carving of Christ enthroned and another of Christ on the cross. Near to the crucified Christ was St Francis, now almost worn away, with an inscription bearing his name and the date 1228, and the information that, in that year, he was canonised and the cloister completed. This means that La Merveille was completed, not in the lifetime of Philip II, but during the regency of Queen Blanche of Castile, mother of the future St Louis IX. His devotion to St Francis he may have learnt from his mother, and her patronage may help to explain Francis' presence here. The inscription and the figure of Francis were fortunately recorded in an early nineteenth-century drawing. He is shown frontally, standing, his arms bent at the elbows and raised, but the hands are missing, presumably already obliterated when the drawing was made. The stigmata are shown in both feet but not in the side.[5]

The earliest surviving fresco of him – a cult object, not a portrait – is in the chapel of St Gregory in the Sacro Speco at Subiaco. It is to the right of the entrance; to the left a second fresco commemorates the consecration of the chapel by Gregory IX before he became pope. An inscription records that the fresco was painted in the second year of his pontificate, so its date is between 19 March 1228 and 18 March 1229. Both appear to

[4] Kirschbaum et al. 1968–76, v, 320–34; VII, 289–97, 374–91; VIII, 158–74. For discussions of the portrait in the central Middle Ages see Morris 1972, pp. 86–95; Gardner 1992, esp. pp. 172–5; Binski 1986.
[5] Brooke and Swaan 1974, pp. 210–18, figs. 24–6 and pls. 329, 334–50, esp. 347–50. The drawing is in Paris Bibl. Nat. MS Franc. 4902, fo. 226, reproduced in Brooke and Swaan 1974, pl. 349. For the inscription see also *Gallia Christiana*, XI, 522.

Plate 13 Mont Saint-Michel, the cloister, early thirteenth century: in the centre, Christ crucified, to the right, Christ enthroned (Photo Wim Swaan Photographic Collection (96.P.21), Research Library, The Getty Research Institute, Los Angeles).

be by the same hand and executed at the same time. Francis is shown standing, facing the viewer, dressed in the habit of his Order, with the knotted cord round his waist, and barefoot. *Frater Franciscus*, brother Francis – not saint – is written by his head, and the stigmata are absent. In his left hand he holds a page bearing the words *Pax huic domui* – Peace be to this house – the greeting which Christ instructed his disciples to use when he sent them out two by two, and which Francis consequently required his friars to use. The abbot of Subiaco kneels at his feet[6] (Plate 14).

Subiaco is also a Benedictine house. We are dependent on chance survivals, but it is noteworthy that two of the earliest representations of Francis, which commemorate his canonisation, were carved or painted not in houses of his own Order but in those of the traditional monasticism. Later in the century the Benedictines were to react against the friars, to show hostility and jealousy towards them, but in the early days relations between the different Orders were generally harmonious. It is likely too that

[6] Krüger 1992, pp. 56–65 and figs. 112–14; Moleta 1983, Frontispiece, pp. 16–17; Scarpellini 1982b, p. 107; Bughetti 1926b, pp. 936–7. Cook 1999, pp. 221–2, dates it later. *Pax huic domui* is from Luke 10.5 – and the *Regula non bullata* c. 14 (Esser 1976, p. 389).

Plate 14 St Francis, Subiaco, fresco of 1228–9 (© www.Assisi.de. Photo Gerhard Ruf).

the friars were not all that quick to disregard their founder's clearly expressed views on poverty and simplicity. Their churches and their living quarters were to be humble and unadorned.

Another very early, and remarkable type of visual image was the monstrance reliquary. There is an exquisite example now in the Louvre, dated c.1228.[7] On the reverse the miracle of St Francis receiving the stigmata is illustrated in flat-painted enamelling. He is shown frontally, haloed, wearing the habit and cord of his Order, standing between olive trees. All five wounds are conspicuous. Above his head the six-winged seraph is nailed to a cross (Colour Plate 1). The quatrefoil reliquary has a wooden core. On the obverse five tiny hollows have been carved out in this, one at the centre, one in the centre of each foil, to create the form of a cross. The wood was then covered with a sheet of gilded copper, with five framed cruciform perforations over the hollows. A hinged chased copper cover was fixed over this, holding five oval carinate crystals, which acted not simply as monstrances but also as magnifying glasses, enabling the relics within to be better seen. Rock crystals and cabuchons encircle each of these. No relics from St Francis' body were allowed to enter circulation. The five tiny receptacles will have contained fragments of cloth that had been used as dressings for Francis' five wounds. The base was decorated with enamelled peacocks – symbols of Paradise – and the stem is so constructed that the top can be swivelled round above the knot with its eight projecting ribs. Apart from the technique and the enamelling, everything about this reliquary is innovative. The goldsmith created it to display the authentic relics of a contemporary saint, with the relics on one side and the picture explaining them on the other; the swivel mechanism meant that either face could be shown as required. It is small enough to be suitable for use as a portable altarpiece. This type of icon reliquary could fulfil more than one function. It could be utilised in public acts of liturgical worship and provide a focus for private devotion. The work of art could be contemplated, the relics venerated. Both provided a visual spiritual link between St Francis and the cross of Christ. This reliquary, and a second surviving example (now in the Musée de Cluny), were both made in the same enamelling workshop in southern France, which produced work in the Limoges manner. Some of its decorative elements, such as the sun, moon and stars surrounding the seraph, and the peacocks, suggest a link with central Italy and the papal court in Rome. It is believed to have come from Palma de Mallorca, where a Franciscan house was established in the second quarter of the thirteenth century.

Francis had been popularly venerated as a saint even during his lifetime, and after his death the news of the stigmata ensured the rapid diffusion of his cult. A little evidence about the proliferation of painted images of him can be gleaned from Thomas of Celano's *Treatise on Miracles*. There was, he wrote, in Rome, a married woman of good life and noble birth, personally known to him, who had chosen St Francis as her patron, and kept a painted image of him in her room. One day, while she was engaged in prayer, it struck her that the picture lacked the marks of the stigmata, and she began to feel unhappy and surprised. It was not really surprising that they were not in the picture,

---

[7] For what follows see Gauthier 1987, pp. 138–40 and pl. 82.

as the artist had omitted them. After some days, during which she worried over their lack, the stigmata suddenly appeared in the picture, just as they are accustomed to be painted in other pictures of the saint. The woman, all of a tremble, called her daughter and asked her whether the picture had been without the stigmata up till then. Her daughter confirmed that it used not to show the stigmata and that now it did. However, an unworthy doubt again entered the woman's mind; perhaps after all the marks had been there from the start. Lest the first miracle should be undervalued God added a second, for the marks disappeared.[8] The so-called miraculous element here may fail to impress, but this story provides evidence that there were pictures of St Francis in the possession of lay people by the beginning of the 1250s, when the *Treatise on Miracles* was written.

Another miracle story from the same collection concerns a cleric called Roger, who was a canon of the cathedral at Potenza in Apulia. One day he entered a church in which there was a painting of St Francis, which showed the stigmata. He began to have doubts about this miracle, as a thing altogether unheard of and impossible. Suddenly he felt a sharp blow on his left hand beneath his glove. Pulling off the glove he uncovered a wound which looked as if it had been inflicted by an arrow. For two days he cried out with the pain. He was healed when he abandoned his doubts and swore he now believed that St Francis had in truth received the stigmata.[9] It is not stated whether the church he entered pertained to the friars. But by the 1250s representations of St Francis bearing the stigmata were to be found in churches of monastic houses and in churches belonging to seculars, as well as in churches connected to the Order. The image he saw may well have been on a simple narrow wooden panel displaying a standing, full length, frontal figure. There seems to have been a ready market for such panels, judging from the number of surviving examples.[10] They were probably designed to hang on church columns. Margarito of Arezzo produced a whole succession. The earliest surviving was painted some time between 1235 and 1245 and is signed. Francis wears a black habit with hood up, and knotted cord. He holds a closed gospel book in his left hand; his right hand is raised in blessing. The stigmata are indicated by tiny black dots in hands and feet. The side wound is not shown. There is no nimbus, but he is captioned 'Sanctus Franciscus'. In another early example, now at Siena, the stigmata are still indicated by tiny dots; the gospel cover is decorated with a cross. The relative inconspicuousness of the stigmata suggests a hesitation in portraying them due to sensitivities aroused by the phenomenon. In an example in the Vatican, of the early 1250s, perhaps commissioned by Innocent IV, the dots are larger. Pious lay people – women as well as men – were instrumental in spreading the cult in places of public worship. In her will, dated 3 January 1250, a lady called Alays stipulated that 'an image of the blessed Francis with the signs of the stigmata of Jesus Christ, with which He wonderfully and uniquely marked his saint, be made in one of the middle windows of the apse' in the Benedictine abbey of Allois, near Limoges.[11] Such windows could be viewed by the public and must

[8] *3 Cel.* 8–9. For discussions of the stigmata, see note 13 and pp. 33–5, 167–8, 234–5.   [9] *3 Cel.* 6–7.

[10] For this and what follows, see Cook 1999, esp. p. 21, and nos. 6, 175, 162. Cf. Krüger 1992, pp. 30–6.

[11] Vauchez 1968, p. 596 n. 2, quoting the edition of F. M. Delorme in *Studi Francescani* 11 (1925), 126–8.

have been agreed to by the communities or priests concerned. They were officially sanctioned.

Canon Roger was not the only cleric to have his doubts. Gregory IX's bull, *Mira circa nos*, addressed to the archbishops, bishops and other clergy, announcing his canonisation of St Francis, actually makes no specific reference to the stigmata.[12] St Bonaventure throws some light on this. He admitted, in his *Life of St Francis*, that the pope himself initially had doubts, though apparently they were confined to the existence of the wound in his side. St Francis reassured him in a vision, and he became active in defence of their genuineness.[13] On 31 March 1237 Gregory IX wrote to the bishop of Olomoue in Bohemia, ordering him to mend his ways. The bishop, Robert the Englishman, a Cistercian, had sent this mandate to the clergy of his diocese: 'Because the son of the eternal Father alone was crucified for the salvation of mankind, and the Christian religion ought to adore his wounds alone with suppliant devotion, neither blessed Francis nor any other of the saints is to be depicted with stigmata in the Church of God, and who asserts the contrary, sins.' The pope personally vouched for the truth of the stigmata, and ordered the bishop to repudiate his false opinion, to preach the opposite publicly in their defence, and to have the saint depicted with the stigmata. A different bull was sent to the Provincial priors and priors of the Dominican Order denouncing one of their friars, Evechardus, who, in a public sermon at Oppava, in Moravia, had declared the stigmata were faked and the Friars Minor 'false preachers'. The pope dispatched yet another letter addressed to all the faithful in Germany, instructing them to have faith in the miracle of the stigmata and the sanctity of Francis, and not to believe

---

[12] Sbaralea I, 42–4.

[13] Bonav., *Miracula*, I, 2, AF X, 627–8. There has been much discussion over the centuries about the authenticity and precise nature of the stigmata: among the most recent and subtle expositions of the view that the form the imprint took developed in the mind and imagination of disciples, biographers and artists in the thirteenth century is Frugoni 1993 – *Francesco e l'invenzione delle stimmate*. Two pillars of her argument are that Francis himself was not deeply stirred by meditation on Christ's physical suffering, and that Bonaventure imported Christ-centred mysticism into the image of Francis (ibid., esp. pp. 115–24, 148–9, 173–82). 2 *Cel.* 10–11 place Francis' lamentations on the Passion at the outset of his conversion. Frugoni bypasses this evidence, while observing that the Crucifix which spoke to him in San Damiano (2 *Cel.* 10) was an image of Christ triumphant, not the suffering Jesus so fashionable later; and she finesses the witness of Francis' own *Officium passionis Domini* (Esser 1976, pp. 338–44): she argues that to Francis the Passion is part of a wider concern with Christ from incarnation to resurrection; Jesus is integral to the Trinity. But the *Officium* contains a deeply moving evocation of Jesus' sufferings, linked to a brilliant vision of the passion as triumph – a reminder that the crucifix at San Damiano represented a paradox which presents itself in vivid colours to an imaginative person meditating on it; and it was by such imaginative meditation that the practice (not new, but newly dominant) of meditating on the events of Jesus' life was inspired (Southern 1953, pp. 237–8; Brooke and Brooke 1984, pp. 139–45, 166).

It is true that Bonaventure added the name of Christ to an account of the stigmata otherwise closely based on Celano – but since Celano refers to 'virum . . . crucifixum' (1 *Cel.* 94), it hardly seems a significant addition. Francis was a more profound and subtle theologian than he has seemed to some critics, and he was perfectly capable of combining deeply orthodox Trinitarian doctrine and sentiment with passionate insight into the sufferings of the human Jesus. His emphatic identification of Christ as 'Verbum Domini' in his second *Epistola ad fideles* (Esser 1976, p. 208) echoes St John's Gospel (cf. esp. Frugoni 1993, pp. 116–18), but that does not make his use of the Gospels specifically Johannine, for there are roughly three times as many citations from the Synoptic Gospels in his writings as from St John (Esser 1976, pp. 466–8). Accounts of the stigmata vary in detail, as we would expect. If the accounts were in origin fictitious a great many people within and without the Order must have connived: his deathbed was a very public place. In general terms the basic facts could hardly be better recorded.

any lying detractors. Less than a week later the same bull was circulated throughout Christendom.[14]

In the same year, 1237, a different approach was undertaken at Assisi: a list of those who had seen the stigmata was drawn up. The Book of St Gilbert of Sempringham reveals the remarkable care that Innocent III had taken to have Gilbert's miracles confirmed by veridical witnesses. The first embassy bringing the petitions of the English Church was sent back to seek out more witnesses and bring them to Rome.[15] A remarkable single sheet of vellum survives in the Archives of the Sacro Convento listing the witnesses to St Francis' stigmata.[16] It was written in at least two campaigns. In the first the scribe wrote: 'In the name of the Lord, Amen. These are they who saw the stigmata of the Blessed Francis while he was alive in the flesh and after death', and he then wrote two names, followed by James 'canon of the bishopric' who 'saw the stigmata of the saint only while he lived'. After this the original scribe left a space of two lines, evidently for other witnesses, and started a new paragraph: 'These are they who saw [the stigmata] after [Francis'] death', and listed about four names. Subsequently to the first list was added 'Albericus notarius' and to the second eight names, including 'Halbericus notarius' – evidently the same man who had seen the stigmata while the saint lived – and ending with John of Greccio, the friend of St Francis who prepared the Christmas crib at Greccio.[17]

It is noticeable that there are no friars in the list; most of those who can be identified appear to be members of leading Assisan families, active in civic government: doubtless it was intended to supplement the witness of brother Elias and the friars by adding trustworthy independent lay witnesses.[18] The witnesses after death include *Dominus Ieronimus*, clearly to be identified with the doubting Thomas recorded by Bonaventure who had to touch the nails before he believed. He was chamberlain of Assisi in 1228–9, and podestà in 1230.[19]

The first campaign was concluded by adding two names near the foot of the parchment whose role is left unclear. The second campaign added eight names to the list of those who had witnessed the stigmata after death – then left ten lines blank and added

---

[14] For the three bulls see esp. Vauchez 1968, pp. 601–2, and references. They are *Usque ad terminos*, variously dated 31 March and 12 April 1237 (31 March in copy in Assisi – the original apparently does not survive; 12 April, not 11th as in Vauchez 1968, according to Wadding: see Potthast, II, nos. 10308 and after 10319; Alessandri 1915, p. 597 no. 23; full text in Sbaralea, I, 211–12, G9 no. 220). *Non minus dolentes* of 31 March 1237 (Potthast, II, no. 10309; Sbaralea, I, 213); *Confessor Domini* of 31 March 1237 (Potthast, II, no. 10307; Alessandri 1915, p. 597, no. 24). A text of *Confessor Domini*, addressed generally, is dated 5 April 1237 (Potthast, II, no. 10314; Sbaralea, I, 214): either this was a reissue a few days later, or address and date have been garbled in transmission.

[15] Foreville and Keir 1987, esp. pp. 168–73.

[16] Bihl 1926 (with facsimile of the recto of the leaf); cf. Vauchez 1968, p. 600. For what follows see esp. Bihl 1926, pp. 931–2 and pl. XXXII, and Bihl's discussion, pp. 933–5.

[17] For John of Greccio, Giovanni da Vellita, see pp. 45–6; 1 Cel. 84–6; 2 Cel. 35; Bonav. X, 7; Cuthbert 1913, pp. 391–4, esp. 391–2 n. 1.

[18] For Elias' witness, see p. 34. Bihl identifies some of the witnesses from the records of Assisi, especially Thomas de Raynerio who is listed as 'tunc camerarius comunis', and occurs as a consul in 1223 and 1228; Iohannes de Guarnerio, who occurs in 1228; Masseus Andree de Preite, perhaps the same as Matheus Andree Preiti who occurs in 1231, and Bartolus and Balierus, who may occur in 1232 (Bihl 1926, p. 932, nn. 4, 6–8).

[19] Bonav. XV, 4; cf. Bihl 1926, p. 932 n. 5; AF X, 624 n. 5. See pp. 35, 408 and Plate 67.

a description of the stigmata almost identical with that in 1 *Celano* 95. This was probably copied from Celano, as Father Bihl, who edited the document, convincingly argued.[20] Much later scribes have added on the verso of the sheet a reference, first to two then to three bulls of Gregory IX defending the authenticity of the stigmata, all originally issued in 1237. Bihl noted pin-holes at the foot of the document and a fragment of thread attached to them; and he argued that the summary on the verso referred to a transcript of these bulls contemporary with the surviving lists.

The witnesses after death must have seen the body in October 1226, or very soon after: by 1228 it is unlikely to have been in a state for close inspection, and after the translation it was inaccessible to all. The witnesses after death included Thomas de Raynerio, 'then (*tunc*) chamberlain of the commune' evidently referring back to 1226[21] from some later date. The description of the stigmata could not have been written till 1228 or later – after 1 *Celano* had been completed. The bulls belong to 1237.[22] The lists themselves must refer to events of 1226, and the process of collecting witnesses which they reflect could not have been undertaken in this sort of way decades or generations later: the hands indeed enforce a date in the first half of the thirteenth century. On two occasions there must have been particular anxiety to collect witnesses to the stigmata: in the very early days, immediately after Francis' death and in the period leading up to his canonisation – between 1226 and 1228, that is; and again in 1237, when Gregory IX was constrained to issue these bulls defending the stigmata against detractors. It is possible that the first campaign belongs to the very early years, the second to 1237. But the informality of the document, which was evidently a draft drawn up for a specific occasion, may suggest that the second campaign followed hard on the first – that both were a part of the defence of the stigmata which had to be mounted in 1237. In either event the list may have been the brain-child of Elias or Gregory, or of both of them; and it is a remarkable testimony to the care that was taken to authenticate this most strange and (to many) incredible of miracles – and to the number of witnesses who had actually seen the body alive and dead.[23]

THE PESCIA ALTAR PANEL

Altar panels designed to celebrate St Francis and foster his cult began to be produced quite soon after his death. They represent a version of a form of visual image, the vita-retable, which emanated from late twelfth-century Greek icons – works of art intended to give public honour to saints.[24] These Byzantine biographical icons, which contained a central image of the saint surrounded by narrative scenes of his or her life and miracles, in the thirteenth century exercised a deep influence over a wide area, notably in Cyprus, Sinai, Russia and Italy. The story of an edifying life presented in

[20] Bihl 1926, p. 935. Bihl noted small verbal changes in the version in the list, and Celano's characteristic prose rhythms in the passage.
[21] Bihl 1926, p. 932.
[22] *Usque ad terminos* and *Confessor Domini* of March–April 1237: see above, note 14.
[23] On the defence of the stigmata see esp. Vauchez 1968; and for the wider context in the authentication of miracles and the elaboration of the processes of canonisation, Vauchez 1997.
[24] For their development and functions, see esp. Krüger 1992 and Sevcenko 1999.

pictures proved an effective 'mode of transmission between cultures sharing the same saints but venerating them in different languages and liturgies'[25] – for example St Catherine of Alexandria, St Margaret of Antioch, St George, St Nicholas. The language of art was international. The genre was adapted in western Europe to promote a range of new saints. Such panels were placed not on high altars but on side altars; some might also on occasion have been carried in processions. St Francis was not the first recent saint to be depicted in this way – the same format occurs in a wall painting, dated c.1200, portraying the standing figure of St Thomas Becket with scenes from his life[26] – but the fame of St Francis and the readiness of the Franciscans to utilise them were important in stimulating the spread and popularity of this form of altar panel.

The earliest surviving altar panel of which St Francis is the subject is at Pescia in Tuscany, between Lucca and Florence. It is signed, Bonaventura Berlinghieri, and dated, 1235[27] (Plate 15). It is a gabled panel showing a full length frontal image of St Francis, on a gold ground. His shoulders are flanked by busts of angels, also facing front. He is barefoot and wearing a habit, with hood and knotted cord. This was to become the standard representation of a Friar Minor, though the colour of the habit might vary, grey or brown or black. The stigmata are conspicuous in hands and feet, but the wound in his side is not shown. He is holding a book, the Gospels, to indicate that he is a preacher.

To either side of him are three scenes, one above the other. They are all taken from Thomas of Celano's *First Life*.[28] Two depict episodes during his lifetime – the stigmata and the preaching to the birds – and four, posthumous miracles. They are to be read beginning on the left from top to bottom, followed by the right from top to bottom.

St Francis' reception of the stigmata is the most crucial episode of his life in the Order's presentation of its dead founder.[29] It is placed top on the viewer's left, that is, on St Francis' right hand. The seraph is based on the description in Isaiah: 'each one had six wings; with twain he covered his face, and with twain he covered his feet, and with twain he did fly' (Isaiah 6. 2, as modified by Celano, who also drew on Ezekiel 1. 5–14, 22–3). According to Celano, Francis was staying in the hermitage on La Verna when he saw, in a vision, a man like a seraph, having six wings, standing above him with his hands extended and his feet joined, fixed to a cross. Two wings were raised above his head, two were extended in flight, while two veiled the whole body. The picture departs in a few details from Celano's description. The seraph has the marks of the nails in hands and feet, but is free standing, not fixed to a cross. The side wound is not shown. He is not looking 'kindly and graciously' on Francis (as Celano claimed); he is staring straight ahead. But a stream of golden light is directed from him straight onto Francis, who is kneeling, gazing at the winged man, with his arms outstretched

---

[25] Sevcenko 1999, p. 165.   [26] At Stow in Lincolnshire (Binski 2004, pp. 165–7).

[27] A great many panels have been lost, but among surviving Italian panels containing narrative scenes flanking the central figure of a saint, this one depicting St Francis is the earliest (see Duffy 1997, pp. 203–4; Garrison 1949, esp. sections xxi–xxii. For lost panels, cf. Garrison 1972).

[28] In Franciscan altar panels narrative scenes 'were always an illustration of an existing text' (Kaftal 1950, pp. 21–2, quoted Bourdua 2004, p. 10).

[29] 1 Cel. 94–5, 112–15.

Plate 15   The Pescia altar panel (© www.Assisi.de. Photo Gerhard Ruf).

in prayer towards him. He is placed near the base of the mountain. The hermitage is on the summit of La Verna, but Celano did not mention this. The scene is a new one, and a challenge to the painter. One of the scenes illustrating Christ's Passion, the Agony in the Garden of Gethsemane on the Mount of Olives, offered a model of prayerful vigil on a mountainside that could be adapted.[30] Celano had provided, in his account of the prelude to the vision, faint echoes of the accounts of the Agony in the Garden in Mark 14. 33 and Luke 22. 45, and had told how, on rising from prayer, Francis had, in his humble desire to know God's will for him so that he might do it, taken the Gospel Book from the altar and opened it three times. Each time he read of the tribulation Christ suffered in his Passion.[31] The visual image makes the point more clearly, whether intentionally or not. The viewer will have received the impression, at least subliminally, that St Francis' experience was akin to Christ's.

Below it comes the scene of Francis preaching to the birds.[32] The incident happened when he was travelling along the road which runs through the valley of Spoleto, and noticed a large congregation of birds. The artist has not grouped them by the roadside, but, the better to display them, has perched them on trees and bushes distributed over the slopes of a steep hill, which rises even higher than La Verna. According to Celano, the birds were doves, crows and a related species – probably either rooks or daws. The birds here are black, of differing sizes, partly to suggest distance, and could be crows and rooks, apart from two recognisable magpies perched on branches of the tree at ground level. All are facing St Francis, who, distinguished by halo and stigmata in hands and feet, and accompanied by two companions, holds a book, the emblem of the preacher. This scene has been chosen not simply because it is a naturally attractive subject for illustration, but to emphasise an important point about Francis' preaching. Here he is confronting the dualist beliefs prevalent among the heretics of his day, who held that material things are inherently evil. He is urging the birds, and with them all created things, to praise God, their Creator.[33] It is an affirmation of the essential goodness of the natural world.

These two scenes serve to reinforce the message of the central image: that Francis bears in his body the Saviour's wounds, and has His authority to preach.

The first miracle to be illustrated is, appropriately, the miracle with which Celano opened his collection of miracles in Part III of his First Life: the healing of a child with a dislocated neck.[34] It was put first because it occurred on the day of Francis' death, when his body was moved from the Portiuncula to San Giorgio.[35] It is depicted bottom

---

[30] Gardner 1982, p. 224. Painted crucifixes with apron panels in which scenes illustrating the Passion flank the central figure of the crucified Christ were another source of inspiration (cf. Frugoni 1993, p. 321; Derbes 1996, esp. pp. 1–34).

[31] 1 Cel. 91–3; cf. AF X, 69 n. 11, 71 n. 1.   [32] 1 Cel. 58; and see p. 44.

[33] Frugoni 1993, pp. 236–53, discusses the various levels of significance that can be read into Francis' preaching to the birds. She notes that in medieval literature different species of birds could denote different strata of society and that the doves and crows specified in 1 Cel. 58 could represent the labourers, could be interpreted as symbols of the poor and marginalised members of society, and could be extended to include the Friars Minor themselves. Duffy 1997, pp. 205–7, suggests that an element of apocalyptic speculation can be read into both this scene and the preceding scene of the stigmata. Apocalyptic speculation was to have an influence in England in Matthew Paris' rendering of these two scenes (see pp. 194–201), but I see no evidence of apocalyptic imagery in the Pescia panel.

[34] 1 Cel. 127.   [35] 1 Cel. 116–18; and see pp. 35–6.

left, below the preaching to the birds. As is quite usual, the miracle is shown in two successive stages within the one picture – rather like a strip cartoon. The mother of the child kneels in prayer, while the little girl with the dislocated neck lies by the altar. One friar comforts and exhorts the mother; the other already holds up his hands in amazement at the miracle. On the left, the mother is going out, carrying her healed daughter on her shoulder.

The next scene, top right, combines a number of miracles of healing. A group of assorted sufferers kneel, among them a crippled boy whom St Francis coaxed to reach out his hand, and presently to gain the confidence to stand up, by offering him pears.[36] Standing immediately behind them, to the right, is a man holding castanets in his right hand and carrying a flask hanging from a stick over his right shoulder, attributes which identify him as a leper.

Below this, in the middle scene, St Francis cures a lame beggar in the waters of a bath.[37] The leg is shown shrunken and thin, as broken or disused limbs become. On the right, the man is shown again, cured, walking away on two stout legs, carrying his crutches.

The fourth miracle scene, bottom right, is again a conflation of a group of miracle stories, relating to people suffering from dementia, which was held to be possession by evil spirits.[38] The exorcised demons are portrayed springing visibly from the mouths of the insane. How the insane were often treated is indicated by the detail that the two women have their hands tied in front of them, and are in the custody of the man on the far right.

THE PISA ALTAR PANEL

An altar panel at Pisa has the same overall shape and layout as the one at Pescia.[39] There are six scenes, but none represents events of Francis' life. They are all posthumous miracles: three the same as in the Pescia panel, though showing one cripple instead of the combined group of sufferers, and a fourth, likewise an exorcism, but a different incident (3 Cel. 153), and two not depicted elsewhere. One is a further miracle of healing – a noblewoman cured of an ulcer between her breasts. She had entered a Franciscan church to pray and noticed a book containing St Francis' life and miracles. She asked about him, and when she had been instructed she wet the book with her tears and laid it open upon the fistula, saying: 'St Francis, just as the things that are written about you in these pages are true, by the same token free me now from this infection by your holy merits.' After more tears and prayers the ulcer healed completely, leaving no scar. Celano must have experienced some feeling of satisfaction as he recorded this particular miracle as the book will have been either his *Vita Prima S. Francisci* or the abridgement of it which he made at the request of brother Benedict, the *Legenda Chori*.[40] But the merits accrued to the subject of the book, not the author. The other relates to a woman who was punished, through her daughter, for getting on with her normal work

[36] 1 Cel. 128–34, esp. 133. [37] 1 Cel. 135. [38] 1 Cel. 137–8.
[39] Frugoni 1993, pl. 34 and pp. 399–406; Cook 1999, no. 143, pp. 169–71.
[40] 3 Cel. 193, AF X, 328 and n. 8. For the *Legenda Chori*, see AF X, pp. xix–xx, 119–26.

on St Francis' feast day.[41] This, the first punitive miracle to be depicted, represents another, to us distasteful, aspect of cult promotion. The friars were naturally keen that people should venerate their founder; his feast day was an opportunity to stress his merits. In 1256 the Franciscans of Pisa secured from Alexander IV the granting of indulgences to those who visited their church, and confessed, on the feast days of their three chief saints, St Francis, St Anthony and St Clare.[42] Of course those who were drawn by the promise of an indulgence brought profit to the house. But the presence of this scene in the panel is evidence that they were prepared to use the stick as well as the carrot. These miracles were recorded by Celano, not in his *First Life*, but in his *Treatise on the Miracles*, written sometime between 1250 and 1252. They were not however included by St Bonaventure in his *Life*, finished in 1263. It would seem therefore that this panel was painted between c.1252 and c.1266, when Celano's writings were replaced by Bonaventure's.[43] The date can be narrowed a little further. Incentives for the faithful not to work on a feast day but to go to church were being highlighted at Pisa around 1256. In 1265, when Archbishop Frederick Visconti preached in the friars' church at Pisa on St Francis' feast day, he drew attention to the miracles of the saint and to his picture, which his audience could look at.[44] So the panel was there and instilling its messages by then. It is attributed to the school of Giunta Pisano.

THE ASSISI ALTAR PANEL

At Assisi there is another early altar panel, now kept in the Treasury of the Basilica[45] (Colour Plate 3). The proportions are different, but this too has as its centre and dominating feature a full length, frontal image of St Francis, with the stigmata in hands and feet. The gospel he holds is open at the words from St Matthew: 'If you would be perfect, go and sell all that you have and give to the poor' – the text that led to the founding of the Order.[46] There are four miracle scenes, two on each side of him. The subjects are the same as in the Pescia altar panel, but the two on the right show one exorcism and one cripple.

In the first scene, top left, in the top left-hand corner is painted what some scholars have identified as a bird's eye view of Assisi itself. Representation of real and specific, as well as symbolic landscape, townscape and interiors, occurred during the medieval period. Ambrogio Lorenzetti's allegory of Good and Bad Government, in the Palazzo Publico at Siena, painted in the second quarter of the fourteenth century, has been taken as one of the earliest authentic pictures of a city and its contado, though there is undoubtedly a strong conceptual element in it.[47] Artists would use conventional symbols to denote backgrounds and buildings, to set the stage – like props employed in dramatic productions. A hill with trees represented the countryside, as in the scene of Francis preaching to the birds in the Pescia altar panel. An altar with a canopy over it represented the inside of a church; towers, gateways and so forth, outside in the streets

[41] 3 Cel. 103.   [42] Frugoni 1993, p. 400.
[43] See pp. 269, 242–4.   [44] See pp. 223–9, esp. p. 225.
[45] Scarpellini 1980, pp. 34–8; 1982b, pp. 94–9.   [46] Matt. 19. 21; 1 Cel. 24.
[47] For discussion and bibliography, see Skinner 1986; Rubinstein 1997.

of the city, as in the first, second and fourth miracle scenes in the Pescia panel. These were symbols which could be easily read and understood. But there was an increasing tendency towards more concrete and naturalistic representation.

St Francis was intimately connected with Assisi. His sanctity and miracles attracted throngs of pilgrims and secured for the city reputation and prestige, an influx of wealth and influence. Assisi was proud of, and grateful to, St Francis, and indeed quite prepared to make the most of this valuable asset. Francis' life story provided a fund of reminiscence, tied to familiar local surroundings, and the burst of artistic creation it inspired encouraged artists to try to depict scenes from it in the specific places with which they could be associated – even earlier than the famous cycle in the Upper Church.

The first scene in the Assisi altar panel, top left, depicts the first miracle, which took place on the very day of Francis' death. The rather unusual appearance of the shrine is due to the painter's attempt to represent the circumstances faithfully. Francis was carried up from the Portiuncula to a place of greater safety, near the walls of Assisi. His body would have been laid temporarily in a wooden mortuary chest, and it is this which has been portrayed, on legs.[48] The little girl has crawled underneath it; only her head, shoulders and arms are showing. On the left is shown a view of part of a city – the rest is to be imagined continuing beyond the frame. It is walled and perched on a hill, packed with houses, churches, towers. High in the distance is a half-destroyed castle. But is it Assisi? Perhaps the most we can say is that the little city shows features Assisi possessed, and that the miracle illustrated occurred at Assisi.

The miracle scene top right is more conclusive (Colour Plate 4). The altar in it invites comparison with a real and still existing altar. The artist has painted, not a conventional altar, but the high altar of the Lower Church of the Basilica, consecrated in 1253, drawn from the life, with its arches and its row of lamps hanging inside them[49] (Plate 16). The miracle illustrated is an exorcism. A girl from Norcia, near Spoleto, became mentally ill; she mutilated herself with her teeth, and lost the power of speech and the use of her limbs. Her anxious parents brought her to Assisi bound to a pallet on a mule. On New Year's Day, as their daughter lay stretched out before the altar of St Francis while High Mass was being celebrated, she suddenly vomited some filth. Then rising on tiptoe she kissed the altar and, fully freed from all disorder, she exclaimed: 'Praise the Lord and his saint!'[50] This miracle is recorded in Celano's *Treatise on the Miracles* shortly before 1253, the year in which Innocent IV consecrated the altars in the Basilica. This scene, therefore, is a representation of a recent cure at the place where it happened; it depicts the very altar in front of which the young woman, brought by her parents – who are there beside her – was freed from her affliction. It emphasises place, the shrine of the saint. St Francis is not depicted; his power is channelled through the altar in his Basilica. Topographical realism is making its appearance, and some sense of contemporary reporting. But this is an isolated instance, though an exciting one. The argument must not be pressed too far. There is not complete commitment to historical accuracy. The

[48] See pp. 35, 464, 466–7.   [49] Cf. Gardner 1981.

[50] 3 *Cel.* 153, AF X, 318 and nn. The miracle occurred on 1 January, the Feast of the Circumcision, not, as Duffy states (1997, p. 210) at Candlemas, the Feast of the Presentation in the Temple, 2 February.

Plate 16 The high altar in the Lower Church (© www.Assisi.de. Photo Stefan Diller).

same altar, only this time draped with an altar-cloth, appears in the scene below, the healing of the crippled Nicholas of Foligno. He had himself carried to the tomb, and after spending the night there in prayer, was able to return home without a stick.[51] But this was one of the early miracles recorded before Francis' canonisation in 1228, and therefore before the building of the Basilica was begun or the high altar commissioned. It must have occurred while the saint's body rested at St Georgio. But such niceties were irrelevant. Celano had asked: 'What can be denied to him, seeing that the stigmata gives him the appearance of Christ himself . . .? Surely he will be heard . . .?'[52] A purpose of these altar panels was to show in pictures, clearly and vividly and dramatically, the kind of things that could happen here and now. We are surely justified in concluding that this panel was painted at Assisi and for the Basilica. Its function? To blazon before the eyes of the sick and afflicted gathered at the shrine, hoping for a cure, some of

[51] 1 Cel. 129.   [52] 1 Cel. 119.

Francis' notable successes. We might call it a thirteenth-century advertisement. It is the work of an artist painting 'in an unequivocally Pisan style' and is probably slightly later than the Pisa panel.[53] The style is Byzantine in inspiration, as is shown by the gold ground, the decorated bands dividing the scenes, the vignette of a city, the high bulbous cranium of the saint, reminiscent of the ascetics in eastern icons, the intensity of emotion, especially noticeable in the mother in the first miracle scene. Her portrayal is very moving. Even if we did not know the subject, we could appreciate that she is urgently beseeching, praying for some boon.

THE BARDI ALTAR PANEL

An altar panel now in the Bardi chapel at Santa Croce in Florence marks a considerable development, though it has close links with the previous panels[54] (Plate 17). It has a frontal image, with the stigmata in hands and feet, but here it is flanked by far more scenes, twenty in all, and more than two thirds of these represent incidents in Francis' life. The central figure and each episode are framed with a border, decorated with arabesques and foliage. Where they join there are circles with little busts of friars. This layout and content reflect the influence of earlier Byzantine icons, such as, for example, an icon honouring St Catherine herself and an icon of St Nicholas, both dating from the twelfth century, found at the monastery of St Catherine of Alexandria at Mount Sinai (Plate 18). The greater number of scenes, their arrangement round the whole of three sides, and their emphasis on what St Francis did in life – thus more specifically holding him up as a role model to be emulated by those seeking a way of life that will lead them to heaven – link the Bardi panel closely to Byzantine prototypes: more closely than the Tuscan variant represented by the Pescia panel[55] (Plate 15).

The first church built for the Franciscans in Florence was dedicated to the Holy Cross, and their next, begun by 1252, was also so dedicated.[56] It is probable that this altar panel was commissioned for the new church. The Franciscan convent at Pisa had acquired

53 Martin 1996, p. 188. Bughetti argues convincingly that this panel and a closely related panel in the 'magazzino' of the Pinacoteca Vaticana depend upon the Pisa panel in their treatment of the miracles they have in common (apart from the lame man cured in the bath in the Rome panel). In the Rome and Assisi panels, and in the Bardi altar panel, which will be considered next, the scenes are in decorated frames, narrower in the Bardi panel, and the horizontal panels wider in the Rome panel than in the Assisi one. But these form a group, together with the Pistoia panel, unfortunately much damaged by restoration (see p. 181); and they represent a new stylistic form. The buildings, too, in the Rome and Assisi panels, have changed style – they are more slender and elegant, more varied than their Romanesque counterparts in the Pescia and Pisa panels. Although they are not yet Gothic, the Romanesque is well on the road towards it. See Bughetti 1926a, esp. pp. 687–700; Kaftal 1952, 1965; Assisi 1999, pp. 54–9.

54 We do not know where the panel was originally. There is a tradition that it was already in Santa Croce in the thirteenth century, in the earlier church on the same site (see Scarpellini 1982b, p. 117; Goffen 1988, pp. 30 and 104–5 n. 8). It was translated to its present position as the retable to the altar in the Bardi chapel in 1595 (Goffen 1988, pp. 29 and 104 n. 5).

55 Krüger 1992, esp. pp. 119–28; Sevcenko 1999, esp. p. 154. There were Greek painters working in the Dominican church of Santa Maria Novella in Florence, not far from Santa Croce, in the 1250s. When Cimabue was attending the school in Santa Maria Novella, which catered for the novices but also for the sons of Florentine citizens, c.1252–5, according to Vasari, he kept slipping away into the church, where Greek artists were working on frescoes in St Luke's chapel (Meersseman 1946, pp. 180–1). If there were Greeks working in Santa Maria Novella, there were probably Byzantine icons there too.

56 Goffen 1988, pp. 1–4.

Plate 17 The Bardi altar panel, Florence, Santa Croce (© www.Assisi.de. Photo Stefan Diller).

Plate 18 St Catherine icon, from the Monastery of St Catherine, Mount Sinai (Reproduced through the courtesy of the Michigan-Princeton-Alexandria Expedition to Mount Sinai).

its altar panel between c.1252 and 1264.[57] There was rivalry between the two cities, and the Franciscans of Florence maybe wished to have one larger and more elaborate than their Pisan brothers. Its shape and proportions, however, make it possible that it did not function as an altar retable originally, but was intended to be hung on a wall behind a side altar, or on a screen.[58] It would have been paid for by a donor, or donors, but the programme, the content, would have been decided, not by the painter or by the donors, but by the friars of the house, increasingly aware of the value of pictures as teaching aids.[59] The design bears the marks of thoughtful, careful planning and is complex; it can be 'read' in a variety of ways, some of which overlap, and on a variety of levels.[60] It provides ample subject matter for sermons and instruction, from commentaries on individual episodes to a range of wider themes.

The dedication of the church to the Holy Cross may have inspired the increased stress on the closeness of St Francis to Christ. In the central figure Francis raises his right hand in blessing in a gesture identical with Christ's blessing as portrayed in some Byzantine icons. The hem of his habit is artificially raised in two folds above Francis' feet, the better to display their stigmata, and his left foot points downwards to draw attention to the scene below, which portrays his reception of the stigmata.[61] In the border which surrounds him, the inward pointing hands of the friars in the roundels, reinforced by those at the four corners being slightly larger and more emphatic, direct the eye to him.

Fourteen scenes from Francis' life are depicted down the left-hand side of the panel and along the bottom, ranged in roughly chronological sequence, beginning top left. First come what were in fact two episodes, condensed within one frame. His mother releases Francis from the chains his father had imposed, and his father, on his return, reviles her. Immediately below, Francis renounces his father, returning his clothes, and the bishop covers his nakedness with his cloak. Francis then adopts a habit recalling the cross. Next he hears the vital words of the Gospel which revealed to him his future way of life, and is shown in the act of taking off his shoes. Below this, he kneels before Pope Innocent III receiving approval of his Rule. Then come the representation of the crib at Greccio, the preaching to the birds and the preaching before the Sultan. In the centre, below the feet of the image of St Francis, are four scenes, two showing his concern for lambs, one above the other, then the stigmatisation, and below this his public penance for eating flesh during Lent when he was ill (Plate 19). The cycle continues from the bottom right with his appearance to the brothers assembled in chapter at Arles. In the scene immediately above, he washes the feet of lepers and cares for them. Then comes his death, with sick and crippled already gathering, hoping for cure. Above this a conflation of early posthumous miracle scenes, his canonisation, a miracle aboard

[57] See p. 173.
[58] Van Os 1974, p. 121; 1983, p. 334. For the screens in Santa Croce and other Italian churches, see Hall 1970, 1978.
[59] See pp. 302–4 and ch. 9.
[60] It has been extensively studied by a number of scholars. For a wide range of views, see Stein 1976; Moleta 1983, pp. 20–3; Goffen 1988, pp. 29–50, 103–11; Krüger 1992, pp. 119–28; Frugoni 1993, pp. 357–98; Duffy 1997, pp. 214–32.
[61] Moleta 1983, pp. 20–2; Duffy 1997, pp. 215–16.

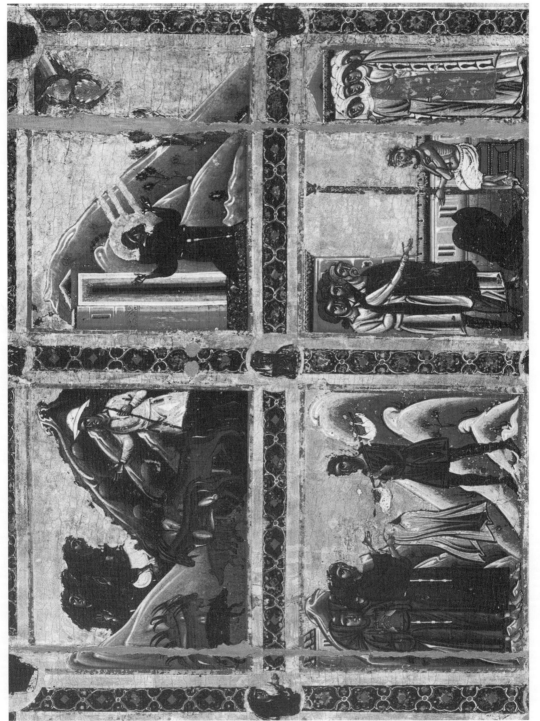

Plate 19 Four scenes from the Bardi altar panel illustrating St Francis' concern for lambs, the stigmata and St Francis doing public penance (© www.Assisi.de. Photo Stefan Diller).

ship, a group of penitents bringing candles to his shrine, and lastly the fourth of the early posthumous miracle scenes.

This is the first surviving major selection of scenes from Francis' life on panel and it shows some interesting and individual features. Some of the scenes chosen for illustration – Francis renouncing his father, the crib at Greccio, the preaching before the Sultan, the appearance at Arles – became popular subjects; but others did not catch on, were rarely reproduced and were replaced by alternative material. The selection of scenes to illustrate, their treatment and content, and their order, can also throw light on the date of this panel.[62]

The illustrations are based on both artistic and literary sources. The artist was aware of the Pescia altar panel, dated 1235, and its associates, and of a panel at Pistoia, which unfortunately cannot be dated as it was profoundly retouched, obscured and confused by a maladroit restoration early in the seventeenth century. The Pistoia panel has four scenes to either side of a full length frontal image of St Francis. The two lower scenes to either side are the same four early posthumous miracles. The two above on the left are St Francis receiving approval of the Rule from the pope, and a scene which has been identified as St Francis preaching.[63] However the general appearance of the scene is not unlike the crib at Greccio in the Bardi panel, and its significance may have been altered by the restoration. The upper two on the right are the stigmatisation and the death of St Francis. The artist of the Bardi panel, as well as seeming to base his design of the crib scene on the Pistoia panel, also used it as the inspiration for his own more developed treatment of the approval of the Rule. His deathbed scene, likewise, shows its influence, though it faces the other way. Immediately next to this, his treatment of two of the early posthumous miracles – the cures of the girl with the dislocated neck and of a demented girl – is a neat conflation of separate scenes in the earlier panels, closest to Pistoia, but with links also to the Pescia panel[64] (Plate 15). The fourth of these miracles – the cure of the lame beggar – is misplaced in the Bardi panel. It should come, like the others, before the canonisation, but for some reason it ends the cycle. Again it depends on both the earlier panels, but is closest to Pistoia. The same miracle also appears, misplaced, between scenes of the crucifix at San Damiano, and the dream of Innocent III, in the St Francis window in the nave of the Upper Church at Assisi. It

---

[62] I laid out my arguments for dating the Bardi panel in lectures I gave in the late 1970s and during the 1980s, but did not publish my results. Several scholars have worked in this field recently, but with two exceptions have dated the panel earlier. Moleta 1983, p. 20, dates it some thirty years after the Pescia panel, i.e. c.1265, but without discussion. In 1997 Eamon Duffy published a paper in which he argues as I do, for a date after 1263 (see esp. Duffy 1997, p. 231). He arrived at his conclusion quite independently: equally, the arguments I present were formulated earlier and are independent of his. Where I have benefited in details of interpretation from his contribution to the subject, I have indicated this in the footnotes. Other scholars have dated the panel as follows: Bughetti 1926a, p. 685 – post 1263; Kaftal 1950, p. 117, no. 6 (errata sheet) – c.1250; Kaftal 1952, col. 385 – c.1240; Stein 1976, esp. p. 294 – 1254–66, probably before 1257; Scarpellini 1982b, pp. 97–8, 117 – 1254–66; Goffen 1988, p. 29 – 1245–50; Frugoni 1993, pp. 206, 339, 386 – 1243; Derbes 1996, pp. 109, 133 – 1240s.

[63] For a discussion of the Pistoia panel and its links with the Bardi panel, see Bughetti 1926a, pp. 664–86 and plates, esp. pls. III, IV, XVIII, XIX and XXII. See also Frugoni 1993, pp. 338–45 and pl. 159.

[64] In both the Pistoia and the Bardi panels the demented girl is fully clothed and stands to the left of the altar. In the Bardi panel the healing of cripples is spread between two scenes: at the deathbed they sit and pray; in the scene above, one stands next to the altar, showing amazement at the demons expelled from the girl, but no doubt also rejoicing in his own ability to stand.

must have had some particular connotations and importance now mysterious to us.[65] The treatment of the preaching to the birds shows no dependence on the Pescia panel. The artist's distinctive design may have been inspired by the text: 'Unto what is the kingdom of God like . . .? It is like a grain of mustard seed, which a man took, and cast into his garden, and it grew, and waxed a great tree; and the fowls of the air lodged in the branches of it' (Luke 13. 18–19). In which case the birds here could represent those destined for heaven, because they hear Francis proclaim the Gospel, good news and salvation. The stigmatisation is differently rendered by the three artists, except that they all portray the seraph as not nailed to a cross. In the Bardi panel Francis is depicted with his arms held open and raised, the first appearance of this *orans* stance, which was to become more common as it had the advantage of making it easier to portray the side wound;[66] though the artist does not avail himself of the opportunity he created (Plate 19).

The literary source for all the scenes in the Pescia and Assisi panels was Celano's *First Life*, written 1228–9. Was the Bardi panel also based on 1 *Celano*, or on St Bonaventure's *Life*, completed in 1263?[67]

One scene has a possible intermediate source. St Francis saving men from shipwreck is first recorded in Celano's *Treatise on the Miracles*. So the Bardi panel can hardly be earlier than c.1252. But this miracle, unlike the two extra ones depicted in the Pisa panel, is included by Bonaventure in his collection, and could have been taken from there.[68]

The scene immediately above it is unusual, because it is the only scene for which there is no specific written source. It shows penitents, naked to the waist, with cords round their necks, bringing candles in their hands to the saint's altar. This would have been a familiar sight. It may represent the fulfilment of the seamen's vow – a thank offering for deliverance – or be simply a general reference to gratitude and penitence. Perhaps a hint to encourage others to follow their example.

The order in which the scenes are displayed is not by itself conclusive. Celano's treatment of Francis' life is basically chronological, Bonaventure's more thematic; but the artist makes his own arrangement. For example, his sequence runs: the crib at Greccio, preaching to the birds, preaching before the Sultan, then, after three intervening scenes, penance for flesh eating and the appearance at Arles. Whereas in 1 *Celano* the stories come in the order: the appearance at Arles, penance for flesh eating, preaching before the Sultan, preaching to the birds, crib at Greccio; and in Bonaventure's *Life*: the appearance at Arles, penance for flesh eating, preaching before the Sultan, crib at Greccio, preaching to the birds.[69] The sequence of three earlier scenes, starting with

---

[65] See pp. 325–6.   [66] Gardner 1993, ch. VI, p. 224.

[67] It has been suggested that there is a close link between the Bardi panel and Julian of Speyer's *Office for St Francis*: cf. Frugoni 1993, p. 389 n. 14.

[68] 3 *Cel.* 85; Bonav., *Miracula*, IV, 5. Frugoni 1993, pp. 380–1, who dates the panel to 1243, argues that this scene is taken not from Celano's *Treatise on the Miracles*, but from an episode in Francis' life, when he became a stowaway on a ship bound for Ancona, and, when the sailors had exhausted their provisions while rowing through a storm, fed them all miraculously throughout the several more days needed to reach port with the food he had received in alms (1 *Cel.* 55). But St Francis is not depicted feeding the sailors, and there is no suggestion that the boat was in danger on that voyage. In 3 *Cel.* 85 the storm threatens to engulf the ship. On the Bardi panel Francis is shown making a gesture of calming the great waves which curl high around the bows and stern, and the mast is broken.

[69] 1 *Cel.* 48, 52, 57, 58, 85–6; Bonav. IV, 10, VI, 2, IX, 7–8, X, 7, XII, 3.

Francis' renunciation of his father before the bishop, is more illuminating. The artist follows Bonaventure's order here. According to Celano, after renouncing his father, Francis spent a few days working in the kitchens of a monastery, then went to live among lepers, serving them (a scene which comes much later in the Bardi panel), and laboured to restore the church of San Damiano. Then he heard the Gospel passage in which Christ instructed his disciples on how they should go out to preach, and consequently took off his shoes. He consequently also designed a tunic for himself. According to Bonaventure, after Francis had given his father back his clothes, the bishop told his servants to provide some, and they brought him a shabby tunic. Francis drew a cross on this with a fragment of chalk. Then come the brief time at the monastery, his stay with the lepers and his care for them, and the restoration of San Damiano, leading up to the hearing of the Gospel passage. But the order is not all. The way the artist represents the middle scene of the three is decisive. The bishop is present. The artist is using Bonaventure's *Life*. However, if he intended to show Francis drawing a cross on the garment with a piece of chalk, he has not made a very good job of it. The central position of the religious habit, standing up stiff and flat in the shape of a cross, with Francis seeming to be laying it out thus with the help of a stick, is very striking. According to Celano, Francis designed for himself a tunic that was the image of the cross. Surely the artist is drawing on 1 *Celano* too for his picture?[70]

This raises a problem. Bonaventure's *Life* was commissioned by the General Chapter of 1257 and written by 1263. The General Chapter of 1266 accepted it as official, and granted it a monopoly, in so far as this was feasible. The friars were ordered to destroy all their copies of earlier *Lives*, and, wherever possible, to recover and suppress such copies as were in circulation outside the Order.[71] Artists were reduced to one official source, St Bonaventure's *Life*. This is the source of the most famous cycle of all, in the Upper Church at Assisi. We can, then, distinguish two periods for the literary sources that provided artists with subject matter: before and after Bonaventure.

But the problem of dating the Bardi panel is finely poised. Bonaventure's *Life* is based upon the earlier sources. Many of the scenes illustrated here could be taken from Celano material as retold by Bonaventure – preaching to the birds, for example, or the crib at Greccio. All the birds are portrayed as lifting their necks and looking attentively at their preacher, and those on the second branch from the top are shown in addition stretching their wings, conforming to reactions ascribed to them by both Celano and Bonaventure in virtually identical wording.[72] In the crib scene painterly requirements dictated one departure from the written sources. Hay was provided, and an ox and ass led in, but Francis did not put an image of baby Jesus on the hay. Only the nobleman, John of Greccio, who had prepared the stage according to Francis' instructions saw a vision of a child lying in the manger.[73] A child wrapped in swaddling clothes, as in scenes of the Nativity, has been painted in to complete the picture and make the

---

[70] 1 *Cel.* 22. For the whole sequence, see 1 *Cel.* 15–22; Bonav. II, 4 to III, 1.

[71] See p. 244.   [72] 1 *Cel.* 58; Bonav. XII, 3.

[73] 1 *Cel.* 84–6; Bonav. X, 7. John is named as the nobleman who prepared the crib in 1 *Cel.* 84, and as the individual who was vouchsafed a vision in Bonav. X, 7. Duffy 1997, p. 223, is mistaken in saying that Francis used a doll: the intensity of devotion Francis succeeded in evoking by staging this scene for a lay audience resulted in John seeing a child lying in the hay.

message clear. Three sermons are encapsulated here in one small frame. Francis, in the robes of a deacon, is censing the book before reading the appointed Gospel from it, after which he will preach on the birth of the baby Jesus in poverty in Bethlehem.[74] But the painting, though it indicates that this sequence will take place, is not stressing the transient spoken sermon, but the memorable enacted sermon, which captured the imagination of its audience, was recorded, and enhanced a tradition of dramatic representations of the Gospel story.[75] The painting itself is a visual sermon, on the Nativity, and on Francis' success in arousing the hearts of men and women to ponder the human experiences of Jesus.

In the preaching before the Sultan the artist could have followed the Celano version. He did not illustrate the great fire that became a popular ingredient in the scene with later artists. It was Bonaventure who introduced the detail of how Francis offered to prove the truth of the Christian faith by going through fire with the priests of Islam.[76] But he could have been using Bonaventure without featuring the fire. The Order was actively engaged in the mission field beyond the frontiers of Christendom. Before this picture was painted, the friars in Florence will have been aware of the accounts written by John of Pianocarpine, after his return in 1247, of the mission he had been sent on by Innocent IV in 1246, which led him and a Polish friar to undertake an exhausting journey of over 3000 miles through Tartar held territory to reach the court of the Great Khan. The picture may have made them spare a thought too for another friar after Francis' own heart. William of Rubruk and Bartholomew of Cremona were sent on another mission to Mongolia in 1253. They first visited a Mongol prince, Sartak, who had been reported to be a Christian but turned out not to be. They were sent on to the court of Mangu Khan, in the Mongolian capital. Here brother William, in his worn habit, was summoned before the Khan. He was treated courteously – as Francis had been by el-Kamil, the Sultan of Egypt – and the two discussed their faiths through an interpreter. But, like the Sultan, the Khan listened, but was impervious to the friar's evangelistic pleadings, and sent him away. In his *Itinerarium*, William ended his description of this deeply Franciscan encounter with the wistful words: 'If I had had the power of working miracles, like Moses, he might have humbled himself.'[77]

Below Francis' right foot are two scenes illustrating his concern for lambs (Plate 19). This is what Bonaventure says on the matter: 'He frequently redeemed lambs which were being led to slaughter, in memory of that most gentle lamb who wished to be led to slaughter for the redemption of sinners.' That is all; a rather bald summary of three chapters in Celano. Celano tells the stories thus, the upper one first. Once

[74] Duffy 1997, p. 223. Moleta 1983, p. 22, states that St Francis was made a deacon when the Rule was approved by Innocent III, i.e. in 1210. Francis and his companions received tonsures and permission to preach repentance then, but this did not constitute ordination. We have no evidence for the date when he was ordained deacon. The detailed evidence is laid out in C. Brooke 1989b, p. 65 and nn.; cf. ibid. pp. 84–5.

[75] The Franciscans were instrumental in promoting such dramas and making them available to the people (instead of just to religious communities) as part of their drive to foster orthodox education among the laity. I owe this point to Dr Johannes Tripps.

[76] 1 Cel. 57; Bonav. IX, 7–9.

[77] For John of Pianocarpine, see Moorman 1968, pp. 232–3 and nn.; Salimbene, H, pp. 206–7, 213; S, I, 297–8; for William of Rubruk, Moorman 1968, pp. 234–5 and nn.

when St Francis was travelling with brother Paul, Minister of the March of Ancona, he saw a shepherd minding a flock of goats. Among the goats was one little lamb. Francis was touched, reminded of how Christ walked meekly and humbly among the pharisees and chief priests. He bought the lamb – a merchant conveniently passing and providing the price, as Francis would never touch money himself – and gave it to some nuns, who cared for it and later sent Francis a habit made from its wool. In the picture Francis is holding the white lamb. Artistic licence has added a couple of pigs to the goats.[78] In the second story, below, Francis and the same companion, brother Paul, met a man carrying two lambs bound over his shoulder, on his way to market. Francis asked what would happen to them and was bluntly told they would be bought, killed and eaten. Francis purchased the lambs by handing over an expensive cloak – in the centre foreground – which had been lent him to keep him warm. Loans to Francis were seldom returned, but were usually donated to a good cause. His friends and admirers learned to expect it. There can be no doubt that these two pictures are based on Celano, not on Bonaventure.

Thus the artist drew his subject matter from both Celano's *First Life* and Bonaventure's *Life*. How could this come about? Santa Croce was an important convent; it was one of the Order's provincial study centres.[79] The friars of Florence could hardly have allowed an artist to study 1 *Celano* after it had been officially suppressed.[80] The answer enables us to date this panel with some precision. When Bonaventure had completed his *Life* he prepared thirty-four copies, one for each province, ready for the General Chapter which was held at Whitsun, 1263, at Pisa. In 1266 at the Whitsun General Chapter, held at Paris, it was determined that each friary should have its own copy of the new *Life* and that all earlier *Lives* should be destroyed.[81] So there was a space of three years when the

---

[78] Bonav. VIII, 6; 1 *Cel.* 77–9. Duffy 1997, p. 225, suggests a thought connection with the story Bonaventure takes from 2 *Cel.* 111, which he tells immediately after his single sentence on the lambs, of the savage sow who bit and killed a new born lamb and whom Francis cursed. But for this incident to be consciously recalled in the picture there should be one sow, and it would introduce a jarring note and blur the message. Frugoni 1993, p. 392 n. 60, also refers to the sow who killed a lamb, arguing (pp. 370–2) that the presence of the malevolent pigs emphasises the bad company in which Francis found the lamb; and she suggests that the scene is intended to recall the Last Judgement. I would interpret it as a pastoral scene with the single, central lamb as a symbol of light and redemption.

[79] Gratien 1928, pp. 133–4. The Order had *studia generalia* at Bologna, Paris, Padua and Oxford. On the terminology see Bihl 1941, p. 72 and n., *Narb.* IV, 12, 16.

[80] Duffy 1997, pp. 231–2, suggests 'that the work of synthesis evident in the panel is the product of fairly sophisticated reflection, and so is unlikely to have been done while the ink was still wet on Bonaventure's pages'. But this is to underestimate the intelligence of the highly educated academics within the community. He also suggests (ibid. p. 232) that 'Santa Croce, with a strongly observant presence among the brethren, might have retained knowledge and perhaps an actual text of Celano's *Vitae* for some years after the official suppression.' There was certainly a strongly observant presence there in the late 1280s: Peter John Olivi was lector to the friars in Florence from 1287–9, and Ubertino was there in the same period (Burr 2001, pp. 47, 62). But the circumstances of the mid-1280s did not pertain twenty years earlier. Artists worked from texts, and the suggestion that the guardian of the convent and other responsible friars would be prepared deliberately to flout one of the Order's statutes, and show an artist a banned book, seems to me highly improbable. Considering that 1 *Celano* was the main *Life* of Francis available between 1228 and the 1260s, surviving manuscripts are few: twenty are listed in *AF* X, pp. ix–xiii, but of these four are lost and four only contain fragments; and only one complete MS and tiny fragments survive in Italian MSS. The majority of the MSS are in northern libraries, and, where the provenance is known, from monastic or secular libraries more often than from friars' convents.

[81] *AF* X, p. lxxii; and see p. 244.

old and the new could be both available on an equal footing, as it were. Santa Croce was the leading house in Tuscany, and Florence is not far from Pisa; as a study centre it is likely to have got access to the Pisan copy of the new *Life* promptly. The Bardi panel was probably painted after Bonaventure's *Life* was launched at Pisa at Whitsun 1263, and before the ruling of the Paris General Chapter at Whitsun 1266, which was to put 1 *Celano* effectively out of circulation, reached Florence.

Between the angels above St Francis' head hangs a scroll held by a hand from heaven, with the message: 'Listen to this man, who presents the teachings of life.'[82] The words, though not a direct quotation, evoke the scene at the Transfiguration, when out of the cloud came a voice, saying: 'This is my beloved Son; listen to him' (Mark 9. 7; Matt. 17. 5).[83] The scroll is proclaiming that St Francis' way of life is the Christian way of life and has divine approval and endorsement. The choice of text explains why so many scenes from Francis' life were displayed. Up to now the Order had concentrated upon putting across the message: 'Listen to this man' through the written word. Celano had been commissioned to write books three times within three decades; reminiscences had been sought, in writing, from friars who had known St Francis; Bonaventure, as Minister General, had officially sifted through all existing material and written his definitive *Life*. Here for the first time members of the Order are trying out the possibilities of a new medium, and presenting Francis' imitation of Christ in paint. What was the message the friars of Santa Croce wished to convey, to their own community, and to the faithful thronging to their church? What particular aspects were highlighted, at this time, during St Bonaventure's Generalate, when there was, as yet, no established norm? The early scenes stress Francis' close links with the Church's hierarchy. All the five scenes that flank St Francis on the viewer's left, from shoulder to foot, illustrate some aspect of this. The bishop of Assisi supports him in the first and second of these scenes; the officiating priest is central in the third and fifth; the pope approves the Rule in the fourth. In a central position opposite on the right, the pope and three cardinals conduct the canonisation ceremony, attended by other ecclesiastics and friars. The message is clear. Francis is an official saint of the Church, and his Order enjoys the Church's blessing.

Scenes along the bottom of the panel show aspects of Francis' ministry and teaching: preaching to the birds and to the infidel, rescuing lambs, setting an example of asceticism and integrity, tending lepers – all supremely characteristic – and his closeness to Christ and Christ-like demeanour. In some scenes these images are intricately interwoven.

Three of these scenes exhibit points of particular interest. The vision brother Monaldo had of Francis appearing at the chapter at Arles while St Anthony was preaching is the only instance, apart from the stigmatisation, of a 'miraculous' element in scenes of the living Francis; later cycles were to increase the number of this genre, most notably the cycle in the Upper Church. Why did the friars in Florence select this episode? Not all its significance is immediately obvious. It links together, on an intellectual level,

---

[82] 'Hunc exaudite perhibentem dogmata vite.' Cf. Frugoni 1993, pp. 357–9.
[83] Krüger 1992, p. 123.

the stigmatisation (diagonally to its left) and Santa Croce. While a Provincial Chapter is taking place at Arles, St Anthony preaches on the text: 'Jesus of Nazareth, the King of the Jews' (John 19. 19), the title written by Pilate and nailed to the Cross. The most appropriate occasion for a sermon on this theme is the Feast of the Exaltation of the Holy Cross, 14 September – one of the two major patronal festivals for Santa Croce, and a likely time of year for holding a Provincial Chapter.[84] While on La Verna, in 1224, fasting from the Feast of the Assumption of the blessed Virgin Mary to the Feast of St Michael – that is, from 15 August to 29 September – Francis saw in a vision a seraph fixed to a cross and received on his body the impression of Christ's stigmata. Bonaventure added a detail to Celano's account: it was in the morning, about the time of the Feast of the Exaltation of the Holy Cross.[85] Maybe it was the receipt of this new information which prompted the first painting of this scene, with its suggestion that on the day he received the stigmata St Francis was present in the spirit in Arles while St Anthony preached on the Holy Cross, at Santa Croce, in Florence. John Bonelli, the Provincial Minister of Provence who summoned the Chapter at Arles, came from Florence. Celano provided the details of his name and origin; they were omitted by Bonaventure, so within a few years knowledge of him would fade. It was a favourable moment when all the sources could be utilised.

In the leper scene – one of those not represented elsewhere – there are some striking features which reflect early traditions about St Francis, not any particular source. Francis is shown twice. On the left he is nursing a leper on his knee, like a mother her child. The image of the friar as mother was fostered by Francis. It is written into the Rule that the friars, being spiritual brothers, should love and nourish each other even more than a mother loves and nourishes her son. His *Rule given for hermitages* restricted the numbers of those living in hermitages to three or four. Two were to assume the role of mothers, and live the life of Martha, two (or one), the role of sons, and live the life of Mary. When Francis himself sent brother Leo a letter, prompted by all the discussion they had had together on the road, he wrote: 'I say this to you, my son, as a mother.'[86] Celano records that brother Elias could exert influence on Francis and persuade him to take medical advice for his eye illness because Francis had chosen Elias to stand in the place of a mother to himself, and had made him father to the other brethren. On another occasion Celano recounts how brother Pacifico called Francis 'mother dearest . . . dearest mother', when he wanted to manipulate him.[87] The lepers look remarkably infectious; one is scratching a sore on his leg. The ghostly object just left of centre is a towel Francis has been using now hanging up to dry. At the Last Supper Christ had taken a towel and poured water into a basin and washed the disciples' feet,

---

[84] I Cel. 48; Bonav. IV, 10. The other major festival, the Invention of the Holy Cross, falls on 3 May. The Franciscans held their General Chapters at Whitsun, and the Provincial Ministers might hold one Provincial Chapter after it was over, later in the same year (*Regula bullata*, c. 8, Esser 1976, p. 369). Frugoni's use of this scene and the sermon to date the Bardi panel to 1243 (Frugoni 1993, p. 386) is too ingenious, and her argument is invalidated by her refusal to admit that the artist knew and used Bonaventure's *Legenda Maior*.

[85] 1 Cel. 94; Bonav. XIII, 3.

[86] *Regula bullata*, c. 6, Esser 1976, p. 369; *Regula pro eremitoriis data*, Esser 1976, p. 409; *Epistola ad fratrem Leonem*, Esser 1976, p. 218, quoted SL 9.

[87] 1 Cel. 98; 2 Cel. 137.

and had told them to follow His example (John 13. 4–15). Over the centuries monks and princes had washed the feet of the poor, particularly on Maundy Thursday, in imitation of Christ, so Francis' act of humility must be seen as conforming to a long tradition. The way the scene is depicted, with Francis girt with a towel and a leper seated with his feet in a basin of water, while a couple more wait their turn, recalls the words of St John's Gospel.[88]

The scene below the stigmata is remarkable (Plate 19). The story, concerning Francis' abhorrence of hypocrisy, originated in 1 *Celano*, but was much elaborated by Bonaventure.[89] The picture is based on Bonaventure's version, but the artist has treated his chosen source somewhat cavalierly in order to make a further, and different, point. Francis had been ill, and he wanted people to know that because of this he had eaten a little meat. He must be proclaimed a glutton! According to Bonaventure, he summoned the people of Assisi to the main piazza. Then he ordered the friars to lead him, in the view of all, with a rope round his neck and naked except for his pants, to the stone on which malefactors were punished. On this stone, although it was bitterly cold and he was still feverish, he preached a sermon with great fervour. The artist has depicted Francis naked except for his pants, with a rope round his neck. To either side of him are grouped the people of Assisi, the women on the right (Francis' left), the men on the left (Francis' right). But he is not standing on a malefactor's stone and preaching to them. Instead he is seated on a red stool: the other end of the rope is tied to the top of a slender column and one of his hands is chained to the column. The leading man holds out his right arm, pointing to Francis. Any further significance of his gesture is not clear, but he could have just thrown down Francis' habit, which is between them; he could be remonstrating, even deriding. For it is clear that the design of the picture is intended to make the viewer connect this scene with representations of the mocking or the flagellation of Christ, tied to a pillar.[90] It is the earliest portrayal in art of the theme of the conformity of Francis' life to that of Christ beyond what was warranted by the facts; a theme the Order was increasingly to emphasise.

The four central scenes along the bottom of the panel create yet another unit of thought-provoking imagery in this amazingly richly textured visual presentation (Plate 19). Francis loved lambs, because they symbolise Christ. 'He was led as a sheep to the slaughter; and like a lamb dumb before his shearer, so opened he not his mouth' (Acts 8. 32). The two scenes featuring lambs are there to call to mind Christ's Passion; and they lead on to the scene recalling the mocking of Christ at the pillar, and culminate in the stigmatisation. Francis is shown entering into and sharing in Christ's agony. As we look, 'our eye will rise to the central figure, drawn upwards by the U-shaped sequence of the four scenes carefully chosen and arranged to fill the space below his feet. The

[88] In the *Regula non bullata*, c. 6, Esser 1976, p. 382, the friars are exhorted to wash one another's feet (John 13. 14).

[89] 1 *Cel.* 52; Bonav. VI, 2. It also occurs, in a fuller form than in 1 *Cel.* 52, in SL 39; but this version would not have been available in the mid-thirteenth century as it was not incorporated by Celano in 2 *Celano*. Celano specifies chicken; Bonaventure renders this simply 'meat'.

[90] As is noted in Moleta 1983, p. 22. Derbes 1996, pp. 107–10, 132–4, suggested a further layer of meaning, seeing a reference to scenes of the mocking of Job. The likeness of St Francis to Job as well as to Christ was a theme developed by St Bonaventure, who also stressed St Francis' humility, a virtue exemplified in this scene.

entire narrative on the Bardi panel, down the left and up the right, is crystalized in the Passion sequence at the lower center of the panel.'[91] Celano had written: 'In actual fact the venerable father was marked in the five parts of the body, with the signs of the passion and the cross, as if he had hung on the cross, with the Son of God'; and: the stigmata give him the appearance of Christ himself, who 'is co-equal with the Father'.[92] Bonaventure wrote: 'the seal of the likeness of the living . . . God, which was marked on his body, confirms it with the impregnable testimony of truth'; and: 'the angelic man Francis came down from the mountain, bearing on him the effigy of the crucified, not fashioned by a craftsman's hand in stone or wood, but scored on the parts of his body by the finger of the living God'.[93] Hard on the heels of Bonaventure's *Life* we have here its complement, the work of an artist painted on wood – a much more developed and self-conscious image than the previous panels. Some recent scholars have claimed that we are seeing here what amounts to a new image: 'the fingers of his right hand impart a blessing and in this more conventional gesture he takes on the mantle of the second Christ intended for him by Bonaventure'. And: 'There can be little doubt that this central image presents us with an enormously high doctrine about Francis as "Alter Christus", a second Christ.'[94] But the central image in the Bardi panel represents one of many stages in a steady progression. The side wound is not shown, which links this image to those of the past. Fully explicit identification of Francis as a second Christ was not realised until propounded in legends circulating in the early fourteenth century.[95] But the typological legends of the fourteenth century grew out of Bonaventure's interpretation of the stigmatisation and its significance; as Bonaventure's grew out of 1 *Celano*. The germ of the image was there from the start.

The deathbed scene, with the sick assembling for cure, the posthumous miracles, the canonisation, the penitents offering candles at the shrine, complete the message, proclaiming the efficacy of the saint's intervention and the popularity of his cult.

Why did the friars at Florence choose to have a panel which so emphatically proclaimed God's and the Church's approval of Francis and his Order? Partly this can be explained by natural pride in their founder and in the continuing work and mission he inaugurated; partly by a desire to record, honour, instruct, advertise. But partly, too, it has a defensive purpose. The very success of the mendicants had caused their Order, and the Order of Preachers, to come under attack. Some secular clergy had become jealous and hostile, but the most fundamental attack was coming from an academic

---

[91] Moleta 1983, p. 22. Frugoni 1993, pp. 382–5, groups the scenes differently: six down the left side, ending with the crib at Greccio, as 1 Cel. 84–7 form the end of Book I; the bottom eight on a sort of predella, divided in the middle, the left-hand four showing Francis' adhesion to Christ in word and example, the right-hand four showing scenes of the Passion (here her matching of the Appearance at Arles with the Last Supper seems far-fetched); six up the right side, beginning with Francis' death, as does 1 Cel. 88, the beginning of Book II. Duffy 1997, p. 218, proposes the following: 'the panel . . . is . . . divided up into five sets of four scenes, thematically rather than chronologically arranged. The fivefold arrangement is almost certainly another reference to Francis' stigmata, a re-emphasis of the *Alter Christus* theme of the central figure. The themes of the five groups are, in order: (A) renunciation of the world and of property (B) mission to preach (C) passion (D) Francis' loving care for his own and (E) canonisation and cult.'
[92] 1 Cel. 90, 119.   [93] Bonav., Prologus 2; XIII, 5.
[94] Cf. Moleta 1983, p. 20; Duffy 1997, p. 216.
[95] Stanislao da Campagnola 1971, pp. 202–5; Van Os 1974, pp. 115–16.

quarter, the university of Paris, led by one of its Masters, William of St Amour. William sought to undermine the ideals and principles on which the mendicant way of life was based. To him, the mendicants were false apostles, forerunners of Antichrist. In 1255 he had published his *Tractatus brevis*, arguing that Christ had not taught that total renunciation of all property was necessary for perfection, and that, although voluntary poverty was laudable, begging was not, and the friars should earn their keep, preferably by manual labour. William's arguments were challenged by Bonaventure in his lectures in the Franciscans' *studium generale* in Paris; and the tract was examined by a committee of cardinals, condemned by papal bull, and burnt on 5 October 1256. In August 1257 the king, St Louis, banished William from France, at the instance of Alexander IV, but attacks on the friars were continued by other secular Masters throughout the 1260s and beyond. In 1269 Gerard of Abbeville mounted a powerful critique of the whole concept of evangelical poverty. The leading theologians of both Orders felt obliged to defend the friars' way of life.[96] The Bardi panel was intended to boost the morale of the community, as well as to edify, inform and enhance the devotion of the faithful to St Francis.

Some scholars who have argued for an earlier dating of the Bardi panel have coupled this with an assumption that the programme presented by the panel seeks to put across a message associated with a particular grouping of opinion within the Order. Stein suggests that it was commissioned while the 'Spiritual' John of Parma was Minister General (1247–57), and that the reason why some of the scenes depicted in it, such as St Francis taking off his shoes after hearing the Gospel reading, and the two recording his concern for lambs, were not subsequently repeated was because they could be interpreted as showing a 'Spiritual' bias.[97] Frugoni too argues that the Bardi panel portrays the Francis of the *zelanti*, the zealots, the forerunners of the Spirituals.[98] Both are tempted to read more into an individual scene than it can properly sustain. Stein detects the influence of St Francis' original companions and their followers in the way in which the Crib at Greccio is portrayed; and Frugoni claims that the scene showing the Chapter at Arles (which took place in 1224) was intended to record the glorious early days.[99] Goffen heads her chapter 'The Bardi Dossal: Celano's Francis', not simply because of her contention that three of his books – the two *Lives of St Francis* and the *Treatise on Miracles* – were the source for its narrative scenes, but, equally important, the way in which these events were depicted was permeated by his distinctive interpretation. Celano's Francis was 'the personification of the Spiritual cause' and moreover at the time they were being painted, 'the Spirituals were influential, if not ascendant, in Santa Croce'.[100] The Celano she is thinking of, who made himself the mouthpiece of 'those who were with' St Francis, was the author of 2 *Celano*; 1 *Celano*, commissioned by Gregory IX, and the *Treatise on Miracles* were used as sources for the Bardi panel, but

---

[96] Thomas Aquinas replied with *De perfectione vitae spiritualis*, Bonaventure with *Apologia pauperum* and John Pecham with *Tractatus pauperis*: Gratien 1928, pp. 216, 218–20, 255–62; Moorman 1968, pp. 128–30.

[97] Stein 1976, pp. 294–5.

[98] Frugoni 1993, pp. 357–98. The running head of her section on the Bardi reads: 'La tavola Bardi, Francesco degli zelanti'.

[99] Stein 1976, p. 281; Frugoni 1993, p. 386.   [100] Goffen 1988, pp. xvi, 28–9, 50.

there is no evidence that 2 *Celano* was used at all.[101] There was a Spiritual presence at Santa Croce in the late 1280s. Olivi was lector there from 1287 to 1289 and Ubertino da Casale was there at the same time. By this date there were two opposing factions within the Order, to which the party labels Spiritual and Conventual could be applied, but these had not emerged as coherent forces until after St Bonaventure's death.[102] There were occasional sporadic and isolated outbursts of unrest. There is no record of Santa Croce's sympathies at an earlier date. There was discontent in the March of Ancona in the 1270s. There had been trouble there in the 1240s; the brothers had rebelled against their Provincial Minister, Crescentius of Jesi. When he was elected Minister General in 1244, Crescentius made a complaint against them in General Chapter 'to those who had zeal for the Order'.[103] 'Zeal for the Order' was not necessarily the prerogative of one group. Eccleston applies it here to the official element – membership of General Chapter was restricted at this date to the Provincial Ministers and one custodian and one elected representative from each province:[104] at least two-thirds of its members were therefore officials, charged with a concern to uphold discipline and obedience, matters on which St Francis himself had maintained a firm line. Angelo Clareno, however, writing c.1323–6, characterised the rebels as friars troubled in conscience by what they regarded as a flood of evils and relaxations; who consulted some of St Francis' companions who were still alive before attempting to appeal to the pope; and whose punishment he highlighted as the 'third tribulation' suffered by those friars zealous to preserve the obligations of the Rule intact.[105] It is inherently implausible to suppose that friars such as these would have sought to further their cause by sponsoring an altar panel such as the Bardi. And on the practical level the creation of such a panel was an exceedingly expensive undertaking, requiring costly pigments and a great deal of gold. It would have been against their principles and beyond their means. It is misleading to view the narrative scenes of the Bardi panel in a polemical context, a context which did not seriously exist until after St Bonaventure's time. To say with Goffen that 'this is Celano's Saint Francis' is a partial statement; as is Duffy's 'this is Bonaventure's Francis, not Celano's', though he quite rightly qualifies this elsewhere.[106] Stein, Goffen and Frugoni make a valid point when they stress Celano's importance as a source. Apart from one scene of impending shipwreck, all the information culled from him is from his *First Life*. In the years 1263–6 1 *Celano* was still a revered source and one with which the Friars Minor would have been thoroughly familiar. Their understanding of their founder, at this date, was firmly grounded in Celano's words and 'spin'. St Bonaventure's *Life* was the latest; and they made use of it, but they felt no compulsion to give it priority. This is best illustrated in the portrayal of two scenes. For the rendering of St Francis preaching before the Sultan, they chose 1 *Celano*, preferring genuine missionary endeavour to legendary histrionics. And, extremely interestingly, for the stigmatisation scene, they chose to retain a rendering of Celano's seraph as depicted in the Pescia panel rather than opt for Bonaventure's more explicit gloss.[107]

---

[101] See p. 138.   [102] Burr 2001, esp. pp. 11–12, 39–41, 43–65; and see pp. 185 note 80, 251.
[103] Eccleston, p. 72.   [104] Brooke 1959, p. 237.   [105] *ALKG* 11, 256–61.
[106] Goffen 1988, p. 50; Duffy 1997, pp. 221, 230–1.   [107] Stein 1976, p. 286.

My dating of the panel to a small window of opportunity in 1263–6 may serve to explain why there have been such widely differing and apparently contradictory interpretations of its message.

MATTHEW PARIS

These early Franciscan altar panels are the work of professional artists. They would have been commissioned by the friars themselves, or by benefactors. But there were artists within the Order. Brother William, an Englishman, who had been a companion of St Francis, was an artist. If he ever employed his talent to portray St Francis, his portrait has not survived; but his friend Matthew Paris, a monk of the Benedictine abbey of St Albans, valued and preserved William's remarkable drawing of the Christ of the Apocalypse.[108] Matthew Paris took the religious habit at St Albans on 21 January 1217 and died in June 1259. He was an accomplished historian and artist. His *Chronica Maiora* took the form of a revised edition and continuation of the *Flores Historiarum*,[109] which began with the Creation, written by his predecessor Roger of Wendover, who died on 6 May 1236. Matthew's original manuscript survives. It is in three parts, of which the second, spanning the years 1189–1253, is relevant to us. It is almost entirely in Matthew's hand, and was written between 1240 and 1250. His own personal contribution starts in the mid-1230s.[110] The account of St Francis occurs under the year 1227. So the text is a copy, slightly adapted, of Roger of Wendover's work. In the margin Matthew penned two drawings of St Francis. He chose for illustration the two most favoured subjects, the preaching to the birds and the stigmata.

After stating that 'About this time [1227] Francis . . . founder of the Order of Minors, began to coruscate with miracles in the city of Assisi', Roger gives details of his conversion and way of life – how he despised his paternal inheritance, put on a cowl and a hairshirt, took off his shoes and mortified his body with vigils and fasts. He chose 'spontaneous poverty'; gave orders that the friars were to have no property at all, and were only to eat the earthly food that was offered to them in alms. If after their 'most meagre meal' there was anything left over, it was all to be given to the poor, reserving nothing for the morrow. Francis slept clothed. He lay on a rush mat and put a stone as a pillow for his head. Francis drew up a Rule which he took to Pope Innocent III in Rome for his approval; and this enshrined his 'saving purpose' – which is to this day most strenuously observed by the brothers.[111] This brief sketch shows remarkable insight into essential principles of the Franciscan way of life. It gives vivid examples of voluntary poverty as lived; and, though the Gospel is not mentioned, it describes how the Minors followed it to the letter, eating what was set before them (Luke 10. 8) and taking no thought for the morrow (Matt. 6. 34). It also provides a glowing testimony of how this new religious Order was regarded when it first arrived and in the early

[108] Little 1914a, pp. 1–8 and pl. IV; Brieger 1957, pl. 55a. For brother William, see p. 74 and Plate 32.
[109] Not to be confused with Matthew's own *Flores Historiarum*, Luard 1890; cf. Vaughan 1958, pp. 36–41 and ch. 6.
[110] Corpus Christi College, Cambridge, MS 16; see Vaughan 1958, pp. 1, 11, 49, 59–61.
[111] Luard 1872–83, III, 131.

years thereafter by a monk of an older Order.[112] It is independent corroboration of Eccleston's witness – which may have been partial, he being an English Friar Minor – to the fervour of the English province. Eccleston entitles one of his chapters 'On the purity of the early friars' (c. 5), and stresses, for example, how keen they were on the observance of the Rule and the integrity of its text, and how they went barefoot even in bitter cold and deep mud.[113]

What were Roger's sources? He ends his piece on Francis with his canonisation and the institution of his feast day, so he wrote after October 1228, but probably not long after, as his work is in the form of annals. He shows no knowledge of 1 *Celano*, and this is not surprising as the probability is that he was writing about the same time as Celano, or at any rate before the *First Life* became available in England.[114] His information would have been oral, coming from the friars themselves. They had arrived to establish a province in England in September 1224 and had acquired places in London and in Oxford by the end of that year. They did not set up a house in St Albans; but members of the Order will have visited the abbey from time to time when travelling, or when attached to the royal household or a noble household, such as that of the justiciar Hubert de Burgh, on their visits.[115]

Roger's account of Francis' adventures in Rome when seeking papal approval for his Rule shares certain key features with the Order's own versions: Innocent III did not immediately agree, thinking the proposed way of life too arduous and impossible to perform, but in a second interview he was persuaded, and did approve the Rule and give Francis and his friars permission to preach.[116] Otherwise it is distinct, and provides a totally different setting for the preaching to the birds. Roger first describes Francis' appearance: his uncouth habit, despicable face, long beard, unkempt hair and black drooping eyebrows created a bad impression.[117] The pope despised him and dismissed him rudely, telling him to go and find some pigs, as he was more fitted to consort with them than with men. 'Roll with them in the slough, give them a rule devised by you for them, and try out the office of your preaching on them.' Francis humbly obeyed – the story faithfully reflects Francis' characteristically eccentric way of getting round those in authority – and returning to the pope covered in filth, told him: 'I have done what you ordered. I beg you now to hear my petition.' The pope felt ashamed, and conceded, and blessed him. Thus endorsed, Francis began at once to preach the Gospel to the people of Rome, but the Romans were 'the enemies of all righteousness' and refused to listen to the man of God. So after some days spent in fruitless endeavour he went out of the city, and in the suburbs found ravens, kites and magpies sitting on carrion, while many other birds were flying in the air. He summoned them with the words: 'I order you in the name of Jesus Christ whom the Jews crucified, whose preaching the

[112] Cf. the welcome recorded by Eccleston: the Benedictines of Fécamp escorted the first Franciscan mission to England across the Channel, and the Benedictines of Christ Church, Canterbury, welcomed them on their arrival: Eccleston, p. 6. Cf. pp. 161–2.

[113] Eccleston, pp. 25–6, 71, 27; cf. also ibid. p. 98.

[114] Luard 1872–83, III, 135. Celano was commissioned to write in 1228 and presented his book to the pope in February 1229: see p. 39.

[115] See Eccleston, p. 14; Vaughan 1958, pp. 12–13. Henry III stayed for five days in 1225.

[116] Luard 1872–83, III, 132–3; see 2 *Cel.* 16–17; 3 *Soc.* 47–52.

[117] Cf. 1 *Cel.* 83 (also, more briefly, SL 103); Brooke 1967, pp. 182–3; and pp. 160–1.

wretched Romans have despised, that you come to me and hear the word of God, in the name of Him who created you and rescued you from the waters of the flood in Noah's Ark.'[118] The birds all crowded round him, fell silent at his bidding, and listened to his preaching for half the day, not moving from the spot, with their eyes fixed on his face. People going to and from the city noticed this phenomenon, particularly as it was repeated three days running. The Romans were now ready to hear him and he was welcomed back into the city with honour.

The margins of the Corpus manuscript are wide. Matthew Paris made use of them, where he considered it appropriate, to include further information, explanation or comment, and to embellish the text with illustrations. His method, almost always, was to make a rough sketch first in lead pencil, and then work it up in a dark brownish-black ink with bold and accurate rapid strokes; some he enhanced with delicate washes, usually of pale green, ochre or brown, to which he added stronger ink outlines and fine detail.[119] On folio 70 verso (formerly 66v) he has penned one of the earliest known representations of St Francis preaching to the birds. It is monochrome, touched up with a soft green wash on the rough ground and stylised tree[120] (Plate 20). The rubric above Francis' head reads: 'Spurned by the city of Rome St Francis sows divine seeds of his sermon to a flock of birds.'[121] In the confined space in front of him, squeezed into four lines of smaller writing, Matthew gives the gist of his sermon: 'Hail birds! Praise your Creator, who feeds you and clothes you with feathers; you do not toil nor spin, plough nor sow, nor gather into barns' (Luke 12. 24, 27). This shows that Matthew had access to Celano's *First Life*: the content is based on 1 *Celano* 58. His further note, below the drawing, confirms this: 'This occurred while he was travelling through the valley of Spoleto, not only concerning doves, ravens or hooded crows, but vultures and birds of prey.' Here he is correcting the rubric and Roger of Wendover's text – Francis preached to the birds not in Rome but in the valley of Spoleto; but he is also emending Celano's, expanding his list of birds to include more feasters on carrion. Matthew was not averse to inserting marginal glosses of this kind. The provision of a second account of an event which differed from the first was intended to enhance the overall effect.[122] The reader is presented with a choice, and a conflation.

Matthew's portrayal of the scene is original – a totally different rendering from near contemporary Italian versions. Francis, dressed in a cowled habit and knotted cord, and barefoot, is leaning on a pilgrim staff as he discourses. He is shown, correctly, without the stigmata, which he received later. As for the birds, Matthew does not attempt a vulture, though his inclusion of this bird in the list was his own contribution. Vultures do not, indeed, occur in English manuscripts of this period.[123] Nor does he depict Celano's doves, or Roger's magpies, or the ravens (or crows) mentioned by both. He does include a bird of prey, not a kite, probably a hawk. But he gives pride of place to a crane, beautifully drawn, evidently from nature. Cranes were among a number of birds

[118] Luard 1872–83, III, 133.   [119] Vaughan 1958, pp. 216–17; Lewis 1987, pp. 56–8.
[120] For what follows see Little 1914a, pp. 1–2; Lewis 1987, pp. 314–16.
[121] 'Dia serit volucrum sermonibus semina turbe.' 'Dia' is clearly what Matthew wrote – though the sense seems to demand 'Divina'.
[122] Lewis 1987, p. 57.   [123] Yapp 1981, p. 27.

Plate 20 Matthew Paris: St Francis preaching to the birds, *Chronica Maiora*, Cambridge, Corpus Christi College MS 16, fo. 7ov (formerly 66v) (Photo by permission of the Master and Fellows of Corpus Christi College, Cambridge).

kept in captivity, so it was possible for artists to observe them closely.[124] There are two indeterminate birds perched on the bottom branches of the tree, but I would suggest that the bird standing confidingly close to St Francis represents a heron. An illustration of the Call to the Birds in a manuscript of Alexander of Bremen's *Apocalypse Commentary*, probably written c.1242, contains reasonably good renderings of the three long-legged species – crane, stork and heron – all labelled. 'Ardea', the heron, is portrayed with distinctly shorter legs than the crane[125] (Plate 21). Matthew Paris' bird has, admittedly, shorter legs still, but it has the long bill and the same feathered short trousers. The presence of a crane in Francis' congregation is a sign that Matthew is deliberately extending the purely artistic possibilities of the subject; but it could also be a sign of something else. Cranes are almost certainly the commonest of all birds in English manuscripts, apart from the symbolic dove and eagle, from the mid-thirteenth century on. As well as appearing as marginal decoration and in scenes of the Creation, they figure in scenes of the Apocalypse.[126] In the Trinity Apocalypse, produced in the same decade, 1240–1250, as Matthew Paris was at work on his *Chronica Maiora* – and one of the earliest English manuscripts in which an attempt is made at an accurate drawing of a variety of birds – a crane occurs in two scenes.[127] One stands on the ruined walls of the city of Babylon, illustrating the verse: 'Babylon the great is fallen, is fallen and is become the habitation of devils . . . and a cage for every unclean and hateful bird' (Rev. 18. 2) along with an owl, a hawk and a jay. In the scene of the Call to the Birds, illustrating the verse 'And I saw an angel standing in the sun; and he cried with a loud voice, saying to all the fowls that fly in the midst of heaven, Come and gather yourselves together unto the supper of the great God' (Rev. 19. 17), a crane is prominent in mid-air, hurtling downwards. Among those already gathered are an owl, a jay and a magpie. These birds were regarded as sinister. It was a ghastly supper they were called to, to feast on the corpses of kings, their armies and their horses, slain in an apocalyptic battle (Rev. 19. 11–21). It is likely that Roger of Wendover was signalling references to the Apocalypse when he staged for Francis a congregation of predatory birds settled on carrion, and emphasised the depravity of the citizens of Rome.[128] That Matthew Paris picked them up is suggested by his choice of birds and his reference to vultures; but the message is not overt. The predatory birds are docile while Francis preaches. None of

---

[124] Yapp 1981, p. 75.
[125] Yapp 1981, pp. 106–7, pl. 14. Cambridge University Library MS Mm. v. 31 and a closely related MS in Wrotzlaw (Breslau) were probably produced in a workshop in Cologne shortly after the author of the Apocalypse commentary, Alexander of Bremen, a Franciscan friar, died in 1271. A number of striking iconographic parallels have been noted between these and Anglo-Norman MSS of c.1250. It has been suggested that an English Gothic Apocalypse could have been brought to Germany by an English Franciscan friar (Lewis 2001, esp. pp. 369–71, 384, a reference I owe to Dr Paul Binski). Brother Peter of Tewkesbury, who is mentioned as being *custos* of Oxford in 1241, was Provincial Minister of Cologne in 1250, a post he did not yet hold in 1245. He was appointed Provincial Minister of England in 1254 (Eccleston, pp. xxii, 71, 91 and n., 100–1). If so, the model for the late thirteenth-century Cologne MS (now MS Mm. v. 31) could have been in England, perhaps in Oxford, in the 1240s, its production closely contemporary with Matthew Paris' drawing, and it or a related MS could have been known to him.
[126] Yapp 1981, p. 13.
[127] Trinity College, Cambridge, MS R.16.2; cf. Klingender 1953, p. 18 and pl. 3B; Yapp 1981, pp. 71, 104 and pls. 13A, 13B.
[128] Klingender 1953, esp. pp. 16–18. His argument is endorsed by Frugoni 1993, pp. 247–8, but discounted by Lewis 1987, p. 503 n. 47.

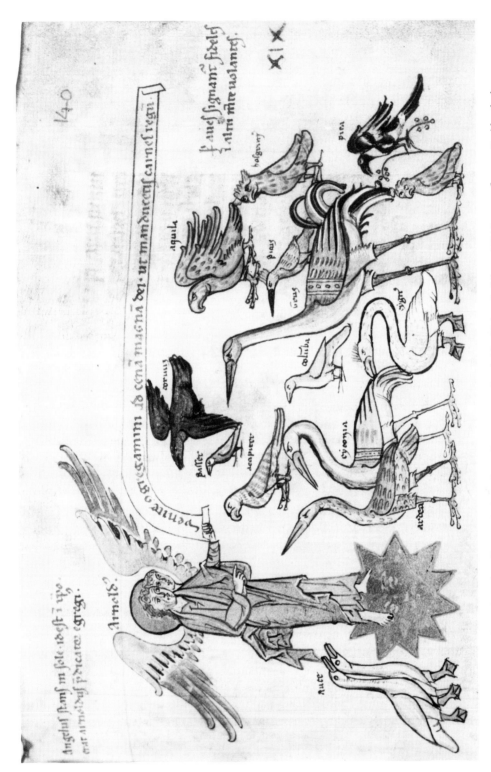

Plate 21 The Call to the Birds in Alexander of Bremen's Apocalypse Commentary, Cambridge University Library MS Mm. v. 31 fo. 140r. Besides the heron, crane and stork, there are two geese, a swan, a dove, a hawk, a sparrow, a raven or crow, an eagle, a woodpecker, an owl, a magpie, all labelled, and an unidentified bird, probably another owl. (Photo by permission of the Syndics of Cambridge University Library.)

Matthew's birds is black or pied. By contrast, all the birds in the Pescia altar panel are black or pied.[129] Birds of this colouring are of predatory or scavenging type. But in the Italian panel there is no hint of apocalyptic overtones; neither is there any in 1 *Celano*; though Celano's mentioning of crows and related birds may carry the message that St Francis had power over birds of ill omen, as well as over doves, with their peaceable and religious associations.

Roger of Wendover interpreted the act of preaching to the birds as an object lesson which jolted the Romans into listening. Francis and his friars then preached the gospel of peace in the city of Rome and its surroundings for many years, as well as preaching to the gentiles and the Saracens.[130] Roger then details the wonderful ending. He likens Francis to a successful money-lender, who restored with multiple interest the talent lent to him by his generous benefactor. As death approached, he received as the reward for his labours the crown of life which God had promised to them that love him. 'For a fortnight before his death wounds appeared in his hands and feet which bled continually, just as they had appeared when the Saviour of the world hung on the cross, crucified by the Jews. His right side appeared so opened and sprinkled with blood that even the inner recesses of the heart seemed visible . . . A great concourse of people, including cardinals, came to marvel at so rare an event . . . They asked: "What does this that we see signify?"[131] Francis told them: "This that you see in me has been manifested to those to whom I have preached the mysteries of the Cross, that you may believe in Him who for the salvation of the world bore on the cross these wounds which you see, and also that you may know me to be his servant, who has preached the Gospel of his cross, death and resurrection. So that you may persevere constant in his faith, remote from all ambiguity, to the end, immediately I am dead these open and bleeding wounds which you see in me will be sealed and healthy, and similar to the rest of the flesh."' He died without any bodily anguish. When he was dead, no wounds of the stigmata in side, feet or hands remained.

This lurid account of Roger's is an interesting example of the success of gossip and rumour in sensationalising a tale in the period immediately after Francis' death, when the only written evidence available was the English Provincial Minister's copy of brother Elias' letter.[132] Particular emphasis is laid on the side wound and its depth. The description illustrates the powerful effect that visual images could have on the imagination. The side wound cut Francis to the heart. Paintings and carvings of the crucifixion showed the wound made by the lance in Christ's right side. When Francis prayed before a crucifix he absorbed this mental image, and when anguished concentration on Christ's sufferings induced the wounds in his own flesh the side wound materialised in his right side.

Matthew Paris' rendering of the stigmata is, again, original, uninfluenced by the type that was being developed at around this period in Umbria and Tuscany (Plate 22). Francis is not kneeling in prayer, but is lying semi-recumbent, asleep on a green

---

[129] See p. 171 and Plate 15.   [130] Luard 1872–83, III, 134–5.

[131] *Visio* here has its original meaning of seeing, sight – not of an extra-sensory 'vision'. Roger does not mention Francis' vision of the seraph.

[132] AF x, 525–8; Jordan, c. 50; see p. 34.

Plate 22 Matthew Paris: St Francis' vision of the seraph, showing the stigmata, Chronica Maiora, Cambridge, Corpus Christi College MS 16, fo. 7ov (formerly 66v) (Photo by permission of the Master and Fellows of Corpus Christi College, Cambridge).

ground. His head is supported on his elbow, a pose which bears a striking resemblance to representations of the recumbent figure of the visionary St John the Evangelist in mid-thirteenth-century English manuscripts.[133] There is a sense, as with the crane pictured further up the margin of the same folio, of an undercurrent of apocalyptic associations. The stigmata are shown, in hands and feet and side, clearly indicated by red dots. Apart from the monstrance reliquaries produced in southern France around the time of Francis' canonisation, this picture is the earliest known to include the side wound.[134] It is not possible to be sure whether there is a sign of any cut in the clothing; there may be, or the red dot may have been just put on. Matthew positioned the figure of Francis at the foot of the left-hand margin of folio 70v (formerly 66v), with a caption at his head, reading: 'St Francis in the penultimate year of his life saw the seraph in this manner.' This is further evidence that Matthew knew Celano's First Life; again he is contradicting Roger – it happened two years, not two weeks, before Francis' death – and adding further information. Roger of Wendover's text makes no mention of the seraph. But Matthew seems also to have drawn on stories about the stigmata that were circulating orally among the friars of the English province. According to Celano (1 Cel. 94), 'St Francis saw a man like a seraph in a vision of God' (cf. Ezek. 1. 1; 8. 3). But brother Leo told Peter of Tewkesbury that the appearance of the seraph was vouchsafed to St Francis in 'a transport of contemplation, and more plainly than was written in his Life'.[135] In the Italian iconography St Francis is on his knees and his eyes are open. In this English version his eyes are closed and he sees the seraph in a dream. According to Celano the seraph stood above him. But brother Leo told brother Warin of Sedenefeld that brother Rufino, who was also present on La Verna, said that the angel had stood upon a stone, which St Francis ordered him to wash and anoint with oil.[136] In the Pescia altar panel the 'man like a seraph' is depicted in the air, hovering with outstretched arms and wings.[137] Matthew Paris' 'man like a seraph' dominates the deep margin at the foot of the folio. He is paying no attention to Francis, but is shown frontally, looking out at the viewer. Matthew, following Celano's indications, has drawn him in such a way as to convey two images in one. He represents the crucified Christ, for his nimbus is marked with a cross and he is nailed to the roughly hewn wood of a cross, coloured green. He stands on what appears to be a block of wood, but which is in fact the foot support (suppedaneum) used on contemporary images of the Crucifixion. The back part of this is coloured green and there is a narrow green line against his left leg (the viewer's right), to indicate that the vertical stem of the wooden cross is attached to this base. There is no sign of physical suffering, but all five wounds are emphasised. They are more conspicuous than Francis' and all have streamers. Each is shown as a large red dot with tears of blood falling from it. He also represents the six-winged seraph of Isaiah's

---

[133] Lewis 1987, p. 318. The same pose, though reversed, was later used to portray Matthew Paris himself on his deathbed, in British Library Royal MS 14 C. VII fo. 218v. Matthew died in June 1259 (Lewis 1987, pp. 5–6 and fig. 1).

[134] See p. 164 and Colour Plate 1. In Italy the earliest surviving portrayals of the side wound are by the Master of St Francis, prominent in a standing figure of St Francis painted on a panel some time in the 1250s, and also, shortly afterwards, in a fresco depicting St Francis' deathbed in the Lower Church: see pp. 296–9 and Plates 31, 30.

[135] Eccleston, p. 75.   [136] 1 Cel. 94; see Isaiah 6. 2; Eccleston, p. 75.   [137] See Plate 15.

vision (Isaiah 6. 2). The side wound fits well with the decorative eyes of the peacock feathers of which these great wings are composed.[138] Each wing is assigned a number, in red. The first and second completely cover the body from the neckline – stylishly decorated with a knotted ribbon – to below the knee. The third and fourth are the flight wings, held poised, flanking the body. The fifth and sixth are lifted up and cross over, framing the head, their feathers intertwined. Each wing is made up of five feathers, and each feather represents a virtue. These are listed in columns to the side. The first wing, which shields the heart, embraces truth, integrity, steadfastness, humility and simplicity; the second wing, devout prayer, liberal almsgiving, bodily mortification, abundant tears and renunciation of sin.[139] The seraph's left arm is labelled 'action', his right 'contemplation'. This type of emblematic figure was inspired by a treatise *De sex alis Cherubim*, ascribed (probably wrongly) to Alan of Lille, and became a standard diagramatic tradition in the late twelfth and thirteenth centuries.[140] A seraph standing on clouds, his feathers inscribed with virtues, closely analogous to Matthew Paris' seraph, occurs in a late twelfth-century manuscript from Sawley Abbey, Yorkshire.[141]

Matthew Paris was not able to fit all his columns of listed virtues to the right of his illustration of the seraph; there was space on the folio only for the feathers of five wings. So he carried on, placing the sixth column at the foot of the next folio. Only he then decided he wanted to include the complete text of the *Regula bullata*, and transcribed it on to a spare leaf which he inserted at this point, thus separating the feathers of the sixth wing from their mates.[142] In the right-hand margin of the inserted folio, beside chapter III of the Rule, Matthew drew, with painstaking care, his friend brother William. William's head is turned towards the words of the Rule he has vowed to obey, but also towards the facing folio, with its illustration of St Francis, whose companion he had been. Matthew has given us a very clear and sensitive picture of how a Friar

---

[138] Not unfortunately discernible in a black and white reproduction. There is some green shading on the nimbus and on the bands surrounding the peacock feathers. In Italy the first seraph to be shown with the side wound is in the stigmatisation scene in the St Francis Cycle in the Upper Church (Plate 64).

[139] Lewis 1987, pp. 317–18; ibid. p. 503 n. 56 completes the lists of all thirty virtues.

[140] A late version is copied in PL 210, col. 268, followed by the text of the treatise ascribed to Alan on cols. 269–80. This was based on the 1654 edition of Alan's works (Alan 1654, pp. 172–80), where the text was derived from a fourteenth-century MS from Saint-Vaast, Arras, now Arras, Bibl. Municipale, no. 891 (*Cat. Générale* IV, 354–5). The list of wings and feathers occurs in a number of MSS, sometimes with, sometimes without the drawing; and in the Arras MS it has an elaborate preface (a different preface occurs in Cambridge University Library MS Mm. vi. 4). Some recent scholars have followed Stegmüller 1940–80, II, 28, 249, nos. 949, 1980, in distinguishing two treatises, one by Clement prior of Lanthony by Gloucester (c.1150–1169 × 74, Knowles, Brooke and London 2001, pp. 172–3), the other by Alan. But the twelfth–thirteenth-century MSS known to Christopher Brooke do not suggest that these were stable or substantial treatises: it looks as if an interpretation of the cherubim by Clement, often copied without attribution, became entangled in Alan's works (as in Oxford, Bodleian E Mus. 82, fo. 80) and attributed to him: it was later attached to the works of St Bonaventure. In two twelfth-century MSS, the earliest known (Hereford Cathedral Library P. I. 1 and Oxford, Bodleian Library MS Auct. D. 2. I), it is attributed to Clement prior of Lanthony, as also in the fourteenth-century Cambridge University Library MS Ii. i. 5. Further investigation is needed, but the MSS make an English provenance likely. (On early MSS cf. also Lewis 1987, pp. 318, 503 n. 58.) The allegorising of seraphs' wings goes back to Gregory the Great: cf. PL 76, cols. 809–10; Frugoni 1993, pp. 163–8, 194–8, esp. pp. 165–6, 195.

[141] Lewis 1987, p. 318, fig. 202, and p. 503 n. 58.

[142] In the MS (Corpus Christi College 16) fos. 62–75 are marked as quire VI, but the strings come after fo. 67, showing that two leaves have been added after fo. 67. That one of these is fo. 71 is established by the appearance of the first five columns of the seraph's virtues on fo. 70v and the sixth on fo. 72r. Fo. 71r–v contains the whole of the *Regula bullata*.

Minor of that first generation looked. 'Matthew has delineated the . . . figure entirely in brown line and wash to maintain a poignant sense of self-effacing humility suggested by the actual colour of his mendicant robes; the delicate monochrome effect is then intensified by the contrasting addition of a rubric in bright vermilion headed by a blue paragraph marker.'[143] He made a sketch in his later style – this time a more generalised representation of a friar – next to the annal for 1207, where Roger first referred to them. His caption reads: 'Note the original poverty and excellence of life of the Friars Minor.'[144] So Matthew Paris seems to have shared Roger of Wendover's good opinion of the Order, at least part of the time; or perhaps he always regarded it as something of a curate's egg. He could be very critical as well.[145] But Francis impressed and fascinated him, and so he dedicated to him two of his most thought-provoking drawings.

KALENDERHANE CAMII

The earliest fresco cycle depicting scenes from the life of St Francis, so far discovered, is not in Italy, is not in the west at all, but in Constantinople. It was unearthed, quite literally, by archaeologists engaged on a joint Turkish-American project to investigate the site of a church complex immediately to the south of Valens' aqueduct, in 1966–7.[146] In the course of the excavations a barrel vaulted hall was revealed, almost filled with black earth, owing to its use, since the seventeenth century, as a sewage settlement tank. Off this hall was discovered a small, hitherto unsuspected chapel. The entrance arch still bore the first part of an inscription from Psalm 25(26). 8: 'Lord, I have loved the habitation of thy house.' On the semi-dome of the apse were several fragments of scenes, of which only one could be immediately identified. But it was conclusive; it was St Francis preaching to the birds (Figure 6). Mixed with the earth which filled the body of the chapel were hundreds of fragments of the frescoes, which had been deliberately hacked off in the sixteenth century, some less than a centimetre in size. They were systematically recovered, and the painstaking work of cleaning, sorting, conserving, assembling and mounting the surviving pieces of this jigsaw puzzle took some twelve years to achieve.[147]

The site is near the centre of old Istanbul, not far from the Forum Taurus, the most important forum of the medieval city. It was continuously occupied by churches and related buildings from the third quarter of the sixth century. Each building phase utilised and adapted parts of existing structures, starting with the first church, which incorporated two arches of the aqueduct into its north wall. In the late seventh century the so-called Bema Church was built to the south of this, on a slightly different axis. It was a timber roofed, galleried basilica, and was associated with a monastery. Its bema and diaconicon complex – against which two small chapels had been added some time

---

[143] Lewis 1987, p. 64; Little 1914a, pl. III, facing p. 3.

[144] Lewis 1987, pp. 66, 314 and fig. 28, p. 63.

[145] Some of Matthew's more offensive comments on the friars, both Franciscan and Dominican – words such as *turpiter, enormiter, indecens, fiunt theolonarii pape* – have been erased in his autograph MSS: Vaughan 1958, p. 120.

[146] Fully described in Striker and Kuban 1997, on which the following is largely based.

[147] Striker and Kuban 1997, pp. 128–9.

between the tenth and twelfth centuries – were among the areas retained when most of this church was dismantled to make way for the Main Church.[148]

This church, most of which survives, was thought to date from the mid-ninth century, but the archaeological excavations established that this major rebuilding occurred at the turn of the twelfth and thirteenth centuries. Twelfth-century pottery was found in sealed deposits under the paving beds of the aisles, and a scattering of coins of Isaac II, 1185–95, under the north cross arm. There were four coins of Alexius III, 1195–1203, under and in the setting bed of the new bema paving which overlaid the paving of the earlier bema incorporated from the Bema Church. This suggests that the Main Church was completed just before the taking of Constantinople by the armies of the Fourth Crusade in 1204. The church was dedicated to the Mother of God Kyriotissa and was attached to a monastery, like its predecessor. It was the last big Byzantine church to be built in the city, and its 20.5 m high dome is the second largest among all the surviving churches of the middle Byzantine period. It was handsomely fitted and adorned, in accordance with its status. The naos was paved with grey/white and *verde antico* marble and included a large porphyry rota, 2.37 m in diameter at the entrance. The paving of the bema included two *opus sectile* medallions depicting six-pointed stars. The walls were faced with polychrome marble, which is notable for its orderly symmetry and is unusually well preserved. At least eight types of marble were used in this revetment. Some of this, and possibly all, was reused marble, cut from columns. There was also mosaic decoration, but only a well-preserved fragment of the archangel Michael survives.[149]

The Main Church was fortunate to escape damage in 1204. The crusaders installed a Latin emperor and a Latin patriarch. The Greek princes, the patriarch and many clergy were expelled or fled to Asia Minor, and an imperial centre was established at Nicaea. There is mention of a Kyriotissa monastery in Nicaea in 1239, and it is likely that it was established by the Greek Orthodox monks serving the Main Church, who had sought refuge in Nicaea. During the Latin occupation no structural changes seem to have been made to the church, and it appears to have been well maintained. Unfortunately there is a dearth of documentary sources relating to Catholic churches in this period and no information as to their location. Because of lack of evidence for the existence of a Franciscan house in Constantinople, named or unnamed, it has even been suggested that the little chapel containing the St Francis Cycle may have formed part of a French Dominican house, which is mentioned in the sources.[150] This is not an acceptable hypothesis.

There can be no doubt at all that there was a Franciscan house, and an important one, in Constantinople. We know that, in 1249, the friars in Constantinople had a

[148] Striker and Kuban 1997, pp. 7–8. The bema in a Byzantine church was the area of the apse and chancel raised one step above the naos, which, in a centrally planned Byzantine church, was the area in front of the bema for the congregation, corresponding to the nave. The diaconicon: Striker calls this irregular complex of rooms and chapels the diaconicon because of its location adjoining the south flank of the bema, not on the basis of evidence that liturgically it served only that function (Striker and Kuban 1997, pp. 4–5, 81).
[149] Striker and Kuban 1997, pp. 16, 71–2, 116–18, 126–7, fig. 68 and pls. 16–31, esp. 16–18, and 37–8, 141, 143–4.
[150] Striker and Kuban 1997, p. 17.

lector, Thomas the Greek, because in that year he was in Lyon, acting as an envoy for the Byzantine emperor Vatatzes in negotiations with Innocent IV, and Salimbene met him. Lectors were Masters of theology, and were attached to convents, where they taught. Lectors in the Order's *studia generalia* were the only friars other than Provincial Ministers and the Minister General who were permitted to have a private room – all the rest were required to share a common dormitory. Thomas returned to the east as a member of the group the pope sent to continue the effort to achieve reunion of the churches under the leadership of the Minister General John of Parma.[151] The first of the series of these embassies – one of the consequences of the Latin occupation of Constantinople – had been sent by Gregory IX in 1233. It consisted of two Dominicans, both Frenchmen, and two Franciscans, the Englishmen Haymo of Faversham and Ralph of Rheims.[152] Discussions took place at Nicaea, with the Emperor Vatatzes and the Patriarch Germanus II acting as joint hosts, and the friars certainly thought they were winning the argument. However, the patriarch proposed an intermission, saying the questions at issue were so difficult of solution that a council attended by his fellow patriarchs of Jerusalem, Alexandria and Antioch should be convened the following March. The friars replied that they did not dare or wish to act beyond the papal mandate they had received. They would return to Constantinople; and the Greeks should hold their council and inform them of the outcome of their deliberations.[153] But the Greeks desired their attendance, and in March 1234 wrote to them, and also to two leading Franciscans, Benedict of Arezzo, Provincial Minister of 'Romania' and James of Russano, who were at that time in Constantinople.[154] The Province of 'New Rome' would surely have had a house in the capital founded by Constantine. We may presume that brother Benedict was staying in it; and that the other Friars Minor visiting the city on business were staying in it too. Franciscans were required to seek food and shelter at houses of their own Order wherever possible when travelling. They were to offer a warm welcome to Dominican travellers, treating them as brothers, but as there is record of the existence of a French Dominican house in Constantinople in 1233 we may take it that the two Dominican envoys stayed there.[155]

Haymo and Ralph and their two colleagues had prepared themselves properly for their mission and had arrived at Nicaea with 'a vast quantity of Greek books from Constantinople'.[156] It is likely that these were loaned to them from the libraries of the two convents. If, as I argue, there was a Franciscan house in Constantinople in 1233–4 containing a substantial library, the obvious candidate is the Main Church dedicated to the Mother of God Kyriotissa, with its complex of monastic buildings and its little chapel. When may the friars have acquired it? They seem to have established a small settlement c.1220.[157] But they would have needed an influential patron to secure such

[151] Salimbene, H, p. 322; S, 1, 468; cf. *Narb.* IV, 16 in Bihl 1941, p. 57. See also Striker and Kuban 1997, pp. 16–17, 73.
[152] Golubovich 1919; Eccleston, pp. 28, 73: 'Frater Radulfus Remensis Anglicus'.
[153] Golubovich 1919, pp. 442–4, cc. 12–13.
[154] Golubovich 1919, pp. 445–6, c. 16; Wolff 1944, pp. 224–8, esp. 226: James (Jacobus) had acted as a papal envoy taking letters to the king of Georgia.
[155] Striker and Kuban 1997, p. 16 and n. 103. Cf. *Narb.* v, 8, IV, 19, in Bihl 1941, pp. 63, 58.
[156] Golubovich 1919, p. 434, c. 7.   [157] Golubovich 1906, I, p. 109; Moorman 1968, p. 227.

a prime site, central and only recently rebuilt, enlarged and refurbished. It is unlikely to have been their initial residence.

John of Brienne was reputed the finest soldier of his time. He had become titular King of Jerusalem by right of his late wife Sybilla. One of his daughters married the Emperor Frederick II, and Frederick took advantage of him, concluding a treaty with the Sultan, al-Kamil, and wearing the crown of Jerusalem himself. Angered, John accepted the command of the papal troops in southern Italy, and it was as the holder of this office that he was in attendance on Gregory IX in Perugia and in Assisi in 1228, and was present at the canonisation ceremony for St Francis. The next year he was made Emperor of Constantinople, and entered the city in 1231. He was a God-fearing man, and St Francis clearly impressed him. Before his death in 1237 he was received into the Order and clothed with the habit by Benedict of Arezzo.[158] It is indeed possible that he gave this splendid church to the Friars Minor on or shortly after his arrival in 1231.

The St Francis chapel projects from the east wall of the diaconicon.[159] It consists of a 2.5 m square forebay defined by four piers carrying arches, originally covered by a fenestrated drum and dome on pendentives; at the east end is a small apse – the span of the semi-dome is only 2.30 m – lit by three windows carried on mullions. When the friars took over the monastery this apse was decorated with mosaic. A small fragment, four courses of tesserae with a stepped geometric motif, probably from a border, was detected under the plaster of the scene of St Francis preaching to the birds.[160] When the archaeologists unearthed the frescoes they found that much was irretrievably lost: 649 fragments were recovered, of which 142 could be joined together into larger units; another 35 were distinctive; the rest were pieces of plain blue background or red frame or nondescript. Together with the pieces of fresco found *in situ* the total that could be usefully assembled amounted to no more than two-fifths of what was originally there. But there was enough to reconstruct the programme. The design was based upon the Romanesque/Byzantine type of altar panel, adapted to the exigencies of a curved surface (Figure 3). In the centre was a large, standing, frontal image of St Francis; above him, in the lunette in the crown of the vault, a bust of the Virgin and child flanked by two flying angels; to either side of him five scenes, arranged in three registers, one in each upper, three in the middle, and one in the spandrel of each outer window arch.

When the frescoes were done must lie between two clear dates: after the canonisation in 1228, as Francis is distinguished by a halo throughout, and by 1261, when the Greeks reconquered Constantinople. It can reasonably be moved forward to after c.1231, when it is likely the Friars Minor were given the monastery. Within this period there are very few relevant altar panels surviving for comparative study. It has been estimated that no more than 5 per cent possibly even fewer, of the altar panels painted in Italy in the thirteenth century survive.[161] For the 1230s we have only the Pescia altar panel, dated 1235; for the 1250s, the Assisi altar panel, and the related Vatican altar panel, and the Pisa altar panel. The Pescia panel showed St Francis preaching to the birds, St Francis

[158] Salimbene, H, p. 43; S, I, 59–60; 1 *Cel.* 124 (AF X, 99 and n. 5); Abulafia 1988, pp. 149–50, 152–3, 180–8; Wolff 1944, pp. 214–21 and nn.
[159] Striker and Kuban 1997, p. 60 and fig. 30. [160] Striker and Kuban 1997, pp. 81–3, 128–9.
[161] Garrison 1972, p. 140, cited Striker and Kuban 1997, p. 140 n. 14.

Figure 3 Istanbul, Kalenderhane Camii, St Francis Chapel; from Striker and Kuban 1997, pp. 130–48: reconstruction sketch, after ibid., fig. 70

receiving the stigmata, plus four posthumous miracles. The Assisi and Vatican panels showed four posthumous miracles, the Pisa panel six posthumous miracles.[162] As the apse frescoes have ten scenes, some must be new introductions; new, that is, as far

[162] See pp. 168–76, Plate 15 and Colour Plate 3. For the Vatican panel see *Assisi 1999*, pl. 1/2, p. 55. The Pistoia panel is too overpainted to be helpful; the Bardi panel is later: see pp. 176–92 and nn., and Plate 17.

as we know. There may have been panels containing additional scenes that are earlier than these frescoes which have not survived.

All the scenes were enclosed by red frames averaging 2.7 cm, trimmed by a white line. Of the ten scenes once there, fragments of seven can be placed (Figures 4, 5). At least four, probably six or seven, possibly eight, were miracle scenes. Faint traces of inscriptions remain in the sky of scenes 5, 6, 8 and 9, and the survival of numerous fragments of white letters against a blue ground indicates that each scene had a caption.[163] Tantalisingly, there is insufficient to be legible.

If the frescoes were painted some time between the mid-1230s and the early 1250s the Pescia panel is the only one available for comparison; and there are links. Both show the presence of two angels. Both contain the scene of the preaching to the birds, similarly designed[164] (Figure 6 and Plate 15). St Francis stands in front of his companions on the left; on the right the assembled birds face him on the slopes of a hill. There are differences of detail: in the panel he has two companions, holds a book and bears the stigmata; in the fresco he has three, and both hands are outstretched; they are well preserved and do not show the stigmata. In the panel the birds are black, apart from two magpies, and are perched on trees; in the fresco they are gathered on rising ground. They are more colourful – brown, black, white – and more lively: most have their beaks open and some spread their wings (Plate 23). The portrayal is quite close to the scene as it is described in 1 *Celano* 58.

The only other scene occurring in Francis' lifetime in the Pescia panel is the stigmatisation. Was it also in the fresco? There is no extant evidence for it; none of the fragments *in situ*, or reconstructed or loose, are applicable. If it was included, it must have been in one of the blank spaces. It is not likely to have been the subject of scene 1, since Striker's hypothesis – that a group of fragments depicting St Francis performing a miracle watched by three friars, taken together with another showing the hems of habits and a length of red frame, belong to this scene – is probably correct.[165] It may have been scene 7, or 10; though scene 10 is an awkward shape for it, it would balance the preaching to the birds. We must not assume it was included.

The Assisi, Vatican and Pisa panels all contain the same selection of type of posthumous miracles as the Pescia panel, but these three replace the more general picture of the exorcism of demons from a group of sufferers with a specific case, that of a young woman from Norcia brought to the altar at Assisi by her parents. This was first recorded in Celano's *Tractatus de Miraculis*, written 1250–2. If the frescoes were painted after 1252, though it is unlikely that this additional source was used, it is not impossible. The *Tractatus* was not widely disseminated. But it was known in Pisa, as well as in Assisi. Three of the six posthumous miracles in the Pisa panel were taken from the *Tractatus*.[166] Pisa had close military and trading links with Constantinople and there were regular sailings between the two cities.

[163] Striker and Kuban 1997, p. 130 and figs. 71–2.
[164] Striker and Kuban 1997, pp. 133–4 and fig. 78, pls. 159, 163.
[165] Striker and Kuban 1997, pp. 136–7, fig. 82A; pl. 168 and fig. 82B.
[166] 3 *Cel.* 153, 193, 103; and see pp. 172–3.

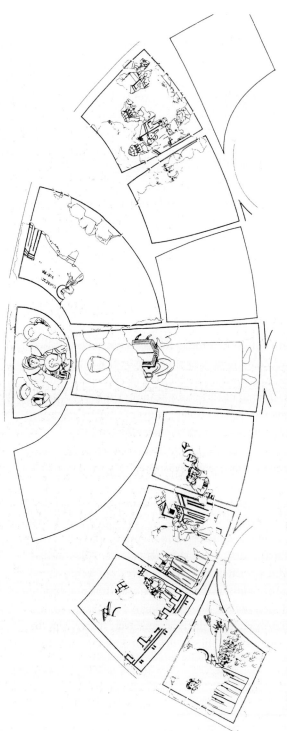

Figure 4 St Francis frescoes: reconstruction of fragments; Striker and Kuban 1997, fig. 71

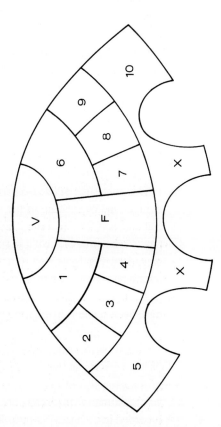

Figure 5 St Francis frescoes: diagram of programme; Striker and Kuban 1997, fig. 72

Figure 6 St Francis frescoes, scene 5: Preaching to the birds; Striker and Kuban 1997, fig. 78

There are also links between the Assisi and Vatican panels and the frescoes. The scenes are demarcated by pronounced borders – those in the frescoes are plain, those in the panels broader and decorated. The painters of the Assisi panel and the frescoes share a mastery in depicting buildings and conveying distance not given to their fellows. The top left scene in the Assisi panel succeeds in evoking the city of Assisi; the architectural background in scene 9 of the frescoes includes two charming Byzantine rotundas, topped with drums lit by windows and domes covered with grey plates[167] (Figure 9). The style of the frescoes, indeed, suggests that they were not painted before 1250. They are not 'Greek' but Latin pictures. Their style is very close to that of the painter of the Paris Arsenal Bible. This MS, a translation of the Bible into Old French, is considered the crowning achievement of miniature painting in the Latin Kingdom of Jerusalem. It was probably commissioned by Louis IX during his stay in the Holy Land while he was on crusade, and is attributed to a new crusader scriptorium or painter working in Acre. Detailed comparison of the Arsenal Bible and the frescoes confirms the closeness of their relationship. The craned-neck posture and gesture of the friar on the right in scene 2 resembles those of David in the Arsenal Bible; the same headdress worn by the woman in scene 3 occurs in the frontispiece to Tobit (Figure 7); the loose fragment of striped dress is similar to the dress worn by Judith.[168]

---

[167] See pp. 173–4 and Colour Plate 3; Striker and Kuban 1997, pp. 135–6, fig. 81 and pl. 160.

[168] Buchthal 1957, and ibid. pls. 77, 76, cited Striker and Kuban 1997, p. 142. For the friar, see Striker and Kuban 1997, fig. 75 and pl. 161; for the headdress, ibid. fig. 76 and pl. 158; for the fragments of dress, ibid. fig. 82G and H, and pl. 167. Cf. also Striker 1983, pp. 117–21.

Plate 23 Istanbul, Kalenderhane Camii, St Francis preaching to the birds, detail (Photo courtesy of C. L. Striker. © Verlag Philipp von Zabern (Mainz)).

Only a fragment of the central standing figure of St Francis is preserved, but enough to show that it differed in details from the panels. He holds an open book in his left hand, the fingers supporting the spine. The clasps are nicely detailed; the pages are blank. We cannot know whether the stigmata were shown. The right hand is missing. It was not holding anything. From the position of the fragment of sleeve and forearm it would appear not to have been raised in blessing; it was more probably pointing to the book.[169] In the Pescia and Pisa panels the book is closed; both hands show the stigmata, and the right hand is raised in blessing. In the Assisi and Vatican panels both hands show the stigmata and the right hand holds a cross. The book is open. It lacks clasps. In the Vatican panel the pages are blank. In the Assisi panel they contain a text from Matthew 19. 12.[170]

[169] Striker and Kuban 1997, p. 131, fig. 73 and pl. 157; and see Figure 4.   [170] See note 162.

Figure 7 St Francis frescoes, scene 3: a healing miracle; Striker and Kuban 1997, fig. 76

It is interesting that among the four posthumous miracles in the Pescia panel only the two in which the patient thought he saw or felt St Francis depict the saint. Francis entices a boy to rise by offering him pears, and lays his hands on Bartholomew of Narni's foot and leg.[171] It is possible that some of the scenes in the fresco cycle where St Francis is present are of this type, or relate to miracles done while he was alive. Scene 3, though fragmentary, shows St Francis, distinguished by his halo from his companions, facing a woman whose right hand is raised in an attitude of beseeching, and who may, from the angle of her left arm and hand, be leaning on a stick. Francis' right hand touches her face (Figure 7). There is no miracle of St Francis healing a blind person illustrated in the Pescia, Assisi or Vatican panels. The Pisa panel illustrates, albeit inaccurately, from the *Tractatus*, the case of the woman whose daughter's eyes fell out of their sockets, but this clearly is not the subject of scene 3. None of the group of

[171] 1 *Cel.* 133, 135; and see p. 172.

miracles of the blind receiving their sight read out during the canonisation ceremony and recorded at the end of 1 *Celano* is appropriate. But a miracle told much earlier in the book, performed by Francis while he was alive, could well be the subject. 1 *Celano* 67 records that a woman of Narni, who had been struck blind, recovered her sight when St Francis made the sign of the cross upon her eyes.

One of the loose fragments shows the head of a woman. 'She has a low brow, pulled back hair, wide open eyes, a pug nose, and open mouth, from which issues a black, stick-like figure. This is obviously from an exorcism scene.'[172] Yes, but which one? The Pescia panel shows a man along with two women with their arms tied being healed at the altar; the Assisi, Vatican and Pisa panels the girl from Norcia, who was also healed before the altar.[173] Celano tells another story that happened during St Francis' life, and he tells it in 1 *Cel.* 69, only two paragraphs after his account of the blind woman in 1 *Cel.* 67, so if scene 3 was based on that, it is not impossible that another scene was based on this companion story. And it is a delightful story. St Francis and three companions were staying with a God-fearing man in San Gemini, in the diocese of Narni. His wife was possessed by a devil, and after urgent entreaties Francis was prevailed upon to help. He stationed his three companions at three corners of the house, taking the fourth himself, explaining that the devil might try to escape by hiding in a corner. After they had all prayed, Francis went up to the woman, who was clamouring horribly, and said: 'In the name of our Lord Jesus Christ, I command you, evil spirit, on obedience, to go out of her and never dare to torment her again.' He had hardly finished when the devil came out so very quickly, angrily and noisily that St Francis thought he had failed, and promptly left the place in shame, only learning later that the woman had been cured. Three friars occur in scenes 4 and 5, and in the fragment probably belonging to scene 1, but together, and two friars together in scene 2, so these are all ruled out. If the exorcism scene does illustrate 1 *Celano* 69, it will have to be placed in one or other of the two scenes that are totally blank, nos. 7 or 10. Among the isolated fragments there happens to be a bit of a friar on his own at the corner of a building.[174] Maybe he and the woman's head belong in the same scene.

Part of scene 6, a single scene occupying the whole of the top register, and therefore one of the two largest, was found *in situ*[175] (Figure 8). St Francis is standing in the sky, above buildings, leaning slightly forward and looking down, his left arm slightly raised. Of a four-line caption in the sky only his name is legible, and indistinct fragments at ground level are no help in interpretation. Striker examines scenes depicted in later thirteenth-century cycles, and quite rightly concludes that there are problems in identifying it with the Apparition at Arles, the Ecstasy of St Francis or the Stigmatisation. Later cycles could not have been models for these frescoes, and the Assisi, Vatican and Pisa panels were probably painted at much the same time as the frescoes. The only extant earlier type is the Pescia panel, and the only certain literary source is 1 *Celano*. We should seek for a possible source of inspiration there.

---

[172] Striker and Kuban 1997, p. 137, fig. 82F and pl. 166.
[173] 1 *Cel.* 137–8; 3 *Cel.* 153.   [174] Striker and Kuban 1997, p. 137, fig. 82E.
[175] Striker and Kuban 1997, fig. 79 and pp. 134–5. See Figures 4, 5.

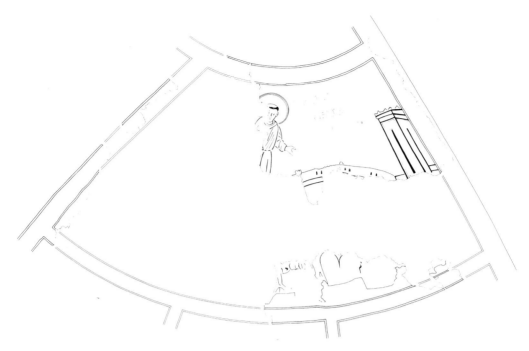

Figure 8 St Francis frescoes: scene 6; Striker and Kuban 1997, fig. 79

Among the posthumous miracles collected at the end is a story about a deaf and dumb beggar boy.[176] One evening he sought shelter at a house door, indicating his need by leaning his head sideways in the palm of his hand. He was taken in, and kept, because he proved a willing and bright servant, understanding sign language. One evening at supper the man remarked to his wife how wonderful it would be if St Francis would give the boy hearing and speech; if he did, he would provide for him for life. The vow uttered, the boy at once spoke: 'St Francis lives.' He continued: 'I see St Francis standing on high, and he is coming to give me speech.' It is only speculation. But we should not confine ourselves to a list of topics contained in panels or other media which chance has caused to survive, when so much has been lost, and when potential themes for illustration are there, encapsulated in a book that was widely available. There may have been greater variety of scenes than we are aware of, depending on the interests of patrons and communities for whom these images were made.

In scene 9 the entire foreground, though fragmentary, appears to be the horizontal surface of a slab of pink breccia marble in tilted perspective (Figure 9). Two friars stand at the left, and three more, only the tops of their tonsured heads remaining, in the centre. Behind, the buildings include two churches. It is not a miracle scene. There is no room for supplicants in front of the slab or to its sides. There are two candles, apparently resting on the slab, to the left; one, possibly two, on the right. There is no sign of St Francis, but the presence of the candles and the slab suggest this could be

Figure 9 St Francis frescoes, scene 9, death of St Francis; Striker and Kuban 1997, fig. 81

his deathbed scene. There is just about room for his body to be laid out in the missing central section.[177]

Scenes 4, 2, 8, and one other, probably 1, whose subjects are not identified, are all probably miracle scenes, because of the presence in them of groups of friars looking on. 'The usual suspects' – the standard four posthumous miracles – may well have been present. We know an exorcism scene was there somewhere.

The decoration of the St Francis chapel was not confined to the apse. There are indications that it was extended to include the dome-covered forebay. This means that the Franciscans in Constantinople were not observing their Order's constitutions regarding church decoration.[178] They actually redecorated the apse, plastering over existing mosaic, evidently in order to enable them to honour their founder. It was not to eradicate Greek Orthodox decoration for the sake of it. This is made clear by the context. On the face of the arch leading in to the apse was the inscription from

[177] Striker and Kuban 1997, pp. 135–6 and fig. 81, pl. 160.
[178] Striker and Kuban 1997, p. 144; and Narb. III, 15–18, in Bihl 1941, p. 48.

Psalm 25(26), and on the soffit, facing outwards, were representations of two Greek Church Fathers. The lower parts of their vestments were found *in situ*, and a fragment of inscription identified one as St Chrysostom. They would have been about 1.60 m tall, almost life-size, and so almost twice the size of the standing central figure of St Francis (Figure 3). There is no doubt that these Greek Fathers were painted at the same time as the St Francis Cycle, and were part of the same programme. The underlying preparation is identical in this area, and the fresco surfaces are continuous. The details of their liturgical vestments are rendered with such great accuracy that it has been suggested that these two Fathers may have been the work of a Greek painter employed alongside the Latin crusader painter responsible for the St Francis Cycle.[179]

It is particularly striking that in the same campaign of decoration, probably in the early 1250s, the life of St Francis was portrayed in the manner of the Italian panels, and is clearly of western, Catholic inspiration; while the figures on the arch leading to the semi-dome portrayed Greek Fathers of the Church. We seem to have a modest reflection here of the attempts to reconcile the two churches.

The Franciscans learnt early on that for their evangelical and missionary work to be effective it was necessary to learn the languages of the people they went among. Their first mission to Germany was a disaster because no one in the group could understand German.[180] Greek was studied at the Franciscan school at Oxford under the aegis of the secular Master Robert Grosseteste, who lectured to them from *c*.1230 to 1235, when he became bishop of Lincoln.[181]

Brother Ralph of Rheims was a Greek scholar. He signed and testified to the report produced by the four mendicant envoys in both Greek and Latin. It was presumably he who, towards the end of the doctrinal debates at Nicaea on the procession of the Holy Spirit, 'unrolled the book of the blessed Cyril on the IX Anathemas and began to read in Greek'.[182] Earlier in the disputations, when the friars were asked to put their arguments in writing, they produced them first in Latin, but, on request, translated them into Greek. When the Greeks then drew up their reply, in Greek, the friars, because it was now night-time, postponed translating it till the next day.[183] They deployed both languages with the aim of better understanding the Greek position, refuting it, and persuading their opponents of the truth of the position of the papacy and the Roman Church. In order to support their arguments with authorities and citations, the friars brought with them, both to Nicaea and to the council at Nymphaeum, copies of the works of the Fathers and a great quantity of Greek books. These were a problem to them when they prepared finally to leave, fearing for their safety. Because they had excommunicated their Greek hosts their promised transport was initially withheld. They felt compelled to set out on foot, though the ground was inhospitable and the sea far away, with just the books they could carry. They had to leave the weightier tomes with an imperial official. Fortunately for them the difficulty was sorted.[184] Probably

---

[179] Striker and Kuban 1997, pp. 129–30, 138–40, fig. 84, pl. 165, and fig. 85; also pl. 155, and p. 140 n. 13, citing Weitzmann 1944. See p. 209 and note 168.

[180] Jordan, c. 5.   [181] Little 1926, pp. 171–4; cf. Southern 1986, pp. 181–6.

[182] Golubovich 1919, pp. 442–3, c. 12.

[183] Golubovich 1919, pp. 425 (misspr. 435) – 426, 436–7, c. 9.

[184] Golubovich 1919, p. 434, c. 7, and p. 465, c. 30.

most, if not all, the Greek books in the Franciscan convent library were inherited from the Greek Orthodox monks whose buildings they occupied.

The convent in Constantinople contained some friars who were Greek or partly Greek. In 1249 Salimbene travelled with the Minister General John of Parma, who had been summoned to Lyon by Innocent IV, who proposed to send him to the Greeks, the Emperor Vatatzes having again indicated a willingness to consider reconciliation with the Roman Church. At Vienne they encountered Vatatzes' envoy to the pope. Salimbene was struck by the fact that he was a Friar Minor with the same name as himself. He tells us that this second Salimbene was half Greek and half Latin; that he spoke excellent Latin, although he was not a priest, and that he also knew vernacular Greek and Latin very well. John of Parma took him with them to Lyon. There Salimbene met another Friar Minor sent by Vatatzes, the lector of the Franciscan house at Constantinople. He was Greek, Thomas the Greek, and he too was bilingual, speaking Greek and Latin excellently. John of Parma took these two friars, plus a number of other suitable friars, with him on his mission to the Greeks.[185]

In 1261 the Greeks reconquered Constantinople. Striker believes that the Greek Orthodox monks returned to reoccupy their monastery very soon after this. But it is, however, likely that the Franciscans were allowed to stay on for the time being. The Latin patriarch, Pantaleone Giustiniani, fled from Constantinople together with the Latin emperor Baldwin II, but he left as his vicar a Franciscan friar, brother Anthony. Anthony's appointment was confirmed by Urban IV in a bull dated 31 October 1263, so it would seem he was still in Constantinople then. The Greek emperor, Michael Palaeologus, was, indeed, concerned to deflect the threat of a crusade against him. Throughout the 1260s he sent a succession of Franciscan envoys to the pope, first to Urban IV, and after him to Clement IV. The next pope, Gregory X, heard the news of his election in Acre, where he was on crusade, and the reunion of the churches was one of his key objectives. In 1272 he sent a group of Franciscans, including Jerome of Ascoli, as envoys to Constantinople. Their efforts were greatly helped by the co-operation of one of the Greek friars resident in Constantinople, John Parastron, who was bilingual and a learned theologian. He instructed the emperor in the articles of faith of the Roman Church, particularly the Latin doctrine of Purgatory, acted as his envoy to Gregory X, and was present at the General Council which the pope summoned to meet at Lyon in 1274, where he played a leading role, acting as an interpreter. Reunion was temporarily achieved, the Greek Church accepting the primacy of Rome, the *filioque* clause, and the use of unleavened bread in the Eucharist. But the schism reopened in 1281. In March 1282 the Sicilian Vespers destroyed the power of Charles of Anjou and removed the danger of a crusade against the Greek emperor. Michael Palaeologus died in December 1282. Not surprisingly, there was a violent reaction against the policy of reunion under his son, Andronicus II, and the Franciscans and Dominicans were expelled from Constantinople. It was probably only then that the Greek Orthodox monks will have been able to reclaim their monastery.[186]

[185] Salimbene, H, pp. 321–2; S, I, 467–8.
[186] Striker and Kuban 1997, p. 143; Golubovich 1906, I, 283–90; Wolff 1944, pp. 224, 230; Kelly 1986, pp. 195–8.

Archaeological evidence has shown that, when they did return, the little apse containing the St Francis Cycle was walled up and the diaconicon complex from which it protruded was redecorated. The reason for blocking it off was probably to provide continuous wall surfaces for a new fresco programme. After the Latins were dislodged and the Greek emperor Michael Palaeologus' dynasty was established, there was an artistic revival, which took its name from the family. The Palaeologan 'volume style' was characterised by solid modelling of the human figure and the organic cohesion of the limbs, so that the figures seem to possess weight, and to create space around and depth behind themselves – developments which had almost immediate repercussions in Italy. In the diaconicon of this monastery, the new decoration consisted mainly of images of male and female saints disposed in one or two registers depending on the space available. Where there was room for two, those in the lower register were full length and almost life size, those in the upper bust length. All were originally identified by inscriptions. Of approximately twenty saints, only Constantine and Helena can now be identified. Running beneath this programme the whole way round the walls was a 1 m high frescoed dado unifying the whole. On the surface of the wall built across the apse the dado was of simulated ornamental marble revetment, but mostly it was comprised of painted hangings. The fresco decoration of the Upper Church at Assisi was to be similarly unified by a continuous dado of painted hangings[187] (Colour Plate 5). Another example of trompe l'oeil decoration survives in a small room known as the Icons chapel because of its row of wooden icons – half length figures of male saints painted complete with their picture frames and iron rings, and the nails from which they hang on the wall. They can be compared with Cimabue's half length angels in a painted arcade in the Upper Church[188] (Plate 50).

The St Francis Cycle had replaced a Greek mosaic. It was not itself visible for long, but was put into storage by the returning Greeks. The Palaeologan fresco programme suffered in its turn. After the Ottoman conquest the east hall of the diaconicon appears to have been disused. Later it was walled off to create a vaulted cess-pit and the inner wall surfaces were covered with a hard waterproof mortar. Mehmet II, as part of his policy of resettlement, designated the church an *imaret*, to be used by travellers and dervishes. The dervishes had helped in the siege of Constantinople in 1453. Given the building, they seem to have used it both for the conduct of religious ceremonies on Fridays and as a soup kitchen for the poor. Later it was transformed into a mosque, Kalenderhane Camii, the mosque of the Kalenders.[189]

---

[187] Striker and Kuban 1997, pp. 144–9 and fig. 90; and see pp. 354, 366 and 378.
[188] Striker and Kuban 1997, p. 149 and fig. 90N; Bellosi 1998, pp. 179, 183; and see pp. 353–4.
[189] Striker and Kuban 1997, pp. 17–19, 87.

CHAPTER EIGHT

THE OFFICIAL IMAGE IN SPEECH AND WRITING

SERMONS

Information and instruction could be conveyed to live audiences in sermons. Among the few, relevant to St Francis, that have survived, particularly influential were those preached by university masters. For example, the Franciscan house at Paris included a prestigious school, one of the Order's *studia generalia*, to which promising friars were sent to take an advanced course in theology, which could qualify them in their turn to become lectors in convents throughout the Order, with responsibility for educating their brothers and training them to preach.[1] The Franciscans in Paris were privileged to be addressed by a succession of distinguished masters of theology of their own Order, who included John of La Rochelle, Eudes Rigaud, St Bonaventure, John Pecham and Matthew of Aquasparta, and also by distinguished secular masters and masters belonging to other Orders. For university sermons were delivered on Sundays in the church of the Dominican convent at St Jacques, and on festivals occurring on weekdays in the Franciscan convent church, dedicated to St Mary Magdalene.[2]

The secular master Guiard de Laon, a great supporter of the friars, later archbishop of Cambrai, preached one such sermon on 4 October 1230, St Francis' feast day, on the text 'We are ambassadors for Christ, as though God did beseech you by us' (2 Cor. 5. 20). God so loved us that he sent his Son to reconcile us to himself, and then the Holy Spirit, and thereafter deputy ambassadors (or legates, *sublegatos*). Guiard chose two as examples, St Paul and St Francis; a striking juxtaposition at this early date, according St Francis the status of an apostle. St Francis had very recently been translated – in May that year – and the First Life by Thomas of Celano had been completed only the year before. Guiard stated that both saints were alike, first, in that both had been 'ambassadors of the devil'.[3] St Paul before his conversion had been a persecutor of Christians; but to say that Francis before his was a 'legatus diaboli' is a slur, a preaching device, based on 1 *Celano*'s conventional, negative characterisation of his upbringing (1 *Cel.* 1–2), further

---

[1] *Narb.* VI, 12–16, Bihl 1941, p. 72; Bougerol 1983; Moorman 1968, pp. 123–39; d'Avray 1985, pp. 132–47.
[2] Bougerol 1983, p. 180 and n. 23; Bougerol 1993, I, 34.   [3] Bougerol 1983, p. 181 and n. 24.

heightened for effect. Francis' previous record amounted to a misspent youth and to belonging to a wealthy merchant family. Secondly, both saints were especially chosen by the Lord and directly instructed by Him. This seems to suggest a knowledge of the Testament[4] as well as 1 *Celano*, from which he also took the story of Francis' dream of armour (1 *Cel.* 5). The sermon is an indication of the immediate popularity of St Francis' cult in Paris. It was also favoured and promoted by the French royal family.[5]

A group of surviving sermons preached by Eudes of Châteauroux, who was chancellor of Paris 1228–44, and cardinal bishop of Tusculum (or Frascati) 1246–73, shed an interesting light on what were deemed Francis' most significant attributes and achievements by a leading churchman who strongly supported the friars, welcomed their recruitment of scholars and approved their influence in the university.[6] In one, preached on 4 October on the text 'The things that my soul refused to touch are as my sorrowful meat' (Job 6. 7) – an appropriate text for a theme illustrating Francis' conversion, with reference to the Testament – he said: [Francis] 'was a great sinner, ignorant and simple, uneducated except in what merchants are accustomed to know. Furthermore he had many impediments to well-doing: his own father and his companions . . . But converted to the Lord he began to hunger after his salvation; and the things which previously had seemed to him bitter were made sweet to him and turned into spiritual food.' In a second on the text 'And the Lord said, like as my servant Isaiah hath walked naked and barefoot' (Isaiah 20. 3), he dwelt on another crucial stage of Francis' conversion, his renunciation of his father and all his father stood for. 'So blessed Francis, not of his own will but by divine inspiration, denuded himself of all that he had . . . before his bishop to mitigate the anger of his father, returning to him not only the money which with such fury he required, but also all his clothes, even his breeches, which it is not the custom of men to take off, and which are in the greatest degree necessary to a man – or reckoned to be all the more necessary to him, for it is easier to bear cold than shame and easier to bear taking off one's tunic and other garments than one's breeches . . . So blessed Francis, ceding his right and succession to his kindred, and all right and worldly goods which he could have and possess, took off not just one shoe but two, and furthermore took off all his clothes and his shoes, and could then truly say to his father, indeed to all men and to all the world: "Do thou make use of my privilege, which I profess I do willingly forego"' (Ruth 4. 6, Douai). The significance of taking off a shoe – a very interesting theological point – is explained by this reference to the story of Ruth. After Boaz had caused the next of kin to yield his right, the passage continues: 'Now this in former times was the manner in Israel between kinsmen, that if at any time one yielded his right to another: that the grant might be sure, the man put off his shoe, and gave it to his neighbour; this was a testimony of cession of right in Israel. So Boaz said to his kinsman: Put off thy shoe. And immediately he took it off from his foot' (Ruth 4. 7–8).[7]

Eudes' style is repetitive, even more repetitive than as I have quoted it, to drive home the shocking thoroughness of Francis' act. This is the first of two recorded occasions

---

[4] Esser 1976, p. 439.   [5] See p. 161.
[6] Bougerol 1983, p. 175; Moorman 1968, p. 131 and n. 8.   [7] Bougerol 1983, pp. 177–8 and nn. 9–12.

on which St Francis performed the symbolic act of stripping completely, intentionally at the beginning and at the end. A few days before his death he struggled to undress himself and sat totally naked on the bare ground. His guardian understood that he wished 'to dispossess himself even of the tunic and breeches which the Rule allowed the friars, that he might be in everything a true pauper and imitator of Christ in life and in death', so he took the tunic and breeches and told Francis they were now lent to him, and he was not allowed to give them away. Francis was satisfied, confirming that: 'it is as poor as this that I wish to die' (SL pp. 296–7, App. c. 3). The account is laden with key words – naked, infirm, poor. The call 'naked to follow the naked Christ' and related formulas first appear in the letters and homilies of St Jerome, though their origins go back to the primitive Church, and were much quoted in the twelfth and thirteenth centuries, not only in monastic circles but also by leaders of apostolic movements, and by academics and by preachers. The challenge was generally understood metaphorically. It implied and involved giving up everything for Christ, and indicated a condition of weakness and vulnerability as well as of economic poverty. Poor, *pauper*, was used in the early Middle Ages as the opposite of *potens*, powerful, and in this context the terms *nudus*, *pauper*, *egenus* (destitute) and *humilis* (humble) were more or less interchangeable.[8] The renunciation required of the monk was threefold. He gave up all his property and took a vow of poverty. He gave up all his family and took a vow of chastity. He gave up his own will – a different type of renunciation, very difficult for some – and took a vow of obedience. The monks took individual vows of poverty, but monasteries could hold property and so could become wealthy in fact. St Francis strengthened the vow of poverty for his Order by requiring the renunciation of corporate as well as individual ownership. He also wished his educated followers to renounce their learning, and study to attain the fundamental virtues of their vocation, namely simplicity, prayer and poverty (SL 70). 'He once said that a great cleric ought, when he joins the Order, in some measure to resign even knowledge, so that stripped of such a possession he may offer himself naked to the arms of the Crucified' (2 Cel. 194). Francis is here using 'nudus' in its then normal, extended, religious sense. But he would quite frequently divest himself of his tunic, either out of generosity or as a form of penance; and the word *nudus* is used in this context in the sources to indicate exposure to the cold. Sometimes Francis gave it in alms to a poor man or to a friar who begged it out of devotion; on one such occasion remaining *nudus* for about an hour before his concerned companions or guardian could find a replacement (SL 52–3). He also took off his tunic when he wished to do public penance for having eaten a little meat and meat broth while he was ill, and insisted that brother Peter Catanii lead him thus 'nudum coram populo' (SL 39). He ordered a friar who disparaged a poor man to take off his tunic and go naked before the poor man and throw himself at his feet and apologise. Indeed he considered this a suitable punishment for all detractors, who had deadly poison in their tongues (James 3. 8). A friar who blackened the reputation of a brother should be deprived of his tunic, that is, his habit, the uniform of the Order, until he had made amends (2 Cel. 182).

---

[8] Constable 1979.

In a third sermon referring to Francis' conversion, Eudes of Châteauroux laid emphasis on his previous occupation, again with a well-chosen text: 'The kingdom of heaven is like unto a merchant man seeking goodly pearls' (Matt. 13. 45). He used the language of commerce, explaining this conversion as a transaction. For the circumstances were exceptional. Jesus had told the rich young man: 'Go and sell that thou hast and give to the poor, and thou shalt have treasure in heaven' (Matt. 19. 21–2). Technically Francis – likewise a rich young man – made restitution: he gave back to his father money that belonged to his father, and also, to his father, the clothes his father had provided. But by so doing he renounced his father and in consequence his inheritance. So Eudes produced this argument as coming from Francis' mouth: 'This saint sold, that is he relinquished, everything he had, but because he gained great profit through this renunciation he called it a sale.' Earlier in the sermon he held out a picture of the merchant state as an exemplary trade. 'By calling blessed Francis to himself the Lord made him a seller of spiritual stuffs, who before had been a seller of worldly stuffs and a merchant . . . St Francis, as it is said, from a purveyor of earthly goods, was made a purveyor of celestial goods.'[9]

In another sermon, preached at the Portiuncula, he developed this theme in a vivid and original way. 'When I arrived here just now I was reminded that when I was a child I tried to understand a story depicted in a window.' It was the parable of the Good Samaritan. A young layman explained to him that this stained glass image discredits clerks and religious in comparison to layfolk, because they showed no compassion to the poor and indigent, whereas laymen shared their sufferings and helped them in their need. After this introduction, Eudes presented St Francis as the type of the Good Samaritan: he was a layman, not a cleric, albeit somewhat educated. Just as the Jews did not mix with the Samaritans, Francis was not familiar with clerics; the Samaritans were intent on making money, and Francis socialised with fellow merchants, accepting the profit motive, sharing their commercial outlook, and their taste for worldly luxuries and comforts. The way of life of the unregenerate youth, castigated in 1 *Celano* (and utilised in a pejorative way by Guiard of Laon), is a generation later, being utilised as a bridge to establish contact with a prosperous urban lay society.[10] Francis can be cast as a role model for merchants. How does this affect his role as a religious leader? Eudes was aware of the stumbling block, and selected the text: 'If any man among you seemeth to be wise in this world, let him become a fool, that he may be wise. For the wisdom of this world is foolishness with God' (1 *Cor.* 3. 18–19). 'Blessed Francis in his youth, absorbed with merchandise, seemed to be wise in this world, increasing riches by lawful and unlawful means, and he was made a fool, rather, he made himself a fool in order to be truly wise.' But did this really qualify Francis for the task he undertook? Eudes stated the objections bluntly. 'For a man who knew nothing about the religious life and had no experience of it to found religious Orders seemed foolishness; and madness to preach to the Saracens, to preach indeed to Christians, a man who knew nothing of the Scriptures and was not in the habit of listening to sermons, because we nowhere

[9] Bougerol 1983, pp. 177–8, nn. 12–13; cf. Little 1978, p. 200; Lambert 1961, p. 39.
[10] Bougerol 1983, pp. 175–6 and n. 7.

read this of him before his conversion – it would seem foolish, positively dangerous especially in regions corrupted by heresy. It would seem highly presumptuous for one newly converted from sin audaciously to rebuke sinners; and so in the manner of his conversion and in the things that he then did he seemed truly to have played the fool. But it was confirmed in this way that to pretend to play the fool is highest wisdom.' Eudes clearly felt the same lively delight in paradox as Francis had done. His conclusion: 'In the fruit which he produced in the Church of God, God showed that the wisdom of this world is foolishness.'[11]

St Francis also succeeded because of his steadfastness; having entered the way, he persevered in it and did not turn aside either to right or left. Eudes applied to him a further text from Job: 'My foot hath held his steps, his way have I kept, and not declined. Neither have I gone back from the commandment of his lips; I have esteemed the words of his mouth more than my necessary food' (Job 23. 11–12), and claimed that in this text 'the Holy Spirit [who was believed to have written the Bible] briefly describes the life and works of blessed Francis, and this is as it were his epitaph'. Eudes then engaged the attention of his audience with an arresting hunting analogy. The Friars Preacher were referred to as dogs – a play on the name 'Dominicans', 'Domini canes', dogs of the Lord. They are so shown in a mid-fourteenth-century fresco in the Spanish Chapel, part of the Dominican house of Santa Maria Novella in Florence, on the wall depicting the Way of Salvation. Christ's flock, appropriately represented by sheep, rest quietly, guarded from harm, that is, heresy, by two dogs, in the Order's colours, black and white. Eudes commandeered the term for Francis. 'Just as when a dog finds a wild animal he chases it, and on his example others follow with loud barking, so this man pursued the Lord as his prey, and on his example very many follow after the same prey through thorns and tribulations and with loud barking; and they come scratched to pieces, and they rejoice, because their leader already holds the prize . . . Some turn aside from the straight way on account of the difficulty of the journey, because it is too steep or stony or muddy or narrow, or on account of the dangers from robbers or enemies. Assuredly this man did not turn aside, neither on account of harshness or depth or height or any other impediment, because he always sniffed the scent of Christ whom he followed, convinced that he was on Christ's track.'[12]

Eudes reached a climax in his praise of Francis in a sermon preached on the text: 'The kingdom of heaven is like to a grain of mustard seed which a man took, and sowed in his field, which indeed is the least of all seeds, but when it is grown it is the greatest among herbs and becometh a tree' (Matt. 13. 31–2). The Church, especially the primitive Church, is so closely assimilated to the kingdom of heaven – in much the same way as a daughter is close to her mother – that it can be called the kingdom of heaven. 'What was, is that which is to come; therefore in our time what was made then is made again and renewed in blessed Francis, and through this repetition faith in what has gone before is confirmed for us. For the well-directed heart (cor) is the one that is not at variance (non discordat) with God's will, which should be the rule of our heart

[11] Bougerol 1983, pp. 178–9 and nn. 15, 17; cf. SL 114; 1 Cor. 1. 20–5.
[12] Bougerol 1983, pp. 178–9 and nn. 14, 16.

(*cordis*)' – a play on *cor, cordis, discordia*. 'So because blessed Francis, after the Lord had visited and enlightened him and converted him to himself, studied to conform his will to the divine will . . . he was thereby brought into conformity with those who are in the kingdom of heaven, just as the men of the kingdom of France are said to be the kingdom of France, and when the great men are gathered anywhere, there is said to be the whole kingdom of France. So therefore the blessed Francis was the kingdom of heaven.'[13] The argument is a sophisticated academic one. The conformity of Francis' life to the mode of the primitive Church was instrumental in forming St Bonaventure's own vocation, and its importance was stressed by him.[14] The idea that a few could represent the whole was one that was rapidly and efficiently developed by the Dominican Order as a tool of government in its early statutes, and was very topical.[15] The representative principle was one that was central to the political thinking of the thirteenth century in the west. Its use in this context is very interesting and striking. To declare that St Francis was the kingdom of heaven is a remarkable claim and invites comparison with the much more widely disseminated claim that he was a 'second Christ', 'alter Christus'.[16] Though extravagant, and inevitably tendentious, it is however reverent and proper, claiming no more than that he is the representative of the saints.

Another Paris master and leading churchman who actively supported the friars was Frederick Visconti, consecrated archbishop of Pisa in 1257. He died in 1277. A member of a Pisan noble family, he was immensely proud of his city. As a student at Paris some time after 1244 he was much influenced by Dominican theologians, and may have attended Albert the Great's lectures.[17] A major intellectual concern shared by both mendicant Orders in Paris at this time was the refining of a moral theology capable of addressing the social problems posed by the commercial activities of an expanding urban economy. Innovative discussion in this challenging area had been inaugurated by Peter the Chanter and his circle near the end of the twelfth century and was pursued in the thirteenth, among others by Alexander of Hales, and by the Dominican Hugh of St Cher, who helped to establish the crucial distinction between honest and dishonest merchants. These theologians taught that the honest merchant deserved the profit he made; it could be regarded as payment for his labour. But he should use it properly. He should not horde it, nor indulge in an unduly extravagant lifestyle for himself and his family. He should provide reasonably for his family's needs and he should be charitable to those less fortunate. Thus merchants could make a positive, useful contribution to society not only by distributing goods but by redistributing wealth as well.[18]

Pisa was a thriving port. Frederick Visconti took his pastoral mission very seriously. Early in his episcopate he moved his official residence from the bishop's palace near the cathedral to San Pietro in Vinculis, close to the central market place. Seafarers and merchants, merchants' wives, grass widows and widows could form a substantial element in the large congregations that attended his sermons, in many of which he

---

[13] Bougerol 1983, pp. 179–80 and nn. 18–21.
[14] Bougerol 1983, p. 179 and n. 19; cf. Bonaventure, *Opera Omnia*, VIII, 336, c. 13.
[15] Hinnebusch 1966, pp. 169–93.   [16] Cf. Stanislao da Campagnola 1971.
[17] Murray 1981, pp. 23, 30–3.
[18] Little 1978, pp. 175, 178–9; d'Avray 1985, pp. 207–16. For Alexander of Hales, see p. 247.

made practical application of the theory he had studied with mendicant theologians in Paris.[19] So it is no surprise that when he preached at the Minors' church in Pisa on Francis' feast day in 1257 he pointed out that the text 'The kingdom of heaven is like unto a merchant man'(Matt. 13. 45) applied to Francis, 'and cerainly he was literally (ad litteram) a trader or merchant of the city of Assisi in the valley of Spoleto, and when he was enriched by trade he wanted to be made a knight, just as the citizens of Lucca and Genoa do; the Pisans used not to, but now they do differently, as you see' – anchoring him firmly in an urban social context familiar to his audience. Later in the sermon he addressed merchants and their womenfolk specifically: 'O blessed the trader or merchant from whose trading there is in this house [the friars' convent] bread and wine or food for the body or silk cloth for the altar or for a chasuble or wet weather cope, or a hanging or woollen cloth for garments, or coarse cloth or skins [?] for coverings, or soles for shoes or money for buying books. O blessed the woman who bestows on them through the work of her own hands a priestly vestment, a surplice with sleeves [?], coverings for the altar or the table.'[20] Such words of commendation were calculated to give satisfaction to listeners who had in such varied ways provided for the friars and to prod others towards giving.

He continued to remind his hearers that St Francis had been a merchant – one of them – in further sermons. Preaching in San Francesco in 1261, he first dealt with his duty as their bishop, when preaching, to urge sinners to confess and make satisfaction. For example, they might go on pilgrimage to the Holy Places, or to St James of Compostela, or to Rome, or to the Basilica. 'O, how many men and women there are today who have visited S. Francesco at Assisi for the remission of their sins and to acquire merit, because the saint has been glorified in our time, and because his church, which our lord Pope Innocent IV endowed and enriched with great privileges and many treasures, is glorious and most beautiful and spacious.'[21] Frederick had been one of Innocent IV's chaplains both before and after he became pope. He went on: 'And that is how the churches of such saints ought to be, so that the spirit takes pleasure in entering and remaining, and also in frequently returning. But if they are cramped, as this church is, men unwillingly stay there to hear divine service and sermons and are even more unwilling to return another time, saying to each other: "I do not want to go to that one because there was such a crush there the other day that I still have a sore head, or foot, or something else wrong."' As it was not capable of holding all those wishing to come to sermons, the archbishop pronounced that the church should be enlarged and that he himself would lay the foundation stone. He offered as an incentive an indulgence additional to the limited one granted to the Franciscan church at Pisa by Alexander IV, to all true penitents for the duration of the construction work;[22] but he was fully aware that the bulk of the costs would have to be borne locally, and that meant from trading profits. 'Of course . . . our (nostri) merchants . . . love this place and honour the friars', but

[19] Murray 1981, pp. 35–7, 40–2, 44–5.
[20] Bihl 1908, pp. 652–3; Murray 1981, pp. 64 n. 171, 41–2 n. 79.
[21] Bihl 1908, pp. 652–3; and see pp. 66–8; in 1252 Innocent IV had granted an indulgence of one year and forty days to pilgrims to the Basilica on St Francis' feast day and during the two weeks thereafter.
[22] Murray 1981, p. 14 n. 92; Bihl 1908, p. 653 and n. 3. The indulgence, dated June 1256, was for 100 days for visiting on the feast days of St Francis, St Anthony and St Clare, and their octaves.

they should give more. To stimulate and organise their involvement, he announced the establishment of a fraternity in honour of St Francis, their peer (*consocius*), to meet here in the church to hear mass and receive communion and fulfil other worthy objectives. 'Bear in mind that it ought to be agreeable for merchants that their fellow, St Francis, was a merchant and was canonised in our time. O how much good hope there must be for merchants, who have such a merchant intercessor with God.' In Pisa at any rate, Francis has been enrolled as the patron saint of merchants.[23]

Frederick also stressed that Francis had had ambitions to become a knight, reckoning this would appeal to the upwardly mobile element among the Pisan middle class. The knightly metaphor continues after his conversion: indeed Francis used it himself. Francis became a spiritual knight and 'Christ willed that the stigmata, the signs of the five wounds, should appear in St Francis' body, just like the new knight of any great lord, who bears the sign [the livery] of the arms of that man who made him a knight.'[24] A third aspect he highlighted was that Francis repaired three ruined churches and thereby merited to found three Orders.[25]

In one sermon, preached on 4 October 1265, he dwelt on Francis as an individual. 'Truly they are blessed who saw St Francis.' He then testified to his own experience. 'We by God's grace saw and touched [him] with our hand in the piazza of the commune of the Bolognesi in a great throng of men. They also are blessed who saw his miracles, as are they who looked, or look daily, with devotion at his image (*picturam*) . . . and they who obey him, that is to say, his doctrine.'[26] However, his succinct account of Francis' life, repeated in sermon after sermon on his feast day, reveals that Frederick, despite having seen him, got close enough to touch him – which suggests he was moved to devotion at the time, particularly as he did not find crowd situations comfortable – venerated Francis not primarily for himself, but because he was the founder of Orders the archbishop considered not merely useful but essential for the improvement and good administration of his own diocese and the Church at large. The climax of his oration on this occasion was the blessedness of those who obey Francis' doctrine, 'which he left in his Rule; they are adorned with the grace of virtues and glory both with God and with men, because thus they are made perfect. With how much honour and grace are the friars of St Francis honoured before God and men!'[27] 'The Order' – he said in 1257 – 'is a precious pearl, a pearl both of great price [Matt. 13. 45], and so cheap, that every man, poor and rich, can have or buy it provided he gives up what he has, and it is the more precious because with this habit all good things are had (*habere, habet, habita habeantur*).'[28]

---

[23] Bihl 1908, p. 654; Little 1978, p. 217.   [24] Bougerol 1983, p. 180 n. 22.

[25] Bougerol 1983, p. 180; cf. Julian of Speyer, cc. 14, 23 (also his *Officium S. Francisci*, 14,v, AF X, 380). A similar point was made by St Bonaventure in a sermon delivered at Paris on 4 October 1267. 'In the beginning of his conversion [Francis] founded three churches . . . and he instituted three Orders, the Order of Friars Minor, the Order of sisters of blessed Clare who were first called the poor ladies of Sts Cosmas and Damian, now, after St Clare has been canonised, they are called the sisters of blessed Clare; and he instituted the third Order of penitents who are called the continent brothers. These three orders – as it were his three daughters – he instituted and ordained to the worship of God' (Bougerol 1993, II, 752–3, sermon 57, c. 4). St Clare was canonised in 1255; the change of name of the Poor Ladies was actually effected by Urban IV in the Rule promulgated on 18 October 1263 (Brady 1976, p. 132).

[26] Bihl 1908, p. 654, and see p. 173.   [27] Bihl 1908, p. 654 (1265).

[28] Murray 1981, p. 66 and n. 178. 'Illa habita' perhaps rather means 'once the pearl is possessed'.

Because of their exemplary lifestyle they are powerful intercessors. The laity carry on their everyday lives, sleep, watch, till the soil, sail the sea unaware that they are being shielded from harm by the friars' prayers. But that is the case. The friars work for the salvation of souls and deserve support. 'We ought, best beloved, to remain in friendship with St Francis and his friars both spiritually and temporally . . . and provide for their needs in food, in clothing, in books, as well as in furnishings and treasures for the church, that we may participate in their prayers and benefits.' He held out the carrot that benefactors might derive the most benefit. Many times their benefactors are defended from adversity. Their business dealings are given a fair wind.[29] But essentially he understood the basis of Francis' trust; if he and his followers depended utterly on God, God would provide for them. They would spend their days in prayer, travelling, preaching, caring for the sick and lepers, helping the poor, responding to need. In return they might accept the necessary food, clothing and shelter and if this was not forthcoming they were to beg from door to door.[30] That is why the archbishop urged his flock to support the friars generously. He even used the same kind of language as Francis had done. The friars were 'knights of Christ' and deserved a knight's 'stipend', which was in their case 'the necessities of life'.[31]

It is clear that Frederick greatly valued the contribution the friars, both Franciscan and Dominican, could make, and he actively supported their ministry. 'We can rejoice . . . that at this eleventh hour God has given us . . . these two Orders, the Preachers and the Minors, who do not cease to propound God's word conscientiously and fully on our behalf on Sundays and feast days and also for the dead both within the city and outside.'[32] 'All the Friars Preachers and Minors who preach in our city or diocese, preach by our authority and in our place and therefore we have commanded that as often as they come and go to preach they are to be honoured as ourself.'[33]

His emphasis on preaching was in part in response to local circumstances. The Pisan commune was strongly Ghibelline. When he was elected archbishop in 1254 the city was under interdict. This had been imposed by Gregory IX as far back as 1241 when the Pisan fleet, at the instigation of Frederick II, had attacked ships taking churchmen from Genoa to Rome for a council, sinking three and capturing twenty-two. Throughout these years, and until 1257, when as a result of Archbishop Frederick's mediation the interdict was lifted, Pisan citizens were denied church services and pastoral care.[34] There was an urgent need for an active campaign of instruction and regeneration led by the archbishop, who bore responsibility for the spiritual welfare of his flock. Nicola Pisano's great freestanding polygonal pulpit for the Baptistery at Pisa is signed and dated 1260. There is no documentary evidence as to who commissioned it, but the Opera of the Baptistery was controlled by the canons of the cathedral, and Frederick Visconti was a canon in the years between his studies in Paris and his becoming archbishop. As archbishop he promoted the construction and embellishment of new churches, notably the Dominican church of Santa Caterina, and the enlargement of others, such

[29] Murray 1981, p. 61 and n. 162 (1257); Bihl 1908, p. 654 (1265).
[30] *Regula bullata*, cc. 5–6, Esser 1976, pp. 368–9.
[31] Murray 1981, p. 61 and n. 159 (1257).   [32] Murray 1981, pp. 67–8 and n. 182.
[33] Murray 1981, p. 68 n. 182; and cf. n. 184.   [34] For this and what follows, see Angiola 1977.

as San Francesco. He was a patron of painters. The name of Giunta Pisano occurs in a list of a group who swore fidelity to Frederick in a document dated 28 August 1254. It is probable that his patronage inspired the Baptistery pulpit. The Baptistery, an integral part of the outstandingly rich and beautiful cathedral quarter, was a symbol of the power and wealth both of the commune and of the Church. In contrast to England, where a city might contain numerous tiny parishes – London, for instance, had over a hundred, and Cambridge fifteen – each parish church having its own font,[35] in Italy it was normal for there to be a single baptistery close to the cathedral, where everyone in the city and its contado was baptised by the bishop. The same proximity of baptistery, cathedral and campanile at Pisa is evident for example at Florence. Frederick described the Baptistery as 'the mirror of this city and the gate of Paradise, for no-one will enter Paradise who has not been baptised in the baptism of blessed John, who baptised Christ'. The sacrament of baptism embraces concern not only with birth but also with Christ's death and resurrection, the whole unfolding of Christ's life on earth. St Paul wrote: 'Know ye not, that so many of us as were baptised into Jesus Christ were baptised into his death? Therefore we are buried with him by baptism into death; that like as Christ was raised up from the dead by the glory of the Father, even so we also should walk in newness of life' (Romans 6. 3–4).[36] The five sculptured scenes on the pulpit display this range: the Nativity, the Adoration of the Magi, the Presentation in the Temple, the Crucifixion and the Last Judgement, when the heavens open to the baptised. The theological programme so innovatively executed by the sculptor is complex and highly structured. It was almost certainly devised by the archbishop himself. The iconography is biblical and the particular way in which the scheme is developed suggests that it may have been based on Hugh of St Cher's *Postilla*; and Hugh was a Dominican theologian who more than any other influenced Frederick Visconti's thinking.[37]

One notable feature of the iconography is the importance of the role assigned to Mary and other women. Mary's serene and monumental figure presides over the scenes of the Nativity and the Adoration of the Magi. In the Presentation she represents also the Church, 'Ecclesia': she is both the mother and the bride of Christ. Among the biblical figures carved in relief at each of the six corners of the pulpit, women are granted their full share: three women, Eve, Judith and Esther, balance two men, John the Baptist and Daniel, and the archangel Gabriel.[38] Frederick's attitude towards women was positive and supportive. He maintained, following Solomon, that many women are good, and will have grace in the present life and glory in the future. He addressed his words to 'sons and daughters' and his references to Christians were inclusive: 'Christian men and women'. He gave instructions that men should set their sons and daughters to reading and writing so that they might think about the good and avoid the evil that the young are prone to. He spoke publicly in praise of St Clare, arguing the case for her sanctity during her canonisation process. She was a role model for women just as St Francis was for men.

---

[35] C. Brooke 1999, pp. 31–2, 73–89, 101; Cattaneo 1970.
[36] Quoted Angiola 1977, p. 7.   [37] Murray 1981, pp. 31–2 and n. 43.
[38] Angiola 1977, esp. pp. 10–19. For what follows, see Murray 1981, pp. 35–6 and nn. 58–61.

A prime aim of preaching was to move the people to penitence and confession, a task particularly important with a population deprived of the sacrament for the previous fifteen years and one the friars were well equipped to fulfil. But their training and way of life were bonuses which could be put to further good use by the archbishop. The interdict had imposed an enforced idleness on his secular clergy, and with the churches closed many had become demotivated, and such skills as they had were rusty; many lacked the education he considered requisite. From the start, in his inaugural sermon in 1257, Frederick held up before his clergy the example of the religious, who process out of their sacristies and approach the altar and behave in choir with devotion, 'like angels of God'.[39] Furthermore, he told them, in another sermon, that they must study, because priests must possess wisdom as well as works and zeal; and excuses, such as that they had no money or books to go to Bologna, would not do. For God had now provided them with teachers in Pisa, that is 'masters of theology of the Orders of Friars Preachers and Minors, who, living in your land [preach] to you for free and without charge'.[40]

The image of St Francis reflected in Frederick Visconti's sermons is to a great extent determined by its specific context of time and place. An active, well-educated and conscientious archbishop selected from St Francis' life those aspects calculated to appeal to the Pisan mercantile society entrusted to him. Merchants, their wives and widows, could be encouraged to lead more Christian lives, to join fraternities attached to his cult or become members of his Third Order. For it was his achievements through others, as the founder who set the seal of his own distinctive holiness on Orders catering for all sections of the community, that Frederick honoured in St Francis. His outspoken admiration for the Friars Minor was also geared to contemporary realities as viewed from his perspective. It was not the Order of the early days but the Order as it was in the mid-thirteenth century that he promoted and that helped him. It had by now become, from a mainly lay, a predominantly clerical and educated Order, and this development, significantly, had been triggered by Paris masters of the previous generation to Visconti's, by Alexander of Hales and John of La Rochelle. They had joined the Minors and focused the opposition to brother Elias, which resulted in the far-reaching constitutional changes implemented during the generalate of Haymo of Faversham, another Paris master.[41] For Frederick, the Minors' convent in Pisa was the home of learned masters of theology; their church needed enlarging so that bigger crowds could attend sermons there;[42] the Dominicans needed a new one, 'for it was unseemly and inconvenient that such wise and religious men in such a city as this should have such a wretched and paltry church'. 'It is fitting that this our honourable city of Pisa and so honourable a convent of friars as this is, where there are more than fifty friars, as you know, most wise and discreet, should have an honourable and beautiful church.'[43] The two Orders were closely associated in the archbishop's mind, frequently referred to together in the same breath. Pisa, in the twenty years of his ministry, from

---

[39] Murray 1981, p. 65 and n. 172.   [40] Murray 1981, pp. 58 and n. 152, 67 and n. 180.
[41] Jordan, c. 61; Eccleston, p. 27; Brooke 1959, pp. 161–6; and pp. 123–4.
[42] For this and what follows, see Murray 1981, pp. 59–72.
[43] Murray 1981, p. 60 and n. 158; cf. ibid. pp. 27–9.

1257 to 1277, offers a concrete example of how both reacted to pressures and demands both shared. The followers of St Francis and St Dominic worked side by side in Pisa.

Academic friendship played a part in fostering harmony. At Paris the Dominican regent master Guerric of St Quentin, the chancellor of Paris, Eudes of Châteauroux, a secular, and the Franciscan regent master John of La Rochelle were close friends. Guerric delivered a sermon in celebration of St Francis on his feast day in 1242. Christ is the way. But because it is difficult, 'He has put a sign for us in the way, blessed Francis, who teaches the way for us to go to heaven, saying: "This is the way, go in it; this is the way of coming to God and following Christ, that is by poverty, by penitence and suchlike."'[44]

John of La Rochelle, taking as his text 'I will give unto my two witnesses' (Rev. 11. 3), preached on the two saints Francis and Dominic jointly, the only known sermon on this theme to survive from the period. 'O what concord there was in the blessed fathers Francis and Dominic, who on the most secure evidence wanted to unite their Orders – to make them one Order. But it was prevented by divine ordinance, because it is better to have two than one: for two will foster one another; if one falls, the other will support it.'[45] John died in February 1245, months after the instruction to gather material about St Francis had gone out at Whitsun 1244, but before Thomas of Celano wrote his *Second Life*, between August 1246 and July 1247.[46] There is no mention of St Dominic in 1 *Celano*. Therefore the 'secure evidence' of a wish to unite the Orders to which John refers must have been available, but not officially recorded, before 1245. His sermon thus enhances the credibility of the account in 2 *Celano*. 148–50 of a meeting between Francis and Dominic in Rome in the presence of Hugolino. The cardinal put to them a proposal to promote friars to bishoprics, recalling the practice of the primitive Church when pastors were poor. The two saints vied in humility as to who should speak first, and Francis won. Dominic spoke first, followed by Francis; both declined. Then they left the great man, and while they were still together, Dominic devoutly asked Francis to give him his cord – and proposed a merger between the two Orders. In this second contest in humility, one cannot but feel that Dominic won. Francis gives no answer – but it is implied that he felt bound to refuse. The story has been widely disbelieved, but it is supported by some evidence from Dominican sources, and has been shown to fit some of the traits of Dominic, who could be intuitive and impulsive – though he could also be logical and highly organised. It is indeed likely that there was such a meeting, and that it played a crucial part in forming Dominic's plan to convert his tiny Order of canons regular dedicated to preaching to heretics into an order of friars.[47] St Bonaventure incorporated a much abbreviated and modified version of the incident into his *Life*. He recorded that the cardinal enquired of Francis whether he would be willing for his friars to be promoted to ecclesiastical dignities, and quoted his incisive definition, taken from 2 *Cel*. 148, that his brothers were called Minors, 'minores', precisely in order that they might not presume to become greater, 'maiores'. The part played by St Dominic is entirely omitted (Bonav. VI, 5). Without

---

[44] Bougerol 1983, p. 183 and n. 29.   [45] Bougerol 1983, pp. 182–3 and n. 28.
[46] AF X, xxvi.   [47] See C. Brooke 1971, pp. 222–7; Brooke 1975, pp. 95–7.

2 *Celano* – supported by John of La Rochelle's sermon – we should have no insight into a crucial moment in the formation of both Orders.

John of La Rochelle preached at least four other sermons on St Francis, of which one, on the text 'God created man in his own image' (Gen. 1. 27), is of particular interest. 'God created the first man, Adam, in his own image and likeness. But Adam destroyed God's image and likeness in himself. Yet through St Francis God's image and likeness are restored. And so it can rightly be said of him "God created a man" – that is St Francis – "in his own image and likeness"'[48] (Colour Plate 2). The claims made for St Francis in 1 *Celano* had been high, but here they are breath-taking. St Francis was created in the image of the divinity of Christ and in the likeness of his humanity. The divinity is considered first. The three Persons of the Trinity each has an attribute: the Father power, the Son wisdom, the Holy Spirit goodness (according to the *Summa* of brother Alexander of Hales), and Francis conforms to all three. He is like to the Father in the two manifestations of control and action: he had command over creatures (fish and birds for example) and he performed miracles – healing the sick and lepers, exorcising demons and resuscitating the dead. He is like to the Son in wisdom, penetrating the secrets of the heart and predicting the future. He is like to the Holy Spirit in goodness – he renounced everything and gave everything out of love, and he sought martyrdom, going so far as to preach to the Sultan. His conformity to the humanity of Jesus is then analysed. He is like Jesus in his life of poverty, humility and mortification, all undertaken in imitation of the life of Jesus. He is like Jesus in death, because he received the stupendous privilege of the stigmata; and like in resurrection since his afflicted flesh, previously blackened, became shining, as if already glorified.

Many of the illustrative details, such as the obedience of creatures to him, his desire to achieve martyrdom, and his miracles, were taken, as we would expect, from 1 *Celano*. A second source was Julian of Speyer's *Rhymed Office of St Francis*, composed earlier than 4 October 1235.[49] Julian was chapel master and director of the student friars in the *studium* at Paris, where he died in 1250. He will have conducted the chant at the service during which the sermon was delivered, and it will have been in part in compliment to Julian that John embellished his address with generous references to the antiphons, responses and hymns of his *Office*. It is likely that John also drew on the letter sent by brother Elias immediately after Francis' death for his description of the state of Francis' body after death. The one extant copy of this letter is that addressed to Gregory of Naples, the Provincial Minister of France. Elias wrote that, while his spirit remained in his body, there was no comeliness in it but his countenance was despised (cf. Isaiah 53. 2–5), and his limbs were contracted and stiff as if already dead. But after his death his appearance was most beautiful, glowing with an astonishing radiance, and his limbs, which were previously rigid, were made exceedingly soft and flexible so that they could be moved about like those of delicate boys.[50]

---

[48] For this and what follows, see Bougerol 1983, pp. 187–90; cf. d'Avray 1985, pp. 140–2; Frugoni 1993, pp. 107, 110, 125–6 n. 18.

[49] AF x, pp. xlii–xlix, 375–88.

[50] AF x, 525–8, esp. 527. The phenomenon of the incorrupt bodies of saints is discussed in Vauchez 1997, pp. 427 ff.

Such extravagant claims as John of La Rochelle voiced had an understandable attraction for the Order. They not only extolled St Francis as an individual; they offered a theological justification for the vocation of the Friars Minor.[51] A very similar sermon, on the same text and theme, and with an identical structure of development, was preached in Paris on 4 October 1262, some twenty odd years later. It was mistakenly attributed to St Bonaventure. It was actually delivered by a cardinal, who, Brady argues, can be identified as Eudes of Châteauroux.[52]

St Bonaventure

Five sermons on St Francis by St Bonaventure have survived which are accepted as authentic.[53] The earliest is in some respects the most interesting. It was a university sermon, preached in the church of the Franciscan convent at Paris on 4 October 1255. It was delivered in two parts, the first, cc. 1–13, in the morning to the whole university master and student body, the second, cc. 14–31, in the evening *collatio* to the more restricted audience of the Friars Minor.[54] At that date Bonaventure was not yet Minister General. He would not then have known he would be asked to write his own *Life of St Francis*. At that date, owing to a quarrel between the university and the mendicant Orders that had been intensifying on a number of fronts since c.1250, St Bonaventure was not recognised as a regent master by the university, although he had qualified; he and his opposite number St Thomas Aquinas were not formally received as regents until October 1257. The unauthorised appearance of brother Gerard of Borgo San Donnino's *Introduction to the Eternal Gospel* in 1254 precipitated a concentrated pamphlet war on the mendicants by some of Paris' secular masters, led by William of St Amour. His *Tractatus brevis*, denouncing the mendicant Orders as false apostles, forerunners of Antichrist, appeared in 1255. Bonaventure immediately countered by holding a series of disputations in the university on the subject of evangelical poverty, and it is in this context that the sermon is to be interpreted.[55]

Its text is taken from the portion of St Matthew's Gospel set for St Francis' feast: 'learn of me; for I am meek and lowly in heart' (Matt. 11. 29). The words are Christ's and succinctly encapsulate the sum of evangelical perfection. They encourage their hearers to accept Christ's doctrine and become his disciples; and they can be applied to his perfect imitator, St Francis, who was a true disciple and a good teacher (c. 1). For Francis, inspired by Christ, relinquished the society of sinful youths and worldly merchants, gave up all possessions, including clothes, left his father and mother, and with continual groans and tears strove to expel vice and sin. By these stages of conversion

[51] Bougerol 1983, p. 189.
[52] Bonaventure, *Opera Omnia*, IX, 582–5, sermo III; Brady 1976, pp. 132–7; also Doyle 1983; Bougerol 1983, p. 188; Bougerol 1993, I, 37–8.
[53] Bougerol 1983, pp. 190–1; Bougerol 1993, I, 11–16, 37–8; II, 604–20, 742–812; d'Avray 1985, pp. 142–4.
[54] Bougerol 1993, I, 7 and n. 11; II, 787–812, Sermon 59 (= Bonaventure, *Opera Omnia*, IX, 590–7, sermo V); Bougerol 1983, pp. 191–3 and nn. How many members of the university will have attended is unclear. See p. 218.
[55] 'Quaestiones de perfectione evangelica', in Bonaventure, *Opera Omnia*, V, 117–24; cf. Bougerol 1983, p. 191 and nn.; d'Avray 1985, pp. 163–203. For the context, see Douie 1973; Gratien 1928, pp. 130–2, 205–21; Moorman 1968, pp. 124 ff; Dufeil 1972, esp. pp. 174–87, 194–6.

Francis achieved true discipleship and wisdom could enter his soul (cc. 2–5). He passed from disciple to good teacher: so receive his teaching, for four reasons. First, he teaches what he learned through revelation, which cannot be other than true, because God is truth. Thus Paul said, in Galatians 1. 11–12, 'I make known to you the Gospel which was preached by me, because it is not made by man – nor did I receive it from man but by the revelation of Jesus Christ'; likewise Francis (The reference is to the Testament): 'How could he teach others when he did not learn from men? Did he find it through himself – *per se*. Hear that it was not so! – The sign of which is that when he was instructed by anyone or prepared a sermon in advance, he forgot what he was going to say, as is written in his Life.' This is actually a reference to Julian of Speyer's *Life of St Francis*, which would have been readily available in Paris, not, as we might have expected, to 1 *Celano*.[56] At this point Bonaventure draws a clear distinction. He realised that his line of argument was potentially dangerous. The inspired unpremeditated words of the saint 'were to be admired and praised rather than imitated. His sons do not learn without being taught, because to know without a human teacher is the privilege not of everyone but of the few. Although the Lord was pleased to teach Paul and Francis himself, he wished their disciples to be taught by human agency' (c. 6). Secondly, Francis teaches 'without guile' (Wisdom 7. 13, Douai); thirdly, by 'not becoming a forgetful hearer but a doer of the work' (James 1. 25, Douai). Francis learned by experiencing sufferings, not delights. At the beginning of his conversion he became acquainted with many obstacles – jibes, blows, chains, prisons and lies, and in these things, like St Paul (cf. Phil. 4. 9) St Francis is to be praised and imitated and followed in discipleship (c. 8). Fourthly, he teaches what he learned, like Paul, in the certainty that his doctrine was saving, since God confirmed it by signs and miracles (1 Cor. 15. 1–3; Mark 16. 20) (c. 9).

'For it pleased God to authenticate and confirm the teaching and the Rule of this holy man, not only by the signs of his miracles but also of his stigmata – so that no-one acting in good faith could contradict either from outward or inward reasoning. It pleased God's divine fatherhood to set his seal of lead (*bulla*) upon the Rule and teaching of Francis, since he did not dare to teach nor write save what he received from God: for he himself bore witness that he had learned the whole Rule by revelation – [Testament again] – and so, just as it is the custom of the pope to confirm his letters with a lead seal, thus too Christ, recognising that Francis' Rule was his, attached the leaden seal of his miracles – and by this token confirmed his teaching inviolably. Certainly Francis' teaching could not have had confirmation among men on his own account, since he was a merchant without letters, an illiterate teacher; and so – to ensure that no wise men belittled his teaching or Rule as the work of an ignorant man, it pleased God to confirm them with manifest signs as if with a heavenly and wonderful seal of lead. In

---

[56] Julian of Speyer, c. 58 (AF x, 362). The story is also told in 1 Cel. 72, but, as Brady argued (1976, p. 139), Bonaventure is here closer to Julian. Although the same word 'praecogitare' is used in both, 'omnino quod diceret non habebat' echoes a phrase in Julian but not in Celano. Brady (1976) showed, on rather slighter but convincing grounds, that in the passages cited below (nn. 62–3) Bonaventure's text is closer to Julian, cc. 37, 62, than to 1 Cel. 81, 95. The presumption is that Julian was Bonaventure's source throughout this sermon. On Julian's connection with Paris, see p. 230. At least two of the surviving MSS of his Life come from Parisian canons' libraries (AF x, pp. xlviii–xlix). For his use in Bonav., see AF x, p. lxiv, and the notes to the texts of Bonav. in AF x.

this it is clear that the height of divine wisdom is to be wonderfully admired, which Christ indicates at the outset of this Gospel [appointed for St Francis' feast day] when he says: "I confess to you, Father, lord of heaven and earth, that you have hidden these things from the wise and prudent, and revealed them to the little children." [Matt. 11. 25]. Who is the little child if not the blessed Francis, humble and despised? He retains his primacy among the little ones, that is the Friars Minor [c. 10].

'He must be thoroughly hard-hearted who doubts that such signs have confirmed that the teaching and Rule of the blessed Francis are the straightest road by which one can come to life – especially as it is many times established that God wonderfully impressed such signs on his body, both by the number of the witnesses and their authority and sanctity. The number of the witnesses undoubtedly creates confidence because the many trustworthy laymen who saw with their eyes exceeded a hundred. If every word may be established by the mouths of two or three witnesses [Matt. 18. 16], how much more by a hundred! The authority of those bearing witness . . . was confirmed and approved by the Roman curia whose authority is supreme in the world . . . The sanctity of those who bear witness indisputably casts aside all doubt, since his companions, men of wonderful sanctity, whose probity of life and sanctity are manifest, asserted most assuredly with all the firmness of an oathtaking, that they had seen those wonderful signs with their eyes and handled them with their hands [1 John 1.1] [c. 11].

'Who ever heard that such very beautiful pearls appeared in anyone's body? . . . since his hands were not scored or pierced, as some instrument of iron or wood could have done this; but nails had grown in the flesh itself, since on one side they had the heads, on the other they were bent and divided, and quite wonderfully distinct from other flesh in hands and feet so that none of the faithful could doubt that such signs could be imprinted otherwise than by an admirable miracle [c. 12] . . . Let all hear and learn the teaching (or doctrine) of Francis as that of a good teacher (or doctor) . . . Let blessed Francis say: "Learn from me" – inspiring others' [c. 13].

Bonaventure continued during the *collatio* of the evening office, developing the second part of his text. St Francis, the perfect imitator of Christ, can also echo Christ's further words, that is, he can urge others to learn from his example to be meek and humble. 'For a man is meek (or gentle) out of brotherly love; humble from a sense of inferiority and of lesser worth. Whence to be meek is to be the brother of all; to be humble is to be less than all (*omnibus minorem*). To be meek and humble of heart is truly to be a lesser brother (*fratrem minorem*). "Learn therefore from me to be meek and humble" means to be Friars Minor (*fratres minores*) [c. 14].[57]

'We ought to learn this most necessary meekness from blessed Francis, who preserved a wonderful meekness not only towards men but also to wild animals. He called all animals by the name of brothers and untamed animals ran to him as to an intimate friend, as is read in his Life' (c. 18) – again a reference to Julian of Speyer.[58]

This sermon was clearly aimed to reassure the Friars Minor that their way of life was soundly based theologically. It also provides valuable insights into St Bonaventure's

---

[57] Cf. Julian of Speyer, c. 23; 1 *Cel.* 38.   [58] Julian of Speyer, c. 37; cf. 1 *Cel.* 81.

own vocation: why he chose to follow Christ in the steps of St Francis rather than in some other way.[59] In another sermon, also preached in Paris twelve years later to the day, on 4 October 1267 Bonaventure returns to the theme of humility. 'I intend to describe to you a spiritual and perfect man, and one whom anyone may strive to imitate – and while preserving the pen [or style] of verity, I intend to make a model of blessed Francis' – adding a revealing personal affirmation and endorsement: 'I admire the humility of blessed Francis above all his virtues' (cc. 1–3).[60] St Bonaventure was personally convinced that he and every other Friar Minor was following in the steps of a perfect man and saint, perfect because he was a perfect imitator of Christ.

In the sermon the humble are equated with the Friars Minor; the humble Francis was granted wisdom. His teaching and Rule are not to be dismissed or denigrated as the work of an ignorant man (a line of attack exploited by the Order's opponents). For Francis himself bore witness that he learned the whole Rule by revelation (c. 10). This is an allusion to the Testament, given in a way which assumes it was familiar to his audience, and so is a further indication that, although not legally binding, this document was still revered, and may well have been kept next to the Rule, as St Francis instructed, and read out loud in all chapter meetings when the Rule was read.[61] Bonaventure's belief and assertion that the whole Rule (totam regulam) was divinely revealed may be based simply on Francis' words, emphasised twice in the Testament, but it is possible that the story contained in the Verba – in which the voice of Christ is heard, declaring, 'Francis, there is nothing of yours in the Rule, but all (totum) which is there is mine' – was already circulating in 1255.[62] Bonaventure then made a further, powerfully argued claim. Using a very imaginative analogy, he suggested that, just as the pope authenticated his letters with his lead seal, his bulla – a transparent allusion to the fact that the Rule had received papal confirmation in a bull and was known as the Regula bullata – Christ authenticated and confirmed the Rule by fixing his bulla on Francis' body, the stigmata, the signs of the Crucified (c. 10).

This claim enabled Bonaventure to move on to another pressing subject of controversy and mount a public defence of the stigmata's authenticity, which was recurrently challenged by the hydra-headed monster of doubt. This defence was reasonably based on evidence – the evidence of eyewitnesses. Bonaventure states that over one hundred trustworthy laymen saw the stigmata. We cannot check this statement precisely. The number of witnesses in the list preserved in the Archives of the Sacro Convento – a draft document probably produced in 1237 – amounts to less than twenty. It names four individuals as having seen the stigmata while Francis was alive and some fourteen as having seen them after his death. None of these individuals were friars; most appear to have been members of leading Assisan families active in civic government – trustworthy, independent witnesses, in fact.[63] Many friars could have seen the stigmata on the night Francis died, but their evidence was open to question as not disinterested. Over a hundred laymen? It is quite possible. Both 1 Celano and Julian of Speyer write that

---

[59] Bougerol 1993, I, 48.
[60] Bougerol 1993, II, 749–52, Sermon 57 (= Bonaventure, Opera Omnia, IX, 575–82, sermo II).
[61] The Testament in Esser 1976, pp. 439, 444; Brooke 1975, pp. 117, 119.
[62] Verba c. 3 = SL 113: see pp. 260–1. [63] See pp. 167–8 and note 16.

there was 'a flocking together (concursus)', of the people; Celano adds that 'the whole city rushed (tota civitas Assisii ruit)'.[64] The figure is the product of oral tradition. But even if it is an exaggeration, the basic validity of this evidence is unaffected. The four named witnesses who saw when he was alive, or the fourteen who saw after death – it could be argued – are sufficient. Bonaventure next added the testimony of the Roman Church. This is warranted by papal bulls issued in March and April 1237, in which Gregory IX personally vouched for the truth of the stigmata and threatened detractors with excommunication.[65] Thirdly he marshalled the best evidence of all: the witness of Francis' close companions, who nursed him during his last two years and so were ex officio aware of all the intimate details of his physical condition, and who were, as he stated, men of 'manifest probity and sanctity'. His words, with their mention of oath-taking, seeing and handling, suggest a possible specific reference to the Minister General John of Parma's recent efforts to dispel doubts. At the General Chapter held at Genoa, probably in 1251 – four years before this sermon – John had ordered brother Bonizo, one of Francis' companions, 'to tell the friars the truth about his stigmata, because many throughout the world were in doubt about this. He responded with tears: "These sinful eyes saw them, and these sinful hands touched them."'[66]

The next point at issue was whether the signs could have appeared naturally or been faked, by scratching for example, or by wounding the flesh with a metal or wooden implement. This was not the case: such wounds would have been superficial. The stigmata were integral to the flesh, the nails growing through and protruding from hands and feet. They were not induced by human agency (c. 12).

Eyewitness testimony might be classified as legal evidence to support the case that the stigmata were a fact and that they were not a natural phenomenon. Bonaventure's defence culminates with an outline of his theology of the stigmata. In c. 13 he gives what he regards as a highly rational account of God's actions culminating in the stigmata. 'The providence of divine rule' wished to convert the merchant into 'a fisher of men and leader of those who might perfectly imitate Christ; and so he handed to him to bear his own flag, that is the sign of the crucified'.

The second of Bonaventure's sermons on St Francis to survive was preached at the evening collatio, probably on 4 October 1262.[67] It was delivered at Paris, and he compliments his audience. 'Among the approved customs this is one of the best that the scholars of this city willingly come to hear the word of God.'[68] The date provides a useful marker as it was composed while he was engaged in writing the Legenda Maior.[69] His text is taken from the portion of St Matthew's Gospel set for St Francis' feast: 'And then shall appear the sign of the Son of Man in heaven' (Matt. 24. 30). In the light of the increased information he had gathered and his reflections upon it while working on the Life, he developed his treatment of the stigmata.

[64] 1 Cel. 112; Julian of Speyer, c. 71.   [65] See pp. 166–7 and n. 14.
[66] Eccleston, p. 74. For the date of the chapter at Genoa, cf. Brooke 1959, p. 257 and n. 2.
[67] Bougerol 1993, II, 771–87, Sermon 58 (= Bonaventure, Opera Omnia, IX, 585–90, sermo IV).
[68] This suggests that members of the university who were not friars had come to hear him. See p. 231.
[69] The Legenda Maior and its epitome, the Legenda Minor, were written at Paris during 1260–2 (AF X, pp. lxx–lxxii).

On this occasion Bonaventure's first concern was to emphasise the exceptional nature of the stigmata. He 'dared' to say it was a 'special, or rather unique, privilege'. He uses similar language in the *Legenda Maior*: 'that most holy flesh . . . bore the image of Christ's passion by a unique privilege, and by the novelty of the miracle foreshadowed the manner of his resurrection' (xv, 1). Again: 'Francis, the new man, shone with a new and stupendous miracle, with a unique privilege not granted in previous centuries' (Bonav., *Miracula*, i, 1). But his 'if I dare say it' was a rhetorical device advancing nothing new. Brother Elias had claimed as much for Francis as soon as he was dead. 'I announce to you a great joy and a novelty among miracles. Throughout the ages such a sign has not been heard of, except in the Son of God, who is Christ the Lord.'[70] He was followed by Thomas of Celano: 'an unheard of joy and a novelty among miracles . . . honoured on earth with a unique gift . . . O an unparalleled gift! . . . O how wonderful and amiable was God's plan to avoid any suspicion, because of the novelty of the miracle, by first in His mercy displaying in Him who "came down from heaven" [John 3. 13] what He would wonderfully perform a while later in him who "was living in the world"' (Col. 1. 20) – an extraordinarily bold conceit! (1 *Cel.* 112–14). Bonaventure is echoing his sources.

The cross is a sign of severe judgement, and also of mercy to all peoples, all nations, on the Day of Judgement (c. 3); the sign of enrolment in Christ's army (the crusaders' emblem). It appeared in heaven to Constantine as a sign of victory (c. 4), and likewise to St Francis (c. 5). In c. 5, as in the prologue to the *Legenda Maior*, Francis is the angel ascending from the east, and there are other references to the Apocalypse in c. 13: but these are metaphors, not developed theological schemas. The theology that is developed here is the symbolism of the cross; and for Bonaventure's interpretation of Francis, the reference in c. 5 to that mark (*signum*), the Tau, imprinted 'upon the foreheads of the men that sigh' (Ezek. 9. 4) – also quoted in the prologue to the *Legenda Maior* – is also significant.

The sign appeared 'in heaven', and Bonaventure develops this part of his text, dwelling on Francis' excellent merits and the properties of heaven they exemplified (cc. 5–12). For example: 'Heaven is beautiful in its ornament' and Francis 'was such a heaven on account of the purity of chastity' (c. 8). The passage invites comparison with one in a sermon preached by Eudes of Châteauroux in which 'blessed Francis was the kingdom of heaven'.[71] Bonaventure's account of Francis' relation to heaven is not a sustained scholastic argument, but rather a model of theological rhetoric.

His concept of heaven derived from the celestial hierarchy of the Pseudo-Dionysius.[72] He envisaged heaven in space as a series of peaks, and the excellence and completeness of his poverty, and the fact that he gloried in it, placed Francis on the highest (c. 6). He accepted that such praise coming from his lips could evoke rebuke, but affirmed that words commending 'ourselves, our Order and our father were warranted . . .

---

[70] AF X, 526. It is clear St Bonaventure genuinely believed the phenomenon unique; he is not aware of other cases; see p. 34.

[71] See pp. 222–3.

[72] The influence of the Pseudo-Dionysius has been illuminated in many articles by D. E. Luscombe: for a general view, see Luscombe 1988b. For his influence on Bonaventure, see *New Catholic Encyclopaedia*, 11, 663 (L. C. Brady); *Dictionnaire de Spiritualité*, IV, 2, 2120–6 (T. Szabó).

The means by which the Holy Spirit has wonderfully confirmed the profession of poverty ought not to be passed over in silence. For . . . at the same time (*eodem tempore*) in which blessed Francis sought the confirmation of his Order from the pope, the stigmata of Our Lord were impressed on him. This confirmation was not from a man but from God. A man can be deceived, and so not only did man set his seal of lead (*bullam*) on the confirmation of this religious rule (*religionem*) in which is the profession of the highest poverty, but the Lord himself wished to apply his own seal of lead to the confirmation of poverty by impressing the stigmata of His passion on blessed Francis' (c. 7). Bonaventure is so keen to emphasise the immediacy of God's approval of the Order, its founder and its Rule, that he downgrades the pope. He is saying, in effect, that the pope is a man, and therefore fallible. He also telescopes events to improve his point, which he sees as essentially a theological, not historical one.

The *Regula bullata* is enshrined in the papal bull *Solet annuere*, dated 29 November 1223. It was addressed to 'brother Francis and the other brothers of the Order of Friars Minor' and it has remained in Assisi ever since.[73] Bonaventure will have had opportunity to study it when he visited Assisi as part of his preparation for writing the *Life*. His whole account of the confirmation of the Rule in the *Legenda Maior* (IV, 11) is very interesting. He notes that it was confirmed by Pope Honorius in the eighth year of his pontificate, and that Francis, to encourage its observance, 'used to declare fervently that nothing had been put in it of his own devising but he had had every word written there as it had been divinely revealed to him. So that it might be more certainly established by God's testimony, after just a few days had elapsed, the stigmata of the Lord Jesus were imprinted on him – as it were the lead seal (*bulla*) of the supreme pontiff, Christ, for a total commemoration of the Rule and a testimonial of its author' (IV, 11). The eighth year of Honorius III's pontificate ran from 25 July 1223 to 24 July 1224.[74] In his chapter on the stigmata Bonaventure states, following his sources (Julian 61, 1 Cel. 94), that it happened two years before Francis' death (XIII, 1). He adds a new specific detail he must have learned orally – it was 'in the morning about (*circa*) the feast of the Exaltation of the Holy Cross' (XIII, 3). This fixes the day as being on or around 14 September 1224. St Bonaventure was a theologian, a philosopher, a mystic; he was not a chronicler, not really interested in chronology. It was in his mind that Rule and stigmata were closely linked; and he associated them in time. Nine and a half months seemed but a few days. It is strange, though, as unity in time implied unity in space. To compose the final Rule Francis went up into 'a certain mountain' with two companions. He received the stigmata on La Verna, a mountain near Arezzo. The mountain where he wrote the Rule is not named in any early source. According to tradition the place was Fonte Colombo near Rieti.[75]

---

[73] See Esser 1976, pp. 363–404; and see p. 92.

[74] By this date papal years were calculated from the pope's coronation, not from his election: Honorius III was crowned on 24 July 1216 (Cheney and Jones 2000, pp. 48–9, 55).

[75] Topographical detail is first given by Ubertino da Casale in his *Arbor Vitae*, 1305, who had the story orally from Conrad of Offida: Burkitt 1932, esp. pp. 47–50; Brooke 1959, pp. 88–95.

In his sermon there is naturally also a strong pastoral preoccupation, to exhort and to encourage. A moving example is his inspirational call to love. Francis' charity was so all-embracing that 'it was not enough for him to preach to Christians and the faithful, but he went to the Saracens to preach to them, to see if anyone would spill his blood and kill him for the faith of Christ . . . Our hearts are not glowing or on fire. It is said that heat is one of the properties of the heart, and the works of him around whose heart there is more warmth are more powerful and more virtuous: thus he who has the glow of love or charity in his heart can by his own efforts perform more virtuous works. Do *you* (*tu*) want to imprint Christ's cross in *your* heart? Do *you* want to transform yourself, in the degree in which you burn with love, into Christ himself? Just as it is with iron, when it is well heated so that it begins to melt, then any form or shape can be imprinted on it: so in the truly fervent heart through love towards Christ crucified the crucified himself and the cross of the crucified is imprinted, and he is wholly transformed into the crucified: as was blessed Francis' (c. 12). Bonaventure uses the personal pronoun singular. He is addressing each and every individual friar.

In a sermon preached in Paris on 25 May 1267, on a text appropriate for the occasion – the feast of the translation of St Francis' body – 'Friend, go up higher' (Luke 14. 10),[76] Bonaventure further developed his concept of the Rule with a sustained comparison of St Francis to Moses. Moses had spiritual grace, because the Lord called him to a special or spiritual conference. There the Lord spoke with him and gave him the Law. 'Thus I say to you of blessed Francis: he was called by the Lord to a special grace, because – when by his prayers he found the Rule of the Order of Friars Minor and afterwards lost it – he returned again to the mountain on which he had found the Rule and prayed there, and there by divine inspiration a second time, by means of his prayers, he found the lost Rule' (c. 5). Bonaventure makes explicit here analogies implicit in his account of the confirmation of the Rule in the *Legenda Maior* IV, 11. In the Book of Exodus God spoke to Moses, detailing the Ten Commandments, 'and he gave unto Moses, when he had made an end of communing with him upon Mount Sinai, two tables of testimony, tables of stone, written with the finger of God' (Exod. 31. 18). While Moses remained on the mountain the people of Israel grew rebellious and persuaded Aaron to make the golden calf. When Moses came down he broke the tables in anger: 'And the Lord said unto Moses: "Hew thee two tables of stone like unto the first; and I will write upon these tables the words that were in the first tables, which thou brakest . . . and come up in the morning unto Mount Sinai, and present thyself there to me in the top of the mount" [Exod. 34. 1–2] . . . And the Lord said unto Moses, "Write thou these words" . . . and he wrote upon the tables the words of the covenant, the ten commandments' (Exod. 34. 27–8). In both cases the Lord spoke to his servant as to a friend; the Law, the Rule, was divinely revealed on a mountain and when brought down from there was destroyed, lost; only to be revealed a second time in the same place, in the same words. Bonaventure was claiming for the Rule a status comparable to the Ten Commandments.[77] He continued: 'And then the Rule was confirmed there [*ibi* – that is, by God, not the pope!]. And then also the stigmata of Christ crucified were

[76] Bougerol 1993, II, 604–17, Sermon 46; Lerner 1974.   [77] Lerner 1974, p. 484.

laid on his body. There also the Lord showed the likeness of a seraph. In the likeness of a seraph the Lord appeared to him so that he could speak with him as with a friend.' It seems that by now the two events had become completely fused in Bonaventure's mind. It does seem that he regarded La Verna, not Fonte Colombo, as the Sinai of the Order. He then pointed the conclusion to his audience: 'I say to you that if we were true friends and faithful followers of Christ, he himself would still speak with us' (c. 5).

In Bonaventure's sermons on St Francis that survive he concentrated on a relatively narrow range of topics. All but the earliest were delivered after he became Minister General, responsible for leading the founder's followers to salvation. These sermons therefore highlight for us the key features of Bonaventure's image of St Francis and the manner in which he projected his inspiration on to the friars as a whole. The stigmata are treated in all five. The likening of St Francis to the 'angel ascending from the rising of the sun, having the seal of the living God' (Rev. 7. 2) and the claim that he signed the foreheads of the elect with the mark of the Tau cross (Ezek. 9. 4) – analogies which Bonaventure introduced in the opening paragraphs of his *Legenda Maior* (Prol. 1–2) – are integral to the theme of the second sermon (no. 58), approximately contemporary with the *Life*, and are repeated in those of October 1266 (no. 56) and October 1267 (no. 57, *collatio*). That St Francis' Rule is sacrosanct is affirmed in three. In the earliest (no. 59) and in that of May 1267 (no. 46), the words of the Rule were revealed to the saint by God. The confirmation of the Rule is endorsed by the imprinting of the stigmata, conceived as *bulla*, in these, and also in the second sermon, where it is specifically linked to the profession of the highest poverty (no. 58, c. 7).

There are occasional details of Francis' early life, such as the fact that he was a merchant (nos. 59, 46). The last sermon, October 1267 (no. 57), mentions several, including that when he had seven brothers, and he was the eighth, he sent them out two by two to the four corners of the earth (c. 4); that 'when he was first converted he had the mud of the piazzas thrown at him by his fellow-citizens, and came naked before the bishop and gave up all his temporal possessions' (c. 7); and that the Lord wished to speak to him 'not as to a stranger but as to a special friend. The cross spoke out loud to him that is preserved by the sisters of San Damiano. Perhaps you will say: "Who was there?" Who was with the blessed Virgin when the Angel said to her "Hail Mary full of grace"?' (*collatio*, c. 2). Francis' service to lepers is spelt out: 'When he was a secular, he especially abhorred lepers; but after his conversion he devoted himself to the service of lepers, washing their feet, binding their wounds, extracting the puss and corrupted blood from their sores and kissing their feet' (c. 5). Bonaventure interjects at this point that humility is greatly to be commended and is better performed in deeds, with the hands; and then tells a delightful story. 'Gregory IX, full of wisdom, on account of his intimate friendship with blessed Francis, became his imitator and kept a leper in his chamber whom he served in a friar's tunic. One day this leper said: "Doesn't the supreme pontiff have anyone except this old man to serve me? He is too worn out." It is good to serve one's neighbour!' (c. 6).[78]

---

[78] Service to lepers is also noted in no. 59, cc. 19, 31, and in no. 56.

Few stories are selected and very few are told at any length.[79] Not surprisingly, none is told in detail in the earliest of the sermons. When he was engaged in writing the *Legenda Maior* Bonaventure had access to a fund of stories and he chose three to illustrate his second sermon. He related brother Pacifico's vision of the thrones in a manner quite close to his account in the *Legenda*, which is itself closely based on 2 *Celano*.[80] He also told a miracle story in which animals were cured after being sprinkled with water that had been used for washing St Francis' hands and feet. His account in the *Legenda* is taken from Celano's *Tractatus de Miraculis*, but in the sermon he says it was told to him by someone who witnessed it.[81] Apart from the stupendous overarching miracle of the stigmata, there is remarkably little emphasis on miracles in these sermons – and this healing of livestock is directly linked to the stigmata.[82] The third story, an example of how severely Francis afflicted his body, is told differently in the sermon. In the *Life* (v, 4) Bonaventure copied from 2 *Celano* 116–17 an account of how, when tempted to lust, Francis, after taking off his tunic and whipping 'brother ass', went out still naked into the snow and made seven figures, a snow 'wife', four snow 'children' and two snow 'servants'. In the roughly contemporary sermon he utilised the mortification to create a comparison of St Francis to St Benedict. His concern was to illustrate how Francis belonged to a long tradition of inspired religious leaders.

The sermons contribute some new information not contained in the written sources we have.[83] Bonaventure had been at pains to acquaint himself at first hand with Assisi and to interview close friends of St Francis who were still alive when he was collecting material for the *Legenda Maior* (Prol. 4), and he occasionally mentions in a sermon that he is relating something he has learned personally.[84] It has been noted that the later sermons contain more apparently legendary material and that this could be due to the proliferation of exaggeration and legend in the oral tradition which Bonaventure tapped.[85] St Bonaventure was a very busy man. He had to preach a great number of sermons, including many on St Francis; certainly a number more than have survived. The later sermons give the impression of having been somewhat more hastily composed; some of the themes are becoming well worn. It must also be borne in mind that these sermons were delivered live to live audiences. Transmission has been through

---

[79] Lerner suggests, of Sermon 46, that this is because they would have been familiar to a Franciscan audience (Lerner 1974, p. 481). But this sermon, and also Sermons 56–9, were university sermons, preached in the Minors' church but attended by a wider audience of university members who were not friars. Bougerol 1993, I, 34; Brady 1976, pp. 132–7. It is also possible that some stories were abbreviated by reporters.

[80] Sermon 58, c. 11; Bonav. VI, 6; 2 *Cel.* 122–3.   [81] Sermon 58, c. 12; Bonav. XIII, 6; 3 *Cel.* 18.

[82] In 3 *Cel.* 18 and Bonav. XIII, 6 the miracle took place in the province of Rieti. In the sermon 'in illa provincia', with the implication that it took place near La Verna. This is another indication that in his sermons Bonaventure consistently retains a unity of place and time for the confirmation of the Rule and the imprint of the stigmata, and subordinates history and geography to simplicity of theological perception and edification. The healing of the loose-living cripple who presently, as Francis foretold, returned to his evil ways and came to a sticky end is told in no. 57, collatio c. 9 (Bougerol 1993, II, 770–1), based on Bonav. XI, 5, which was based on 2 *Cel.* 41. These two healing miracles, though separated in Celano and in the *Legenda Maior*, are told next to each other in SL 57–8.

[83] Lerner 1974, pp. 481–2, lists new information and sayings contained in the sermon dated 25 May 1267 (Bougerol, no. 46).

[84] Sermon 58, c. 12; Sermon 46, c. 6.

[85] Clasen 1962, pp. 161–2, 189–90, quoted in Lerner 1974, p. 483 and n. 62.

transcripts or notes taken by a secretary.[86] Minor inconsistencies and inaccuracies in the sermons as we have them are probably mainly due to reporters' or copyists' errors.

In the last of his recorded sermons, delivered in Paris on 4 October 1267, there is a lively account of Francis' meeting with the Sultan and his challenge to test the truth of the two faiths by fire (no. 57, c. 15). Among stories highlighted in the sermons, this dramatic encounter, the fiery chariot, Pacifico's vision of the thrones, the stigmata, were scenes later depicted in the St Francis Cycle in the nave of the Upper Church. All these occur in this last sermon, which was particularly rich in material illustrated in the cycle; it referred, though briefly, to Francis renouncing all his temporal possessions naked before the bishop (no. 57, c. 7), the crucifix at San Damiano speaking to him (c. 7 and *collatio* c. 2), his preaching to the birds (*collatio* c. 2), and his preaching before Honorius III (*collatio* c. 6).

Bonaventure has words of praise for holy poverty. 'Voluntary poverty, which has conformity with Christ and imitation of Christ conjoined together, that is the furnace testing the elect, in which furnace the young men were put [Daniel 3] . . . Poverty which is with the cross and has the life of the Gospel attached to it is the testing furnace . . . This is the way a man follows Christ naked in the furnace of poverty' (no. 57, c. 13).[87] This is a vital defence of the friars' Rule and way of life. But the fundamental virtue in his eyes, emphasised time and again in these sermons, which were primarily addressed to his friars, is humility. 'Blessed Francis had true humility, whence he also wished his Order to be named after it: for it is called the Order of Minors which simply means what it says . . . A great weight is laid on us, I tell you, in that we are called Minors, because we ought to reckon ourselves inferior and more despised than all others' (no. 58, c. 11). The overriding impression left by these sermons is of St Bonaventure's own sanctity. He had achieved the humility he so much admired in St Francis. The seraphic doctor held up for veneration and emulation a 'non litteratus doctor', a man who received his teaching directly from God.[88] Nor did St Bonaventure reserve his deference just for St Francis. A notable example of his humility and generosity of spirit is to be found in a sermon he composed for Easter Eve, the third of a trilogy which contain a coherent theological meditation on the paschal mystery which is very personal. The cross reveals the mystery of love, a theme to which he returned in the *Itinerarium mentis in Deum*.[89] We are invited to supper on Maundy Thursday, to the cross on Good Friday, on Easter Eve to rest (no. 21, c. 1). For Easter Eve, using the text, 'Come unto me all ye that labour and are heavy laden, and I will give you rest' (Matt. 11. 28), there is a section on contemplation. On the analogy that Jacob served seven years for love of Rachel (Gen. 29. 20), Bonaventure concludes that 'it is necessary for a man to work seven years that he may have rest. These seven years are the seven steps of contemplation, which blessed Bernard expounded in one way, Richard of St Victor another way, and other holy men in various other ways' (no. 21, c. 4). But he chooses to elaborate on none of these. Instead, he chooses to speak of in the same breath, and to give pride of place to the mystical

---

[86] Bougerol 1993, I, 8–10, 11, 604, 742, 749, 771, 787. The secretary chiefly responsible for recording sermons was brother Mark of Montefeltro (ibid., I, 8; Salimbene, H, p. 308; S, I, 448–9).

[87] Cf. Sermon 46, cc. 8–9.   [88] Sermon 59, c. 10; see p. 232.

[89] Bougerol 1993, I, 43, 48, and Sermon 21, pp. 307–16.

insights of one of St Francis' companions. 'But there was a certain lay brother who for thirty years had the grace to fall into a trance, and who was most pure, a virgin, and the third brother after St Francis.' This identifies him clearly as brother Giles.[90] 'This man stated it thus: the seven steps of devout contemplation are these: fire, unction, ecstasy, contemplation, savour, consolation, rest, and the eighth that follows is glory' (no. 21, c. 4). Brother Giles was among Francis' earliest followers singled out for praise in the *Legenda Maior*. 'The holy father Giles won the third place, a man filled with the divine presence and worthy of great fame. He was later eminent in the exercise of lofty virtues, as God's servant foretold of him. Although he was unlettered and simple, he was raised to the summit of lofty contemplation. For over long periods he was ceaselessly intent on sublime activities, so frequently rapt in divine ecstasies, to an extent to which I myself have been an eye-witness, that one might think he was rather leading the life of an angel than of a man' (III, 4). Brother Giles became a contemplative in the year St Francis died. His great vision began just before Christmas 1226, and from then on he ceased to go among men. He died at Perugia on the night of 22–23 April 1261, so Bonaventure must have gone to Perugia on purpose to visit and commune with him shortly before his death.[91]

THE *LEGENDA MAIOR* OF ST BONAVENTURE

Why were Celano's Lives superseded? One reason was liturgical. Haymo of Faversham had undertaken a scholarly revision of the liturgy aimed at providing the Order with concise, straightforward, small books appropriate to their needs. His new Ordinal for the gradual, missal and breviary was so outstanding that it became a model for subsequent reforms within the Church at large. In 1249 John of Parma sent a letter to the Tuscan province demanding strict observance of the liturgical books. At the General Chapter of Metz in 1254 this was made obligatory on the whole Order, and a lengthy series of liturgical statutes was issued.[92] At the next General Chapter, held at Rome in February 1257, in which Bonaventure was elected Minister General in his absence, he was *ex officio* entrusted with the correction of the books for the Divine Office, and it was also ordained that 'out of all the legends of St Francis, one good one should be compiled'.[93] A similar sequence had been taking place in the Dominican Order. A decision taken at the General Chapter in 1244 to initiate measures to unify the Divine Office led to the setting up the following year of a commission of four friars charged with correcting and unifying the text, notation and rubrics of the liturgical books; and a series of revisions was undertaken.[94] Then in 1254 Humbert of Romans, who had probably been a member of the earlier commission, was elected Master General and authorised to revise all the offices for day and night and correct the liturgical books. The constitutions approving his revision received the three necesessary consecutive

---

[90] Cf. my edition of Brother Leo's *Life of Brother Giles* in SL pp. 307–49.
[91] SL pp. 307, 310–11, 349n.
[92] Van Dijk 1963, I, 117, 144, 163–4; cf. Brooke 1959, pp. 208–9 and 209 n. 1, 262–4 and nn.
[93] Van Dijk 1963, II, 417.
[94] For this and what follows, see Hinnebusch 1966, I, 347–9; MOPH III, 29, 33.

confirmations in 1254, 1255 and 1256. To meet the expense of producing a master copy, which was to be kept at Paris, all the provinces were taxed.[95] In 1257 and 1258 the friars were instructed to ensure that all transcripts and newly written office books were carefully corrected against this exemplar. In 1259 this was reinforced, but with a reassurance: the priors were to take steps to provide copies of the new correction of the office – they can be sure that the Master will not make any further changes.[96] In 1260 Humbert ordered the friars to use the *Life of St Dominic* inserted in the lectionary and not to write any new Lives. This *Legenda S. Dominici* Humbert had himself written while Master specifically for liturgical use.[97] The correction of Franciscan liturgical books in accordance with Haymo's triple Ordinal and the provision of exemplars for the provinces took a number of years. The gradual with its preface must date from before 1254. Copies of the missal may have been distributed at the General Chapter of 1257, or may have gone out in 1260 together with those of the breviary, which were ready by then. A definition of the Chapter of Narbonne required the provincial ministers to have texts of their existing breviaries and missals corrected against the best exemplar they could obtain.[98]

In 1259 St Bonaventure made an agreement with the Cistercian Order. The Cistercians enhanced their liturgical commemoration of St Francis to a feast of twelve lessons, and in return the Friars Minor solemnly celebrated the feast of St Bernard 'on its proper day'. The Dominicans had entered into a similar agreement in 1255, the Cistercians including in their liturgical calendar feasts of twelve lessons for St Dominic and St Peter Martyr, in return for Dominican veneration of St Bernard. Such reciprocal arrangements were one of the means by which the mendicant Orders propagated the cults of their saints.[99] However, they required the provision of suitable liturgical *Legendae*. The *Legenda S. Francisci liturgica* based on Celano provided only nine lessons.[100] Celano's *First Life* was the Life most generally acquired by houses of other Orders – by Benedictine houses for example – and Julian of Speyer's *Life* was also used by some.[101] A desire to introduce uniformity is evidenced by the ordinances of 1257.[102] The Dominicans laid a strong emphasis on uniformity. The Prologue to their Constitutions of 1228 opens with the words: 'Our Rule commands us to have one heart and one soul in the Lord, so it is right that we who live under a single Rule and by a single profession should be found uniform in the observance of our canonical religion, so that the unity we are to maintain inwardly in our hearts will be fostered and expressed by the uniformity we observe outwardly in our behaviour.' Humbert began to write a *Commentary on the Constitutions* in which he rehearsed the benefits of uniformity and regretted that the Order's vow of poverty made its achievement in the matter of buildings and clothing for example more or less impossible.[103] The leadership of both Orders in these years sought to foster a common

---

95 MOPH III, 68, 71, 73, 78, 81–2.   96 MOPH III, 88, 92, 98 9.
97 MOPH III,105; Walz 1935, pp. 353–68, text, pp. 369–433; Hinnebusch 1966, I, 349; II, 289–90 and 327 n. 60.
98 Van Dijk 1963, I, 115–19; Delorme 1910, p. 502, no. 2.
99 Vauchez 1997, p. 122 and n. 45; Van Dijk 1963, I, 128–30 and nn.
100 AF X, 531–2.   101 AF X ix–xiii, xlviii-xlix.   102 See p. 242 and note 93.
103 Tugwell 1982, pp. 141–2, 456; Hinnebusch 1966, II, 290. The wording of the Prologue is closely based on the Constitutions of the Premonstratensian Canons.

policy, faced as they both were by attacks from the secular masters of Paris and the secular clergy on their way of life. In 1254 John of Parma and Humbert of Romans took identical measures to cope with the crisis in Paris, and in 1255 they issued a joint letter to their friars exhorting them to peace and concord. Both men shared an interest in music and introduced in their Orders' antiphonals and graduals a system of notation that was probably derived from or inspired by the musical practices within the church at Paris, where both had graduated Master and where both Orders had a *studium generale*.[104]

Why was St Bonaventure asked to write the new Life? One reason was probably the fact that Humbert of Romans, the Master General of the Friars Preachers, had just completed his new *Life of St Dominic*. So it was appropriate to ask Bonaventure, not so much because he was the most distinguished academic in the Order as because, as Minister General, he would add the weight of official authority. The first copies of the *Legenda Maior*, one for each province to act as exemplars, were transcribed at Paris under St Bonaventure's supervision and presented by him to the General Chapter at Pisa in 1263 for distribution. The plan of the book was clearly defined and functional. It consisted of a Prologue and fifteen chapters, listed in a brief table of contents at the end of the Prologue (Prol. 5).[105] It was programmed to be read in the refectory during the octave of the feast of St Francis. Bonaventure also produced the *Legenda Minor*, an epitome, a *Shorter Life*, designed to produce the lessons for the Divine Office during the octave, and therefore divided into seven chapters, each with nine paragraphs.[106]

A definition of the next General Chapter held at Paris in 1266 'ordered on obedience that all the Legends of blessed Francis formerly made be destroyed'.[107] This followed in the footsteps of a previous definition passed by the General Chapter of Narbonne in 1260. To this, the first General Chapter over which he presided, Bonaventure brought a draft of a new edition of the Order's constitutions, which he had personally undertaken with the aim of clarifying them so that they could be better enforced. The Chapter endorsed this and decided that the guardian of every house was to have a copy and to see that the constitutions were read out loud once a month, especially the first seven chapters which applied to everyone. These constitutions having been published, the old were to be destroyed. This curt and unambiguous directive was supported by a further definition which clearly bears the stamp of Bonaventure's personal authority. 'The Minister General revokes all the edicts and commands of the Ministers General his predecessors, whether written or oral.'[108] The instruction seems to have been scrupulously obeyed. No copy of 'the great multitude of constitutions' promulgated in 1239,

[104] Van Dijk 1963, I, 118–19; see Brooke 1959, pp. 230, 269–70 and nn.
[105] The text of the *Legenda Maior* is in AF x, 555–652, of the *Legenda Minor* in ibid. 653–78. There is an English translation of the *Legenda Maior* in Habig 1979, pp. 627–87.
[106] D. Vorreux in Habig 1979, pp. 622–3 and n. 2; AF x, pp. lxx–lxxi. Humbert de Romans' *Legenda* for St Dominic (Walz 1935, pp. 369–433) survives in the Prototype MS, now preserved in the Archives of the Dominican Generalate in Rome: it is divided into six lections for the feast of the saint, made up to nine by three 'de omelia evangelii "Vos estis sal terre"', followed by a group of lessons for weekdays and Sunday in the octave (cc. 7–24); then a larger group which 'can be read in the refectory' (in *mensa*) (cc. 25–60), nine lections for the octave (cc. 61–9, plus 70) and an Appendix of lessons for the feast of the saint's Translation (cc. 1–62).
[107] Little 1914b, p. 678.   [108] Diffinitiones I, 17, in Delorme 1910, pp. 502–4.

or the constitutions added in the course of the intervening years before 1260, seems to have escaped the guardians' vigilance.[109]

Why did they deliberately destroy their records? As far as the constitutions were concerned, there was a good practical reason: the aim was to bolster observance and avoid confusion, since later constitutions frequently modified or even contradicted earlier ones. It was also sensible and in accordance with the lifestyle of an Order vowed to poverty not to hang on to documents or books which they no longer used, because they had been superseded. They would simply take up space. And it is not as if there was no continuity. In the letter Bonaventure wrote to the Provincial Ministers and custodians when news of his appointment reached him in Paris, he stated that it was not his intention to load them with new chains. Very few statutes can confidently be assigned to him. He weeded the constitutions; those he retained, numbering just over 250, he arranged into twelve chapters according to subject. The Constitutions of Narbonne provide a major edition of existing legislation.[110] The intention of the 1257 Chapter was that 'out of all the legends of St Francis one good one should be compiled'. There was no suggestion that earlier lives should be destroyed and then a new one written from scratch. In 1257 a friar who wished to acquaint himself with Celano's account of St Francis needed to consult three separate books. The tables in the Preface to the Quaracchi edition of the *Legenda Maior* and the marginal references to the text display how faithfully Bonaventure discharged his brief; he made close and constant use of Celano's *First* and *Second Life* and his *Treatise on Miracles*, and of the related *Life* by Julian of Speyer.[111] Though interestingly it was not these legends that were acknowledged when the work was done. Bonaventure's formal acknowledgements were to the saint's companions. 'To the end that the true story of his life transmitted to future generations should be more surely and clearly known to me, I went to the place where he was born and lived and died, and I held a careful discussion on these matters with those of his close friends and associates who are still alive and especially with some who knew him and followed him most eminently, in whose word trust is undoubtedly to be placed, on account of their known probity and virtue' (Prol. 4). The definition of the 1266 Chapter echoes this line as official. Bonaventure is persuasive and in control. All the former legends are to be destroyed, 'and where they can be found outside the Order, the brothers are to take care to withdraw them, since that legend which has been made by the Minister General has been compiled just as he had it from the mouths of those who were with St Francis virtually all the time and knew everything with certainty – and what is set down there has been carefully established'.[112] In the 1240s and 1250s an Order already led by an educated clerical élite preferred Celano's style to that of the early companions; and in the 1260s St Bonaventure's to Celano's. The value St Francis had

[109] Salimbene, S, I, 233; H, pp. 158–9; Delorme 1910, p. 492; see Brooke 1959, pp. 210–79, esp. pp. 210 12, 274–9 and nn.
[110] Bonaventure, *Opera Omnia*, VIII, 468–9; Brooke 1959, pp. 274–7.
[111] See tables in AF x, pp. lxvi–lxvii; Moorman 1940, pp. 149–51; and Habig 1979, pp. 1638–48. Bonaventure's use of Julian was carefully noted by Bihl in the margins of Bonaventure, and summarised (AF x, p. lxiv) as contributing to Bonaventure's phraseology, not to the substance, of his versions of Celano. For the *Miracles*, see pp. 269–79.
[112] Little 1914b, p. 678; AF x, p. lxxii. The order to recover copies of the superseded Legends in use outside the Order would have had a liturgical aim and they would have been replaced by Bonaventure's.

put on spelling and grammatical mistakes as indicative of humility and of fellowship with the uneducated poor was no longer shared by his followers.

From 1266 until the end of the century, Bonaventure's *Life* was unrivalled as a written text, but about the turn of the century some writings, attributed by then to Leo alone rather than to the companions as a group, resurfaced. The Spirituals used him as an authority during their controversies with the Conventuals over St Francis' intentions on the observance of the Rule, and on the *usus pauper*. In 1309 Pope Clement V set up a commission to consider the dispute and both sides contributed a number of polemical pamphlets. In preparation for the Council of Vienne, in his last *Declaratio* of August *c.* 1311, Ubertino, who by then had succeeded in acquiring some of what he believed to be Leo's manuscripts, based his arguments squarely on their authority.[113] The Conventuals also seem to have appreciated the need to equip themselves with a copy of the Leonine stories when preparing their case. I have demonstrated already that the Perugia MS 1046 (**P**), containing a collection of papal bulls, the Leonine stories and Bonaventure's *Legenda Maior*, was compiled in 1310 or 1311, 'very likely in preparation for the vital discussions on the Order at the Council of Vienne in 1312'.[114] One consequence of the feud between the Spirituals and the Conventuals was the bringing back into the public domain of some of the earlier source material with its distinctive image of St Francis.

Thus in the early fourteenth century a small number of copies were made of SL and a larger number of its offshoot, the *Speculum Perfectionis*, completed at the Portiuncula in 1318. This led to the proliferation of stories and legends and to that remarkable work of historical fiction, the *Actus beati Francisci et sociorum eius* – better known in its Italian dress as the *Fioretti*, the *Little Flowers of St Francis*. These works were popular in the fourteenth and fifteenth centuries; and from the late fifteenth century on a variety of versions of the *Speculum Vitae*, a daughter of the *Speculum Perfectionis*, were available in print. Yet none of these works could compete in popularity with Bonaventure. His *Legenda Maior* remained the official and the most widely read life of the saint until the nineteenth century. But since the revival of his predecessors by the Bollandists – and even more, since the renaissance of Franciscan studies from the time of Paul Sabatier on – Bonaventure's *Life* has lost something of its pre-eminence.[115] Yet it is a major document, of fundamental importance. It represents a carefully devised presentation of the literary image of the saint, as it appeared to one of the most notable, dedicated and powerful minds of Paris and the western Church in the mid-thirteenth century.

Bonaventure was born *c.*1217 at Bagnoreggio, a small hill town in the Papal States, in the region of Orvieto and Viterbo. His father was a doctor. When he was about eight years old he was sent to the local Franciscan convent, presumably to school. In 1235 he went to Paris, where he studied philosophy in the Faculty of Arts. He joined the Friars Minor probably in 1243, and from then on studied theology in their *studium* under their Masters John of La Rochelle (d. 1245), Eudes Rigaud (1245–8, when he became archbishop of Rouen) and William of Melton (1248–54). He probably heard

---

[113] *ALKG* III, 168, quoted in SL p. 55; see SL, Introduction, esp. pp. 51 ff; Burr 1989, p. 193; Lambert 1961, chs. 7–9; and p. 125.
[114] See pp. 105–6.
[115] Cf. e.g. Sabatier 1893/4, pp. 391–8; Burkitt 1926; Moorman 1940, pp. 136–48.

the Dominican Master Albert the Great, who also taught in Paris 1245–8, and Hugh of St Cher. He succeeded William of Melton in 1254, though he was not officially accepted by the university as a regent master till October 1257.[116] As he had lived in close association with the Friars Minor since childhood, it seems likely that he retained some contact with them in Paris while he was an arts student. He will certainly have heard of Alexander of Hales' decision to join the Order, which caused a sensation, and probably occurred soon after his arrival in the city; and he may well have been aware of the moves to oust brother Elias which ensued, initiated by Alexander of Hales, John of La Rochelle and Haymo of Faversham at an unauthorised meeting held in Paris probably some time in 1236. He certainly sat at the feet of Alexander of Hales, who, although he ceased to be sole Regent Master in 1238, remained an active scholar and teacher until his death in 1245.[117] In 1241–2, Alexander of Hales, John of La Rochelle, Eudes Rigaud and another Franciscan academic composed their commentary on the Rule, the *Exposition of the Four Masters*.[118] The issues they considered in the *Exposition* they will surely have discussed, and continued to discuss in the next few years, with their students, including Bonaventure who joined them *c.*1243.

He joined the Order then at just the time when it was settling into a new mould and at the place where crucial influences shaping that mould were articulated. He belonged to a new generation faced with new challenges and expectations. The Order had been growing rapidly, its composition was changing, and it was being asked to take on more tasks, which it felt itself obliged, and qualified, to fulfil. Two of the determining factors which induced Bonaventure to join were its vitality and its potential. 'Let it not disturb you [he wrote], that the brothers were in the beginning simple and illiterate; rather this very fact ought to confirm in you a faith in the Order. I confess before God that it is this which made me most greatly esteem the life of St Francis because it is similar to the beginning and perfection of the Church, which first began with simple fishermen and afterwards advanced to the most illustrious and learned doctors. Thus you will see in the Order of the blessed Francis that God shows that it was not contrived through human prudence but through Christ; and because the works of Christ do not fail but increase, this was shown to be the work of God when wise men did not disdain to descend to the company of simple folk.'[119] This ringing endorsement of the legitimacy of the current situation forms the climax to the *Letter concerning Three Questions*, which Bonaventure wrote, it seems, while he was regent master at Paris, that is between 1253 and 1257. Burr suggests that it was probably addressed to a potential desirable recruit who was having second thoughts because of adverse criticism directed at the Minors by, apparently, an English Dominican, who accused them of not conforming to their Rule in accordance with the intention of their founder.[120] Alongside the attempts of the leadership of both Orders to encourage fraternity a range of tensions and jealousies

---

[116] Bougerol 1984, pp. 11–12; *Dictionnaire de Spiritualité*, I, 1768–9 (E. Longpré).

[117] Alexander of Hales probably joined the Order in 1235–6: cf. Brooke 1959, p. 162 and n. 1; Greenway 1968, p. 54. Bonaventure himself tells us that Alexander was his master – 'patris et magistri nostri' (Doucet 1951, I, 20*); and ibid. pp. 18*–19* cites evidence that his death left the *second* chair vacant.

[118] See pp. 78–81.

[119] Bonaventure, *Opera Omnia*, VIII, 336; Brooke 1959, pp. 273–4.

[120] For this and its context, see Burr 1989, pp. 148–54.

simmered, as both were necessarily in competition for recruits, sites for convents, and public support. Franciscan claims to superiority, as followers of Gospel perfection, some Dominicans found irritating. The three specific questions referred to receiving money, to manual labour and to learning.

On the question of money Bonaventure explained that if a donor committed money to his servant, ownership remained with him, as if it was still in his own hands, and this remained the case even if it was passed on through any number of 'interposed persons'. 'If you say that the lord intends to give to the friars simply and absolutely, I say that no-one in his right mind intends to give the friars otherwise than in accordance with their profession and Rule. For who would give them alms in order to make them lose eternal life? He gives therefore in a way that is expedient to the friars, that is by committing [the money] to someone who spends it on his behalf on things which the friars are allowed to receive. Thus that money, through whomsoever's hands it passes, in no way reverts to the friars, because it is always the first donor's. They do not receive it either themselves or through an interposed person.'[121] This answer Bonaventure lifted virtually word for word from a passage in Hugh of Digne's *Exposition of the Rule*. Indeed, he concurred with many of Hugh's arguments and quoted from him extensively, though without acknowledgement.[122] On the related question of who owned the buildings and the things the friars used, he again echoed Hugh: 'whoever it may be it is not the Order and that suffices for the purity of conscience'.[123] Especially striking is the defence of learning for friars, which incorporates extensive quotations from Hugh. Thus 'the pomp of mastership is condemned but the office and study approved'. It would be absurd for the learned not to use their gifts: 'Who of sane mind would say that Master and Brother Alexander [of Hales – at whose feet Bonaventure himself had sat] ought to have preached "Blessed are the poor in spirit" when he was rich; but when he became a poor man to have stayed silent?'.[124] On these themes Bonaventure and Hugh were wholly at one.

Bonaventure was held in great esteem by friars in the élite circles in which he chiefly moved, for his personal holiness, his academic distinction and his leadership qualities. The author of the Catalogue of Ministers General of c.1304 recorded that 'he was endowed with such a good abundance of innate integrity, that that great master, Alexander [of Hales], sometimes used to say of him that in him it seemed Adam had not sinned'.[125] Bonaventure was a mystic, not an ascetic. During the bitter contoversy which erupted, after his death in 1274, over issues connected with the observance and the practice of poverty, he was accused of having lived 'very laxly' – an aspersion indignantly repudiated by Peter John Olivi, a leading protagonist on the side of poverty, revered by the Spirituals. 'It was hitherto customary to cite pious men as examples of perfection; yet today, alas, they are cited as examples of laxity . . . I say, therefore, what I know of [Bonaventure]. He was of the best and most pious inner disposition, and in

[121] Bonaventure, *Opera Omnia*, VIII, 332; Flood 1979, p. 42.
[122] Bonaventure's dependence on Hugh was demonstrated by Esser 1940; his quotations are set out in full in Flood 1979, pp. 41–7. For Hugh's *Exposition*, see pp. 81–96.
[123] *Opera Omnia*, VIII, 333; Flood 1979, p. 44; see p. 89.
[124] Bonaventure, *Opera Omnia*, VIII, 334–5; cf. Flood 1979, pp. 45–7; see pp. 91, 93.
[125] Salimbene, H, p. 664.

his words he always endorsed whatever is consistent with perfect purity . . . Yet he had a frail body and was perhaps a bit self-indulgent in this respect, as I often heard him humbly confess.'[126]

Bonaventure was appointed Minister General on the personal recommendation of John of Parma. The circumstances were exceptional. John himself seems to have been outstandingly well qualified to lead the Order. He was devout, prayerful; he set an example of goodness and holiness; he was a gifted preacher and a great teacher of theology. He was also strong and healthy, able to shoulder the burdens of administration and study and the daily life of a friar.[127] He exemplified the ideals of the élite dominant in the Order in the 1240s, a combination of example of life, and learning. His appeal and acceptability were wider even than this implies. Elected by the officials, he could equally have been the choice of the early companions. His Achilles heel was his ardent Joachism, unacceptable in the wake of Gerard of Borgo San Donnino's excesses. He was obliged by Alexander IV to resign. The friars were extremely unwilling to release him, and as a mark of their confidence in him asked him to nominate his successor. John promptly designated Bonaventure, saying that in the whole Order he knew of none better than he.[128]

When news of his appointment reached him in Paris, he sent out a letter to all the Provincial Ministers and Custodians outlining the policy he proposed to adopt, and appealing to them for their co-operation.[129] Right at the outset of his generalate he showed himself conscious of the importance, indeed the necessity, of the active co-operation of his colleagues. I have taken most careful advice, he writes, as to what is amiss and how it should be corrected. Know the causes why the splendour appropriate to our Order has become in some measure obscured. Money, above all things enemy of the Order's poverty, is avidly sought, incautiously received and even more incautiously handled. Some of the friars are idle, and idleness is a stupefying vice, bilgewater, a monstrous state between the active and the contemplative life. So too instability: many are wandering excessively, inconveniencing and scandalising those they pass among. Begging has become so importunate that travellers are as loath to meet with friars as with robbers. The construction of sumptuous and overnice buildings disturbs the peace of the brethren, burdens their friends and incurs litigation. Familiarity, prohibited in the Rule, arouses suspicion and scandal. The imprudent appointment to office asks too much of men insufficiently proved, who are neither mortified in the flesh nor spiritually robust. Avid interest in wills and burials greatly disturbs the parish clergy. Frequent and extravagant change of place, sometimes involving disturbance, carries the danger of inconstancy and prejudice to poverty. As to extravagant expenses: if the friars will not be content with little, and charity cools, we become a burden on all, and will become a greater burden in the future unless a remedy is applied quickly.

---

[126] Burr 2001, pp. 59–60. For the dating and development of the controversies that were to divide the Order into Spiritual and Conventual parties, see Burr 2001, esp. pp. 12, 41 and chs. 3 and 4.

[127] From Salimbene, H, p. 297–8, quoted Brooke 1959, p. 256.

[128] Peregrinus of Bologna in Eccleston (1909 edn), p. 144; Salimbene, H, pp. 309–10; cf. Brooke 1959, pp. 255–71, esp. pp. 270–1; also Eccleston (1951) p. 74.

[129] Bonaventure, *Opera Omnia*, VIII, 468–9. This and the next two paragraphs resume a passage in Brooke 1974, pp. 82–4.

Bonaventure considers that the problem is that of a badly behaved minority. The habit of the vices listed must be checked, even though it will seem difficult. A first step must be the restriction of entry, so that unsuitable recruits are not admitted. Then, the lazy must be stimulated to action, the wanderers restrained, the importunate silenced, the aggrandisers of houses abased, the seekers after familiarity shut up in solitude. The offices of preaching and confession are to be given only on examination, the constitutions relating to wills and burials are to be more strictly observed, and no places are to be moved without his special licence. The friars must learn to be content with what is moderate and modest, whether they like it or not.

Bonaventure ends: 'if you are obedient, and I learn of this through the visitors, whom I wish to be diligent and vigilant in correcting faults in head and members, I give thanks to God and to you. If not . . . I must in conscience extirpate these evils with all my force, as they evidently impugn the truth and purity of the Rule which we have professed and which we must observe to be saved.'

Olivi quotes from this letter in support of his own view of the obligations inherent in the Franciscan vow.[130] This illustrates a point which it is important to emphasise. Bonaventure was aware of two challenges to the Order's integrity which had to be faced, one external, one internal. Both concerned the matter of evangelical poverty. External criticism, led by William of St Amour and Gerard of Abbeville, Paris secular masters, sought to undermine the validity of the Rule by arguing that Christ and the apostles had not lived in absolute poverty or rejected money, and that the Franciscan way of life was therefore not particularly meritorious; was indeed dangerous and impracticable. This required a theoretical, theological response, which was undertaken chiefly by Bonaventure and Pecham.[131] Malpractices and shortcomings within the Order required practical administrative reform. Hence his letter to the Provincial Ministers and Custodians. All friars of good will wished for standards to be maintained. It was just that it was becoming more difficult to achieve. The problems caused by the Order's increasing size, diversification, usefulness and popularity proved intractable.[132] But this did not lead to Bonaventure being a target for criticism from a 'spiritual wing' within the Order during his lifetime.[133] He was criticised retrospectively. As a new wave of controversies gathered and swelled, threatening to engulf the Order, and attitudes hardened, he came to be regarded by some among the Spirituals, and by some among the Conventuals, as having been a defender of relaxation.

Olivi was in the Order during most of Bonaventure's generalate, and he actually vouched for Bonaventure's zeal from his own personal knowledge in his *Tractatus de usu paupere*, written after October 1279 but probably before Easter 1283.[134] 'He was so

---

[130] Burr 1989, pp. 59–60 and nn. 9–10.

[131] See esp. *Quaestiones de perfectione evangelica*, in Bonaventure, *Opera Omnia*, v, 117–24; cf. Bougerol 1983, p. 191 and nn.; d'Avray 1985, pp. 163–203; and the literature quoted above, p. 231 n. 55.

[132] For an excellent recent account of the dilemma inherent in the Franciscan ideal, see Burr 2001, chs. 1–2.

[133] It was a contention of my doctoral thesis, 'Brother Elias, and the Government of the Franciscan Order 1217–1239' (Brooke 1949), written over fifty years ago, and published in a revised and extended form as Brooke 1959, that to interpret the early history of the Order in terms of parties is a mistake (see esp. Brooke 1959, pp. 4–5), and that Bonaventure's 'Generalate was the last before the period of conflict and schism between Conventuals and Spirituals opened' (ibid. p. 182).

[134] For this and what follows, see Burr 1989, pp. 49–87.

distressed at the widespread laxity of this age that, in full chapter, in my presence, he said that there was no time since he became Minister General that he would not wish to be pulverised if it would help the Order to reach the purity of St Francis and his companions, and to that state which he intended his Order to attain. Thus the holy man stood excused from much if not all of which he could be charged. For he was not of the number who defend relaxations and impugn the purity of the Rule, nor among those who seem to enjoy wallowing in these impurities.'[135]

Ubertino da Casale entered the Order c.1273, so at the very end of Bonaventure's life. In his *Arbor Vitae Crucifixae Jesu*, written in 1305 on La Verna, he criticised Bonaventure for being economical with the truth in the *Legenda Maior*. 'These stories [said to be contained in some *rotuli* written in brother Leo's own hand] were purposely omitted by brother Bonaventure, who did not wish to write them for all to see in his *Life*, especially because some of them openly showed how they were departing from the Rule at that time, and he did not wish to disgrace the brothers prematurely before those outside the Order.'[136] Bonaventure, in his opinion, failed to own up to the extent to which the Order had declined, by the 1260s, from the standards originally set; and moreover, by suppressing stories illustrative of tensions between St Francis and some ministers and learned friars, presented a misleadingly favourable picture of the situation that developed during St Francis' later years. Ubertino and Angelo Clareno believed that they could trace the germs of the early fourteenth-century conflict with the Conventuals right back to the days of St Francis. They saw themselves as Francis' direct heirs, dedicated to preserving his true legacy, as handed down through brother Leo and the Leonine tradition.[137]

Angelo Clareno probably entered the Order at some time during Bonaventure's generalate. When he came to write his *History of the Seven Tribulations of the Order of Friars Minor* c.1323–6 he still harboured bitter feelings of rancour against Bonaventure, whom he regarded as a hypocrite because of his treatment of John of Parma after his abdication, but even he did not class Bonaventure's generalate as one of the tribulations suffered by the friars.[138]

After 1274 localised disputes and unrest, which had hitherto surfaced intermittently, intensified and merged, and two factions crystallised. From this time on, the word 'spiritual' acquired distinctive polemical overtones and Spiritual Franciscans could be identified as adherents of a party.[139]

In 1259, two years after his appointment as Minister General, Bonaventure left Paris for Italy and prepared himself to write a definitive Life of St Francis. At the beginning of October – 4 October is St Francis' feast day – he went to La Verna, the scene of Francis' supreme mystical experience, to pray and reflect.[140] St Bonaventure's faith was Christ-centred and he found inspiration in the example of Christian discipleship St Francis had given. His thought was profoundly influenced by his perception of

[135] Olivi, *Tractatus de usu paupere*, MS Assisi 677, fo. 28ra–rb, quoted in Burr 1989, p. 86, n. 69, translated ibid., p. 78 (here slightly adapted).
[136] Ubertino de Casale 1485, v. 5, fo. E. iii, quoted SL p. 54; cf. Burr 1989, pp. 26, 36 n. 104.
[137] Brooke 1959, pp. 3–8; Potestà 1980, pp. 130–1, 134–5, quoted Burr 2001, pp. 99–100, 363 nn. 98, 99.
[138] Burr 2001, pp. 11 (and 349 n. 1), 32–6; Burr 1989, pp. 26–7, 30.
[139] Burr 2001, esp. pp. 11–12, 39–43.   [140] For this and what follows, see Gilson 1924, pp. 71–9.

St Francis' spirituality. In the solitude and in the charged atmosphere of La Verna he wrote a meditation, his *Itinerarium mentis in Deum*, 'The journey of the soul to God', which is signposted by the Gospel, and by the Franciscan way of life based on the Gospel. Its goal is the peace Jesus promised to his disciples: 'Peace I leave with you, my peace I give unto you' (John 14. 27).[141] That promised peace is not of this world; it is equated with ecstasy, to be sought through contemplation of the divine. 'Our Lord Jesus Christ gave and preached the good news of that peace; our father Francis repeated his preaching, in all his preaching announcing peace at the beginning and at the close, in every greeting choosing peace, in every contemplation sighing for ecstatic peace, just as the citizen of that Jerusalem of which that man of peace speaks . . . "Pray for the peace of Jerusalem" (Psalm 121(122). 6).'[142] 'The six wings of the seraph can be understood as six illuminations to which the soul is led as to steps or journeys, so as to arrive at peace' through penitence and active loving service to one's neighbour. They are necessary paths, as is the constant practice of meditation and prayer.[143] Divine illumination is a gift of the Holy Spirit and comes through grace; ecstasy and the joys and insights accompanying it are not reserved for the privileged or the learned, but may be granted to the simple and the ignorant – to the like of brother Giles for example – and were granted pre-eminently to St Francis. Therefore Bonaventure himself 'on the example of the most blessed father Francis would seek this peace with panting breath', and went to La Verna 'as to a quiet place, inspired by love of the search for the peace of the spirit'.[144]

It has been said that Bonaventure did not seek to convey a portrait of St Francis that was historical.[145] His own Prologue to the *Legenda Maior* lends support to this view: he has not always woven a narrative of events in the order in which they occurred 'to avoid confusion', but rather has organised a number systematically according to subject matter (Prol. 4). Yet he was deeply concerned to set St Francis into a historical context. Only his attitude towards the past, present and future was based on different presuppositions to ours. Thirteenth-century interpretations of the ways in which the divine providence worked its will throughout history had been powerfully stimulated by the prophetic message of Abbot Joachim of Fiore (c.1135–1202).[146] His doctrine of the three states was based on his mystical experiences and upon deep and prolonged study of the Scriptures, and was steeped in numbers, concords and patterns, the fruit of spiritual intelligence. The course of history reflected the nature of the Godhead, both in a twofold relationship, that of the Father and the Son, and in a threefold, that of Father, Son and Holy Spirit. The Old Testament, the age of the Father, prefigures the New Testament, the age of the Son and the Christian centuries which have succeeded it. The relationship is Trinitarian, and the three states overlap and infuse each other, as the Holy Spirit proceeds both from the Father and from the Son. The third age is still to come, but the first and second ages would continue, like two parallel streams, and the Old and

---

[141] *Itinerarium*, Prologue, 1; cf. Gilson 1924, pp. 76–7.
[142] *Itinerarium*, Prologue, 2; cf. Gilson 1924, pp. 76–7.
[143] *Itinerarium*, Prologue, 3 and vii, 3, quoted Gilson 1924, pp. 77 n. 3.
[144] *Itinerarium*, Prologue, 2, quoted Gilson 1924, pp. 76–7.
[145] Bougerol 1984, p. 24.   [146] For this and what follows, see Reeves 1969.

New Testaments would last till the end of time. Joachim associated the first age with the order of matrimony, the second with the priesthood and the third with the monastic order, while stressing that the second and third have their origins in and proceed from the first. So the monastic order has its seed in Elijah, and its germination and growth it owes essentially to St Benedict, whose Rule is an instrument of the Holy Spirit. The transitional period leading into the third age will see the appearance of spiritual men, contemplatives enlightened through spiritual understanding, which equips and calls them to be preachers of the truth.[147] A number of Franciscans, not unnaturally, fancied that this prophecy referred to them.[148] A dramatic and dangerous twist was given to Joachim's pattern of threes, however, by Gerard of Borgo San Donnino's irresponsible and misguided public declaration that the third age was imminent, and that, with its advent, the Old and New Testaments would be abrogated and authority would pass to the Third Testament, which was none other than the Eternal Gospel of the Holy Spirit contained in Joachim's works.[149] Gerard's book, *The Introduction to the Eternal Gospel*, was condemned in 1255, and the scandal it generated compromised his Minister General, John of Parma, a convinced Joachite.[150] We have no first-hand evidence of John's beliefs, but some of his sayings were recorded by leaders of the later Spirituals. Ubertino da Casale, who fell under his influence after his return to Italy from Paris in 1284, and who regarded him as a saint 'with the face of an angel', wrote: 'He most categorically asserted this – as I heard from his holy mouth with my unworthy ears – that the sixth seal takes its rise in Francis and his Order.'[151] And according to Angelo Clareno: 'He said that since the highest state of gospel perfection has been promised by the brethren, God requires of them the highest faith, charity and good works . . . He also said . . . that the brothers ought to hold the Testament in the utmost reverence, both because it was the saint's command and blessing, and because Christ's spirit spoke in him, who lived in Him very fully and perfectly after that wonderful impression of the holy stigmata . . . And just as the whole law and the prophets and the gospel hang on the command and sacrament [or mystery, *sacramentum*] of charity, so all perfection and regular intention and faith and spiritual intelligence are enclosed in the Testament of St Francis . . . And because it is necessary for the gospel life, renewed by Francis on Christ's order, to be reformed, for the same reason, after the Rule, the Holy Spirit through Francis finally published the Testament.'[152]

St Bonaventure was obliged to interrogate John of Parma, to whom he owed his office. It was not an enviable task: 'it is doubtful if even a future saint could emerge with credit from the task of judging one who was later to be beatified'.[153] John apparently defended Joachim's doctrine from the charge of heresy. He was sent into retirement to the hermitage at Greccio. Gerard of Borgo San Donnino was also interrogated,

---

[147] Reeves 1969, pp. 136–44. The Carmelites claimed Elijah as the actual founder of their Order, a theme which caused much later controversy (Jotischky 2002).

[148] See pp. 82–3.   [149] Reeves 1969, pp. 59–61.

[150] On John of Parma as 'maxima Joachista', see Salimbene, H, pp. 232–3, 294, 301–4; S, I, 334, 428, 439–40.

[151] *Arbor Vitae* in Ubertino da Casale 1485, fo. ccvi v, quoted Reeves 1969, p. 186 n. 2.

[152] Angelo Clareno, *Historia Septem Tribulationum* in *ALKG* II, 271–6, quoted in Reeves 1969, p. 186.

[153] Brooke 1959, p. 271, citing Gilson 1924, p. 25

and condemned to perpetual imprisonment. Gerard was punished for drawing logical but unacceptable inferences about the third age. Joachim would have repudiated his conclusions absolutely.[154] It was inevitable however, that his Trinitarian conception of history was discredited. At a provincial Council held at Arles in 1263 the whole 'pernicious doctrine' of the three states, as maintained by the Joachites, was condemned, together with those of Joachim's writings, such as his *Liber Concordie*, on which it was based. Only the *Joachitici* were named; Abbot Joachim himself was not.[155]

It was in the same year 1263 that Bonaventure presented his *Life of St Francis* to his Order. He seems never to have subscribed to Joachim's Trinitarian doctrine of history. He had repudiated it already in his *Commentaries on the Four Books of the Sentences* delivered in Paris as lectures in 1250–2; and at the other end of his specifically academic involvement, in his *Collationes in Hexaemeron*, delivered in 1273, likewise to students of theology in the university at Paris, he sets a pattern not of three periods but of four: the time of nature before the law, the time of the law, the time of the prophets – all under the wing of the Old Testament – and the time of grace.[156] The fourth period embraces the whole of history from Christ's advent till his Second Coming, thus expressing Bonaventure's firm conviction of the centrality of Christ in history. But he also set out a double-sevens pattern.[157] Such patterns divide both the Old and New Testaments into seven parallel periods, with those of the Old Testament prefiguring those of the New. Joachim had proposed just such a pattern, in addition to his doctrine of the three states, though the idea can be traced back earlier than him.[158] Bonaventure's divisions do not coincide with Joachim's, but, like Joachim, he uses the symbols of the seven days of creation for the ages of history, and summarises the seven ages in language very similar to Joachim's. He, too, places the seventh age between the destruction of Antichrist and the Last Judgement and distinguishes it from the eighth. 'Thus there will be a time of peace at the end. For when Antichrist, after very great destruction of the Church, shall be killed by Michael – after the supreme tribulation of Antichrist – there will come before the day of judgement a time of peace and tranquillity unparalleled since the beginning of the world, and there will be found men of such sanctity as in the time of the Apostles.'[159] He shared the expectation that there would be a culminating period of spiritual illumination. 'Just as the world was made in six days, and Christ came in the sixth age, so, after six ages of the Church, at the end the contemplative Church will be born.'[160] 'And it was necessary that in that time an Order should come, the prophetic manner of life, like to the Order of Jesus Christ, whose head would be the angel ascending from the rising of the sun, having the seal of the living God, and conforming to Christ.'[161]

These statements are taken from his *Collationes in Hexaemeron*, but already in the opening words of his *Life of St Francis*, St Bonaventure pinpoints the place he believes

---

[154] Reeves 1969, pp. 186–9.   [155] Reeves 1969, p. 61 and n. 3.

[156] For this and what follows, see Reeves 1969, pp. 66–8, 179–81; d'Avray 1981, esp. pp. 468–74.

[157] See table in Ratzinger 1971, p. 21; d'Avray 1981, p. 469 n. 1.

[158] Cf. Southern 1972, pp. 164–5; d'Avray 1981, p. 465 n. 1.

[159] *Collationes in Hexaemeron*, in Delorme 1934, p. 185, quoted Reeves 1969, p. 180.

[160] Delorme 1934, p. 265, quoted Reeves 1969, p. 181.

[161] Bonaventure, *Collationes in Opera Omnia*, V, 405, quoted Reeves 1969, p. 180.

St Francis occupied in the sequence of temporal events. 'The grace of God our Saviour has appeared in his servant Francis in these last times' – 'novissimis', a word with eschatological as well as purely historical meaning; and he claims an eschatological role for St Francis: it is Francis who is being referred to when, after the opening of the sixth seal, St John sees in his vision 'another angel ascending from the rising of the sun, having the seal of the living God' (Rev. 7. 2). The claim is clearly deliberate, and, given the circumstances of the time, courageous. The wording is unambiguous and categorical: we learn 'by a faith free of all doubt' through 'a prophecy full of truth', furnished by no less an authority than the Apostle and Evangelist St John, that 'this messenger of God . . . was Francis the servant [or slave] of God' (Prol. 1–2). Historical speculation of this kind forms part of a long tradition of orthodox apocalyptic stretching back to the Book of Daniel. John of Parma had linked St Francis with this very prophecy, and by repeating it so publicly St Bonaventure gives his countenance and blessing to legitimate expectations and understanding of the role and mission of St Francis and of his Order widespread among its members. The friars, as they read the *Life*, will have appreciated that their Minister General was not prepared to allow them to be driven off course, or to have their confidence undermined, by heretical deviants.

Bonaventure's likening of St Francis to the angel entrusted with the task of sealing the foreheads of the elect (Rev. 7. 2–8) comes as the climax to a series of images culled from the Order's earlier literature, signifying the retention of a reassuring thread of continuity. 'The morning star in the midst of a cloud' was part of the text chosen by Gregory IX for his sermon on the occasion of Francis' canonisation, a ceremony vividly described by Celano in his *First Life*. 'The rainbow giving light in the clouds of glory' comes from the same passage of sustained poetry in Ecclesiasticus.[162] His resemblance to John the Baptist had been stressed in 2 *Celano* 3–4, a comparison with Elijah hinted at in 1 *Celano* 47. Throughout the passage, the analogies are linked to angels and to prophecy. Francis was 'an angel [or messenger] of true peace' (Isaiah 33. 7), he was 'filled with the spirit of prophecy and also entrusted with angelic office, wholly inflamed with seraphic fire'. For Francis also has his place in the hierarchy of angels, among the seraphim, whose wings were visualised as fiery red. Hence his association with the prophet Elijah, who was transported into heaven in a fiery chariot drawn by horses of fire (4 Kings (2 Kings) 2. 11). Bonaventure's angelology was based on the Pseudo-Dionysius.[163] The Old Testament story of Elijah's miraculous ascent was interpreted as a prefiguration of Christ's Ascension. Francis, while he lived, 'was an imitator of angelic purity, which is why he has been set as an example for the perfect followers of Christ . . . The sign of the likeness of the living God, that is, Christ crucified, which was imprinted on his body, gives confirmation with the unbreakable testimony of truth; imprinted not through natural causes nor through human skill, but rather through the admirable power of the spirit of the living God' (Prol. 1–2). This is a superlative opening.

---

[162] Eccles. 50. 6–8; 1 *Cel.* 125; see pp. 37–8.
[163] See Bihl's note, AF X, 557 n. 16; and on Pseudo-Dionysius and his influence, see p. 236 and note 72. See also the texts quoted in Reeves 1969, pp. 180–1.

Later in the *Life*, as the conclusion to his account of St Francis as prophet, Bonaventure assigns to him a pivotal role in a span of sacred history which on this occasion he divides into three. 'For the heavenly Doctor is wont to reveal his mysteries to the simple and lowly, as first appeared in David, most distinguished of prophets, and later in Peter, the prince of the Apostles, and later still in Christ's poor little servant Francis. Although they were simple men in their limited skill in letters, they became illustrious by the teaching of the Holy Spirit: the first a shepherd to pasture the flock of the Synagogue which had been brought out of Egypt; the second a fisherman, to fill the Church's net with believers of many kinds; the third a merchant, to buy the pearl of the evangelical life, having sold and dispersed all he had for Christ's sake' (XI, 14). In a sermon he preached in Paris on the feast of St Francis' translation on 25 May 1267, he repeated this remarkable historical statement.[164]

The plan of the book appears at first sight to be based on the pattern of Celano's *Second Life*: after the Prologue there is a comparatively short biographical section, taking the story up to the confirmation of the Rule (I–IV), followed by a much longer collection of stories and examples grouped under headings (V–XIII). The final chapters (XIV–XV) are closer in conception to 1 *Celano* (109–50), covering Francis' death, canonisation, and afterlife of miraculous interventions.

The first section is of much the same length as the equivalent Book I of 2 *Celano*, but that was only a supplement to the more detailed narrative already provided in 1 *Celano*. Chapter 1 deals with Francis' life in the world. It is very selective. The incidents that are mentioned are condensed. They are not so vividly told as in Bonaventure's sources; they are made less interesting, and give a less clear picture of Francis as an individual, though they emphasise his virtues and his spiritual progress. They afforded, however, three stories destined to be dramatised in fresco in the nave of the Upper Church. First, a very simple man prophetically spread his cloak under the young Francis' feet out of reverence, a detail not recorded elsewhere – one of the few traces of Bonaventure's oral enquiries in and around Assisi.[165] Second, Francis gave his clothing to a poor knight.[166] Thirdly, he had a dream of a palace full of armour bearing Christ's cross.[167] In spite of its brevity the initial impression gives prominence to two categories of people whose role in Francis' upbringing was crucial: beggars and lepers. The condition, the lifestyle, of the beggar stirred the imagination of this pampered young man, by an attraction of opposites. In the first paragraph of chapter 1 Bonaventure chooses to tell how Francis dismissed empty-handed a beggar who approached him while he was busy trading. A common enough situation; but in this particular encounter Francis' conscience was aroused by the appeal 'for the love of God' and he rushed after him and gave him a fistful of money. It was a defining moment. He promised God he would never again, if at all possible, deny anyone who begged with these words, a promise he kept. In the final paragraph of this short chapter Bonaventure returns to the theme. 'To the poor and also to beggars he yearned to give not only his goods but himself, on occasion

[164] Bougerol 1993, II, Sermon 46, c. 10.
[165] Bonav. I, 1; Moorman 1940, pp. 142–3.
[166] Bonav. I, 2; the comparison with St Martin is made explicit in 2 *Celano* 5.
[167] Bonav. I, 3.

taking off his clothes, or ripping them up or tearing pieces from them to give to them, having nothing else to hand' (I, 6).

Francis himself attributed his change of heart to his meeting with a leper. 'The Lord granted me, brother Francis, to begin to do penance in this way, that when I was in sin, it seemed to me very horrible to see lepers, and the Lord himself led me among them and I helped them. And when I left them that which had before seemed to me horrible was transformed into sweetness of body and soul. After that I remained only a little time before I left the world.' These are the opening sentences of his Testament.[168] Bonaventure's account of Francis' actions (I, 5–6) is very similar to 2 *Celano* 9. He details Francis' instinctive repulsion; how he dismounted, pressed money into the leper's hand and kissed it, and how this experience of self-mastery spurred him on so that, instead of going out of his way to avoid lepers, as he had hitherto done, he now frequently visited their houses, gave them liberal alms, kissed their hands and mouths. But he goes further, and gives the reason for this new devotion, humility and compassion: it was because the prophet Isaiah (in the Vulgate version) foretold that Christ crucified would be despised as if he were a leper. To modern English readers familiar with Handel's *Messiah* or with the Authorised Version, 'He is despised and rejected of men . . . We did esteem him stricken, smitten of God and afflicted' (Isaiah 53. 3–4), the full significance of Isaiah's words may not be brought home. The Vulgate is clear: 'et nos putavimus eum quasi leprosum'. The connection is not made in the early sources;[169] nor does St Francis spell it out. Bonaventure understood that when St Francis was confronted by the leper face to face he saw Christ. His handling of this theme shows him attuned to St Francis' spirituality.

The subject of chapter II is the period of education that ensued under the tutelage of Christ. Christ began by instructing him, through the painted crucifix at San Damiano, to repair his ruined house. Francis took this literally, and behaved like the trained merchant he was. Church repairs cost money; so he sold some cloth; only the priest would not accept his cash. Francis chucked the coins on to a window ledge, suddenly seeing that if money could not be used to mend a church it must be absolutely useless – just dust (II, I). His, to his family, eccentric behaviour precipitated a breach with his father. Bonaventure says very little about Francis' family. Neither of his parents is named. His father comes across as violent, harsh, bad-tempered and grasping. His mother receives no word of praise (II, 2–3).[170] This is surprisingly ungenerous at the time of writing, since, throughout Bonaventure's generalate and beyond, the lay proctor of the Basilica and Sacro Convento was a member of the family, Picardo Angeli, one of St Francis' nephews. The Order undoubtedly benefited greatly from the legal and business skills he devoted to its service. In particular, in 1259, he masterminded the consolidation of the Order's landholdings on the Collis Paradisi.[171] Bonaventure must have had personal dealings with him while he was in Assisi researching materials for the *Life*. Francis now experienced something of the reality of being poor. He spent

---

[168] Esser 1976, p. 438; Brooke 1975, p. 117.   [169] 1 Cel. 17; 2 Cel. 9; Julian of Speyer, c. 12.

[170] Bonaventure's account is based on 1 Celano and Julian of Speyer. For the treatment of the family in 1 and 2 *Celano* and 3 *Soc.* see pp. 43, 49–50, 153.

[171] See pp. 153–5.

some time among lepers, tending and washing their ulcers and kissing them, acquiring skills of healing (II, 6). Then he returned to Assisi to obey the command to repair San Damiano in the only way open to him, the hard way. He forced himself to overcome the embarrassment of begging and to endure physical hard labour. He continued along this restricted path, repairing a church dedicated to St Peter, and then settled at the deserted Portiuncula. Bonaventure's account in praise of the Portiuncula is brief, but it contains all the essentials. Francis loved the Portiuncula more than any other place in the world, because it was dedicated to the Virgin mother of God and because it was visited by angels. Here he began humbly, here he progressed in virtue, here he died. This is the place where St Francis, guided by divine revelation, founded the order of Friars Minor, and the place he commended to the friars as he lay dying (II, 8). Francis progressed from material things to spiritual things, from lesser to greater. His repair of three churches (a literal and visible rebuilding) prefigured his foundation of three Orders[172] – a spiritual and theological threefold renewal of Christ's Church. Using a phrase from 1 *Celano* 37, 'the triple militia of the saved', Bonaventure ends on a note of triumph: 'as we now see it fulfilled' (II, 8).

This is a very good example of Bonaventure's adroit handling of his subject. His last sentence in chapter II is addressed to Francis' followers living in the mid-century, now – 'we now see'. It is a rallying call from their present leader, to hearten any daunted by the experiences and challenges of the recent past. They should look beyond any immediate, material horizon, any menacing clouds of hostility and jealousy, and instead raise their sights to heaven, where with the eye of faith they can perceive a numerous company of all three ranks of St Francis' followers, friars, penitents and virgins, who have already passed on into glory. Yet to say that Bonaventure writes 'essentially' as Minister General[173] is an oversimplification, and a belittlement of his achievement. He writes also as a theologian and as a mystic. It is also clear, not simply from his own admission in the Prologue, but from numerous examples from his writings and his sermons I have already cited, that he writes out of personal devotion to St Francis and his memory. On a different level he is a compiler and synthesiser, and analyst, of others' writings and reminiscences. It is not a first-hand or contemporary account. Over thirty years have passed since Francis' death. That is still quite close, within the living memory of a few. But inevitably this *Life* is conditioned by the actual context in which it was written, by its own *Sitz im Leben*.

Chapter III provides a narrative of the founding of the Order up to the approval of the Rule. It begins with a full account of the impact made on Francis by the Gospel passage (Matt. 10. 9–10) detailing Christ's instructions to his disciples when he sent them out to preach; indeed it is fuller on Francis' response than either 1 *Celano* 22, which mentions his discarding shoes and staff, or Julian of Speyer 15, which adds 'bag or wallet'. Bonaventure spells it out: Francis took off his shoes, put down his staff, repudiated wallet and money (III, 1). He is not in any way toning down what commitment to the Gospel involves. Three of his earliest followers are named, Bernard, Giles and Sylvester. The manner of Bernard's initiation is described in detail: Francis took him to the church

---

[172] See IV, 5–6.   [173] Moorman 1940, pp. 143–4.

of St Nicholas, where they sought God's help by opening the Gospel book three times. The point is made that right from the start, with the Order's first recruit, the Rule is God-given, and is based on a literal and spiritual obedience to Gospel texts. The paragraph on Sylvester, the first priest to join, provides an insight on the nature of Bonaventure's selectivity. He omits all the revealing details contained in 2 *Celano*'s account of his conversion (2 *Cel.* 109), but does not omit his vision. Bonaventure appreciated visions and their interpretation. He has included several already, and Sylvester's, far from condensing, he expands (III, 5).[174]

Chapter IV begins by summarising their manner of life after their return to the valley of Spoleto, praising especially their prayerfulness and their poverty. It includes one striking story about Holy Poverty (IV, 7) which does not occur in any of his written sources. Some friars who had reached the regions of the infidels and were obviously destitute were offered money by a Saracen, which they refused. When he understood that they had made themselves poor for the love of God he was so impressed that he offered to supply all their needs for as long as he had the means. 'O the priceless quality of poverty, by whose wonderful virtue a mind imbued with barbarous savagery could be turned to such sweet mercy! It would be a horrid and a wicked deed for a Christian to trample on this noble pearl which a Saracen elevated with such veneration' (IV, 7). Here the pearl of great price, the kingdom of heaven (Matt. 13. 45–6), is equated with voluntary poverty.

Chapter IV, the last in the narrative biographical section, reaches its climax in an account of the rewriting and confirmation of the Rule. Bonaventure's treatment here of the themes of the Rule's divine dictation and its double sealing, papal and divine, was a reworking of ideas and material he had already used in his 1255 sermon.[175] His researches when preparing the book provided him with further material which led him to introduce this important topic with a vision. Francis dreamed that he was surrounded by many starving friars and must gather crumbs of bread from the ground. But they were so small he was afraid they would slip through his fingers. A voice from above said: 'Francis, make one host out of all the crumbs and give to those willing to eat.' He did so and those who did not receive it devoutly were presently afflicted with leprosy. Francis did not immediately understand the meaning of this, but while he was at prayer he heard a voice from heaven explain: 'the crumbs are the words of the Gospel, the host is the Rule, leprosy wickedness' (IV, 11). The words of the Gospel are the bread of life; but still it is a bold claim. The Rule is likened to the Eucharist; failure to observe the Rule properly is wicked, blasphemous. However, Bonaventure did not invent the metaphor. He lifted this story virtually word for word from 2 *Celano* 209. Thomas of Celano is here again the source, the fountain head of Franciscan imagery.[176] Bonaventure does, though, omit one significant detail of the context. According to Celano the dream occurred at the time when there was discussion among the friars about the confirmation of the Rule and Francis was extremely agitated over this business. The Rule 'written down simply, in few words', sanctioned by Innocent III in 1210, had grown over the years and become

---

[174] For Sylvester's great serpent see Daniel 14. 22.
[175] See pp. 232–4.   [176] See AF X, 576.

unwieldy, overladen with exhortations and biblical quotations.[177] Admonished by the dream, Francis accepted it needed pruning and revision.

Ubertino criticised Bonaventure for not including stories believed to have been written down by brother Leo, in particular this story concerning the writing of the *Regula bullata*, for which Leo was a first-hand witness, for he was present and wrote the Rule[178] – that is, he acted as Francis' secretary.

'While St Francis was on a mountain with brother Leo of Assisi and brother Bonizo of Bologna to make the Rule – because the first, which he had written on Christ's instruction, was lost – many ministers came to brother Elias, who was St Francis' vicar, and said to him: "We have heard that this brother Francis is making a new Rule. We are afraid that he may make it so severe that we will not be able to observe it. We want you to go to him and tell him that we do not want to be bound to that Rule. Let him make it for himself and not for us." Brother Elias replied to them that he did not want to go, as he feared St Francis' reproof. But they were so insistent that he should go, that he said he would not go without them. So they all went. When brother Elias, with the ministers, was near the place where St Francis was standing he called to him. St Francis answered and, seeing the ministers, said: "What do these brothers want?" Brother Elias replied: "These men are ministers who have heard that you are making a new Rule and fear that you are making it too strict; they say and protest that they do not want to be bound to it. You are to make it for yourself and not for them." Then St Francis turned his face towards heaven and addressed Christ thus: "Lord, did I not tell you that they would not believe you?" Then the voice of Christ was heard in the air replying: "Francis, there is nothing of yours in the Rule, but all which is there is mine. I want the Rule to be observed as it is to the letter, to the letter, to the letter, and without gloss, and without gloss, and without gloss." He continued: "I know how much is possible to human frailty and how much I wish to help them. Let those who do not wish to observe it leave the Order." Then St Francis turned to the brothers and said to them: "Do you hear? Do you hear? Would you like me to have it said to you again?" Then those ministers retired abashed, blaming one another' (SL 113 = *Verba* c. 4).[179]

This dramatic confrontation forms part of a small group of stories that circulated as an independent tract, titled the *Verba S. Francisci*, in the early fourteenth century. It is ascribed to Leo alone, not to Leo, Rufino and Angelo, the three companions. No detectable use is made of it in 2 *Celano*. I have argued elsewhere that it was written not until after 1247, and probably before 1260.[180] I suggested tentatively then that it might have been written in 1257, prompted by the fall of John of Parma, but I incline now to think it was most likely written in the early 1250s, a time when there was much earnest and anxious discussion in the Order concerning the Rule, its observance, and the attitude that should be taken towards papal privileges. At the General Chapter held at Genoa in 1251 decisions were taken to abstain from taking advantage of both Innocent

---

[177] Esser 1976, pp. 439 (Testament), 377–402 (*Regula non bullata*).
[178] Ubertino da Casale 1485, *Arbor Vitae*, v. 5.
[179] Quoted from SL 113. Ubertino's version in the *Arbor Vitae* shows some variants as it comes not from a text but from oral tradition.
[180] SL pp. 57–66.

IV's privilege *Quanto studiosius*, which gave the friars virtual control over their properties and finances, and of his bull *Ordinem vestrum* with its more lenient interpretations of the Rule, a decision reaffirmed at Metz in 1254.[181] If Ubertino's statement that Leo entrusted his 'rotuli' to the Poor Ladies of Santa Chiara is true, it could be that he gave them along with St Francis' breviary c.1259.[182] If so, Bonaventure could have had access to them. He could also have known these stories through oral tradition – Ubertino's version of *Verba* c. 4 comes from Conrad of Offida, who heard it from brother Leo's mouth – or indeed he too could have learnt them from Leo himself. Ubertino believed that Bonaventure was aware of these stories and deliberately chose not to incorporate them in his *Life*. However, from Bonaventure's account of what transpired it is clear that he was by now aware of the story contained in *Verba* c. 4. Francis retired to a mountain with two companions to pray, and, fasting on bread and water, dictated the Rule 'at the prompting of the Holy Spirit'. Coming down from the mountain, he entrusted it to his vicar, who, a few days later, claimed it had been lost through negligence. So the saint once more returned to the place of solitude, 'and there restored it in the form of the earlier version, as if he received the words from God's mouth' (IV, 11).

There are indications that he used material from two other stories in the *Verba*. In IV, 10 Bonaventure states that 'sometimes over five thousand brothers' gathered at General Chapter – an exaggeration no doubt. The figure five thousand occurs in two independent accounts of incidents that took place at a General Chapter, in Eccleston's *Tractatus* and in *Verba* c. 5 (= SL 114). The actual number may not have been accurate but there was evidently a pleasingly high turnout, and it is likely to have been a record. Another chronicler, Jordan of Giano, estimated the number attending the General Chapter in 1221 at three thousand. Francis used to summon all his brothers to Chapter, as Bonaventure acknowledges in IV, 10. With the confirmation of the *Regula bullata* in 1223 membership of the General Chapter was drastically reduced, to officials only (chapter VIII). I have argued elsewhere that the two incidents connected to a Chapter hosting five thousand probably relate to one and the same Chapter.[183] Bonaventure will not have known Eccleston's *Tractatus*. It is likely that he plucked the figure of five thousand from *Verba* c. 5 (SL 114). But he completely omitted its story of what happened at that crowded Chapter, during which a number of wise and well-educated friars lobbied Cardinal Hugolino to get him to use his influence to persuade St Francis, in private, to listen to their advice and accept the teachings of an existing monastic rule. Francis would have none of it. Taking the cardinal by the hand, he confronted all the friars in Chapter, where his impassioned and uncompromising outburst left Hugolino speechless and the friars afraid.[184] This story is inherently convincing. It sits adjacent to the story of the writing of the *Regula Bullata* in SL (113, 114) and the *Verba* (cc. 4, 5), and the mention of the presence of over five thousand friars at General Chapters in Bonaventure's *Life* (IV, 10) is adjacent to his account of the writing of the Rule (IV, 11).

[181] Brooke 1959, p. 264 and n. 3. For the dates of these two General Chapters, see ibid. p. 257 and nn. 2, 3.
[182] SL p. 8.
[183] Eccleston, p. 32; Jordan, cc. 16–18; Brooke 1959, pp. 286–91.
[184] Part of his speech is quoted pp. 8–9.

Bonaventure comments that although there was a dearth of everything one needed at these Chapters attended by such a multitude, 'nonetheless divine mercy provided and there was enough to eat and there was health of body and overflowing spiritual joy' (IV, 10). The *Verba* c. 2 (SL 112) tells how when the ministers tried to persuade St Francis to allow some things in common so that the greatly increased numbers of friars might have something to fall back on St Francis called upon Christ in prayer. 'Christ at once replied that He would take away all their possessions held individually and in common, saying that this is His family and He was always ready to provide for it, however much it grows, and will always foster it so long as it puts its hope in him.' Bonaventure has surely incorporated this story too, but drawn its sting. He included the detail of the loss of the Rule because it evoked a comparison between St Francis and Moses – a comparison he elaborated in one of his sermons.[185] Chapter IV, 10–11, provides a good example of Bonaventure's treatment of some of his material. He has used a controversial source, but omitted all traces of criticism and conflict. In his conclusion he emphasised the divine inspiration of the Rule with a quotation from the Testament, attributed to Francis though the Testament itself is not named.

The next nine chapters (V–XIII) contain a collection of stories. As in 2 *Celano* Book II these are presented analytically, grouped under headings. The general headings are more rationally arranged in Bonaventure's *Life*, although in some sections, especially that on poverty, 2 *Celano* has a much clearer organisation of the material – with sub-heads. This seems partly to be due to Celano's readiness to expand very much on some topics. Bonaventure is more restrained or constrained.

Bougerol has traced a theological progression throughout these chapters. It is certainly not chronological: thus, for example, at VII, 10, soldiers are escorting a terminally ill Francis back to Assisi. According to Bougerol, Bonaventure systematised his material in conformity with the theory of 'the triple pathways' expounded in his *De triplici vita* and repeated in other works, from his *Postilla in Lucam* to his *Collationes in Hexaemeron*.[186] The paths of virtue that Francis followed began with 'the way of purgation', *via purgativa*: penitence, and austerity of life (V); humility and obedience (VI); love of poverty (VII). His way forward was next by 'the way of illumination', *via illuminativa*: compassion (VIII); charity (IX); prayer (X). These virtues led on upwards to 'the way of unity', *via unitiva*: the spirit of prophecy (XI); preaching (XII); the stigmata (XIII).

Not all the stories fit comfortably into the pattern: The miracle of the spring (VII, 12) only creeps into chapter VII on poverty because it is a story of Francis miraculously quenching the thirst of a poor man. The crib at Greccio does not seem to illustrate the efficacy of prayer – rather the effect of preaching: it is Francis' sermon which leads John of Greccio to see the vision of the baby asleep in the crib before Francis takes him in his arms. It ought to be in chapter XII, and seems almost to be stuck on the end of chapter X. Bonaventure specifically adds that Francis asked for and obtained papal permission for the ceremony, so that he could not be accused of being an innovator. It may be that questions had been raised and that Bonaventure had considered omitting it. By contrast, the opening of chapter XII on prayer and solitude versus preaching and

[185] See p. 238.   [186] Bougerol 1984, pp. 36–46.

the active life is very interestingly presented; as is chapter XI on knowledge of Scripture: here Bonaventure is on home ground.

Bonaventure leads into his display of Francis' virtues with a military metaphor. 'When Francis perceived that by his example very many people were taking up the cross of Christ with fervour, he himself was inspired as a good leader of the army of Christ to pursue the palm of victory by way of the summit of unconquered virtue' (V, 1). He describes his austerities, how he ate and drank very little, and if he ate cooked food mixed it with ashes or diluted it with water to make it tasteless. He includes Celano's story of how he once rolled in the snow and made seven snowmen to quench the fire of lust,[187] though altering Francis' claim to know only two women by sight to: 'he once told his companion he recognised almost no woman at all' (V, 5). Yet Bonaventure has interesting and original references both to Clare and to Jacoba. It is true that he reduces St Clare and her vocation to five ecstatic and uninformative lines (IV, 6) and omits the story of Jacoba visiting Francis on his deathbed. But he is our first and best source for the story that Francis consulted both brother Silvester and St Clare as to whether his vocation should be to a preaching life or to a life of contemplation (XII, 2); and he brings the saint's body to San Damiano for Clare and her sisters to lament over it – and makes Clare and her sisters witnesses of the stigmata (XIII, 8; XV, 5). In VIII, 7 he has a charming story of how Francis gave Jacoba a lamb who used to rouse her from sleep when it was time to go to church by bleating and butting her with its horns. Bonaventure's treatment of the problem of women is as ambiguous as Francis' own.

Francis used to call his body 'brother ass' because it bore heavy burdens, was frequently beaten and was fed on vile food (V, 6). He shed so many tears of contrition that he damaged his eyes (V, 8). Bonaventure then tells how Francis addressed brother fire before braving cauterisation,[188] and how water was turned into wine to strengthen him when ill (V, 10). He concludes: 'Consider how wonderful was the purity of this man and how great his virtue, at whose nod fire tempered its heat, water changed its taste, angelic melody brought comfort, and light divine brought guidance, so that thus the whole structure of the world was shown to serve the sanctified senses of the holy man' (V, 12). This chapter is clearly didactic, addressed pointedly to the friars.

Chapter VI is mainly on humility, with obedience as a manifestation of humility. Bonaventure declared in a sermon: 'I admire the humility of blessed Francis above all his virtues';[189] and he opens the chapter with the words: 'humility the guardian and lustre of all the virtues.[190] Francis overflowed with humility. In his own estimation he was nothing but a sinner, though in truth he was a mirror and glorious image of all sanctity.' He wanted his brothers to be called Minors, and the prelates of his Order Ministers, using the words of the Gospel which he had promised to observe; his disciples should come to the school of the humble Christ to learn humility. Maintaining the scholastic image – Jesus Christ, the Master of humility, said, in order to teach his pupils perfect humility: 'whosoever will be great among you, let him be your minister' (Matt. 20. 26) (VI, 5). The later sections instance rewards his admirable humility won for Francis.

---

[187] 2 Cel. 112; and see p. 145.   [188] V, 9; and see p. 114.
[189] Bougerol 1993, II, 749–52, Sermon 57; see p. 234.   [190] Echoing St Bernard: see AF X, 582 n. 3.

'The wisdom of the poor man, that is, Francis' humility' – he had sent brother Sylvester as his herald to expel the devils from Arezzo – 'restored peace and saved the city' (VI, 9). A friar (Pacifico) had a vision of a fallen angel's resplendent throne, reserved for Francis because Francis saw himself 'as the greatest of sinners'.[191] But the most extravagant claim concerned relics abandoned in a deserted church. St Francis ordered the friars to take them reverently to the friary; they forgot. But when they withdrew the altar cloth in preparation for celebrating mass, most beautiful sweet-smelling bones were revealed. The friars humbly confessed their negligence and St Francis said: 'Blessed be my Lord God, who has himself fulfilled what you ought to have done.' Bonaventure, following 2 *Celano*, comments: 'Consider diligently the care of the divine providence for our dust, and the excellent virtue accorded the humble Francis in God's eyes. For when man failed to obey his orders, God obeyed his wishes' (VI, 7).[192] This chapter too ends with an exhortation: 'Francis' humility is worthy of imitation.' Bonaventure is making use of his position as Minister General and his task as author to preach.

Chapter VII, on Francis' love for the highest poverty, is culled almost entirely from 2 *Celano*'s rich store, exploiting the range from romantic poetry through cautionary tales to miraculous provision.[193] He really attempts to do justice to this theme. He includes Francis' insistence that anyone entering the Order should give everything he had to the poor, and his dismissal of brother Fly (VII, 3); the bulging purse that disgorged a snake (VII, 5); the three poor women – whom Bonaventure interpreted as symbolising Francis' perfect observance of the three monastic vows of chastity, obedience and poverty – who greeted him: 'Welcome, Lady Poverty' (VII, 6); Cardinal Hugolino's embarrassment when Francis, his guest at dinner, brought bread he had begged to the table (VII, 7).[194] He even includes Francis' saying, hard for such as him: 'Whoever wishes to attain this summit should renounce in some measure not only worldly prudence but also skill in letters – so that, shorn of every such possession, he may enter into the powers of the Lord and offer himself naked to the arms of the Crucified' (VII, 2);[195] and another in which he avows that he is sure the Blessed Virgin would prefer her altar to be stripped bare rather than that goods of postulants should be retained as a precaution against emergencies (VII, 4). Bonaventure made some additions: a saying to sum up the section on poverty in buildings, which must never be appropriated or sumptuous; Francis 'used to call evangelical poverty the foundation of the Order: on it the whole structure of the Order rested, first and foremost – so that it is strengthened by its strength – but if poverty is uprooted, so is the Order' (VII, 2); the detail that Francis used to go begging whenever possible on the major festivals because bread begged for the love of God was angels' food (Ps. 77(78). 25) (VII, 8). His next story on begging provides a good example of how Bonaventure could completely rewrite his source. According to Celano, one Easter at Greccio the friars decked the table festively. Francis, displeased, stealthily went outside disguised as a pilgrim and begged for alms. The astonished friars gave him a dish and he sat down alone, putting

[191] VI, 6; see 2 *Cel.* 122.   [192] Bonaventure's source for all these stories was 2 *Celano*.
[193] He makes use of 2 *Celano* 55–6, 61, 66–7, 71–3, 77, 80–1, 83–4, 93, 194 (AF X, 587–92).
[194] See p. 119.   [195] Cf. Constable 1979; Ps. 70(71). 16.

the dish in the ashes. 'Now', he said, 'I am sitting like a Friar Minor' (2 Cel. 61). And Celano spells out the analogy of Christ at Emmaus making the hearts of the disciples burn (Luke 24. 18, 32). According to Bonaventure, one Easter Sunday, staying at a hermitage too remote to make his begging possible, Francis, remembering that Christ appeared to the two disciples on the road to Emmaus on that day disguised as a pilgrim, himself begged alms from the friars as a poor pilgrim, and preached to them on the theme that they should travel through the world as 'strangers and pilgrims' (1 Peter 2. 11) (VII, 9).[196] Bonaventure here omits all the vivid dramatic detail and all suggestion of criticism of the friars. Then there are some miracles, selected to support a message of reassuring hope: Christ's poor need have no fear. Poverty enabled Francis, on occasion, miraculously to provide food, drink or essential house repairs necessary to those who helped him. Bonaventure ends thus: 'If, I say, at the behest of the poor man dry rock yielded an abundant drink to a thirsty and impoverished pauper, in every way he will not deny his support to those who have left all for the Author of all' (VII, 13). As a piece of rhetoric and word play – and not Bonaventure at his best – it is revealing as to how his mind worked. Up to this point the whole of this middle section is geared to encouraging the friars to tread the paths of virtue in the steps of their founder. The emphasis now shifts to the reverence Francis' exceptional virtues must inspire, and the number of miracles included continues to multiply.

Chapter VIII is about attitudes, *pietatis affectus*, about feeling, affection, compassion. Strikingly, Bonaventure compares St Francis to 'a mother in Christ', and discusses some of his attitudes – the things he disapproved of and the things which reflected his *pietas*. Francis disapproved of conceited preachers. He used to say that a simple, inarticulate friar could convert more sinners, beget more children for Christ, by his private prayers and good example of life (VIII, 2). He strongly disapproved of detractors, who are more impious than thieves because they destroy souls with their tongues (VIII, 4). 'This most Christian poor man saw in every poor person the image of Christ himself', and so would give anything he had to anyone in need (VIII, 5). The rest of the chapter deals with his attitude, his affection towards creatures, whom he called 'brothers and sisters'. He was drawn especially to any referred to in the Bible as images of Christ, and so responded with particular compassion to lambs. He cursed a sow that attacked and killed a new-born lamb (VIII, 6). Living creatures brought to him for food he released – a leveret, a water fowl, a fish, a pheasant – but they were reluctant to leave him without his blessing. Others, a sheep, a flock of birds, a cicada, a falcon, either instinctively or at his invitation, joined in his worship and praise of God.

Chapter IX develops the intensity of feeling from affection to the fervour of charity. It opens with a 'theological hymn' celebrating St Francis' passionate, glowing love for Christ his spouse.[197] Bonaventure's ecstatic language is, however, mainly taken from Celano, especially from 2 Celano. 'In beautiful things he beheld Beauty . . . He followed

---

[196] 2 Celano 61 is based on SL 32, though in Celano the occasion is Easter, not Christmas. Celano may have changed it to make his theological point, though more than one version may well have been circulating. There is a thorough and interesting discussion of this story in Kleinberg 1992, pp. 126–33.
[197] Bougerol 1984, p. 40.

the Beloved everywhere' (2 *Cel.* 165; IX, 1). He exhorted all creatures to praise God in the harmony of the virtues and performances given to them by God, perceiving a celestial symphony – a reference to the Canticle of brother Sun. Because of his love for Christ crucified he received communion often, and so devoutly that he inspired others to devotion (IX, 2). His love for Jesus' Mother, who made the Lord our brother, was intense, as was his love for the angels – especially St Michael, because it is his office to present souls to God – and for the saints, especially St Peter and St Paul. He kept Lents, fasts of forty days, in honour of Christ, the Virgin and St Michael (IX, 3; 2 *Cel.* 201, 197–8). He considered the salvation of souls of paramount importance. It was out of charity towards his neighbour that he prayed and preached as he did and strove always to be a living example to others. This ardour culminated in his longing for martyrdom, and Bonaventure describes his efforts, all unsuccessful, to court death for Christ.[198] Bonaventure concludes, as did Celano, that God reserved for St Francis a singular privilege – the stigmata – equivalent to martyrdom (IX, 9; 1 *Cel.* 57).

Francis sought consolation and guidance through ceaseless prayer. 'Walking or sitting, at home or away, working or at leisure, he was so intent on prayer that he seemed to have dedicated to it not only his heart and body but his work and time' (X, 1). He could concentrate his mind on prayer even in crowded places, but preferred seclusion and the night time, retiring to remote places or abandoned churches. He often experienced transports of contemplation and ecstasy, when he was totally unaware of all that was going on around him, and penetrated mysteries beyond human understanding.[199] His tireless application to prayer, coupled with his ceaseless exercise of the virtues, led Francis to such serenity of mind that, although he was not taught theology, 'inspired by the rays of holy light he could penetrate the depths of Scripture with a wonderfully sharp intelligence . . . Where academic learning stayed outside, the affection of the lover entered in.'[200] He had a tenacious memory and meditated constantly on what he read. Asked if he was prepared to allow learned men entering the Order to continue to study Scripture, he replied that he was happy for them to do so, provided that they did not neglect the study of prayer, following the example of Christ, who is recorded to have prayed more than he studied. 'I want my friars to be disciples of the Gospels, proficient in knowledge of the truth and growing in the purity of simplicity, not separating the simple dove from the wise serpent, which the excellent Master joined with his blessed lips' (Matt. 10. 16). Bonaventure then tells, much abbreviated, the story, taken from 2 *Cel.* 103, of the learned theologian – he omits to say that he was a Dominican – who consulted St Francis on the interpretation of a difficult passage (in Ezekiel) and was so impressed with the clarity of his doctrinal response that he exclaimed in admiration: 'Truly, the theology of this holy father, carried high on the wings of purity and contemplation, is a soaring eagle; our learning crawls on its belly on the ground' (XI, 2). The rest of the chapter concentrates on St Francis' spirit of prophecy, with stories illustrating his power to see into the hearts of men, and to read their thoughts and desires.

---

[198] See p. 238 for Bonaventure's treatment of the themes of this chapter in a sermon delivered on 4 October 1262.

[199] Ch. X is based on Celano, esp. 1 *Cel.* 71–2 and 2 *Cel.* 94–6, 99–101.

[200] XI, 1; 2 *Cel.* 102.

Francis' talents as a preacher were likewise the product of prayerful meditation and divine inspiration, not of any formal training. St Bonaventure's first example of the efficacy of Francis' preaching is the story of his preaching to the birds.[201] He also tells the story of his preaching before Honorius III and the cardinals, but he leaves out the charismatic element, how Francis, in his fervour to convey spiritual joy, danced before them.[202] At some of his sermons miracles occurred, and Bonaventure has no hesitation in declaring that this was a reason why people listened to what he had to say 'as if he were an angel of God' (XII, 12). He records a number of miracles. When preaching on the sea shore at Gaeta, because of the crowds Francis got into a small boat which moved out to sea, and he addressed those assembled on the beach from there (XII, 6). This recalls Christ's delivery of the parable of the sower from a boat to the multitude standing on the sea shore (Matt. 13. 1–3). Another miracle, taken from 1 *Celano* 67, Bonaventure altered so as to turn it into a Gospel parallel. Francis cured a woman's withered hands, and she promptly went home and prepared food for him and the poor, 'like Simon [Peter's] mother-in-law' (Matt. 8. 14–15) (XII, 10). But Bonaventure has gone off at a tangent. Two miracle stories mention a flock of swallows whose twittering interrupted Francis' sermon (XII, 4, 5), but the chapter becomes a catalogue of assorted miracles, mainly of healing, which are not specifically linked to preaching – they are not said to have occurred during or after sermons. Two took place in private houses where Francis was given hospitality (XII, 9, 10); others were effected through water his cord was dipped in, bread he had touched or the reins of a horse he had ridden (XII, 11). This chapter is not well organised.

Chapter XIII, on the stigmata, is told by St Bonaventure as the climax of St Francis' spiritual journey.[203] St Bonaventure regards the miracle as unique: Francis' 'holy flesh . . . bore the image of Christ's passion by a unique privilege' (XV, 1). He bases his contribution on the widest possible foundations: on the written sources, Celano's *First* and *Second Life* and *Treatise on Miracles*, on the fruits of his own personal pilgrimage to La Verna, and on the information he gained from his interviews with some of Francis' companions who were still alive. He describes in detail Francis' period of preparation, fasting and praying and meditating on Christ's Passion, the vision of the seraph with six fiery wings, the imprint of the nails, and their physical appearance. Francis never spoke of the mysteries revealed to him during his ecstasy, and endeavoured to conceal the wounds, but friars who tended him and a few others caught glimpses of them. A number of these testified on oath to the reality of the phenomenon. Pope Alexander IV in a sermon he preached to the people, at which many friars, including Bonaventure himself, were present, affirmed that he also had seen the stigmata while Francis was alive. When Francis died they were seen by over fifty friars, St Clare and her sisters, and innumerable lay people, and were kissed and touched by many – further proof of the truth of their existence.[204]

---

[201] XII, 3; 1 *Cel.* 58.
[202] XII, 7; 1 *Cel.* 72–3.   [203] Bougerol 1984, pp. 43–5.
[204] Bonaventure's treatment of the stigmata is discussed at length earlier in this chapter, pp. 232–9, and from a different angle in chapter 9, pp. 401–4.

Chapters XIV and XV deal with his final illnesses and death, and, after further description of the stigmata, with his canonisation and translation. During life the signs illuminating Francis' virtues had been brilliant; after his death, glorified by God's power, he shone throughout the world, glittering with yet more splendid miracles.

Bonaventure's chief motive was 'to gather together the virtues, acts and words of Francis' life – as it were collecting fragments, partly neglected, partly scattered, though not complete, yet as best he could', as Jesus had said of the remnants of the barley loaves, 'lest they be lost' (John 6. 12). It is a remarkable achievement, and – if we forget his predecessors – a notable evocation of the saint. It will be clear from our investigation of the earlier lives and legends that stories about Francis could be – and were – grounds for argument about how the friars should live and work, about how the Order should be run. Bonaventure had to compose a life which would not stimulate controversy – yet which brought the saint vividly and accurately to life. It has been said that his Life was hagiography not biography in the modern sense or history;[205] but the contrast is misleading. A Life of St Francis which failed to portray a living saint could not satisfy, could not replace Celano and the other early legends. The Francis of Celano's Life is here, almost complete; very little is missing. The Francis of the Scripta Leonis is less complete – the wayward, anxious Francis, not at ease with all the world, ready to argue with Hugolino himself, is almost entirely omitted. Bonaventure sets out with care and subtlety to tell the truth, but not always the whole truth. It is also said that he wrote a work of theology rather than a biography – a great theologian interpreting a divinely inspired, creative life.[206] But this too is true only to a limited extent.

It has seemed to some readers that the fragments of barley loaves represented an economical, or even disingenuous, description of the early legends which provided the bulk of his material. There were twelve baskets full, no mean quantity. He did his best. Virtually every known source was tapped here or there.

Bonaventure inevitably saw the life of Francis in a theological context – as he saw everything in this world and the next. There are hagiographical elements throughout; some have argued that Bonaventure made him appear so saintly he could no longer be imitated.[207] But the saint is given no new saintly attributes, the qualities emphasised in earlier writers are there in abundance, the miracles are virtually all taken straight from Celano. It is indeed striking that the section of miracles at the end contains the least new material, the least rewriting, in the book.

In a paradoxical sense, the surgical operations which Bonaventure performed on the material he inherited were made necessary by the conjunction of two principles not always in perfect harmony: that the saint was the model friar, a perfect representation of the Order in action; and that he must be portrayed as he really was, as a historical character. It was not a new dilemma: the evangelists had faced one very like it; and with the lives of St Francis, as with the Gospels, the truth is obscured, not illuminated, by refusing to allow that they are at once human biographies and works of theology.

---

[205] E.g. in Clasen 1961–2.   [206] See e.g. Stanislao da Campagnola 1971, pp. 173 ff.
[207] Cf. Moorman 1940, p. 147, citing Goetz 1904, p. 251.

THE MIRACLES OF ST FRANCIS

The early altar panels emphasised Francis' miracles[208] (Plate 15, Colour Plates 3, 4). The Pescia altarpiece of 1235 was clearly based on Celano's *First Life* of 1229, and in portraying the stigmata, the preaching to the birds and a group of posthumous healing miracles it anticipated, in a way, the programme of Thomas of Celano's *Treatise on Miracles*, of the early 1250s. For in *3 Celano*, among the early wonders, Francis' stigmata and his power over animals were to precede the catalogue of healing.

The early lives of St Francis contain much that is wonderful; but miracles treated specifically as such are gathered only in three of the main sources: in the catalogue of miracles read out to Gregory IX at the canonisation process in 1228, given by Celano in *1 Celano* 127–51; in his *Tractatus de Miraculis*, of 1250–2; and in the *Miracula* appended to St Bonaventure's *Legenda Maior*, of 1260–3.[209] Extensive as these sections are, they do not leave us with the impression that either author thought miracles essential to the sanctity of Francis. Brother Leo and his colleagues observed that they 'were not content simply to narrate miracles, which do not create, but only demonstrate holiness' – a well worn cliché; and Celano, echoing their Introductory Letter in his Prologue to *2 Celano*, simply stated that 'some miracles are inserted as opportunity offered to give them a place' – though indeed there are very few in *2 Celano*. Celano gives the impression in the same Prologue that wonderful events of St Francis' life matter more to him than miracles. Bonaventure avoids giving any definition of miracles at the outset of his collection – or any special excuse for compiling an inventory of them. How Celano viewed his task is obscured for us by the loss of his Introductory Letter to *3 Celano*. Arnald of Sarano in the late fourteenth-century *Chronicle of the Twenty-Four Generals* tells us that Celano wrote on the orders of the Minister General John of Parma, and cites the opening words of the dedicatory letter, which was evidently attached to the copy he read, though it is missing in the only complete manuscript of *3 Celano* which survives.[210] The facts that his *Second Life* was virtually miracle-free, and that he was most probably pressured to make good the deficiency by writing *The Treatise on Miracles*, are indicative of a pervading attitude towards miracles among the friars in the early decades of the thirteenth century that was the exact opposite of what we might presuppose. The Dominicans did not exploit their founder's early miracles at Bologna; quite the contrary: they downplayed them. In his testimony recorded for the canonisation process for St Dominic, in 1233, brother William of Montferrat stated that 'after the translation [of St Dominic] many people of various states of life said that they had received graces of healing'. And concluded:

---

[208] See pp. 168–76.

[209] All the early sources of the miracles are in AF x; and Bihl's notes to *3 Celano* and Bonaventure's *Miracula* and his use of small print for quotations and echoes of earlier sources make it easy to identify the known sources of these two collections. Moorman 1940, pp. 150 1, has a useful table giving the relations of Bonaventure's *Miracles* to *3 Celano*. This shows no source in *3 Celano* for Bonav., *Miracula*, i. 2, iii. 1, ix.1, x. 8–9. Of these, x. 8–9 are Bonaventure's comments, not separate stories; i. 2 is Gregory IX's testimony to the stigmata, iii. 1 is in fact based on *3 Cel.* 52; and ix. 1 is a genuine addition: see pp. 272–3. See also note 213. Paul 1983, pp. 257–9, has maps of Italy and Sicily showing the places named in *3 Celano*

[210] AF III, 276, quoted by Bihl in AF x, pp. xxxvi–xxxvii. For the surviving MS, see ibid., pp. xxx–xxxi, xl, and for the fragments, pp. xl–xli.

'But I do not remember their names, because I was a diffinitor at the Chapter and was too caught up in other things to pay attention to them.'[211]

Celano opens the surviving text of 3 Celano by saying that the creation of the Order – a vine stretching from sea to sea – was the greatest wonder of all, a valid point; and after the stigmata, which both he and Bonaventure place in the forefront of their collections, he goes on to list instances of Francis' control over the natural world, fire, water and animals, including his preaching to an attentive audience of birds. Bonaventure regarded these as part of his saintly attributes, and did not include them in his collection of miracles, because he had already included many of them in his account of Francis' life.[212]

Bonaventure's collection is almost entirely dependent on Celano's: there are only about three miracles in Bonaventure not in 3 Celano, one of them told in most summary fashion.[213] Of the others, c. ix. 1 tells a story from near Poitiers, and indicates that there were other similar events in the neighbourhood: this reminds us that Bonaventure had been a professor in Paris and had more access to French sources than Celano. The third, c. iii. 4, describes a scene when Cardinal Rainaldo, bishop of Ostia – Cardinal Protector of the Franciscan Order and the future Pope Alexander IV – was preaching in the Basilica in the presence of the Roman Curia. This most likely occurred in 1253, when Innocent IV and the Curia were in Assisi from May to October[214] – that is to say, after the compilation of 3 Celano. While he was preaching, a stone fell from a height on to a woman in the congregation, and stunned her. She was thought to be dead, and was covered with a cloak until the sermon was finished. Then it was discovered that she not only was alive, but had been cured of the almost continuous headaches from which she had long suffered.

In most cases there is a close verbal similarity between the versions in Celano and Bonaventure, though Bonaventure tends to abbreviate and rephrase, in this as in the rest of the Legenda Maior. A striking difference is the number of miracles recorded by Celano omitted by Bonaventure. Bonaventure has sixty-eight sections, whereas 3 Celano has 198. Taken by themselves, these figures are misleading: not every section in Celano contains one miracle, and some of Bonaventure's contain more than one: thus 3 Celano. 183–6 and 189–92 are compressed into two sections by Bonaventure, Miracula x. 3 and 2. Four chapters on the stigmata, nine healing miracles and almost the whole section in Celano on Francis' power over fire, water, birds and other animals have been transferred by Bonaventure into the body of his Legenda.[215] If we leave out the twenty-six stories in 3 Celano in these categories and two chapters of general discussion, then approximately 170 sections remain, of which eighty-eight are not represented in Bonaventure. The first collection in 1 Celano. 127–50 was the source of thirty-five sections in 3 Celano:

---

[211] Tugwell 1982, p. 71. See also the testimony of the prior of Bologna (ibid., p. 69), and pp. 75–6.

[212] The exception is 3 Celano 16, on his miraculous provision of water to a thirsty woman who invoked his aid. This is repeated in Bonav., Miracula, x. 1.

[213] Bonav. Miracula, iii. 11, conflating a story from Catalonia unique to him with one from Ancona in 3 Cel. 52.

[214] The only alternative dates after Rainaldo's promotion as cardinal bishop in 1231 are brief visits by Gregory IX in 1235 and by Innocent IV in 1254 (Mas Latrie 1889, col. 1118, summarising data from Potthast). 1235 is probably too early for the event; 1253 is much the most likely.

[215] Celano had some of them in 1 Cel. and repeats them in 3 Cel.

thirty of these are not in Bonaventure. Why Bonaventure was reluctant to reproduce miracles from that first collection is a puzzle. There are large groups of stories in *3 Celano* which are told in extremely summary fashion – 62–80 and 136–45: both contain much from *1 Celano*. Another group, 155–7, 160–72, likewise has much material from *1 Celano*. These are almost all omitted by Bonaventure, and the effect is somewhat to reduce the number of healing miracles. One group, *3 Celano* 110–15, relate to diseases of the bowels and genitals, and may have been omitted as indelicate. There was maybe a prudish element in Bonaventure; and this may account for the omission of *3 Celano* 193, the moving story of the noblewoman who was cured of a fistula between her breasts by pressing against it a book containing the life and miracles of St Francis – very probably *1 Celano*.[216]

It is also possible that he tended to avoid stories which emphasised Francis' friendly relations with women. He told in very abbreviated form Celano's story of a cure in a household of three pious women in Bevagna, mother, sister and cousin[217] of one of his friars, whom Francis often visited: on one of these visits he cured the cousin from blindness by putting spittle on her eye (*3 Cel.* 124; Bonav. XII, 10).[218] Francis had above all to set an example his friars could safely follow. The friars were reluctant to admit that St Francis had friendships with women, and Celano himself told the story that the saint claimed only to know two by sight (*2 Cel.* 112). We owe our knowledge of his relations with the Roman aristocrat Jacoba dei Settesoli to three passages in the early sources: in one, Bonaventure himself tells the story of the lamb which Francis entrusted to her for safe keeping. 'The lamb, instructed, as it were, in spiritual matters by the saint, attended the lady as she went to church, stood by her there, and stayed close to her as she returned. If at the hour of Mattins the lady was slow to rise, the lamb rose up and butted her with its little horns and roused her with its bleating, exhorting her with nods and gestures to hasten to church.'[219] The other passages are SL 101, and *3 Celano* 37–9, which tell the story of her visit to Francis' deathbed. The friars were troubled because the entry of women to the house was forbidden: 'that regulation is not to be observed with this lady' is the version of the reply in SL. 'God be blessed who has brought our brother Jacoba to us', is Celano's version. The story is not to be found in Bonaventure.

He does not otherwise display a prejudice against women. Many of the miracles were performed on women. But he sometimes omitted significant details. For example, in viii. 7 he repeats the miracle performed for Sister Praxedis, the Roman recluse; but he does not follow *3 Cel.* 181 in saying that Francis had received her into his obedience, and given her – and to no other woman – the friar's habit, tunic and cord. Likewise, in viii. 3 he only mentions in passing the girl from Norcia near Spoleto, who *3 Celano* 153 tells us was brought by her parents tied to a litter to mass in the basilica, and when she was cured, kissed the altar of St Francis (Colour Plate 4).

---

[216] See p. 172. But Bonaventure records the cure of two women with issues of blood (*Miracula*, viii. 6, from *3 Cel.* 148–9).

[217] She is referred to as the mother's *neptis*, and in the context this probably means niece in accordance with normal medieval usage.

[218] Cf. p. 211 and fig. 7.   [219] Bonav. VIII, 7. For what follows, see p. 126.

More numerous, and more puzzling, omissions are the stories which involved visits to the tomb of St Francis. All but one of those in *3 Celano* come from the group of very early miracles in *1 Celano*, and clearly involve visitors to his tomb in San Giorgio before his translation into the Basilica.[220] At the time of the translation *3 Celano* 109 describes, and Bonav. *Miracula*, viii. 2 repeats, how brother James of Iseo had been cured. After 1230 Celano has only one reference to a visit to the tomb (*3 Cel.* 188), which can be dated in 1234: Transmundus Annibaldi, podestà of Siena, brought his friend and aide Nicholas to Assisi, and 'received him instantly cured before the tomb (*ante tumbam*) of St Francis'.[221] In 1230 brother Elias had buried Francis' body in the rock: his tomb was hidden and inaccessible. 'Before the tomb' must be an anachronism – or a periphrasis for 'before the altar, *coram altari*', where the girl from Norcia received her cure.[222] Indeed, the literature of Francis' miracles is curiously reticent on the subject of pilgrims to Assisi. In *3 Celano* 89 a prisoner's chains are brought to Assisi after his release (a detail not repeated in Bonav., Miracula, v. 2); *3 Celano* 115 sends a beneficiary from Sicily 'to visit his home', that is, the Basilica. Both Celano and Bonaventure, though with differences of detail, describe a dramatic incident that occurred near Rome. A nobleman and his devout wife gave hospitality to some friars out of reverence for St Francis. That night the guard on top of their high tower went to sleep at his post and fell on to the roof of the palazzo, and thence to the ground. He was picked up – after some commotion, as the noise at first made the nobleman think he was being attacked – to everyone's amazement, still living. But he was indignant at being woken from a delightful dream in which he was carried in the arms of St Francis. When he understood what had happened he did penance and with his lord's permission went on pilgrimage – we are not told where, perhaps to Assisi; and the lord's wife gave the friars a beautiful vestment.[223]

But the best story is one of Bonaventure's own contribution. The priest of Le Simon near Poitiers, who held St Francis in devotion, told his parishioners that Francis' feast day was a solemn festival. One of them, ignorant of the saint's power, went into the country to cut wood, in spite of hearing a voice telling him three times: 'This is a holy day; work is not permitted.' He held a pronged tool in one hand; as he raised the axe held in his other hand to begin work, both hands stuck to the tools and he could not relax his fingers. Stupefied, he hastened to the church, where a number of priests had gathered, called to celebrate the festival. One of them advised him, penitent before the altar, to vow himself humbly to St Francis. He made three vows, as he had heard the voice three times: he would observe his feast day, go to church on his feast day wherever he happened to be, and personally visit the body of the saint. Wonderful to relate! – one vow taken, one finger free, the second vow, another released; after the third vow, a third finger, and then the whole hand. By now crowds of people had gathered to view the marvel, and while all prayed devoutly to the saint for mercy, the other hand was

---

[220] The relevant miracles are 1 *Celano* 127, 129–30, 132–4, 136–7, 145, 149.

[221] *3 Celano* 188 is dated to 1234 by Bihl, AF x, 327 n. 3. This is not repeated in Bonaventure.

[222] *3 Cel.* 153.

[223] *3 Cel.* 49, Bonav., Miracula, iii. 1. Bonaventure omits mention of the pilgrimage; as well as a detail revealing a mortal feud between the nobleman and his wife's brother – perhaps because it was not relevant to the miracle, perhaps because it was not edifying.

freed. The man, praising God and the saint who could so wonderfully strike and heal, himself offered his tools. Those tools hang to this day before the altar built there in St Francis' honour.[224]

In the miracle collections of Thomas Becket (d. 1170) and Gilbert of Sempringham (d. 1189) there are numerous references to visits to the tomb of the saint, and the benefits accruing: a number such are shown in the twelfth- and thirteenth-century glass in Canterbury cathedral, so that the form of his tomb and shrine is well represented.[225] After the archbishop had been brutally murdered in his cathedral, he considerately made available as an added inducement ample supplies of blood, which the monks mingled with water to provide phials of a most efficacious nature. The contrast between the throng of pilgrims to Canterbury and Sempringham in the miracles of St Thomas and St Gilbert and the handful of pilgrims to Assisi in Celano and Bonaventure is very striking, especially since by this time the Basilica was a great pilgrimage church.

The characteristic modes by which Francis acts in his miracles are by appearing in dreams and visions or by answering prayers or accepting vows and dedications. The stories of the guard who fell from a tower enjoying a delicious dream that he was in Francis' arms or of the boy of eight, presumed dead, whose father promised he would become a friar if his life was saved (3 Cel. 54), are vivid examples of a characteristic pattern. A less appealing model is that of the man or woman who ignores Francis' feast day or refuses to call a child Francis, or, in a more extreme case, blasphemes against him, and is punished.[226] Even these stories have happy endings, and Francis is never portrayed as vengeful in the manner of St Martin who, in the eyes of his devotees, could destroy robbers stealing property from a church containing his relics, or St Cadoc of Llancarfan, who was portrayed as the hammer of his enemies;[227] but this group of miracles strays from the generous image of the saint which infuses the majority.

Here are two examples of his kindness. An eighty-year-old woman's daughter died, leaving a baby. Destitute and helpless, she implored St Francis' help. He told her to put the baby to her own breast and God would give her plenty of milk. She did so and the child thrived. The wife of a judge in Tivoli bore him six daughters. This upset her as she longed for a son. Hating the thought of producing any more girls, she made a complaint to God. She told her husband she would abstain from intercourse, and indignantly did so for a year. After having been ordered to do penance and be reconciled to her husband, she was persuaded by her confessor to ask St Francis for a boy, to whom the name Francis would be given. She duly conceived and gave birth to twin sons, christened Francis and Blaise, though she had only asked for one.[228]

Once the saint reprieved an ox. Martin's ox broke a leg a long way from home. As he could not move it, he left St Francis to look after it and see that it was not eaten by wolves; when he returned in the morning the saint had not only protected it but cured it. This story appealed not only to Celano, but also to Bonaventure.[229]

---

[224] Bonav., Miracula, ix. 1.
[225] Robertson and Sheppard 1875–85, I–II; Caviness 1981; Foreville and Keir 1987, pp. 92–117, 264–335.
[226] 3 Cel. 100–5, 107, 128–9; cf. Bonav., Miracula, ix. 1–4.
[227] Krusch and Levison 1951, pp. 184–5; C. Brooke 1986, ch. III, esp. pp. 86–7.
[228] 3 Cel. 182, 99; Bonav., Miracula, x. 4, vi. 3.
[229] 3 Cel. 183; Bonav., Miracula, x. 3.

The miracles of Thomas Becket were mostly performed on British suppliants, though there was a fair sprinkling of French and an occasional German pilgrim;[230] Gilbert's were more local: his Order never spread beyond Lincolnshire, the north-east and the midlands of England, and almost all who sought his aid came from those regions. Francis' miracles were performed in many parts of Italy – Tuscany, Umbria, the Marches, Lazio, Rome and Apulia; several were in Sicily. Umbria is well represented, naturally enough, though surprisingly not Assisi itself. North Italy is much less well represented, and only one of Celano's occurred north of the Alps, a miracle in Germany recorded by Gregory IX, and repeated in Bonaventure.[231] *3 Celano* 100 takes us to Le Mans; Bonaventure referred to a small group round Poitiers (ix. 1); his iii. 11 takes us to Catalonia. Celano included one from Spain and two from Greece (*3 Cel*. 11, 48, 118); *3 Celano* 95 (Bonav., *Miracula*, vi. 1) introduces a countess from *Sclavonia*.[232] But there is no suggestion that the cult of Francis' miracles spread in the way his Order had – to England, Ireland, Germany, Poland and central Europe: these regions are not represented either in Celano or in Bonaventure.

Comparison with Becket and Gilbert is revealing in a number of other ways. Their processes are the supreme evidence for the changing pattern of attitudes towards the miracles necessary to establish a case for canonisation. Alexander III speedily accepted the case for Becket: the manner of his death and some report of the early miracles sufficed to win St Thomas the crown in a little over two years. Before attending to the case for Gilbert, Innocent III had tried out the process when canonising Homobonus of Cremona in 1199 and the Empress Kunigunde, wife of the Emperor Henry II, in 1200. When an impressive delegation from England came in 1201 to request Gilbert's canonisation, the pope insisted that it return to England and set in motion a more exacting inquiry. This was accomplished later in the year and at the turn of 1201 and 1202 a new delegation, including sworn witnesses and carrying sworn testimony authenticated with seals, waited on the pope – and Innocent, after a satisfactory dream, accepted the case.[233] In comparison, after a developing tradition of such strictness, the canonisation process for Francis seems almost casual – for the pope himself was the chief witness.[234]

Even in Celano the miracles of Francis are not so numerous or impressive as one might expect from so prestigious a saint. William and Benedict, the Canterbury monks who recorded Becket's miracles, had each scored well over two hundred within the first four years after the martyrdom.[235] Gilbert was a much less exciting figure; yet his biographer records some seventy-six: twenty in his lifetime, thirty after his death in the formal catalogue submitted to Pope Innocent III; twenty-six less formal (but several of them provided with quite an impressive list of witnesses) – all these reported within twelve or thirteen years of his death.

---

[230] See esp. Abbott 1898, I, 311–14.
[231] *3 Cel*. 22, 157 relate to Parma; no. 48 and Bonav., *Miracula*, ii. 8 to Germany.
[232] *3 Cel*. 102 may be located in Spain. *Sclavonia* refers to some part of the Balkans, presumably Croatia or Bosnia, in *1 Cel*. 55 and parallel passages (see AF x, Index).
[233] Foreville and Keir 1987, pp. 168–79; cf. ibid. pp. xciii–xcvii for the sequence of canonisations from Becket to Gilbert.
[234] See pp. 36–9.
[235] Robertson and Sheppard 1875–85, I–II. Cf. the very full analysis in Abbott 1898. William and Benedict commonly recount the same miracles, but not invariably – so that the total is well below 400.

There is one very specific link between Gilbert's miracles and Francis'. In Gilbert's, it is common for the patient seeking for a cure to offer a wax candle of large dimensions, sometimes as tall as the petitioner, to the saint. In *3 Celano* 65 a large candle is offered in a church of St Francis in Calabria. In *1 Celano* 146 and also *3 Celano* 146 the story is told of a man with a son who was a leper; he arranged for the boy to offer a candle of exactly his own height every year to St Francis – and at the moment when the boy was measured for the purpose, the leprosy disappeared. Bonaventure (viii. 5) repeats the story, emphasising Francis' special love for lepers; but he omits the candle.

A curious feature of Benedict's account of Becket's miracles is a section on the saint's little jokes or tricks, *ludi*. He has two cases in which kindly persons found that the small change they gave from their pockets in alms was multiplied, so that they had more to give.[236] Francis was not credited with such tricks.

A significant contrast between these earlier collections and Francis', is that a large number of Becket's, and the large majority of Gilbert's, were authenticated by named witnesses. In *3 Celano* 54 a boy of eight is saved from being crushed to death by being vowed to the saint; and he duly became a friar and told his story to Celano, who thus refers to himself as a witness; but most of the miracles have no other authentication than the story and the names of the participants.

In the light of this, it would not be surprising if Bonaventure was a good deal concerned about the authenticity of what he recorded – and this doubt may well account for many of his omissions. He was indeed very discreet. Celano had told the story of a mad woman of Narni to whom Francis appeared in a vision, instructing her to make the sign of the cross – and when she said she could not, he made it himself upon her, and she was cured. 'But because deceiving falsehood will often trap this kind of people, passing briefly by them, let us go on to greater matters.' This is *1 Celano* 138, one of the very few stories in the miracles in *1 Celano* repeated by Bonaventure, who concludes, however, that to give further details of such troubles and cures 'would take a long time' (Bonav., *Miracula*, viii. 4). The mild scepticism of Celano has been sanitised.

Yet Bonaventure had no doubts regarding Celano's tales of rescue from shipwreck. A ship in difficulties off Barletta in Apulia put out anchors, but the ropes broke. When the storm ceased they struggled all day to retrieve their anchors, whose dangling ropes reached the surface. They called on all the saints in turn, but failed to recover one. A crew member called Perfectus – though he was far fom perfect – mockingly suggested: 'Let us call on this Francis, who is a new saint, that with his hood he dive into the sea and recover the lost anchors. We will give an ounce of gold to his church, newly built in Ortona, if we reckon he has helped us!' The others rebuked him and invoked St Francis in all earnest. The anchors promptly floated to the surface as if the property of iron had turned into light wood. Sailors have a reputation for telling tall stories. One cannot help feeling that Bonaventure, like Celano before him, was prepared to swallow stories involving water. Apparently brother James of Rieti and a number of other friars crossed a river in a small boat. The others got out, but as he made to follow them the boat capsized and he sank. With the help of St Francis he walked along the bottom as

[236] Robertson and Sheppard 1875–85, ii, 209; Abbott 1898, i, 315.

if it were dry land, took the sunken boat and came with it to the bank. His clothes were not wet; no drop of water had touched his tunic. Another friar, called Bonaventure, and two other men, were crossing a lake when their boat sprang a leak, and went down with them. From the depths of the lake they appealed to St Francis; the boat resurfaced full of water, and they were brought safely to land. Bonaventure's conclusion to the chapter could hardly be more positive. 'I do not for a moment believe it to be possible to describe in detail how greatly this blessed father has shone and shines in mighty prodigies of miracles on the sea, or how often he has brought help there to those in despair. No wonder if he who now reigns in heaven has been granted authority over the waves, who even in this mortal life was wonderfully served by "every kind of creature fashioned again as from its beginning" [Wisdom 19. 6].'[237]

One of the most remarkable contrasts between *3 Celano* and Bonaventure's *Miracula* is in their transmission. Of the *Legenda Maior* and its attendant *Miracles*, 400 copies or so are known, and these are survivors of an army which no one could number. Of *3 Celano*, apart from some fragments, only one manuscript survives, and even that lacks its Introductory Letter.[238] In the similar case of *2 Celano*, of which only two more or less complete manuscripts survive (one of them the unique manuscript of *3 Celano*), it has been suggested that it was from the first unpopular with the less rigorous elements in the Order.[239] But no such explanation can be offered for the paucity of manuscripts of *3 Celano*, and it is much more probable in both cases that the decree for the destruction of manuscripts was effective, and that only a handful escaped the ban. In any case it may never have been widely disseminated, as it was completed only a decade before it was superseded by Bonaventure. None the less, *3 Celano* survived through Bonaventure in carefully edited form. Bonaventure often abbreviated, but essentially Celano's subject matter, his treatment, even his wording are preserved. Bonaventure ends his chapter on the raising of the dead with an example from Germany, which was made known by Gregory IX in letters to all the friars gathered in Chapter at the time of St Francis' translation: he concludes with the words, 'I have not written down the details of this miracle, because I have no knowledge of them, believing that the testimony of the pope surpasses the corroboration of any other testimony.' The wording in Bonaventure and Celano is identical. Here as elsewhere in his writings, if Bonaventure agrees with the statement of another writer he is content to copy and does not waste his time searching for another way to put it.[240]

Miracle collections could be read by the educated, and were consulted by preachers for sermon material, and in that way passed on to a much wider audience. Time could be devoted by a friar to an individual unable to read, as Celano records. A sick woman who went into a friar's church to pray noticed a little book of the life and miracles of St Francis, and enquired what was in it. When instructed, she bathed the book with tears and laid it on her infected place, saying: 'Just as the things written of you in these

---

[237] *3 Cel.* 81, 83, 86; Bonav., *Miracula*, iv. 1, 3–5.
[238] See p. 269 and note 210. The MS is Rome, Archivum Fratrum Minorum Capuccinorum, Arm. 1.1.1, of c.1300 (Bihl in *AF* X, pp. xxx, xl). For the fragments, see ibid. pp. xl–xli. Four hundred is the approximate figure of MSS of Bonaventure's *Legenda Maior*, given by Bihl in *AF* x, p. lxxix n. 2.
[239] Moorman 1940, p. 127; see p. 107.   [240] *3 Cel.* 48; Bonav., *Miracula*, ii. 8; see p. 248.

pages, St Francis, are true, so may I now be freed of this affliction by your holy merits' (*3 Cel.* 193). When a wonder occurred, news could spread by word of mouth. Crowds of men and women flocked to see the old woman enabled to breast feed her orphaned grandson. In cases of emergency, crowds could gather quickly and play their part. As well as watching fascinated as their neighbour's fingers were one by one released, the people of Le Simon prayed hard. The faith of such crowds could even affect non-Christians. A boy playing with other children on the bank of the Volturno fell in and was sucked under the mud at the bottom. A swimmer dived down and dragged him out, but he was already dead. The children and the crowds who gathered were all crying and shouting: 'St Francis, give the boy back to his father!' Some Jews who were at the scene demonstrated their solidarity by joining in the cry: 'St Francis, give the boy back to his father!' Devotion to St Francis and belief in his power were fostered, then, in a whole variety of ways. A noblewoman who suffered from a flow of blood for twenty-three years was moved to pray to him by hearing a young man singing about his miracles in the Romance vernacular.[241]

A range of images of St Francis emerges from the miracle stories. To the seaman Perfectus he was a newcomer, a novice, unlikely to succeed where long-established and experienced saints had failed: he needed to prove himself. For the Frenchman who knew nothing at all about the details of Francis' life, and was not prepared simply to accept his parish priest's word that he merited a solemn festival, when his conscience pricked him, reminding him that it was a holy day, it was probably his subconscious fear of the power of the saints in general that made his hands seize up. People's attitudes towards the saints could be complex. They could fear their power certainly, and yet expect them to use their power in a good cause. The tone then could be peremptory, especially where a crowd was involved – as when the children and grown-ups, including Jews, gathered on the river bank, joined in clamouring: 'St Francis, give the boy back to his father!' It was St Francis who was importuned in this instance because he was the saint to whom the drowned boy's family was particularly devoted. His father and grandfather had been active in the construction of the local church in his honour in their city, Capua. Celano's version of the chant went: 'St Francis, give the boy back to his father and grandfather, your indefatigable servants' (*2 Cel.* 44). They had earned his help and he should hurry up and do something. To friends of the Friars Minor, already familiar with his cult, it was natural to turn to him in an emergency, especially if it occurred when they were with the friars, or working for, or helping them.

St Francis' attribute from early on was the stigmata, and some of the miracles of healing stress the holiness of hands that draw their power from Christ's wounds. St Bonaventure spells it out. 'In fitting manner the blessed father – now dead to the flesh and living with Christ – granted a cure to a man mortally wounded by the wonderful revelation of his presence and the gentle soothing of his sacred hands. For he bore in his own body the stigmata, the marks of Christ [cf. Gal. 6. 17], who in his mercy died

---

[241] Bonav., *Miracula*, x. 4, ii. 5, viii. 6; *3 Cel.* 182, 44, 148.

and wonderfully rose again, and thus cured the human race left half-dead [echo of the Good Samaritan, Luke 10. 30], by the virtue of his own wounds'[242] (Plate 59).

In the modern world mention of St Francis conjures images of preaching to the birds and promoting peace. Celano incorporated many stories of Francis' relations with the natural world and as an animal lover, and Bonaventure only slightly fewer. But we must be careful not to attribute modern attitudes to either. Martin did not entrust his ox to Francis because he considered him an appropriate choice in a context of animal welfare. He hoped Francis would protect it from wolves as he was anxious its hide should not be damaged, and lose its value. He reckoned the beast was a write-off and returned in the morning with the implement necessary for flaying it.[243] As to peace, despite its importance throughout society, it is an issue conspicuous by its absence. In these recorded miracles St Francis resolves no conflicts, effects no reconciliations between family members, though there was clearly scope for this – for example, when the sleeping guard fell from the nobleman's tower and, in the dark, the nobleman drew his sword and rushed at him and his wife thought he was about to kill her brother.[244]

Finally, in view of recent discussions on the varied social origins of the beneficiaries to be found in miracle collections, it can be said that Francis' suppliants came from every walk of life, and his charity was open to both clergy and laity, to men and women of every kind, without respect of persons or age. They include members of noble families and their households; there are knights, priests, sailors, workmen carting stone, children, women in labour, the falsely accused and victims of ambush and attack, lepers, a debtor, a heretic, a recluse.[245] The embrace is wide. Appropriately, there are several poor folk, from the poor woman who dedicated her son to Francis, who cured him from blindness, to the poor man of Parma who grumbled ceaselessly to Francis that his son had a twisted foot, until eventually the saint put it right (3 Cel. 133, 157). Francis was ready to relieve their lesser problems and humble daily needs as well. He alerted a man to the fact that a beast of his, stolen three years ago, was in Spoleto; he mended a snapped ploughshare so that a ploughman should not lose a day's work. He smoothed a domestic crisis. A man of the people bought a beautiful bowl and gave it to his wife. Her maid put into it some clothes to wash with lye, but the lye became so hot in the sun that the bowl cracked and was no use any more. Trembling and in tears she brought it to her mistress. She was no less alarmed, terrified of her husband's anger and most certainly expecting blows. St Francis was invoked, the pieces joined together and the bowl became as good as new.[246] Although friars and friars' churches figure in the stories quite often, very few – surprisingly few – of those who were helped

---

[242] Bonav., *Miracula*, ii. 5; see pp. 272–3. Cf. also iii. 3, 8; viii. 7, and x. 6–9. Bonav., *Miracula*, ii. 5 conflates details from 3 Cel. 11–13, concerning a miracle in Castile, with a story of a miracle at Lerida in Catalonia from another source.

[243] 3 Cel. 183; Bonav., *Miracula*, x. 3. See p. 273.

[244] 3 Cel. 49; Bonav., *Miracula*, iii. 1. Cf. p. 272 and note 223.

[245] E.g. 3 Cel. 81, 85 = Bonav., *Miracula*, iv. 1, 5 (sailors); 3 Cel. 57–8 = Bonav., *Miracula*, iii. 6–7 (workmen carting stone); 3 Cel. 44, 47, 51 = Bonav., *Miracula*, ii. 5, 7, iii. 3 (children); 3 Cel. 88, 91, 94 = Bonav., *Miracula*, v. 1, 3, 5 (the falsely accused); 3 Cel. 89 = Bonav., *Miracula*, v. 2 (debtor); 3 Cel. 93 = Bonav., *Miracula*, v. 4 (heretic).

[246] 3 Cel. 185, briefly summarised in Bonav., *Miracula*, x. 3.

or cured were themselves friars. Brother James of Iseo's hernia was healed, and two other brothers likewise, and a brother Robert's sight was restored.[247] One group of recorded interventions eased the difficulties friars faced on the journeys their peripatetic lifestyle required them to undertake. Crossing water – even rivers and lakes – could be hazardous.[248] Another group related to boys or young men who experienced cures and joined the Order. We have encountered the little boy of eight who became a friar when he was fourteen and told his story to Celano; as did the nobleman's son, blind from birth, renamed Illuminatus, when he came of age; and the poor woman's son may have become a friar.[249] Bonaventure's own life had been saved by Francis. 'As a boy I was rescued from the fangs of death, as I keep fresh in my memory, by his intercession and merits.'[250]

[247] 3 Cel. 83, 86 (2), 109; cf. Bonav., Miracula, iv. 3–4, viii. 2.
[248] 3 Cel. 83–4, 86; cf. Bonav., Miracula, iv. 3–4.
[249] 3 Cel. 54 = Bonav., Miracula, iii. 5; 3 Cel. 123 = Bonav., Miracula, vii. 6.
[250] Bonav., Prologue, 3.

CHAPTER NINE

THE OFFICIAL VISUAL IMAGE:
THE DECORATION OF THE BASILICA

INTRODUCTION

The way the Basilica came to be decorated provides a stark example of a sea change that transformed the friars' attitude towards embellishment. They came to appreciate that colour and pictures could play a positive role in attracting congregations, providing subject matter for sermons and stimulating devotion. Adherence to poverty was subtly undermined by desire for conversions.

Brother Elias had commissioned a great crucifix painted by Giunta Pisano in 1236, now unfortunately lost. The Assisi altar panel, painted roughly twenty years later, has survived. This is a gorgeous piece of craftsmanship, very expensive to produce and flaunting its cost, with its brilliant colours and solid gold ground. It has been assigned on stylistic grounds to the 1250s, and it has been suggested that it was made for the official formal dedication of the altars by Innocent IV in 1253.[1] It is highly plausible that its existence was linked to that ceremony. But was it painted in advance, in honour of the occasion? Or was it painted subsequently in response to the pope's clearly expressed displeasure at finding the church so unadorned? In other words, who was responsible for its creation? We can only speculate, but musing on the question is worthwhile because the Assisi altar panel seems to have set in motion an ongoing flow of commissions: it became as it were the core of a snowball. If it was painted to be displayed at the ceremony, John of Parma, Minister General at the time, must at least have authorised its production. But such an action would have been uncharacteristic of him. When he visited England in 1248, the year after he became Minister General, he confirmed provincial constitutions on frugality and poverty in buildings, and he may himself have passed statutes against extravagance in the dimensions and decoration of buildings.[2] He had the reputation for being true to St Francis in spirit. Activities flagrantly at odds with public statements and stances can occur, but I confess to being

---

[1] See Cook 1999, pp. 62–3. If, as seems probable, it is later than the Pisa panel, it is unlikely that it was painted before the ceremony (see pp. 173–6 and note 53).
[2] Eccleston, p. 98; Brooke 1959, p. 261.

wary of accepting the hypothesis that John of Parma was responsible for this beautiful object. In his bull *Decet et expedit* of 10 June 1253 Innocent IV bluntly announced that the fabric and appearance of the Basilica should be improved, any statutes of the Order or prohibitions of the Minister General or any of its officers or members notwithstanding; and he entrusted the task of implementing his directive to the Cardinal Protector.[3] Was not the Assisi altar panel the first-fruits of this initiative? And is it not, then, most likely that the man responsible for inaugurating the whole lengthy programme which transformed the previously plain surfaces of the Lower and Upper Churches was Pope Innocent IV, acting through the Cardinal Protector, Rainaldo de Segni, nephew of Gregory IX, another key figure? Perhaps, indeed, it is he who deserves the chief credit, as it was he who took charge of the project. For Innocent IV in any case had little remaining time or opportunity to interest himself personally in the Basilica. He died in December 1254, having quarrelled with the friars in his final months. Rainaldo succeeded him, as Pope Alexander IV. He was so devoted to the Friars Minor that he was unwilling to relinquish the office of Cardinal Protector on his elevation, but continued to exercise it until his death in 1261.[4] Close partnership between a succession of popes and Cardinal Protectors was, in the event, to continue, the links occasionally being even further strengthened. Another Cardinal Protector, Gian Gaetano Orsini, became Pope Nicholas III, and a Minister General, Jerome of Ascoli, became Pope Nicholas IV; and papal and curial patronage could go a long way towards explaining how the project was financed. Though we cannot be sure because we have no accounts.

THE DECORATION OF THE LOWER CHURCH

The earliest surviving painted decoration in the Basilica of any substance is the fresco cycle in the nave of the Lower Church.[5] It is not intact as in the early fourteenth century the walls were pierced to enable the creation of a series of side chapels. There are two sequences of scenes, facing each other in pairs across the nave, beginning at the entrance end and culminating nearest to the high altar. On the right-hand side approaching the altar are five scenes taken from the Passion and Resurrection of Our Lord; on the left-hand side, five scenes covering the life and death of St Francis.

When were they painted? We have a few clues which help to determine the date before which they were done.

The first is the way the seraph is portrayed in the scene of Francis receiving the stigmata (Plate 24). The figure, youthful and golden haired, floats in the sky near the mountainside; two wings fully cover the body, two frame the outstretched arms, two rise above the head, which is inclined, looking kindly down, originally at Francis, a tiny portion of whose habit is all that survives of him. The hands and feet show the marks of nails but they are not fixed to the wood of a cross. The gesso patterned halo includes no cross. This iconography is close to that of the earliest known representation in the

---

[3] See pp. 66–7.   [4] Philip of Perugia in Salimbene, H, p. 681.
[5] Cook 1999, pp. 33–6, no. 11. Fragments of fresco at the east end include part of St Francis' head; he may have been surrounded by small scenes from his life, and a few other fragments survive in the narthex. Cook 1999, p. 33, no. 10; *Assisi* 1999, pp. 33–4.

Plate 24 Assisi, Basilica of St Francis, Lower Church nave, the Seraph of the Stigmata
(© www.Assisi.de. Photo Stefan Diller).

Pescia altar panel of 1235 and to that in the Bardi panel.[6] All three are based on Celano's description of how Francis saw in a vision a man standing above him, like a seraph with six wings, two raised above his head, two extended for flight and two wrapped round his body.[7] All three follow a pictorial tradition which leaves out the cross, though Celano clearly stated that his hands were extended and his feet joined together and fixed to a cross. Celano went on to record Francis' great joy at seeing himself so graciously regarded by the seraph. St Bonaventure subtly amended 'seraph' to 'Christ in the guise of a seraph'.[8] The *Legenda Maior* led to an amended iconography. In the Stigmatisation scene in the Upper Church cycle the seraph has a nimbus marked with a cross, and the two covering wings start below the chest so as to expose the side wound[9] (Plate 64). It has been argued, therefore, that the frescoes were painted before Celano's *Lives* were suppressed in 1266. This argument alone is not conclusive because anachronisms are possible.[10]

Captions originally elucidated each scene, but are mostly illegible now, and interpretation is not helped by the fact that we are partly dependent on transcripts made by seventeenth-century antiquaries which are not entirely accurate. With this caveat, the captions accompanying the first two episodes of Francis' life are both closer to 2 *Celano* than they are to Bonaventure.[11]

A further clue is provided in the scene of Innocent III's dream (Plate 25). This is a new scene, represented here in the Lower Church for the first time. The pope reclines, still wearing his mitre, on a gorgeously draped feather bed, and is dreaming. The story first occurs in 2 *Celano* 17 as part of the additional information relating to the saint's visit to Rome to ask for papal approval of his nascent Order. The balance was finally turned in Francis' favour by the pope's recollecting a dream. He had seen in his sleep the Lateran basilica in imminent danger of collapse, when an unknown religious, a man 'small and despised' (Isaiah 16. 14, 53. 3), supported it, by putting his own back under it, lest it fall. In the fresco Francis is supporting a heavy burden with his right shoulder, his left knee bending under the strain: the Lateran unfortunately is missing. The story of Innocent III's dream was clearly circulating in the early 1240s. St Francis had died in 1226, St Dominic in 1221. Friars in both Orders, some twenty years on, acted on an awareness that first-hand reminiscences of their founders would not remain recoverable indefinitely, and so it happened that in 1244 the General Chapters of both Orders sent out a request for information. The resultant material was written up, Celano composing his *Vita Secunda S. Francisci*, and Constantine of Orvieto his *Legenda S. Dominici*, in the same years 1246–7. Both authors appropriated the story for their own sainted founder.[12] In visual terms the Franciscans, who naturally thought the story was properly theirs, seem to have got in first, with this fresco. The painter

---

[6] See pp. 169–71 and 182, and Plates 15, 19.   [7] 1 Cel. 94.   [8] Bonav., XIII, 3.   [9] See pp. 401–4.

[10] E.g. Cannon 1982, p. 66; Goffen 1988, p. 101 n. 9; Cook 1999, p. 35.

[11] Frugoni 1993, pp. 286–7 and p. 313 n. 117. First scene: 2 Cel. 12 closer than Bonav., II, 4; second scene: there is nothing to choose between 2 Cel. 17 and Bonav., IV, 10, unless REC[TUS . . .] (Frugoni 1993, p. 287), which makes no sense, should be amended to REL[IGIOSUS], as in Celano – Bonaventure has *pauperculus*.

[12] 2 Cel. 17; Constantine of Orvieto, *Legenda S. Dominici*, c. 21, in Walz 1935, pp. 301–2; for the date, ibid. pp. 281–3.

Plate 25 Lower Church nave, Pope Innocent III's dream (© www.Assisi.de. Photo Stefan Diller).

experimented with the problem of how to tackle the pose in an atlas figure supporting a decorative frieze in the spandrel of one of the Lower Church vaults.[13] The Dominicans preferred sculpture. One of the scenes in the Arca di San Domenico in San Domenico at Bologna illustrates their version. St Dominic is holding up the corner of the Lateran with his right hand and right shoulder; his left shoulder is hunched and his head pokes forward, as he takes the weight on his left leg, his left arm held close against his body, his hand clutching his knee. The pose resembles that of St Francis in the fresco. The pope also holds up his hand in surprise, as in the fresco. Joanna Cannon has suggested that, as the Dominicans had as yet no tradition of depicting narrative scenes from Dominic's life, they may well have looked to the Basilica for inspiration, especially as they were using the same story. Work on the Arca was already in progress in 1265 when the General Chapter called for funds to complete the tomb, and St Dominic's body was translated to the Arca in 1267. Her argument that this would support a date of 1260–5 for the Lower Church cycle is a convincing one. She comments further that the composition was better managed at Bologna. The Arca was created by Nicola Pisano and his workshop, which consisted of his two pupils, Arnolfo di Cambio and Lapo, and his own son Giovanni. During the same period he was also engaged in working on another important commission, for on 29 September 1265 Nicola signed a contract to provide a new marble pulpit for Siena cathedral. This was completed by 1268.[14] It is indeed possible that while working at Siena these sculptors may have paid a visit to Assisi to view the new frescoes. The distance is not great, and they may have been further motivated to go by a shared cultural bond. Nicola Pisano's presence in Tuscany is first recorded in 1258, but he must have been an established master by then to have been awarded the commission for the marble pulpit in the Baptistery at Pisa, which is signed and dated 1260.[15] Such magnificent embellishments were a symptom both of a revival of prosperity and of an extraordinary civic pride, characteristic of Italian cities. Pisa's status as a great centre of maritime power sprang from a pirate raid on Palermo in 1063; a number of Muslim ships were destroyed and much booty taken. As a thank offering the citizens set aside a whole corner of their city, just inside the walls, for church building. Pisa's Duomo, separate Baptistery and campanile, their outside walls faced with costly green, red and white marble, begun in the mid-eleventh century, were not completed till the thirteenth (Plate 26). Pisa controlled the marble quarries of Carrara and could afford to nurture sculptors; she also boasted a famous guild of metal-workers. As a great trading centre she was also a natural meeting place for a rich variety of cultural influences. By sea she was in regular contact with Byzantium; by road with northern Europe, whence penetrated Romanesque and later Gothic influences. To these must be added her local heritage. Italians lived and still live surrounded by visible and tangible signs of their past history. This is pre-eminently true of Rome, but it is true of a great number of Italian towns and cities which have remained in continuous occupation of their present sites. Ancient sarcophagi and statuary were reused

[13] Cannon 1982, pp. 66–9.
[14] Cannon 1998, pp. 30–4, 42–5 nn. 26–62 and figs. 20–6; Von Matt and Vicaire 1957, pl. 102; Ayrton 1969, pp. 37, 42.
[15] Ayrton 1969, p. 26.

Plate 26 Pisa: duomo and campanile (Photo C. N. L. Brooke).

and available in Pisa as elsewhere. Nicola Pisano could study classical Roman relief sculpture as well as contemporary French and Byzantine models.[16] Pisan workshops had a reputation and were in demand. An artist, and craftsmen, from Pisa had worked at the Basilica already in the time of brother Elias, who had employed Giunta Pisano, and the bellfounder Bartholomew of Pisa and his son.[17] And the link continued. The painter of the nave frescoes in the Lower Church received his artistic training either in Pisa or in one of its neighbouring towns, Pistoia or Lucca.[18]

Who commissioned these frescoes? And, a related and most important question, who determined their content?

One obvious possibility is the Minister General himself, St Bonaventure. St Bonaventure was lector at the Franciscan convent at Paris when John of Parma nominated him as his successor as Minister General in February 1257; he did not immediately return to Italy, but managed to spend a considerable part of the next years in Paris, continuing with his studies and his writing. In 1259 he kept a retreat at La Verna, where he wrote one of his best-known works of mystical theology, the *Itinerarium mentis in Deum*. Between his nomination in 1257 and the General Chapter of Narbonne, held at Whitsun 1260, over which he presided, he drafted a new edition of the Order's constitutions. It is unlikely that he devoted any attention to such matters as the decoration of the Basilica before the summer of 1260. However, the General Chapter, as well as approving the Constitutions

[16] Ayrton 1969, pp. 30–4 and figs. h–o.   [17] See pp. 60, 62.
[18] Martin 1996, pp. 177–91, esp. pp. 185–9.

of Narbonne, commissioned him to write a new Life of St Francis, and St Bonaventure spent time in the next three years in and near Assisi. He could have organised a decorative programme in this period 1260–3. It has been argued that he would not have done so because the Constitutions of Narbonne, for which he was responsible, contained statutes forbidding such decoration, but the situation was more complex. The Order's constitutions – for Bonaventure simply edited existing constitutions, adding little that was new – had been over-ridden by Innocent IV's bull.[19]

Another main contender is the pope, who retained his role as Cardinal Protector, Alexander IV. There is one detail in particular that seems to link the depiction of St Francis with him. In the scene of St Francis' death the side wound is shown for the first recorded time in fresco (Plate 30). It is possible that the side wound was similarly shown in the stigmatisation scene, but unfortunately almost the whole of the figure of Francis is missing from the scene. Alexander IV was extremely active during his pontificate in defending the existence and the validity of the side wound.[20] It can also be said that, while Cardinal Protector, he had been commissioned by Innocent IV to exert himself to beautify the church. What did he do if he did not get this done, or at least started? This is a theoretical argument, but not necessarily to be despised on that account. Against it, however, it must be said that from the time of his election as pope, in Naples, in December 1254, we have no record of his ever afterwards being north of Viterbo – except perhaps for one fleeting visit to Genoa in late September 1260 – until May 1261, the month in which he died, in Viterbo; so it seems unlikely that he was able to involve himself personally in the iconography.[21] Alexander IV's main contribution to the decoration of the Basilica was the provision of stained glass windows in the apse of the Upper Church, itself an expensive and lengthy process.[22]

After his death there was probably a short hiatus as far as the Order was concerned. His successor, Urban IV, 1261–4, was a Frenchman, as was his successor, Clement IV, from early 1265 to 1268, the only two popes in office within the probable deadline of pre-1266 for the execution of the Lower Church frescoes. Both were mainly preoccupied with the bitter struggle in which the papacy engaged with Frederick II's heirs.[23] The Order had no Cardinal Protector for about two years. But at the General Chapter at Pisa in 1263 St Bonaventure and the Provincial Ministers decided to ask Urban IV to appoint John Gaetano Orsini, then cardinal deacon of San Nicola in Carcere Tulliano, the future Pope Nicholas III.[24]

He is a third possibility. He was a member of a powerful and wealthy Roman family. The achievement with which he was mainly associated as pope was his enrichment of his family: his nepotism was notorious. 'He edified Zion in his blood-relations', Salimbene commented; and Dante consigned him to hell for nepotism and simony. But he spent

[19] Brooke 1959, pp. 274–5; Marchini 1973, pp. 23–4, 88; see pp. 66–7, 244–5.
[20] Cook 1999, p. 35; Frugoni 1993, pp. 209, 280–4. See p. 299.
[21] For the papal itinerary, see Mas Latrie 1889, col. 1118; Potthast, II, pp. 1286–1472.
[22] See pp. 312–13.
[23] See summary in Kelly 1986, pp. 194–7, and fuller account in Waley 1961, pp. 165–81. Gregorovius 1906, v, 2, 343–451, is still useful.
[24] Philip of Perugia in Salimbene, H, p. 681; cf. Gratien 1928, p. 533 and n. 7.

large sums of money too on art patronage.[25] And he had the highest regard for, and devotion to, the Friars Minor. Elected pope in November 1277, he delayed to appoint a Cardinal Protector. In 1279, after the General Chapter at Assisi had replaced Jerome of Ascoli with his friend and companion brother Bonagrazia as Minister General, Bonagrazia and the Provincial Ministers went to Soriano, near Viterbo, which the pope had refurbished as his summer residence, to ask him for Jerome, whom Nicholas had made a cardinal in March 1278. Instead, Nicholas III gave them one of his nephews, Matteo Rosso Orsini, cardinal deacon of Santa Maria in Porticu. The speech he made when introducing him to them was recorded by brother Philip of Perugia, who was there. It affords us a remarkable and precious insight into the pope's feelings: '"Our words are addressed to you [Matteo]. If we would count up the benefits which have come to you through us, they would be found to be great and useful and numerous. But in nothing at all similar have we given you the earnest of life eternal so much as in this, which we now grant you. For we give you that which leads you to paradise, namely the prayers and merits of the holy friars of this Order. We give you the best gift that we have. We give you the desire of our heart, the pupil of our eyes." Then with these words such sweetness of love poured forth from the heart of the pope, such a flood of tears poured from his eyes – I who tell the tale was a witness of it – that . . . he became speechless and could not keep his voice from wailing. [He gave his own ring to the cardinal, kissing his hand] "We commit to you the Order of Friars Minor . . . The Order does not need your governance [referring to the passage in the Rule on the Cardinal Protector], because it abounds in men of such great wisdom and prudence, that it is fully equal to govern itself. [Similarly correction is not your business.] In one respect, however, it has need of your patronage. They are weak and poor and they have many [enemies] who frequently disturb their peace unduly . . . and so they need the strong arm of a protector. This is the point in which your care for them can help most powerfully."'[26]

He was certainly a generous patron when he was pope. His arms were emblazoned by Cimabue in the crossing of the Upper Church.[27]

Gian Gaetano Orsini was probably with the Curia in Perugia – where Urban IV died – from 2 October 1264 to 19 April 1266.[28] He would then have had ample opportunities to be in Assisi during a crucial period, so he is also a strong candidate.

It looks as though the frescoes were done in Bonaventure's generalate. The juxtaposition of St Francis' life and Christ's Passion is certainly a Bonaventuran theme;[29] yet 2 Celano was preferred for the captions. Surely at the Order's headquarters St Bonaventure's Legenda Maior would have been used if it was ready? So it looks as if they were begun before 1263. But the cardinal who is most likely to have taken a hand was only appointed Cardinal Protector in 1263. The evidence is not tidy, and we can only speculate. St Bonaventure and his colleagues asked for Gian Gaetano Orsini, so they probably knew him quite well already. For an ambitious decorative scheme of this kind two things

---

[25] Salimbene, H, p. 498; S, II, 728; Dante, Inferno, canto xix, 31 ff.
[26] Philip of Perugia in Salimbene, H, pp. 682–3; cf. Salimbene, H, p. 498; S, II, 728; Gratien 1928, pp. 533–5.
[27] See pp. 346–8.   [28] Potthast, II, pp. 1540–84, 1649.   [29] See pp. 231–41.

were needed: a religious community which knew the message it wanted to put across and was well equipped to devise the programme; and a patron to provide the money. Martin suggests an appeal by Innocent IV provided the money.[30] But donations from the public were unlikely to have been enough. Orsini had wealth, and enthusiasm for art. It could be that he was already a donor before 1263. The office of Cardinal Protector, which carried with it responsibility for the decoration of the Basilica, could then be seen not just as appropriate for such a man, but as his reward for services rendered, in much the same way as wealthy supporters can be given political honours today. It was an office worth having. The first two holders had ascended the papal throne, and in due course its third holder was to follow suit. We know the high value he set on it – his speech when handing it on to his nephew has already been quoted.[31]

The theme of St Francis' conformity to Christ in pictorial language is there in embryo in the scene of his stigmatisation in the earliest known altar panel, dated 1235.[32] The idea of developing this in juxtaposed scenes derives from the parallel cycles depicting foreshadowings in the Old Testament of themes and happenings in the New Testament.[33] But the whole conception of this cycle in the Lower Church is none the less innovative and highly original.

Let us begin with the first pair of facing scenes. The series on Francis' life begins with his repudiation of his father and his father's values. He is in the act of raising his hands and his eyes to heaven. It is clearly the moment when he announces: 'Henceforth I may freely say: "Our Father who is in heaven", not father Peter Bernardone.'[34] He and the bishop stand centrally. He is already naked and the bishop is holding part of his cloak around him to cover his private parts. Peter Bernardone is standing to their left – the viewer's right. Unfortunately only a vertical segment of his figure survives, but presumably he is clutching Francis' discarded clothes.

The scene opposite to it, the first of the scenes of the Passion in this cycle, is of quite exceptional interest and importance (Plate 27). Again, it is defective, and it is the most significant area that is either missing or surviving, but hard to make out. Christ is standing to the right of the cross – on the viewer's left. Only his arms remain. He is in the act of handing his garments to the foremost of a group of Jewish priests standing to the left of the cross, that is, on the sinister side.

In the Bardi altar panel, painted at around the same time as this fresco cycle, there are scenes illustrating St Francis' conformity to Christ.[35] Below the central figure of the saint is the stigmatisation scene, with its obvious comparison. Immediately to the right of this, and immediately before the scene of Francis' death, is a scene depicting Francis washing the feet of lepers. Its placing so late in the story – at a time when he was needing others to wash him, rather than at a much earlier stage in his spiritual journey, where it would have fitted more naturally – has surely been chosen to prompt the viewer to associate Francis' washing of the lepers' feet with Christ's washing of

[30] Martin 1993, p. 120.
[31] Salimbene, H, p. 498; S, II, 728; above, p. 288.   [32] See pp. 169–71, and Plate 15.
[33] There was an early and outstanding example in the nave frescoes in the Basilica of San Paolo fuori le mura in Rome, now known only from seventeenth-century watercolour copies (Kessler and Zacharias 2000, pp. 167–72 and pls. 160–73).
[34] 2 Cel. 12; cf. Frugoni 1993, p. 286.   [35] See pp. 186–9, and Plates 17, 19.

Plate 27 Lower Church nave, Christ stripping himself before the crucifixion (© www.Assisi.de. Photo Stefan Diller).

the disciples' feet shortly before His death.[36] Immediately below the stigmatisation is a scene purporting to illustrate Francis' self-imposed penance for eating meat and broth while he was ill, but the details of the written accounts of this incident have been deliberately altered in the pictorial account so as to approximate the image of Francis' penance to pictures of the Flagellation of Christ.[37]

In the first Lower Church Passion scene, to my astonishment, the opposite occurs. There was no standard format for Passion cycles. They might begin, for example, with the Raising of Lazarus, the Entry into Jerusalem, the Last Supper, the Betrayal, or one of the Trial scenes.[38] In the Lower Church the Passion begins with Christ stripping off his clothes at the foot of the cross. Christ was stripped three times after his arrest. First, He will have been at least partially stripped for the scourging. After this, the soldiers took him into the hall, 'and they stripped him and put on him a scarlet robe . . . and after that they had mocked him, they took the robe off from him, and put his own raiment on him, and led him away to crucify him'.[39] 'And when they had crucified him, they parted his garments, casting lots upon them, what every man should take.'[40] So He will have been stripped a third time at the site of the crucifixion. But none of the four Gospels gives details, though all four give various details as to the division of His clothes among the soldiers responsible. So the stripping of Christ at the foot of the cross is not directly based upon the Gospel narratives. It is a new scene. It appears here for the first time.[41]

Why the new scene? And why is it portrayed in this way? It is inherently more likely that Christ was stripped by his executioners than that He stripped Himself. Throughout the succession of trials He had remained steadfastly passive; he had patiently borne abuse, mockery, blows. It looks as though this scene was devised specifically to complement the scene of Francis voluntarily stripping himself painted opposite.[42] If so, the story, not simply of Christ's life, but a detail of His Passion, has been deliberately adjusted to bring it into line with an incident in Francis' life! This is truly astonishing. Who can have been responsible for conceiving, or countenancing, such a daring innovation?

Derbes has combed the writings of St Bonaventure for material relevant to the Passion. She quotes from his *Vita mystica* on the disrobing of Christ: 'Our most loving Lord Jesus Christ is stripped of his clothes . . . Alas, the Lord is stripped . . . He is *made a spectacle and a shame to the world.'*[43] There is no suggestion here of self-stripping.

My first reaction to taking in the full significance of the juxtaposition was to dismiss out of hand the supposition that the painter might have been responsible. The programme will have been devised, conceivably by the Cardinal Protector, or by the Minister General, or – which I believe the most likely – by consultation between the two, and the painter will have had it explained to him what was required. However,

[36] Cf. Duffy 1997, pp. 227–9.
[37] See p. 188 and ref., and Plate 19. It has also been interpreted as resembling another Passion scene, the Mocking of Christ: cf. Derbes 1996, pp. 109–10, 132–4.
[38] Cf. Derbes 1996, pp. 1–11.   [39] Matt. 27. 26–31; cf. also Mark 15. 15–20.
[40] Mark 15. 24; cf. also Matt. 27. 35, Luke 23. 33–4 and John 19. 23–4.
[41] Derbes 1996, pp. 138–42. Ibid. p. 139, fig. 83, shows a similar version, of similar date, in San Sebastiano, a convent of Poor Clares near Alatri.
[42] Cf. Cook 1999, p. 35.
[43] Quoted Derbes 1996, p. 150 from De Vinck 1960, 1, 164–5; the italics echo 1 Cor. 4. 9.

291

he may have been left to some extent to his own devices as to the exact rendering of a scene. It is well known that painters' workshops could devise their own distinctive renderings of specific themes and then reproduce them over time as required. If instructed to paint a scene of Christ disrobed at the foot of the cross, the painter will have had no direct model on which to base his design. Meditation on Christ's human life and experience had developed in the twelfth century. St Aelred's meditation on 'Jesus at the age of twelve' was an early and striking example. This mode of contemplation was greatly enhanced by Francis' own example and teachings, was encouraged by the friars and elicited a ready response.[44] It was in harmony with the piety of the time. One of the themes emphasised was the voluntary nature of Christ's sacrifice of His life for our salvation. It may be that the painter is concerned not so much with the exact words of the Gospel as with conveying, in the medium of paint, this message: Christ chose suffering, and shame, and nakedness for our sakes – and was unaware of the fine line he had crossed in confronting the two scenes. This supposition is reinforced by a detail in the scene not yet mentioned: there is a ladder behind the figure of Christ, propped up against the cross. This alludes to a second scene, likewise without foundation in the Gospel narrative, that entered the vocabulary of Passion scenes at about this time – the Ascent of the Cross. A visually arresting and clearly explicit representation of the theme is found in Guido da Siena's panel of c.1275–80, in which Christ nimbly and purposefully mounts the ladder two rungs at a time.[45] Such pictures are intended to convey a spiritual truth, not a factual one. It would be difficult for an executioner to crucify a victim from the top of a ladder. Crucifixion as a form of public execution was practised during the Roman Empire, but was forbidden by the Emperor Constantine after his conversion to Christianity. Thirteenth-century men and women may not have been familiar with the details of this particular brutal punishment. The upright post was fixed firmly in the ground, the condemned had his hands nailed or his wrists bound to the crossbeam while this lay on the ground. It was then hauled up with ropes until the sufferer's feet were off the ground, when it was fixed in place and the feet nailed or tied.[46] The source for the painted ladder may have been the use of a ladder leaning against the cross in the staging of Passion plays.[47]

The next pairs in the cycle do not succeed in maintaining the remarkable standard of correspondence achieved by the first pair. The facing scenes support the general idea of St Francis' conformity to Christ, and also the concept that the whole of St Francis' life is focused on looking at Christ's Passion. But relating scenes from his life and death to a Passion cycle does not offer great scope for close comparisons. And options that might appear obvious were not taken. The Crucifixion and the Stigmatisation are both portrayed, but not opposite to each other; the Lamentation and Francis' deathbed also, but again, not opposite. It may be that the majority of pilgrims took in the general

---

[44] Cf. Brooke and Brooke 1984, pp. 141–4, 166.

[45] Derbes 1996, pp. 145–9; ibid. fig. 89 for Guido da Siena; and fig. 88, for detail from Coppo di Marcovaldo's historiated cross, dated c.1261, from Santa Chiara, San Gimignano.

[46] See *Oxford Classical Dictionary*, s.v., 2nd edn, p. 300; 3rd edn, p. 411.

[47] Thier and Calufetti 1985, p. 278 and n. 24.

impression without too much further reflection once they had assimilated the clear message provided by the first pair they passed. Yet parallels can be and have been found, some of them very ingenious.

The second scene on the right is the Crucifixion; but of the crucifixion itself only Christ's left arm remains. It is astonishing that the Order was so cavalier in its treatment of its earliest decoration, and especially of this subject. Extant is a group of pious women, the Virgin Mary and St John. The caption at the foot gives Christ's words entrusting His mother to him.[48] Opposite, Pope Innocent III lies dreaming of St Francis supporting the weight of the Lateran to prevent it from collapse. A symbolic interpretation highlights the Virgin, taken to represent the Church. Her swooning body is supported by St John, while an unsteady Lateran – which can also be taken to represent the Church – is held up by St Francis.[49]

The third pair of scenes – Francis preaching to the birds and the Deposition from the Cross – make it clear that the scenes are to be read in sequence while moving up the nave. Though the third of five, they are not central. If they were, the Crucifixion should have occupied this position, which could easily have been arranged, for example, by including a scene of Christ carrying his Cross after the Stripping. The depiction is a striking composition. Joseph of Arimathaea stands centrally on a vestigial ladder holding the limp body horizontally – the head and shoulders would have been supported by Mary, now missing apart from a fragment of blue gown. The legs sag in a curve, the bleeding feet still fastened to the cross. Nicodemus kneels, about to extract the nails with a pair of pincers and a hammer[50] (Plate 28). The scenes of Francis' life unfold in chronological order, and with space only for a meagre five, Francis preaching to the birds was probably already an inevitable choice (Plate 29). It was an established popular favourite, appreciated by viewers and artists alike. Its beautiful rendering here foreshadows the design of the better-known example in the Upper Church, with olive trees, and the birds nearly all on the ground. Both scenes provide much food for thought, but there is no clear link between them.[51]

Next come the Stigmatisation and the Lamentation. There is a link, certainly. All five bleeding wounds are visible on Christ's dead body; the seraph shows four of the stigmata, and the kneeling figure of Francis probably originally showed all five wounds. But the correspondence should not be exaggerated. The Virgin, the women, St John and St Peter grieve bitterly over a tortured corpse. It is a deeply moving and distressful scene. We do not know how Francis' expression was rendered. According to 1 *Celano* 94, his first reaction was of the utmost astonishment, his second a powerful feeling of joy at finding himself so kindly and graciously looked upon by this seraph of inestimable beauty. It is this moment that the painter has sought to capture. The seraph's face is indeed beautiful; the expression is gentle and kind and calm; there is no suggestion of pain or suffering. In Francis' vision the seraph was fixed to a cross, and the meaning of the suffering involved presently frightened him. So the vision left him glad and sad, joy and sorrow alternating within him.[52]

---

[48] John 19. 26–7; Frugoni 1993, pp. 287–8.   [49] Cook 1999, p. 35. See p. 283 and Plate 25.
[50] See p. 301 and Colour Plate 6.   [51] *Pace* Frugoni 1993, pp. 288–90.   [52] 1 *Cel.* 94; see Plate 24.

Plate 28 Lower Church nave, Deposition from the cross (© www.Assisi.de. Photo Stefan Diller).

Plate 29 Lower Church nave, St Francis preaching to the birds (© www.Assisi.de. Photo
Stefan Diller).

The final scene on the left is of Francis' deathbed. He is surrounded by mourners. A kneeling friar draws the attention of the friar behind him, and so the viewer, to the saint's side wound. Francis' face looks up, drawing the eye aloft to where tiny angels carry his soul straight to heaven (Plate 30). The scene opposite is so badly damaged that it was only quite recently securely identified. A man is seated at a laden table – it represents the Supper at Emmaus. So the last pair are both recognition scenes – Francis had concealed the stigmata, the outward and visible signs of his conformity to Christ, during his life – and are also both resurrection scenes, a fitting and triumphant conclusion to the cycle.[53]

There is no record of the painter's name. He acquired the designation, the Master of St Francis, or the St Francis Master, because he had also painted a panel 'portrait' of St Francis at the Portiuncula (Plate 31). This panel is different from those discussed earlier, and is of exceptional interest. Tradition alleged it was painted on a board St Francis had slept on. By the time blessed Angela of Foligno saw and meditated on it, it had become a cult object, with something of the status of a relic.[54] The standing figure of St Francis is unusually tall. It bears some resemblance to the figure in the Assisi panel – a similarly elongated body, witness to the artist's familiarity with Byzantine art, and he holds a cross in his right hand and supports an open book on his left forearm.[55] The inscription on this book reads: 'Hic michi viventi lectus fuit et morienti', 'This [book] was read to me while I was alive and when I was dying.'[56] The book was, of course, the holy Gospel, which the Friars Minor promised to observe; and the copy of the Gospel that this painting illustrates and refers to survives. It was bound in with the breviary which brother Angelo and brother Leo deposited for safekeeping at Santa Chiara.[57] All five wounds of the stigmata are prominently displayed, the side wound particularly so. There are no scenes from his life flanking him. Instead, his body, from his shoulders to his knees, stands against a square background painted deep blue, with a patterned border imitating cosmati work along its top and both sides, lined with red. This again shows the influence of Byzantine art. There are exquisite decorated borders on the pope's cloak, and the cross on his tiara is similarly decorated in the fresco of Innocent III's dream in the nave of the Lower Church by the same artist.[58] Above this solid square is a gold background with Francis' large halo etched in the centre. To either side is the bust of an angel, each holding a pattern encircling a cross. They thus draw attention not just to Francis's present abode among the angels, but to the link between the crucifixion and the Eucharist – Christ gives his crucified body in the sacrament – and emphasise the stigmata that Francis' body bears and his devotion to the Eucharist. In the balancing space below the central square, the message is spelt out in a lengthy

---

[53] Cook 1999, p. 35. See Poeschke 1985, pl. 41.

[54] Thode 1885, p. 77; Assisi 1999, p. 71; Krüger 1992, pp. 50–6; Frugoni 1993, p. 297 and nn.

[55] See Colour Plate 3.

[56] This inscription has been mistranslated by some modern scholars. Thus Frugoni 1993, p. 297: 'This was my bed while I lived and when I was dead', relating it to blessed Angela of Foligno's concept of the cross as a bed. Cook 1999, pp. 67–8, no. 32, states that 'bed' refers not to the board on which the image is painted but to the cross Francis holds, and echoes Jacopone de Todi's *Lauda* LXXI. The mistake goes back to Faloci-Pulignani, cited Goffen 1988, p. 96, nn. 12–14. Goffen 1988, pp. 15 and 96, translates it as 'I chose him while I lived and as I died.'

[57] See p. 109.　　[58] See Plate 25.

Plate 30 Lower Church nave, St Francis' death, showing side wound: angels carry his soul to heaven, top right (© www.Assisi.de. Photo Stefan Diller).

Plate 31 The St Francis panel at the Portiuncula (© www.Assisi.de. Photo Gerhard Ruf).

inscription to either side of St Francis. It is difficult to decipher, but has been made out to read:

left:	'Me Jesus expresse	right:	'Nemo causetur
	Dilectum me comprobat esse		Sed Christo glorificatur
	Cuius sic me stigmata		Cui placuit dignis
	Stigmata meque decorant'		Me sic attollere signis'

'Jesus expressly proves me to be beloved, whose stigmata thus decorate me. Let no one dispute it, but give glory to Christ who has been pleased to exalt me thus with worthy signs.'[59] 'Sanctus Franciscus' is written at the foot.

So here, at the Portiuncula, the place most dear to St Francis, we are faced with a panel proclaiming an overtly polemical message. The purpose of the panel was to advertise the stigmata and assert their authenticity. The wording of the inscription is close to that of Gregory IX's bull, *Usque ad terminos*, of which the Order had a copy at the Sacro Convento dated 31 March 1237. To counter a mounting threat of scepticism Gregory IX had issued a series of bulls that year, in which he personally vouched for the truth of the stigmata and urged the faithful to accept the miracle, and the sanctity of Francis.[60] There was another wave of criticism and disbelief a few years later. At a General Chapter meeting held at Genoa, probably in 1251, John of Parma called on brother Bonizo, who had been one of St Francis' companions, 'to tell the friars the truth about his stigmata, because many throughout the world were in doubt about this'.[61] Thomas of Celano, compiling his *Tractatus de Miraculis* at the behest of John of Parma at around the same time, 1250–2, introduced his chapter on the stigmata with a straightforward appeal to faith: 'The reason is not to be asked, because it is a wonderful thing, nor is a model to be sought, because it is unique' (*3 Cel.* 2). Alexander IV next weighed in with a series of bulls, starting with *Benigne operatio* of 29 October 1255, in which he notes that he had had the privilege of knowing St Francis during the time when he had been in lesser orders in the household of Gregory IX (when Gregory had been Hugolino, Cardinal Protector of the Friars Minor). Alexander was Gregory's nephew, and in his bulls he repeats Gregory's endorsement of all five wounds, and his instruction to include them all in images of the saint, and to preach in their defence. Alexander exhorts the faithful: 'We wish to signify before your eyes, to be recollected frequently and greatly admired, those joyful insignia of the Lord's Passion which the heavenly hand imprinted on the saint's body.' Detractors were warned that no one was to infringe his prohibition, or dare to contradict his confirmation and will.[62]

The panel fits into this context. It was clearly commissioned either by the Order or by the Cardinal Protector, Rainald dei Segni (either before or after he became Pope Alexander IV). It can be dated sometime in the 1250s.[63] It has the distinction therefore of being the first surviving painted image in Italy to depict the side wound. The Master

[59] Thode 1885, pp. 86–7; Frugoni 1993, pp. 298 and 318 n. 169. Frugoni suggests emending the first 'stigmata' to 'signant', and omitting the second 'me' to improve the metre.
[60] See pp. 166–7.
[61] Eccleston, p. 74 (for the date, see Brooke 1959, p. 257 and n. 2). See p. 35 and note 14.
[62] Sbaralea, II, 85–6, A4, no. 120.   [63] On this I agree with Scarpellini 1982b, p. 108.

of St Francis went on, shortly afterwards, to paint the side wound again in his frescoes in the nave of the Lower Church.

After he had finished work in the Lower Church, the Master of St Francis was given an important commission by the Franciscans in Perugia. Brother Giles, the third friar to join St Francis, died there on St George's day, 23 April 1261. He was buried in the church of San Francesco al Prato in an antique early Christian marble sarcophagus on whose sides the story of Jonah was carved. He performed no great miracles after his death, but he was venerated by the citizens of Perugia, who guarded his dying body to prevent his removal to Assisi, as they knew that if he could choose he would wish to be buried near St Francis. Brother Leo regarded him as a saint and wrote his life.[64]

The Master of St Francis painted a magnificent crucifix to hang above the altar. St Francis is kneeling at Christ's feet, the place traditionally assigned to St Mary Magdalene. The background emphasising the link between St Francis and Christ has the same criss-cross diamond pattern and narrow red border as the artist used on the St Francis panel at the Portiuncula more than ten years earlier.[65] The crucifix is dated 1272.

That he also painted a truly splendid and innovative double-sided altarpiece for the same church has been established thanks to the researches of a number of scholars, culminating in the meticulous study of Dillian Gordon.[66] Some of the panels are lost, and the surviving panels are scattered, but enough remains to reconstruct its essential features. The painted and carved architectural details on the panels reflect the carved decoration of the sarcophagus. Gordon's arguments that it was designed to stand on the altar above brother Giles' tomb are convincing. The altarpiece was exceptionally wide, and the measurements fit. The back of the altarpiece depicted the twelve apostles, together with St Francis (and probably St Anthony of Padua), apostles of the new apostolic Order of Friars Minor – a juxtaposition analogous to the stained glass windows in the nave of the Upper Church, on several of which the same artist was to work after he returned to Assisi from Perugia.[67] Its six surviving panels show St Francis, SS. Bartholomew and Simon combined, St James Minor, St John the Evangelist, St Andrew and St Peter, in that order, and make up the complete left-hand section, with St Francis on the outside at the far left and St Peter at the centre. The right-hand section presumably would have contained the remaining six apostles and St Anthony of Padua in a matching sequence, with St Anthony on the outside right, then two apostles combined, three further apostles, and St Paul at the centre.[68] The central panel may probably have contained a Virgin and child. In all the panels on this side the saints stand against a gold ground framed by slender columns painted to represent red marble, with gilded acanthus leaves on the bases and blue acanthus leaves on the capitals, surmounted by a round arch with an inscription including their names. St Francis carries a cross in his right hand and supports with his left arm an open book, displaying a text from one of St Paul's Epistles: 'Christus confixus sum cruci, vi' – of which the '*vi*' is part of the next phrase: 'vivo autem iam non ego . . .'; 'I am crucified with Christ; nevertheless I live; yet not I but Christ liveth in me

---

[64] SL pp. 307–49; Salimbene, H, p. 557.   [65] Cook 1999, p. 162, no. 137 (detail); Goffen 1988, p. 22.
[66] Gordon 1982.   [67] See pp. 321–9 and Plate 37.
[68] Assisi 1999, pp. 70–5, pls. 6/7, 6/2, 6/4, 6/3, 6/6, 6/5; Cook 1999, pp. 162–3, no. 138.

(Gal. 2. 19–20).[69] The front of the altarpiece contained beautiful scenes of the Passion, framed at each end by a Franciscan saint, and at the centre by a prophet. The four surviving panels show Isaiah, the Deposition, the Lamentation and St Anthony of Padua. On this side there is again a gold ground, but the architectural framework is different; the columns are squatter, there are trilobe framing arches, prophets' and saints' names are at their feet, and the whole composition is joined along the bottom by a band of cosmatesque decoration.[70] Gordon has established by examining the grain of the wood at the back of the panels that the St Francis, SS Bartholomew and Simon, and St Andrew had been cut from the same piece of wood as the St Anthony, the Lamentation and the Deposition, so they must have been placed directly back to back. The ten surviving panels, therefore, make up one complete wing of the altarpiece, front and back.[71] The centre panel on the front would clearly have been the Crucifixion. On the left-hand side, looking at it from the front, presumably Jeremiah came next, balancing Isaiah, and at the far end St Francis, balancing St Anthony of Padua; between them will have come two more Passion scenes. We do not know which they would have been; there was a choice. They might have included an Entry into Jerusalem, a Betrayal, or Christ carrying His cross; or conceivably the only pre-crucifixion scene painted by the artist in his Lower Church fresco cycle – Christ stripping himself before mounting the cross.[72] The Deposition scene on the Perugia altarpiece enables us to gain a much clearer picture of what the artist's earlier version in fresco will have looked like before it was cut through[73] (Colour Plate 6). The design is very similar. Nicodemus kneels, about to extract the nails with a pair of pincers and a hammer; St John holds Christ's limp hand against his cheek. The ladder leans at a diagonal, strengthening the line of a beautiful and most moving composition, but rendering Joseph of Arimathea's position untenable. The scene captures a split second of equilibrium in suspense, more fraught than the tensions in Keats' Grecian urn. In the Perugia panel we can admire the lovely columnar figure of Mary, and smile at the incongruous but thoughtful touch which provides her with a footstool. Probably such a footstool was a stage prop in the Passion plays. Part of a footstool can be made out below the fragment fold of Mary's gown in the fresco. The Lamentation scene on the Perugia altarpiece offers similar opportunities for comparison.[74]

Gordon argued that the altarpiece should be dated after 1266, when Bonaventure's *Legenda Maior* was declared the official Life, because, on it, the stigmata on Francis' hands and feet are painted black, to represent nails, and the side wound red, as described in Bonav. XIII, 3, and that Celano did not make this distinction. This is not in fact so. When describing the imprint of the stigmata, Celano likened the appearance of the hand and foot marks to nails and said the right side was as though pierced by a lance and the wound frequently bled (1 *Cel.* 95), so was presumably red. He states this specifically later in the book, when describing how St Francis' body looked immediately after death – the hands and feet showed the nails themselves formed out of flesh and showing the blackness of iron, 'and his right side was red with blood' (1 *Cel.* 113). However her

---

[69] Cf. *Assisi* 1999, pl. 6/7; Frugoni 1993, p. 299.   [70] *Assisi* 1999, pls. 6/1, 6/9, 6/10, 6/8.
[71] Gordon 1982, pp. 71–2.   [72] See Plate 27, and pp. 291–2.   [73] See p. 293 and Plate 28.
[74] See *Assisi* 1999, pl. 6/10, and Poeschke 1985, pl. 38.

dating, between 1266 and c.1272, is surely correct.[75] The Master of St Francis would have painted both altarpiece and crucifix in Perugia as part of the same commission. And what a prestigious commission it was; the crucifix one of the largest and finest of the century to survive, and the splendid double-sided altarpiece representing an enormous advance on the smaller single altarpieces that were the norm at the time. Just as the Bardi altar panel may have been the answer of the Franciscans at Florence to the Pisan altar panel – civic pride and inter-city rivalry urging them to order one larger and more elaborate;[76] so maybe, this crucifix and altarpiece were Perugia's response to what had been going on during the previous two decades in nearby Assisi. They employed the same artist, sanctioned the most lavish use of gold, and altogether did the blessed brother Giles proud. Perugia was wealthier than Assisi, but Assisi was not to let matters rest there.

Cimabue: Virgin and child enthroned with angels and St Francis

Some few years after the Master of St Francis painted the frescoes in the nave of the Lower Church, Cimabue painted the Virgin and child with angels, attended by St Francis, on the east wall of the north transept. The fresco is badly deteriorated, only fragments of the original splendid colouring remaining. The Virgin is seated on a wooden chair throne of Byzantine type (Plate 32). The throne is painted using the foreshortened frontal setting, in which one side is left undistorted, aligned with the flat two-dimensional surface of the wall, while the second side appears foreshortened and recedes. It has been suggested that Cimabue is not yet wholly successful in solving the problems of the perspective – the left side is splayed out towards the plane and is awkwardly related to the steps. He also painted six thrones in the Upper Church – for each of the four Evangelists, for the Lamb, and for the Virgin and Christ. With so many thrones available for comparison in one building it is possible to trace a process of progress and development which suggests that the one in the Lower Church was the earliest to be painted. This conclusion is reinforced by the treatment of the haloes. In the Lower Church they are gilt. In the Upper Church, haloes with gilded relief radiating patterns occur on the upper walls of the north transept, the first to be decorated – by the Northern Master and his associates – and when Cimabue took over from them he made use of this more modern type that they had introduced.[77]

In the early fourteenth century the east wall of the north transept vault of the Lower Church was redecorated by Giotto and his workshop. Cimabue's Maestà was spared, but was cut down on all sides, especially on the left, to make it fit into the new scheme. Originally, St Francis will have been balanced by a standing figure of St Anthony of Padua, the other shining example of the new apostolic Order of Friars Minor. For by this time both the two main Orders of friars had convinced themselves that the needs of their apostolate required them to offer and provide instruction through images as well as by words and deeds. They ought therefore to admit religious art into their churches, while

---

[75] Gordon 1982, p. 76.   [76] See pp. 176–9.
[77] White 1987, p. 179; White 1967, p. 27; Bellosi 1998, pp. 227–30 and plates, pp. 230–2; and see pp. 337, 344–6, 356–7, 361–2.

Plate 32 Cimabue, Virgin and child enthroned with angels and St Francis. Below the fresco
is the site of the tomb of five friars, including Bernard, Sylvester and William the Englishman.
(Photo Wim Swaan Photographic Collection (96.P.21), Research Library, The Getty Research
Institute, Los Angeles.)

of course guarding against notable superfluities and curiosities through legislation. They needed to have representations of Christ, the Virgin, the saints on their altar panels; and presently on their walls with frescoes, in their windows in stained glass. The Orders' own saints had their proper place in these representations, and both Orders chose to concentrate on two. In 1254 the Dominican General Chapter ordered images of St Dominic and St Peter Martyr to be painted in all their convent churches. Peter, an Inquisitor who actively and very successfully preached against heretics, had been assassinated in 1252 and canonised in 1253. By the time of St Bonaventure the Franciscans officially permitted the portrayal of crucifixes, the Virgin, St John, and St Francis and St Anthony, in stained glass windows behind high altars.[78]

The portrayal of St Francis is the most distinctive of all that survive from the thirteenth century (Frontispiece). It is not a portrait. But it succeeds in evoking what I can only call something of the essence of Francis' spirituality in a way that the earlier iconic centrepieces of panels and the later, smoother, more substantial actor shown in the scenes of the nave cycle do not even attempt. He is of roughly the same height as the angel he stands beside: a slight figure in a torn habit, with a sensitive face. He clasps the Gospel book close with long thin fingers. Poverty and humility are shown to stand with the company of heaven, with the Virgin and child and the angels of God. It is an image of the holy.

THE DECORATION OF THE UPPER CHURCH

By about the end of the thirteenth century the Upper Church was decorated throughout – apse, choir, crossing, transepts, windows, walls, vaults. It was a riot of colour; spaces which were not decorated with figures or scenes were painted with fictive architectural features and furnishings. But what was the thirteenth-century worshipper and pilgrim actually able to see? Lighting fluctuated according to the season and the time of day. Visibility was dependent on the position and strength of sunlight, and on flickering rush lights and candles; also on the position of the pictorial material. The sequence of scenes of the St Francis cycle was at eye level in the nave, and could be followed the most readily. The scenes above it had their shapes dictated and their flow punctuated by the windows, which had their own separate agenda, quite distinct from the frescoed narrative, and whose beautiful coloured glass must have cast its own reflection and patterns on frescoed surfaces when the sun shone. The roundels in the vaults must always have been difficult to distinguish from the floor with the naked eye. It may be that some thirteenth-century people had excellent eyesight, but some will have been shortsighted, and we know from the great frequency with which they are mentioned in miracle collections that many people suffered from eye afflictions.[79] A number of the pilgrims who flocked to the Upper Church will have been partially sighted.

[78] Farmer 1987, pp. 350–1; Creytens 1948; Dondaine 1953; Narb., III, 15, 18, Bihl 1941, p. 48.
[79] Finucane 1977, pp. 106–7, 147–50; cf. e.g. Foreville and Keir 1987, p. ciii and Index s.v. diseases, blindness.

Plate 1 Monstrance reliquary of St Francis, c.1228, reverse: St Francis receiving the stigmata – see p. 164. Paris, Louvre (Photo RMN. © Daniel Arnaudet).

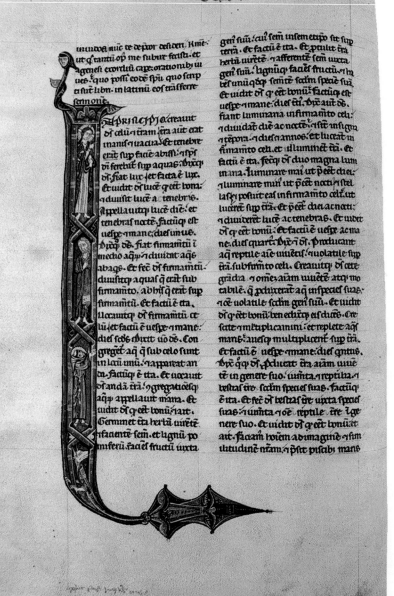

Plate 2 Christ, Adam, St Francis and a dragon in the initial I of Genesis: Assisi MS 17, fo. 5v. This page comes from the first part of a two-part Bible – comprising Genesis to Job – produced by an Umbrian scriptorium for the Sacro Convento, probably not long after Francis' canonisation. According to oral tradition it was used by John of Parma, Minister General 1247–57. Francis is portrayed with a halo, and with stigmata in hands and feet. The volume is listed first in the inventory of the library of the Sacro Convento drawn up in 1381, with a note that passages from it were read out loud to the friars in the refectory (*Assisi 1999*, p. 134). (© www.Assisi.de. Photo Gerhard Ruf.)

Plate 3   Assisi altar panel (© www. Assisi.de. Photo Gerhard Ruf).

Plate 4   Assisi altar panel, detail showing the Lower Church altar (©
www.Assisi.de. Photo Gerhard Ruf).

Plate 5   View of the interior of the Upper Church from the apse (Photo Ghigo Roli).

Plate 6   Deposition from the cross, by the Master of St Francis, from the double-sided altarpiece, originally in S. Francesco in Prato, Perugia (© www.Assisi.de. Photo Gerhard Ruf.)

Plate 7   Innocent III's dream of St Francis supporting the Lateran Basilica, Cycle no. 6
(© www.Assisi.de. Photo Stefan Diller).

Plate 8   Guccio di Mannaia, Chalice, given to the Basilica by Nicholas IV: Basilica,
Museo-Tesoro (© www.Assisi.de. Photo Gerhard Ruf). Of the figures in the quatrefoils
round the base, the crucifixion is centre foreground, with, to the right of it, St John
the Evangelist and St Francis receiving the stigmata, to the left the Virgin and St Clare.
In the centre of the node stands the Redeemer blessing, between St Peter and St Paul.
See pp. 440–1.

So, how much, and what, did they see? The question cannot be precisely answered. If we take as an example Cimabue's Evangelists in the crossing vaults, they are hard to make out in detail because they are so high up. The friars will have been made familiar with them. Lay congregations seem to have been permitted to enter the sanctuary on high festivals. The blessed Angela of Foligno came on pilgrimage to Assisi in the Jubilee year 1300 to participate in the Portiuncula indulgence.[80] On the Sunday before the feast she attended a Mass celebrated at the high altar in the Upper Church, dedicated to the Virgin. It would have been a very crowded occasion, and her gaze, as of other devout worshippers, would have been concentrated on the altar and the host, but they will have gained some impression of the frescoes on the walls and vaults.[81] Those privileged to raise their eyes to see the Evangelists in their brilliantly foreshortened settings will have had their understanding enhanced by the descriptions and expositions of guides and mentors. They will have left having perceived more than they could have actually seen. We cannot know what the guides may have told them, but we can be sure that the message was put across, even in this most visually explicit of churches, in a manner in which channels of transmission are blurred. Three media are involved: pictures, written text and oral exposition. To take the St Francis Cycle: the starting point is the visual image in fresco, but this is firmly based upon a written text, St Bonaventure's *Legenda Maior*; and the viewer will have had it explained and commented on through the medium of an oral interpreter.

Not everyone had need of an interpreter. When Angela of Foligno first visited the Upper Church about the time of St Francis' feast day in 1291, as she genuflected, her eyes focused on an image in the stained glass window nearest on her left to the door through which she entered. In the lowest section are two imposing standing figures: on the right the Virgin Mary holding the Christ child, beside her on the left, Christ holding St Francis. Above them are six great angels[82] (Plate 39).

The Franciscans at Foligno had allowed her to make her profession as a member of the Third Order in the summer and she had come to Assisi on pilgrimage with some companions, probably also tertiaries. She was in a state of prayer all the way from Foligno. She prayed St Francis to intercede with God for her that she might feel Christ's presence, receive grace to observe well the rule of St Francis she had newly promised, and most of all that He would make her truly poor from now until the end. At the junction of three roads (a symbol of the Trinity), where the narrow path leading up to Assisi diverged from the route to Spello, she experienced within her the presence of the Holy Trinity, and she heard a voice. '"I am the Holy Spirit, who has come to you to give you consolation such as you have never tasted . . . I will not leave you until the second time you enter St Francis's church; then I will depart from you so far as this consolation goes . . . My daughter and my sweet spouse . . . I love you more than any other woman in the Valley of Spoleto . . . You besought my servant Francis, and because my servant Francis loved me much, I did much for him. And if there were some other

---

[80] Thier and Calufetti 1985, pp. 486–8; see p. 72.   [81] Cf. Aston 1990, esp. pp. 241–4, 269–81.
[82] Thier and Calufetti 1985, pp. 33–4, 184; Martin and Ruf 1998, pl. 193. This window is in this position now, where it is believed to have been originally: see pp. 307–8, 326–31.

person who loves me more, I would do more for that person. I will do that for you which my servant Francis received, and more if you love me . . . I am he who was crucified for you, and experienced hunger and thirst for you, and poured out my blood for you, so much I loved you." And he uttered the whole of his passion.'

When they reached Assisi it would seem they first visited the Lower Church and then went out to have a meal, the Holy Spirit still accompanying her, as promised. The group then returned to the Basilica, but this time went to the Upper Church. 'On this my second visit, I genuflected at the entry of the church, and at once I saw St Francis pictured in the bosom of Christ, and he said to me: "thus will I hold you tight, and much more than can be seen with the eyes of the body. Now is the hour when I fulfil, sweet daughter, my temple, my beloved, what I said to you, that as far as this consolation is concerned I leave you – but I do not ever leave you if you love me." . . . Then I perceived that I could see both with the eyes of the body and of the mind.' Asked later by her confessor: '"What have you seen?" she answered: "I have seen a fullness, an immense majesty which I cannot express, but it seemed to me to be All Good. And it spoke many words of sweetness to me with immense gentleness when it departed, and it plainly hesitated to depart."'

'And then after its departure I began to scream and cry out at the top of my voice. I screamed without shame, and cried saying: "You love, not known before, why do you leave me – why – why?" I could do and say nothing at all but cry out, without any shame: "You love, not known before, why do you leave me?" But my voice so strangled this saying that it could not be understood. I was left then with the certainty, and without any shadow of doubt, that he had most assuredly been God. And I cried out and wished to die, and it was very painful to me that I could not die . . . – and then all my faculties were scattered.'[83]

As it happened the friar who had earlier been her confessor in Foligno was at that time resident at the Sacro Convento. He has described the conclusion of this remarkable episode from his point of view. 'She was sitting at the entrance to the [Upper] Church, screaming. Because of this, I, who was her confessor and blood relative . . . was greatly ashamed, most especially as many friars had come to watch her screaming and shouting who knew both of us. Although that holy man, now dead . . . who wanted to expropriate himself at the same time as her, and was at that time her companion on the journey, humbly sat on the ground inside the church on the tiled floor not far from her, regarding her . . . with the utmost reverence and sadness . . . I did not approach her . . . When she stopped that strident clamour, got up from the door and came to me, I could hardly speak calmly. I told her never to dare to come to Assisi again . . . and I told her companions never to bring her.'[84]

This vivid account, written subsequently by her confessor, is an isolated but valid indicator of what the direct impact of a visual image could be on a highly intelligent, sensitive and receptive woman. It seems her sudden first sight of the window inspired her vision. She sought St Francis' intercession because St Francis was the saint whose

[83] Thier and Calufetti 1985, pp. 33–4, 176–84.   [84] Thier and Calufetti 1985, pp. 168–70.

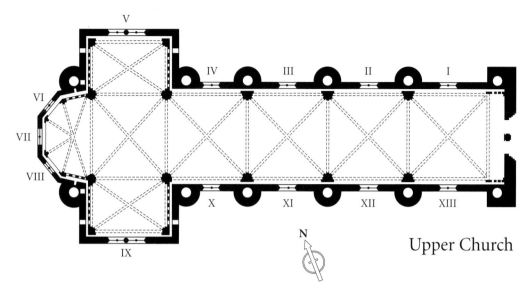

Figure 10 Assisi, Basilica of St Francis, Upper Church: Plan of windows

example was leading her to Christ. She aimed high and was very competitive. She longed to be where St Francis was shown to be – held in Christ's loving embrace.[85]

THE STAINED GLASS WINDOWS IN THE UPPER CHURCH

There are four pairs of Gothic windows in the nave of the Upper Church, each consisting of two lancets surmounted by a quatrefoil lunette. To the left of the entrance is the remarkable window that produced such a powerful effect on Angela of Foligno on first viewing, XIII (Plate 39; Figure 10[86]). Above the tall standing figures of Christ holding St Francis and the Virgin Mary holding the Christ child are six great angels, three to each lancet.[87] Opposite it on the right is a window celebrating St Francis

[85] See chapter 11. In 1995 Jacques Dalarun published his provocative article, 'Angèle de Foligno a-t-elle existé?' He conceded that there was such a person, but argued that her mystical writings were the work of a group of Spiritual Franciscans. In a characteristically judicious and fair-minded review of Dalarun's and other scholars' attempts to convert Angela's *Memoriale* into Spiritual propaganda, Burr shows conclusively that, although she had links with the Spirituals – Ubertino himself greatly respected her – the *Memoriale* also points in quite a different direction (Burr 2001, pp. 334–46, 393–4). In my view, Dalarun's hypothesis fails on two counts: the external evidence of Ubertino which shows the respect in which a formidable witness of the spirituality of the age held the actual Angela, and Dalarun's failure to appreciate the nature of the mysticism of the age, especially as we meet it in the female mystics of the twelfth and thirteenth centuries. I am convinced that the Angela of the *Memoriale* was a genuine historical character, though a very unusual one. Dalarun has since reflected, with the help of colleagues, and now accepts not only her existence but the authenticity of her teachings: 'Ainsi y a-t-il une Angèle, *mulier religiosa* de Foligno; un moment de rédaction de ses dires par *frater A.*; un moment d'édition des notes du scribe au Sacro Convento; une phase d'oubli; un instant de résurgence du *codex* dans la Bibliothèque assisiate; un temps de résurgence du texte dans le courant de l'Observance, un autre dans le contexte de la *devotio moderna*' (Barone and Dalarun 1999, pp. 5–6).

[86] Figure based on Marchini 1973, p. 20. I follow Marchini's enumeration.

[87] See pp. 326–31.

and St Anthony, I (Plate 37). St Anthony stands to the right, nearest the door, thus opposite Christ with St Francis; St Francis, in the left lancet as you face the window, is opposite to the Virgin and child. The lights above the standing figures are filled with scenes taken from their lives.[88] The further six windows were devoted to the twelve apostles. There has been damage, some caused by earthquakes – the serious earthquake of 1997 is only the most recent – and much dislocation. Fortunately repairs have been carried out conservatively, and Assisi seems to have been largely spared the problems caused, for example, at Canterbury, by nineteenth-century fakes. Still, some glass is missing and some may not be in the right place. An agreed order, so far as could be known, was reinstated in a major restoration and conservation campaign after the Second World War, in 1948–51.[89] Originally all the standing figures of the apostles were surmounted by stories from their lives, taken from *The Golden Legend*, to be read from bottom to top. The stories above St James the Great and St Andrew, in the window nearest the right transept, IV, are lost, and have been replaced with modern geometric decoration. But these two apostles have retained their heads. The heads of the rest – St John the Evangelist and St Thomas, III; St Bartholomew and St Matthew, II; St Simon and St Judas Taddeus, X; and St Philip (?) and St James the Less (?), XI, are modern. So are the heads of St Francis and St Anthony, in I, and of Christ, St Francis, the Virgin and child, and all the angels above them except the topmost two, in XIII, so it rather looks as though at some point an overzealous restorer targeted heads.[90] The whole of what was in window XII is lost.[91] Checking the list of apostles and presumed apostles, St Peter is conspicuous by his absence. So he was probably one of the two placed in this window, which is in an honourable position, adjacent to the Virgin, Christ and St Francis, in XIII. Various options could be chosen for the replacement of the traitor Judas Iscariot, but as St Paul is depicted as the twelfth apostle in the ranks frescoed in the right transept, St Paul was probably associated with St Peter in XII.

The glazing of the nave was tackled from the western end – that is, from the crossing – eastwards. The last windows to be glazed would have been the two nearest the entrance. Angela of Foligno described one of these – XIII – when she visited the Basilica on pilgrimage in the autumn of 1291. So the programme was complete by that date.[92] The Basilica was clearly not adorned with stained glass when Innocent IV consecrated her altars, so the glass is later than the summer of 1253. The date of the nave glass can be refined a bit further, as stories illustrating the lives of the apostles were taken from *The*

---

[88] See pp. 323–6.

[89] Marchini 1973, pp. 22–3. For the Canterbury restorations, see Caviness 1981, esp. pp. xxxvii, 2.

[90] Marchini 1973, pp. 46, 64, 67, 77, 79, 86. The figures as well as the heads of Judas Taddeus in xb and James the Less in xib are modern (Marchini 1973, pp. 77, 79). Cf. now Martin and Ruf 1998, pp. 262–6, 280–4.

[91] Marchini 1973, p. 80. Before the restoration of the 1940s, window XIII was sited where XII now is. Cf. Martin and Ruf 1998, pp. 231, 284–5.

[92] See pp. 305–6. Marchini thought this window, now XIII, was stylistically earlier than I opposite it (Marchini 1973, p. 87); but he also reckoned that the glazing of the nave was effectively the work of a single campaign.

Golden Legend. This was compiled by a Dominican friar, James of Voragine, by 1265 so these windows were designed after *c.*1265.[93]

The glazing of the Upper Church was begun in the apse. There is general agreement that there was no stained glass in the church when Innocent IV came to consecrate the altars on 25 May 1253, and that the apse glass was installed in direct response to his bull, *Decet et expedit*, of 10 June 1253.[94] The decision to make stained glass a priority has been attributed to the pope's personal initiative. Martin, for example, has drawn attention to the period of the pope's exile. He assumes that Lyon was in France, and that Innocent familiarised himself while based there with French Gothic architecture. Based on these assumptions he suggests that the pope, when he contemplated the plain surfaces of the Gothic Upper Church at Assisi, was less struck by the lack of wall paintings that were customary in Italy, than by the absence of the stained glass he had become familiar with in the French Gothic sanctuaries he had frequented during the previous seven years.[95]

But it is not quite as simple as that. Sinibaldo Fieschi was a Genoese nobleman, son of the Count of Lavagna. He was a distinguished canon lawyer, who had studied and taught at Bologna. Made a cardinal by Gregory IX, he was governor of the March of Ancona 1235–40. There is no evidence that he ever travelled north of the Alps before his election as Pope Innocent IV on 25 June 1243. As a cardinal he had been on friendly terms with Frederick II, but, as has frequently proved to be the case, the mantle of office profoundly influenced the attitudes and actions of the office holder, and, as pope, he continued the fight with the Empire engaged in by his predecessors. Almost a year to the day later, while pretending to negotiate with the Emperor, he fled, sailing with a Genoese fleet provided by his Fieschi relations, to Genoa in June 1244. Thence he made his way over the Alps and up the Rhône, reaching Lyon on 29 November 1244.[96] Lyon was chosen because he could hope for the protection of the French king there, though it was just outside the French border.

During the almost seven years he spent there in exile, Innocent IV had naturally no opportunity to visit any of the Gothic cathedrals in northern Europe within the confines of the Empire. Nor does he seem to have indulged in sightseeing over the border into France. His only recorded excursion was a brief visit to Cluny in November 1245. His mobility was more circumscribed than might be imagined. There is no evidence that he was personally acquainted with any of the glorious stained glass that was being installed in cathedrals and churches throughout northern Europe during this period. Still, he could certainly have heard its praises sung, and may have indicated that that

---

[93] ODCC 1997, pp. 689, 861. James of Voragine (Varazze) was Provincial Prior of Lombardy, 1267–77 and 1281–6. In 1292 Pope Nicholas IV with difficulty persuaded him to become archbishop of Genoa. The earliest papal candidate who can be considered as a possible patron for the second phase of stained glass decoration in the Upper Church is therefore Clement IV, pope 1265–8.

[94] Sbaralea, I, 666, 14 no. 489; see pp. 66–7, 287.

[95] Martin 1993, pp. 120–3; Martin 1996, p. 177.

[96] There is a useful summary of Innocent's career in Kelly 1986, pp. 192–3, with references to modern literature; cf. Abulafia 1988, pp. 354–406. Gregorovius 1906, v, 1, chs. 6–7, still provides a helpful narrative. For Innocent IV's itinerary see Potthast, II, pp. 943–1283; Mas Latrie 1889, cols. 1117–18.

was what he wanted. He returned to Italy, travelling by barge down the Rhône in April 1251 and then by sea from Marseille to Genoa.

In the event his command that the church of St Francis should be 'decorated with the peak of splendid workmanship', was, over time, obeyed to the letter, the entire building, walls, vaults, windows, receiving lavish decoration, but it seems that the apse windows were done first.[97] The Order's statutes on the observance of poverty strictly prohibited 'curiosities and superfluities' in the matter of 'pictures, carvings, windows and columns' in their buildings, and forbade the putting in of 'historiated or painted glass windows . . . except that in the principal windows behind the main altar in the choir they may have images of the crucifix, the Virgin, St John, St Francis and St Anthony; any others are to be removed by the visitors'.[98] These statutes were peremptorily overruled in the same bull. The setting of no less than fifty-four painted scenes from the Old and New Testaments into the windows of the apse of the Basilica at Assisi, the birthplace and headquarters of the Order, was a flagrant violation of the Order's Rule and principles: it highlights the part played by popes and cardinal protectors of this period in forcing through and accelerating change – and in fuelling it, for without papal and curial patronage it could not have been achieved on the scale it was. The faithful were exhorted and given incentives to give, but their donations alone would have been quite insufficient for such an enterprise.

The idea of having stained glass was unfamiliar in Italy, and must have come from north of the Alps. It could easily have been suggested by any one of a number of leading Franciscans familiar with the universities and cities of northern Europe who may have been consulted as to the best way of implementing Innocent's orders. It used to be thought that glaziers were summoned from Erfurt. The Franciscan church at Erfurt still retains some of its thirteenth-century stained glass. The medallions include scenes from the life of Christ, from a Jesse window, and two scenes from a life of St Francis – the Approval of the Rule and the Stigmatisation. There are also fragments from the scene of Francis' death in the museum.[99] The windows were thought to date from 1230–5, and so were considered the source for the apse windows at Assisi, but Martin has argued that, on the contrary, they show the influence of Italian models and must be dated twenty years later.[100] Indeed they may be later still. Frugoni has succeeded in

[97] *Decet et expedit.* See pp. 66–7; Martin 1996, p. 177.

[98] *Narb.*, III, 15, 18, Bihl 1941, p. 48. These statutes are likely to have been in force well before Bonaventure's time. Regulations governing the construction of buildings and their decoration are recorded early. Eccleston, p. 38, records that brother John of Malvern, who conducted the second visitation of the English province, bringing with him a copy of Gregory IX's bull *Quo elongati* of 28 September 1230, took stern measures regarding the windows in the chapel of the friars' convent at Gloucester. He also deprived a friar who had painted a pulpit of his hood, and imposed the same punishment on the guardian of the convent for allowing it to be done. *Narb.*, III, 18 must be later than the canonisation of St Anthony in 1232, and seems to be earlier than Hugh of Digne's *Dialogue on Poverty* (see p. 94), as he echoes its wording. Bonaventure produced a new and revised edition of the Order's constitutions, but added little new. However, the words 'de cetero', 'henceforth', in *Narb.*, III, 18, may be an editorial insertion in an attempt at a cover up, or to forestall wrath. Cf. Brooke 1959, pp. 274–9; also Salimbene, H, pp. 158–9; S, pp. 232–4.

[99] The Erfurt glass is discussed in detail in Martin 1993, pp. 61–95, with drawings of three reconstructed windows on p. 62, and Martin's suggestions for the original order – with the tree of Jesse surmounted by the life of Jesus in medallions on the left, and scenes from Francis' life on the right (see p. 94). There are excellent plates showing the main medallions and details, ibid., pls. 99–109.

[100] Martin 1993, pp. 93–5.

deciphering almost all of the lettering framing the scene of St Francis receiving the stigmata, and has noted a coincidence in the use of an unusual word in the inscription and in St Bonaventure's *Legenda Maior*. The Erfurt glass may therefore perhaps be dated after 1263.[101] Another provenance for the apse glass must be sought.

Martin distinguishes two styles in the Assisi glass, the first showing marked affinities with Austrian book illumination, the second with mid-thirteenth-century German art from the region of Cologne or Mainz. The affinities of the first style are the more difficult to pinpoint, since there were close links between Austrian book illumination – especially as represented by the mid-thirteenth-century Seitenstretten Missal – and Venetian work of the same period and slightly earlier. Martin has little doubt that craftsmen travelled from Austria and Germany to paint the glass in Assisi; and argues that one of these artists had worked in the workshop that produced the Seitenstretten Missal, which was probably at Salzburg.[102]

The apse in the Upper Church has three Gothic windows, each consisting of two lancets, with a quatrefoil lunette flanked by two small triangles above. The right-hand lancets show New Testament scenes bearing on the life of Christ; the left-hand lancets scenes from the Old Testament chosen because they were thought to foreshadow or illuminate the Gospel stories. The iconographic programme is organised in the way that was normal in northern Europe. It is to be read from left to right and from bottom to top. Some scenes are difficult to identify, which has led to scholars offering different interpretations. With the exception of the right-hand lancet of the window left of centre, VIIIb, which is almost entirely modern, the glass is well preserved. Almost all the lead is original.[103] The original order cannot be worked out archaeologically. It has had to be reconstructed from knowledge of the Bible, and by comparison with other similar biblical cycles.[104] The sequence begins bottom left with the usual starting scene, with Jesse lying down on the ground with a tree sprouting out of him, and the quotation from Isaiah 11.1: 'And there shall come forth a rod out of the stem of Jesse, and a branch shall grow out of his roots', which was interpreted as prophesying both the coming of the Messiah and the birth of Jesus. It ends top right with Pentecost.

As examples of the correspondences perceived between the Old and New Testaments: in the left hand window, VIIIa&b, the visit of the Wise Men at Epiphany is foreshadowed by the visit of the Queen of Sheba to Solomon; the presentation of Jesus in the Temple by the offering of the infant Samuel in the Temple; the Apocryphal story that when the Holy Family was in Egypt the idols of the Egyptian gods collapsed, with the fall of the god Dagon. In the central window, VIIa&b, the Transfiguration is matched by Moses' vision of God from behind; Christ washing the disciples' feet with Abraham washing

---

[101] Frugoni 1993, pp. 129–30 n. 60; Bonav., I, I.   [102] Martin 1993, pp. 96–119.

[103] Marchini 1973, pp. 22–3. The panels showing Jesus' origin and birth, from the meeting of Joachim and Anna to the Flight into Egypt, VIIIb, and the Crucifixion and Burial of Jesus, VIb, are modern.

[104] The problem is especially acute in windows composed of roughly equal panels or medallions, and made for lancets of approximately identical dimensions, as in the Upper Church. See Marchini 1973, pp. 22–3, with plan; with more detail, Martin 1993, pp. 16–40, esp. the plans on pp. 16, 40. But in fact, Martin's reconstruction, p. 40, differs little from the present arrangement, p. 16, which is essentially the work of the art historian Giustino Cristofani, adviser of the reconstruction which began in 1946, though partly based on earlier evidence and the work of previous scholars (Martin 1993, pp. 31–3). See also Bonsanti 2002a, II. pp. 1012–22, pls. 1941–2001, IV, pp. 578–91.

Plate 33 LEFT Apse window VI, a8, Elijah taken up into heaven in a chariot (© www.Assisi.de. Photo Gerhard Ruf). RIGHT Apse window VI, b8, the Ascension (© www.Assisi.de. Photo Gerhard Ruf).

the angels' feet; the Last Supper with the Feast of King Ahasuerus (Xerxes) (Esther 1); Christ prays in the Garden of Gethsemane with Elijah's prayer on Mount Horeb; the kiss of Judas with Joab kissing Amasa before slaying him (2 Sam. 20. 8–10). In the right hand window, VIa&b, Christ carrying his cross is paired with Isaac led to sacrifice; the Resurrection with Jonah spewed out by the whale; Jesus revealing himself to doubting Thomas with Joseph revealing himself to his brethren; and the Ascension with Elijah taken up into heaven (Plate 33).

The bottom New Testament scene of the central window, VIIb, Christ in the midst of the doctors, contains an open book. Kleinschmidt thought that what was written on it could be fleshed out to read: 'Nicolaus pulcro modo me fecit picturari.' This would have required a date in the late 1270s for the windows, as Nicholas could only have referred to Pope Nicholas III, but this reading cannot be substantiated. Leading palaeographers have concluded that there is no message: it is fictive writing.[105]

The apse windows, when first installed, were the only ornament in the Upper Church, and must have looked particularly impressive and beautiful while unchallenged by competition, forming shafts of light in glorious, vivid colours rising behind the high altar. There seems no doubt as to who was the person responsible for them. He was the Cardinal Protector of the Order, now also pope, Alexander IV.[106] His choice of theme for their narrative scenes was quite conventional. There was much to be said in its favour: as well as its inherent decorative and dramatic interest and its didactic potential, it was desirable to select an iconographic programme with which glaziers from northern Europe would be familiar. It may also reflect a more particular concern. The apse windows have been dated to c.1255. It was in 1255 that Alexander IV formally

[105] Marchini 1973, p. 30, citing Kleinschmidt 1915–28, II. Supino 1924, pp. 200–1, cited Kleinschmidt and the rival interpretation of B. Marinangeli. But, as Marchini observes, neither carries conviction: he cites (p. 30) expert palaeographers who have agreed that the writing makes no sense. The inscription is reproduced in Marchini 1973, pl. XII b, and the only letters entirely clear read (at the outset) NCO – or just possibly NICO – and in the penultimate line ME FECIT. It is tempting to make something of it, but no weight can be attached to any reconstruction.

[106] See pp. 67–8, 287 and 446.

condemned as heretical Gerard of Borgo San Donnino's *Introduction to the Eternal Gospel*, which argued that the Old and New Testaments would be superseded by a Third Gospel, the Gospel of the Holy Spirit. The rash and unwarranted opinions of this one individual friar seriously compromised the Order. It would have seemed an opportune moment for the pope, by commissioning a typological juxtaposition of Old and New Testament scenes, publicly to endorse his confidence in the Order's theological orthodoxy in its Basilica. It was the duty of the Cardinal Protector to act as 'governor, protector and corrector' of the friars.[107]

Some little time elapsed before further windows were tackled.[108]

The windows in the left transept, IX, were created by a workshop characterised as *Francesizzante*, Frenchified, and were probably the work of French artists or of Italians much influenced by French masters. They are notable for the clarity of their scenes. The colours are paler than those used in the two nave windows, IV and III, also made by the same workshop, with touches of white: style and colour suggest links with north-eastern France and possibly England. At the same time, the borders and medallions of the Genesis stories clearly derive from the decorative world of the Cosmati.[109]

There are two windows, each of two lancets surmounted by a quatrefoil lunette. There is a main rose above in the centre (Plate 34). No doubt influenced by what was already in the apse windows, the designer began to enlarge upon the Old Testament background as a prelude to the Gospel story depicted in the apse. Although twenty-seven Old Testament scenes occur there as foils to the New Testament, they could be regarded as a haphazard collection. The transept series is systematic, so far as it goes. In the left-hand window, the left lancet shows the seven days of creation, starting at the bottom with the creation of heaven and earth, and ending with God the Father resting on the seventh day. The right lancet continues the story with Eve and original sin, above it a lovely rendering of Adam and Eve driven from Paradise, followed by both of them at work, Adam chopping and Eve spinning, then the offerings to God of Cain and Abel, surprisingly, and incorrectly, both corn, whereas the younger, Abel, offered a first-born lamb from his flock (Gen. 4. 2–4); above, Cain kills Abel with a flail, and then God questions Cain: 'Where is your brother?' At the top Cain is shown weeping over his dead brother.[110]

The right-hand window is quite different. It is composed of a group of female saints, identically presented. Each lancet has a kneeling angel at its apex and shows four saints, each sitting upon a throne under a canopy. St Clare is there, and seven virgin martyrs, St Agatha, St Lucy, St Catherine, St Barbara, St Margaret, St Cecilia and St Agnes. The central rose has a geometric pattern. The lunette on the left, above the early Genesis window, has the figure of Christ, seated, at its centre. On Christ's right, the viewer's left, is the head and upper body of St Francis, with the side wound prominent; on Christ's left, St Anthony of Padua. The lunette on the right, above the female saints,

---

[107] *Regula bullata*, c. 12, Esser 1976, p. 371; cf. Martin and Ruf 1998, pp. 40, 237–52.
[108] Martin 1996, p. 177.   [109] Marchini 1973, p. 53.
[110] Marchini 1973, pp. 40–1. The scene does not appear to be biblical, and its identification must be in doubt.

Plate 34 Left transept window IX. The quatrefoil above the two right lancets shows the Virgin and child between the prophets Isaiah and Jeremiah. The one above the two left lancets shows Christ blessing St Francis and St Anthony. (© www.Assisi.de. Photo Gerhard Ruf.)

has the Virgin and child at its centre, flanked by two prophets, Isaiah and Jeremiah, each holding a scroll with a text foreshadowing the incarnation.[111]

The right transept window, v, was the creation of none other than the Master of St Francis, whose frescoes adorn the nave walls of the Lower Church, and his workshop[112] (Plate 35). He took advantage of the situation that had arisen, in which a shortage of workers in stained glass in Italy coincided with a major glazing job opportunity at the Basilica. He learnt and mastered the art of glass painting. It was not uncommon for medieval artists to acquire multiple skills. At León in Spain, famous for its glass, the chapter records show that two named glass painters were at work on the windows in 1263, joined by a third the following year, who worked for fifteen years. In 1281 Juan Pérez, who succeeded Master Enrique as master mason, is recorded as being engaged in painting glass.[113]

The right-hand window echoes the left-hand window of the opposite transept in that it continues the theme of the apse Gospel cycle. That ended with Pentecost. This adds to the number of Resurrection scenes. Unlike its opposite window, but following the apse windows in this, it juxtaposes, with one exception, Old Testament and New Testament scenes; but departs from the apse layout, and from the norm, by reading from top to bottom, and by providing no correlation between the series of juxtaposed scenes.

The left lancet depicts a number of angelic visitations – thus picking up the theme of the Annunciation, near the beginning of the apse Gospel cycle.[114] They have been interpreted as follows: first, at the top, an angel announces to Sarah, aged ninety, that she will bear a son (Gen. 18. 2–16); then the angel Gabriel appears to Zacharias and foretells that his wife Elisabeth, though well stricken in years, will bear a son (Luke 1. 5–20); an angel appears to Gideon (Judges 6. 11–22); Tobias encounters the angel Raphael;[115] then an angel sent by God joins Shadrach, Mishach and Abed-nego in the burning fiery furnace (Dan. 3. esp. 25 & 28); and lastly, an angel sent by God shut the lions' mouths to protect Daniel in the lions' den (Dan. 6. esp. 21).[116]

The right lancet begins with the resurrected Christ's appearance to the two Marys, and ends with His appearance among the apostles. Both medallions are based on Byzantine models, and demonstrate the Master of St Francis' familiarity with and skill in integrating the *maniera greca* into his repertoire when he chose. In between are Christ appearing to St Peter – a simple dialogue scene – and three scenes detailing the Emmaus story (Luke 24. 13–35). For these, more complex, scenes, the Master of St Francis relied on models, models which Martin has convincingly shown came from the region of Pisa

---

[111] Marchini 1973, pp. 40, 43; Cook 1999, pp. 42–3 and pl. 19.

[112] See pp. 288–302; Marchini 1973, pp. 59–62; Martin 1996, p. 179.

[113] Swaan 1969, p. 272. In such cases the glass was installed as the building was erected.

[114] Marchini 1973, pp. 26–7, shows the Annunciation as VIIIb no. 2; Martin 1993 shows it as VIIIb no. 2 in the plan on p. 16, but as no. 3 in his own reconstruction on p. 40.

[115] In Tobit 5, esp. 4–5, Tobias does not realise that his companion is an angel, which is perhaps why Raphael is shown without wings. In the Genesis example the three men entertained by Abraham and Sarah are taken to be angels.

[116] Marchini 1973, pp. 60–1, and Martin 1996, pp. 179–80 (see also Martin and Ruf 1998, pp. 269–73), agree on the content, but the identification of some of these scenes, which rely on a simple dialogue composition and sparse details, seems to be based on little evidence – the iconography is so simplified.

Plate 35 Right transept window v (© www.Assisi.de. Photo Gerhard Ruf).

and its environs. The first two scenes, the meeting of Christ and the two disciples on the road to Emmaus, and their journeying on together, bear a remarkably close resemblance to a relief on a pulpit in San Bartolomeo in Pantano, in Pistoia. An inscription on the pulpit gives the date of 1250 and the name of the sculptor, Guido Bigarelli. The third scene, the Supper at Emmaus, very closely resembles the last in a series of eight Passion scenes on the apron of a painted wooden crucifix, probably of Tuscan provenance, attributed either to Coppo di Marcovaldo or to a Lucchese-Berlinghieriesque Master.[117] This scene, the Supper at Emmaus, the Master of St Francis had already depicted in fresco as the final scene in his Passion cycle in the Lower Church.[118]

Both lancets of the left-hand window are filled with geometric patterns in vivid colours.

The upper part of the right transept window is rich in meaning (Plate 36). In the central rose, within a hexagonal frame, Christ sits enthroned in a mandorla supported by two angels, his right hand raised in blessing, his left holding a book. The angels look down upon the apostles crowded into two circles attached to the lower sides of the hexagon. The four other circles contain an angel or archangel. The apostles are looking up at Christ in such wonder that the tops of their circles have opened up like lids – each furnished with a little triangular handle decorated with a rose. Adapting the design to fit into a stained glass rose window clearly presented difficulties. The opening lids, while allowing the apostles a better view, put pressure on the smaller central linking arc, directly under Christ's feet, containing the head and shoulders of the Virgin. Her expression suggests her astonishment at being so squeezed. The iconography of this scene again points to Pisa and its surrounding area as the source of the Master of St Francis' inspiration. Master Guglielmus' pulpit for Pisa cathedral, carved 1158–62 – replaced by Giovanni Pisano's pulpit in the early fourteenth century and now in Caglieri cathedral – displayed on its short side the same distinct components, a horizontal inscription separating the apostles with the Virgin in their midst from Christ in a mandorla supported by angels. At Lucca, c.1250–60, the same workshop that carved the reliefs on the pulpit at San Bartolomeo in Pantano, carved at the cathedral, on the tympanum above the doorway, Christ enthroned in a mandorla supported by two angels, and on the lintel below a row of standing apostles with the Virgin in the centre. Yet another example can be found in the façade mosaic on the church of San Frediano in Lucca, dated to the second half of the thirteenth century. Here again Christ is seated on a throne in a mandorla supported by two angels and is separated from the apostles ranged below by an ornamental band and an inscription.[119] The last words of this inscription, 'nube levatus', 'raised on a cloud' (cf. Acts 1. 9), make it clear that these portrayals – though their essentials hark back to representations of Pentecost, as for example on the mid-twelfth-century tympanum at Vézelay[120] – are of the Ascension.

---

[117] Martin 1996, pp. 180–3 and nn., with clear and ample illustrations. The crucifixion is no. 434 in the Uffizi in Florence.

[118] See p. 296. Martin has not noted this.

[119] Martin 1996, pp. 183–7, with notes and illustrations. He cites a further example of a possible Pisan model for this type of Ascension painted on a crucifix in San Pierino, Pisa, c.1255–60.

[120] Brooke and Swaan 1974, pl. 113. It is clear that Pentecost is represented, since Christ and the apostles are encircled by the peoples of the world.

Plate 36 Right transept window v, detail (© www.Assisi.de. Photo Gerhard Ruf).

But not just of the Ascension. Christ is not being transported up to heaven by the angels. He is already there, seated on his throne. It is a Christ in Majesty as well. And Christ in Majesty also imparts a warning: it resonates of Christ's Second Coming and the Day of Judgement. The outlying prophet medallions reinforce these messages. In that on the left (Christ's right), the text of King David's scroll reads: 'God is gone up with a shout, the Lord [with the sound of a trumpet]' (Psalm 46. 6 (47. 5)). In the opposite medallion Isaiah's scroll reads: 'Who is this that cometh from Edom with dyed [garments]?' The next verse makes clear that the dye is red, and in the centre of the rose window Christ is wearing a brilliant red mantle.[121]

[121] Isaiah 63. 1–2; Martin 1996, pp. 183–5.

Both transept windows pose problems, the left transept window in particular. Its content is much less richly charged. Why? The first puzzle is why the Virgin Mary receives so little honour in the sanctuary. The high altar is dedicated to her, but she is portayed only in small scale: where appropriate in the life cycle of Christ in the apse, in a confined space between the apostles in the north transept rose, and in the right lunette in the left transept. The central rose window in the left transept would have been an appropriate place to honour her, either with an Assumption of the Virgin – to balance the Ascension element in the north transept rose opposite, or with a Coronation of the Virgin – to balance the Christ in Majesty element.[122] But this rose window does not honour her, or anyone else, or send out any message other than to admire its beauty and craftsmanship: it is filled with geometric patterns.

The dating of the glass has depended hitherto on three kinds of evidence. First, on style, but while style can be helpful in determining sequences, it generally fails to establish firm or absolute dates. To take but one example from the Upper Church itself, scholars differ widely in their dating of the nave frescoes.

Allied to style is the related topic of working practices. Hueck, Martin and Belting all agree that the apse and transepts were glazed before the start of any painting in the Upper Church. Belting goes further – the nave windows were also finished before painting began.[123] But he gives no evidence at all in support of his argument. One can understand the practical advantages of segregation, preventing different groups of workmen from getting in each others' way and splashing paint all over each other, and the ensuing quarrels, which lends support to the hypothesis that those in charge wanted the transept glazing finished. Marchini has suggested that an original, more complicated programme was modified, and geometric designs inserted in the two lancets of the left-hand window of the right transept and the rose window of the left. But the lancets may have been part of the original design – such windows were very popular in northern Europe; and they are very beautiful, with glowing colours, and seem, as he points out, to derive from the Roman tradition of cosmati work and interest in the antique. I see no reason why the nave glazing could not have been proceeded with while the painters and decorators were let loose in the sanctuary. In any case, in practice, it would seem that the workshops frescoing the upper walls of the right transept must have worked at least partly at the same time as the glass painters, so if there was a theory, theory and practice diverged.[124]

Secondly, on the supposed views of a Minister General. Marchini might have preferred to date the windows of the left transept earlier, but he felt constrained by his understanding of St Bonaventure's policy to postpone their date until after his death in 1274. He believed that Bonaventure himself drafted the statutes relating to buildings and their decoration in the Constitutions of Narbonne, and that he would not have permitted breaches of them during his generalate.[125] However, these statutes are earlier;

[122] Marchini 1973, p. 38, suggests that an Assumption was probably intended; but on p. 40 that some of the friars may have wanted an Exaltation of St Francis.
[123] Hueck 1969, p. 131; Martin 1993, pp. 126, 133–4; Belting 1977, p. 184; Binski 2002, p. 104.
[124] Marchini 1973, pp. 59–75, esp. 72–5, 88; Binski 2002, p. 106.
[125] Marchini 1973, p. 58.

they were edited by Bonaventure, who added little that was new; and both building activity and decorative work took place at Assisi while St Bonaventure was General. At the Sacro Convento the friars' living quarters were enlarged and a new refectory built, and at the Basilica the fresco cycles on the nave walls of the Lower Church were under way.[126] We must conclude that Bonaventure accepted papal policy and concurred in it. If he had not, the authority of the Minister General and all other authorities of the Order in this area had been pre-empted into the hands of the pope and Cardinal Protector. The statutes could have been simply overridden. None the less, there is a good argument on stylistic grounds for postulating a hiatus between the glazing of the apse windows and the start of glazing of the transept windows. Why there was this gap we do not know, but it may be connected with the lack of local Italian glazing workshops. Time may have been needed to 'head hunt' the 'Frenchified' workshop that began with the left transept window; and the Master of St Francis needed to acquire his training in a new skill. He, we know, went on to work on an important commission in Perugia after he had finished his work in Assisi in the 1260s – his great crucifix in Perugia is dated 1272 – and he probably did not turn his attention to glass painting until after that date.[127]

Thirdly, on evidence of patronage. This has been used to date Cimabue's work on the crossing vault, where the Orsini arms and the buildings of Rome enforce a date during the pontificate of Nicholas III.[128] But evidence of patronage needs to be more extensively and systematically researched if we are to make any serious progress in precise dating of windows and frescoes.

The right-hand window in the left transept, its two lancets occupied by female saints, is a case in point. Martin finds no problem in integrating them into the overall scheme in the sanctuary: 'The introduction of the virgins . . . reiterates the typological design of the apse windows, symbolising the Heavenly Jerusalem.'[129] The design was the work of men, and I doubt whether thirteenth-century men would have envisaged the population of the Heavenly Jerusalem as best represented entirely by women. Marchini described their introduction as an 'inexplicable interruption'.[130] The window subject gives the impression of having been imposed by some remote and autocratic patron ready and powerful enough to interfere with the arrangements of what is otherwise a reasonably coherent programme. Throughout the years when the left transept window is likely to have been created there was continuity in the overseeing and implementation of the decorative programme provided by the Cardinal Protector. Gian Gaetano Orsini had been appointed to that office in 1263, and retained it up to and even beyond the time when he was elected pope in 1277. Between the years 1263 and 1277 the only individuals with undisputed authority to override his judgement were the popes, of whom there were six in these years – three of them extremely short lived. The 'odd one out' among the female saints is St Clare – the others are all martyrs (or were held to be).[131] If any one of these popes had a particular devotion to St Clare he would be a likely candidate for patron of this window. Alexander IV had canonised St Clare in 1255, but he died in 1261,

---

[126] See p. 310 and note 98, and pp. 286–8.   [127] See pp. 300–2.   [128] See pp. 346–50.
[129] Martin 1996, p. 179.   [130] Marchini 1973, p. 38.
[131] Nothing historical is known about St Barbara, St Catherine of Alexandria or St Margaret of Antioch, and almost nothing about St Cecilia (Farmer 1987, pp. 31, 77–8, 281–2, 79–80).

which is too early. Of the six popes of the period the most favoured candidate seems to be Clement IV.[132] One argument in favour of his involvement is that he was French, and this glass shows French influence. Another possibility is Innocent V. He was a Dominican theologian and a man of austere piety. He was a friend of St Bonaventure, and preached his funeral sermon at Lyon in 1274. His dates, 21 January to 22 June 1276, though very short, could fit quite nicely.[133] But this is simply speculation.

The right transept window probably dates to c.1275, the left transept window to about the same time. Both were finished before Cimabue started to paint in the sanctuary. The workshop responsible for the left transept window went on to do two in the nave, IV and III, while the Master of St Francis and his workshop went on to do the remaining six in the nave, I, II, X, XI, XII and XIII. Creating stained glass windows is a lengthy process, so the Master of St Francis probably did not complete his assignment until into the 1280s.[134]

The sanctuary windows would have been seen, and could have been reflected upon, by the friars resident in the Sacro Convento, and by those visiting it, several times every day, when they assembled to sing the Offices. The windows of the nave would have been viewed by the laity and other clergy. Their fundamental message was perfectly clear. They showed the twelve Apostles and St Francis and St Anthony. Here Francis and Anthony are not simply celebrated as thirteenth-century saints. They have both been promoted to the rank of apostle. This claim the Franciscans had been emboldened to make because of their understanding and appreciation of the prophecies of a revered Calabrian abbot and hermit, Joachim of Fiore, who died in 1202. Joachim taught that the history of the world should be divided into three ages, to correspond to the three persons of the Trinity. The period before the birth of Christ, recorded in the Old Testament, was the age of God the Father; the period since, that of the New Testament, the age of God the Son, had existed until now, but was about to be superseded by the third period, the age of the Holy Spirit. This third age would be heralded by the appearance of two new religious Orders, living in apostolic poverty. Joachim's writings came to the attention of the friars in the 1240s, and both the Franciscans and the Dominicans were tempted to identify their Orders with the two of Joachim's prophecy. Some Franciscans became very enthusiastic and eagerly sought out copies of Joachim's works; they included Hugh of Digne, Salimbene and the Minister General, John of Parma.[135] Unfortunately some got carried away. In 1254 Gerard of Borgo San Donnino, a lector in theology at the

---

[132] Poeschke 1985, p. 19; Lunghi 1996.
[133] Kelly 1986, pp. 198–9; Mas Latrie 1889, col. 1120; Potthast, II, 1704–8. He was elected at Arezzo on 21 January, was at Viterbo on 7 February, crowned in Rome on 22 February, and died at Rome on 22 June 1276. On stylistic grounds Martin in Martin and Ruf 1998, p. 82, dismisses everyone before the mid-1270s.
[134] Martin 1993, pp. 126–7, 133–4; Martin 1996, p. 177; Marchini 1973, pp. 21–88, esp. 23–4, 54; Martin and Ruf 1998, pp. 253–89. Frugoni 1993, pp. 209, 283–4, 293–6, states that the nave windows were in place by 1258–9, and that the Master of St Francis worked on them at about the same time as he was working on the fresco cycles in the Lower Church. This dating would require a continuous programme of glazing, with no gap in time between the apse and the transept glass, and even then it is not likely that such a major project could be devised and executed in such a short space of time as six years (1253–9).
[135] Salimbene, H, pp. 232–3, 236, 717 s.v. Ioachim; S, I, 334–40; cf. Moorman 1968, pp. 114–15; Reeves 1969, esp. pp. 45–58, 175–90.

Franciscan convent in Paris, produced a sensational book, *The Introduction to the Eternal Gospel* – a garbled, provocative and heretical travesty of Joachim's ideas. The book was formally condemned by Alexander IV in 1255. John of Parma's known Joachite views were now an embarrassment, and the pope advised him to resign, which he did, at a General Chapter held early, on 2 February 1257. However, Alexander IV was careful not to condemn Joachim's work, only the heresies of his misguided disciple.[136] Joachim's thought remained influential. In these nave windows the Joachite ancestry of the concept of St Francis and St Anthony as apostles, and as shining representatives of the new apostolic Order of Friars Minor which was ushering in a spiritual revival, is proudly presented, and must have been obvious to many.

St Anthony was Portuguese. Born *c*.1195 at Lisbon, he joined the Order of Augustinian canons at the age of fifteen, and studied theology at Lisbon and then at Coimbra. But when, in 1220, he heard of the martyrdom of five friars in Morocco, he sought leave to transfer to the Franciscans. He became a famous preacher. His sermons attracted such crowds that there was not enough room to hold them all in a church, and he preached in the market place. When he was preaching the shops shut, having no customers, and when it came to harvest time, he left off preaching and retired to the woods, so as to ensure that the harvest was gathered; when it was all safely in, he resumed his sermons. He died in 1231 and a great many miracles were recorded at his tomb. Gregory IX canonised him on 30 May 1232, the process being concluded even more quickly than it had been in the case of St Francis.[137]

St Anthony had been a man after St Francis' own heart. Francis wanted his friars to give up everything, not simply their worldly possessions, but their own personal will, and their learning if they possessed any. Celano records how Francis once said that the educated should forsake even their learning, so that, stripped of all their possessions they might offer themselves naked to the naked Christ. 'Learning robs many people of their gentle characters', he said, 'and does not allow them to bend their stiff necks to humble tasks . . . I would wish an educated man first to offer this prayer to me: "Brother . . . grant me a home far removed from the bustle of the world, in which I can recall my years passed in sorrow, recollecting the distractions of my heart, and reshape my soul to better ends." What kind of man . . . would you reckon he will become who made such a beginning? Surely he would set forth . . . strong as an unchained lion, and the blessed savour he had savoured at the start will grow in him with continual profit. He could be securely assigned to the true ministry of the word, for he would pour out what bubbles up within him.'[138] St Anthony had given just such an outstanding example of humility. After the General Chapter of 1221 he was assigned to a hermitage near Forli. The other friars there believed him a simple brother – though with a smattering of Latin – and he performed menial tasks. It was only a visit to Forli, where he was unexpectedly required to preach, that alerted them to his intellectual

---

[136] Reeves 1969, pp. 59–71; cf. Gratien 1928, p. 214; Brooke 1959, p. 270; and see pp. 252–4.
[137] Moorman 1968, p. 65–6, 93; Robson 1997, p. xxiii, ch. 7; Farmer 1987, pp. 23–4; Paciocco 1990, pp. 44–7; Gamboso 1981, p. 436.
[138] 2 Cel. 194.

stature and preaching abilities.[139] St Francis held theologians in honour, writing in his Testament: 'we ought to honour and revere all theologians and ministers of the divine word, as those who minister to us spirit and life.' And so he honoured St Anthony, addressing a letter to him, authorising him to teach theology to the friars, 'To brother Anthony my bishop'.[140]

St Anthony was the perfect role model for the new generation of friars – a priest and scholar, a preacher who could preach doctrine as well as repentance with outstanding success. The union of wisdom and holiness, of theology and the Gospel way of life, was an ideal that naturally exercised a strong attraction for learned men – men like Hugh of Digne, John of Parma, St Bonaventure himself.

The Constitutions of the Order permitted pictures of St Francis and St Anthony in churches. Both are portrayed, one to either side of Christ, in a quatrefoil lunette in the left transept, and a standing figure of St Anthony probably originally balanced the figure of St Francis on the other side of the Virgin in Cimabue's fresco of the Virgin and child in the Lower Church.[141] In the nave window the two saints are allotted a lancet each (Plate 37). St Anthony receives almost the same distinction as St Francis, though not quite. Above the standing figure of the saint are six scenes. The original first scene is lost and has been replaced by a modern figure.[142] The second is said to show him confronting or admonishing Ezzelino III da Romano, dressed in armour, holding his shield and brandishing his sword.[143] The family stronghold was at Bassano, near Vicenza. It was only after St Anthony's death that he became the ruler of a substantial territory with the help of the Emperor Frederick II, but he already held Verona. Within his territories – when it suited him, which was most of the time – proceedings against heretics were not tolerated, and Cathars could live and move freely. It is uncertain whether he was a Cathar himself, but his sister was posthumously condemned as a heretic and 'his passion for astrology, his interest in magic, his relations with Arabs are straws in the wind'. His father had tolerated heretics and died excommunicate. St Anthony went on a number of preaching tours directed against heretics both in the south of France and in northern Italy. On a visit to Verona he met Ezzelino. But did he confront him on the issue of heresy? Ezzelino was captured many years later, after an attack on Milan in 1259, and died of his wounds.[144] This scene is the only pictorial representation of him, and he could be taken as a notorious representative of powerful men who sheltered heretics. The only account of the incident is in Rolandino of Padua's Chronicle, which ends in 1262. 'Whether because the holy man had faith in God's help, or because he was moved and urged by the count of San Bonifacio's friends, he went to Verona and uttered

---

[139] Gamboso 1981, pp. 302 ff, cc. 6–8; cf. Smalley 1982.

[140] Esser 1976, p. 439 and p. 153 (cf. pp. 147–54); 2 *Cel.* 163.

[141] *Narb.*, III, 18 (p. 48); Cook 1999, p. 36 no. 12; and see Plate 34.

[142] Marchini 1973, pp. 67–8.

[143] Frugoni 1993, p. 294; Cook 1999, p. 43. In September 1231 Gregory IX sent two letters to Ezzelino ordering him not to continue to protect heretics or he would be considered one himself, and threatening him with excommunication if he did not comply (G. Saranzo, 'Sant'Antonio da Padova ed Ezzelino III da Romano', *Il Santo*, I, 2 (1961), 3–12, cited Frugoni 1993, p. 316, n. 152).

[144] During the brief ascendancy of the Dominican revivalist preacher John of Vicenza in 1233, Ezzelino allowed the enthusiasm of the Alleluia to run its course and acquiesced in an orgy of burning of heretics in the Roman amphitheatre, which lasted three days. Lambert 1998, pp. 129–30, 183–7 (the quotation is from p. 186); Robson 1997, pp. 170–2; Frugoni 1993, pp. 294–5.

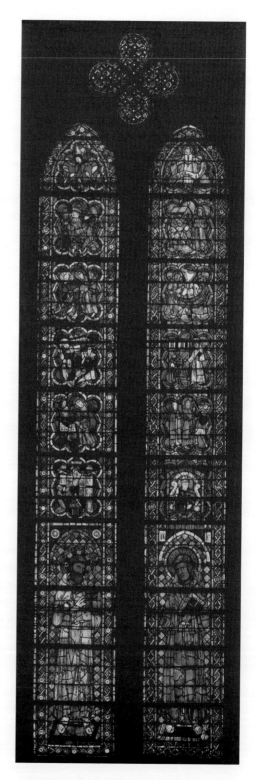

Plate 37 Nave window 1, St Francis and St
Anthony, with scenes from their lives above
(© www.Assisi.de. Photo Gerhard Ruf).

many, many prayers to the rectors of Lombardy, the podestà and the lord Ezzelino and his counsellors of Verona, to free from prison the count and his friends, whom they held captive in Lombardy. But prayers are without fruit even when just, where there is not the smallest shoot of charity.'[145] This links St Anthony, Ezzelino and prisoners, but the subject is related not to heresy but to politics; St Anthony did not confront or admonish Ezzelino – he came before him as a suppliant – and his efforts to secure the release of prisoners in Ezzelino's power were unsuccessful. Contemporaries no doubt comprehended the messages better than we can. It may be that they took the scene to indicate St Anthony's tender compassion for prisoners. It is generally held that one of the scenes shows St Anthony releasing prisoners.[146] The next two scenes are both miracle stories. The first looks more like St Anthony healing a cripple (also among the scenes listed by Frugoni and Cook), than rescuing a prisoner. In the second he is saving a ship in a storm. Among the miracle stories in the *First Life of St Anthony* there are a number recording him healing cripples and the sick; one of a rescue of a storm-tossed ship and its passengers; none relate to prisoners being released. The final scene – St Anthony preaching at a Provincial Chapter at Arles – occupies two lights. Its position has been deliberately chosen. In the lower, he preaches to the assembled friars in the open air; behind them is a little chapel. Above, in the top light, the complete standing figure of St Francis is shown frontally. It has been said that he appears with his arms open as if he were on the cross, but Plate 37 shows clearly that his arms are half raised in an informal act of blessing, and he holds a scroll which probably contained the words: 'Benedicat vos Dominus', 'May the Lord bless you.'[147] St Francis' arms are not raised to the horizontal or above, as in a crucifixion – compare his posture with that of the seraph in the adjacent lancet. But he is none the less exalted, though the theme of crucifixion is not stressed in this lancet. In his appearance at Arles he appears without the stigmata. But by placing him in the top light on St Anthony's side he is raised to the same level, and by implication, to a similar status, as the seraph. The Order is claiming a great deal for him, and the message is easy to read.

In the left lancet, devoted to Francis' life, the Master of St Francis was able to reproduce in glass three of the scenes he had already depicted in his nave frescoes in the Lower Church: the dream of Innocent III, Francis preaching to the birds, and Francis receiving the stigmata. He begins with a scene not previously portrayed: Francis kneeling before the crucifix in San Damiano, when the painted image of Christ spoke to him, an incident first recorded in 2 *Celano* 10. Next comes one of Francis' posthumous miracles, his healing of the lame beggar. This was clearly a very popular scene. It occurs in all the surviving early altar panels. It occurs, misplaced, in the Bardi altar panel.[148] It occurs, again clearly misplaced, here. It seems so out of context that it has been argued that it has been misidentified, and really represents St Francis curing a leper. But the exposed parts of the sufferer's body show no ulcers, and his leg is clearly being straightened by the saint. What is more, he is holding two crutches. A supporting argument, that the man is not shown walking away carrying his crutches after cure, and that there is

[145] Frugoni 1993, pp. 295–6, 316, nn. 152–3.
[146] Marchini 1973, p. 68; Frugoni 1993, p. 294; Cook 1999, p. 43.
[147] Frugoni 1993, p. 294; cf. Péano 1983.   [148] See pp. 172, 181–2 and Plates 15, 17 and Colour Plate 3.

no pool, shows a lack of appreciation of the different requirements and framework of glass painting. To make a clear visual impact a scene might be rendered in simplified form, and yet be identifiable. The same Master represented the scene of Shadrach, Mishach and Abed-nego in the fiery furnace in the left lancet of the right window in the right transept in just such a highly simplified form, ruthlessly omitting normal iconographic elements helpful for identification – even the flames and the furnace.[149] Pilgrims would have recognised the subject without difficulty – many would be familiar with the earlier version on the altar panel on display downstairs in the Lower Church. In this sequence this miracle symbolises Francis' fulfilment of the Christian's duty to love his neighbour as himself, to help the poor and care for the sick and afflicted.

Christ's words from the cross had been: 'Francis, go, repair my house, which as you see is entirely ruined.' These link the first scene naturally to the third: Innocent III's dream of Francis supporting the leaning Church on his shoulder. The Master of St Francis has drawn inspiration from his fresco – the figure of the pope is closely related (Plate 25). His are the first two representations of this scene, and in different media, but because of the confined space in the glass panel the Master has moved the Lateran to the centre so it is between Francis and Innocent.[150]

The two scenes above are the standard favourites: Francis preaching to the birds, with a variety of richly coloured birds, listening attentively; and the Stigmatisation (Plate 38), arranged on two levels, to balance the appearance at Arles in the St Anthony lancet. Technically, this is the earliest surviving portrayal in Italy of Francis showing the side wound in this scene, but it is virtually certain that the Master of St Francis will have included it in his fresco in the Lower Church, in which almost the whole of St Francis is now missing. His way of depicting the wound in the glass, with the hole in the tunic drawn in the shape of a little door, is identical to that he used in the scene of St Francis' death.[151] As in the Lower Church (Plate 24), the seraph's outstretched arms are outlined by his outstretched wings. The theme of the cross is emphasised in this lancet. Francis meditated on the Passion throughout his life, from his first crucial encounter with the crucified Christ at San Damiano till the imprint of the stigmata on his flesh on La Verna.

On the other side of the nave is the window which commanded Angela of Foligno's attention (Plate 39). The iconography of this window is absolutely exceptional. The two lancets correspond with each other in a symmetry which is not purely decorative. The tall figure of Christ, sumptuously dressed, stands on a ceremonial footstool. Directly in front of him, a smaller standing figure of St Francis seems suspended in mid-air, his feet not touching the floor. Christ's left hand is resting on Francis' shoulder, while his right hand supports Francis' elbow. Francis carries a cross, the book of life; and a book, the Gospel, the good news, which signifies that he is a preacher of the Gospel. He bears the stigmata in hands and feet, corresponding to Christ's wounds. His head is framed in a cruciform nimbus, as is Christ's; and the vertical through the crosses

---

[149] Cook 1999, pp. 44–7, no. 21; Martin 1996, pp. 179–80 and fig. 2.
[150] 2 Cel. 10; Marchini 1973, pp. 66, 72.
[151] See p. 296 and Plate 30. The side wound was included much earlier in this scene in French monstrance reliquaries, Colour Plate 1, and in Matthew Paris' drawing, Plate 22.

Plate 38 Nave window I, a9-10, Stigmatisation of St Francis (© www.Assisi.de. Photo Gerhard Ruf).

Plate 39 Nave window XIII, Christ and St
Francis, Virgin and child, with angels above
(© www.Assisi.de. Photo Gerhard Ruf).

of both haloes and the cross Francis holds visually underlines Francis' union with Christ in his sufferings. Beside Christ, and equally tall and resplendent, stands the Virgin Mary, depicted as *theotokos*, 'Mother of God', but many of the details of the traditional image have been modified with the evident purpose of achieving symmetry and correspondence. She is normally represented seated with the child on her lap, but here she too stands on a ceremonial footstool, and the child seems to float before her relatively unsupported. Her right hand rests on his shoulder in a gesture similar to Christ's, though reversed; her left hand supports his leg. The child's arms are similarly positioned to Francis'. Above Christ and Mary in each lancet are three standing angels, clothed in long robes and byzantine stoles, each carrying a mace and a globe marked with a cross.[152]

The image is dramatic, and may seem superficially a simple one. The window is clearly devoted to the glorification of St Francis. But its full significance and theological implications have been the subject of varying interpretations. In an important article, Poulenc has drawn attention to hitherto unnoticed links between the window and devotional works exploring mystical themes of union with God popular in the second half of the thirteenth century.[153]

In the window St Francis, though physically adult, appears as a child in the bosom of Christ, corresponding to the infant Christ, and calling to mind Christ's saying: 'Except ye be converted and become as little children, ye shall not enter into the kingdom of heaven' (Matt. 18. 3).[154] Christ then assumes the role of mother. Some biblical texts convey the tenderness of God towards his chosen people under the image of a mother who will not abandon her child and carries him lovingly in her arms (cf. Isaiah 49. 15; 66. 11–13). St Paul called the converts he had won for Christ his little children for whom he travailed in birth again (Gal. 4. 19). This type of spirituality spread during the twelfth century both in monasteries and among the faithful thanks to the wide diffusion of collections of the prayers of St Anselm. St Anselm invoked St Paul and the other apostles by the title of mother, and considered Christ, the source of eternal life, as pre-eminently our mother, for Christ has begotten us through his suffering and death, and, according to the Gospel, he gathers us as a mother hen under her wings (Matt. 23. 37; Luke 13. 34). In the middle of the thirteenth century the theme of Christ as mother was reinforced in the Postills on Isaiah of the great Dominican biblical commentator Hugh of St Cher.[155]

One devotional text in particular, James of Milan's *Stimulus amoris*, enjoyed a great success in the second half of the thirteenth century, and was broadly representative of Franciscan piety. Such treatises could make theological themes accessible to a wide audience, to the friars themselves, to the faithful and to artists. Its chapter on meditation on the Passion urged its readers to meditate constantly on the sufferings of the Saviour, and enumerated the spiritual benefits that would ensue. Some passages seem especially relevant to our understanding the iconography of the window: 'He whose thought dwells on Christ's torments does not consider himself, he only sees . . . his suffering

[152] Poulenc 1983, pp. 701–2.   [153] Poulenc 1983, pp. 701–13.
[154] P. Magro, *Assisi, storia, arte, spiritualità* (Assisi, n.d.), p. 77, cited Poulenc 1983, p. 704 and n. 3.
[155] Poulenc 1983, pp. 710–12 and references, esp. to Bynum 1982.

God; he wants to carry his cross with him . . . and the angels honour him and the Virgin Mary adopts him as her son. He wants to grieve with Christ, and he is in joy . . . he wants to hang on the cross with Christ, and Christ embraces him with a wonderful sweetness.' Again: '"It is good to be" with Him, and in Him. I wish "to make three tabernacles" [Matt. 17. 4], one in his hands, one in his feet and the third perpetually in his side. There I wish to rest and sleep, eat and drink, read and pray . . . In this manner let me follow in the footsteps of my most sweet mother whose soul was pierced by the sword of the Passion of her son . . . Not only will I appear crucified with her son. I will also return to the crib and lie there with him as a little child. And there with her son let me be worthy to drink the milk from her breast. Then I will mix the mother's milk with the son's blood and make for myself the sweetest of drinks . . . He who was formerly enclosed for sinners in a Virgin's womb, deigns today to carry me, miserable me, in his entrails . . . If he gives me birth he will have like a mother to nourish me on his breasts . . . and enfold me in his embraces . . . His wounds are always open; I will always return into his breast until the time I become inseparably enfolded in him.' And again: 'O how blind are the children of Adam! . . . Are you not aware that Christ is the joy of the blessed? . . . The beatitude of the angels is before you, the wall set about him is broken open, and you neglect to enter . . . O soul created in the image of God, how can you still hold back? . . . Your most sweet spouse, wounded for you, now in glory, desires to embrace you . . . and you neglect to hasten to him. It is because of his unbounded love that he has opened his side in order to give you his heart. Moreover he has wanted his hands and feet pierced . . . so that your hands may penetrate his hands and your feet his feet, and that your union may be inseparable. I beg you then . . . strive to prove this . . . and do not depart from there any more; I doubt not if you put this to trial that you will reckon as bitterness all else beside Him.'[156] The bright angels in the upper part of the window symbolise Francis' ascent to the realm of the angels, and the homage the angels now pay him. Francis in Christ's arms, with its affectionate gesture of Christ's hand on his shoulder, represents his soul's embrace by the divine spouse. The parallelism of his positioning with that of the infant Jesus evokes the maternal love in which the Redeemer enfolds him.

Poulenc concluded that the extent of correspondence between images and text could not be coincidence. The devisers of the programme for the window must have been influenced in their choice of iconography by the popularity of the type of devotion encouraged by such texts. He felt justified in claiming that passages such as those selected from the *Stimulus amoris* provided the theological foundation on which the artist was instructed to base his representation of St Francis in glory.

The theme which dominates the composition, then, is the greatness of the grace given to Francis. On one side, Mary and the child portray the divine condescension which stooped to take on our human nature to save us from sin; on the other, Francis in Christ's bosom exalts the tenderness of him who raised human nature to its highest degree of union with him through the mystery of the cross. Viewed through the mysteries of the

---

[156] James of Milan 1905, pp. 67–76, esp. pp. 70–5, quoted (from reprint of 1949) in Poulenc 1983, pp. 705–7.

incarnation and the Passion, Francis' glory does not appear as the excessive exaltation of an individual, nor as the triumphant affirmation of his conformity to Christ. It presents itself rather as an invitation addressed to everybody to welcome eagerly the Lord's gifts. To souls who, like Francis, know how to let themselves be moved and guided by meditation on the mystery of the double abasement of the Saviour in his nativity and on the cross, Christ accords the grace to live in him and to be born to eternal life. He will lavish on them the caresses both of a mother and of a spouse.[157]

Angela of Foligno immediately understood the message as an invitation. Christ promised to embrace her as tenderly as he did St Francis and held out the prospect of even more exquisite delights. Her response, and the witness of her own spiritual growth and teachings, provide powerful backing for the view that Poulenc's reading of the window's iconography is valid and in tune with contemporary attitudes of mind. They also provide new insights on the Order's spiritual and pastoral concerns and policies, especially with regard to their representation of their founder.[158]

Also a salutary corrective: it is gratuitous to suggest, as Belting does, that Angela, with six years' education already in Franciscan spirituality, was deceived, and misread the message.[159]

Yet images are susceptible to a range of interpretations which are not necessarily mutually exclusive. The iconography of the window may legitimately be explained in more than one way. The correspondences – the vertical line through the haloes and cross, Francis' stigmata and Christ's wounds – have been taken to be the result of a deliberate policy on the part of the Order to exalt the conformity of St Francis to Christ. As the Virgin presents her infant son to the veneration of the faithful, so does Christ present St Francis as His son, made in his image, marked with his wounds. Poulenc dismisses this interpretation as unsubstantiated hypothesis.[160] But it too is based on valid contemporary evidence and attitudes. Once he was dead, the overwhelming importance of Francis' stigmata was publicly proclaimed with reiterated emphasis throughout the thirteenth century.

This conspicuous visual image in the Upper Church will have been seen by countless pilgrims, local people, and visiting friars and officials. Startlingly comprehensible – as Angela bears witness – it can be 'read' in varying degree according to the capacity of the individual, and taken in more easily than a book. It was an ideal medium for conveying messages to a wide and varied audience.

But though this type of visual image was a most efficient and cost effective vehicle for disseminating the Order's propaganda on Francis' unique position among the saints (though the initial capital outlay was expensive), the visual image was not the only, or the earliest, means employed. Both oral and written strategies were used. Thomas of Eccleston records how one of the leading friars of the English province, brother Augustine, gave an account to the community in London of a sermon preached on the

---

[157] Poulenc 1983, pp. 707–8.
[158] Cf. pp. 305–7, 472–88; Poulenc 1983, pp. 712–13.   [159] Belting 1977, p. 47.
[160] Cristofani 1912, pp. 25–7; Kleinschmidt 1915–28, 1, 208–11; Marchini 1973, p. 84; Belting 1977, p. 47; Poulenc 1983, pp. 702–4.

feast of St Francis by Pope Gregory IX in Assisi, probably in 1235.[161] 'The pope described in that sermon how two leading heretics had been converted at Venice, and were sent to him with letters from the cardinals who were legates there, containing an account of how both the heretics on the same night at the same hour saw [in a dream] Our Lord Jesus Christ in the form of a judge, seated with his apostles and all the Orders which are in the world; but they nowhere saw the Friars Minor, nor St Francis, whom one of the legates had said in his preaching was superior to St John the Evangelist because he had received the stigmata.[162] But they saw the Lord Jesus himself reclining on the bosom of John, and he likewise on His [John 13. 23, 25]. When they reckoned for sure that this was shown them to confirm their own opinion – for they thought that the legate had spoken blasphemy and were gravely scandalised by what he had said and spoke ill of his preaching – lo! gentle Jesus opened the wound in his side with his hands, and St Francis appeared within his breast most clearly; and gentle Jesus closed his wound and shut him wholly within. And so the heretics, when they awoke and met each other next day, and each described to the other his vision, made public confession to the cardinals, and were sent (as has been said) to the pope and by him fully reconciled.'

The pope's sermon was preached to a large audience, which will have included a great many friars. They in their turn will have reported it back to the houses in the provinces from which they came – as brother Augustine reported it in London – and the friars in these audiences could have passed the information on to friars in other houses. And all of these friars qualified to preach could have used it in sermons to the faithful. So the pope's sermon could have been very widely disseminated orally, though we cannot quantify its impact. Certainly the pope gave the story all the publicity he could. It has come down to us in only one written record – Eccleston's chronicle, which circulated only in the English province[163] – but it may have been written down in other regions and the record not survived.

The impetus to exalt St Francis, to claim that he was uniquely close to Christ and beloved by him, because he genuinely bore the marks of Christ's wounds, was essentially created by his friend and admirer Cardinal Hugolino, when he became Pope Gregory IX.[164]

THE DECORATION OF APSE AND TRANSEPTS

The north transept

The fresco decoration of the Upper Church began in the north transept. Here an artist known as the 'Northern Master', together with groups of associates, painted the vault and the upper regions of the three walls as far down as the dog-tooth string-course

---

[161] Eccleston, pp. 89–90 and nn. See p. 62.
[162] This will have been Rainaldo, the pope's nephew, cardinal bishop of Ostia and Cardinal Protector of the Order, who was one of the two legates assigned to the Veneto at that time.
[163] Eccleston, p. 90; and for the surviving MSS, ibid., pp. xi–xx.
[164] Bonav., *Miracula*, i, 2; cf. pp. 36–9, 166–8.

beneath the wall passage and triforium.[165] The windows on the north wall had already been glazed, and their content was taken into account when the fresco decoration was designed. In the central rose Christ sits enthroned in a mandorla, and the apostles crowded below the frame look up at him in wonder.[166] This window is made, as it were, the central panel of a triptych. To its right, in a lunette on the east wall, nearest the nave, is painted a large image of the Transfiguration; to its left, on the west wall, nearest the apse, a balancing image of Christ in Majesty. On both sides, the back wall of the triforium passageway is painted with the figures of six apostles, who face each other through the arcades (Plate 40).

The transfigured Christ stands in a mandorla high up at the apex of the wall rib. Below are the two Old Testament figures seen with him by the apostles Peter, James and John: Moses kneels on Christ's right, Elijah on his left. Today we can see only a shadow of what was originally there: the brilliance of the colours is gone and the oxidisation of the lead white has reversed Christ's shining white robes, so that they show black as in a negative. The head of God the Father, his face showing, appears, surrounded by cloud, on Christ's right, the index finger of his right hand pointing across the mandorla to his Son. The inclusion of the Father in this scene is most unusual in Italian or Byzantine art, but there is an example in a nearly contemporary thirteenth-century mural in Gurk Cathedral in Carinthia, in Austria. There, a Transfiguration on the west wall of the west gallery includes a bust of God holding a scroll inscribed *filius dilectus*. It is not itself the model for Assisi as the bust of God is placed above the Son and is separated from Him by an oculus, but artistic influences could well have come from that region via the Veneto, possibly from Venice itself, where representations of the Transfiguration were unusually common. Binski suggests that the Father's explicit presence here in the Basilica witnesses to the importance of the devotion to the Trinity in Franciscan spirituality, citing St Bonaventure's interpretation of the Transfiguration as a revelation of the mystery of the Trinity, and its glory a prefiguration of the Resurrection.[167] Here, however, as at Gurk, the presence of God the Father is primarily due to the painter's effort to render the Gospel account faithfully: 'a voice came out of the cloud, saying, This is my beloved Son: hear him' (Mark 9. 7; also Matt. 17. 5). The different, and eccentric, placement of the figures in the transept can be attibuted to the exigencies of the pictorial space.

The Christ in Majesty at the apex of the wall rib opposite is much damaged; only some details are legible. Christ sits on a throne surmounted by a Gothic tabernacle, and flanked by the symbols of the Evangelists. This iconography is unusual. The combination of a tabernacle with a Majesty carries distinct apocalyptic overtones. 'Behold, the tabernacle of God is with men' (Rev. 21. 3). The presence of the beasts that St Jerome assigned to the Evangelists as their symbols also originated in St John's vision (Rev. 4. 2, 6–8).

[165] This section is closely based on Dr Paul Binski's British Academy lecture, 'How northern was the Northern Master at Assisi?' (Binski 2002), delivered on 29 March 2001. I am most grateful to him for allowing me to study this prior to publication.

[166] See pp. 317–18, and Plates 35, 36.

[167] Bonaventure, *Lignum Vitae*, in *Opera Omnia*, VIII, 73–4; Binski 2002, p. 87; cf. also Belting 1977, pp. 52–3.

Plate 40 Upper Church: general view of the north transept. (Photo Istituto Germanico di Storia dell'Arte, Florence.)

The imagery of the three walls overlaps and coalesces to convey a powerful message fraught with meaning. As was explained earlier, when discussing the significance of the stained glass windows, the glass on the north wall of the north transept refers to Pentecost, and represents the Ascension, but not just the Ascension. Christ is not being transported up to heaven, he is already there, seated on his throne. It is a Christ in Majesty as well. It also warns of the Second Coming and the Day of Judgement, messages reinforced by the outlying prophet medallions. The right lancet below portrays appearances of the Risen Lord.[168] The theme of Christ's dominion is reinforced in the treatment of the Transfiguration on the right. There, somewhat exceptionally, but not surprising in this context, Christ holds in his left hand a globe of T-O form, a globe, that is, which is divided by a Tau cross into three segments of different colours, to signify Europe, Africa and Asia.[169] Christ will also have held either a globe or a book in the Majesty, but the paint has gone. In this scene Christ enthroned in heaven, under a tabernacle highlighting the Second Coming and the Day of Judgement, symbolises the fulfilment of the Transfiguration, itself the sign that the Kingdom of God will come with power (Mark 9. 1), achieved by means of the Resurrection and Ascension, in the central window image.

Indeed, the theme of Christ's dominion permeates the entire transept, as Binski has demonstrated.[170] The blue vault, conventionally stencilled with gilt stars, like the vault of the papal oratory in the Sancta Sanctorum in the Vatican restored by Nicholas III in the late 1270s, has a series of eight bearded crowned heads painted in the lower corners of the webs (Plate 41). Cimabue was to paint Atlases at the corresponding points on the crossing vault. What do these striking masks signify? They are too few and too dispersed to represent the twenty-four Elders of the Apocalypse. Binski has suggested they might 'signify those earthly dominions over which Christ is to hold sway. In his exposition of the eternity of Christ's kingdom, the twelfth fruit of the *Tree of Life*, St Bonaventure says that "He indeed is king who has on his garment and on his thigh a name written King of kings and Lord of lords [cf. Rev. 19. 16] . . . whose kingdom will not be destroyed and whom all tribes and peoples and tongues will serve [cf. Daniel 7. 14] throughout eternity." Thus Christ is the prince of the kings of the Earth (Rev. 1.5). The role of these royal [quasi-]corbel heads in supporting Francis's and Christ's church makes expository sense as a corollary of Christ's dominion, the natural end of the evangelical, and Franciscan, mission. Christ transfigured holds up the World, and the Evangelists accompany His Majesty opposite; the Apostles stand in the triforium beneath. On the adjacent great crossing vault the Evangelists reappear in Cimabue's work at the corners of the Earth addressing their Gospels to Judea, Italy, Greece and Asia; and Cimabue finished the lower walls of the right transept with the Acts of the Apostles. The fundamental continuity with Cimabue's work needs therefore to be

---

[168] See pp. 315–18.

[169] Other representations of the Tau cross beloved by St Francis in the Basilica include one in a full-page miniature of the Christ of the Apocalypse in a Missal possibly given by St Louis, of 1255–6, *Assisi* 1999, pp. 136–7, pl. 35, and another in a Christ in Majesty on the rear face of a late thirteenth- or early fourteenth-century reliquary, also the gift of a member of the French royal family, ibid. pp. 160–2 and pl. 46; see Binski 2002, p. 90 and n. 41.

[170] Binski 2002, pp. 89–95; *Assisi* 1999, pp. 137, 163.

Plate 41 A head on an eastern corner of the vault in the north transept. The face, large, with prominent staring eyes, big protruding ears and abundant corn-yellow flowing beard, which tapers into the lower corner of the web, is Gothic in style, though wearing a cylindrical, Italian or Byzantine-style crown. See Colour Plate 5. (Photo Istituto Germanico di Storia dell'Arte, Florence.)

stressed. These apparently marginal heads contribute meaningfully to what stands as one of the most powerful assertions in medieval art of the spread of Christ's mission to the ends of the Earth since the great Romanesque portal of the narthex at Vézelay.'[171]

The Upper Church itself was an early example of Gothic style in Italy, and in the decades from the 1250s to the 1280s it pioneered the use of stained glass in its windows, until then a predominantly northern medium. Continuing this tradition, the first programme of frescoes was unlike anything to be found in central Italy at that time, and its relatively marginalised position on the upper walls of the darker of the two transepts served to increase the impression of its Gothic origins. Close study of the walls made possible by the major restoration work of 1979, and more recently by the restoration

[171] Binski 2002, pp. 92, 95, quoting Bonaventure from Cousins 1978, p. 169; Bonaventure, *Opera Omnia*, VIII, 84.

made necessary by the earthquake in 1997, has revealed that the situation is complex, that the frescoes are surprisingly heterogeneous, suggesting that the work was carried out by artists of different national origins or of different training. Stylistic criteria suggest that, in general, one team of painters, allied to artists who worked on the portico of Old St Peter's in Rome, produced the figures of the apostles, the gables and the angel roundels of the east triforium; and the painter who collaborated on the north wall was also Italian, possibly Roman. The 'Northern Master' was responsible for the two lunettes and two of the vault masks, and a related team did the apostles and roundels of the west arcade.[172] But there seems to have been a surprising amount of collaboration. There is a mixture of styles, and also a mixture of techniques, which weave and criss-cross over the walls and galleries. Incised drawing has been found in the Transfiguration, especially in the figure of Moses – a method of preliminary treatment practised in both Italian and Greek painting. Haloes with gilded relief radiating patterns, associated with Italo-Byzantine decorative methods, were consistently used in these 'Gothic' murals. Variations in the delicacy and number of striations show that the painters who set the haloes of the Transfiguration also set those of the apostles in the west gallery opposite, but not those of the apostles below the Transfiguration, which are the work of a finer hand. All the painters unfortunately used lead white, and not chalk white, grounds, which have caused a blackening and reversal of tones. Cimabue also used lead white, which suggests that there was an important element of technical continuity between this workshop and its successor. Oil paint was also used. Traces of oil have been found on primed plaster. The technique of painting with oil is typical of important Gothic painting in northern Europe but was unusual in thirteenth-century central Italian painting. Its presence in Assisi, therefore, is evidence that some of the artists had trained in the north.[173]

Some of the paintwork is out of key with the preliminary drawing. The apostle galleries and angel roundels are the most complicated areas, 'not least because it is here that much of the underdrawing of the figures has been exposed by the decay of pigment applied *secco*. Though poorly preserved, the apostles in the east gallery are generally agreed to have been Romanizing in style. The figures, broad and classical in stature . . . were set on a single pale blue ground [Plate 42]. The drawing of the faces of the angels in the roundels above them agrees with them in style, with pretty, finely drawn features, hair arranged in proto-Cimabuesque curls with a hair-band, and the same delicately-wrought haloes [Plate 43]. The west gallery figures are . . . better preserved and strikingly different . . . They are set on a red-blue counterchanged ground studded with large gilded five-petalled rosettes . . . The haloes more closely resemble those in the Transfiguration. The drawing of the angels also differs from those opposite . . . The features of one of the angels, the first from the left, are amongst the most Gothic of any in the transept, with large feline eyes . . . The west gallery apostles

---

[172] Binski 2002, pp. 74–7 and nn. 4, 9–11, 96–104; Hueck 1969, pp. 115–44; Belting 1977, pp. 91, 112–18, 192–3, 195–6; White 1984, pp. 127, 135–6, 144–5. See now also Bonsanti 2002a, II, pp. 1036–41, pls. 2045–61; pp. 1048–9, pls. 1068–73; IV, pp. 592–601.

[173] The technique of oil painting is described in the twelfth-century treatise on *The Various Arts* (i. 25) by a German Benedictine monk using the pseudonym Theophilus, who is probably to be identified with Roger of Helmarshausen (Dodwell 1961, p. 24).

Plate 42 North transept, east wall arcade: the fifth apostle from the left, next to St Peter
(Photo Istituto Germanico di Storia dell'Arte, Florence).

are especially problematic. Again the paintwork is out of key with the preliminary
drawing . . . The apostle on the far right has two left ears clearly indicating reworking
if not total repainting, and several of the apostles, including Paul, have facial features
which do not quite fit the profile of the head.' Unlike the east gallery apostles, who
appear to have their feet placed firmly and classically on the ground, those on the west
'have a Gothic hovering tiptoe stance'[174] (Plate 44).

A mixture of Gothic and Italian treatment is apparent too in the painted architecture surrounding these figures. Extremely steep gables were painted above the trefoil-
headed arches of the triforia. The faces of those on the west wall contain alternating
trefoils and quatrefoils ornamented with bar tracery inscribed in circlets, with pointed
trefoils in the spandrels (Plate 45). On the east wall, all six gables contain a trefoil, but
their faces are painted as if they were of marble, with trefoils set into them; and the

[174] Binski 2002, pp. 101–2; cf. Belting 1977, pp. 197–8.

Plate 43 North transept, east wall arcade: second angel roundel from the left
(Photo Istituto Germanico di Storia dell'Arte, Florence).

spandrels have simulated triangles of cosmatesque inlay (Plate 46). To each side of the
fictive Gothic gables slim pinnacles rise on points – architecturally implausible but very
decorative – from the centres of the real carved and painted French-style crocket capitals. Their vertical stress is stylistically appropriate to the gables, but these obliquely set
pinnacles look rather like Italian campaniles. Binski concludes that Gothic-influenced
designers probably provided a basic gable model with lateral pinnacles at the preliminary drawing stage, perhaps for use as a repeat pattern. Those on the west wall were
finished by artists connected with the Northern Master, those on the east wall by a
Roman group.[175]

Some such assortment of painters – some conversant with the Gothic idiom, some
not – could explain the idiosyncrasies that have been noted. That the overall design
was conceived by a master familiar with Gothic was argued in detail by Belting.[176]

[175] For this and what follows see Binski 2002, pp. 125–9.   [176] Belting 1977, pp. 112–18, 183–9.

Plate 44 North transept, west wall arcade: first apostle from the left, St Paul
(Photo Istituto Germanico di Storia dell'Arte, Florence).

The extension of the north transept window tracery on to the adjacent wall surfaces
has a large standing figure on each side framed in a pointed arch with fictive window
tracery above; and figurative schemes framed by pointed lunettes, with affinities both
to tympanum sculpture and to stained glass windows, on both walls: these are Gothic
architectural motifs. The Gothic tabernacle over the Majesty is decorated with true
Rayonnant pinnacles – though an Italianate townscape background has been somewhat awkwardly juxtaposed. The concept, and much of the execution, can be attributed
to a Northern Master. But what region of northern Europe did he come from? Architectural sources have been perceived over a wide range, in France – in the Ile-de-France,
Champagne and Burgundy – and in England.[177] However, the fictive gables above
the triforium on the west wall may prove significantly helpful in indicating a further

[177] Binski 2002, esp. pp. 129–34; Volpe 1969, pp. 22–4; Marchini 1973, pp. 50–8; Belting 1977, pp. 184–9,
194, 198–202; Romano 1982, p. 112; Romano 1984, pp. 72–5; White 1987, p. 181; Martin 1993,
pp. 128–30.

Plate 45 North transept, west wall arcade (Photo Istituto Germanico di Storia dell'Arte, Florence).

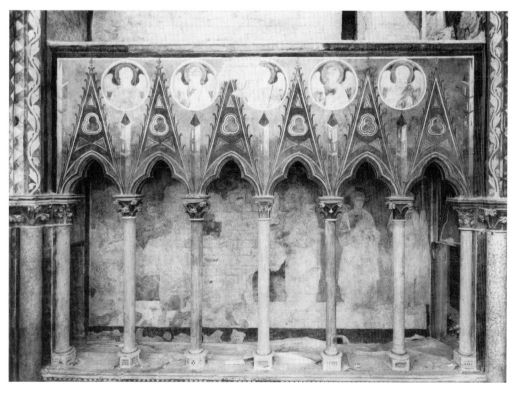

Plate 46 North transept, east wall arcade (Photo Istituto Germanico di Storia dell'Arte, Florence).

possibility. Binski has reminded us that 'painter's architecture' could follow closely on the heels of innovation in built architecture.[178] He draws attention to the relevance, for comparative purposes, of stained glass production in the upper Rhineland, in the area between Colmar and Worms, and he finds an exact counterpart in the clerestory glazing in the nave of Strasbourg cathedral. The nave was begun in the 1240s and was still under construction in the 1260s. 'The extraordinarily ambitious canopies developed in the nave clerestory at some point between the 1260s and about 1275 include the earliest instances of the inscribed alternating quatrefoils and trefoils, and pointed trefoil spandrels [illustrated in the painted gables on the west transept wall] at Assisi. Exactly these motifs characterise the drawings prepared probably around 1277 or slightly later for the west façade of the cathedral, notably the interior triforium of the tower bays . . . which are to all intents and purposes identical to the Assisi instances, not least in being both steep and linked by intervening turned pinnacles, and having exactly the same configuration of tracery on the gable faces . . . The windows and architecture are marked throughout by the same dry spare detailing as at Assisi . . . Strasbourg's nave triforium glazing, very heavily restored as it is, nevertheless also offers a suggestive Gothic parallel for the combination at Assisi of standing figures under arcades with roundels above containing bust-length figures of angels with unusual radiating haloes.'[179] Binski therefore favours a date c.1280 for the decoration of the right transept. 'Even at a date of c.1280 the Assisi work is tellingly up-to-date.'[180] A date in the late 1270s, up to c.1280, would seem to me consonant with the progress of the glazing and decoration of the Upper Church as I understand it.[181]

Some features of the fresco decoration of the north transept were crucially influential in determining the basic structure of the entire decorative programme of the Upper Church. Its star-spangled blue vault was repeated alternately with vaults having figurative representations in each of their four fields. And the integration of architecture and painting begun here was continued and developed throughout.[182] The implementation of a policy decision not to be content with stained glass windows, but to maximise the use of colour with wall painting, was inaugurated here.

CIMABUE

Cimabue was a Florentine artist. We know very little about him, other than that he was the most famous Italian painter of the generation before Giotto. The story goes that as a boy he was fascinated by Greek painters working at the Dominican convent of Santa Maria Novella, and watched them instead of attending to his grammar.[183] We know that he was in Rome in 1272, as he appears as a witness – *Cimabove*

---

[178] Binski 2002, p. 125.   [179] Binski 2002, pp. 134–6 and figs. 24, 30.   [180] Binski 2002, p. 136.
[181] Suggested dating has ranged from Cadei 1983 (1250s), through Poeschke 1985, pp. 19–23, Pace 1983, Romano 1984 (1260s – though Prof. Romano has recently revised her dating of the Northern Master to nearer 1280), and Hueck 1969 (1270–5), to Martin 1993, p. 125 (1275–80), Belting 1977, p. 193 (1277–80) and Bonsanti 2002a (see note 172) (1275–80): see Binski 2002, pp. 77–8 and n. 14, 136.
[182] Cf. Belting 1977, pp. 112–18, 183–9.
[183] Dante, *Purgatorio*, xi, 94–6; Meersseman 1946, pp. 180–1 (from Vasari).

pictore de Florencia – in a document dated 8 June 1272, which is preserved in the archives of Santa Maria Maggiore.[184] He was in Pisa 1301–2. His only documented work is the figure of St John the Evangelist executed in mosaic in the apse of Pisa Cathedral in the last months of his life.[185]

Cimabue was a great artist, who was prepared to study the works of other artists and to learn from a wide range of expertise, in mosaic and marble as well as paint; who took a pride in his craft; and who continued to develop and refine his skills throughout his life. His contribution to the decoration of the Basilica began in the north transept of the Lower Church, where his tender image of the Virgin and child with angels, attended by St Francis, survives.[186] He was then transferred to the sanctuary of the Upper Church, where initially, it seems, he and his workshop worked alongside the painters who were decorating the upper walls of the north transept.

The actual working practices underlying the fresco decoration have been revealed to us thanks to the meticulous and painstaking studies of White and Zanardi.[187] Their analysis has been further refined as a result of the reconstruction work necessitated by the 1997 earthquake. The process can be followed right from the start through the staging of the scaffolding. The first scaffolding was confined to the north transept. Before this was dismantled, however, further scaffolding, fixed at slightly different levels, was erected in the apse.[188] The scaffolding for the crossing and south transept was erected in one operation, and as its levels coincide with those in the apse, it is quite likely that the whole of this large area was under scaffolding at the same time.[189]

A wall surface is prepared for fresco painting first by covering it with a layer of plaster – the *arricio* – on which guide-lines and preparatory drawings can be marked out, and then adding a thin layer of plaster over the area to be worked next. As the programme of decoration progressed at Assisi the process was refined, and it became the practice to apply the pigments on to fresh, damp plaster, which meant only applying the final thin layer of plaster over an area that could be painted in one session. This technique is known as *buon fresco*, and the individual plaster section as the *giornata*, the day's work. The division of fresco into a number of *giornate* was first used at Assisi in the nave. Cimabue was still employing the less advanced technique. He covered larger areas at a time with the final layer of plaster, and applied the pigments, mixed with glue to bond them to the surface, *a secco*, on to a wall which was already dry.[190] The sequence of the work-stages can be traced because of the slight overlapping which takes place every time a succeeding section of plaster is laid on. With Cimabue, a close examination by hand and eye is needed, because of the very high level of craftsmanship he required from his workshop. Great care was taken to smooth the joins within the pictorial fields, even in the crossing vaults which are some 18.5 m (62 ft), above the floor.

---

[184] Bellosi 1998, pp. 66, 91 n. 1, 290.   [185] Bellosi 1998, pp. 9, 256–7, 291–2, and plate, p. 8.
[186] See pp. 302–4, Plate 32 and Frontispiece.   [187] White 1984, chs. V, VI.
[188] Romano, forthcoming; Binski 2002, pp. 74–5 and n. 4, 77.
[189] White 1984, chs. V, pp. 116–17, VI, p. 145.   [190] Lunghi 1996, p. 58.

The Northern Master initiated the decoration of the apse, making a start at the top level, only to be replaced by Cimabue. He began by completing its upper walls, as far down as the arcading and passageway, with figures of angels, prophets and saints, and scenes from the life of the Virgin, and giving the vaults of the south transept a blue star-spangled sky and decorated ribs to correspond to those already in the north transept and apse. He then tackled the crossing vaults.

The four Evangelists

'The Rule and life of the Friars Minor is this, to observe the holy Gospel of our Lord Jesus Christ.' So begins St Francis' Rule as confirmed by the pope, and it ends on the same note.[191] So, centrally, and directly above the high altar, are painted the Evangelists, engaged in writing the Gospels to be sent to the four corners of the earth. They sit on thrones against a background not of blue starry sky but of pure, shining gold: they are in glory[192] (Plate 47).

The scaffolding contained platforms at four levels and, on each, trestles would have been stood on the main planking to enable the topmost areas to be covered. It must have been a highly dangerous assignment. The most important work was all tackled from the highest platform. In each of the four webs the field containing the Evangelist was done first. This was then framed with broad putti-inhabited acanthus borders, and the ribs were decorated last. This whole area is relatively horizontal, but since the ribs support the vault their surfaces are lower than those of the webs, and by working downwards the risks of splashes of plaster or paint falling on to finished parts was minimised. The downward progression was then transferred to the next platform, while the bottom two covered the almost vertical run down to the main piers.[193]

The curved triangular webs were awkward and challenging. White and Zanardi's studies have enabled us to study Cimabue's learning curve.[194] The sequences of the plastering indicate that the St John was painted first, followed by St Luke, then St Matthew, and lastly St Mark. Evidence of progress in overcoming compositional problems point to the same conclusion. All four succeed in projecting a powerful image. All share the same basic pattern – an imposing seated figure faces a walled city representing the part of the world he evangelised. An angel flying down from heaven lays a hand on the head of each, directly imparting divine inspiration. Their attributes, the four winged beasts of Revelation 4. 6–8 – St John's eagle, St Luke's bull-calf, St Matthew's man, St Mark's lion – are at their feet. The carved wooden chair thrones of Byzantine type are all painted in the foreshortened frontal setting with the side on the left receding, like the Virgin's throne in the Lower Church.[195] In order to fit the field St John's reading desk and lectern have been positioned behind him, though he

---

[191] Esser 1976, pp. 366, 371.
[192] The high altar was originally in the centre of the crossing. Most of the gold leaf has flaked off.
[193] White 1984, ch. V, pp. 112–17 and fig. 1. There are splendid colour plates in Bellosi 1998, pp. 172–6.
[194] White 1984, ch. VI, pp. 136–43; cf. ch. V, pp. 112–15.   [195] See p. 302, and Plate 32.

Plate 47 Cimabue: Upper Church, crossing vault: the Evangelists. The vault is shown with the apse, at the west end, at the top. St Luke is in the web next the apse; opposite him is St Matthew at the entrance of the nave. In the north web (the viewer's left) is St John, in the south, St Mark. It appears back to front because one is looking upwards. The decorative scheme framing the webs, with its ribbons of painted mosaic cosmati work, flanked by bands of ornamental acanthus scrolls rising out of pot-bellied amphorae, uses motifs similar to those developed in the Sancta Sanctorum. For an impression of the colours, see Colour Plate 5. (© www.Assisi.de. Photo Stefan Diller.)

W

N + S

E

could clearly do with their support for his heavy book, and the relationship between the legs of the throne, the footstool and his feet is not well co-ordinated. For St Luke, the arrangement has been much improved. He sits at his desk writing his Gospel, but the desk is parallel to the picture plane and the throne recedes, so he appears in some danger of losing his balance. For St Matthew there are further improvements. He can sit more comfortably, resting his left elbow on his desk, his feet more relaxed on their supporting platform, but the angle of the back of the throne still shows an exaggerated forward thrust. Finally, with St Mark, this problem is resolved. His throne is actually similarly positioned to St John's – the limitations of the almost parallel alignment with the web of the two intervening experiments having been recognised – but his desk is now convincingly, and usefully, integrated in front of it. The walled cities are also painted in the 'Greek manner'. In St John's 'Asia' the buildings are awkwardly huddled and the gate is at an unconvincing angle. A similar picture was probably painted for St Luke's 'Greece', but did not satisfy; almost the whole of its area was replastered and done again, with a group of buildings in much better perspective, with just one building, preserved from the original and painted from a different view-point, sticking out on the left like a sore thumb. St Matthew's 'Judea' is similar, but narrower and taller, because his throne and desk, the largest, take up more of the space. It boasts the most imposing of the gateways. The domed building in the centre is probably intended as a stylised representation of the Temple of Jerusalem.

But in St Mark's 'Ytalia' we are faced with something quite remarkable and new. In all the webs there are delightful realistic touches – like the carafe promising refreshment in St John's bottom cupboard. In 'Ytalia' realistic details abound (Plate 49).

In the top left-hand corner, between two towers and directly under the word 'Ytalia', is the Palace of the Senate. Its façade and wall are hung with shields, alternately bearing the letters SPQR – (*Senatus populusque Romanus*, the arms of the Romans and their Senate) – and the arms of the Orsini family (Plate 48). The senators were the secular rulers of medieval Rome. They bore the title 'senator' rather than consul as in other cities in honour of Rome's unique past. The link between ancient and contemporary Rome was, in the eyes of its citizens and rulers, at once very deep and quite superficial. Its depth is reflected in the ancient formula of Roman republican authority, SPQR; its superficiality by the absence of any effective long-term constitution for the city. At one time or another there could be one senator or two or even fifty-six. The name was bandied about in the endless tension, often conflict, between pope and citizens – sometimes with the emperor as a third participant – or between rival factions of citizens, for temporal authority in the eternal city. Its superficiality was clearly demonstrated in the political appointment of Charles of Anjou as sole senator for ten years from 1268 to 1278.

Gian Gaetano Orsini, a member of an illustrious Roman family, was elected Pope Nicholas III at Viterbo on 25 November, and consecrated at Rome on 26 December 1277. He negotiated with Charles, who agreed to step down at the end of his term of office, and on 18 July 1278 he issued the bull, *Fundamenta militantis Ecclesiae*, which laid down a constitution for the city, with a Senate presided over by a single senator, to be elected

Plate 48 Cimabue: Ytalia detail: the Senate with the SPQR and Orsini arms (© www.Assisi.de. Photo Stefan Diller).

annually. No emperor, king, prince or other outsider might hold the office without express papal consent. Only Roman citizens were eligible. With the strong backing of his family and other Romans, Nicholas III was duly elected sole senator in September 1278 – and for life. This provides a very firm date. Linked SPQR and Orsini arms cannot have been displayed on the Senate before September 1278, since for the previous ten years the senator of Rome was Charles of Anjou. Nor are they likely to have been painted on a representation of the Senate on the vault in Assisi after the death of Nicholas III in August 1280. There would have been no specific point in drawing the attention of Martin IV to this achievement of his predecessor by painting Orsini family heraldry in another pontificate; and the same is true for his immediate successors, Honorius IV and Nicholas IV, though all continued the tradition inaugurated by Nicholas III of holding sole senatorship for life. None of these three popes was a member of the Orsini family. During the two and a half year vacancy, interrupted only by the short pontificate of Celestine V, August to December 1294, which followed the death of Nicholas IV on 4 April 1292, the senatorship was shared, briefly, around 1293, by an

Orsini and a Colonna; but this fact bears no known relevance to Assisi and 1293 seems an unacceptably late date for the painting of the crossing vault.

The full significance of the Orsini arms on the Senate appearing in fresco on the crossing vault – the one firm piece of historical evidence we have before the 1290s – has not been appreciated by some scholars partly because of some confusion over the status of senators. Nicholas III established a papal signoria in Rome. But he did not carry out the duties of the office of senator himself. He assigned them to a series of vicars, who were given the title of senator, the first being his brother, Matteo Rosso Orsini. His successors acted likewise, Martin IV handing it back to Charles of Anjou.[196]

The alternate SPQR and Orsini arms link Cimabue, Assisi, Rome and Nicholas III. Other buildings in 'Ytalia' also have much to contribute to our understanding, as Andaloro's study has demonstrated[197] (Plate 49). Next the Senate, to its right, is the Vatican Basilica of St Peter, showing Christ, the Virgin and St Peter, part of the middle register of its façade, which had been renovated by Gregory IX. To its right is its bell-tower, its five storeys and spire clearly detailed.[198] Earlier popes when in Rome had resided in the Lateran palace. Their bulls are given from the Lateran – *Dat. Laterani*. Nicholas III transferred the papal residence and the papal administration to the Vatican. His bulls are given from the Vatican – *Datum Rome apud sanctum Petrum* – thus emphasising the Primacy of Peter. So the Senate and the Vatican are painted on a level, side by side, at the apex of the city, twin symbols of the temporal power over the city and the spiritual power over the Church uniquely conjoined in the person of Nicholas III – and reinforcement of the evidence for the dating of 'Ytalia' to Nicholas III's pontificate.

In the right foreground is the Castel Sant'Angelo, which the Orsini had acquired from the Pierleoni earlier in the century. Above it, on the right, wedged between it and the bell-tower, is a monument, pyramid-shaped at the top, known as the Meta Romuli. It was traditionally held to mark the tomb of Romulus, one of Rome's twin founders, but had come also to be regarded as the signpost marking the site of St Peter's martyrdom. To its left, in the centre, stands the Pantheon. In this case too the classical building has been given a changed role. It is now a church, Santa Maria Rotunda – there is a cross at the top of the pediment. To the left of the Pantheon is the tall Torre dei Milizie, the property of the Annibaldi. The basilica in the bottom left-hand corner and the house adjacent to it cannot be identified with certainty, but are probably the Sancti Apostoli and a Colonna residence.[199]

The vignette of 'Ytalia', then, can be shown to encapsulate two overlapping images. First, it is a clear statement of the bases of Nicholas III's personal authority: the Senate – he is sole senator, supreme executive of the civic government; the Vatican – he is the successor of St Peter, vicar of Christ; the Castel Sant'Angelo – he is a member of the Orsini, a Roman family which owns this crucial strategic property and much

[196] Waley 1961, pp. 181, 190–1, 225; Gregorovius 1906, v, i, 48–9, 194–5, ii, 489, 517; cf. White 1984, ch. IV, pp. 107–8.
[197] Andaloro 1984.
[198] Andaloro 1984, pp. 154–7 and pls. 11–13. For bulls dated at St Peter's (below), see Sayers 1999, nos. 793–5, 801–24.
[199] Andaloro 1984, pp. 157–9, and plates esp. 1, 18–19.

Plate 49 Cimabue: crossing vault detail, Ytalia (© www.Assisi.de. Photo Gerhard Ruf).

else besides. Second, it reveals to us Nicholas' vision of Rome. Christian Rome is represented by the Vatican and its campanile, the Meta Romuli, the Pantheon/Santa Maria Rotunda, and the basilica (?) of the Sancti Apostoli. Civic Rome is represented by the Palace of the Senate – and all Roman citizens technically at least elect their senator – and by the presence of representative landmark structures belonging to leading Roman families: the Castel Sant'Angelo (Orsini), the Torre dei Milizie (Annibaldi), the town house (?Colonna).

It was Nicholas III's deliberate policy to glorify Rome and the Romans. They were a 'chosen people'; Rome a 'priestly and royal city . . . made head of the whole world through [being] the sacred seat of St Peter'.[200] In a bull of 3 February 1279, which significantly begins 'Civitatem sanctam Ierusalem novam', he declares that Rome is the new Jerusalem, 'which according to the prophet is built as a city, that is, in the likeness of that city', and underlines his awareness of the responsibilities that lays on him. 'This is the city over whose walls we recognise with fear that God has given us charge.'[201] These are the walls, too, that with their gateway and five towers, ring 'Ytalia'. 'Ytalia', through its representation of what is recognisably Rome, symbolises the new Jerusalem.

This walled city, as has been shown, is no haphazard collection of buildings, and is in a totally different category from the three stylised cities painted to represent Asia, Greece and Judea. Cimabue was in Rome in the early 1270s and will have studied its monuments; and some monuments, such as the Meta Romuli with its simple pyramidal structure, could have been recognisably indicated from memory. But the range and quality of the detail deployed in 'Ytalia' could not have been conjured from memory. He must have known what buildings he was to include, and made studies of them and sketches of individual features. In so doing Cimabue introduced a new degree of 'realism' into central Italian painting. He did not attempt photographic exactitude. Some contours were adjusted and proportions altered to make the pieces of his jigsaw fit together. The Pantheon, for example, is more elongated and slender. The silhouette of the dome with its great oculus would be enough to identify it, but it is enriched with details, including the capital of a column and the letters of an inscription.[202] The most striking proof that he must have made drawings from life is provided by the accuracy of details included in his picture of the Castel Sant'Angelo: the marble facing of the rectangular base and, most of all, the frieze along the cornice of the podium, with its bull's heads and festoons. A fragment of the actual cornice discovered in 1891 enables a comparison.[203]

All this points to one conclusion. Nicholas III commissioned the work and stipulated what he wanted. To dismiss the evidence, as Bellosi does, because it does not fit with his theories regarding Cimabue's artistic development, simply will not do.[204]

The Orsini were a wealthy family who held lands in the Campagna and were powerful in Rome itself. In addition to the Castel Sant'Angelo they owned two fortresses and

---

[200] Potthast, II, no. 21362, quoted Andaloro 1984, p. 146.
[201] Potthast, II, no. 21531, quoted Andaloro 1984, p. 156 and nn. 107–12.
[202] Andaloro 1984, pp. 161–3 and pl. 18.   [203] Andaloro 1984, p. 159 and pls. 14–17.
[204] Andaloro 1984, pp. 172–7; Bellosi 1998, pp. 88–9, 161–2, 170.

palaces on the opposite side of the Tiber in the regions of Ponte and Pariona and so controlled the bridge crossing the river. As pope, Nicholas III had access to other than family wealth. In his time the financial administration of the Papal States was under firm control. Surviving documents indicate that, in the years 1278–80, at least 5000 l was drawn in taxation and fines from just a handful of towns in the March of Ancona. He also increased the area and resources of the Papal States, for in 1278 he acquired the Romagna, one of the most fertile and prosperous provinces in Italy, until then a zone of imperial administration.[205]

He spent lavishly. The sheer number and variety of his ambitious projects suggest an elderly man in a hurry. At the Vatican he built a new papal residence for himself, and contributed to the importance and extent of the Vatican city by redeveloping the area and laying out gardens, which he surrounded with walls and towers. He also had a covered passageway constructed along the top of the Leonine wall to link the Vatican with the Castel Sant'Angelo. For the summer months he acquired a country house at Soriano, near Viterbo.[206]

From Innocent III onwards, most of the thirteenth century popes had contributed to the restoration and embellishment of churches in the city. Nicholas III continued the tradition on a grand scale. While still a cardinal he restored San Niccolò in Carcere, his titular church. As pope he undertook an extensive renovation of the Basilica of St Peter and completely rebuilt and decorated the papal chapel at the Lateran, the Sancta Sanctorum. He was responsible for funding a major refurbishment of the late Antique mural paintings in three Basilicas. At San Paolo fuori le mura roundels containing images of the popes were restored and the two-row cycle of the Acts of the Apostles; and similar restoration work was done at Old St Peter's and St John Lateran.[207] The frequent presence of the Curia in Rome promoted prosperity and jobs. Though Nicholas III may not have offered circuses, he certainly 'brought to many the means of buying more bread'.[208] He was the patron of a range of craftsmen, of two architects, the Dominican friars Sisto and Ristoro, whom he summoned from Florence, of the marble cutter and mosaicist Master Cosmatus, the painters Cavallini, Jacopo Torriti, Cimabue, and many more whose identity we do not know.

The decorative programme at the Sancta Sanctorum and Cimabue's work in the Upper Church at Assisi were undertaken during the same years for the same patron and share comparable features. Both include costly items. An inscription at the Sancta Sanctorum proclaims it the work of Master Cosmatus, a member of a famous Roman family firm. He is responsible for the marble facings of the walls, the marble benches, the porphyry columns, the outstandingly sumptuous and graceful floor, with its twelve porphyry and serpentine disks, all the cosmatesque inlay, and the alternating braided and twisted spiral white marble columns of the blind arcades with their trilobe arches. These last explicitly recall the real triforium arcades of the transepts at Assisi.[209] At Assisi the backgrounds of the webs of the great crossing vault were of gold leaf, which

[205] Waley 1961, pp. 93, 189–93, 199; Gregorovius 1906, v, ii, 661–2.
[206] Gregorovius 1906, v, ii, 632; Kessler and Zacharias 2000, p. 187 and fig. 188.
[207] Gardner 1993, ch. 11, pp. 240–8; Tomei 1995.   [208] Waley 1961, p. 191.
[209] Andaloro 1995; Kessler and Zacharias 2000, pp. 40–3 and figs. 35–8; and see Plate 50.

was only exceptionally used in fresco painting because of its expense. The vault of the Sancta Sanctorum is blue with gold stars, to represent the firmament, and so are the vaults of the transepts and apse at Assisi. The symbols of the Evangelists holding open books, each with an appropriate gospel text, are painted in the four webs at the Sancta Sanctorum, a simpler design than at Assisi, but bearing the same significance.[210] Of the eight scenes within the lunettes at the Sancta Sanctorum, five depict the marytrdoms of saints and apostles, whose relics are venerated there. Two, the crucifixion of St Peter and the beheading of St Paul, also occur in the north transept at Assisi.

As well as shared content there are shared decorative elements. 'The motif of the acanthus scrolls is almost identical, with wide, elegant volutes fretted . . . with a white edge that is lobed and saw-toothed . . . very similar . . . is the presence of . . . amphorae out of which the acanthus heads grow' – though those at the Sancta Sanctorum are more classical. At the Sancta Sanctorum the real cosmatesque mosaic work in the floor and in the lintel of the sanctuary is replicated in the painted cosmatesque ribbons in the cornices of the lunettes, probably executed with a stencil.[211] At Assisi the keystone of the crossing vault has a circle of real mosaic round its central ring, and the ribs are painted with imitation cosmatesque decoration. Cimabue even experimented with a more elaborate method of simulating mosaic. Right by St John's lectern cupboard, between and beside its open doors, is an area which has been deeply incised with a regular rectangular grid. A similar area has been found on the diagonal face of the secondary rib near the rockscape of St Luke's city. Cutting these cubes in the plaster must have been time-consuming, and the result would have been indistinguishable from stencilled squares when looked at from the ground, so it is not surprising that this method was abandoned. But the test patches show that it was tried, and bear witness to 'the urge for decorative splendour'.[212]

One of the painters employed by Nicholas III at the Sancta Sanctorum was Torriti. The splendid wings of the St Matthew symbol he painted there are very close in inspiration and technique to those of Cimabue's angels in the left transept at Assisi.[213] It looks as if there was a little group of painters at Rome in the 1270s who shared ideas and sources of inspiration, and also their experiences and experiments with techniques; they were aware of what others were doing. During Nicholas III's pontificate Torriti and another painter worked at the Sancta Sanctorum; Cimabue worked at Assisi. It has already been argued that Cimabue made close studies of particular buildings in Rome specifically in connection with his commission at Assisi. If so, he is likely during his one, or several, such visits to Rome also to have visited the Sancta Sanctorum to see the work in progress there. Similarly, Torriti may well have visited Assisi; may even have lent a hand.[214] For one gets a strong impression at Assisi, throughout the extended period that the whole programme took to complete, that the decoration was a collaborative, as well as a successional, effort. They may have been rivals for reputation, but painters

---

[210] Kessler and Zacharias 2000, fig. 39, p. 47; and see Plate 47.
[211] Bellosi 1998, pp. 74–7 and plates on pp. 76–9; Romano 1995; Kessler and Zacharias 2000, pp. 41–6 and figs. 37–8, 42–3.
[212] White 1984, ch. VI, pp. 153–4.   [213] Bellosi 1998, p. 71 and plates, pp. 72–3.
[214] Bellosi 1998, pp. 67–90 and refs.

from different workshops, from different parts of Italy, indeed of Europe, were ready to work together from the same scaffolding platform, to borrow one another's paint pot.[215]

The decoration of the sanctuary walls

When the ribs of the crossing vault were completed, the wall arches of the south transept were plastered and decorated.[216] Unfortunately these frescoes are badly deteriorated and much is lost. In the lunette on the east wall, next to the nave, there seems once to have been a figure of Christ enthroned, surrounded by cherubim and seraphim. On the south wall, three tremendous full-length angels once stood to either side of the stained glass windows, and two half-length angels in each of the two deep arcades. In the lunette on the west wall, in the upper, apex half, against a background of a segment of seven concentric circles – representing the heavenly spheres – the archangel Michael and two supporting angels, all wearing armour and brandishing long lances, attack, in the lower half, a large central winged dragon, and a host of part bat-like, part monkey-like, demonic figures, who are being thrust hurtling downwards headfirst, with their long arms outstretched. But again only fragments of this once dramatic scene survive.[217] On the passage walls behind the east and west triforium arcades are three full-length angels with wide-spread wings. Above them, in a painted architectural gallery of six recessed arches on short fluted columns, are six half-length angels, each holding a mandorla on which is painted a small throne (Plate 50). In the spans of the arches are half-length angels in frames; those on the south wall are clearly holding sceptres (Colour Plate 5).[218] So, while the upper walls of the north transept opposite show the Transfiguration, Ascension and Majesty of Christ, with Pentecost and the apostles, the upper walls of the south transept seem to show Christ in heaven attended by the choirs of angels. Seraphim with their fiery wings and cherubim are there; thrones can be identified by their emblematic thrones, dominions by their sceptres. St Michael and his companions – presumably Gabriel and Raphael – are archangels. The two types of full-length angels and the unidentified half-length angels between them could account for three more ranks in the hierarchy – the virtues, powers and principalities – making eight. The ninth, the lowliest, the angels, appear in abundance in the scenes below on all three walls.[219]

All the wall surfaces of the sanctuary were now complete down to the level of the passageway, and Cimabue proceeded to paint the scenes on the lower walls. The work-stages in the plastering make clear that there was a steady onward progress from left to right, taking in the intervening columns, and beginning at the junction of the east

[215] White 1984, pp. 144–5, 158; Binski 2002, esp. p. 77. See pp. 336–42.
[216] White 1984, ch. VI, pp. 145; ch. V, pp. 121–2.
[217] Carlettini 1993, pp. 107–10 and figs. 4–8.   [218] Bellosi 1998, pp. 175–81.
[219] Beatrice expounds the angelic hierarchy to Dante as consisting of Seraphim, Cherubim, Thrones, Dominions, Virtues, Powers, Principalities, Archangels and Angels, listed according to the order given them by the Pseudo-Dionysius (*Paradiso* xxviii, 97–132). Belting 1977, pp. 62 ff., considered all the angelic choirs were represented. Christe 1980–1, p. 158, suggested that St Michael's companions are powers, but the iconography of St Michael and the dragon is quite clear, and the altar in the south transept is dedicated to him. Dionysius names three archangels; Jewish apocryphal writings add Uriel.

Plate 50 Upper Church, south transept, west wall arcade, showing the real arcading of the passage way with the fictive, painted arcade above, and the row of painted corbels which seem to support an architrave, below (Photo Luigi Artini, for Istituto Germanico di Storia dell'Arte, Florence).

wall of the south transept and the nave. The east wall is devoted to a monumental crucifixion scene, which occupies the entire width between the columns, and rises from immediately above the door to the sacristy (on the extreme right), to the painted cornice below the passageway, an area measuring some 7.2 m wide and 4.8 m high.[220] The sequence closes on the corresponding east wall of the north transept with a second great crucifixion scene (Colour Plate 5). Sadly both have suffered very badly. The original colours have almost all gone, leaving only the ochre preparation, and what should have been the lightest areas and the highlights now appear black through the oxidisation of the lead white. But though shadows of their former selves they still succeed in conveying a powerful and arresting sense of drama and agony. Together the two dominated the sanctuary. There is a dado beneath them decorated with painted hangings, so they are positioned a little higher than the height of a man, in clear view. All the friars will have been confronted by them several times every single day, when they gathered for worship.[221]

Both compositions are symmetrically balanced. The central wood of the cross is buried in the rock at the base and touches the cornice at the top. The figure of Christ

[220] White 1984, ch. V, pp. 122–7; ch. VI, pp. 144–52.   [221] White 1967, p. 24; Bellosi 1998, p. 183.

is magnified, the sagging curve of his body more than life-size. The figures nearest to the cross create a triangle and draw the eye upwards to the sacrifice. Massed figures stand to either side, and the air above their heads is alive with angels. The inspirational source of these frescoes is the Byzantine tradition of painting in which Cimabue was initially trained. Especially noteworthy are the flying half-figures of angels, their bodies ending in a flourish of draperies, and the crowds, with a few full-length figures at the front, most of them seemingly treading on others' feet, while a massed crush of heads behind is quite unsupported by legs; the entire grouping is not anchored to the ground. But the Byzantine is not the only influence. In the crucifixion scene in the left transept the treatment of the crowd on the right also shows awareness of Nicola Pisano's crucifixion panel on the Baptistry pulpit at Pisa, which owes much to Roman relief sculpture.[222] Cimabue's ability to fuse a weightless crowd derived from the Greek manner of painting, with insights derived from classical Antiquity via the solid achievements of contemporary sculptors, is characteristic of his mastery. And in the context in which he uses it here this tension between solidity and weightlessness is totally appropriate.

This crucifixion scene is a masterpiece, perhaps the most tragic representation of Christ's Passion in medieval western art. It captures a dramatic moment. Christ is dead. It was after his death that one of the soldiers pierced his side with a spear, while others broke the legs of the two crucified with him, and out of the wound came blood and water (John 19. 32–4). As it flows it is being collected in a cup by one of the angels. The anguished figure of Mary Magdalene, her arms thrown up in a gesture of uncontrollable despair, is the most striking of all. There is a bond between the two, a line linking her arms and hands up through the right side of Christ's body to his bowed head. We seem to hear her scream, and Christ seems to look at her though his eyes are closed. Cimabue has caught the vivid sensibility of Franciscan meditation on the Passion, one of St Francis' lasting legacies to his three Orders and to Christendom. His painting is as moving and dramatic as any acted play. St John has moved from his traditional position on the opposite side of the cross, and stands beside Mary, clasping her hand. Before he died Christ had consigned his mother to John's care and he will now take her to his home (John 19. 26–7). The atmosphere is fraught with emotion and movement, with tension between earth and heaven. The earthquake that immediately followed his death (Matt. 27. 49–51, 54) will have caused the wind that rips Christ's loincloth sideways. The swirling angels are arriving in haste and agitation. They emphasise the intimate connection between the crucifixion and the Eucharist, three of them holding cups to catch the blood from His hands and side, blood 'shed for many for the remission of sins' (Matt. 26. 28).

In the crucifixion scene that balances it across the crossing in the north transept the basic overall structure of the image is repeated; only some details are varied, to avoid it appearing a mere copy. The Virgin swoons in St John's arms. The sides of the triangle pointing up to Christ's body on the cross are composed of two figures, the

---

[222] Bellosi 1998, pp. 48–52 and plates, pp. 51, 54, 184; Aubert 1907, p. 36, cited Bellosi 1998, pp. 183, 241 n. 67; Ayrton 1969, p. 35 fig. k.

one, the soldier who wielded the spear, the other, the man who raised on a hyssop wand the sponge filled with vinegar for Jesus to drink (John 19. 28–34). But both have fulfilled their allotted tasks. Jesus is dead. Blood and water gush into the cup. Lance and wand are at 'half mast'. They are symbols, instruments of the Passion; here because functional to the design. This stylised element renders this alternative less harrowing.

The dual concentration on Christ crucified and on the Eucharist is overwhelming. The two thieves are omitted. They would distract. At the foot of the cross St Francis kneels in prayer, and in a cleft in the rock directly underneath the cross is Adam's skull. These details can hardly be made out in the north transept version, it is so badly damaged, but they were there. St Francis drew a cross planted in a head as part of the special blessing he wrote for brother Leo (Plate 12). When he died, in 1271 or 1272, Leo bequeathed his cherished parchment to the Sacro Convento. To explain the context he annotated it: 'Two years before his death, St Francis kept Lent in the house on La Verna in honour of the blessed Virgin Mary, the mother of God, and of the archangel Michael, from the feast of the Assumption of the blessed Virgin Mary until the feast of St Michael in September. And the hand of God was upon him. After the vision and speech of the seraphim and the impression of Christ's stigmata on his body he composed these praises that are written on the other side of the leaf, and wrote them with his own hand, giving thanks to God for the benefit conferred on him. St Francis wrote this blessing with his own hand for me, brother Leo. Likewise he made this sign Tau and the head with his own hand.'[223] Leo's note connects St Francis, through this fast, with the Virgin, St Michael, the crucifixion and the stigmata. The creased autograph epitomises major themes enshrined in the sanctuary, both in its liturgy and in its decoration. By painting Adam's skull at the base of the cross on both transept walls Cimabue presented all the friars with a large-scale visual reminder of a precious relic of their founder they had acquired only a few years earlier, at the start of the decade. But that is not all. It is a reminder too of the role of brother Leo, whose testimony was already prized and disseminated by a flourishing oral tradition. Allusion to him here, at the very centre of the Franciscan Order and the Franciscan liturgy, surely reaches out to those many friars for whom brother Leo was a venerated link with St Francis himself, the companion who pre-eminently articulated the pristine authentic image of the saint. It is an official gesture of recognition and inclusion. It provides a corrective to the all too common tendency to assume that the bitter divisions between the conventual and spiritual wings of the Order were already hardening by this date. After St Bonaventure's death 'a variety of battles [with definable issues and contestants] . . . gradually began to emerge', but in the 1270s the vast majority of friars still shared a wide degree of consensus.[224]

The crucifixion scene occupied the whole of the east wall. The remaining two walls of the south transept were devoted to scenes from the Book of Revelation. Three scenes of equal size were painted on the south wall. The first to be done, that on the left, nearest to the crucifixion, was based on Revelation 4–5, and represented the Adoration of the Lamb. Top centre, in a mandorla, is the throne John saw in his vision. Lying upon it is

[223] See pp. 73 and 109–11.
[224] Burr 2001, esp. p. 43; and see p. 106 note 14. For St Bonaventure's discussions with brother Leo on La Verna in October 1259, see p. 401 and note 334.

the lamb. The book with its seven seals rests against the back of the throne. Supporting the mandorla are the symbols of the four Evangelists. Ranged around, following the shape of the mandorla, are the twenty-four elders and, framing them on all sides, ranks of angels. The lamb, lying as if on an altar, has a cruciform nimbus, and looks with open eyes leftwards towards the crucifixion on the adjacent wall, linking the two scenes and underlining the acceptance by Christ the Lamb of sacrificial death, which enables the opening of the seals. 'And when he had taken the book, the four beasts and four and twenty elders fell down before the Lamb, having every one of them harps, and golden vials full of odours, which are the prayers of saints. And they sung a new song, saying, Thou art worthy to take the book, and to open the seals thereof: for thou wast slain, and hast redeemed us to God by thy blood out of every kindred, and tongue, and people, and nation' (Rev. 5. 8–9).[225]

The next scene illustrates what happened after the Lamb had opened the sixth of the seven seals. John saw four angels stationed at the four corners of the earth holding back the four winds so that they should not blow on the earth or the sea or any tree (Rev. 7. 1). Cimabue portrays them as strange winged figures, with mops of untidy hair, naked except for a long fold of cloth draped diagonally from the left shoulder so as to cover the right hip and leg down to the calf and then up over the left shoulder again to fall in a long fold. Each supports a large horn with the left arm. They stand with their backs to a battlemented wall, positioned like the four parts of a hinged screen. Showing above the battlements are houses and towers and behind these rise hillslopes with trees, all as yet undamaged by the winds. The angels' bare feet may be standing beside, or on, water, but the fresco is badly deteriorated, especially along the bottom and at the top. John then saw another angel rising from the east, having the seal of the living God, who cried with a loud voice to the four angels not to hurt earth or sea or trees 'till we have sealed the servants of our God in their foreheads' (Rev. 7. 2–3). Only part of the angel, flying towards the centre, and part of the sun, top left (which is east), survives.[226]

The right hand scene follows on from this. The seventh seal has been opened, and Christ sits in a mandorla, top centre, blessing with his right hand and holding the opened book in his left. Around him fly seven angels blowing trumpets. Central, below Christ's feet, is an altar, and another angel censes this with a golden censer. Below are two massed groups of kneeling men and women – conspicuous among them Franciscans – who clearly represent God's servants whose foreheads have been sealed (Rev. 8. 1–4).[227]

In John's vision the angels did not blow their trumpets all together, but one at a time, and each sounding trumpet heralded calamities – storms, earthquakes, fires, shooting stars, eclipses, wars and plagues. Then there was war in heaven, and Michael and his angels fought against the dragon and his angels and cast them out (Rev. 12. 7–9) – the very scene depicted in the lunette of the west wall. Below is the culmination of the apocalyptic conflict, the Fall of Babylon; a scene which occupies more than half

---

[225] Hueck 1981, pp. 283–6; Carlettini 1993, pp. 110–15; Bellosi 1998, pp. 194–6 and plate p. 195.
[226] Bellosi 1998, p. 196 and plate p. 198.   [227] Bellosi 1998, p. 197 and plate p. 199.

the lower wall space. An angel announces this twice. Cimabue illustrates the second, more detailed description. 'Babylon the great is fallen, is fallen, and is become the habitation of devils, and the hold of every foul spirit, and a cage of every unclean and hateful bird . . . Come out of her, my people, that ye be not partakers of her sins' (Rev. 18. 2, 4). The angel flies in top left. Along the bottom, the line of battlemented walls is again depicted as a screen, like part of a stage set. Above the battlements the buildings of the city are convulsed from the centre (unfortunately missing), the two halves falling outwards to left and right, 'as in a slow motion explosion'.[228] From many windows and doors come writhing dragons and snakes. In front of the wall screen, in the centre, are hairy demons, including monkeys, and a bird, probably an ostrich, symbol of heresy or of evil, or a wading bird, most like a heron.[229] On the right a crowd of monkey-like fire-raising demons with bat wings approaches an open doorway in which stands a taller hairy demon holding a flaming torch and sounding a horn. Through the open doorway on the left people are fleeing to safety.

In the final scene John and the angel are sitting on a small island, shaped roughly like a mandorla, surrounded by a sea swarming with shoals of fish. John, who had shared in the trauma and sufferings of the early Christians in Rome during and after the Neronian persecution, was banished by Domitian early in AD 70, and released by Nerva in AD 71. He spent his exile on the island of Patmos and it was there that the God-given Revelation of Jesus Christ was signified to him by an angel (Rev. 1. 1, 9).[230] The angel is shown talking to John and pointing with his right hand. It has therefore been argued that this must be the first scene. But Cimabue actually painted it last in the cycle, and the individual scenes have followed the unfolding of the vision so far in sequence; it presumably therefore is intended to come last. It does represent St John on Patmos, but not at the outset, when he saw, not an angel, but 'in the midst of the seven candlesticks one like unto the Son of man' (Rev. 1. 13). In the final chapters John 'saw a new heaven and a new earth . . . and . . . the holy city, new Jerusalem, coming down from God out of heaven, prepared as a bride adorned for her husband. . . . And there came unto me one of the seven angels, which had the seven vials full of the seven last plagues, and talked with me, saying, Come hither, I will show thee the bride, the Lamb's wife. And he carried me away in the spirit to a great and high mountain, and showed me that great city, the holy Jerusalem, descending out of heaven from God' (Rev. 21. 1–2, 9–10).[231]

The four scenes on the lower walls of the apse – two to either side of the papal throne – complete the cycle of the life and death of the Virgin. The scenes are based on James of Voragine's *Golden Legend*. On the south wall the dying Virgin is propped up in bed, with the twelve apostles seated in a circle round her, and one of the apostles, probably

---

[228] Bellosi 1998, p. 200 and plates pp. 177, 203. [229] Monferini 1966, pp. 30–1.

[230] Bellosi 1998, plate p. 204. The details of the life of 'John' are controversial and the reconstruction accepted in the text is conjectural: see Robinson 1976, pp. 249–53. Early tradition attributed John's exile on Patmos to Domitian: some modern scholars have argued cogently that this occurred – not when Domitian was sole emperor (AD 81–96) – but when he was a Caesar subordinate to his father Vespasian, in charge in Rome in AD 70.

[231] Hueck 1981, pp. 283–4, argues that it is the introduction to the apocalyptic cycle not its conclusion. Carlettini 1993, pp. 107–9, Monferini 1966, pp. 31–2 and Bellosi 1998, p. 201, in my view correctly, argue that it is the last.

St Paul, 'the least of the Apostles' (1 Cor. 15. 8–9), edifying them all with a sermon.[232] This, and the next scene, the Dormition, are both framed by a wide, heavy, rounded trilobate arch, supported on Corinthian columns, which dominates their design.[233] The entire space within the arch, and spilling over the front of it in places, is filled with lines of haloed figures, one row standing in front of the bier, others to the sides and around and above to form a solid half-circle. The iconography is most unusual. The dead body of the Virgin is laid out horizontally in the centre and, forming a vertical central axis with her, Christ appears, standing and blessing, and holding lovingly to Him in his left arm a baby wrapped in a shawl, representing the blessed Mary's soul. The fresco is much damaged but it is still possible to work out that He and she together were positioned to form the cross-piece and head of the cross. It is also extremely rare for Christ to collect even His mother's soul personally. It was normally the duty of an angel to fly down to catch a saved soul as it left the body and carry it up to heaven.[234]

In the very centre of the apse is planted the papal throne. To either side of it is a frescoed roundel containing the half-length figure of a pope, wearing tiara and pallium, haloed, in the act of blessing, and holding a book. No recent popes had been officially canonised, and these will represent two among the many early popes traditionally revered, most probably St Leo the Great and St Gregory the Great (Plate 51).

On the north-west wall, next to the papal throne, is the Assumption of the Virgin. Belief in the bodily assumption into heaven of the mother of God arose in the eastern Church, became accepted in the west, where it grew in popularity during the eleventh and twelfth centuries, and was a devotion greatly encouraged and promoted by the friars.[235] The bottom half of the scene is composed of massed horizontal lines, focused on the empty coffin, with Mary's discarded robes and winding sheet lying in graceful folds over its rim; to either side crowd kneeling saints, some of them women, in an attitude of prayer and adoration. Above the coffin, filling the whole span from side to side, are serried ranks of saints, with conspicuous raised and radiated haloes, interspersed with rows of Hebrew patriarchs and prophets wearing distinctive headgear. In the top half, against a background of blue sky, four flying angels transport, not simply the Virgin, but the Virgin and Christ together. Again, the iconography is most unusual. They are enclosed in a mandorla; the Virgin rests her head on Christ's shoulder, her hand on his arm, while He is sustaining her in a tender, loving embrace. The image is inspired by the Song of Songs, and is a wonderful evocation of Franciscan spirituality. It would have looked enchanting when it was first painted (Plate 52).[236]

[232] Maggioni 1998, II, 779–82, esp. p. 782; Ryan and Ripperger 1941, pp. 449–51. James (p. 781) quotes 'Dionysius Pauli apostoli', i.e. the Pseudo-Dionysius (De divinis nominibus, i, 3) to the effect that all the disciples came together 'in dormitione uirginis', and that he himself was there, and each made a sermon in praise of Christ and the Virgin. Cf. Bellosi 1998, p. 202 and nn. 86–8 and plates pp. 206, 208.

[233] White 1967, p. 25; Bellosi 1998, pp. 202, 207.

[234] Maggioni 1998, II, 779–82; Ryan and Ripperger 1941, pp. 449–51; Bellosi 1998, plate p. 208.

[235] For an excellent account of the history of the feast of the Assumption and the cult associated with it, see Fulton 1998.

[236] Bellosi 1998, pp. 202, 205, 207; Henderson 1981, p. 22. According to the Golden Legend Christ raised her body from the tomb after three days: Maggioni 1998, II, 782–3, cf. pp. 783–6; Ryan and Ripperger 1941, p. 451–2, cf. pp. 452–4.

Plate 51 Upper Church: the papal throne in the centre of the apse. The lion, asp, basilisk and dragon carved upon the base can be symbols of the resurrection. Each armrest is a lion standing over a bull. (© www.Assisi.de. Photo Stefan Diller.)

Plate 52 Cimabue, Assumption of the Virgin, Upper Church apse, next to the papal throne on the viewer's right (© www.Assisi.de. Photo Gerhard Ruf).

The Marian cycle ends with a scene of Christ and the Virgin Enthroned. The horizontal lines of the Assumption culminate in the verticals of an impressive contrasting composition. The wooden throne, beautifully carved and inlaid, is tall and stately, rising from the floor right up into the sky. Unlike the five thrones Cimabue had already painted in the Upper Church, and a sixth, in the Fall of Simon Magus yet to come, this throne is of a new type, which was to become the norm, presented frontally. Vestiges of old habits linger however; the footstool is askew, seen from the right, in the foreshortened frontal setting. The Virgin, gorgeously attired in the rich robes in which her body ascended in the previous scene, sits on Christ's right hand, side by side on the one throne. She stretches out her right hand towards Franciscan friars who kneel at the base of the throne. They wear no haloes; they represent the living and recently departed friars for whom she is interceding. The narrow space to either side of the throne is thronged with representatives of the hierarchies of heaven, angels, patriarchs, martyrs, confessors and virgins.[237]

The lower walls of the north transept focus on the apostles, chiefly on St Peter and to a lesser extent St Paul. On the west wall the first scene depicts St Peter, accompanied by St John, healing the lame man who sat begging for alms at the gate of the Temple at Jerusalem (Acts 3. 1–11). The background scenery has reverted to the 'stage set' in this and the next two scenes. The buildings and the treatment of space derive from Byzantine painting. The central building in the first scene, representing the Temple, is crowned with a cupola, and there is a little cupola on a roof to the right. The eye is first caught by the Temple and then is drawn outwards by the receding lines of the buildings making up the wings. The three viewpoints implied by this grouping lead to the Temple appearing hexagonal. The sense of movement achieved in this scene is heightened by Cimabue's incorporation of the little door which provided access from the convent to the church and also to the gallery of the triforium and the passageway. St Peter steps over the arch of the real doorway to seize the cripple's hand and lift him up.[238]

The second scene shows St Peter, accompanied by two other apostles, healing the sick and casting out devils, for 'believers . . . brought forth the sick into the streets, and laid them on beds and couches, that at the least the shadow of Peter passing by might overshadow some of them. There came also a multitude out of the cities round about unto Jerusalem, bringing sick folks and them which were vexed with unclean spirits: and they were healed every one' (Acts 5. 14–16). Rays of light shine down on the scene from above the cupola of a church tower.[239]

The first of the three scenes on the north wall, which all took place in Rome, depicts the Fall of Simon Magus, a story taken from the *Golden Legend*. Simon, a magician who had the favour of Nero, claimed he could fly and climbed a high tower, here portrayed as a slender wooden trestle scaffold, such as might be used in building or decorating works, or in a play. Peter stands before it, his right hand raised in denunciation, while St Paul kneels behind him, praying fervently. Simon is still airborne, upheld by flying devils. Nero, dressed in antique Roman armour, his head crowned with a laurel wreath, sits on a carved wooden throne.[240] Nero took revenge for Simon's fall by ordering the execution of the apostles.

So the next, which can be regarded as the centre of a triptych, is a crucifixion scene, the Crucifixion of St Peter. The composition is of an extraordinary stark simplicity. A

[237] Bellosi 1998, pp. 207, 210; Maggioni 1998, II, 785–6; Ryan and Ripperger 1941, p. 454.
[238] For a detailed discussion and assessment of Cimabue's use of the foreshortened frontal setting in this scene see White 1967, pp. 28–30; see also Bellosi 1998, pp. 52, 55 and plate p. 55, also pp. 212–14, 217 and plate p. 215. There is a corresponding door on the west wall of the south transept.
[239] Bellosi 1998, pp. 212–13, 217 and plate p. 216.
[240] Bellosi 1998, pp. 213, 220 and plate p. 218; Maggioni 1998, I, 561–9; Ryan and Ripperer 1941, pp. 332–7.

pyramid, the Meta Romuli, which was traditionally held to mark the site of St Peter's martyrdom, is on the left. Balancing it on the right is a nearby pyramid, Nero's Terebinth. The crowd on the left and the guards on the right, martyred because they were converted by the apostles, are confined within the outlines of these Roman monuments, so that the central space is reserved for the martyrdom alone, the cross standing out against the blue sky, with St Peter's body, upside-down as he requested, lifted high, the outstretched arms above the heads of the standing figures in the foreground (Plate 40).[241] The third and final scene depicts the martyrdom of St Paul.[242]

The pictorial programme of the sanctuary was inspired by the needs of worship and the liturgy.[243] The focus of Franciscan devotion was Christ's sacrifice on the cross and the Eucharist. The two great frescoes of the crucifixion offered a powerful stimulus to spiritual meditation and prayer. Each acted as the reredos of an altar (Colour Plate 5). The altar in the south transept was dedicated to the archangel Michael; that in the north transept to St Peter and St Paul, and possibly to the other apostles. The high altar was dedicated to the Assumption of the Blessed Virgin Mary. Its consecration had taken place on the feast of her Nativity. All the Marian feasts would have been celebrated here, including the regular Saturday Mass in her honour. This had been raised to the status of a double feast by the liturgical constitutions passed at the General Chapter held at Assisi in 1269. Michaelmas likewise was raised to a double feast by the same Chapter.[244] The double feast of St Peter and St Paul was on 29 June. The Marian scenes in the apse surrounding the papal throne highlight the symbolism of Mary as *Ecclesia*, the Church.

The dedication of the altar in the south transept to St Michael emphasises St Francis' devotion to the archangel, and the part this devotion played in his spiritual preparation for the reception of the stigmata.[245] The only reference to St Michael in the New Testament comes in the Book of Revelation 12. 7–12. 'There was war in heaven: Michael and his angels fought against the dragon; and the dragon fought and his angels, and prevailed not; neither was their place found any more in heaven. And the great dragon was cast out, that old serpent, called the Devil, and Satan, which deceiveth the whole world: he was cast out into the earth, and his angels were cast out with him. And I heard a loud voice saying in heaven, Now is come salvation, and strength, and the kingdom of our God, and the power of his Christ: for the accuser of our brethren is cast down, which accused them before our God day and night. And they overcame him by the blood of the Lamb, and by the word of their testimony; and they loved not their lives unto the death. Therefore rejoice ye heavens, and ye that dwell in them.' This text sheds light on the messages delivered by the scenes in this transept. St Michael and his companions vanquish and cast down the dragon and his demon angels on the west wall, so that on the opposite wall the Saviour Christ sits enthroned in power attended by the angelic host. In the first scene on the south wall the sacrificial Lamb is adored by the elders and the angels. The central figure in the row of imposing angels at the

[241] White 1967, p. 24; Bellosi 1998, pp. 220–1.
[242] Bellosi 1998, plate p. 223; Maggioni 1998, I, 578–82; Ryan and Ripperger 1941, pp. 342–5.
[243] Mitchell 1971, pp. 118, 120; Hueck 1981.
[244] Hueck 1981, pp. 283 and 321 n. 11, 292 and 322 nn. 26–7; Van Dijk 1963, II, 441.   [245] See p. 109.

base of the picture possibly represents St Michael, who is identified with the 'mighty angel' in the antiphon for the Magnificat for Michaelmas.[246]

The upper half of the second, central, scene on this wall was dominated by the figure of the 'angel ascending from the east, having the seal of the living God' (Rev. 7. 2), of which unfortunately only fragments survive. No friar will have been unaware of the claim made by St Bonaventure in his Introducton to the *Legenda Maior* that, through the image of this angel, St John the Apostle and Evangelist was referring to St Francis (Prologue 1). The task of the angel was to mark the foreheads of the servants of God, who merited salvation, and reassuringly, and predictably, Friars Minor are prominently placed in the third scene kneeling in prayer below the golden altar before the throne (Rev. 7. 3–17; 8. 2–4); in the iconography of these frescoes altar and throne are one. Illustrating scenes from the Book of Revelation both honours St Michael and provides an opportunity to highlight St Francis' eschatological role.

The overwhelming urge to praise God that found expression in the Psalms is also evident in this last book of the New Testament. The four beasts who became the symbols of the Evangelists 'rest not day and night, saying, Holy, holy, holy, Lord God almighty' (Rev. 4. 7–8). It is most improbable that the author of Revelation was John the Apostle, but this was widely, though not universally, believed in the Middle Ages. It was attributed to him by Irenaeus as early as the late second century. In a letter written in the 1160s to satisfy the intellectual interests in biblical questions of Henry, count of Champagne, John of Salisbury declared: 'Some hold that the Apocalypse was described by John the Apostle, others by a most holy priest of Ephesus called John, as St Jerome the father of learned men tells us; but in the general belief of the Church the Apostle has it.'[247] Among those who accepted the attribution was St Bonaventure. In his fresco of the Adoration of the Lamb Cimabue places John's eagle in prime position. His symbol had already been similarly placed in the lunette of the Majesty of Christ in the north transept. Thus in the sanctuary of the Basilica one of the sons of Zebedee is shown getting what his mother asked for for him, to sit at Jesus' right hand in his kingdom (Matt. 20. 20–3).[248] The messages implicit in the decorative programme here are directed primarily at the friars. Narrative illustration is loaded with theological exposition. St John, in the opening chapter to his Gospel, wrote: 'No man hath seen God at any time; the only begotten Son, which is in the bosom of the Father, he hath declared him' (John 1. 18); and Bede expounded this text: 'In the bosom of the Father means in the secrets of the Father, to which human understanding cannot reach.'[249] St John himself was the disciple 'whom Jesus loved' (John 13. 23). So he came to be credited with a privileged understanding of divine mysteries. The Book of Revelation,

---

[246] Some details of these frescoes were taken from lections in the breviary, as Hueck has shown: 1981, p. 284.

[247] Millor and Brooke 1979, pp. 332–3 and n. 43, based on Isidore and Jerome.

[248] Bellosi 1998, plate p. 195. The Majesty is poorly preserved; Matthew's symbol is legible top right (Christ's left) and Luke's bottom right, implying that John's was top left and Mark's bottom left. 'This order of Jerome's symbols, though known in German and Italian medieval art, departs from that usual in northern European Majesties of the period in exchanging John and Matthew' (Binski 2002, p. 58 and n. 33 and fig. 3, p. 82).

[249] Bede, *Opera homiletica* in Hurst 1955, pp. 11–12, quoted in Henderson 1981, p. 34 and n. 38; for this and what follows see ibid. pp. 32–5 and nn.

supposedly by him, revealed the secrets of heaven, 'because at the Last Supper he had lain on Christ's bosom, in which "were hidden all the treasures of wisdom and knowledge, from which deep fountain he was worthy to draw"'.[250] It was for the friars an impeccable apostolic source.

The series of scenes from the lives of St Peter and St Paul serve both to approve the casting of St Francis and St Anthony as new apostles, carrying on their mission to preach the Gospel, and to reflect the status of St Francis' burial church as a papal Basilica. During his brief pontificate, Nicholas III sponsored the restoration of fifth-century cycles illustrating the Lives of the two apostles in the basilicas of San Paolo fuori le mura and Old St Peter's; and scenes of their martyrdom are portrayed in the Sancta Sanctorum, the papal chapel at the Lateran he rebuilt and decorated. The close iconographical similarities linking these with the corresponding martyrdom scenes at Assisi make probable the hypothesis that these four visual narratives formed part of an ambitious programme, the project of Nicholas III and his entourage, to reaffirm the primacy of the papacy through the revival of the ancient apostolic tradition on which the Church of Rome had always based its authority.[251]

THE DECORATION OF THE NAVE OF THE UPPER CHURCH

The decorative scheme of apse and transepts is complex; in contrast, the decoration of the nave follows a series of relatively simple patterns. There are four elements or registers.

1 The glass: here Francis and Anthony are set among the apostles.[252]
2 Of the frescoed surfaces, the vaults comprise the highest layer. If we include the crossing, there are five bays in all, two of them painted blue and stencilled with gilt stars, thus continuing, and echoing, the decoration in the vaults of apse and transepts. In the centrepiece Francis is depicted with the New Testament characters to whom he was specially devoted: Christ himself and Mary, with John the Baptist, to highlight Francis' role as a witness and as a new forerunner, preparing the way of the Lord[253] (Plate 56). The exalted company he keeps makes this a sort of apotheosis or transfiguration of St Francis, although it is not portrayed as a transfiguration, but as a circle of busts. To the west, over the crossing, are the four Evangelists; to the east, next the entry, are the four Doctors of the Church, Ambrose, Jerome, Augustine and Gregory.
3 Along the north and south walls, high up around the windows, are magnificent series of biblical scenes (many of them now sadly fragmentary). On the north side, in two lines in sequence one above the other, starting at the top, is the story of Creation as

---

[250] Henderson 1981, pp. 34–5 and n. 40, quoting Berengaudus, *Expositio super septem visiones libri Apocalypsis*, PL 17, col. 765.
[251] Gardner 1993, ch. 11; Tomei 1995.
[252] See pp. 307–9, 321–31. In what follows I describe the nave and crossing as they were before the earthquake of 1997: for its consequences, see the summary in Bellosi 1998, p. 271; and see also Bonsanti 1997, pls. 64–9; 2002a, II, pp. 1244–63, pls. 2377–2405, III, pp. 261–7.
[253] Bonav., Prologue, i, echoing John 1. 7 and Mark 3. 3.

told in the Book of Genesis – Creation to Cain and Abel above, Noah building the ark to Joseph revealing himself to his brothers below. On the south side, similarly in two lines, is the story of the Gospels – the childhood of Jesus culminating in his baptism above, and his ministry and death, from the Marriage at Cana to the Passion and burial, below, concluding not with the resurrection, but with the empty tomb, which the women visit in the final scene. But the series is continued over the east portal (where there are no Old Testament scenes) with the Ascension and Pentecost occupying both registers. The childhood narratives mingle stories from Matthew and Luke; the two scenes from Jesus' ministry, the Marriage at Cana and the raising of Lazarus, are both from John; the Passion evidently reflects a knowledge of all the Gospels; the Ascension and Pentecost come from Luke and Acts, with Mary added (as so often in medieval painting) to Pentecost.[254] It is interesting to compare the selection of scenes to the 153 panels in the ceiling of the church at Zillis in Switzerland, painted a century earlier.[255] As at Assisi, a full half of the scenes are taken up with Jesus' birth and early life; but thereafter the large majority are scenes of his ministry. The Passion is amply portrayed as far as the crown of thorns – but there is no crucifixion or resurrection. Zillis concentrates on the living human Jesus; at Assisi there is the same concentration on Jesus as a human child; but his ministry is reduced to two token miracles, a highly strange and surprising disproportion.

4 Below the biblical scenes is the cycle of the life of St Francis, painted in a continuous series starting at the north-west corner, at its junction with the north transept, passing right round the east end and continuing to the south-west corner. The scenes are at the optimum level for viewing: below them, on the same panels, is a purely decorative band of fictive drapery hangings, which serves to lift St Francis above the heads of pilgrims standing in the nave – and to make the cycle all the more clearly visible to them if they came in large throngs.

Two points are immediately clear in the planning of the north and south walls. First of all, the biblical and Franciscan scenes were not designed to be viewed and studied all at once. The story of Francis proceeds in orderly fashion, as doubtless it was followed by many gatherings of pilgrims, the whole way round the north, east and south walls. The Creation story starts at the same point, but has to be followed in two stages – west to east, then west to east again. Similarly with the Gospel story – Jesus from Annunciation to Baptism takes the viewer from west to east along the south wall, then he or she must return to the west and start again on the second line of pictures. The series of biblical scenes was designed to echo and recall the decorative schemes adorning the nave walls of Roman basilicas. At both San Paolo fuori le mura and at Old St Peter's a continuous narrative of Old Testament scenes on two registers faced its counterpart of New Testament scenes, all rows beginning at the apse end. These fresco cycles date from the fifth century, and honour these apostles in the churches built as shrines to house their tombs. Their importance was stressed by Nicholas III, who commissioned

---

[254] In the account of the women visiting the empty tomb on Easter morning, John 20. 1–2 only mentions Mary Magdalene – but Ruf 1974, p. 120, gives reasons for thinking that John's account has influenced the scene. All the biblical scenes are most helpfully illustrated and described in Ruf 1974, pp. 24–127.

[255] Murbach and Heman 1967; Brooke and Brooke 1984, pp. 134, 137–9 and pls. 29–32.

lavish programmes for their restoration.[256] The arrangement at Assisi lends majesty to the whole conception, but is inconvenient – especially for those contemplating the story of St Francis who wish also to follow the biblical scenes. Standing in the middle, the viewer may contemplate an assortment of scenes in each bay, on three levels and on opposite sides. For example, the first bay contains, on the north wall, the creation of the world – light and darkness, land and water, fowl, fish and beasts – and the creation of man; Noah instructed to build the ark and his three sons engaged in the work, the ark itself – not a boat, but an unseaworthy chest (a play on the word *arca*, used both for Noah's ark and for the ark of the covenant, and so a symbol of the Law), a chest beautifully inlaid with marquetry, its lid propped open, while in the bottom left corner a crouching lion eyes a ram crossing the drawbridge; St Francis honoured by a simple man, who lays his cloak on the ground for him to tread on, Francis gives his cloak to a poor knight, and has a vision of a palace filled with Christian armour – all read from left to right (Plate 53). On the opposite wall are the Annunciation and Visitation, the Marriage at Cana, the raising of Lazarus – these four read from right to left; three of Francis' posthumous miracles – a mortally wounded man healed, death cheated long enough for a woman to complete her confession, a prisoner accused of heresy freed – to be read from left to right (Plate 59). Three of these scenes inaugurate their respective cycles. The first creation of the world is opposite the new creation heralded by the Annunciation; and Francis stepping on to the cloak heralds the coming of the new saint who follows in Christ's footsteps. But there is no immediately obvious detailed coherence. It is clear that a methodical viewing of the scheme of decoration bay by bay is not an easy option.

Secondly, the nave of the Upper Church is a large open space, designed for the accommodation and instruction of lay congregations, a meeting point for the friars and the rest of the world, focused on St Francis. On the surface, we are offered a straightforward historical, literal representation of the story in Genesis and of the life of Jesus, with the life of Francis beneath. It is indeed the case that the history is divided into three ages – of the Father, the Son and St Francis – superficially similar to the Joachite scheme as interpreted by some Franciscans. But there is no hint here of the wayward elements in the Joachite scheme, nothing of the prophecies of Daniel which inspired it.[257] It may seem strange and controversial to call the schemes historical or label them as plain narratives, since modern critics hardly look to Genesis for history; much of the life of Jesus at Assisi concentrates on stories widely considered legendary – the infancy narratives and the miracles at Cana and Bethany – and the life of Francis has more visions and miracles in it than would be fashionable today. But to a viewer around 1300 the three narrative elements, taken from Genesis, the Gospels and St Bonaventure's *Life of St Francis*, would stand out as representing a historical approach. They were designed in such a way that they could be read and understood as unfolding dramatic stories directly and straightforwardly.

I am aware that this view is currently unfashionable. The recent trend has been to argue that the biblical and the Franciscan stories are not intended to be interpreted in

---

[256] See p. 351.   [257] Daniel 7; Reeves 1969.

Plate 53 Upper Church nave, first bay, north wall, with Cycle nos. 1–3 (© www.Assisi.de. Photo Stefan Diller).

the historical sense at all: they are theological.[258] This is a misleading dichotomy. It has indeed often been said that the Gospels are not historical narratives, but works of theology. But at the heart of the theology of the Gospels lies the claim that Jesus really existed, that the story is genuine history. This is an inescapable element in Christian theology: the story must be true. The truth (as he understood it) was expressed very dramatically by the author of St John's Gospel at the outset – 'In the beginning was the Word' is a grand theological statement (John 1. 1); but in the next breath we are told that 'There was a man sent from God whose name was John' (John 1. 6) – facts, such as the Baptist's name and that John baptised in Jordan, and the theology of the Word are inextricably interwoven in the Fourth Gospel.[259] For St Paul the core of the Gospel was the death and resurrection of Christ. He preached 'how that Christ died for our sins according to the scriptures; and that he was buried, and that he rose again the third day according to the scriptures'. Paul gave a list of the witnesses to the risen Lord: 'he was seen of Cephas (Peter), then of the twelve. After that he was seen of about five hundred brethren at once; of whom the greater part remain unto this present . . . After that, he was seen of James; then of all the Apostles. And last of all he was seen of me also . . . the least of the apostles.' He emphasised to the Corinthians his apostolic credentials: 'I delivered unto you first of all that which I also received . . . Therefore whether it were I or they, so we preach, and so ye believed.' Paul received and shared in the apostolic tradition in the very early days of the Church. His visit to Jerusalem when he stayed with St Peter was not more than seven years after the crucifixion. There is other early evidence. St Peter spoke of Christ's life as well as of his death and resurrection when he visited the centurion Cornelius – his speech as recorded in Acts seems based on an Aramaic source earlier than Acts itself. 'That word . . . began from Galilee, after the baptism which John preached. How God anointed Jesus of Nazareth with the Holy Ghost and with power: who went about doing good, and healing all that were oppressed of the devil; for God was with him. And we are witnesses of all things which he did both in the land of the Jews, and in Jerusalem; whom they slew and hanged on a tree: him God raised up the third day, and shewed him openly; not to all the people, but unto witnesses chosen before of God, even to us, who did eat and drink with him after he rose from the dead. And he commanded us to preach unto the people, and to testify that it is he which was ordained of God to be the judge of quick and dead.'[260] Jesus of Nazareth lived. If he had not lived he could not have been put to death under Pontius Pilate, and 'if Christ be not risen, then is our preaching vain' (1 Cor. 15. 14). As has been succinctly observed about the Christmas message and the Nativity stories (even if they have legendary elements in them) – 'no baby, no Church'.

The wall paintings in the nave of the Upper Church have indeed a theological content; but the heart and core of their theology is a plain statement to their lay audience: the story

---

[258] This is a major theme of Ruf 1974: see esp. p. 218, 'unicamente dal punta di vista teologica'.

[259] The fullest and most convincing study is still Dodd 1963. Robinson 1985, chs. 1–6, expounded the point very fully – though he oddly proposed that the Prologue was a later addition (ibid. pp. 158–9 and refs.). I am well aware that many scholars do not accept the genuineness of the historical element in John, but it is inescapable that the author or authors meant us to do so – 'we know that his witness is true' (John 21. 24).

[260] 1 Cor. 15. 3–11; Acts 10. 37–42; Dodd 1944, pp. 7–35, esp. pp. 7–24.

of God's creation of the world; the story of Jesus' birth, life, death and resurrection; the story of the life and miracles of St Francis – these are all historically true. The modern interpreter will not believe in the historical truth of everything there presented; but the historical message is none the less powerful for that.

The distinction between letter and spirit dates back to Patristic times. In the central Middle Ages commentators generally thought of Scripture as a letter addressed to mankind by God. The Evangelists were traditionally represented as writing at the dictation of an angel or of the Holy Spirit – as on the crossing vault in the Upper Church at Assisi.[261] A variety of senses might be discerned – literal, historical, allegorical, symbolic, parabolic, mystical, moral, doctrinal. In the ninth century John Scotus Eriugena postulated a twofold division. First, mystery or allegory, which embraced historical events and institutions, and has both a literal and a spiritual meaning, the one for the simple, the second for the wise; thus the old Law prefigures the new. Second, symbol, which includes metaphor, parable and doctrinal teaching. This must be accepted by all Christians; the simple must believe, even if they cannot understand. Difficulties arose because Patristic tradition was not agreed as to the meaning of 'literal' and 'historical'. For example, Jerome said that Abigail, the girl brought to King David in his old age to warm his bed, was a symbol only, while Augustine held that Bathsheba was a real historical person. By the second half of the thirteenth century biblical scholarship had advanced considerably and a clear definition was given by St Thomas Aquinas. 'His *Summa* opens with a statement of the whole problem of the literal and spiritual senses and their relationship . . . God is the principal author of Holy Scripture. Human writers express their meaning by words; but God can also express his meaning by "things", that is by historical happenings. The literal sense of Scripture, therefore, is what the human author expressed by his words; the spiritual senses are what the divine author expressed by the events which the human author related. Since the Bible is the only book which has both a divine and a human authorship, only the Bible can have both a literal and spiritual sense.' This offered a solution to the question of what senses should be assigned to the 'letter'. 'But if the "letter" is defined as the whole intention of the inspired writer, it makes no difference whether he expresses himself in plain language or symbolically or metaphorically. The literal sense, as St Thomas explained, was not the figure of speech, but its content, that which it figured. The spiritual senses were not derived from the words of the writer, but from the sacred history in which he was taking part, and whose meaning at the time was known only to God, its author.'[262]

At the turn of the twelfth and thirteenth centuries, theological studies at the University of Paris seem to have concentrated on moralities and questions. The arrival of the two main Orders of friars altered the emphasis. The Dominicans opened their *studium generale* in Paris in 1229, the Franciscans theirs in 1231. The *raison d'être* of the Dominicans was doctrinal preaching: they regarded study, scholarship and disputation as essential qualifications for their mission as evangelists. St Francis and his early friars were penitential preachers, but many students, and their professors, chose to enter the Order,

---

[261] See above, pp. 344–7 and Plates 47, 48.
[262] Smalley 1952, *passim*, esp. pp. 41–2 – quotations from p. 300.

and their abilities made them influential. The value of a fitting academic education for Franciscan preachers was soon promoted. In both Orders the Bible was given a central role in the curriculum. Learned friars compiled concordances, and studied languages in order to amend and correct corrupt and defective texts. The Dominican Hugh of St Cher, who held one of the two chairs of theology at Saint-Jacques from 1230 to 1235, produced postills – that is continuous glosses interposed between the lines of the text – no doubt with the help of his pupils, for the whole Bible. His fellow Dominican Albert the Great made use of Hugh's postills in his own teaching and concentrated on the literal sense. In his Commentary on the Book of Lamentations, he explains its fourfold division as being due to its historical subject matter. It is a lament for the loss of property and of glory, for present misery contrasted with memories of past happiness. He criticises other commentators for providing explanations such as 'that man and the world consist of four elements, or that there are four seasons in the year: "but our custom is not to concern ourselves with divisions which cannot be deduced from the letter." His commentaries on the Gospels . . . show his purpose at its clearest. The story of St Peter's denial had lent itself easily to moralisation; St Peter signified the sinner, the servants and bystanders three stages of sin: temptation, consent, misdoing. St Albert remarks: "all this can be expounded morally, but it does not seem profitable to me to distract my readers' minds from the piety of faith; so we pass over such expositions." In commenting on the temptation of Our Lord in the wilderness to change stone into bread, he says: "this is the literal truth", and goes on to reject the conventional comparisons between the hard stone and the Law, or the sinner's heart: "I think it an absurd exposition, and contrary to the mind of the author."[263]

St Bonaventure used Hugh of St Cher's postills extensively; it looks as though he may have attended Hugh's lectures before he decided to join the Minors. Bonaventure's own postill on Ecclesiastes, written between 1253 and 1257, contains some spiritual exposition, but its emphasis is on the literal. Already in the prologue he confronts the difficult question: in what sense are we being taught to despise all worldly things as vanity, when we know (from Genesis) that the world reflects the goodness of God, its creator? 'The postill, prologue included, is a magnificent monument to the literal interpretation of a book having a specific aim and raising specific problems.'[264] A literal, historical reading, as defined by Aquinas, of the cycles in the nave is, then, in harmony with St Bonaventure's outlook and teaching.

In the frescoes in the Lower Church there was some attempt to make parallels: the stripping of Francis has opposite to it the stripping of Jesus; the death of St Francis and the raising of his soul to heaven face the revelation of Jesus at Emmaus, a resurrection scene. The stained glass windows in the apse select scenes from the Old Testament which were considered to prefigure the New.[265] Scenes from the Old Testament (or the old Law) are called 'types', and the related New Testament scene (the new law), the 'anti-type'. Typology originated in Old Testament times: the Jews tended to view the events of their history in terms of prophecy and its fulfilment. Christ was conscious

---

[263] Smalley 1952, pp. 264–300, esp. pp. 299–300.
[264] Smalley 1952, p. 298; cf. pp. 273–5.   [265] See pp. 289–92, 296, 311–13.

of living out a pattern of prophecy which went back to the patriarchs. When certain scribes and Pharisees asked him for a sign, Jesus answered: 'No sign shall be given . . . but the sign of the prophet Jonas. For as Jonas was three days and three nights in the whale's belly, so shall the Son of Man be three days and three nights in the heart of the earth' (Matt. 12. 39–40). From the very beginning of the Church, the preaching of the Gospel was linked at many points with the words and deeds of the Old Testament. St Peter made frequent references to the patriarchs, and St Stephen offered the Council (the Sanhedrin) a distilled history lesson from the time of Abraham, through Joseph and Moses to Solomon and the prophets, before he was stoned to death (Acts 1–7). St Paul preached and wrote 'that Christ died for our sins according to the scriptures; and that he was buried, and that he rose again the third day according to the scriptures' (1 Cor. 15. 3–4). In Christian art the pairing of type and anti-type can be traced back to the catacombs. Types could be prefigurations, or symbolic parallels, or opposites.[266]

The Old Testament cycle in the Upper Church is restricted to the Book of Genesis, which relates the early history of mankind up to the advent of Moses and the Law. It provides some standard prefigurations. Christ is the second Adam – though the creation of Adam is not directly opposite the Nativity. Instead, the creation of Eve faces the Nativity, highlighting the role of Mary, who restores what Eve lost, and whose reclining figure dominates the scene (Plate 54). The sacrifice of Isaac prefigures Christ's sacrifice – it is opposite the kiss of Judas, which precipitated the events of the Passion: Abraham's obedience to God prefigures Christ's obedience, Isaac's submission, Christ's non-resistance. Joseph as saviour of his people is a precursor of Christ the saviour of us all. The decorative programme chosen includes symbolism and typology, but the main emphasis is on narrative. The narrative is significant, and rigorously selective. It is not overburdened. Only one Old Testament book is illustrated: Genesis. So standard prefigurations from later books of the Old Testament, as for example Jonah remaining three days and nights in the belly of the whale, are of necessity all omitted. Specific references in the New Testament scenes to their opposite numbers are likewise incomplete – what was foretold by the prophets being outside the scope of the scheme. Jesus' ministry is not elaborated. No scene records the sermon on the mount, the sending forth of the disciples, the draught of fishes. Their absence allows ample scope for the unfolding of three themes: the Nativity, the Passion, and the role of Mary. These three themes had been central to St Francis' personal spirituality. They continued central to the piety the Franciscans fostered among the laity.[267] 'The humility of the incarnation and the charity of the Passion so especially occupied his memory that he scarcely ever wanted to think of anything else', Celano wrote in his First Life of St Francis, and he had an especial devotion to the Virgin. The Salutation Francis composed for her begins: 'Hail Lady, holy queen, holy Mary mother of God, who art the virgin fashioned as the Church, and chosen of the most holy Father from heaven, whom he consecrated with his most holy Son, the beloved, and the Holy Ghost the Paraclete, in whom is all plenitude of grace and everything good.'[268] Mary is at the beginning and the ending of the cycle;

---

[266] Wayment 1972, p. 7.
[267] Cf. Delaruelle 1975, section II, esp. pp. 229–73; Poulenc 1983.
[268] 1 Cel. 84; Esser 1976, p. 418.

Plate 54 The Nativity, the second bay, south wall. This image also shows the decoration of the ribs and spaces between the scenes, framed by curved bands of painted cosmatesque ornament and a curved band of fictive cornice; also the wide band in which 'marble' polygonal frames surrounding stylised flowers alternate with oval frames containing busts of saints. Top right, a putto holding a flower springs from the mouth of an amphora. (© www.Assisi.de. Photo Stefan Diller.)

addressed by the archangel Gabriel; presiding over the apostles at Pentecost. In the upper register she is a major figure in the first six of the eight scenes: the Annunciation, the Visitation, the Nativity, the Adoration of the Magi, the Presentation in the Temple, the Flight into Egypt – she was probably also in the seventh, Christ at the age of twelve in the Temple in the midst of the doctors (Luke 2. 42–51), but the fresco is badly damaged and the surrounding figures are indecipherable. In the lower register she appears in four of the eight scenes, in the Marriage at Cana, Jesus carrying his cross, the Crucifixion and the Lamentation. In this scene Mary clasps her son's dead body, her right arm supporting his head and shoulders, her left arm embracing his waist. Mary Magdalene kneels at his feet, holding and kissing his left foot; St John kneels at his side, grasping his left hand, while another Mary weeps. Behind the chief mourners stand more of the women who followed Jesus, and Joseph of Arimathaea and Nicodemus on the right.[269]

A narrative presentation did not preclude meditation, or commentary; indeed provided opportunities for those inclined to avail themselves of them, as well as subject matter for sermons. The very orientation of the biblical cycles can be interpreted as symbolic. The Old Testament scenes move from west to east along the north wall, aligned with night time and the moon, while the New Testament scenes are on the south wall, and the sun streams through the windows on its side by day, casting light on the north wall. 'As the moon receives her light from the sun, so the Old Testament is illumined by the New.'[270]

A typological scheme of facing scenes is not the only method of displaying relationships. Links can be drawn on the same wall, both vertically and diagonally. Both occur at Assisi. For example, the Old Testament scenes in the fourth bay illustrate different consequences of jealousy between brothers. In the case of Cain and Abel it results in fratricide. In the case of Joseph and his brothers it ends in forgiveness and the saving of lives. God sent Joseph as he was later to send Jesus.[271] On the opposite wall there is one example linking the Francis Cycle to the New Testament series. Francis kneeling before the seraph of the stigmata draws the eye up in the direction of the Crucifixion above, in the middle register of the next panel, and Francis dies immediately below the death of Jesus on the cross (Plate 65). But the lives of Jesus and Francis pass as ships in the night, since on the south wall the story of Francis is unfolding in a westerly direction leading to the altar, and the story of Christ's incarnation and Passion is heading in an easterly direction towards the door.

Biblical parallels can also be indicated within the framework of the design of an individual scene. In the Crucifixion, for example, the cross is raised over Adam's grave. In the Francis cycle two scenes have references to later books of the Old Testament. The eighth scene shows Francis portrayed as a second Elijah. The typology of Elijah

---

[269] Ruf 1974, pp. 116–19, with plate, p. 115, rejects its designation as a Lamentation and argues that the scene represents the burial of Christ. But, although damaged, the main components of the scene are quite clearly recognisable. The rock is there in the background, but the new sepulchre carved within it is not visible. Christ's body is not yet being prepared for burial with spices and linen cloths (John 19. 39–42), or committed to the tomb; it is being grieved over. See Plate 65.

[270] Bonaventure, *Hexaemeron*, xiii. 29, *Opera Omnia*, v, 392, quoted Ruf 1974, p. 28.

[271] Gen. 4. 1–15; Ruf 1974, pp. 38–9, 64–9.

prefiguring the Ascension was already present in the Upper Church in the stained glass windows of the apse (Plate 33). The fourteenth scene, on the east wall, records how St Francis' urgent prayers for the relief of a thirsty peasant, who had provided an ass for his use, caused running water to flow from the solid rock. Francis is being likened to Moses, who, when the Israelites in the wilderness complained that they and their children and cattle were like to die of thirst, struck the rock with his rod and water came out.[272]

Perhaps the most interesting, because of the richness of its imagery, is the scene of St Clare grieving over his dead body (Plate 55). On the morning after St Francis died, the crowds of friars and the clergy and citizens of Assisi who had gathered round his deathbed accompanied his body from the Portiuncula back to the city, bearing tree branches and candles, and singing hymns and praises. They carried the bier via San Damiano, where Francis had installed Clare and the Poor Ladies. In this twenty-third scene St Clare makes her only appearance in the cycle. Directly opposite her, in the top register, is the Fall of Eve. This implicit association of her with the Virgin Mary is made explicit in the scene itself. The design of the lower right-hand sector is closely based on a Lamentation; many of its details can be compared to those of the Lamentation depicted on the same wall two bays down. Clare has her left arm round Francis' waist, while her right arm is under his shoulder; her hand must be supporting his head, for it is raised, and the two haloed heads incline towards each other. One of the nuns, in a position analogous to St John's, leans over his side, raising his left hand which she kisses, while another nun recapitulates the role of Mary Magdalene, kneeling at his feet, and holding and kissing his left foot.[273]

In the left-hand half of the scene citizens and clergy and friars are gathered. Some in the background hold olive branches, clergy and friars hold candles, and one of the friars is singing. It looks entirely appropriate, though the composition is based on the left side of a Triumphal Entry into Jerusalem, including the boy shown climbing a tree to gather more branches (a scene, incidentally, omitted from the life of Jesus above). The artist has achieved his overall effect by successfully integrating elements from a conflation of two scenes in the Passion sequence. But on the right, instead of an imposing gateway into Jerusalem, there is an imposing church. What is it? What does it represent? Certainly it is not an attempt to depict the humble church of San Damiano, which Francis repaired with his own hands and which will have been familiar to the friars and to many of the pilgrims who visited the Basilica. Nor is it a picture of Santa Chiara, begun in 1257 and consecrated in 1265, whose architecture is based on the Upper Church; nor of the church of the Holy Sepulchre in Jerusalem. The church has a lofty nave and two aisles, the façade is faced with marble, with coloured marble decoration; it has Romanesque arches and two rose windows, but also a Gothic pointed arch, lunette, niche, pinnacles, and snail crockets. A carved Romanesque tympanum shows Christ with two kneeling angels, with a Madonna and child in a Gothic niche above, adored by six carved angels; there are statues in the pinnacles, two more kneeling angels with

---

[272] Bonav., VII, 12–13; Exod. 17. 1–6; cf. Kleinschmidt 1915–28, II, 123 and n. 2; Clasen 1961, p. 210; Ruf 1974, pp. 174, 250 and nn. 118–20; and see pp. 238–9, 411–13 and Plates 58, 68.

[273] See above, p. 374 and note 269; and see Plate 65.

Plate 55 St Clare grieving over St Francis' dead body at San Damiano on its way to Assisi, Cycle no. 23 (© www.Assisi.de. Photo Stefan Diller).

scrolls flank the lunette, and at the very top is perched an eagle with outstretched wings. It seems that an attempt has been made to enrich and embellish this church with every possible extravagance. It surely represents an idealisation, intended to glorify St Clare, a suggestion of the glorious habitation prepared in heaven for her and her companions. Sabatier wrote: 'Which is the more beautiful, the ideal temple of the artist's fancy, or the poor chapel of reality? No heart will be in doubt.'[274] This fresco is an exceptionally good illustration of the role that images can play, and of the way interpretation of them can alter over time.

The language St Bonaventure used to describe the manner in which St Francis' body was carried to Assisi consciously evoked Christ's Triumphal Entry into Jerusalem, but he did not introduce the analogy; it had already been made by Celano in his *First Life*.[275] But it is Assisi that St Francis is entering in triumph; Assisi, his native city and the headquarters of his Order. As well as all its other significations, this scene is redolent of local civic pride.

The fifth scene, the central scene of the second bay, illustrates the dramatic moment, decisive in Francis' life, when he renounced his father and his father's values, declaring: 'henceforth I can say with confidence "Our father who is in heaven"' (Bonav. II, 4) (Plate 57). Directly opposite, the twenty-fourth scene depicts Francis' canonisation. There is a clear connection between them. Francis' decision to give up everything for the love of God receives its reward. Both scenes take place in Assisi, though the city is not identified by realistic detail in either. The first was staged in the piazza before the bishop of Assisi. On the right two clerics attend the bishop, who is protecting Francis' modesty with his cloak. A central space separates the son from the substantial figure of his irate father, dressed in yellow, who holds Francis' clothes over his left forearm. His right arm is thrown back, his fist clenched, but it is firmly held by the restraining hand of a friend or relative. A crowd of citizens are witnesses, while in the left foreground two children wonder what is going on. The hand of God blesses Francis from on high. The canonisation ceremony took place probably in the Piazza San Giorgio.[276] The fresco is unfortunately badly damaged. Part of the specially erected papal throne remains, but not the pope, who will have been the dominating figure. Great crowds are in attendance, bishops and clergy, friars and citizens. The foreground is most charmingly portrayed. The places at the front and near the altar table are assigned to women. A mother holding two children stands just to its left, her graceful head bowed, while numerous women, several with children, sit on the ground to the right. Under the table a young woman reclines, awaiting cure.

Directly overhead, in the vault, Francis is resplendent in glory. His bust looks down in the company of those of Christ, the Virgin and John the Baptist. The bust of Christ is encircled with the inscription: 'IESVS CRISTUS REX GLORIE' (Jesus Christ the king of glory); the Virgin's reads: 'SANCTA MARIA ORA PRO NOBIS' (Holy Mary pray for us); the Baptist's: 'SANCTE IOHANNES BAPTISTA ORA PRO NOBIS' (St John the

---

[274] Sabatier 1893/4, p. xxxiii. I owe the precision of the architectural nomenclature to Dr Paul Binski.
[275] Bonav., xv, 5; 1 *Cel.* 116. Cf. AF x, 116 n., showing an echo not only of the Gospels but also of the Palm Sunday hymn 'Gloria laus et honor'.
[276] See above, pp. 37–8.

Baptist pray for us); and Francis': 'ORA PRO NOBIS SANCTE FRANCISCE' (pray for us, St Francis) (Plate 56).

By showing him thus glorified, his Order is claiming that by virtue of his renunciation of the world to follow Christ, and his canonisation, Francis has become one of the most powerful of intercessors.

The positioning of the facing scenes of Francis' repudiation of his father, and his canonisation, so that they are linked with his apotheosis in the vault above, and also the link we have observed between the kneeling Francis of the stigmata and the crucifixion, are hardly likely to be coincidence; and if not, they presuppose that some sketching out of the life of Francis had been prepared before the scenes in the vaults and the Bible scenes had been set in place. This is likely in any case. The Upper Church has no aisles. One consequence of this was to provide the space on which the life of Francis was later painted – in a form ideal for this purpose, all the more so because the lofty windows stop sufficiently above ground level to leave ample room for a continuous line of frescoes. In contrast, the biblical scenes have to make do with spandrels – with the awkward wall spaces not usurped by the windows – though admittedly they are broad and ample spandrels. When a major campaign of decoration for the nave was embarked on in the church built to house his relics, but in which for security reasons these relics were hidden and invisible, there was scope for a narrative cycle of St Francis' life and miracles, of the type familiar from altar panels, on a spectacular scale.

THE ST FRANCIS CYCLE

The story is told in the form of a narrative horizontal strip the whole way round the nave, along the wall surface below the triforium passage. It is integrated into the overall design by means of the remarkable range of painted architectural and decorative devices used to frame the images. A pattern of drapery hangings, echoing though distinct from those of the choir, creates a unified dado (Colour Plate 5). The scenes are grouped between the structural clustered columns which support the vaults, three scenes on each side in the three bays nearest the altar, four in the fourth bay nearest the door. Each individual scene is immediately framed by a plain red border, as in some panel paintings, with an inner band of pale blue[277] (Colour Plate 7). They are further surrounded by a complete fictive architectural setting composed of a series of beautiful coloured and decorated simulated marble twisted columns, topped with foliage capitals supporting a coffered architrave (Plate 57). The painted corbels, together with the architrave and the band of cosmatesque decoration above it, serve to unify the space and emphasise the horizontal. All these elements reinforce the links with the earlier decoration in the choir, recapitulating the rich profusion of illusionistic motifs introduced there by Cimabue. The functions of the row of painted corbels are developed further in the nave. Those responsible for the design of the cycle could have chosen simply to draw the eye down both sides to focus on the centre of the entrance wall, which would have

---

[277] For this and what follows see White 1967, pp. 23–47; Bellosi 1998, pp. 184–94, 210 and refs. See also pp. 176 and note 53, 205, 207 and Plates 59, 61.

Plate 56 Apotheosis of St Francis, Upper Church nave, second bay, vault. Christ is in the west web, nearest the high altar; opposite him is St Francis; in the south web (viewer's right) the Virgin Mary; and in the north John the Baptist. It appears back to front because one has to view the vaults from below. (© www.Assisi.de. Photo Stefan Diller.)

W

N + S

E

Plate 57 Upper Church nave, second bay, north wall, with Cycle nos. 4–6 (© www.Assisi.de. Photo Stefan Diller).

mirrored the apse; instead they decided to provide a focal point for each bay. The device was most effective in the bays with three scenes, where it highlights the centre of the central scene. The corbels are deployed in the opposite direction to that employed by Cimabue, fanning out from the centre, those on the left seen from the right, those on the right from the left. The orthogonals of the capitals and of the bases of the columns, and the pattern lines of the coffering, are all made to recede in similar fashion. The result is to create not just a splendid frame for each group of scenes, but a frame that itself makes a positive contribution to the way in which the scenes are viewed. The most successful symmetry, and visual enhancement of the layers of meaning, is achieved in the second bay of the north wall containing scenes 4–6. The explanatory text below the central scene 5 reads: 'When he restored everything to his father, he discarded his clothes and renounced his father's goods and earthly possessions, saying to his father: "Henceforth I can securely say 'Our Father who art in heaven'" since Peter Bernardone has rejected me.' The eye of the beholder is drawn to focus on the empty space – the henceforth unbridgeable gap – symbolising the divide created by the son's deliberate decision to change his life dramatically. The two groups of figures and the stylised buildings behind them stand opposed and balanced. Below the left-hand scene 4 its message is likewise spelt out: 'When St Francis was praying before the image of the Crucified, a voice came down from the cross saying three times: "Francis, go, repair my house which is totally in ruins," by this signifying the Roman Church.' Francis experienced this call in the church of San Damiano just outside Assisi, which was in danger of collapse through age and neglect. No attempt is made to portray the little church which Francis repaired with his own hands, with stones that he begged, with the help of the citizens of Assisi (Bonav. II, 1, 7). Instead we are shown both the outside and the interior of a symbolic church. Details of the outside emphasise the dilapidation: half the roof tiles are missing; there are jagged fractures in the walls. Inside, the screen and furnishings show that Francis is in the chancel kneeling before the altar above which hangs the painted crucifix. Written below the right hand scene 6 is: 'How the Pope saw that the Lateran basilica was near to ruin; and a little poor man, that is, St Francis, had set his own back under it to prevent it falling, and he was holding it up.' In this scene the portico of the Lateran, symbol of the Roman Church, is recognisably portrayed[278] (Colour Plate 7). Francis has taken up his position where the corner column, essential to the stability of the structure, should be. His upright but relaxed stance suggests he is supporting it confidently and easily. But for him, it looks as if the church and the campanile would come crashing down on the sleeping pope. The lesson – that St Francis has been chosen and instructed by Christ to restore the Church – is explicit in the images and their accompanying texts; and is harmoniously underscored by the composition and setting. 'The fact that the building in the left-hand fresco is meant to be seen, within the symmetrical framework of the whole bay, as the formal counterpart of that in the right, is unequivocally emphasised by the heavy, rich, red bands that stress the baselines of the two buildings. These run in towards the centre at an identical angle to the lower border. Even in photographs the effect is so striking

[278] See p. 428.

that it seems impossible to deny that the formal elements of the three scenes have been carefully manipulated to create a single, balanced pattern on the wall.'[279]

The cycle can be approached in a variety of ways. It can be followed straightforwardly, from its beginning, at the corner where the nave joins the north transept, down, then across by either side of the entrance doors, and up the nave again to its close at the corner joining nave and south transept. The groupings within the bays – some more profitably than others – can be further studied as coherent units. Or the main story can be deemed to start at scene 5, Francis' renunciation of his father's goods, and culminate in his canonisation, with the first four scenes forming a prologue and the last four an epilogue. Such a reading also draws attention to the many evident relationships between facing scenes and bays.[280]

All the scenes are taken from one written source, St Bonaventure's *Legenda Maior*. A narrow band of script, sandwiched between two narrow red bands going the whole way round underneath the scenes provides a running commentary. Though much is no longer legible, enough remains to establish that it consisted of extracts, some direct quotations from the *Life*, some summary, some paraphrase where it was necessary to tailor the information identifying and expounding the images into the space available.[281] With three exceptions the sequence of scenes follows the order in which the incidents depicted are related in the *Life*.

What considerations governed their selection? Early altar panels seem not to have been very influential. These commonly, though not invariably, included the stigmata and the preaching to the birds, and a group of posthumous miracles. Though the cycle ends with posthumous miracles, these are different from those in the surviving panels. The Bardi panel, which is the most extensively illustrated survival, has twenty scenes and the cycle twenty-eight, but there is remarkably little overlap: in addition to the stigmata and the preaching to the birds, both have the Christmas crib at Greccio, preaching to the Sultan, the appearance at Arles, Francis' death and canonisation, a total of seven.

Analysis of the subject matter reveals a high proportion of dreams and visions. While still a layman Francis had a vision of a palace full of arms signed with the cross (scene 3; Bonav. I, 3); and the painted crucifix spoke to him (scene 4; II, 1). Innocent III dreamed that Francis, now a youthful friar, saved the Lateran from collapse (scene 6; III, 10); Francis appeared to the friars in a fiery chariot (scene 8; IV, 4). Next comes the vision of thrones (scene 9; VI, 6); the vision of Francis raised from the ground in ecstasy (scene 12; X, 4); and the vision of the Christ child in the Christmas crib prepared by Francis (scene 13; X, 7) all on the north wall. On the south wall, the appearance of Francis at

---

[279] White 1967, p. 42.   [280] Cf. Ruf 1974, p. 220, and pp. 372–8.

[281] Full texts, so far as they are known, are given in Ruf 1974 and Zanardi 1996. The pioneer study was Marinangeli 1911, based on a careful transcription of what was then visible, supplemented by the antiquarian notes of fra Ludovico di Città del Castello, MS 148 of the *fonds moderne* of the Sacro Convento. Some sections of text can be made out in the excellent plates in Poeschke 1985, e.g. pls. 173, 192–3, 196–7. For scene 21, the only scene in the cycle to attempt to portray two incidents within one frame, the caption is especially long. By keeping the caption relating to St Francis' death (scene 20) very short, space was provided for it to begin early, below St Francis' knees, but it still extends beyond its own limits into scene 22: ibid. pls. 180–1, 184. A revised version of Ruf 1974 has recently appeared in Ruf, Diller and Roli 2004.

Arles (scene 18; IV, 10); and Francis' vision of Christ in the form of a crucified seraph (scene 19; XIII, 1). Lastly, there are two visions of Francis at the time of his death (scene 21; XV, 6), and Gregory IX's dream of St Francis showing him the side wound (scene 25; *Miracula* i, 2) – eleven all told. There are also six miracles: three during Francis' life – devils are driven from Arezzo (scene 10; VI, 9); Francis causes water to flow from the rock (scene 14; VII, 12); and foretells the death of his host (scene 16; XI, 4); three posthumous (scenes 26–8; *Miracula* i, 5; ii, 1; v, 4).

Francis is compared to saints, to Old Testament figures, and to Christ. Scene 2 shows Francis giving his cloak to a poor knight. Bonaventure does not name the role model (I, 2), though the comparison with St Martin of Tours' charity in sharing his cloak with a beggar was discussed in some detail in his source (2 *Cel.* 5). But the analogy was well known and would have been picked up. There is, however, a further veiled and more subtle reference. The composition of this central scene, indeed the composition of the three scenes of this first bay (Plate 53), invites comparison with the three scenes from the lives of St Peter and St Paul depicted on the end wall of the north transept, just round the corner (Plate 40). 'The centre of the three compositions is not now the crucified St Peter, but the young St Francis. The V-shape of the Roman monuments fades into Umbrian hills which no less firmly run the eye towards the focal point, the haloed head of the young saint. The patterns of the falling hillsides are caught and echoed in the falling folds of the cloak. The balanced masses of the background are the natural counterpart of the balanced foreground figures, with the cloak and the poor nobleman on one side, and the ass upon the other, evenly weighted round the axial figure of St Francis . . . It is . . . no exaggeration to say that this opening bay is composed in quite firm symmetry about the central figure of St Francis.'[282] Here again the formal structure of the design is involved positively in evoking resonances to assist interpretation of the image. In the opening scenes of the cycle, as in other places in the Basilica, St Francis is being presented, visually, as a new apostle.[283] The subject of scene 8 proved difficult to explain briefly. The wording used was mostly St Bonaventure's, somewhat clumsily rearranged. 'When St Francis was praying in a hut and when the brothers were in another hut outside the city, some asleep and some persevering in prayer, and he was absent in body from his sons, behold, a little later they saw St Francis in a fiery chariot all lit up, flying through the house at about midnight, while the hut shone with a great light; which amazed those who were awake, and awoke and terrified those who were asleep' (IV, 4). This was already long, so St Bonaventure's main point, that St Francis was 'transfigured', 'like another Elijah he was made by God chariot and charioteer' (4 Kings 2. 12), was left out. The artist too had difficulty in realising this scene (Plate 58). The hut is represented by a conventional prop, highly unconvincing in this context, and no attempt is made to accommodate the vision within it. Instead, chariot and horses and rayed globe, coloured red to indicate their fiery nature, are silhouetted outside, seemingly resting on a section of flat roof, their stance suggesting that the group was modelled on a classical frieze. They are painted as seen from above and from the right, while the building and the friars are looked at from the left and from below. The same

[282] White 1967, p. 41.   [283] See pp. 302–4, 321, 365.

Plate 58 Upper Church nave, third bay, north wall, with Cycle nos. 7–9 (© www.Assisi.de. Photo Stefan Diller).

dichotomy occurs in the adjacent scene 9, the vision of the thrones, only the opposite way round. The thrones are viewed from above from the left, the figures and apse from below from the right (Plate 58). The change of viewpoint suggests a deliberate attempt to differentiate between the earthly and visionary realms.[284] The fact that the chariot is depicted surmounted by a globe with sun-like rays resting on it, a detail noted in Bonaventure's Life but omitted from the caption, is evidence that the designs were planned by men thoroughly familiar with the Life, and that the artists either knew the Life or were well briefed. In scene 14, the mountain spring from which the peasant drinks gushes out specially for him in response to Francis' prayer; the rock there yielded water neither before nor since. Reference to Moses is not made in the caption, but is in the Life (VII, 12–13; Exodus 17. 1–6). The last four scenes display distinct overtones of Christ's resurrection appearances. Gregory IX had doubts about the side wound. This was quite convenient, as it enabled a public affirmation similar to that provided by the doubting apostle Thomas. In both cases the 'proof' contained a physical dimension. Jesus, though he came to his disciples through closed doors, invited Thomas to reach out his hand and thrust it into his side (John 20. 24–9). Francis, looking stern, appeared to Gregory IX in a dream, raised his right arm to expose the wound, and demanded a vessel to receive the blood which was pouring out of his side. In his dream Gregory held out a vessel, which was filled up to the brim (scene 25; Miracula i, 2). There are eucharistic overtones here as well, though the main intention of the scene is to add papal confirmation of the miracle of the stigmata to the local layman's tangible verification of the wounds, including the side wound, already depicted in scene 22.[285] It comes in the Life immediately after the treatment of the stigmata itself, with which St Bonaventure introduces his concluding chapters on the posthumous miracles. 'To the honour of almighty God and the glory of blessed father Francis, after his glorification in the heavens, I am beginning . . . with that miracle in which the virtue of the cross of Jesus is revealed and its glory renewed.'

Francis as a new man shone in a new and wonderful miracle, with a unique privilege not granted in former ages. He appeared signed, decorated indeed, with the holy stigmata, and fashioned in this mortal body like unto the body of the Crucified.'[286] In scene 26 St Francis, accompanied by two angels, heals a mortally wounded man (Plate 59). This miracle also concerns the stigmata, this time the hands. The physical presence is stressed in both the Life and the fresco. Francis loosened the bandages and seemed to anoint all the wounds with ointment. Immediately the injured man 'felt the soothing touch of those holy hands, which had the power to heal by virtue of the Saviour's stigmata, the infection disappeared, his flesh was restored, his wounds closed, and he was wholly restored to his former health' (Miracula i, 5). Francis is depicted as standing bodily at his bedside, with his hands undoing his bandages. Christ's physical presence after the resurrection is attested in the Gospels and in Acts. In some of his appearances he shared a meal with his disciples (John 21. 1–15; Luke 24. 41–3; Acts 10. 39–41).[287] The link to Christ is strengthened if the identification of the very seriously

---

[284] White 1967, p. 33.   [285] See pp. 35, 166–8, 233, 235, 408 and Plate 67.
[286] Bonav. Miracula i, 1. The final clause echoes Phil. 3. 21 with a phrase from Romans 7. 24.
[287] See p. 296.

Plate 59 Upper Church nave, first bay, south wall, with Cycle nos. 26–28 (© www.Assisi.de. Photo Stefan Diller).

damaged fresco immediately above as the miracle of the raising of Lazarus is correct.[288] In scene 27 St Francis revives a dead woman for long enough for her to complete her confession to a priest. He is shown, small scale, top left, interceding personally with Christ (Plate 59). Christ's hands display the wounds as does Francis' hand, and one foot which peeps out from under his habit especially to show the stigmata. It illustrates St Francis' power as an intercessor. He is acting here in the role primarily associated with Mary, appealing to the Son in the function specifically attributed to him by St Peter: 'Him hath God exalted with his right hand to be a Prince and a Saviour, for to give repentance to Israel, and forgiveness of sins' (Acts 5. 31). In the final scene 28 St Francis releases a prisoner accused of heresy who fasted on the eve of his feast day. According to Bonaventure's account, Francis entered the prison in which he was confined by the bishop once darkness fell, calling him by name to arise quickly. The chains on his feet broke and fell off, the keys of the prison's doors sprang out, and the doors opened, so that the way was open for him to go. But he, astounded, clamoured at the door, and the frightened guards informed the bishop, who acknowledged God's power. The chains were brought before Pope Gregory IX and the cardinals (*Miracula* v, 4). This story is reminiscent of two apostolic adventures. First it recalls details of the freeing of St Peter, imprisoned by King Herod. The angel of the Lord told him to arise up quickly; and his chains fell off from his hands. The angel led him past the guards, and the iron gate leading into the city opened to them of its own accord (Acts 12. 3–11). There are details too from the imprisonment of Paul and Silas (Acts 16. 23–8). Their feet were made fast in the stocks. At midnight they prayed and sang praises to God. Suddenly a great earthquake shook the foundations; all the doors were opened and all the prisoners' bonds loosed. The jailer in despair drew his sword to kill himself, but St Paul called to him, saying: 'Do thyself no harm: for we are all here.' In the fresco, the prisoner is stepping through the open door. The bruises to his ankles caused by his confinement are clearly visible. He holds out the broken fetters, which are indicated to the bishop by one of the guards (Plate 59). The implicit link between St Francis and the fortunes of the two apostles St Peter and St Paul ties in with that linking him with St Peter in scene 2 on the opposite wall. The figure of St Francis is flying upwards towards the east with arms outstretched; his pose is very like that of Christ himself in the Ascension scene on the entrance wall (Plate 68).

All but one of these seven scenes in which St Francis is compared to others is also either a dream, vision or miracle, but the one, scene 2, brings the number of what may be classed as supernatural scenes to eighteen, very nearly two-thirds of the total. On a more mundane level we have ten, most of which fall into two clusters around the beginning and the end of his career. Three are concerned with his early life, up to Innocent III's approval of the Rule; four with his death and reactions to it, culminating in his canonisation.[289] We are left with only three to represent sixteen years of his ministry. All depict him preaching – preaching to the Sultan (scene 11), preaching to the birds (scene 15) and preaching to Honorius III (scene 17). Preaching to the Sultan encapsulates Francis' abiding enthusiasm for missionary endeavour and his personal

[288] Ruf 1974, pp. 101–2; Kleinschmidt 1915–28, II, 74.   [289] Scenes 1, 5, 7; 20, 22–24.

ambition to experience martyrdom. His Order continued to be actively committed in the mission field. In 1291 Nicholas IV sent brother John of Montecorvino, who had already worked for the pope in Persia, on a mission to China.[290] Preaching to the birds illustrates the all-embracing nature of the preacher's task, as St Francis understood it. The scene is placed under the scene of the Ascension on the entrance wall (Plate 68). In St Mark's Gospel, just before he ascended Christ said to his apostles: 'Go ye into all the world, and preach the Gospel to every creature' (Mark 16. 15). St Bonaventure begins his chapter on the efficacy of Francis' preaching with an account of the doubts St Francis felt as to whether it would be more pleasing to Christ for him to devote his time to prayer or to running about preaching. He sent messengers to brother Sylvester, who was then devoting his time to constant prayer up on Monte Subasio above Assisi,[291] and to St Clare asking for their prayers and advice. 'The venerable priest and the virgin dedicated to God, by the revelation of the Holy Spirit from on high, agreed wonderfully on this: that it was God's pleasure that he should go out as God's herald to preach' (XII, 2).

Francis wasted no time, setting out at once. Near Bevagna a large flock of birds was gathered, and he hastened to them, calling on them to hear the word of God as if they were rational creatures. 'My brother birds, you ought greatly to praise your Creator, who has clothed you with feathers, given you wings to fly, granted you fresh air and who saves you from any anxiety by his guidance.' The birds played their part by listening attentively, and only flying away after he had blessed them with the sign of the cross (XII, 3). Preaching to Honorius III and the cardinals demonstrates the deep respect and veneration in which he was held at the Curia. Preaching was only one element in Francis' calling, but a vital one.

Some potential topics are conspicuous by their absence. There is not a leper in sight. Francis washing the feet of lepers was depicted in the Bardi panel (Plate 17). Such a scene, with its clear message of Francis' imitation of Christ, would have been appropriate to the context of the cycle.[292] The scene in the Bardi panel of Francis doing public penance in the piazza in front of the cathedral of San Rufino, which was based on Bonaventure's account (VI, 2), was another which might have been thought worthy of inclusion. It was dramatic, and capable of conveying the same message.[293] The omission of any illustration of Francis' fondness for lambs is probably due to Bonaventure's brevity.[294] He did however tell stories about Francis' love of poverty and his abhorrence of money – such as his meeting with the three identical poor women who greeted him with 'Welcome Lady Poverty' (VII, 6), and the cautionary tale of the abandoned purse which contained a snake (VII, 5), either of which could have inspired a striking picture. No details of the very beginning of the Order – the decision of Bernard of Quintavalle to join him, for example – are shown. Indeed life in the early days is shown only incidentally. The caption to scene 8 states that Francis and his friars were staying in huts, but the portrayal of Rivotorto is not evocative – except in its indication

---

[290] Moorman 1968, pp. 226–39, esp. p. 236.
[291] He was probably staying at one of the little cells at the Carceri: see Plate 2.   [292] See pp. 187–8.
[293] See p. 188 and Plate 19.   [294] See pp. 184–5, 188 and Plate 19.

that the quarters were cramped, and the sleeping friar used a stone for a pillow (Plate 58). The contribution of St Clare and her sisters is restricted to one scene[295] (Plate 55).

Francis' life story is anchored in its local setting. It opens in Assisi, recognisably in the Piazza del Comune (Plates 53, 5). Many of its incidents took place in or near Assisi. He encountered the poor knight when he was out riding, recently recovered from a long illness – the encounter is staged in the plain below San Damiano. Part of Assisi is indicated on the hill on the left – the Porta Santa Chiara faces us, with behind it the Romanesque apse and campanile of San Rufino. On the right is Monte Subasio with its Benedictine monastery (scene 2).[296] That night, at home in his father's house, he dreamed of the palace full of arms (scene 3). Christ spoke to him at San Damiano (scene 4) and he divested himself in the piazza in front of the bishop (scene 5). He appeared to his brothers in the disused hut at Rivotorto, not far from the Portiuncula, where they first stayed when they returned from Rome with Innocent's approval of their Rule in 1210 (scene 8). Pacifico's vision of the thrones (scene 9) happened at the deserted church of San Pietro di Bovara, near Trevi, which is in the valley of Spoleto, a little south of Foligno.[297]

Francis' representation of the Nativity (scene 13) is not portrayed as it occurred in its original setting at Greccio, complete with live animals and real hay, but in the Basilica itself, the shrine church holding his relics and the 'head and mother' of the Order (Plate 60). It looks like the friars' annual liturgical commemoration of that scene, presented as religious drama. Both the celebrating priest and St Francis are wearing the white vestments appropriate for Christmas Mass. The friars are in the presbytery, intent on a crib, by which lie what look like small terracotta figures of the ox and the ass. Some laymen have been admitted to view the ceremony, while the ladies are looking in through an opening in the screen which cordons off the sanctuary from the nave. Something very like this screen, complete with a little pulpit and with similar marble and cosmati adornment, is still in the Lower Church, against a side chapel.[298] The 'certain knight' of the caption was Francis' friend, John of Greccio, whom he had charged with the preparation of the original tableau in the woods (X, 7; 1 *Cel.* 84–6). He is portrayed in a privileged position, standing at Francis' left, between the lectern and the altar, gazing devoutly at the infant his vision has conjured. Francis, as deacon, sang the Gospel. At the point in the service portrayed the friars are singing. Francis encouraged joyous singing. The voice is a God-given instrument, a natural vehicle for thanksgiving. Unlike other aspects of liturgical worship, song presented no conflict with poverty. The Franciscan movement and the Franciscan cult stimulated the composition of hymns and sequences, as well as religious drama. Each convent will have had its choir master. Salimbene has left us descriptions of two who taught him. Brother Henry of Pisa had a marvellous voice, powerful and sonorous, which could fill the whole choir; he could also produce a treble falsetto, delightful beyond measure.

---

[295] See pp. 375–7.
[296] Scarpellini 1978, p. 100 and n. 49; see Plate 4. According to another reading, the landscape divides to suggest the valley that originally separated Assisi, represented on the left, from the hill, the Collis Inferni, renamed Paradisi, on the right, on which the Basilica was built in his honour: Smart 1978, pp. 32–3.
[297] SL 23 and n. 1. [298] Scarpellini 1978, pp. 101–8.

Plate 60 The Christmas crib, Cycle no. 13 (© www.Assisi.de. Photo Stefan Diller).

He was also a composer in both plainsong and harmony. At least one of his hymns was inspired by a vernacular song. Brother Vita of Lucca was another who composed many harmonies. The secular clergy, right up to the bishops and the pope, Gregory IX, loved his music and his singing. His voice was better fitted for the chamber than the choir. If a nightingale was singing in a thicket it would cease if he sang, and listen, not moving from the spot; then it would resume, and so their sweet voices would sound antiphonally. The Minister General, John of Parma, had a good knowledge of music and sang well. He was so energetic in visiting the Order's provinces that he wore out twelve companions. Most of them exhibited a similar range of talents. They were good preachers and good singers; they wrote a good hand; some could illuminate manuscripts; they were learned.[299] They epitomise the standards approved in the Order in the mid-thirteenth century. The qualifications for membership had been revised but much that St Francis had instilled had not been lost.

The 'crib at Greccio' is the last scene on the north wall of the nave, nearest to the door. It could be held to be out of context in that it occurs neither as part of the, up till now, ordered sequence in which the chosen scenes appear in the *Life*, nor in its chronological setting, which would come after 'St Francis preaching before Honorius III'. For Francis staged the crib at Greccio at Christmas 1223 (X, 7). Yet it is most appropriately placed. The fresco in which Francis is shown holding the Christ child in his arms comes in the bay in which, on the opposite side, the stained glass window shows Christ holding St Francis in his embrace (Plate 39).

The site where Francis first preached to the birds (scene 15) was in the valley of Spoleto, near Bevagna, about three miles south of Assisi.[300] Francis died at the Portiuncula (scene 20). The caption to scene 22 states, correctly, that the verification of the stigmata took place at the Portiuncula, but the painted image above it seems to have transported the scene up the hill and into the Upper Church, identifiable by its rood beam – whose supporting corbels can still be seen today[301] (Plate 67). Here is an example of an exceptionally exciting and memorable local occasion – the night Francis died crowds gathered, the air was filled with songs of praise and the light of candles, and many citizens of Assisi were admitted to behold and kiss the stigmata[302] – portrayed in a recognisable local setting, but portrayed anachronistically. The Basilica was not yet built. The sequence continues. The next morning Francis' body was carried in procession up to Assisi, pausing on the way at San Damiano to permit St Clare and her sisters to see him for the last time (scene 23),[303] and laid temporarily in the church of San Giorgio. Gregory IX performed the canonisation ceremony either in this church or in the piazza just outside it (scene 24).[304] Thirteen local scenes, not all labelled or specifically portrayed as such, but all capable of being readily identified by local people.

[299] Salimbene, H, pp. 182–4, 297–8, 551–2; S, I, 262–6, 434, 802–5.
[300] See AF X, 44 n. 7, for the identification of the traditional site.
[301] Towards the end of the thirteenth century a church was built over the Portiuncula for its protection; this was replaced by the present Santa Maria degli Angeli in the sixteenth century (Moorman 1968, p. 155). For the interior of the Portincula see Von Matt and Hauser 1956, pl. 59.
[302] 1 *Cel.* 112–13, 116; Bonav., XV, 4–5; and see pp. 34–5.
[303] See pp. 35, 375–7 and Plate 55.   [304] See pp. 35–8.

Some local dignitaries and people are given prominence. The bishop of Assisi is portrayed in scenes 5, 21 and presumably 24,[305] St Clare in 23. Two laymen are named in captions – Francis' father, Peter Bernardone, in 5, and Jerome, a knight and distinguished lawyer and judge, in 22.[306] A few friars are portrayed as individuals, but not named – brother Pacifico, brother Sylvester and brother Illuminato, in a group of three scenes running 9, 10, 11 – and brother Leo in 19. Very few friars with no particular connection with Assisi are included. St Anthony, the Order's other chief saint, who is honoured throughout the Basilica, is portrayed and named in scene 18, as is brother Monaldus; and scene 21 features the Minister of Terra di Lavoro, a province south of Rome centred on Naples. The bishop of Tivoli portrayed in scene 28 was Jacopo Antonio Colonna, bishop c.1209–c.1245.[307]

One of the striking circumstances to which the cycle bears witness is the amazing accessibility of the popes. It was Francis who took the initiative. He led his small group of followers to Rome to ask Innocent III personally to approve their way of life. He impressed some of the cardinals, who offered him support and hospitality.[308] Francis was in Perugia in 1216 when the pope and cardinals were there and was with Innocent III when he died on 16 July.[309] When he encountered difficulties in regulating the rapidly growing Order – the potentially serious consequences of which became apparent while he was in Syria – Francis hastily returned to Italy and went straight to Rome, where he positioned himself strategically outside the pope's door, waiting until he emerged. He asked Honorius III to grant him a special protector, a particular cardinal, Hugolino, later Pope Gregory IX, with responsibilities to guide, protect and correct the Order.[310] Informal friendly relationships clearly developed. When Francis was staying with a poor priest awaiting eye treatment, Honorius III and some of the cardinals who were at Rieti, close by, visited him nearly every day.[311] The three popes are portrayed, Innocent III twice, in scenes 6 and 7, Honorius III in 17 and Gregory IX twice, in 24–5. Rome is the location for four scenes: 6, 7 and 17 take place at the Lateran; 28 includes a recognisable portrayal of Trajan's column, which is situated very close to the church of Santa Maria in Aracoeli. This church, together with its convent, which enjoyed a prime central site on the Capitoline Hill had been given to the Friars Minor by Innocent IV.

Francis' sanctity is stressed throughout. The *topos* of a misspent youth preceding conversion is wholly omitted. The handsome, rich young man is already haloed. The opening scene is crucial in presenting a bold but clear and comprehensible message in both image and text. In the fresco a man is shown performing an act of homage, ceremoniously laying his cloak before Francis for him to tread on (Plate 53). In the caption it is stated that this simple man was taught by God that Francis was worthy of all reverence, since he would soon be doing mighty things and so be honoured by all. The wording echoes the Gospel passage: 'And as he went, they spread their clothes in the way' (Luke 19. 36). Here the visual image focuses attention on an aspect of the

[305] Scene 24 is the most damaged in the cycle.   [306] See pp. 381, 408.   [307] Gams 1873, p. 733.
[308] 1 Cel. 32–3; AP 32–42; SL 61, 92.   [309] Eccleston, p. 95.
[310] Jordan, cc. 11–14; Brooke 1959, pp. 56–76.
[311] SL 25. Hymns, responses and possibly antiphons to Julian of Speyer's Office for St Francis were contributed by Cardinal Hugolino, by then Gregory IX, and two other cardinals, Thomas of Capua and Rainerius Capocci: AF X, 376–88.

incident only quite subtly suggested in Bonaventure's telling of it in his *Life*[312] and inaugurates the cycle with what is on one level an Assisan re-enactment of Christ's triumphal entry into Jerusalem. Already we are made aware that this is no ordinary life story. The pace of events is fast and exciting and Christ intervenes personally to direct developments at an early stage. Francis' compassionate generosity to a poor knight is promptly rewarded. That night he dreamed. In the fresco Christ stands prominently by Francis' bed; with his right hand he has just lightly touched his shoulder to rouse him; with his left he is showing him the magnificent palace with all its equipment dedicated to his service (Plate 53). The caption contains the military metaphor – the crusading arms were all destined for him and his knights. The friars are therefore by implication included in the promise; theirs is a glorious calling. Next, the painted image of the crucified Christ instructs Francis to repair his church – a different metaphor here, of building, construction. This leads to Francis making his public declaration of allegiance to his heavenly Father – his hands raised in prayer and his raised eyes drawing the eye of the beholder upwards to where the hand of God appears, blessing him, from the sky (Plate 57). As a consequence of his choice Innocent III has a dream – clearly divinely inspired, though Christ is not shown (Plate 57 and Colour Plate 7). The pope's dream leads directly to the approval of the Rule and the granting of the tonsure to the friars, which enabled them to be granted authority to preach repentance and the word of God (Plate 58). So far the series of scenes together with their running commentary have expounded a progressive sequence of cause and effect.

But at this point the narrative takes an unusual turn. After the climax of the papal approval of the Rule we might have expected a group of scenes illustrating their Gospel mission in practice: scenes for example in which Francis and his companions tend lepers, minister to the sick and poor, preach to the people, beg their bread. Instead we are presented with the glorification of Francis in a way quite beyond normal human experience. He is pictured as a prophet, as a second Elijah; and Elijah was taken to represent a prefiguration of Christ.[313] The subject of the adjacent scene, 9, is the vision that Francis' companion (brother Pacifico) had of thrones in heaven, among which one, adorned with precious stones and radiant in glory, stood out as more honourable than the rest. He was told that this throne had belonged to one of the fallen angels, and was now reserved for the humble Francis.[314] The grouping of these three scenes provides a good illustration of the way in which the design expounded, in the language of painting, religious themes emphasised in Bonaventure's *Life* – the sanctioning of Francis' ministry by the Church, and the spiritual significance of his life. The pattern of ascending and descending movements carries the eye from the saint kneeling humbly before the pope up to his transfiguration as a second Elijah, and down to him humbly kneeling before the cross on the altar. The 'primitive' use of perspective actually promotes understanding. The Gospel way of life confirmed in the Rule points to glory; the slanting lines of the thrones and the angel's pointing finger

---

[312] Bonav., I, 1; cf. AF X, 560 n. 10.　　[313] See pp. 255, 383–5.

[314] Bonav., VI, 6. Bonaventure used this story more than once in his sermons. In two he identified the friar as Pacifico, and in one he upgraded the throne as being that of Lucifer: Bougerol 1993, II, 755–6, 781 (sermons 57, c. 8; 58, c. 11); and Plate 58.

Plate 61 Brother Sylvester at Arezzo and St Francis preaching before the Sultan, Cycle nos. 10 and 11 (© www.Assisi.de. Photo Stefan Diller).

indicate that it is Francis' exemplary humility which leads to his enthronement high among the angels.[315]

In the first scene in the next bay, Francis performs a miracle through the agency of another companion, brother Sylvester, whom he tells to go and stand before the gate of Arezzo and order the devils plaguing the city, on obedience, to depart immediately in God's name (VI, 9) (Plate 61). In scene 11 Francis is again cast in the role of the prophet Elijah. Elijah discomfited the priests of Baal, calling down fire from heaven (3 Kings (1 Kings) 18. 23–40); Francis offered to enter a great fire with the Sultan's priests to test which of Christianity and Islam was the true faith (IX, 8). The elderly priest on the left is the embodiment of discomfiture as he slips away. The faces of these high-ranking Muslims are finely drawn. They are in no way caricatured or demonised. There is no attempt here to convey a pejorative image of the infidel (Plate 61). These two scenes both succeed in conveying a message relevant to the Gospel calling as well. The devils in scene 10 represent civil discord, and Francis succeeded in restoring harmony and peace, the citizens of Arezzo being persuaded to reform their civic laws without further factional fighting. The promotion of peace was a fundamental element in Francis' preaching.[316] Francis and brother Illuminato bravely crossed enemy lines and reached the Sultan with the aim of trying to convert him and his subjects by preaching. Francis' offer of a trial by fire, a detail Bonaventure had added to the story, provided the artist with an opportunity to paint an arresting portrait of 'brother fire'.

Scene 12 is another that lends itself to interpretation on more than one level. It can be 'read' straightforwardly as an illustration of St Francis in ecstasy while at prayer: 'he was seen praying at night with his hands stretched out in the form of a cross, his whole body raised up from the ground and surrounded by a glowing little cloud, so that the wondrous radiance about his body bore witness to the wonderful illumination within his mind' (X, 4) on which the caption is based (Plate 62). It has been argued that the cycle was designed to proclaim Francis' mystic union with Christ and that the scenes were intended to be interpreted theologically.[317] Certainly this scene, and scene 19, the reception of the stigmata, are powerful illustrations of Francis the mystic. For Francis, prayer, communion, communication with God, was the spiritual food of the soul (2 Cel. 96). He concentrated his whole being, 'not so much praying as becoming himself a prayer' (2 Cel. 95). St Bonaventure, himself a mystic and expert in mystical theology, described ecstasy as the third stage on the path of contemplation, 'where the soul feels itself filled with the unction of the Holy Spirit, right down to the entrails'.[318] The inclusion of this scene gives expression to what was an integral part of Francis', and through him of Franciscan, spirituality. There are several indications that alterations were made after the fresco was first painted. The presence of holes for scaffolding poles, filled in and made good, cut into the painted columns framing both sides of the scene are a sign that a small temporary scaffold was erected – an expedient resorted to only rarely in the cycle – and Francis' face and hands and the spaces between were

[315] Smart 1978, pp. 33–6.   [316] See pp. 20–4, 28.
[317] Belting 1977, pp. 35–7; Ruf 1974, p. 218.
[318] Bougerol 1993, I, 314 (Sermon 21); Ruf 1974, p. 166.

THE OFFICIAL VISUAL IMAGE

Plate 62 St Francis in ecstasy, Cycle no. 12 (© www.Assisi.de. Photo Stefan Diller).

redone.[319] Also, it is highly probable that the cloud, in its present form, is a correction of the initial iconography of the scene. Traces of the lower part of Francis' body, including his feet, in the act of levitation, can be made out. The dark band where Francis' habit emerges from the cloud, the thicker dark band at the base of the cloud, and the very numerous dark areas on the folds and sleeves of the friars' habits, were all finishing touches added *a secco*. Intended to indicate the brightness of the light emanating from the cloud, these highlights, done in lead white, have turned black.

In the top right-hand corner Christ is leaning down from heaven. He is blessing Francis; he could also be talking to him. In the bottom right-hand corner, below Christ, is a miniature representation of a mountain, with small trees on its slopes, another small tree and a toweringly large tree on its summit. Could this be intended to evoke Fonte Colombo, the Sinai of the Order? If a scroll had issued from Christ's mouth, might not the words have been: 'Regula et vita Fratrum Minorum hec est' – 'The Rule and life of the Friars Minor is this.'[320] This interesting suggestion was inspired, in part, by an argument put forward by Sabatier, that the artist depicted the occasion vividly described in the *Mirror of Perfection*, c. 1 (= SL 113), when St Francis confounded the ministers (represented by the four friars) who objected to the new Rule that he was making, by appealing to Christ, whose voice was heard proclaiming: 'Francis, there is nothing in the Rule of yours but the whole of what is in it is mine: and I wish that the Rule be kept to the letter, to the letter, to the letter, without gloss, without gloss, without gloss.'[321] St Bonaventure omitted all mention of ministerial opposition and this dramatic encounter. The only hint of dissent that survived was in a story from 2 *Celano* he included, possibly because it concerned a vision. When Francis was preparing to seek permanent confirmation of the Rule from Honorius III, he dreamt that he should form tiny crumbs into a host (*hostiam*) to feed his friars. Those who did not accept it with reverence, but rejected or despised it, became infected with leprosy. The crumbs were the words of the Gospel, the host the Rule (IV, II; 2 *Cel.* 209). There are clear eucharistic overtones. The Rule is sacramental. Bonaventure fully subscribed to Francis' conviction that the Rule was, essentially, dictated by God. I would amend Burkitt's words and suggest that the subject of scene 12 is a conflation of two themes: it is both Francis in ecstasy (X, 4), and Francis in ecstasy when Christ revealed the Rule to him (IV, II).[322]

It does seem strange that the Confirmation of the *Regula bullata*, so important for Bonaventure's thought, teaching and defence of the Order and its way of life, is not among the scenes chosen.[323] Was it perhaps because it had been already upstaged? Innocent III's approval of the Rule, scene 7, happens to be another of the scenes that was altered while work on the cycle was in progress. The whole of the area occupied by the figures, apart from the heads of the pope and the three prelates at the far right of the fresco, has been redone. Originally, Francis seems to have been standing, facing

---

[319] For this and what follows, see Zanardi 1996, p. 186 and the diagram on p. 187.

[320] Burkitt 1932, esp. pp. 51–5.

[321] Sabatier 1910, esp. pp. 355–62. Sabatier subsequently accepted that the fresco was based on Bonaventure's *Legenda Maior*, though he still harboured the feeling that artists could and did exercise a degree of freedom and initiative in interpreting subjects assigned to them (Sabatier 1914–19).

[322] Burkitt 1932, p. 54.   [323] See pp. 232–4, 237–9, 259–61, and Plate 58.

Plate 63 St Francis preaching before Honorius III and the Chapter at Arles, Cycle nos. 17 and 18 (© www.Assisi.de. Photo Stefan Diller).

the pope. Now he is kneeling. In the revised version the pope is giving the parchment containing the short Rule to Francis with his left hand, and blessing him and the group of eleven friars kneeling behind him with his right.[324] Bonaventure's statement that they numbered twelve (III, 7) – not included in the caption – is derived from his sources (1 Cel. 29–31; Julian 19–20). Celano makes it clear that Francis himself made the deliberate decision to write a short Rule based on the Gospel, and to take it and his followers to Rome to obtain papal approval, once they reached this significant number, symbolic of the apostles (1 Cel. 32). Francis' petition was discussed by pope and cardinals, but there is no suggestion of formality in the sources. Innocent III's approval was verbal. He had studied the document. He may have handed it back to Francis. There is no evidence of a ceremony. But it is a formal ceremony that is portrayed in the fresco. The uninitiated will have got the impression that the Order was officially approved right at the start. And in a sense that was the case. St Francis certainly understood it that way. He was not interested in legal niceties. But for the designers it presented a problem. A second, similar, scene could cause confusion. It could also draw attention to the anomalous constitutional position experienced by the Order during the period between the Fourth Lateran Council of 1215 and the promulgation of the *Regula bullata* in 1223.[325] Sensitive to such considerations, they may have approached the subject indirectly.

Directly opposite the scene in which Christ is speaking to Francis, quite possibly about the Rule, is St Francis preaching before Honorius III, scene 17 (Plate 63). In this scene too the original figure grouping was revised. The figures in the two symmetrical groupings of cardinals and other clerics to either side of the pope have all been lowered.[326] This has the effect of increasing the distinction given to Francis, placed at the extreme left of the scene, and opens up a clear line of vision between pope and saint. It was a solemn and important occasion for St Francis, and Cardinal Hugolino had persuaded him to prepare and learn by heart a sermon in advance. But he forgot these studied words. The caption, loosely based on Bonav. XII, 7, goes out of its way to emphasise that Francis' sermon was so devout and efficacious that he clearly spoke 'not in the learned words of human wisdom, but with the Holy Spirit'. Bonaventure's source, 1 *Celano* 73, tells the story a little differently and more fully. Hugolino was anxious that Francis should make a good impression because 'he had been set as a father over his family'. I have argued elsewhere that Hugolino was appointed Cardinal Protector during the winter of 1220–1.[327] According to Celano, Francis was in Rome because 'the business of the Order required it'. The purpose of this visit could well have been the presentation of the final version of the Rule to the pope, who approved it in the bull *Solet annuere*, issued at the Lateran on 29 November 1223.[328] Honorius III's replacement of the earlier versions of the Rule by the *Regula bullata* was of vital importance for the Order, and his role could not have gone unacknowledged. He is not portrayed performing a ceremony; he is portrayed looking at St Francis with rapt attention in an

---

[324] Zanardi 1996, pp. 51, 130, and diagram, p. 131.
[326] Zanardi 1996, pp. 51, 244 and diagram, p. 245.
[328] Esser 1976, pp. 366–71.

[325] See SL pp. 204–5 n. 3.
[327] Brooke 1959, pp. 59–67.

official setting; the scene contains deliberate echoes, inviting comparison with that starring his predecessor Innocent III.

It has often been noted that the next scene, 18, showing St Francis appearing at the Chapter at Arles while he was physically elsewhere (Plate 63), is one of only three not illustrated in the order in which they occur in Bonaventure's *Life*. Its placing where it is, therefore, may have significance. It strengthens my argument that scene 17 is intended to convey an implicit as well as an explicit message. Bonaventure's account of the confirmation of the Rule ends his chapter IV (IV, 11). His account of the appearance at Arles comes immediately before it in the same chapter (IV, 10). This might have led to its insertion before Honorius III – but then Honorius III would not have been opposite St Francis in ecstasy – and besides, the Appearance at Arles could perform more than one function. The iconographic ramifications were quite complex. St Anthony was preaching on the title Pilate wrote and put on the cross: 'Jesus of Nazareth, the king of the Jews' (John 19. 19), during a Provincial Chapter. The feast of the Exaltation of the Cross is celebrated on 14 September. It is possible the Chapter was held in 1224.[329] It was in 1224, one morning around the time of the Feast of the Exaltation of the Holy Cross, that St Francis had the vision of the seraph and received the stigmata (XIII, 3). At Arles brother Monaldo saw St Francis with his arms outstretched in the form of a cross (IV, 10). Bonaventure repeated this information in his chapter on the stigmata, and here he made his understanding of the sequence clear. Seven visions of the cross of Christ were marvellously seen by Francis, or concerning him. Of these the sixth vision was seen by Monaldo when St Anthony was preaching; the seventh was the sublime vision of the crucified in the seraph (XIII, 10). This links the Appearance at Arles closely with the stigmata, which is the next scene. It is positioned as appropriately as possible between the two scenes, 17 and 19. There are four scenes in this bay, and the juxtapositioning of two scenes set in ecclesiastical interiors at its centre works satisfactorily artistically. They share the theme of preaching, both attempting to express the spoken content of a sermon visually; not so successfully, it must be said. The artists were developing and experimenting with the exciting possibilities of deploying figures in interior space in ways which enhanced the impression of depth. It was natural that they would want to introduce a variety of poses. But the result was that some members of the audience do not appear to be attending and one or two look as though they are dozing off. The adjacent scenes epitomise the two facets, complementary and contrasting, of Franciscan preaching: a point made clear in the captions. St Francis' is what we might call charismatic – inspirational, penitential. St Anthony's is doctrinal, grounded in the discipline of the schools. It is worth remarking that both ends of the spectrum are afforded equal weight here. The Appearance at Arles has the distinction of being the only scene in which the Order's two iconic saints both play a role. The position of the scene has the further advantage that it faces the stained glass window commemorating the lives of St Francis and St Anthony in its two lights, on the north wall of the bay

---

[329] Péano 1983. The Quaracchi editors, Abate and Clasen, dated the Chapter 1224, the year of St Anthony's probable arrival in France, but it is not easy to establish the chronology: ibid. pp. 244–8.

(Plate 37). Its composition suggests comparison with Christ's resurrection appearances to his disciples within a room (John 20. 19 and 26).[330]

The Stigmatisation, scene 19, is the most lyrical in the cycle (Plate 64). This scene, and scene 14, the Miracle of the spring (Plate 68), are masterpieces of medieval Italian landscape painting, brilliant in composition, brilliant in execution. A comparison of this scene in the Pescia altar panel (Plate 15) – the earliest surviving – with this in the cycle indicates the extent of the development that has taken place. Development has likewise occurred in the written accounts. Generally speaking, the closer an account is to the event described, the more likely to be accurate it is considered to be. 1 *Celano* was completed in February 1229, a little over four years after the event; the *Legenda Maior* before Whitsun 1263, nearly forty years after. St Bonaventure has been accused of profoundly altering the substance of the episode, and subtly distorting its significance.[331] His account is closely based on his written sources;[332] he has made alterations, but are these distortions or perhaps corrections? In October 1259 he sought the solitude of La Verna to prepare himself spiritually to write the *Life*. Also staying on La Verna was brother Leo. Brother Leo had not been an eyewitness: St Francis had been alone, in secluded, private prayer. But he had been one of Francis' closest companions at the hermitage, in close contact with him. Leo's testimony was fundamental, and continuing. He had not felt entirely satisfied with Celano's account of the vision, and he talked about this with friars who came to visit him.[333] To have at, of all places, La Verna, the Minister General, a Minister General furthermore deputed to write the definitive *Life of St Francis*, presented brother Leo with a golden opportunity to make sure that the record was put straight. The setting was ideal. St Bonaventure was taken to the exact spot where St Francis saw the seraph.[334] There are caveats. Our information is not at first hand – Eccleston records that brother Leo told two English friars, the Provincial Minister Peter of Tewkesbury and brother Warin of Sedenefeld, probably Peter's companion, about the vision and about what Francis had said to brother Rufino.[335] And when Leo enlightened Bonaventure in 1259, thirty-five years had passed. He was thirty-five years older. His memories were still vivid, but were they still accurate? It is hard to believe that St Bonaventure would have deliberately falsified information given to him on such an important issue by friars whose trustworthiness he went out of his way to praise (Prologue 4); or that if he had it would have gone unremarked. Many others were gathered with him at the site on La Verna, witnesses to what Leo then said.[336] His *Life* was presented to the Order in 1263, and all its chapters were read out loud in

[330] Ruf 1974, p. 192. For the positioning of another of the 'out of order' scenes, on the opposite wall of the same bay, see p. 391.

[331] Frugoni 1993, pp. 174–80.   [332] 1 *Cel*. 91–5; Julian 61–2; 2 *Cel*. 135–6, 138; 3 *Cel*. 2–5, 18.

[333] Eccleston, p. 75.

[334] Bonaventure, *Itinerarium mentis ad Deum*, c. 7, 3, in *Opera Omnia*, V, 312: 'ut ibidem a socio eius, qui tunc cum eo fuit, ego et plures alii audivimus'. That Bonaventure and Leo were together, and talked together, at that time is proved by a letter Bonaventure wrote to the abbess and sisters at Santa Chiara from La Verna: 'We recently learned, most beloved daughters in the Lord, by our very dear brother Leo, formerly a companion of the holy Father, what pains you take as spouses of the Eternal King to serve Christ, the poor man crucified, in all purity . . . Given on the Holy Mount of La Verna' (Bonaventure, *Opera Omnia*, VIII, 473–4, Ep. 7).

[335] See note 333.   [336] See note 334.

Plate 64 St Francis receives the stigmata on La Verna, Cycle no. 19 (© www.Assisi.de. Photo Stefan Diller).

the convents regularly.[337] Brother Leo lived on until November 1271, or possibly a year longer.[338] He would have had time and opportunity to let it be known if he had been misrepresented. St Bonaventure's account of the stigmatisation may not be right, but its credentials could not be better.

The model continues to be the Agony in the Garden as adapted for the scene of the stigmatisation by earlier painters. The two buildings in the Pescia example are now clearly humble chapels, marked with the cross. Through the open door of the one behind St Francis can be seen the corner of the altar from which he took the gospel book. According to St Bonaventure he told his companion – who will have been either Angelo or Leo[339] – to open it three times.[340] Brother Leo sits in front of the other chapel. He is studiously avoiding looking at the dramatic encounter, and a fissure in the rock is clearly intended to indicate that he is physically separated from it by some distance. This is his first recorded appearance in the scene, and can be interpreted as a recognition of the vital contribution he made to his Order's knowledge and understanding of what took place on La Verna that September day. His written record, noted on St Francis' autograph letter to him, bequeathed by him to the Sacro Convento, was both evidence and relic.[341] St Francis is praying in the 'orans' position, rather than, as in Pescia, with extended hands pressed together, which was then more usual.[342] The 'orans' stance had been employed by the painter of the Bardi panel, but now advantage is taken of it to portray the side wound.[343] Two delicately painted plants with blue flowers spring from the bare rock in the foreground below the hem of his habit.[344] A particular criticism of Leo's had been that the seraph's appearance was manifested a good deal more clearly than was recorded in 1 *Celano*. Bonaventure described how, when the seraph had flown near enough to St Francis, there appeared within the wings the effigy of a man crucified, Christ in the guise of a seraph (XIII, 3). This vision has been beautifully rendered by the artist. It is most graceful, conveying a remarkable impression of suspended flight and weightlessness. Christ's naked upper body, his head framed with a cruciform nimbus, emerges sufficiently through the softly ruffled feathers to expose the side wound.[345] The only departure from Bonaventure's text is an adherence to the convention of omitting the wood of the cross.

Francis' figure was painted in stages. First his head and halo were done, on a very small area of fresh plaster. Then, on a much larger area, which also embraced most of the lower part of the painted column shared with the previous scene 18, and the chapel behind him, his kneeling body. Next, on two tiny areas of fresh plaster, his right hand and his left. The rocky foreground with its flowers, together with brother Leo's right hand and left foot, was then painted, followed consecutively by Leo's head and his body. Two more tiny areas, his right foot and his left, and St Francis and the scene were complete. But one alteration was immediately made. The small area containing

[337] See p. 244. [338] Langeli 2000, pp. 92–3; and see p. 107 note 15. [339] See pp. 109–12.
[340] See p. 171 and Plate 51. [341] See p. 109 and Plate 12. [342] Gardner 1982, p. 224.
[343] See p. 182 and Plates 17, 19. [344] See the detail in Zanardi 1996, plate, p. 271.
[345] Compare with the renderings in the altar panel from Pisa, now in the Louvre – with Giotto's signature, though the attribution has been questioned – and with the Gothic fresco over the entrance to the Bardi chapel in Santa Croce in Florence. Gardner 1982, esp. pp. 231–6 and figs. 1, 6, 22; Frugoni 1993; and her colour plates 20, 21.

the seraph's feet was cut out, replastered and redone, and a post hole in the adjacent painted column, indicating the use of temporary scaffolding, was made good.[346] What could be the significance of this? I suggest tentatively that perhaps the feet may have been originally painted joined together (as described in 1 *Cel.* 94), that is, one above the other and pierced by one nail.[347] The feet are separate in all earlier surviving images of the seraph, and they may have been separated here because of a decision to introduce an innovation among the finishing touches after the plaster was dry. Rays of gold were applied that sprang from 'the effigy of the man crucified' and struck the kneeling figure below, straight lines of light linking right hand and foot with right, left with left, side wound with side wound. A reason for this new addition to the iconography of the scene – which must have created a powerful impression when it was first done – may have been a concern to make it clear, visually, that St Francis' wounds were not self-inflicted. Doubts were still being expressed about the stigmata, doubts related both to its possibility and to its propriety. An English peasant who had allowed himself to be crucified, so that Christ's wounds appeared on him, had been sentenced to life imprisonment by a provincial council at Oxford in 1222, very close in time to when St Francis received the stigmata.[348] Yet another inquiry into the evidence for the stigmata was held within the period when the Upper Church was being decorated, at Santa Croce in Florence, on the order of the Minister General Bonagrazia, in 1282.[349] Celano wrote that Francis was filled with wonder and, having risen from prayer, was struggling to understand the meaning of the vision, when the signs of the nails in his hands and feet began to appear, just as he had seen them in the crucified man above him a little while before (1 *Cel.* 94). The implication is that the interval could have been some hours. Leo declared that the vision came to Francis 'in a rapture of contemplation'.[350] Bonaventure interpreted this as meaning that the signs of the nails began to appear immediately the vision disappeared (XIII, 3). The painter could not convey this within the frame of a single, still, picture; it was not susceptible of being translated accurately into a different medium. So the fresco inevitably bears the message that the vision and the imprint of the stigmata were simultaneous.

Francis lived for two more years, but for St Bonaventure the stigmisation was the culminating achievement of St Francis' life. In his *Life* the chapter on the stigmata (XIII) is followed immediately by the chapter on the death (XIV); and in the cycle likewise St Francis' death, scene 20, follows. The design of the wall integrates the scenes superbly (Plate 65). The kneeling Francis looks diagonally up to 'Christ in the guise of a seraph', and higher still to Christ crucified. Christ's drooping head, although his eyes are closed, draws the eye of the beholder downwards to where Francis lies dead beneath Christ's bleeding feet. There are a number of differences between this scene and those that have gone before. It was done by a different group of painters, using a different

---

[346] Zanardi 1996, p. 266 and diagram, p. 267.

[347] See Frugoni 1993, pp. 161–2 and 193 n. 110. Christ's feet are pierced by one nail in the Santa Maria Novella crucifix (Ciatti and Seidel 2002, p. 18, pl. 1; p. 28, fig. 7). If the seraph's feet originally showed this new iconography, the probability that both were painted by the same artist is strengthened. See pp. 424–6.

[348] Powicke and Cheney 1964, I, 103; Gardner 1982, p. 221 and nn. 13–14.

[349] Gardner 1982, pp. 222–3 and nn. 22–3; Vauchez 1968, p. 618.   [350] Eccleston, p. 75.

Plate 65 The link between stigmatisation, crucifixion and St Francis' death, south wall, with Cycle nos. 19 and 20 (© www.Assisi.de. Photo Stefan Diller).

Plate 66 Cycle nos. 20–22, third bay, south wall (© www.Assisi.de. Photo Stefan Diller).

working method.[351] They adopted a new archetype for heads – the fourth employed in the course of the cycle – which was smaller, appropriate here as the whole picture was almost entirely filled with figures and required a general diminution of scale. Most of these figures were tackled individually, so that the actual creation of this scene was particularly complicated and time-consuming. This is one indication of how important it was considered to be. Detailed study of the plaster surface has revealed a jigsaw of sixty-two *giornate* – the greatest number in the cycle; scene 9 opposite had the least, only six. *Giornata* in relation to fresco painting has been assigned a technical meaning, indicating the area of plaster an artist could paint while the surface was still moist. In practice, in the nave cycle, there was considerable variation. Some straightforward horizontal decorative strips were very long. For example, the top cornice framing the scenes of the stigmata and St Francis' death, and including a band across the clustered columns supporting the vault that interrrupted it, was completed seamlessly in one *giornata*; it would have taken two men, one beginning at the left end and one starting in the middle, both working towards the right, to achieve all this within one day. At the other extreme, heads, hands and feet, some of them corrections, were tiny *giornate*, and one artist would have been able to do several of these in a day. Figures and bits of figures were not parcelled out consistently. St Francis' head and halo, done in one *giornata*, was followed by the friar sitting by his head with his back to us, in two, neatly outlined, divided at the waist (Plate 66). The friar in the middle of the foreground, kneeling with his back to us, was also painted in two *giornate*, but his head was one and the whole of his body the other. The model for the scene is the Death of the Virgin. The dead figure is laid out horizontally in the lower part of the scene. In the foreground and at head and feet are the chief mourners, the friars taking the place of the apostles, with an overt suggestion that the members of the Order are continuing the apostolic mission. In the middle of the scene massed friars mourn and venerate, the front row consisting mainly of friars in vestments engaged in performing the last rites. Above, the soul is carried aloft by angels, to heaven in this picture, but also, looking up to the scene above it, to Christ. The caption states that one friar saw his soul ascend like a shining star. The artist ignored this guidance and painted a bust, though he did include the white cloud mentioned in the *Life* (XIV, 6). Bonaventure described this friar as a disciple. He may be brother Pacifico, whose earlier vision, in which St Francis was to inherit a fallen angel's glorious throne, is depicted in scene 9 directly opposite.[352] He is shown in the left foreground, kneeling behind St Francis' head, looking up and raising his arm to point.

In the next scene, 21, another friar also sees and points towards the soul with both arms outstretched. He is the saintly Provincial Minister of Terra di Lavoro. On his deathbed, and long deprived of speech, he calls out to St Francis to wait for him. In a separate building Bishop Guido is asleep in bed. Absent from Assisi, on pilgrimage to the shrine of the archangel Michael on Monte Gargano, also in southern Italy, in the

---

[351] For this and what follows, see Zanardi 1996: for *giornate*, see detailed discussion on pp. 19–24, with illustrations 1, 2, 4; for i *patroni*, the archetypes, pp. 32–50 with copious illustrations; for scenes 19, 20, esp. pp. 266, 274, and diagrams pp. 267, 275; Zanardi 2002, esp. pp. 62–6, 85–91; and see pp. 444–5.
[352] C. Frugoni in Zanardi 1996, p. 271.

same hour he 'saw' St Francis, who said to him: 'Lo, I am going to heaven' (XIV, 6). All this information is contained in the lengthy caption explaining this double scene, necessary because of the inherent difficulty of conveying incidents dependent on direct speech in pictorial terms.[353]

The lower two-thirds of the next scene, 22, follow the same basic model as scene 20 (Plate 67). St Francis is still laid out on the bier. Behind him stands a massed crowd, but this time its composition is mixed. Friars, some of them in surplices, the officiating priest in a cope accompanied by a deacon carrying holy water, some holding tall candles, as before, stand nearest to him, but behind them a number of lay people are mingled with the friars. In the foreground, again, a few individuals are painted with their backs to us. The one standing by Francis' feet is a friar, but balancing him on the left is a well-dressed military official, who also uses his sword as a swagger stick, thus enhancing by its angle the effect of the long straight line of the candle at an angle over Francis' head. When St Francis became terminally ill the civic authorities of Assisi had sent soldiers to escort him home to the city, where he was lodged in the bishop's palace. There their precautions were not lessened. They decreed that he should be diligently guarded at night by men all round the palace walls.[354] He was guarded still in death. The civic guards are most conspicuously present, close to the body. On the right a second military official, similarly well dressed, faces us, bearing a shield. On the extreme left an armed man bearing a shield stands equally close to the bier. In the centre foreground one man kneels in splendid isolation. The caption identifies him as Jerome, a knight, and a distinguished lawyer and judge (XV, 4). St Bonaventure is the first to record his intervention, at the same time indicating his function in the story. He performs the role of Thomas in the Gospel (John 20. 24–9), whose doubts, proved to be unfounded, serve to contradict and dispel the doubts of others. A respected local dignitary and a layman, Jerome provides independent witness. He has enlarged the tear in Francis' habit, and in full view of the assembled throng is probing the side wound with his fingers.

This third bay on the south wall enjoys a unity of time and of design (Plate 66). All its three scenes take place within a single night. The first and third obviously balance each other, in their upper as well as in their lower horizontally defined zones. The ascension image in the first – St Francis' soul carried to heaven by angels – is directly related, in a compositional sense, to the crucifix on the rood beam in the third. On a technical level the scenes were carefully integrated. One large *giornata* took in the lower part of the painted column between scenes 20 and 21, the figure of the white-robed friar standing next to this column in scene 20, and the wide band of architectural features, slightly curved in shape, that ran the whole way across scene 22. This *giornata*, in effect, was given the role, and to some extent the form, of a bridge between the scene of Francis' death and the verification of the stigmata.[355]

It has been remarked that the position within the fresco cycle of the stigmatisation does not give it undue emphasis.[356] It is important to distinguish between the

[353] See p. 382 note 281.   [354] SL 59, 64.
[355] Smart 1978, p. 35; Zanardi 1996, pp. 274, 286, and diagrams, pp. 275, 287.
[356] Gardner 1982, pp. 226–7.

Plate 67 The verification of the stigmata, Cycle no. 22 (© www.Assisi.de. Photo Stefan Diller).

significance of the phenomena before and after Francis' death. St Francis' spiritual transport, at once terrifying, blissful and agonising, left him permanently physically disabled, and a living, wonder-working, exemplary saint. On death his body with its five wounds became a sacred relic. The architectural configuration of the nave, with three bays of three scenes and a fourth with four, does not lend itself to a central climax. There is an odd number of scenes, and the 'middle' scene on this wall is scene 22, the Verification of the stigmata. Immediately above it is the scene, now sadly damaged, of Christ carrying his cross on the way to Calvary. The Stigmatisation is the prelude, a pointer towards the crucifixion. The third bay concentrates on the cross, the wounds, and the salvation won thereby. In so far as there is a central focus to the south wall, it is here.

Yet, moving further along, the scenes can regroup. The overall design is so subtle, so allusive, so meaningful, that its student can pursue a seemingly inexhaustible range of nuances and perceptions. The group of three bays with three scenes have their own central scene, 24, the Canonisation. It no longer conveys its message adequately, it is so damaged, but its importance in the story is twofold. Francis received the highest accolade the Church can bestow, and this official recognition of their founder gave the Order supreme confidence in the power of his reflected glory and underpinned their mission. The previous scene, 23, the Lamentation of the Poor Clares, maintains continuity with the previous bay both in its design features and in its context in time, happening within hours of Francis' death (Plate 55). So the canonisation scene is flanked on one side by four scenes covering the obsequies, and on the other by four scenes picturing miracles post-mortem.[357]

A central focus for the decoration of the whole of the Upper Church, as viewed from the choir end, is provided by the counter-façade (Colour Plate 5, Plate 68). It is dominated by two great images which conclude the series of New Testament scenes on the south wall. On the right is the Ascension. A majestic figure of Christ is shown rising from out of a cloud, his outstretched hands reaching up to the outer concentric golden circles of the heavenly spheres (Acts 1. 9). The lower part of the scene is heavily damaged. It used to contain a row of standing apostles; hovering behind them were probably two angels with beautiful outspread wings. They may represent the two men clad in white who foretold Jesus' second coming, and caused the apostles to return to Jerusalem (Acts 1. 10–12). The Gospel teaches that Jesus died for our sins and that his resurrection from the dead won triumphant victory over death (1 Cor. 15). This vivid picture of Him ascending to glory generates a powerful impulse of hope.

The risen Lord instructed his disciples to remain in Jerusalem until they were endued with power from on high (Luke 24. 44–53). This promised coming of the Holy Spirit at Pentecost is the subject of the final scene. The apostles are gathered in an upper room, with Mary in their midst. The Holy Spirit is descending in the form of a dove from a circle framed with clouds, from within which shafts of fire are directed onto the head of each. Filled with the Spirit, the apostles experienced the gift of tongues, equipping them to communicate with people of all nations. They were instructed to

357 Moleta 1983, p. 72; and see pp. 385–7.

Plate 68 The counter-façade, with Cycle nos. 14–15: the miracle of the spring and St Francis preaching to the birds (© www.Assisi.de. Photo Stefan Diller).

be witnesses to Christ, and to preach repentance and the remission of sins (Acts 1–2). On the same level of the adjoining bay of the north wall the stained glass window depicts St Francis and St Anthony as new apostles, taking their place in the series of nave windows devoted to the apostles.[358] There is a clear message here. The Friars Minor are entrusted with the task of carrying on the apostolic mission St Francis and St Anthony had reinvigorated.

In the two small triangular spaces, curved because the area for decoration was controlled by the presence of the beautiful rose window in the centre,[359] are roundels containing the busts of St Peter and St Paul. In the central space above the double doorway nestles a roundel of the Madonna and child. The Virgin's expression is serious and sad; in contrast the child in her arms is happy and playful. In roundels to either side is the bust of an angel. The one on the right did hold a little bird with wings spread, probably a robin redbreast, symbol of the Passion, but this was corrected and the bird was painted out.[360] The change in the iconography, however, was not extended to the Virgin's countenance. She looks over the heads of pilgrims and congregations up the nave to the high altar dedicated to her, and beyond to Cimabue's great frescoes of her death, assumption and enthronement in the apse.[361]

On the lower level of the cycle are two scenes, narrower than the rest because of the width of the doors. The same framing and the continuous fictive cornice maintain continuity. Scene 14, on the left, is set in summer. Sunlight streams down the mountain side. St Francis is on his way to a hermitage, where he will be free to devote himself to contemplation; as he is ill he has borrowed a peasant's ass (VII, 12). The mountain is not identified, but it represents Fonte Colombo (the Sinai of the Order), and also seemingly La Verna as well.[362] Francis is praying fervently, indeed importunately; he did not cease from prayer until it was answered, and the thirsty peasant could drink his fill. The incident is laden with meaning. In the Book of Revelation John described the heavenly Jerusalem. 'He that sat upon the throne . . . said unto me . . . : "I will give unto him that is athirst of the fountain of the water of life freely" . . . And [the angel] showed me a pure river of water of life, clear as crystal, proceeding out of the throne of God and of the Lamb' (Rev. 21. 5–6; 22. 1). Celano had developed this imagery already in his *First Life*. 'The new evangelist, like one of the rivers of Paradise, by his pious irrigation spread the waters of the Gospel over the whole earth, and by his works preached the way of the Son of God and the doctrine of truth.'[363] So water can also symbolise apostolic preaching, preaching to all nations. Christ offered his living water to the Samaritan woman at Jacob's well, assuring her that 'whosoever drinketh of the water that I shall give him shall never thirst; but the water that I shall give him shall be in him a well of water springing up into everlasting life' (John 4. 4–14). Moses struck water from the rock for the people and their cattle (Exodus 17. 1–6). Hopefully the ass quenched his thirst too. St Francis used 'brother ass' as a metaphor for the body. 'Brother ass' is a

---

[358] See pp. 321–6 and Plate 37.

[359] Rose windows were very fashionable in the mid and late Middle Ages, and where their glass survives it is very varied in theme and motif. The glass in this rose is modern (Martin and Ruf 1998, p. 290), so no attempt can be made to conjecture its role in the decorative scheme of the counter-façade.

[360] Zanardi 1996, p. 218.   [361] See pp. 358–62 and Plate 52.   [362] See pp. 237, 239, 397 and Plate 64.

[363] 1 Cel. 89, AF X, 68 and nn. 7–10; C. Frugoni in Zanardi 1996, p. 206; and see p. 46.

beast of burden, and in the design of this scene he performs the task of drawing two walls together. The little ass by the crib at Greccio, scene 13, has grown, and the device of painting only the front half of the animal creates the impression that he is travelling from one scene to the next, and imparts a sense of movement. Vasari, writing in the 1560s, was particularly impressed by the vividness and beauty of this scene, 'in which a man lies flat – his thirst for water as it were all alive – and drinks, lying on the ground by a spring, with such a very great and truly marvellous effect that it is as if a living person is drinking'.[364]

The design of the entrance wall as a whole is dynamic. This is most marked on the diagonal projected from the Miracle of the spring. The dominant mountain slope thrusts upwards. The stance of St Francis at prayer links him with the Virgin and child and also encourages the viewer to look up higher to the risen Christ, so brilliantly painted that he seems literally to ascend before our eyes. The diagonal in the opposite direction, impelled by the dove downwards, is less obvious, but clearly implied.[365] That St Francis' preaching was divinely inspired is explicitly stated in the caption to scene 17, almost adjacent – next but one – on the south wall. Having endowed the apostles with the inspiration and talents fitting them to preach the Gospel, the dove will fly on down to where St Francis is preaching to the birds, scene 15, to bestow the gift on him. And there, surely, she will join the other birds to listen to the word of God she has herself inspired, in perfect symbiosis.

It is an idyllic scene, the most reproduced in the cycle. The birds are mainly clustered on the ground, as they are in the fresco in the Lower Church (Plate 29) which seems to have served as a model for this design. The fresco is not in good condition, especially the lower part, and most of the detail has been obliterated. But it is still clear that a great variety of birds was represented. They are said to have included goldfinch, chaffinch, jay, turtle dove, thrush, quail, green and greater spotted woodpeckers, jackdaw, great tit, hawfinch and robin.[366] St Francis' preaching to the birds has been labelled a work of supererogation. This is to misunderstand his motivation. The Gospels do not provide a detailed code of day-to-day conduct. Christ did not come to make the way easier or even to make it plain. He gave particular examples by which we can recognise the good life, the life of the kingdom of God, and said: 'Go and do thou likewise.' Francis was single-minded in his discipleship. In everything he did he sought to follow in Christ's footsteps, to try to enter imaginatively into what Christ would have done.[367] For him there was no such thing as a work of supererogation.

Christ said to his disciples: 'Behold the fowls of the air' (Matt. 6. 26); that is, watch birds and study them. By their living example birds can be teachers and preachers. The first of their lessons is the need to have faith. Wild birds are totally dependent on God; they trust in him to clothe them with feathers and make food available to them[368] Allied to faith is repentance. The prophet Jeremiah illustrated repentance in terms of bird migration. Migratory birds fly away in the autumn but return the next spring.[369]

---

[364] Vasari 1568, I, 121; cf. Smart 1978, p. 30. [365] Ruf 1974, p. 180.
[366] Yapp 1981, p. 78, quoting Howe 1912. [367] Brooke 1975, pp. 33–9.
[368] See St Francis' sermon to them, 1 *Cel*. 58 and p. 194.
[369] For this and what follows, see Stott 1999.

'The stork in the heaven knoweth her appointed times' (Jeremiah 8. 7). Many birds have a highly developed homing instinct, not only the 'homing pigeon' but, for example, the Manx shearwater. A bird transported from the island of Skokholm, off the Welsh coast, across the Atlantic and released in Boston, flew home to its burrow, a journey which took it twelve and a half days. A comparable spiritual homing instinct would lead to a return to God, the true home of the human spirit. Gratitude is another virtue birds exemplify. St Francis recognised their song as an outpouring of thanksgiving and praise. A different detail of bird behaviour is interpreted in a similar way in another continent, in Africa. According to a Ghanaian proverb: 'Even the chicken, when it drinks, lifts its head to heaven to thank God for the water.'[370]

St Bonaventure's image of St Francis was very effectively disseminated in three media: through the spoken word, the written word and the visual image. He delivered a number of sermons on St Francis, some of which have survived.[371] Though preached to restricted audiences in the first instance, the leading members of the Order and the student friars whom he addressed will have attended to their message, and some, possibly many, will have made use of parts of them in their own sermons. Though they originated as occasional pieces, marking for example St Francis' feast day or the feast of his Translation, they were not ephemeral; they were recorded and collected by secretaries.[372] The *Legenda Maior* was officially commissioned and approved, and in so far as this was humanly possible was protected from rivals.[373] When it was decided to commission a visual counterpart, all the material included in the cycle was taken from this book. The illustrated version had necessarily to be highly selective. One criterion was clearly the artistic potential of a story. But it is interesting that eight of the scenes depict incidents favoured by Bonaventure in his sermons.[374] Stories selected by him as suitable subject matter for sermons were also selected by the designers as suitable illustrative material for the cycle. They were in tune with St Bonaventure's thinking.

Celano had attempted a description of St Francis in his first *Life*.[375] Bonaventure, though he made great use of Celano as a source, chose to include no details of the saint's appearance. Moorman criticised Bonaventure for making Francis 'respectable' and this tendency has been carried further in the cycle, which contains no scenes on poverty. Here 'the dirty patched tunic of St Francis [has been] washed and ironed';[376] not only that, the patches have gone; he has been given a new one, ample and of good-quality cloth.

Members of the Order, members of the Third Order, citizens of Assisi, pilgrims from far and wide, many diverse groups of people will have visited the Basilica and seen the fresco cycle. But opportunity to see it in its context was limited to those who lived close at hand or who chose to make the journey. In the decades after it was painted it will have reached a much smaller audience than could be targeted by the written word. It is the opposite today; more people flock to the Basilica to view the frescoes in their

---

[370] Stott 1999, p. 40.   [371] See pp. 231–42.
[372] Cf. the role of brother Mark of Montefeltro in recording Bonaventure's sermons, noted by Salimbene, H, p. 308; S, 1, 448–9.
[373] See pp. 242–4.   [374] See p. 241.   [375] 1 *Cel*. 83; see pp. 40–1 and Brooke 1967, pp. 182–3.
[376] Moorman 1943, p. 352.

restored state than read St Bonaventure's *Life*: and restoration work, improved lighting and sophisticated photographic equipment enable us to study the frescoes in more detail than ever before in a range of beautifully produced and illustrated books. The visual image is no longer confined to a specific physical location.

At the time the decoration of the Basilica was an exceptional and ambitious project, but it could be imitated elsewhere on a more restricted scale. It stimulated commissions within the Order itself where a convent wanted a replica, or at least an epitome, with adjustments, of scenes frescoed in the mother church.[377] An early example is in the choir of the friars' church at Gubbio, where St Francis and St Anthony are depicted as apostles in the company of Christ, St Peter and St Paul, and two scenes survive – St Francis' renunciation of his father and Innocent III's dream – closely copied from those in the earlier cycle in the Lower Church, but reversed.[378] In the choir of the church of San Francesco at Rieti six scenes survive, out of what were presumably originally twelve. They are: Innocent III's dream, the vision of Francis as Elijah at Rivotorto, the vision of the thrones, the crib at Greccio, the healing of the wounded man from Lerida and the freeing of Peter the converted heretic; all executed in close imitation of the cycle in the Upper Church by a painter trained in Rome associated with Cavallini.[379] There are a few other surviving examples, including a series of frescoes in the choir of San Francesco at Pistoia where some of the scenes are close copies of those in the Upper Church while others have been redesigned.[380] Although visual images were then less easy, and far more expensive, to reproduce than books, scenes commemorating St Francis were widely copied – though how widely is now uncertain, so much has been lost.

DATING THE DECORATION OF THE NAVE

Nicholas III died on 22 August 1280. What effect did this have on the progress of the decoration? It would seem that Cimabue left Assisi on the death of his patron. A succession of different artists took over in the nave. But was there an interruption in the work? It has been argued that there was.[381] Innocent IV's bull *Decet et expedit* of 10 July 1253 sanctioned the expenditure of offerings on the Basilica and its embellishment for a period of twenty-five years. On 28 March 1266 Clement IV, when confirming this, extended the time limit by three years, that is, up to 1281. There is no record of similar bulls being issued until Nicholas IV's bull of 14 May 1288.[382] If indeed papal authorisation was denied during this apparent gap, and if the programme of decoration depended on this mode of funding, then work would have been suspended for seven years. Our reconstruction of what may have happened is hampered, however, by lack of evidence. It is surprising that no continuation of the indulgence under Nicholas III is recorded, and the most likely reason lies in the accidents of survival. A great many papal bulls that were issued have been lost. Another possible factor may be the publicity

[377] Gardner 1974, pp. 232–3.   [378] Blume 1983, pp. 23–5, 32–6 and pls. 34–48.
[379] Blume 1983, pp. 42–7 and pls. 89–102.   [380] Blume 1983, esp. pp. 49–54 and pls. 104–17.
[381] Tomei 1990, pp. 48–57; cf. Belting 1977, pp. 88–9.
[382] Sbaralea I, 666, 14 no. 489; III, 76–7, C4 no. 75; IV, 23, N4, no. 29; Eubel 1908, nos. 671, 1258, 1631.

attaching, from around 1268 onwards, to the Portiuncula Indulgence, which St Francis was believed to have been granted by Honorius III. This was a plenary indulgence, and may have affected somewhat the attraction of limited indulgences. Nicholas IV's privilege of 14 May 1288 applied both to the Basilica and to the Portiuncula, and as the latter was administered by the Sacro Convento, monies collected there could be spent on the Basilica. Successful fundraising benefits from 'matching' in the twenty-first century and probably did in the thirteenth. Papal patronage was also helpful as 'enabling' further giving; that is, it encouraged others to give by, for example, the granting of indulgences, thus producing more than its own financial contribution. We do not know how much Nicholas III gave, but the amount will have been substantial. He was wealthy both personally and through his office. He was a notably generous patron in Rome, and in Assisi too he had every incentive to be a principal benefactor himself. He had the very greatest respect for the Order, and a keen sense of the spiritual benefits that association with it would have for him.[383] Orsini patronage did not end with him in either city. The fresco decoration he initiated in the Vatican palace was probably finished after his death by his nephew Matteo Rosso Orsini, who succeeded him in the office of archpriest of the Vatican. Nicholas had appointed the same nephew to take over from him as Cardinal Protector of the Friars Minor in 1279, and one of the responsibilities of this office, since *Decet et expedit*, was the control and oversight of expenditure on the Basilica. Particularly after his uncle's death, Matteo Rosso Orsini had a duty to fulfil. The two popes who reigned between Nicholas III and Nicholas IV were both favourably disposed towards the friars. Martin IV, 22 February 1281 to 28 March 1285, granted them full permission to preach and to hear confessions anywhere they chose in the bull *Ad fructus uberes* of 31 December 1281, thus providing them with increased opportunities to acquire funds for themselves at the expense of the secular clergy.[384] In his will he declared his wish to be buried in the Basilica, but he died in Perugia and the Perugians kept him.[385] Honorius IV, 2 April 1285 to 3 April 1287, upheld the privileged position granted to the friars by his predecessor. He may have been responsible for erecting the magnificent tomb for his father Luca Savelli, in the family chapel which was in the right transept of Santa Maria in Aracoeli, given to the Franciscans by Innocent IV. It boasted a reused early third-century Roman sarcophagus, was ostentatiously decorated with Savelli coats of arms in relief and mosaic, and culminated in a Gothic gable. Luca Savelli was a Roman senator, a layman. Such a monument encouraged a fashion for burial in mendicant churches, and such status burials were accompanied by appropriately generous legacies and gifts.[386] We would be unwise to assume the Basilica lacked funds during these years.

A degree of continuity is suggested by the decoration itself. A group of Roman orna-mental painters who had been working under Cimabue's direction probably carried on, doing the two arches adjacent to the crossing vault, with their busts of prophets,

[383] Tomei 1995, pp. 192–201; for the Portiuncula Indulgence, see esp. Pagnani 1959 with ref. to 1268 on pp. 168–70; and bibliography in Bihl 1940.

[384] Gratien 1928, pp. 339 ff; Moorman 1968, pp. 182–4.   [385] Belting 1977, p. 28.

[386] Honorius IV's own effigy by Arnolfo di Cambio, now in the Aracoeli, was originally in St Peter's, near the tomb of his great-uncle, Honorius III. Gardner 1992, pp. 76–8, 102–4, and figs. 45, 97, 98.

and the first vault of the nave; but without his inspiration the result was more simplified and traditional.[387]

Closely related to the dating of the decorations is the question of their design. When was this drawn up, and by whom? There seems now a consensus that a coherent, unified plan for the Upper Church in its entirety was established in principle right at the start.[388] It was to be frescoed throughout, the vaults as well as the walls – even the ribs of the vaults and the clustered piers of the walls were decorated. The real features of the architectural structure, fictive architectural elements, purely ornamental motifs, statuesque figures of saints, prophets, clergy, narrative scenes, were all harnessed to produce a visually integrated whole, a riot of brilliant colour that would have been awe-inspiring (Colour Plate 5). A project on this scale provided an opportunity for artists to experiment and develop their skills, and as the work progressed individuals and workshops could study, imitate and improve upon aspects of their predecessors' achievements, thus creating a remarkable anthology of late thirteenth-century Italian painting. For example, Cimabue devised the insertion of a row of painted corbels that seem to support an architrave just below the triforium passage, to create the illusion that the lower wall surface is further back than it actually is (Plate 50; Colour Plate 5). His device was continued above the St Francis cycle, and in both transepts and nave 'it is quite difficult to tell where painted mouldings give way to the real stonework of the diaper-patterned cornice which lies just below the passage'[389] (Plates 57, 60). Cimabue's corbels converge in the apse into a central corbel which is shaped rather like a trapezium because it is painted as being viewed from both sides at once (Plate 51). This oddity does not happen in the nave as the device was deliberately reconfigured.[390]

If, as I and others have argued, the transepts and apse were decorated in the latter half of the 1270s,[391] the overall design must have been prepared during that decade. Whose was the inspiration behind a concept at once ambitious, costly and artistically significant, which transformed St Francis' image? The initiative was most likely to have been taken by Gian Gaetano Orsini, and probably while he was still Cardinal Protector, responsible for implementing the embellishment of the Basilica. In Rome he had already shown evidence of a willingness to involve himself in architectural and artistic patronage by commissioning the restoration of San Niccolò in Carcere, his titular church, before he became pope.[392] The inclusion of so many key elements which deliberately invite comparison with the decoration of Roman basilicas must surely be attributed to him. The upper walls of the nave show a series of frescoed scenes from the Old and New Testaments in two registers beginning at the apse end, as in Old St Peter's and San Paolo fuori le mura, both restored by Nicholas III. There is an obvious iconographic connection between the lost images of San Paolo and the Assisi Genesis material, particularly notable in the Creation scene (Plate 53): the separation of light and dark, and the creation of man, are Roman.[393] The decorative architectural framing

---

[387] Belting 1977, pp. 214 ff, quoted Tomei 1990, pp. 57–8; Bellosi 1998, p. 155 and n. 16.
[388] White 1967, p. 23; Mitchell 1971; Belting 1977, pp. 31–45, 155 ff, 214 ff; Hueck 1981; Tomei 1990, pp. 56–9; Bellosi 1998, pp. 152–8.
[389] White 1967, p. 105.   [390] Bellosi 1998, p. 55; and see pp. 378–81.
[391] See pp. 342, 347–50.   [392] Gardner 1993, ch. 11, p. 246.
[393] Rome, Biblioteca Apostolica Vaticana, MS Barberini Lat. 4406, fo. 23 = Rudolph 1999, p. 5, fig. 1.

of the scenes of the St Francis cycle, with its massive twisted columns, is closely related to that in San Paolo fuori le mura, where the scenes of the narrative cycle were divided by fictive twisted columns, and similar to the twisted columns between the frescoes on the side walls of Santa Cecilia in Trastevere in Rome, of c.1293, attributed to Cavallini.[394] The scenes from the lives of St Peter and St Paul in the north transept of the Upper Church, and many decorative elements employed by Cimabue in the sanctuary and repeated with variations in the nave, recall the glories of the Sancta Sanctorum, also rebuilt and decorated by him.[395]

But leading members of the Order were probably involved as well. When Nicholas III handed over the duties of Cardinal Protector to his nephew he asked the Minister General, Bonagrazia, if there was anything he could do to help the friars. A definitive Exposition of the Rule was requested, and a commission was appointed which included two Franciscan cardinals, one of whom was Jerome of Ascoli, as well as the Minister General and several Provincial Ministers, who advised him.[396] It is likely he sought similar advice on the important matter of the decoration of the Upper Church of St Francis' shrine.

Preliminary discussions may have taken place while St Bonaventure was alive, but it is unlikely that he was at all closely involved.[397] In his last year he worked hard to assist Gregory X in preparing for the Council of Lyon, and he died at Lyon on 15 July 1274. He was however responsible for forging the link between Gian Gaetano Orsini and the Friars Minor in the first place, by petitioning Urban IV to appoint him Cardinal Protector; and he left a legacy: a group of loyal friends and colleagues deeply imbued with his thought. He was succeeded by Jerome of Ascoli, Minister General 1274–9, who was therefore head of the Order when the implementation of the decorative programme was set in motion. He is one of those whose name has been put forward as 'the most likely deviser of the programme'.[398] The extent of his contribution to the design will be discussed in detail later, in the context of his active furtherance of the project when he became pope. He was promoted cardinal by Nicholas III in 1278, and was succeeded as Minister General by Bonagrazia in 1279. Bonagrazia had accompanied Jerome in 1274 when he led a delegation to Constantinople to conduct negotiations with the Emperor Michael Palaeologus, which resulted in the short-lived reunion of the Western and Eastern Churches at the Council of Lyon. Shortly after becoming Minister General, Bonagrazia, with the support of the Provincial Ministers, asked Nicholas III to make

---

[394] The San Paolo frescoes were destroyed in the fire of 1823, but the designs of the individual scenes are preserved in water colour copies made for Cardinal Francesco Barberini in 1634. Their general arrangement is recorded in a number of prints and paintings. The surviving fragments of the fresco decoration of Santa Cecilia are sufficient to show that the original arrangement must have been a close development of that at San Paolo. White 1987, pp. 106, 146, 148, 155; cf. White 1956; 1967, pp. 40, 54 n. 36; Belting 1977, pl. 90b.

[395] See pp. 351–2, 362–3, 365.　　[396] See p. 97.

[397] Romano 1984, pp. 137–8, suggests that Bonaventure may have wanted the decorations.

[398] Mitchell 1971, pp. 130–3. The suggestion that Peter John Olivi supervised not only the iconography of the apocalyptic cycle, but the whole decoration of the transepts, the vaults and perhaps the apse (Monferini 1966, esp. p. 38) is implausible. Olivi studied theology in Paris, but was back in southern France by the mid-1270s. Jerome of Ascoli, while he was Minister General, asked to see some of his controversial questions on the Virgin, and ordered them to be burnt (Burr 2001, pp. 50, 355 n. 22).

Jerome Cardinal Protector. The pope consented to relinquish the office, which he had previously continued to hold in his own hands; but appointed his nephew.

Another man suggested is Matthew of Acquasparta (in Umbria), a celebrated theologian and philosopher, a regent master at Paris of the same cast of mind as St Bonaventure. He was teaching at the papal Curia when elected Minister General in 1287. Nicholas IV made him a cardinal in the following year. That he took a perceptive interest in the arts, and in artistic techniques, can be inferred from his sermons and also from the refined quality of his seal matrix, engraved by Guccio di Mannaia.[399] He was a generous benefactor to the Basilica and the Sacro Convento. In 1287 he donated half his well-stocked private library, as well as vestments and goldsmiths' work.[400] His conspicuous tomb, produced by the workshop of Giovanni di Cosma shortly after 1302, is still in its original setting in the Franciscan church of Santa Maria in Aracoeli in Rome. Above the sculptured effigy is a frescoed scene by Cavallini's workshop, in which the small figure of the kneeling cardinal is presented to the Virgin and child by St Francis.[401]

The impressive, permanent success of the design for the decoration of the Upper Church, so stimulating and so satisfying that it has been described 'as a single work of art, growing towards its own completion and perfection',[402] can reasonably be attributed to its being the brain-child not of any one individual but of a group of friends and colleagues who valued and respected each other: the product of intense, committed collaboration. And this collaboration extended beyond the design stage into a lengthy period of implementation. Two men, Gian Gaetano Orsini and Matteo Rosso Orsini, successively exercised the office of Cardinal Protector for some forty-four years, from 1261 until 1305.[403] This in itself will have provided a quite remarkable degree of continuity. After the death of his uncle in 1280 the chief responsibility for ensuring that work was carried out will have fallen on the shoulders of Matteo Rosso. The employment of Roman artists and their workshops after the departure of Cimabue is likely to have been due to his interpretation of his role as Nicholas III's executor.[404] Jerome of Ascoli held the highest offices in the Order and in the Roman Church at two crucial periods: he was Minister General 1274–9 and Pope Nicholas IV 1288–92. Matthew of Acquasparta was Minister General 1287–9, and an influential cardinal from 1288 till his death in 1302. They were natural allies of the Cardinal Protector in this enterprise, and the survival of this powerful group helps to explain the fidelity of its fulfilment.

The sequence of the vaults and upper walls of the nave down to the triforium passage has been established by examination of joins in the plaster. The overlapping of the plaster on the main arch separating nave and transepts shows conclusively that the decoration of the first bay of the nave followed that of the crossing vault.[405]

---

[399] Lunghi 1996, p. 56; Gardner 1992, p. 83 and n. 108.

[400] Gardner 1992, p. 83 and n. 108, citing Kleinschmidt 1915–28, III, Inventory of 1338, nos. 19, 128, 169, 186, 198, 201; Lunghi 1996, p. 57.

[401] Gardner 1992, pp. 51–3, 79, and figs. 54, 57, 59.   [402] White 1967, p. 23.

[403] Gratien 1928, p. 533 and n. 8.   [404] Belting 1977, pp. 33, 89–94.

[405] White 1984, ch. VI, pp. 154–7. Some scholars, including myself, number the bays from the apse end, where the decoration of the nave started; others number them from the entrance to the church.

Plate 69 Torriti, preparatory design for the Creator (© www.Assisi.de. Photo Stefan Diller).

Successive similar overlapping confirms that, as might be expected, each bay was decorated in turn, ending at the counter-façade.

The Roman painter who headed the team that began the cycles of Old and New Testament frescoes was a great draughtsman. The first of the Creation scenes is attributed, with justification, to Jacopo Torriti because of the close resemblance of the head of the Creator to the head of Christ in the apse mosaic of Santa Maria Maggiore, which bears his signature[406] (Plate 53). The playful vivacity of the animals, birds and fish is also comparable to their handling in the apse mosaic. Restoration work on the fresco in the late 1950s revealed the preparatory design[407] (Plate 69). The creative process of design begins with the *sinopia*, the general outline to be followed, traced in red chalk directly on the plastered wall surface, the *arriccio*; this is then covered with a thin layer of plaster, the *intonaco*; the detailed preparatory design is drawn on this and painted over. The Basilica houses the most complete and important thirteenth-century examples of preparatory drawings that have up till now come to light. The drawing enables us to appreciate the quality of Torriti's talent to a degree not possible in the finished fresco. The broader brush of colours overlaid the refinement of the technique, and dulled the expressiveness and sensitivity of the features. The busts of Christ, the Virgin, John the

[406] Tomei 1990, p. 61. Bologna 1969 and Belting 1977 assign it to Rusuti. And see p. 417 and note 393.
[407] For this and what follows see Tomei 1990, pp. 61 ff, 73 n. 84; *Assisi* 1999, pp. 80–1.

Baptist and St Francis on round shields in the vault of the second bay are also attributed to him (Plate 56). The face of the Creator and the face of Christ are so alike that he probably used the same cartoon.[408]

Torriti was assisted by a team of collaborators which included other gifted draughts-men who adhered to the distinctive executive practice and technique established by him. One of them may well have been James of Camerino, who worked with him on the apse mosaic in St John Lateran.[409] Torriti himself probably did the preparatory designs for the rest of the Creation scenes in the upper register – the Creation of Adam and Eve, Original Sin and the Expulsion – but left the painting of them to his collaborators (Plates 53, 57, 58). The scenes of Noah, the Ark and the Sacrifice of Isaac in the lower register of the first two bays are the work of a painter influenced by Cimabue, while the angels in the damaged fourth scene, the Hospitality of Abraham, probably are by Torriti. The one on the right bears a significantly close resemblance to the angel above the Martyrdom of St Stephen in the Sancta Sanctorum, attributed to him.[410]

On the opposite wall, the first scene in the lower register of the first bay, the Marriage at Cana, is the work of an old-fashioned painter, bound to Byzantine iconographic models (Plate 59). The bride looks like a Byzantine empress. This is the first of a succession of interiors attempted in the nave. Several abrupt changes of viewpoint are noticeable. The building is viewed from the right, the table and footstool from the left; the servants and water jars, which are set in front of the columns, from the right.[411] The development in the handling of space which took place within the period when the nave was being frescoed may be gauged from a comparison of this scene with scene 16 of the St Francis cycle, the death of the knight of Celano, at the opposite end of the same wall, which also features a laden dining table.[412] The quality of the central figures in the third scene of this register, the first of the second bay, has led to the artist becoming known as the Master of the Arrest. The discovery of the preparatory drawing shows that he belonged to the group of painters led by Torriti. The scene of the Nativity, above it, may also be assigned to him (Plate 54). In both scenes assistants were employed to do the paintwork of the less important parts, for example many of the soldiers in the Arrest.[413]

Work on the third bay was begun by the same group of painters but there seems to have been a change at this point. In the scene of the Presentation in the Temple, on the south wall in the top register, to the right of the window, there is definite evidence of overpainting. Beneath the cosmatesque ciborium there are traces of an earlier, differently constructed ciborium above the Virgin's head and across and beneath the left-hand capital and curtain of the replacement structure, and some of the heads, including the Virgin's, have been redone. This suggests that there was an interruption in the work. Torriti and at least some of his team have left. A new Master arrives, probably after an interval, possibly of months, possibly longer, and notifies a fresh start by

---

[408] Poeschke 1985, pls. 94, 96.   [409] Tomei 1990, pp. 77–8 and figs. 93, 94; and see pp. 447, 451.
[410] Tomei 1990, p. 64; Bellosi 1998, pp. 82–3.   [411] White 1967, p. 32 and fig. 4c; Poeschke 1985, pl. 114.
[412] Poeschke 1985, pl. 172.
[413] Tomei 1990, pp. 65–7, 74–5 nn. 121–4. The preparatory design is published in Romano 1984, cited Tomei 1990, p. 74 n. 121. For details see Poeschke 1985, pls. 118, 119.

repainting an existing scene.[414] The difference he makes is immediately apparent in the two scenes in the lower register of the north wall (Plate 58). These portray Isaac's Blessings. According to the biblical story Isaac had twin sons by Rebecca. When he was old and blind, wishing to bless his first-born, Esau, he sent him to hunt and to bring him a dish of game. With the encouragement and help of their mother, the younger twin, Jacob, impersonated his brother. She told him to take two kids from the herd of goats, which she cooked. She dressed Jacob in some of his brother's clothes, and put the skins of the kids over his hands and round his bare neck, because Esau was 'a hairy man'. The fresco is much damaged, but the figure of Rebecca can still be made out, seated on the bed behind Jacob, supporting him in a sitting position. Jacob, who is holding the dish of meat in his left hand, has stretched out his right and Isaac is feeling it with his hand and blessing him. In the fresco the deceit is not minimised; the hairy skins envelop his hands and lower arms like gloves; the thin line of a leg and a little hoof dangle close to the line of a fold in the cloak, like a fashion accessory; another little leg and hoof are draped over its shoulder folds to anchor the scarf. Yet the deceiver wears a halo.[415] In the second scene Esau stands before his father eagerly proffering the dish he has prepared; Rebecca's expression and gesture reveal her anxiety; Jacob has escaped from the room just in time – the figure stepping through the doorway is much damaged, but can be identified by the halo. The imposing head and figure of the blind old man succeed in conveying bewilderment, authority, and acceptance of the *fait accompli* (Gen. 25. 19–34; 27. 1–40)[416] (Plate 70). The two scenes emphasise their unity of space and time. The design and the details are faithfully repeated: the slender architectural frame, the bed rails, the bedding, the curtains. The artist, known as the Isaac Master on account of his achievement here, shows awareness of the innovatory experiments in fresco decoration stimulated by the major programmes of refurbishment and redecoration which have been, and are, taking place in the basilicas and other churches in Rome, and has studied ancient Roman monuments and artefacts. His work also draws on a variety of other rich sources of contemporary inspiration, notably mosaic, sculpture and religious drama. The illusion that the action takes place in an actual interior is much increased, and the figures are rounded, they and their draperies carefully modelled, with subtle gradations of light and shade, the light falling from a single source. The narrative is presented like a play. In the first scene the maid is pulling open the curtain to allow Jacob to approach the bed; in the second she has just drawn it almost closed and is following him from the room. There is a sense of movement, and the emotions and reactions of those taking part in this drama are marvellously portrayed. The tension is palpable.[417]

The Isaac Master is also credited with the intensely tragic composition of the Lamentation over the Dead Christ on the opposite wall, above the Stigmatisation (Plate 65). He and his workshop were responsible for completing the third and fourth bays of the nave and for the Ascension and Pentecost scenes on the counter-façade. Meticulous study of

[414] White 1984, ch. IV, p. 107.
[415] Jacob, like Isaac, was one of the Patriarchs; renamed Israel, he became father of the chosen people. The supplanting of Esau, the first-born, by Jacob was interpreted as signifying the replacement of the Old Law of Moses by the New Covenant of Christ.
[416] Zanardi 1996, pp. 364, 372–5 and pls. 365, 373, details 376, 377, 379; Poeschke 1985, pls. 103–9.
[417] White 1967, p. 32; Smart 1978, pp. 23–9.

Plate 70 Isaac and Esau: third bay, north wall (© www.Assisi.de. Photo Stefan Diller).

certain practices and techniques of fresco painting have greatly advanced knowledge and understanding, and improved the ability to recognise workshops and hands.[418] One tool of the trade was the pattern (il *patrono*), a shape cut in paper rendered transparent with hot wax or oil, and rigid with a mixture of a type of clay and albumen. In the St Francis cycle Zanardi has identified four patterns utilised for creating heads. Pattern

[418] Zanardi 1996, 2002.

I was used consistently at first, that is from scene 2, Francis giving his cloak to a poor knight, the first in the cycle to be painted, to scene 6, the Dream of Innocent III (Colour Plate 7). Pattern 1 had also been used for the heads of Jacob and Esau.[419] Zanardi has also closely examined the manner in which the features and flesh of the faces were created: the number of colours used, the order in which the various tints were applied, the type of brushes and brush strokes. In the St Francis cycle he distinguishes four 'modes of execution'. The first mode was employed for all the heads in scenes 2, 3 and 4; in scenes 5, 6 and 7 a variant of the first mode was used for many of the heads, the first mode for the rest. The first mode had been used for the heads of Jacob and Esau, and also for some of the heads in the vault of the Doctors of the Church in the third bay.[420] The Isaac Master and the Master of the St Francis cycle were one and the same. It means, furthermore, that there was no interruption in the programme of decoration between the completion of the upper surfaces of the wall and the start of work on the St Francis cycle by the same workshop.

The recent restoration of the great crucifix in Santa Maria Novella in Florence has revealed a remarkable resemblance between the head of the mourner, St John, on the arm of the crucifix, and the head of Jacob in the first of the Isaac scenes in the third bay of the Upper Church (Plate 58). Comparison with one of the tracings made by Zanardi, proportionately reduced in size, establishes that their facial features and their profiles are incredibly similar, although St John's head is inclined slightly further.[421] The crucifix is attributed to Giotto, so its restoration seems to strengthen the arguments identifying the Isaac Master/St Francis Master with Giotto. However, there is a difference between the drawing in St John and the other mourner, the Virgin, and the drawing of Christ, though Ciatti asserts very firmly that they are by same master.[422] There has long been disagreement among art historians over the attribution of the St Francis cycle to Giotto. Acceptance of the attribution encounters three main stumbling blocks: style,[423] chronology[424] and technique.[425] It is difficult for a historian to judge. The attribution of the crucifix to Giotto rests primarily on documentary evidence: the testament of Riccuccio son of Puccio dated 15 June 1312 includes a bequest 'to give and pay to the sacristy of the Friars Preachers of the Church of Sta Maria Novella 5 pounds of small florins for the purchase annually of two jars of oil, one of them to keep alight continuously the lamp of the crucifix in the same church of Sta Maria Novella painted by the eminent painter named Giotto Bondoni, who is of the parish of Sta Maria Novella; before the crucifix is a bone lantern bought by the same testator. The other jar is to relieve this Society [of the Laudesi] of the expenses they were wont to incur in buying oil for the lamp of the great panel on which is painted the image of the Blessed Virgin Mary: the panel is in the same church of Sta Maria Novella and the

[419] Zanardi 2002, p. 35 and figs. 5–7; Zanardi 1996, p. 366.
[420] Zanardi 1996, esp. pp. 42–4 and figs. 36–41.
[421] Ciatti and Seidel 2002, pp. 283, 285–6, figs. 28–31.
[422] Ciatti and Seidel 2002, p. 43; also Bonsanti 2002b, pp. 138 ff, esp. pp. 141–2; but see Zanardi 2002, pp. 257–60. Unfortunately Bonsanti 2002b reached me too late for me to be able to study it fully.
[423] E.g. Offner 1939–40; White 1987, pp. 207–24, 344–8, esp. pp. 346–7; Zanardi 2002, p. 259.
[424] E.g. Gardner 1984, III, p. 46 n. 112: 'The attribution to the young Giotto faces insuperable chronological difficulties.'
[425] Esp. Zanardi 1996; 2002 ; and see p. 434.

lamp should burn continuously before the panel . . . To the convent of Friars Preachers of Prato 20 shillings of little florins to be paid about the time of the burial of the testator, to be invested in oil to illuminate the beautiful panel in the church of the same convent which Riccuccio himself had painted by the eminent painter named Giotto Bondone of Florence.'[426] Riccuccio was evidently proud to record his association with his co-parishioner's achievement and fame.

Riccuccio was a member of the Society of the Laudesi attached to Santa Maria Novella, and appointed its officers among his executors. The Society's account books include records of many payments in accordance with his bequest.[427] One, dated 16 February 1314, enters a payment 'for a jar of oil to be put in the lamp of the great crucifix made by Giotto bequeathed by Riccuccio Pucci' (doc. 2, c. 5v); another, dated November 1332, is 'for oil for the lamp of the high altar and for the lamp of the panel of the Madonna from the money left by Riccuccio Pucci' (doc. 2, c. 43). Other entries over the years link Riccuccio's bequest to the crucifix, to the high altar and to the panel of the Madonna, which is Duccio's Rucellai Madonna, commissioned by the Society of the Laudesi in April 1285, which hung in their chapel until 1335.[428] The entry of November 1332 is crucial evidence as to the original location of Giotto's crucifix.

The surviving crucifix is a massive object. It measures 530 cm (over 17 feet) in height, 400 cm (over 13 feet) maximum width at the arms, and the planks are 5 cm thick.[429] It weighs about 300 kilograms. It was too large and too heavy ever to have stood on the high altar or to have been suspended above it. It was constructed in such a way that most of the weight was borne by the base, and damage to a lower join, and a slight downwards curvature, confirmed that it had once rested on its base, tilted slightly forward. It was designed to stand on a rood screen – in the position illustrated in scene 22 of the St Francis cycle[430] (Plate 67). A triangle of support rings at the back on reinforced cross-pieces held the ropes which controlled the angle.[431] This crucifix was presumably commissioned for the rood screen of the new nave designed by the Dominican architects brothers Sisto and Ristoro in 1279.[432] The rood screen was set a third of the way down the nave so as to allow ample space for the friars, making the distance between the screen and the high altar in the sanctuary longer than usual (Figure 2). The dating of the crucifix to c.1288–9 would fit quite well.[433] Ciatti attempts to reconcile the physical evidence of the carpentry of the surviving crucifix with the documentary evidence linking Giotto's crucifix with the high altar by conjecturing that the account entries might refer to an altar by the rood screen.[434] But this is not the obvious or normal meaning of *altare maggiore*: *altare magnum, maius* was the normal phrase throughout the Middle Ages for the altar of the apse or sanctuary. Thus *altare maius* occurs ten times in this sense in the *Monastic Constitutions* of Lanfranc, written at Canterbury by an archbishop of Italian origin – he came from Pavia – admittedly in the eleventh century;[435] but the phrase was common throughout later centuries. Zanardi

---

[426] Ciatti and Seidel 2002, pp. 179–80.   [427] Ciatti and Seidel 2002, pp. 227–38.
[428] White 1979, pp. 32–45.   [429] Ciatti and Seidel 2002, p. 247.
[430] Ciatti and Seidel 2002, pp. 57–8, 33–6.   [431] Ciatti and Seidel 2002, p. 249 and figs. 5, 6, 11.
[432] Meersseman 1946, pp. 185–6.   [433] Ciatti and Seidel 2002, p. 59.   [434] Ciatti and Seidel 2002, p. 58.
[435] Knowles and Brooke 2002, p. 229; cf. Latham 1975, s.v. *altare* 2b; Prinz et al. 1967, col. 505.

feels he must accept the attribution of the surviving crucifix to Giotto because it is difficult to believe that the crucifix mentioned in Riccuccio's will of 1312 was another cross, now lost.[436] However, it is not impossible that the community at Santa Maria Novella acquired two crucifixes, one for the rood screen, one for the high altar, for their splendidly and imaginatively enlarged and refurbished church. The evidence is perplexing, but the attribution of the surviving crucifix to Giotto must remain doubtful.

The questions of the dating of the cycle and of its attribution are inextricably linked. We have very little information, not many clues even. Giotto's great reputation was partly based on his work at Assisi. The earliest reference is in a document, filed under the year 1309 in Assisi, which suggests that Giotto borrowed money in Assisi before that date. Headed: 'Repayment of Palmerinus and Giotto', it notes that: 'On 4 January . . . Iolus Iuntarelli for himself and his heirs made fine and quittance etc. to Palmerinus Guidi, acting for himself and Giotto Bondoni of Florence, concerning £50 of Cortonese pence which he was bound to give and pay to him on account of a loan.'[437] The literary evidence exhibits a progression from the unspecific to the circumstantial which is not unusual. Ricobaldo da Ferrara, in a passage written between 1312 and 1319, recorded that 'Giotto is recognised as an eminent Florentine; works done by him in the churches of the Friars Minor at Assisi, Rimini, Padua, and those he painted . . . in the Arena church at Padua, bear witness to his quality as an artist.'[438] Ghiberti, writing c.1450, gives a little more detail: 'In the church at Assisi, of the Order of Friars Minor, [Giotto] painted almost all the lower part (*quasi tutta la parte di sotto*).'[439] The humanist Aeneas Sylvius Piccolomini, who was Pope Pius II 1458–64, visited Assisi in 1459 and recorded his impressions. 'Francis, the rich inventor of the Order of Minors, in whose eyes nothing was richer than poverty, made noble this city [of Assisi]. A noble temple was built for him, in which they say his bones lie; and it is a double church, one above the other, adorned with the paintings of Giotto the Florentine.'[440] Vasari, writing a century after Ghiberti, altered a phrase. The first edition of his *The Lives of the most excellent Italian Architects, Painters and Sculptors*, 1550, stated that Giotto painted 'the whole church of the lower sector' (*tutta la chiesa dalla banda di sotto*)'. As a result of his visit to Assisi in 1563 he both expanded and clarified his account in the second edition of 1568. Giotto went to Assisi to finish the work begun by Cimabue, being summoned there by the Minister General of the time, John of Murrovalle. He frescoed scenes from the life of St Francis on both sides of the church, below the corridor which crosses the windows, 'so perfectly that he thereby acquired great fame'. After he had finished this he painted more 'truly beautiful and praiseworthy' pictures in the Lower Church.[441] John of Murrovalle was elected Minister General in 1296.

Another piece of evidence is provided by a polemical document whose relevance has only recently been appreciated.[442] In 1309 Clement V called for position papers from both Spirituals and Conventuals on the *usus pauper* question, in preparation for

---

[436] Zanardi 2002, pp. 257–60.   [437] Martinelli 1993, quoted Zanardi 2002, pp. 249, 254 n. 1.
[438] *Compilatio historica*, col. 255, quoted Zanardi 2002, pp. 249, 254 n. 2; Murray 1953, pp. 58–61.
[439] Ghiberti 1998, p. 84, quoted Zanardi 2002, pp. 249, 254 n. 3.
[440] Aeneas Sylvius Piccolomini, *I Commentarii*, quoted Gatti 1983, pp. 149–50; cf. Zanardi 2002, p. 249.
[441] Vasari 1550, I, 141; 1568, I, 121.   [442] Burr 2001, pp. 113–22, 145–50; Cooper and Robson 2003.

the Council of Vienne. Ubertino da Casale produced *Sanctitas vestra*, probably at the beginning of 1310. The community spokesmen replied to the charges he listed there in a tract, *Religiosi viri*, drawn up at some time between 1310 and the pope's ruling on the issues in *Exivi de Paradiso* on 6 May 1312. After much special pleading on the size and contents of Franciscan churches, they continue: 'nor have we seen in the friars' churches great sumptuousness of pictures, except in the church at Assisi, pictures which Pope Nicholas IV ordered to be done out of reverence for the saint, whose bones lie there'.[443]

The pictures themselves have been made to furnish a few clues, some more promising than others. Giuliano da Rimini's altar panel of the Virgin and Child with Angels and Saints shows the scene of the stigmatisation in its top left-hand corner. The pose in which St Francis is portrayed is directly dependent on scene 19 of the St Francis cycle. The way in which he kneels on one knee, leaning slightly backwards, the position of his hands, with only the further one breaking the silhouette of the body, and the position of his feet, all exactly repeat the pattern of the fresco. The panel is signed, and dated; and the fact that the final number is spelt out – *AD millesimo CCC septimo* – avoids any ambiguity.[444] If the dependence is agreed, it follows that the cycle was not painted later than 1307; and the conclusion has been generally accepted. The attempt is still made to push the *terminus post quem non* back a little further. The height of the tower of the Palazzo del Capitano del Popolo in the Piazza del Comune was raised – an inscription records it was finished in 1305. In scene 1 of the St Francis cycle, which was painted last, the tower has not yet been heightened.[445] But such an argument cannot be relied on as proof.[446] Scene 1 is set recognisably in the Piazza del Comune, and it does indeed contain details that reflect contemporary practice – the two tiny barred windows remind us that the Temple of Minerva was then used as a prison. But within scene 1 itself the aim is clearly not 'photographic accuracy'. The Temple of Minerva is pictured beautifully, but not precisely; it lacks a column, and its massive classical columns have become slender (Plates 53, 5). The artist has brought together a variety of diverse elements and depicted them in a variety of styles – Roman, Tuscan, Umbrian – creating out of this assortment a brilliantly successful evocation of a local focus point.[447]

Internal evidence has also been sought to help to determine the *terminus ante quem non*. The four webs of the vault in the fourth bay contain representations of four Doctors of the Church, St Jerome, St Augustine, St Gregory and St Ambrose. Designed to balance the Evangelists on the crossing vault, each sits enthroned beside a desk, but in place of a city each is provided with a friar, acting as his secretary, an endorsement of the value the Order now attached to learning. The institution of the feast day of the Doctors was promulgated in 1298 in the *Liber sextus* by Boniface VIII, and it has been argued that the vault was therefore decorated after that date. But the formal institution of the festival was the culmination of a process; it gave sanction to a cult already flourishing.[448]

---

443 Rome, Collegio S. Isidoro, MS 1/146, fo. 263r; Cooper and Robson 2003, pp. 32–3 and nn. 18, 21.
444 White 1984, ch. iv, pp. 96–105.   445 Frugoni in Zanardi 1996, p. 66.
446 White 1987, pp. 217–18, 344.   447 Scarpellini 1978, pp. 96–9.
448 Smart 1971, pp. 30–1; White 1987, p. 202; Poeschke 1985, pls. 135–41.

Scene 6 illustrates Innocent III's dream of St Francis supporting the Lateran (Colour Plate 7). The left-hand area containing the detail of the façade and part of the portico is unfortunately completely destroyed, but enough remains of the decoration of the portico to indicate that what is represented here is the Lateran portico as rebuilt and adorned by Nicholas IV.[449] The evidence for the connection is excellent. At the Lateran Basilica is still preserved a marble slab richly inlaid with mosaic, containing a lengthy inscription in gold letters on a ground of intense blue, which was once embedded in the portico. It begins: 'The Church's father, Innocent III, at the hour when he had gone to sleep, saw this church tottering in ruins: but soon a ragged, rough and contemptible man put his shoulder to support it – and held it up. But when the holy father woke up he saw Francis, and said: "Truly this is the man whom we saw. He will bear the Church and the faith as they falter." Thus Francis was granted all he had sought, and went on his way free and happy. Jerome, chief offspring of Francis in the order of Minors, rising to be Roman pontiff with the name of Nicholas IV, observed that parts of the church were falling into certain ruin. He raised it before and behind; he re-shaped what had been destroyed and adorned it, and part of it he restored from the foundations.' It ends with the date 1291.[450] The inscription repeats the points made about Innocent III's dream in Bonaventure's *Life* (III, 10). The Church is about to collapse and a ragged, contemptible man supports it. When the pope sees Francis he recognises him as the man in his dream, foretells that he will sustain the Church, and grants his petitions; that is, he approves his Rule. The iconography of scene 6 indicates that it was not painted before 1291, when Nicholas IV's restored portico was completed.

A leading scholar's assessment of the dating evidence led him to conclude that the St Francis cycle 'was carried out almost certainly after 1290–1, not necessarily after 1296, and very probably before 1307'.[451]

Let us next consider arguments against a date for the cycle after 1296.

Nicholas IV died on 4 April 1292. There was then a vacancy lasting twenty-seven months. The college of cardinals, divided by family feuds, could not agree. In October 1293 the conclave moved from Rome to Perugia, where finally, bombarded by political and personal pressures – including disorders in Rome and the unexpected death of Cardinal Napoleone Orsini's young brother, Gian Gaetano – on 5 July 1294 they elected an eighty-five-year-old hermit, Peter del Morrone, who approached his coronation as Celestine V symbolically riding on an ass. Napoleone Orsini, deeply distressed by his brother's early death, determined to enlarge and redesign the chapel at the end of the north transept in the Lower Church and transform it into a funerary chapel for his brother. The fresco decoration on the inner surface of the entrance wall to the chapel, above the arch, shows a standing figure of Christ in the act of blessing. On His right, St Francis presents the kneeling Cardinal Napoleone to Him, while on His left St Nicholas presents the youthful Gian Gaetano. Napoleone dedicated the chapel

---

[449] Murray 1953, pp. 71–4.   [450] Tomei 1990, pp. 77–8.

[451] White 1987, p. 344. The date 1296 was scratched on the painted plaster in the passageway between the north triforium and the nave. The decoration of this area was done earlier than this (Lunghi 1996, p. 48). Perhaps a workman 'signed off' here after a final party to celebrate the completion of the Upper Church decoration – but this is pure speculation.

Plate 71 Lower Church, St Nicholas chapel, entrance wall (© www.Assisi.de. Photo Gerhard Ruf).

to St Nicholas because Nicholas III was his uncle, and Nicholas IV had promoted him cardinal deacon of Sant'Adriano in 1288. Behind each Orsini kneel three cardinals (Plate 71). This suggests that some of the cardinals present in Perugia for the conclave when the young man died were persuaded to contribute to the foundation of the chapel. Two of the cardinals, Giacomo and Pietro, were members of the Colonna family.

Celestine V had not wanted to be made pope. Naive, ill-educated, incompetent, easily manipulated by Charles II of Naples, five months were enough, and he longed to return to his mountain retreat. He consulted a noted canon lawyer, Cardinal Benedict Caetani, as to whether it was lawful for a pope to abdicate voluntarily, and was advised that there were precedents. So he abdicated on 13 December 1294; and on 24 December 1294 Benedict Caetani was elected Pope Boniface VIII. On 3 May 1297 Stefano Colonna attacked a convoy carrying papal treasure from Anagni to Rome and made off with it. Boniface VIII, a cruel and arrogant man, was incandescent with rage. Although the treasure was returned, he attacked and razed the Colonna fortresses, including their stronghold at Palestrina, and confiscated their lands. The two Colonna cardinals were deprived of office and excommunicated. It is difficult to follow their movements during the period of their disgrace. Giacomo may have taken refuge in the mountainous districts of Umbria; Pietro may have sought safety with friends in Padua. It would not have been acceptable to depict two excommunicate ex-cardinals on the wall of a papal basilica. A fresco including them must have been painted before May 1297. Not long after, all six attendant cardinals were painted over with a good coat of blue and they were only uncovered during a twentieth-century cleaning and restoration programme. By 1298 most of these cardinals had died and the financial burden of patronage passed to Napoleone Orsini alone; but the most likely reason for their being painted out would have been the presence among them of the disgraced Colonnas. The process of their re-establishment was slow. In December 1303 Benedict XI revoked the sentence of excommunication, but did not restore their titles, benefices or rights, and they appealed to the French king, Philip IV. The support of the royal court proved decisive during the pontificate of Clement V. In December 1305 the cardinalate was restored, but their full reinstatement was not achieved until 1311–12.[452]

The north transept was not the only area of the Lower Church where building work was taking place in the mid-1290s. More space was needed. Crowds of pilgrims were visiting the shrine, causing serious congestion, especially near the altar; some powerful and wealthy people were eager to be buried near to the tomb of St Francis; the friars needed more side chapels. So a row of three side chapels was built alongside the north wall of the nave. The date of their construction is not documented, but study of the masonry indicates that the first of them, the Magdalene chapel, abutting the transept, was built before Napoleone Orsini's St Nicholas chapel. They are not so splendid or elaborate architecturally as his. In ground plan they are simple squares connected by a narrow passage. A stone in the passageway between the Magdalene and St Anthony chapels bears an inscription recording that brother Hugh of Hartlepool, formerly Minister Provincial of England, died on 11 September 1302 and is buried there.[453] If the stone is in its original position, it is helpful evidence for the date of the passage. The entrances to the three chapels cut through the nave wall. In the process the frescoes of the Master of St Francis were mutilated[454] (Plates 27, 28). The Cardinal Protector,

[452] Kelly 1986, pp. 206–10, 212–13; Martin and Ruf 1998, pp. 96–7, 114–15 and nn.; Assisi 1999, pp. 42–3; Zanardi 2002, pp. 194–5; Waley 1982a and b.

[453] Little 1943, pp. 194–5. I am much indebted to Dr Michael Robson OFM Conv for confirming that Hugh of Hartlepool died in Assisi on 11 September 1302 while on embassy from Edward I to the Holy See. His epitaph reads (or read): 'Hic iacet frater Hugo de Hertilpol Anglicus Magister in Sacra Theologia quondam Minister Anglie qui obiit III Id. Septembris anno Domini MCCC secundo. Orate pro anima eius' (Little 1943, pp. 149–50, citing Misc. Fr. II, 92). Martin and Ruf 1998, p. 102 and n. 220, following an article by Irene Hueck which I have not seen, suggest that the epitaph reads '1300'; they also point out that the present situation of the epitaph is only recorded from 1839.

[454] Martin and Ruf 1998, pp. 100–3 and nn.; Assisi 1999, p. 42.

Matteo Rosso Orsini, was responsible for overseeing building work and decoration. He must have sanctioned the switching of Orsini funds, even though not his personally, from the decoration of public space in the Upper Church to a private family chapel in the Lower Church, which involved structural alterations to the end wall of the transept. He must have permitted the friars to spend money on building the side chapels, and permitted the damage to the Lower Church nave frescoes. The scenes on the north wall showed Christ's Passion, not the St Francis scenes, but ruining one side disprized the whole iconography. It seems to me inherently unlikely that the Lower Church would become the focus of attention and funds if the decoration of the nave of the Upper Church was still unfinished, with its lower walls bare. Lack of appreciation for the cycle of frescoes in the Lower Church becomes more likely when the friars have a brand new, bigger, better, more fashionable cycle upstairs.

Boniface VIII initially was not unfavourable to the friars. He had been involved with the affairs of the Orders and familiar with their leaders over many years. He had been a member of the commission chosen by Nicholas III to help draw up *Exiit qui seminat* in 1279. In 1290 Nicholas IV sent him to Paris as one of his papal legates. While there, as well as conducting successful peace negotiations between the king of France and the kings of England and Aragon, he uncompromisingly defended the privileges of the mendicant Orders, forbidding the masters of Paris to dispute them.[455] In 1291 Nicholas IV promoted him cardinal priest. After becoming pope he appointed a number of Franciscans to bishoprics. On 21 January 1296 he issued two bulls in favour of the Basilica. These were basically reissues of two bulls of Nicholas IV dated 27 September 1288 and 4 May 1289. The first granted indulgences to visitors on St Francis' feast day and within the octave; the second to visitors on any day. Boniface VIII was not as generous as Nicholas IV had been. Festival visits now earned one year and forty days instead of three years and forty days, visits on other days, one hundred days instead of one year.[456] Nevertheless these bulls will have provided an incentive. He is not likely to have been a major patron of the Order himself. His personal inclinations favoured St Peter's and his family. Shortly after his election he planned a splendid tomb for himself inside St Peter's, within the reliquary chapel of Pope Boniface IV, 608–15, whose name he took.[457] He commissioned the Florentine mason and sculptor Arnolfo di Cambio, and the artist and mosaicist Jacopo Torriti. Both signed their work, which unfortunately does not survive, but was recorded both in drawings and in descriptions. The monument, which was complex and innovative, was probably designed by Arnolfo. Boniface's effigy, with ministering angels at his head and feet, was inserted into a rectangular niche cut into the wall behind and above the altar. The interior of the niche was draped with curtains; at the base of the decorated bier a mosaic band contained five Caetani shields. Above the architrave a large mosaic showed the pope, holding the keys, presented by St Peter and attended by St Paul, in prayer before the Madonna

---

[455] Gratien 1928, pp. 327–8, 352–4.

[456] Nicholas IV: Sbaralea IV, 43, N4 no. 61; Eubel 1908, no.1659 (27 September 1288); Sbaralea, IV, 73–4, N4 no. III, corrected in Eubel 1908, no. 1688 (4 May 1289). Boniface, VIII: Sbaralea, IV, 379–80, B8 no. 49; Eubel 1908, no. 2052 (21 Jan. 1296); Sbaralea, IV, 380, B8 no. 50; Eubel 1908, no. 2053 (also 21 Jan. 1296). Cf. discussion in Zanardi 2002, pp. 213–15.

[457] For this and what follows see Gardner 1992, pp. 36, 57, 78–9, 107–9, and figs. 106, 107.

and child in a roundel. The whole was surmounted by an elaborately carved baldachin. It was almost certainly ready by May 1296, and had an immediate influence on the development of Italian tomb design, encouraging a fashion for ostentatious tombs. The obit book of St Peter's records his generosity. In the course of the nine years of his pontificate he gave lands and rents valued at 36,173.5 gold florins, as well as major gifts of metalwork, such as reliquaries, *opus anglicanum* – that is, embroidered textiles, such as tapestries, altar frontals, vestments – and books.[458] During the same period he transformed the holdings of his family, buying up castles and villages at an estimated cost of between half and three-quarters of a million gold florins.[459]

Boniface VIII's attitude towards the Spiritual groups among the Franciscans was influenced by the propaganda against him put out by some Italian zealots. At the suggestion of the Minister General Raymond Gaufridi, an Italian group which included Angelo Clareno had sought the protection of Celestine V, who permitted them to observe the Franciscan Rule as they interpreted it, that is according to Francis' intention as enshrined in the Rule, Testament and Leo sources, but under the name of the Poor Hermits of Pope Celestine. When Celestine was replaced by Boniface, who rescinded most of Celestine's legislation, many of the group, including Angelo, prudently retreated to Greece, but some stayed in Italy and sided with the Colonna family. They questioned the legitimacy of Boniface VIII's election, arguing that it was invalid because a pope could not abdicate. As a result Boniface sanctioned disciplinary action against Spiritual groups in Italy and southern France, regarding them as a threat to good order.[460] But he upset the community as well by changing his mind on the issue of mendicant privileges, which he had come to realise were excessive and provocative. In the bull *Super cathedram* of 18 February 1300, he safeguarded the rights of the secular clergy, while permitting the friars to continue their pastoral work – preaching, hearing confessions and burying the dead – a sensible compromise, but bitterly resented by the friars.[461] Boniface VIII made many enemies. A long-running quarrel with the king of France, Philip IV, escalated to his undoing after his issuing of the bull *Unam sanctam* on 18 November 1302, which restated the principle of the supremacy of the spiritual over the temporal power.[462] A plot was devised by a handful of Italian conspirators, including some of the Colonna exiles at the French court, and in the spring of 1303 William of Nogaret, a lawyer and royal counsellor, was sent to Italy to put it into effect. A force of over a thousand mercenaries was raised. The pope was at Anagni. The gates were opened by traitors inside and he was seized. The plan was to take him to France where he would be put on trial before a council. But the next day the people of Anagni rose, expelled the insurgents and rescued him. He was escorted back to Rome by Cardinal Napoleone Orsini, but died on 12 October 1303, broken by shock and anger.[463]

Ten days later a learned Dominican cardinal was elected as Benedict XI. He was the son of a notary of humble family. He was therefore without private fortune. He had been Master General of his Order, and created three Dominican cardinals. He annulled

---

[458] Gardner 1993, ch. v, p. 71 and n. 87.
[459] Partner 1972, pp. 287–90 and n. 5.   [460] Burr 2001, 69–70, 108, 265.
[461] Potthast, II, no. 22664; cf. Gratien 1928, pp. 254–9; Moorman 1968, p. 202.
[462] Kelly 1986, pp. 208–10.   [463] Partner 1972, pp. 293–6.

Super cathedram, thus restoring to both mendicant Orders opportunities to obtain fees at the expense of the secular clergy, but he had no inclination to become a patron of the Friars Minor. He died of dysentery at Perugia on 7 July 1304. There, after eleven months of bitterness and intrigue, the cardinals elected in his absence the archbishop of Bordeaux, a Gascon who took the name Clement V, 5 June 1305 to 20 April 1314. He was crowned at Lyon. He created a number of French cardinals – four of them nephews – reinforcing the French domination of the Curia. He spent several years moving about in Provence and Gascony, though seriously intending moving to Rome. A decision to hold a church council in Vienne resulted in his taking up residence at Avignon in March 1309. Avignon was not on French soil, but it was near to France and subject to the French dynasty of the Angevin kings of Naples, vassals of the French king. The unintended consequence of Clement V's election was the transfer of the Curia to Avignon, where it was to remain for seventy years.[464] During that time papal and curial patronage in Rome and the Papal States was in abeyance. Already by 1300 Arnolfo di Cambio had shifted the centre of his activities back to Florence. The French royal accounts show that Filippo Rusuti and his son Giovanni were working for Philip IV from 1 November 1304. Pietro Cavallini was in Naples by June 1308.[465] Giotto was working in Padua for the wealthy Enrico Scrovegni probably *c.*1304. The history of the papacy in this period makes it extremely unlikely that patronage was available for funding such a major undertaking as the St Francis cycle in the Upper Church between 1296 and 1307.

That Giotto and his workshop worked at Assisi is not in doubt. The question is, what and how much did he do, and when? It is clear that by the middle of the sixteenth century the tradition was established in Assisi that Giotto had painted the St Francis cycle in the Upper Church, that this had made him famous, and that he had then produced more beautiful frescoes in the Lower Church.[466] All this was explained to Vasari in 1563, and spelt out in his second edition. It has been generally assumed that he was just adding more detailed information, but was he actually correcting his first edition? And is his 'banda di sotto' significantly different from Ghiberti's 'parte di sotto'? There is an ambiguity. Murray argued that Vasari's phrase 'can only mean the Francis cycle' and that in Vasari's time, Ghiberti's phrase 'was understood in its obvious sense – "almost all the lower range of frescoes" – and not as meaning "lower church"'.[467] To Zanardi, Ghiberti's words obviously refer to the Lower Church, not to the lower part of the nave walls of the Upper Church.[468] The frescoes in the St Nicholas chapel in the Lower Church, including the entrance arch, with its Annunciation scene, and two scenes depicting the miracle at Suessa where St Francis restored to life a young man killed when a house wall collapsed and buried him (*Miracula* ii, 6),[469] are by Giotto and his workshop. Because the fresco on the inner surface of the arch originally included

---

[464] Kelly 1986, pp. 210–14; Partner 1972, p. 287.

[465] Gardner 1987, pp. 381–3; Gardner 1992, pp. 110–11 and nn. 3, 15. Filippo Rusuti was employed by the Colonna. His signed mosaic on the façade of Santa Maria Maggiore, as recorded in a sixteenth-century drawing, contained representations of the two cardinals Giacomo and Pietro Colonna, kneeling at the feet of the angels supporting the central mandorla encircling Christ in Majesty. Kessler and Zacharias 2002, pp. 127–31 and figs. 123, 125, 128.

[466] For this and what follows, see p. 426.   [467] Murray 1953, p. 66.

[468] Zanardi 2002, p. 207.   [469] See Poeschke 1985, pls. 224–5, 238–9.

the two Colonna cardinals, this wall at least was done by May 1297[470] (Plate 71). John of Murrovalle replaced Raymond Gaufridi as Minister General in 1296. It could be that the tradition, recorded by Vasari, that it was he who summoned Giotto to Assisi was well based; but he summoned him, not to paint the St Francis cycle, but to decorate the St Nicholas chapel, a funerary monument commemorating a young man who met an untimely death in 1294.

The obit book of St Peter's records the death and the generosity of 'Giacomo Gaetani Stefaneschi, cardinal deacon of S. Giorgio and our fellow-canon, who conferred many benefits on our Basilica . . . In the Paradise [atrium] of the same Basilica he had made by the same unique (*singularissimi*) painter [Giotto] in mosaic the story of how Christ lifted blessed Peter the Apostle when he was drowning in the waves, for which work he paid 2200 florins.' This important commission took Giotto to Rome in 1298, according to a charter now lost – the payment is entered in the obit book under 1300. His *Navicella*, a huge mosaic which must have been a replacement for a late fourth- or early fifth-century predecessor, is only known from drawings.[471] A fresco in the Benediction loggia of the Lateran palace – of which a surviving fragment is now in the Lateran – has been attributed to him. The loggia was commissioned by Boniface VIII, and the fresco depicted him on the balcony, conspicuously decorated with the Caetani arms, attended by the college of cardinals, blessing the people below. But the attribution is doubtful; it may be by a Roman painter influenced by Giotto.[472]

Giotto was a successful businessman as well as a great artist. He could by now afford to employ a number of assistants, and was able to undertake commissions at more than one place at a time. One reason why his pictures were so appreciated by his contemporaries was his introduction of a new method of applying paint. Zanardi has made a close study of the way in which Giotto painted faces in the St Nicholas chapel. The colours were applied in a sufficiently diluted, sufficiently liquid state that they shaded into each other. The various tones used to build up the flesh, usually four and always applied in the same order – light, medium, dark, lighter – were put on quickly one after the other so that they blended as they were applied, thus eliminating traces of brush strokes and creating a soft effect, a final result of great verisimilitude.[473] His assistants were trained in the technique, so that when it suited him Giotto could outline a scene, draw the detailed preparatory design, paint some figures if he chose, such as donors, and then leave them to carry on and finish it. Between 1304 and 1312–13 he was responsible for covering the entire interior of the Arena chapel at Padua with frescoes, creating a masterpiece of decorative unity and dramatic narrative.[474] From c.1305 he was also working on further commissions in the Lower Church at Assisi. The document recording the repayment of a debt in 1309 is related to this second phase of his activities there. All the frescoes produced by Giotto's workshop in the Lower Church in both the first and second phases display an identical method of flesh painting.[475]

[470] See p. 430.
[471] Gardner 1993, cf. v, pp. 57–8; Zanardi 2002, pp. 193–5; Kessler and Zacharias 2000, pp. 217–18, and figs. 223, 225.
[472] Boskovits 2000; Kessler and Zacharias 2000, pp. 28–33 and figs. 25–8.
[473] Zanardi 2002, pp. 142–4.   [474] White 1987, ch. 24.   [475] Zanardi 2002, pp. 146, 197.

Giotto's chief patron, in the Lower Church, continued to be Cardinal Napoleone Orsini, who was made papal legate in Italy on 15 February 1306 by Clement V in recognition of his services in procuring his election to the papacy. He now entrusted Giotto with the important commission of continuing with the decoration of the most sacred space around St Francis' shrine. Some more work was first done in the chapel of St Nicholas. Above the entrance arch on the inside the kneeling figures of Napoleone Orsini and his young brother were repainted, after the attendant cardinals had been painted over, and some changes or finishing touches were made to the two scenes of the miracle at Suessa. The chapel's frescoes were probably finished before 1307. The figure of St Clare in Giuliano da Rimini's altar panel, dated 1307, is copied from the depiction of her on the entrance arch; and a legal document drawn up in St Nicholas' chapel on 6 March 1306, recording brother Ercolano's renunciation of his inheritance, has been taken as an indication that it was by then free of workmen and scaffolding.[476]

The political importance of the Orsini family and Napoleone's status as patron are both emphasised in the chapel. The design of his young brother's tomb reflected the very latest fashion, being based on the recently completed tomb of Boniface VIII. The stained glass windows and the fresco decoration surrounding them conspicuously display the Orsini arms. The central window, directly above the sculpted tomb and its panel depicting the Virgin and child flanked by St Nicholas and St Francis, represents St Francis presenting Gian Gaetano to Jesus Christ; below Christ stands St Nicholas, below St Francis and his brother stands the cardinal, his eyes and hands raised towards Christ. An inscription running to either side of his waist states that Cardinal Napoleone was responsible for this work.[477] This window directly faces the inner wall of the entrance arch, where the same theme is illustrated in fresco, with the variation that St Francis presents the cardinal to Christ and St Nicholas presents Gian Gaetano[478] (Plate 71).

Most of the wall surfaces in the north transept in front of the St Nicholas chapel were then decorated by Giotto and his workshop. On the east wall Cimabue's beautiful fresco of the Virgin and child with angels and St Francis was retained, though cropped. Any other of Cimabue's work that may have been there was erased.[479] The theme continued that heralded by the Annunciation scene over the entrance arch to the St Nicholas chapel which had been painted during the first phase – scenes of Christ's nativity and childhood. On the east wall the Visitation and Nativity are on the top register, the Visit of the three kings and the Presentation in the Temple in the middle, but with a crucifixion scene (including figures of kneeling Franciscan saints, and of a living Franciscan which looks as if it may be a portrait, perhaps of the Minister General), on the lowest, to the left of Cimabue's fresco. On the west wall on the top register are the Flight into Egypt and the Massacre of the Innocents, in the middle register the twelve-year-old Jesus in the Temple in the midst of the Doctors and the return of the Holy Family to Nazareth. On the bottom register there is a miracle scene in which St Francis restores to life the seven-year-old son of a notary who jumped from a window, wishing to follow his

[476] Martin and Ruf 1998, pp. 97–8; Zanardi 2002, pp. 193–200; Poeschke 1985, pl. 212.

[477] Martin and Ruf 1998, pp. 96–7, 112–15, 294, Catalogue no. 172, figs. 35, 46, pls. 202, 206; Poeschke 1985, pls. 201, 210.

[478] See pp. 428–9.   [479] See pp. 302–4, Plate 32 and Frontispiece.

mother to church (*Miracula* ii, 4). This scene, not usually portrayed, was presumably especially chosen by Cardinal Napoleone as companion to the two scenes narrating the miracle at Suessa on the entrance arch to the chapel, the raising from the dead of a child and a youth seeming a fitting subject to grace the funerary chapel he created for his brother, who died young.[480]

Giotto's workshop also decorated the webs of the crossing vaults above the high altar, with allegories of the virtues of poverty, obedience and chastity in a Franciscan context, and with St Francis in glory;[481] and may have gone on to depict saints in glory around the crucifixion in the apse, but this part of the scheme has not survived.

Napoleone Orsini was traditionally believed also to be the patron of the chapel at the end of the south transept dedicated to John the Baptist, supposedly as a thanksgiving for his capture of Gubbio on 24 June, the Baptist's feast day, in 1300, and to have intended it to be his own mortuary chapel. It is certainly a chapel under the patronage of the Orsini. The family coat of arms is displayed in the central stained glass window – the only original window to survive – and on the marble revetment of the socle. The decoration is probably to be dated 1318–19.[482]

Teobaldo Pontano, bishop of Assisi 1296–1329, contributed about 600 gold florins for the construction of the Magdalene chapel. He too was a patron of Giotto, who, with his workshop, decorated the entire chapel. Again, as in the St Nicholas chapel, the patron chose to have his patronage emphasised. The bishop is portrayed twice, in one scene, on the west wall, kneeling in his episcopal robes at the feet of San Rufino, his predecessor, patron saint of the diocese of Assisi, who is looking down on him kindly and resting his right hand upon his mitre in blessing. In the balancing scene on the east wall, he is kneeling, dressed as a pilgrim, at the feet of St Mary Magdalene. He is looking up at her face and his left hand is clutching the fingers of her right hand. His coat of arms is displayed six times, twice on each of the side walls and twice on the window arch. The two 'portraits' of the donor may well be Giotto's own work.[483] The date of the frescoes is uncertain. A petition sent to the communal authorities of Assisi by the custodian of the Basilica on 16 July 1311 begging them to control the flow of water from the city and prevent it from pouring into the Lower Church, because, apart from other inconveniences, it was damaging the decorations there, has been taken to imply that Giotto had completed his work in the Lower Church by that date.[484] But this argument is not convincing. The complaint does not refer specifically to frescoes, and this type of decoration was in any case well above floor level. And the Lower Church received decoration susceptible to damp long before Giotto was summoned – and continued to be adorned by a number of artists after he had left. However, it is generally agreed that Giotto had finished work in the right transept, the crossing vaults, the apse and the Magdalene chapel by 1319. In that year the Ghibelline captain, Muzio di Francesco, attacked and took Assisi. He succeeded in breaking into the strong room where the

---

[480] Poeschke 1985, pls. 223–37; Assisi 1999, pp. 42–6; Zanardi 2002, p. 196; and see p. 428.
[481] Poeschke 1985, pls. 241–57.
[482] Assisi 1999, pp. 43–4; Poeschke 1985, pl. 213; Martin and Ruf 1998, pp. 315–18, pls. 283–90.
[483] Martin and Ruf 1998, pp. 100–2, figs. 36–9; Poeschke 1985, pls. 214a–b, 215; Zanardi 2002.
[484] Zanardi 2002, pp. 131, 200–1.

papal treasure had been deposited for safe keeping. Pope John XXII excommunicated the thief and laid the city under an interdict, but he also held the unfortunate bishop personally accountable. He even confiscated the vestments Teobaldo Pontano had donated to the Magdalene chapel. This evidence – that vestments had been supplied – suggests that the chapel was functioning, its decoration completed, by that date: besides, after that date, the bishop would not have been in a position to afford the commissioning of frescoes. A letter of John XXII dated 4 September 1322 refers to him as 'oppressed with the burden of great poverty'.[485]

Thus known patronage, after 1296, was focused on the Lower Church, and stressed the importance of family connections.

Giotto's work in the Lower Church could explain the linking of his name and fame with Assisi as well as with Rimini and Padua. The question remains: had he, as Vasari stated in his second edition of 1568, already acquired great fame by painting the scenes from the life of St Francis in the Upper Church?[486] The attribution and the dating of the St Francis cycle have been the subject of prolonged and intensive study.[487] It is a subject which continues to be very controversial, but a great deal of progress has been made and on some points there is now a degree of consensus. The first point to make is that the cycle was not the creation of a single artist, whether Giotto or anyone else. It was a collaborative endeavour. Workshops were quite efficiently organised. Masters were responsible for designing models, creating the preparatory designs and painting the most significant figure parts. They employed journeyman assistants with a variety of competences, some equipped only to carry out basic tasks such as plastering, filling in background colour and stencilling patterns, others with more specialised skills, such as the ability to paint buildings and architectural details. Many operations required the co-operation of several people, for example the holding and fixing of the 'snapping cords' with which they traced the numerous and often long straight lines, horizontal, vertical and diagonal, that outlined architecture, fittings and cornices. The hands of four principal masters have been distinguished in the course of the cycle. Their diversity has not undermined the unity of theme as their styles were closely related. Three of them were responsible for distinct sequences. The Master of the St Francis cycle – who has been shown to be also the Isaac Master – began with scene 2 and was chiefly responsible for the north wall, but was then joined by a second, unnamed painter, who seems to have contributed the two scenes on the counter-façade, 14 and 15, and the first on the south wall, 16, and to have collaborated on other scenes in the fourth bay. A third master, the Master of the Obsequies, was responsible for bays three and two of the south wall, scenes 20–25; and the cycle was finished by a fourth, known as the St Cecilia Master on account of the altar panel he painted for the church of St Cecilia in

---

[485] Martin and Ruf 1998, pp. 101–6. [486] See p. 426.

[487] The bibliography is vast. Useful bibliographies may be found, for instance, in de Wesselow 2005, n. 2; for the earlier literature, see also Meiss 1967; White 1987, pp. 653–4. For the defence of Giotto's authorship of the cycle, see e.g. Longhi 1948, esp. pp. 49–51; Oertel 1968, pp. 65–78; Bellosi 1985, pp. 41–102; Flores d'Arcais 1995, pp. 32–86; Bonsanti 2002b, esp. pp. 144–63. For the arguments against the attribution to Giotto, see e.g. Smart 1971; Stubblebine 1985; White 1987, pp. 344–8; Maginnis 1997, pp. 79–125.

Florence, now in the Uffizi, who did scenes 26–28 on the south wall and scene 1 on the north, all in bay one.[488]

His fresco decoration of the Arena chapel at Padua provides the basis for study of the essential characteristics of Giotto's style and its development. A number of scholars have elaborated at length the stylistic difficulties encountered in any attempt to attribute the frescoes at Padua, undoubtedly by Giotto, and the frescoes of the St Francis cycle, to the same master.[489] As a historian I am not going to risk any detailed discussion of the radical differences of approach to a whole range of related issues – compositional methods, painted architectural framing, dramatic narrative, portrayal of people and of landscape – discernible in the two cycles. But there is also a discrepancy of a technical kind. Zanardi has made a comparative study of the ways heads were drawn and flesh tints painted. In the St Francis cycle he has identified four patterns for heads and as many 'modes of execution'. Significantly, throughout the cycle the sequence in which the flesh colours were applied followed an identical order in all four modes of execution and their variants. The initial colour was always yellow ochre, and there were always three tones of a colour, whether it be green shading to brown or rose shading to reddish. In contrast to Giotto's practice, these three shades (and Giotto used four) were put on from darker to lighter. Their application was always preceded by the definition of the centre of the cheek with the appropriate reddish tint – a practice which never occurs in Giotto's workshop. The paint used in the St Francis cycle is thicker, has more 'body'. The brush strokes are therefore more evident. The method of painting flesh adopted by Giotto and those who worked with or for him in the Lower Church, which has already been described, was innovative, an expression of his 'dolce stil nuovo'. Taken together, the seemingly fundamental differences of style and differences of painterly technique combine to rule out the likelihood of Giotto's participation in the St Francis cycle.[490]

One argument used by some who favour a fourteenth-century date, after the Paduan cycle, for the St Francis cycle, whether or not they attribute it to Giotto, relates to the borrowing of motifs. A striking example is the 'boy in the tree' in the Lamentation of the Poor Clares, scene 23 (Plate 55). A boy pulling off branches from a tree was a familiar component of the traditional iconography in scenes of Christ's triumphal entry into Jerusalem. In the Upper Church the boy is set in an imaginative context, and the way he is portrayed, actively climbing, with his back to the mourners crowding towards San Damiano, concentrating on what he is doing, is new. In the Arena chapel Giotto has painted Christ's entry into Jerusalem, with, of course, in the tree, the boy – whose silhouette is almost identical. Because of Giotto's great reputation, it has been suggested that it was he who invented the pose.[491] However, White has demonstrated that this argument 'is not wholly convincing. Where both the masters concerned are of the receptivity and inventiveness of the designers of the frescoes at Assisi and at Padua, and it is not even a matter of the relationship between a major and a minor

[488] Zanardi 1996, pp. 42–4, 50 and figs. 36–41; Zanardi 2002, pp. 90–3; Smart 1978, p. 31; White 1987, pp. 215–18; and see p. 445.
[489] For example, Smart 1971; White 1987; Maginnis 1987.
[490] Zanardi 1996, pp. 42–4; Zanardi 2002, pp. 142–7, and figs. 1–9, 42, 44, 46, 51, 53, 55, 57, 59, 70, 72, 74, 76, 78, 80.
[491] Fisher 1956.

figure, there seems to be no way of excluding the very real possibility that the painter at Assisi, in transferring an old idea to a new context, created an original pose.'[492] He has also pointed out that in this particular instance there is a distinct possibility that both are based on a lost prototype in Rome; he instances, for example, Cavallini's activities in Old St Peter's, where there was a cycle of the Life of Christ, and in Santa Cecilia in Trastevere, where there was originally a complete New Testament as well as an Old Testament cycle.[493]

Nicholas IV

It is time to turn to the man claimed by the Order's authorities to have authorised the 'great sumptuousness of pictures', brother Jerome of Ascoli, Pope Nicholas IV.[494] Jerome was born on 30 September 1227 at Lisciano, near Ascoli Piceno, in the March of Ancona. The son of a notary, he joined the Friars Minor as a young man. He was elected Provincial Minister of Dalmatia in 1272. In the same year he was sent to Constantinople by Gregory X on an embassy to Michael VIII Palaeologus to negotiate the attendance of Greek representatives at the Second Council of Lyon, held in 1274, which achieved a temporary reunion of the churches. In 1274 he was elected Minister General. His time in this office was punctuated by interruptions as successive popes required his services. At the next General Chapter, held at Padua in 1276, he offered to resign as the pope was sending him on another mission to Constantinople, but the friars refused to release him. In 1277–8 he was sent as papal legate on a peace mission to France. In 1278 Nicholas III named him cardinal priest of Santa Pudenziana, a small early Christian church close behind the apse of Santa Maria Maggiore, and he was allowed to resign as Minister General in 1279. Martin IV made him cardinal bishop of Palestrina in 1281. After the death of Honorius IV in April 1287 the cardinals, meeting in Rome, could not agree. In the course of an intensely hot summer six died and most of the rest fell sick

---

[492] White 1984, ch. IV, p. 105.

[493] White 1984, ch. IV, p. 106. Recently Thomas de Wesselow, in a brilliant and original article (de Wesselow 2005), has drawn attention to two further examples. He compares the hanging lamps in scenes 9 and 22 of the St Francis cycle, Plates 58 and 67, with the more accurately drawn lamps in frescoes by Giotto in the Arena chapel at Padua. He also compares the right and left vaults of the papal chamber in scene 17, Plate 63, with those in the fictive wall-tombs placed to either side of the chancel arch in the Arena chapel, in which the paired lamps hang. As the fictive wall-tombs are site-specific, he argues that the vaulting and lamps originated in Padua and were copied in Assisi. 'There is . . . a straightforward explanation for the detailed correspondences . . . the presence of a drawing at Assisi of Giotto's left-hand fictive chamber and lamp' (ibid. p. 35). But with literary texts, although there are exceptions, if one is dependent on the other, the less sophisticated version is likely to be the earlier. By analogy, the more accurate and sophisticated version of the same image is likely to be later. All the lamps look as if they have been drawn from the life. They are not identical. It seems rather that the artists at Assisi attempted to draw a lamp that was hanging in the Basilica, and that Giotto, more successfully, drew another, similar lamp made in Padua. Zanardi uses the details of the vaults in the scene of St Francis preaching before Honorius III as an illustration of artists' working practices. The fresco still bears traces of the fine threads and the points fixing them to create straight lines, and curved lines, indicating the complexity of the task of aligning the ribs (Zanardi 1996, p. 31, figs. 22–3). I am thus not convinced by de Wesselow's argument that the Assisi cycle must be later than the frescoes in the Arena chapel; but I regret that space does not permit a fuller account of his arguments, and I am very grateful to him for allowing me to study his paper before publication.

[494] See p. 427. For what follows, see Kelly 1986, pp. 205–6; Moorman 1968, pp. 178–9; Brooke 1959, pp. 233–4; Gardner 1997.

and fled the city. When they reassembled in February 1288 they found that Jerome alone had stayed there patiently. They elected him unanimously on 15 February. He declined. They re-elected him on 22 February. He took the name Nicholas IV in tribute to Nicholas III who had promoted him cardinal, but also as an indication of his intention to follow Nicholas III's example.

We can glean some impression of the man from this sparse outline. He was clearly very capable. He was a linguist with at least a working knowledge of Greek, and an accomplished diplomat. He was well respected and valued by his colleagues. He seems to have fostered an atmosphere of consultation, collaboration and friendship. It is significant that on 18 July 1289 he issued the bull *Celestis altitudo*, allocating half the temporal revenues of the papal lands to the college of cardinals and granting it a share in their administration.[495] He was steadfast – a quality he showed during the conclave that elected him – and did not shrink from risking his own health and safety in the cause of duty. When dedicating Orvieto's new cathedral in October 1290 he descended to bless the foundation stone, 'though the foundations . . . were terrifyingly deep'.[496]

Immediately after his coronation he sent to the Basilica, 'out of his great and continuing affection . . . several sets of different coloured vestments, pontifical silks, silver vessels, a sum of money and other gifts included in a schedule attached to the bull'.[497] He remembered his birthplace too, giving the cathedral at Ascoli a magnificent cope of *opus anglicanum*,which may well have been the gift of the English King Edward I to his predecessor Gregory X.[498] He continued to dispatch lavish gifts to the Basilica. Among them was a remarkable reliquary of very high quality probably produced by a goldsmith in Rome. It consists of a silver-gilt casket decorated with arches and enriched with rock crystals and red cabochons with, rising from it, a support for a rock crystal jewelled cross which originally contained a relic of the True Cross. The casket contained a number of relics, including fingers of St Peter, St Paul and St Andrew and part of St James' stole. As the engraved arches decorating the short sides frame St Francis and St Pudenziana on the right and St Anthony and St Agnes on the left side, it has been plausibly suggested that Nicholas IV commissioned it during the years 1278–81, while he was cardinal priest of Santa Pudenziana.[499]

The most splendid of his gifts was a chalice of exceptional importance and quality, the earliest surviving example of the use of translucent enamel (Colour Plate 8). It is described in the Basilica's inventory of 1370 as: 'A precious silver chalice, gilded, with enamels and figures, which Pope Nicholas IV of the Order of Minors sent; in token of this the said Pope is there portrayed and his name inscribed; and it weighs

---

[495] Langlois 1886–1905, p. 391, no. 2217; Potthast, II, no. 23010; cf. Waley 1961, pp. 223–4; Partner 1972, p. 284.

[496] Gardner 1997, p. 4.

[497] Sbaralea, IV, 4, N4 no. 2; Potthast, II, no. 22605 (25 February 1288). The schedule unfortunately does not survive.

[498] Gardner 1997, p. 4 and nn. 44–6, pls. 1, 7.

[499] Assisi 1999, p. 164, quoting the inventories of 1338 and later, and citing Hueck 1982, and plate p. 165. For Nicholas IV's gifts to the Basilica see Ciardi Dupré dal Poggetto 1991, cited Cooper and Robson 2003, p. 34 nn. 7, 12.

45 ounces.'[500] The inscription, in gold letters on an enamelled ground at the base of the stem, reads: 'NICHO(L)AUS PAPA QUARTUS / GUCCIUS MANAIE DE SENIS FECIT.' It is the only known work signed by the Sienese goldsmith Guccio di Mannaia. The design of the chalice is basically octagonal. Round the edge of the base are eight equally spaced figures set in quatrefoil panels. The crucifixion is opposite the Madonna and child; St Francis receiving the stigmata and St Clare, the founders of the two Orders for men and women, are opposite each other, so that these four panels form a cross. The Virgin and St John the Evangelist flank the crucifixion; St Anthony is placed between St Francis and the Madonna and child, while Nicholas IV is next to St Clare. The pope is shown half-length, standing, wearing a mitre and a cope over his Franciscan habit. The figures are interspersed with smaller circles containing the symbols of the four Evangelists, diffusers of the word, two fauns, symbols of sacrifice, and two lions, symbols of divine justice. The next grouping consists of prophets and angels, who inspired their prophecies. Round the centre of the node are roundels enclosing Christ and seven of his apostles. At the base of the bowl, in which through wine is celebrated the mystery of the Eucharist, are angels and archangels, revealing it like the opening petals of a flower. Interspersed between each group of figures are panels enclosing birds of prey, symbols of God. The iconographic programme is rich and complex, and the artefact itself innovative and an influential model as well as extremely valuable. His gifts bear witness to his devotion to St Francis and to his Order, and to his taste. He wanted the best for them, and to do his best for them.

This explains his issuing of two bulls – one addressed to the Minister General – on 14 May 1288 confirming privileges for the Basilica and the Portiuncula and sanctioning the expenditure of offerings on their conservation, repair, enlargement, adaptation, embellishment and so forth, for, as he states, he knows that the maintenance costs of the Basilica are extremely high, and that it is essential both to conserve the church and to support the friars flocking there.[501] A string of indulgences for the Basilica and other Franciscan churches followed. In the four years of his pontificate he issued over 600 bulls for the Friars Minor, the Poor Clares and the Third Order, a prodigious number.[502] It is evidence that he actively promoted an ongoing programme of decoration in the Basilica and the interests of the Order generally.

Before his elevation Nicholas IV was cardinal bishop of Palestrina, a Colonna stronghold. Not himself a member of an aristocratic Roman family, he chose to rely on the Colonnas to their mutual advantage. He promoted members of that family to positions of power in both the Church and the Papal States. Nicholas III had made Giacomo Colonna a cardinal. Nicholas IV made Giacomo's brother Giovanni, first, Rector of the March of Ancona, then, in 1290, sole senator, so that he ruled Rome. Giovanni's son Pietro he made a cardinal, and another son Stefano he made count of the Romagna. The family reciprocated by aiding the pope's enthusiasm for adorning the Roman basilicas

---

[500] Alessandri and Pennacchi 1920, p. 11; *Assisi 1999*, p. 182 and pl. p. 183.
[501] Sbaralea, IV, 22–3, N4 nos. 28–9; Eubel 1908, nn. 1630–1; cf. Cooper and Robson 2003, p. 34 n. 13.
[502] Sbaralea, IV, *passim*: the indulgences for visitors to the Basilica are Sbaralea, IV, 43, 73–4, 254–5, N4 nos. 61, 111, 475; Eubel 1908, nn. 1659, 1688, 1931, of 27 September 1288, 4 May 1289, 13 June 1291; cf. Cooper and Robson 2003, p. 34 n. 14.

of the Lateran and Santa Maria Maggiore, the Franciscan church of Santa Maria in Ara-coeli in Rome and, it would certainly seem, the Basilica at Assisi, with their own money and patronage. Salimbene described Giacomo Colonna as 'totally friendly towards the Order of Friars Minor'.[503] Nicholas IV's reliance on the family was so marked that he was caricatured in a lampoon as stuck fast in a column (the family coat of arms) with only his mitred head emerging, wedged between two other columns, the two Colonna cardinals.[504]

He was a close student of St Bonaventure's writings. While he was Minister General he actually added three paragraphs to the *Legenda Maior* – which was the literary source on which the St Francis cycle was based – and he was the only person to make alterations to the text. The first expanded the account of St Francis' visit to Rome to seek approval of his Rule. When Innocent III first saw him he repulsed him, but a vision of a fine palm tree growing between his feet caused him to send his servants to seek out the beggar (III, 9a). This story Jerome learned from Cardinal Riccardo Annibaldi, who sprang from the same branch of the counts of Segni as Innocent III, and so he was a good witness, likely to have spoken from personal knowledge. Cardinal Riccardo died in 1276.[505] The scene of Innocent III's dream in the St Francis cycle (Colour Plate 7), introduced a new iconographical form, depicting the Lateran portico as rebuilt by Nicholas IV. Peter Murray therefore dated this scene to the last years of his pontificate, from c.1291, noting that 'it is clear that Nicholas himself thought of his work at the Lateran as the fulfilment of a prophecy'.[506] I would say that he deliberately fulfilled the prophecy.

His other two additions are miracles. In one, St Francis cured a novice who had gone mad and suffered paralysis as the result of a frightening experience (*Miracula*, x, 5a). The other is a gruesome story, and one which Jerome retold in more detail in two letters, both sent from Rome, the first, dated 1 May 1276, addressed to the Friars Minor at Assisi, the second, dated 5 May 1276, addressed to the General Chapter of the Order, due to gather on 20 May at Padua.[507] A man falsely accused of stealing the podestà of Assisi's cloak was condemned by Octavian, then a judge at Assisi, to lose his sight. His eyes were plucked out and the nerves cut by Otto, a knight. Protesting his innocence, he was carried to the altar of St Francis, whose mercy he implored. Within three days he received new eyes. They were smaller, but no less efficient. The knight Otto bore witness to this stupendous miracle on oath before James, abbot of San Clemente, who was investigating the miracle by the authority of Jacopo, bishop of Tivoli. The Minister General, brother Jerome, commanded another witness, brother William of Rome, to tell the truth about what he knew of the matter under pain of excommunication. He therefore affirmed before a number of Provincial Ministers and other very worthy friars that he had formerly, while he was still a layman, seen this man while he had eyes; after the punishment had been inflicted and the eyes thrown on the ground, he had out of curiosity used his stick to roll them over; and he saw the man, after by divine grace he had received the light of new eyes, seeing most clearly (*Miracula*, vii, 7a). The way in

[503] Gregorovius 1906, v, 2, 511; Gardner 1973; Salimbene, H, p. 169; S, 1, 245.
[504] Gregorovius 1906, v, 2, 514–15 and n. 1. [505] AF x, 570 n. 2; *Chron. 24 Gen.* in AF III, 365.
[506] Murray 1953, p. 72; and see p. 428. [507] AF x, 643–4 n. 5.

which this story is laid out is a little confusing. The knight Otto and brother William did not testify during the same inquiry; their witness was separated by a number of years.The fact that Jerome of Ascoli, while he was Minister General, took active steps to reinforce the findings of an earlier investigation and then, in 1276, publicised the miracle, now provided with a new witness, complete with circumstantial detail, is, I believe, significant. It suggests, already at this stage of his career, an intention to please the Colonnas. The bishop of Tivoli was Jacopo Antonio Colonna. The miracle is thought to have occurred in 1231.[508]

This same bishop experienced personal involvement in a miracle – perhaps the reason why he interested himself in another of St Francis' miracles. Gregory IX had entrusted him with the custody of an accused heretic, on pain of forfeiting his see if he escaped. The prisoner fasted and entreated St Francis, who caused his chains to break and fall off and his prison wall to open (*Miracula*. v, 4). This miracle is not known to have been illustrated before its inclusion in the St Francis cycle, scene 28 (Plate 59). Ending the cycle with the bishop of Tivoli, Jacopo Antonio Colonna, in the centre of the scene with his arms raised in prayer and his eyes raised towards heaven, to which St Francis is rapidly ascending, is surely a calculated compliment to the Colonna family. The most likely person to have selected this scene, as well as to have stipulated the iconography of scene 6, Innocent III's dream, is surely Nicholas IV. I am not aware of this suggestion being previously made in discussions about attribution and dating. The content of the cycle together with the rest of the decorative scheme is likely to have been planned during Jerome of Ascoli's generalate; the apse and transepts were mostly frescoed then and probably finished under his successor as Minister General, Bonagrazia, who had been his companion and remained his friend.[509]

This still leaves unsettled the question as to when the nave decorations were done. Some scholars argue that work stopped in 1281 and was not resumed until 1288 when Nicholas IV became pope. Torriti then embarked on the frescoes on the upper nave walls, starting with the creation, but was presently summoned to Rome by Nicholas IV to work on the apse mosaic of St John Lateran.[510] The problem with this hypothesis is that it squeezes the decoration of almost the whole of the nave into a very short space of time, if the arguments that it was completed by 1296 are accepted.[511] Such a time scale may well be feasible. Estimates of the time required are hampered by our lack of information about such practical details as the number of men employed in the workshops, and whether they did or did not work through all or part of the winter.[512] But the sheer extent of stylistic diversity and development on display in the nave would be easier to explain over a somewhat longer period, and there was not necessarily an absence of funding between 1281 and 1288.[513] It has been suggested that Torriti may have belonged to the workshop of the Roman painter working alongside the Gothic workshop in the north transept. Whether that was the case or not, he may have come with a workshop to Assisi shortly after Cimabue left. Some scholars have argued that Cimabue's frescoes in the transept and those of Torriti and his collaborators in the

[508] AF X, 644, nn. 1–4.   [509] See pp. 342, 417–19, 447–8, 450.
[510] E.g. Tomei 1990, pp. 48–66; Lunghi 1996, p. 48; and see pp. 446–8.
[511] See pp. 428–33.   [512] Zanardi 2002.   [513] White 1984, ch. IV, p. 107; and see pp. 415–16.

nave were done very close together in time.[514] I favour this hypothesis as it fits quite well with some facts which may be relevant. In the third bay there are clear signs that there was an interruption in the work. 'This break may well, on stylistic grounds, have been of some duration.'[515] Bonagrazia died on 3 October 1283. The timing highlighted a flaw in the constitutions governing the election of the Minister General. Had he died before Michaelmas a General Chapter would have been called in 1284, but as he died after Michaelmas, a General Chapter to elect his successor was not held the next year as one was not due, but met in Milan in 1285. The Order was nearly two years without a head. This was considered so damaging that the friars decided that in future a Vicar General should be appointed during a vacancy. The new Minister General had little time; he died in 1286. The Provincial Minister of Aquitaine then acted as Vicar General.[516] One of the 'damaging consequences' of a lack of leadership during these years may have been a difficulty with the decorators. Perhaps a workshop left and there was a failure to find a replacement. But the situation was about to change dramatically. In May 1287 the General Chapter elected Matthew of Acquasparta Minister General; in February 1288 the papal conclave elected Jerome of Ascoli Pope Nicholas IV. The two men were colleagues and friends of long standing. They had co-operated in drawing up the decorative programme for the Upper Church in the 1270s. They now had the opportunity together to pour new life into the enterprise. One of the two bulls issued by Nicholas IV on 14 May 1288 sanctioning the expenditure of offerings on the decoration of the Basilica was addressed to the Minister General, that is, to Matthew of Acquasparta. It is possible that this was the spur that prompted the engagement of the Isaac Master. The same year Nicholas IV made Matthew a cardinal, which obliged him to resign as Minister General. The General Chapter was due to meet at Assisi in 1289, but it met instead at Rieti at the special request of the pope, who attended, accompanied by two Franciscan cardinals, Bentivenga Bentivengi and Matthew of Acquasparta. Nicholas IV was there because he had a candidate in mind. But his presence failed to influence the outcome. Against his wishes Raymond Gaufridi, who was sympathetic to the Spirituals, was elected.[517] Raymond will not have been a willing promoter of lavish decoration, but he was not in a position to prevent it. The pope, and the Cardinal Protector, could command. And sufficient momentum had been generated for the work to proceed. When the Isaac Master had finished the upper regions of the third and fourth bays and the counter-façade he carried straight on into the St Francis cycle.[518] At one point his progress can be determined. He did not reach scene 6 before 1291, the year in which the restored Lateran portico he painted in Innocent III's dream was recorded as finished.[519]

Nicholas IV never travelled to Assisi to inspect or admire the decoration that was undertaken during his pontificate. He spent his time in Rome, apart from two stays in Rieti from May to October 1288 and May to October 1289, a visit to Orte in May 1290 and a stay in Orvieto from June 1290 to October 1291.[520] It is unlikely that the St Francis cycle was finished before his death on 4 April 1292. His death may have led to

[514] Hueck 1969, pp. 126–7; Tomei 1990, pp. 48–56; Bologna 1960, pp. 18–20, etc., cited Tomei 1990, pp. 55, 72 n. 61.
[515] White 1984, ch. IV, p. 107.   [516] For the sequence of Ministers General, see Gratien 1928, pp. 361 ff.
[517] Moorman 1968, p. 193 n. 1.   [518] See pp. 421–4.   [519] See p. 428.   [520] Potthast, II, pp. 1826–1914.

a speeding up of procedures. Perhaps, concerned by the ensuing political turbulence, the Cardinal Protector, Matteo Rosso Orsini, may have introduced efficiency targets. Certainly there were changes in working practices.[521] On the north wall the painters deputed to do the horizontal decorative framework above and below the scenes also tackled some small areas within scenes. The outlines of the *giornate* were irregular and might, for example, include areas of sky or the tops of buildings, or feet on the ground. This relaxed approach is encountered for the last time in scene 14, the miracle of the spring, in which *giornata* no. 181 contains both the bottom part of the scene and the dado cornice. In scene 15, St Francis preaching to the birds, the scene and dado are kept distinct. On the south wall, and in scene 1, the scenes were cordoned off with very few exceptions and the *giornate* above and below were synchronised with the horizontal straight lines of the framing. This made the task of the painters of the frames simple, more mechanical and more monotonous, but it meant they could cover longer stretches in a day. A particularly long stretch comprised the top cornice of scene 19, the Stigmatisation, the top section of the architectural pillar, the cornice of scene 20, St Francis' death, and the beginning of scene 21 (*giornata* 209) (Plate 65). The reason for this was to enable scene 20, which was to be frescoed by a new workshop led by the Master of the Obsequies, and was the most complex of all the scenes in the cycle, to be tackled before the preceding scenes in the fourth bay were completed. To facilitate this still further, scene 19, the Stigmatisation, the last scene of the fourth bay, was done first and the painters then went back to the beginning of the bay and frescoed scenes 16, 17 and 18 in order. By this means the two workshops could be at work in the two bays simultaneously, both groups working from left to right without getting in each other's way.[522] Further rationalisation was then introduced. At the beginning of the second bay and at the beginning of the first there was a vertical break between the architectural pillar and the flat surface of the bay. And the same procedure of frescoing the right-hand end first and then going back to the beginning was employed. In the second bay it seems that scene 25 was finished first, then scene 23, the Lamentation of the Poor Clares, and the central scene 24, the Canonisation, last. In the first bay the final architectural pillar was frescoed first, then the top cornice of scene 26, followed by the top cornices of scenes 27 and 28.[523] Some members of the Master of the Obsequies' workshop could have been painting bay two while at the same time the St Cecilia Master was painting bay 1. Indeed theoretically and perhaps in actuality groups of painters could have been at work in all four bays of the south wall at the same time. It seems abundantly clear from Zanardi's researches that these changes in working practices were designed to hasten the completion of the cycle.

The friars who drew up *Religiosi viri*, between 1310 and 1312, in asserting that they had not seen 'great sumptuousness of pictures' in the Order's churches apart from the Basilica in Assisi, were disingenuous.[524] In the friars' headquarters in Rome, the church of Santa Maria in Aracoeli housed the Savelli family chapel in its right transept, and, since shortly after 1302, the conspicuous tomb of their Minister General, Cardinal Matthew of Acquasparta, with, above his sculptured effigy, a scene showing him

---

[521] For this and what follows, see Zanardi 1996, pp. 19–24, 50–2; Zanardi 2002, pp. 85–106.
[522] Zanardi 1996, p. 266; and see pp. 403–7.   [523] Zanardi 1996, pp. 316, 334.   [524] See p. 427.

presented to the Virgin and child by St Francis, frescoed by Cavallini's workshop.[525] That Pietro Cavallini and his workshop were already active in the church earlier, in the 1290s, is indicated by surviving fragments of the apse decoration, and recent restoration work has uncovered further evidence of more frescoes.[526] The church was also embellished externally with scenes in mosaic, of which fragments identifiable as Innocent III's dream survive on the wall facing the Senate.[527] Because of their subject matter these mosaic decorations may have been commissioned by Nicholas IV, and so may Cavallini's frescoes, if they can indeed be dated to c.1290. It seems that Santa Maria in Aracoeli was sumptuously decorated within and without. A lost fresco cycle which, according to Ghiberti, Cavallini painted in the church of San Francesco a Ripa, also in Rome, occupied the nave walls and the transepts, and included 'many miracles of our holy Father'.[528] A number of Franciscan churches acquired fresco cycles in the 1290s and early fourteenth century, which, though on a more restricted scale than at Assisi, breached the spirit of the Rule and the Order's constitutions and justified Ubertino's accusations of extravagance and relaxation.[529]

Ubertino's opponents also oversimplified, attributing the sumptuous decoration to Nicholas IV. They might have generalised their argument, and their excuse, claiming that the popes were responsible. The decision that the Basilica ought to be decorated was taken by Innocent IV. The first command to proceed with it came from him. The final stages of the decoration of the Upper Church were initiated by Nicholas IV. But he was also a Friar Minor and had been an elected Minister General. The Order could not shrug off all responsibility. It would not be true to say that the decoration of the Basilica, as it developed, was forced on the Order against the will of Ministers General in post at crucial moments. The Order's outstanding intermediate patron was Nicholas III, who had been its Cardinal Protector – and he had been specially asked for by St Bonaventure. Among his predecessors Alexander IV had also been Cardinal Protector, responsible for implementing Innocent IV's command. It is possible to trace a long thread of continuity and shared purpose.[530]

Nevertheless, although an oversimplification, the friars had some justification for singling out and naming Nicholas IV. The first Franciscan to become pope, he took advantage of his elevation not only to reactivate the decorative programme in the Upper Church but to promote the image of St Francis in Rome, at the heart of the Roman Church. He made it a priority to rebuild and embellish those parts of the Lateran Basilica in need of restoration. He considered it incumbent on him, and his privilege as St Francis' successor, to fulfil, literally, the prophecy in Innocent III's dream. He made this clear in the inscription inserted in the restored portico.[531] The apse and transept were in part rebuilt on the foundations and, with slight variations, on the plan of the Constantinian basilica. The apse was circular inside, polygonal outside; and Torriti was employed to restore and complete the mosaic decoration. The venerated bust of Christ, set in a blue sky with multi-coloured clouds, supported by angels, which was considered

[525] See p. 419.   [526] Gardner 1992, p. 83; cf. Tomei 1990, pp. 142–5.
[527] Tomei 1990, pp. 142–5, 310–11, figs. 157–60.   [528] Smart 1978, p. 30.
[529] Blume 1983; Burr 2001, pp. 121–3; and see p. 415.   [530] See pp. 281, 287–8, 346–53.
[531] For this and what follows, see Tomei 1990, pp. 77–99, esp. pp. 78–9 and fig. 98; and see p. 428.

Acheropita ($\alpha \chi \varepsilon \iota \rho o \pi o \iota \eta \tau o \nu$ – not made with hands) was carefully preserved. Executed on a slab of travertine, this fifth-century icon was fixed to the apex of the apse with metal clamps. Torriti probably reused some of the original tesserae in reconstructing the iconography. The centre of the semidome was dominated by the vertical line of a great jewelled cross beneath the *Acheropita*. At its central crossing was a medallion showing Christ's baptism. The cross rose from the hill of Paradise down which four rivers flowed, from which two stags and two sheep drank. On the slope of the hill were the jewelled walls of the heavenly Jerusalem, guarded by the angel with the flaming sword (Gen. 3. 24; Rev. 20–2). St Peter and St Paul looked out over the battlements, while above them the dove, the Holy Spirit, perched on top of a tree. So far the iconography adhered to a long devotional tradition dating back to the fifth century. But when it came to the choice of figures flanking the central composition, very significant changes in the iconography were introduced. The original apse mosaic probably portrayed three apostles to either side, headed by St Peter and St Paul.[532] In Torriti's mosaic, against a background of gold tesserae, on the right of the cross (the viewer's left), the Virgin presented the donor, the small kneeling figure of Nicholas IV, her hand on his tiara; close behind her stood St Francis, behind him St Peter and St Paul. On the other side of the cross stood John the Baptist, with behind him St Anthony of Padua, St John the Evangelist and St Andrew. All are identified by name. They stood in a field studded with plants and flowers, cherubs and birds, which formed the bank of a classical river scene, representing the Jordan, teeming with a great variety of birds, and with people fishing, boating and disporting themselves. At the extreme left of the river, Torriti inscribed his signature: 'Iacobus Torriti / pictor hoc opus feccit' (*sic*); and at the opposite end the date, 1291.[533] The horizontal line of Nicholas IV's dedicatory inscription divided the semidome from its base, whose four windows provided the frames for three single standing apostles, while to either side there was space for three more apostles. On the left, between the second and third apostles, was the small kneeling figure of a friar, the architect, holding the set square and compass of his craft; balancing him on the right, between the seventh and eighth apostles, a mosaicist, holding hammer and scalpel, the instruments for creating tesserae from a slab of marble. He knelt by the inscription: 'brother James of Camerino, the master of the work's companion, recommends himself to the mercy of Christ and the merits of blessed John'. The inclusion of recently canonised, 'modern', saints in the apse mosaic of a Roman basilica, was an innovation. That Nicholas IV should include St Francis in his embellishment of the restored Lateran should not surprise us. St Francis had been divinely appointed to save the Lateran and thereby the Church from ruin. This had been revealed to Innocent III in a dream, and justified his presence. Important elements of the new iconography were already on display in the Basilica at Assisi. The vault of the second bay in the nave bears shields, frescoed by Torriti, depicting St Francis in the company of Christ, the Virgin and John the Baptist

---

[532] Tomei 1990, pp. 91, 97 n. 84, citing Christe 1970, pp. 197–206.

[533] Tomei 1990, pp. 77, 94 n. 4. The date is given incorrectly in the modern mosaic as 1292. Torriti's mosaics were damaged in a fire in 1308 which practically destroyed the basilica and the Lateran palaces. Restoration and reconstruction work took place over the centuries, but copies of the medieval iconography survive and tracings were taken before the mosaics were taken down in the late nineteenth century.

(Plate 56). This correspondence lends strong support to the suggestion that Jerome of Ascoli was among the group who drew up the decorative programme for the Upper Church; indeed it suggests that he was responsible for the iconographic scheme of that vault. But Nicholas IV's bold innovation in the Lateran did not simply glorify St Francis; it was intended to do much more. The Lateran apse iconography conveyed not one but two images of St Francis. As a person St Francis had scaled the heights of sanctity. His conformity to Christ, signed and sealed by the stigmata,[534] had earned him an incomparable place in heaven. But he was also the founder of the Order of Friars Minor; the image is given a wider context. His mission to renew the Church was not to be achieved single-handed. His personal exemplarity was the inspiration for a movement of renewal which was absolutely necessary to sustain and continue the momentum. This explains the presence of St Anthony. The Order's two saints were the two new apostles, entitled to stand alongside Christ's apostles. Their positioning is extraordinarily explicit in making this claim visually; the humble are indeed exalted here. Though they are portrayed smaller than the other main figures, St Francis is placed in front of St Peter, St Anthony in front of St John the Evangelist. The same message is conveyed in the enamels decorating the chalice Nicholas IV gave to the Basilica, though on it, it is widened to include St Clare, St Francis' colleague and the head of the Second Order[535] (Colour Plate 8). On the chalice, St Francis receiving the stigmata, St Anthony and St Clare (and Nicholas IV as on the Lateran apse) consort with Christ, the Virgin, St John the Evangelist, St Peter, St Paul and five other apostles, supported by prophets and angels. The same message had begun to be sent out earlier, in the stained glass windows of the Upper Church; also in the fresco decoration of its walls; all of it decoration discussed, and some of it implemented, while Jerome of Ascoli was Minister General, but the richness of that decoration meant that it shared the space with other themes. Nicholas IV was devoted to his Order – though his outlook was very different from that of St Francis and the early friars; he was also official head of the Church, and by reason of his office held service to the Church a top priority. The band of decoration below the semidome of the apse contained an affirmation of the Order's mission that is quite remarkable. The small kneeling figures both wear the habit, cord and open sandals of the Friars Minor. They represent two individual craftsmen – one is named – pictured hard at work between the apostles' feet. They are engaged, literally, in the rebuilding and embellishment of the Lateran. They are also the embodiment of the ordinary Friars Minor, the rank and file of the Order, whose task it is, as followers of St Francis, to renew the Church. Their role is acknowledged and honoured by Nicholas IV in the Lateran.

Nicholas IV's second major project in Rome was the restoration of the papal basilica of Santa Maria Maggiore. The two were not undertaken consecutively; both were equally ambitions determined on by Jerome of Ascoli when his unexpected election to the papacy enticed him with exhilarating scope and opportunity. Both were initiated during the first year of his pontificate, as a group of papal bulls makes clear.[536] Two, addressed

---

[534] See pp. 232, 236–7.   [535] See pp. 440–1.
[536] For this and what follows see Tomei 1990, chs. III–IV and pp. 153–6, pls. XVIII–XXX and figs. 87–144.

to Cardinal Giacomo Colonna, archpriest of Santa Maria Maggiore, and the prior and chapter, and dated 11 August 1288, continue and extend previous indulgences. They were followed by a third, dated 27 September 1288, encouraging visits on any day of the year with the offer of a forty-day indulgence. A fourth bull, issued the same day and addressed to all the faithful, stated explicitly that because of his desire to restore the basilica he was offering an indulgence of one year and forty days for each and every alms or other help given towards its conservation and repair. The structural alterations at Santa Maria Maggiore were more extensive than at the Lateran. Santa Maria Maggiore had no transept. So the fifth-century apse was entirely demolished and rebuilt 6.5 m further back to allow room for a substantial transept to be built between it and the nave. The ancient apsidal arch was retained as a triumphal arch. As at the Lateran the apse was circular inside, polygonal outside. The rebuilding work took longer; so Torriti began decoration after he had finished his mosaics in the Lateran in 1291. In the bottom left-hand corner of the apse he put his signature: '+ / Iacobus Tor/riti pictor / hoc opus mosiacum [sic] fecit', and at the opposite end the date, 1296.[537] So it was not completed until four years after Nicholas IV's death and most of the expense will probably have been borne by the Colonna. Immediately after finishing in Santa Maria Maggiore, early in 1296, Torriti went on to do the mosaic panel on Arnolfo di Cambio's sculptured tomb monument for Boniface VIII in Old St Peter's.[538]

Nicholas IV took a personal interest in the iconography of the mosaic decoration. Already in his bull *Propter veritatem* addressed to Cardinal Giacomo Colonna on 11 August 1288, in his praise of the Virgin, God's 'humble handmaid', he writes: 'This is the lady clothed with sun and moon under her feet, who with fertile virginity bore the Saviour. This is she who as mother and virgin had God for her son, and was raised to the heavenly kingdoms above the choirs of angels.'[539] She is duly depicted in heaven above the choirs of angels and with sun and moon under her feet. That Nicholas IV sent detailed written instructions to Santa Maria Maggiore specifying what he wanted adds weight to the argument that he is likely to have sent written guidance to Assisi. It is noteworthy that he interpreted an apocalyptic passage from the Book of Revelation as applicable to the Virgin, perhaps because of its artistic potential. 'And there appeared a great wonder in heaven; a woman clothed with the sun, and the moon under her feet, and upon her head a crown of twelve stars. And she being with child cried, travailing in birth, and pained to be delivered' (Rev. 12. 1–2). In his bull *Mulier generosa* of 27 September 1288, likewise addressed to the cardinal, he emphasised his conception of his responsibilities as pope; he outlined his wishes and implicitly indicated his expectation that the Colonna would aid him in financing them. Jerome of Ascoli had a particular devotion to the Virgin Mary. From October 1288, whenever he was in Rome he resided at his palace adjacent to Santa Maria Maggiore, and he chose to be buried in this basilica.

The scene, in the centre of the apse, is the Coronation of the Virgin. The background is entirely composed of gold tesserae. Christ and the Virgin are both seated on a wide jewelled throne placed inside a disc of intense blue dotted with stars to symbolise

---

[537] Tomei 1990, p. 13 and figs. 1–3.
[538] Tomei 1990, pp. 14, 127–30 and figs. 139, 141; and see p. 431.   [539] Tomei 1990, p. 154, no. 2.

the highest heaven. The Virgin is on Christ's right; the moon is under her feet, the sun under Christ's. He is in the act of placing a jewelled crown on her head with his right hand, while in his left he holds an open book with the text: 'Come my chosen one, and I will set you upon my throne' – a paraphrase from the Song of Songs 4. 8, 6. 8, used in the liturgy on the day of the Assumption.[540] Outside the disc, to either side, below the arms of the throne, stand representatives of each of the nine choirs of angels, and below it are two lines of inscription, repeating the visual image in words: 'Mary the Virgin has been raised to the heavenly chamber in which the king of kings sits on a throne of stars: / the holy mother of God has been exalted over the choirs of angels to the heavenly kingdoms.'[541] From ground level at either side spring vigorous shoots of acanthus whose branches rise upwards in swirls, home to a variety of birds of evident symbolic significance – the eagle, the heron, the dove, peacocks (symbols of Paradise)– typical of medieval religious imagery. Above the decorative vegetation, in the top centre, the semicircular multicoloured canopy of heaven, rich with jewels, spreads out like a fan.

On the level of the choirs of angels are ranged, on Christ's and the Virgin's right, St Peter, St Paul and St Francis, and on their left John the Baptist, St John the Evangelist and St Anthony, all identified by name, standing on a flowery strip of meadow. St Francis and St Anthony are thinner than the apostles and slightly shorter. Kneeling in front of St Peter is Nicholas IV, in front of the Baptist Cardinal Giacomo Colonna, his co-patron, sharing in the offering of the rebuilding, conservation and redecoration to the Virgin and her Son (Plate 72). The strip of meadow forms the back of a classical river scene graced with sporting cupids, similar to that at the Lateran. The waters flow from an amphora at either end held by a classical river god and from the four rivers which flow from the hill of Paradise at the centre, from which two stags drink. The jewelled walls of the heavenly Jerusalem are guarded by the angel with the flaming sword.

A jewelled cornice separates the Coronation from the decoration beneath, which is devoted to scenes from the life and death of the Virgin. The exterior of the apse is five-sided, but windows were only pierced in the outer four walls; the central section was left windowless to allow room for a large mosaic. In the spandrels of the windows are four small scenes from the Virgin's life: on the viewer's left the Annunciation and the Nativity, on the right the Adoration of the Magi and the Presentation in the Temple. In the centre, intentionally misplaced so as to be positioned directly beneath her Coronation, is the much wider scene of the Dormition of the Virgin.[542] She is laid out on a richly draped bier, with the apostles ranged to either side, attended by devotees and angels. Top left the walls of Sion stand on a hilltop, balanced on the right by the Mount of Olives. Christ in a mandorla stands at her side at the centre, clasping her soul to him in his arms. The concept is identical to that visualised in Cimabue's rendering of the same scene in the apse of the Upper Church. Indeed the Marian iconography of the apse mosaic in Santa Maria Maggiore invites comparison with its counterpart in the Basilica at Assisi, designed while Jerome of Ascoli was Minister General.[543] Marian devotion

---

[540] Tomei 1990, p. 100 and p. 120, n. 13.   [541] Tomei 1990, p. 100.
[542] Tomei 1990, pls. xxv–xxvii, figs. 116–18.   [543] See pp. 361–2.

Plate 72 Detail from the Coronation of the Virgin, Rome, Santa Maria Maggiore, apse mosaic: St Francis, St Paul, St Peter with Pope Nicholas IV: signed 'Jacopo Torriti painter' (Photo Abbrescia Santinelli for Face2Face Studio-Roma).

was likewise fostered by his two colleagues as Minister General, St Bonaventure and Matthew of Acquasparta. In his sermon on the Feast of the Assumption of the Virgin St Bonaventure laid emphasis on her regality and coronation. Matthew of Acquasparta in his sermons defended the simultaneous bodily and spiritual assumption of the Virgin. Both leaders spelt out the direct progression from dormition, through assumption to coronation.[544]

In the centre foreground, kneeling in front of the bier, are three small figures, two friars and one layman. It has been suggested that the friars represent Torriti and his assistant, James of Camerino.[545] However, in none of his signatures does Torriti designate himself as a friar, whereas James of Camerino does. I would suggest that, if these small figures do indeed represent humble craftsmen, then the two friars depict the architect and James of Camerino, as in the Lateran mosaic, and the layman, Torriti. The claim, then, that St Francis and St Anthony are the two new apostles and that

544 Bonaventure, *Opera Omnia*, IX, Sermon V, pp. 699–700, cited Gardner 1973, p. 10.
545 Wilpert 1916, I, 506.

the Friars Minor are charged with continuing their mission to sustain the Church, is identical to that visually conveyed in the Lateran mosaic.[546]

The fresco decoration of the transept which Nicholas IV had added to the building was probably begun soon after the apse mosaic was finished in 1295.[547] Work on it was abruptly interrupted, probably owing to the fall of the Colonna in 1297, and never restarted. In the left transept the upper level is decorated with roundels linked by a plain red band, above which runs a heavy frieze of fictive corbels ornamented with cosmati inlay. Below is the beginning of a series of biblical scenes, of which only a fragment of the first, the Creation, survives. If, as seems probable, there were two registers, 'such a conjunction of scenes would offer striking similarities to that at Assisi, where an Old Testament cycle leads into a New Testament series, and where also the apse is devoted to scenes from the life of the Virgin'.[548] The evidence of close connection is strengthened by the remarkable resemblance of the heads in two of the roundels to heads in scene 11 of the St Francis cycle, St Francis preaching before the Sultan – they have the same chiselled look (Plate 61). The style of the roundels indicates the activity in Rome c.1295–7 of artists trained in the circle of the Isaac Master.[549] The transept decorative scheme will have formed part of the programme projected by Nicholas IV and faithfully continued by Cardinal Giacomo Colonna.

Torriti's artistic achievement, both in fresco in the Upper Church at Assisi and in mosaic in the Lateran and Santa Maria Maggiore in Rome, bears witness to his profound knowledge of late Antique and palaeochristian Roman monumental painting, which, allied to a strong influence from the recent developments of the Palaeologan 'volume style', coalesced to create his own original and recognisable individual style.[550] This Byzantine component may be one reason why Nicholas IV entrusted him with important commissions. While he was Provincial Minister of Dalmatia he will have had opportunity to see some of the contemporary Byzantine murals painted probably by Greek artists who migrated to that region after the sack of Constantinople in 1204. He may have seen the exceptionally fine wall paintings at Sopoçani, where the scene of the Dormition of the Virgin dominated the lower register of the apse in a way not unlike it was to do in his own scheme in the apse of Santa Maria Maggiore. His appreciation of Byzantine art will have been further enhanced during his embassy to the Palaeologan court.[551]

It seems clear that, once he had been persuaded to accept, Nicholas IV considered his elevation to the papacy as providential. The exclusive group, St Peter, St Paul, St Francis and himself, placed on the Virgin's right in the apse mosaics of both the Lateran and Santa Maria Maggiore, constitute an arresting image (Plate 72). It emphasises in visual language that St Francis is an apostle, worthy to stand beside Rome's chief apostles, and that Nicholas IV, previously Minister General of the Order founded by St Francis, is now Peter's successor, Christ's vicar on earth. St Francis as the man destined to support a church 'tottering in ruins' both literally and metaphorically – 'He will bear the Church

[546] See p. 448.   [547] For what follows, see Gardner 1993, ch. III.
[548] Gardner 1993, p. 18.   [549] Gardner 1993, pp. 18–19, figs. 9, 14; Tomei 1990, p. 102, figs. 134–5.
[550] Kitzinger 1966, pp. 45–6 = 1976, pp. 376–7; Demus 1970, pp. 205 ff; Tomei 1990, pp. 46–7.
[551] Gardner 1997.

and the faith as they falter' – and 'Jerome, chief offspring of Francis in the Order of Minors, rising to be Roman pontiff with the name of Nicholas IV' are linked again, verbally, in the inscription Nicholas had inserted in the restored Lateran portico.[552] St Francis supporting the Lateran portico restored by Nicholas IV is illustrated in the Upper Church fresco cycle, scene 6, and the significance of the image is spelt out verbally in the inscriptions underneath scenes 4 and 6[553] (Colour Plate 7). Several previous popes had given strong support to St Francis and his Order, but Nicholas IV was the first publicly and durably to affirm in Rome the importance to the Church of St Francis, St Anthony and the Friars Minor.[554] The manner in which he fulfilled his vocation as a friar presents us with a paradox. He was a devout and dedicated friar; but he had two role models, St Francis and Nicholas III, and when it came to the restoration, rebuilding and decoration of churches his taste and inclinations, and his office, weighed in favour of the example of Nicholas III.

I suggest that Nicholas IV took the initiative in commissioning the Isaac Master to restart the decorative programme in the nave of the Upper Church in 1288, with the active co-operation of Matthew of Acquasparta; and that the St Francis cycle may have been under way by 1291 and was completed in or before 1296.

[552] See p. 428.   [553] See p. 381.   [554] Tomei 1990, pp. 89–90.

CHAPTER TEN

THE REDISCOVERY OF
ST FRANCIS' BODY

As St Francis' tomb was closed and rendered inaccessible, so that the truth of stories and exaggerations could not be checked or disproved, legend developed.[1] Pious meditation on the miracle of the stigmata led some to suppose that Christ would not have wished, and therefore would not have allowed, the wondrous signs of his Passion imprinted on Francis' flesh to be subject to natural decay. A tradition grew up, gathering momentum from the mid-fifteenth century, that Francis' body had remained incorrupt, the five wounds visible and fresh, with the nails, black and protruding, exactly as described by Bonaventure[2] – an example of the powerful effect of verbal description upon subsequent fantasies. Mysterious visits by a few favoured individuals to an underground third church were alleged to corroborate the marvel.[3]

EXCAVATIONS

From time to time attempts were made by the curious or the relic seeker to take up the pavement of the Lower Church or investigate the high altar and its vicinity. But those who tried to find St Francis' body either died within the year, or soon abandoned the search as too difficult.

In 1607 a workman discovered a hole and rumour quickly suggested that this was the entrance to a stairway leading to the tomb. St Francis, Assisi's most precious treasure, was in danger. The body might be damaged or removed. The civic authorities appealed to Rome, with remarkable success. The Cardinal Protector of the Conventuals, Alfonso Visconti, formally and absolutely forbade, on the authority of Paul V, any future attempt by anyone, of whatever rank, to find the body or the tomb on any pretext whatsoever, on pain of excommunication.[4]

[1] What follows is inspired by the researches and scholarship of P. Isidoro Gatti, OFM Conv. His book, *La Tomba di San Francesco nei secoli* (Gatti 1983) was kindly made available to me by the Reverend Dr Michael Robson, OFM Conv. and the Franciscan Central Library, University of Kent.
[2] Gatti 1983, pp. 124, 194–5 and n. 144, 197 and n. 151.
[3] Gatti 1983, pp. 150–2, 199 ff and nn., 227–8; Wadding 1731–1933, II, 235, anno 1230, no. IV.
[4] Gatti 1983, pp. 234–7.

It was not until almost 150 years had elapsed that a new opportunity occurred. Among the friars resident at the Sacro Convento was Ubaldo Tebaldi, a distinguished scholar and a close friend of Benedict XIV. On the strength of this friendship he obtained from the pope a private, personal authorisation to undertake a secret excavation, which he began at Christmas 1755.[5] He chose three lay friars, the master of the bellchamber, the sub-sacrist and the mason to assist him, and they worked in the early hours, from Matins, because the nights were long. He selected as their starting point the floor in front of the seventeenth-century altar in the transept. They at once encountered solid rock, which they needed to break through little by little until they reached a great subterranean wall under the tribune of the high altar. To penetrate this was 'a labour beyond description' because it was composed of dressed stones and almost impenetrable cement; and nothing was found there. They then dug down to the base of the wall and found nothing but pure rock and water. So they began to work upwards over against the high altar and at a certain point Tebaldi felt the whistling of air through a fissure in the rock. He held the lantern to it – and promptly called off the whole enterprise.

When Tebaldi was an old man he wrote a letter to the Minister General describing in vivid detail his excavation of thirty years before. But its contents and indeed its existence were not divulged, but were kept a closely guarded secret.[6]

In 1806 the Minister General Nicola Papini successfully petitioned Pope Pius VII for permission to try to find St Francis' body, the only proviso being that the search should be conducted with the utmost secrecy.[7] Papini enlisted the co-operation of the Custodian of the Sacro Convento, and they selected for the actual work involved eight well-disposed and discreet friars – 'di buon cuore, e senza lingua'. The point chosen to begin the excavation was the pavement directly underneath the papal throne set against the south wall of the nave of the Lower Church between the pulpit and the high altar. The throne was mobile and the entrance to the excavation was concealed during the daytime by putting the throne back to cover it. All the excavated material was dumped in a room behind one of the chapels. They started towards the end of November 1806, working during the night, and as soon as they had raised the paving stones encountered the rock. It took them about sixty nights to open up a passage large enough for a man which reached to below the altar steps. There they came upon the mass of hard cement. Much encouraged, they continued their labours and presently broke into a cavity, but their initial hopes were rapidly dashed when this proved only to lead to a passageway. This disappointment – they had in fact come upon Tebaldi's excavation – decided Papini to call a halt for the time being. The nights were getting shorter and the political situation had become menacing. Napoleon's victory at Austerlitz enabled him to exert increasing pressure on Italy and on the pope. The French army occupied most of the Papal States in November 1807 and entered Rome in February 1808. Pius VII refused to accede to all the Emperor's demands and lived as a prisoner in the Quirinal until in July 1809 he

---

[5] Gatti 1983, pp. 240–3.
[6] Gatti 1983, p. 242 n. 34, from a note made by P. Antonio Contarini, to whom the Minister General entrusted Tebaldi's letter (*Misc. Fr.* 18 (1917), 94–5, quoted Gatti 1983, p. 242. Cf. ibid. p. 158 and n.).
[7] Gatti 1983, pp. 243–5.

was arrested and escorted over the Alps to Savona. In August the Minister General of the Conventuals, Giuseppe Maria De Bonis, who had succeeded Papini, showed his loyalty to the pope by following him into exile. He was arrested and taken to France under armed guard for refusing to take the oath of loyalty to the Emperor. In June 1810 Napoleon decreed the suppression of the religious Orders.

After the battle of Waterloo, pope and Minister General were able to return to Rome. De Bonis' energies were fully absorbed by problems of reconstruction. The Conventuals suffered particularly badly from the effects of revolution. Although the suppression did not last long, many ex-friars had found satisfying work as parish priests or as schoolmasters. When the Restoration came very many chose not to return to their former Order. In 1773 the Conventuals had had 25,000 members. In 1850, despite revival, they had not reached 1,500.[8] Yet the suppression was indirectly responsible for focusing attention on St Francis' remains. Some friars had managed to remain unofficially at the Basilica and it was rumoured that they had succeeded in finding the tomb and had seen St Francis, in very truth uncorrupt in glory.[9] The early nineteenth century witnessed the culmination of the legends, the logical climax of the earlier tales. When, in August 1818, the Procurator General of the Conventuals came to Assisi for the feast of the Indulgence and enquired as to the foundation of the rumours, a young friar, Giuseppe Rossignoli, undertook to enlighten him. He could show him the way: entrance was effected by lifting a stone in the floor in front of the altar of the Conception, situated by Cimabue's Maestà. He had himself been down, and was very ready to furnish a written statement, full of circumstantial detail, mostly drawn from the by now familiar material. He said that he had received the necessary permission from Pius VII while the pope was in exile in Savona, and had made two attempts, in 1812 and 1816, as a member of a group, some of whom he named, but they had died of typhoid a year ago. The first attempt had failed, but in 1816 they were able to open the great door of the subterranean third church and view the miraculous glorification of St Francis. As further proof he produced relics, small pieces of hood and tunic, which he assured the Procurator he had snipped from Francis' garments. In so doing he overreached himself. The Procurator hastened back to Rome to inform the Minister General of this wonderful and exciting development; and the Minister General believed him and thought the opportunity to recover this marvellous body and display it had at last arrived. Pius VII, who had authorised Papini's excavation twelve years before, willingly gave his permission, with the customary stipulation of secrecy. On 5 October, the day after St Francis' feast day, the Minister General, the Procurator General and the other high-ranking officials of the Order who were gathered together in the Sacro Convento prepared to share in the expected triumph. During the night the stone indicated by Rossignoli was lifted and the soil below, which contained a number of bone fragments, was dug out and removed. When morning came the stone was replaced. The following night the work was resumed and presently solid rock was reached. There was no entrance to a third church here; no third church. Rossignoli was summoned to the Minister General to explain himself. Why had he presumed to write, and sign, a story altogether without

[8] Chadwick 1981, pp. 592–3.   [9] Gatti 1983, pp. 246–50.

foundation? He could only confess, with shame, that he had made it up, but he had exaggerated rather than deliberately intended to mislead. De Bonis felt a fool. He foresaw an embarrassing interview with the pope. The Order would be discredited, a laughing stock. It was at this juncture that a friar who had helped in this misconceived enterprise volunteered a suggestion. Giacomo Amelio, now sub-sacrist, was one of the friars who had previously taken part in Papini's excavation.[10] He explained how this had been abandoned prematurely because of the political situation and that he believed they had not dug there sufficiently deep. His hopeful words were warmly welcomed and the Custodian of the Sacro Convento, Bonaventura Zabberoni, was deputed to reopen the earlier tunnel, which started below the papal throne. He afterwards described the whole course of the operation in detail.[11] The tunnel was narrow. Space was so restricted that they had to work stooping, and in places crawling on all fours. Removing the infilling was tedious and tiring, and it took them many nights to reach the mass of hard cement, which they found behind a stone wall underneath the high altar. They chipped away at this with sharp irons, heavy mallets, hammers and picks and broke so many tools that they often sent some to be repaired by blacksmiths at the Portiuncula and at Foligno as well as at Assisi so as not to arouse too much comment. Eventually they removed sufficient to expose three walls of finished stone, the other three sides of a chamber. They smashed one of the stones in the wall facing them, which had clearly never been disturbed, and behind it was the solid rock. They tested both side walls and found the same. So they set about removing the residual mass of petrified concrete below their feet, with the help of a second mason co-opted from the city because of the difficulty of the work. In the end they uncovered part of a polished stone. By chipping away yet more of the cement they exposed more of the surface of the stone. Zabberoni continued: 'I promptly ordered the piercing of the stone, which proved to be about a hand's breadth in thickness. Below it was a layer of more cement, some two to three fingers thick. Below this was another smooth stone, which I likewise ordered to be pierced. This disclosed a piece of iron about the thickness of one finger. At this stage I instructed them to penetrate no further . . . as by now some reverberation could be heard as if it was hollow further down. Instead they were to widen the area by breaking up both stones. When this was done we discovered yet another smooth stone beneath the iron bar. I ordered this to be bored through with care.' Working from the edge about the mid-point of one of the longer sides they carved out a roughly semi-circular hole.[12] 'This revealed a small portion of an iron grating and through the holes of this was lowered with care and caution a tiny candle fixed to a piece of wire, by the light of which we could just make out that there was a corpse there. I instantly urged them to enlarge the hole slightly and then by the light of the same little candle the body could be better seen, with a good view of the head and the feet. Our next care was to finish disposing of the two upper stones which we found had been built into the two side walls. Now we could see the final stone in all its size. It too was embedded in the wall on one side and was also fastened by three iron bars equidistant from each other. I ordered these three iron bars to be cut out, which made it easier to withdraw it from the wall. With

---

[10] Gatti 1983, pp. 250 ff.   [11] For what follows, see Gatti 1983, pp. 251–3 and nn.   [12] Gatti 1983, pl. 3.

the help of an iron ring it could then be levered upwards about two or three hands' breadths to reveal the whole length of the iron grating, which was of square section with very small holes. Once more we approached a small candle and viewed the sacred corpse.'

It was 12 December 1818: the work had occupied some fifty-two nights. The abrupt return of unaccustomed quiet at night suggested to the people of Assisi that a find had occurred. The noise of the pickaxes striking the rock had reverberated outside the Church and they had got into the habit of gathering in front of the doors of the Basilica to listen. The 'secret' excavation had become the main topic of conversation throughout Umbria and beyond. But was it conclusive? The Minister General was disposed to believe that the tomb constructed with such evident precaution directly underneath the high altar dedicated to him did indeed contain the body of St Francis. But not everyone was immediately satisfied. Perhaps the body was that of one of Francis' companions. It might, for example, be that of brother William, an artist and friend of Matthew Paris. Matthew Paris drew a little sketch of him in the margin of a page of his *Chronica Maiora*, with a caption, in red: 'brother William, an Englishman, companion of St Francis'. William returned to Assisi and was buried near to St Francis in the Basilica, where he worked miracles.[13] According to the *Chronicle of the 24 Generals*, compiled c.1369, brother Elias took exception to this, as introducing undesirable competition, and ordered him to desist, which he obediently did.[14] The story was popularised by Mark of Lisbon and familiar to many. The wonderful third church might still await discovery, situated even deeper within the rock.

Pope Pius VII ordered an official inquiry to establish the identity of the corpse, appointing as his Apostolic Delegates the bishops of Assisi, Nocera Umbra, Spoleto, Perugia and Foligno. The legal process was conducted at Assisi.[15] It began with the cross-questioning of all those directly concerned, most notably the Custodian of the Sacro Convento, Zabberoni, the friars who had helped and laboured, among whom were included the sub-sacrist Giacomo Amelio, whose timely intervention had inspired the resumption of work, the master of the bellchamber and the cook, and the two masons from Assisi, the brothers Cesare and Antonio Mariani. The recording of all their depositions occupied four days, 18–21 January 1819. An architect prepared a detailed description of the excavation with measurements (Figure 11). The hole in the floor of the Lower Church measured 135.91 cm by 89.34 cm, and descent was by a rather steep wooden ladder into the passageway, which was irregular, with an average width of about 67 cm, and a height of about 134–56 cm. As it would be uncomfortable, to say the least, for the five bishops to descend together for their inspection, the passageway was now widened and deepened considerably. The first full session of the process took place on 26 January. In addition to the five bishops, the Minister General of the Conventuals, De Bonis, was present, together with experts qualified in the wide range of expertise that would be needed: two notaries, two architects, two doctors, two surgeons, two archaeologists, one blacksmith. Two days later they were joined by a physical chemist,

---

[13] See pp. 201–2 and Plate 32. [14] AF III, 217; Gatti 1983, pp. 254–5 and nn. [15] Gatti 1983, pp. 257–75.

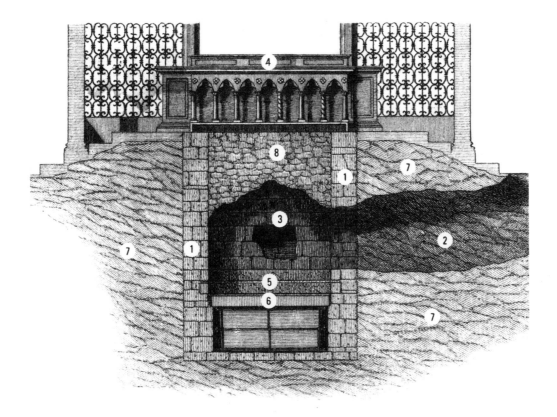

Figure 11 Giovanni Acquaroni, engraving of the tomb of St Francis under the high altar of the Lower Church in the Basilica of St Francis at Assisi, based on the design of the architect B. Lorenzini, made during the excavations of 1818–19: Archivio Generale OFM Conv., Fondo Sacro Convento (Assisi), fasc. an. 1819; Gatti 1983, plate 21

1: The walls of the burial chamber; 2: tunnel cut through the rock in 1819 to extract the third stone, the sarcophagus and the iron cage; 3: passageway created by Tebaldi's excavation of 1755; 4: the high altar of the Lower Church; 5: the two upper stones of travertine; 6: the third stone, set above the iron cage and sarcophagus; 7: the rock of the hillside; 8: cement infilling.

Dr Luigi Canali, brother of the bishop of Spoleto, whose letter to his son provides us with vivid insights into the working conditions with which this galaxy of talent had to contend.

Not without difficulty, on the afternoon of 26 January, the bishops, architects and notaries were shepherded along the passageway by the light of a torch and into the rectangular burial chamber. The architects measured everything. The stone covering the coffin was 178.2 cm below floor level. It measured 2.34 m × 0.97 m with a maximum thickness of 16 cm, and as it was considered desirable to preserve it without further damage (a semicircular hole had already been cut in it) its removal presented a problem. It was decided to cut through the north wall of the chamber, and under the direction of the two architects twelve masons worked day and night to cut a second passageway

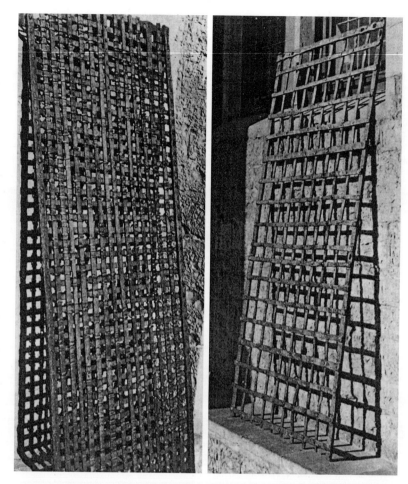

Plate 73 The tomb of St Francis: the two gratings of the iron cage, photographed during the restoration of 1978 (Photo Gerhard Ruf, after A. Mallucci, Sacro Convento, Assisi).

which surfaced in the north transept. This offered the additional advantage of improving the ventilation underground. Further amenity was introduced by enlarging the hole in the western wall of the chamber created by Tebaldi's excavation to accommodate two benches on which the bishops could sit, albeit not in comfort. On 28 January the party was able to descend once more. The stone was slowly raised and winched to the surface. It had no inscription. The iron grating which covered the open coffin could now be inspected. It measured 2.33 m by 0.97 m. There were no fewer than forty-four bars spanning its length, crossed by sixteen along its width. The spaces between them were thus very small, not identical in size, the largest being 3.72 cm and the smallest 2.32 cm[16] (Plate 73). Peering through them the doctors could say no more than that the skeleton was that of a human adult. So the blacksmith was asked to cut it free from the ten vertical iron bars, one to each side of each corner and one in the centre of each of

[16] Gatti 1983, pp. 41, 102.

the longer sides, to which it was attached. It was then taken to the surface as the stone had been. It was very heavy, weighing 143.3 kg. It too bore no inscription.

The doctors and surgeons could now study the skeleton by torchlight. The body had lain untouched in a horizontal position ever since it had been deposited in the tomb, the only disturbance occurring very recently, when the inspection hole had been made in the covering stone, allowing the air for the first time to penetrate the previously sealed cavity. This had caused the hands, which had been crossed low over the breast, to collapse together with the stomach, and some bones of the feet. From the narrowness of the pelvic area it was judged to be the body of a man. The skull was not in good condition. A stalactite incrustation, including some actual crystals of carbonate of lime, had formed on the bones, rendering them very fragile. Six teeth remained among the fragments of the lower jaw. A number of the bones were sound; some had shattered. When they were re-examined in 1978 St Francis' height was calculated at 157–8 cm, based on the measurements of his right humerus and femur, 27.9 cm and 40.2 cm respectively.[17] The excavation and the inquiry exposed Francis' remains not simply to the air but to an atmosphere that was extremely damp. Dr Canali, in a letter to his son, dated 30 January, wrote: 'We are confined inside the mountain at a depth of about [2.45 m] in an excavation [1.11 m] wide and [2.45 m] long. I fear for these Monsignori, for myself and for all of us, on account of the very high humidity which we experience here, since our sessions in this cavity last from seven to eight hours continuously.'[18] Canali agreed with the other doctors that if the bones were not taken out of the stone coffin immediately the existing deterioration would accelerate rapidly. He suggested as a further precaution that they should be grouped according to their state of preservation and recommended that the dust, the fragments and the bones that were more or less intact should be conserved separately for the time being in three wooden boxes, lest the worse contaminate the better preserved. And this was done.

Meanwhile the archaeologists had been examining the various objects, mostly surprising, found in the coffin.[19] Very close to Francis' head, on his right side, was a piece of stone some 20.46 cm high, its dimensions at maximum 17.67 cm, at minimum 11.16 cm, uncut and uninscribed, of local provenance. Twelve coins, covered with verdigris, were found along the side of the coffin and among the bone fragments. They proved to be all of the same quality, silver with a lot of alloy, and from the same mint, from Lucca. From 1167 the coinage of Lucca was accepted as equivalent to the coinage of Bologna, and it was current in Assisi in the twelfth and thirteenth centuries. These particular coins were struck after 1181 and not later than 1208.[20] At the bottom end of the coffin, beyond the feet, was a ring, and under the bones of the feet, which had fallen forward, a little heap of beads. The ring consisted of an oval red cornelian, incised with the figure of the goddess Minerva, set in silver. It was taken to Rome, where it was studied by two antiquarian scholars. They reported that the stone was antique, of good colour. On stylistic grounds they attributed the armed Minerva, depicted standing helmeted, carrying lance and shield in her right hand and holding a figurine of Victory in her left,

---

[17] Gatti 1983, p. 454.   [18] Quoted Gatti 1983, p. 271.
[19] For what follows, see Gatti 1983, pp. 266–8 and nn.
[20] Gatti 1983, pl. 26, and p. 267 and n. For the first eleven coins, see ibid. p. 267; for the twelfth, p. 308.

to the second century AD. The silver setting they dated to the end of the twelfth century. The ring has unfortunately since disappeared.[21] In all, thirty beads were found, thirteen of amber and seventeen of ebony. Their small size is illustrated by the fact that the thirteenth amber bead only came to light when Francis' dust, which had been deposited in a pine box in January 1819, was put through a sieve prior to being restored to the rest of his remains when these were rehoused in an approximately natural arrangement in a rich metal coffin specially made for their reception, in November 1820.[22] Each ebony bead had a hole bored through it, and it was thought most likely that all the beads belonged to a necklace.

The coffin itself, now empty, was winched up into the Lower Church with great effort as it was very heavy, weighing 12 quintali (1200 kg). It was of local travertin, in one piece, rather roughly cut and without any carving or inscription. It was judged to date probably from Roman times and to have been reused more than once. That it had been first used as a sarcophagus was suggested by two details. The base inside had a raised portion at one end, roughly 12.8 cm high, presumably to support the head of a corpse, though it had not been so utilised for St Francis. The rim was recessed all round to accommodate a lid, and this was missing. Subsequently it would seem to have been converted into a drinking trough for animals. A hole for the discharge of water had been bored through one of the longer sides, 10 cm by 8 cm on the outside though narrower within, 10 cm from the base and 20 cm from the corner. It is still visible, though filled with cement, at the right-hand bottom side of the coffin as it is now displayed above the altar in the crypt.[23] The reuse of sarcophagi as drinking troughs or fountains, and of troughs as coffins, was not uncommon during the Middle Ages. The removal of the coffin revealed that it had rested upon another iron grid which had been fixed to the one covering the coffin by means of those ten iron bars the blacksmiths had cut through. This lower grid measured 2.19 m by 1.02 m. It was made up of ten longitudinal bars, crossed by eighteen latitudinal, fixed together with iron studs. It was thus more open than the upper grating, the rectangular holes being roughly 3.44 cm by 11.16 cm with a few exceptions, and therefore lighter, weighing 67.7 kg[24] (Plate 73). The ten vertical bars had been reinforced by a horizontal bar running half-way up all round. The coffin had been completely enclosed within a strongly made iron cage (Figure 12).

The floor of the burial chamber was composed of ten rectangular slabs, some of travertin, some of the solid rock. Did those great slabs hide anything further? Another burial? The famous third church? The bishops ordered the work to continue. 'It would be a fine thing', wrote Dr Canali to his son that day, 30 January 1819, 'if brother Elias in order to make safe the body of St Francis had, after burying him, superimposed upon him as many more graves as the saint had companions. In that case we shall spend Carnival, Lent, Easter and the summer as well in Assisi . . . The enormous fatigue of spending the day in the vault, the night at my desk, is beginning to demoralize me.'[25]

---

[21] Gatti 1983, p. 268 and n. Sketches of the ring published in C. Fea, *Descrizione ragionata della sagrosanta Patriarcal Basilica e Cappella Papale di S. Francesco d'Assisi* (Rome, 1820), p. v, are reproduced in Gatti 1983, pl. 24.

[22] Gatti 1983, pp. 305–12. For the thirtieth bead and the twelfth coin, see ibid. p. 308.

[23] Gatti 1983, pls. 3, 12, and pp. 36–7. For the lifting of the sarcophagus, see ibid. p. 271.

[24] Gatti 1983, pl. 15, and p. 41.

Figure 12   Giovanni Acquaroni, engraving, based on the design of the architect B. Lorenzini, of the iron cage, the sarcophagus and the third stone: from Rome, Archivio Generale OFM Conv., Fondo Sacro Convento (Assisi), fasc. an. 1819; Gatti 1983, plate 13

But the strain and the hardships were almost over. That very afternoon the masons dug up the floor in three places and breached the side walls in four. At all points the burial chamber was proved to be in contact with the solid rock. No one else had ever been buried either below or alongside the individual they had found.

The final session of the process of inquiry took place on Monday, 1 February. It was held, not in the papal apartments in the Sacro Convento, their usual venue, but in the bishop of Foligno's room. He was unwell. Laid low by the lengthy investigations in the chill damp of the underground chamber, he had retired to bed. The absence of any inscription or other incontrovertible means of identification left a degree of uncertainty. The bishops referred the final decision to the pope. Pius VII asked for a scholarly summary of the evidence and opinions, which was prepared by the Conventual friar Francesco Guadagni. He set out the wealth of written evidence, from papal bulls and Franciscan sources, affirming that St Francis was buried in the Basilica constructed in his honour, and that his body had remained there ever since his translation to it in May 1230.[26] The hanging lamps which were kept burning day and night under the arches of the high altar in the Lower Church also bore witness to the unbroken tradition that it was there that St Francis was buried (Plate 16). Yes, but some scholars suggested this could indicate that Francis lay inside the altar rather than under it. During the process no one had recollected this possibility. It was necessary to check. Its table is a monolith supported on four great slabs of red stone from Monte Subasio, forming a recessed quadrilateral. Around this solid frame runs a row of twenty colonnettes.[27] On 20 April

[25] Quoted Gatti 1983, p. 272.   [26] Gatti 1983, pp. 249, 276–9.
[27] Scarpellini 1982a, p. 257; cf. Scarpellini 1978, pp. 85–6; and see p. 62.

the bishop of Assisi conducted an official investigation.[28] Masons moved one of the four slabs out sufficiently to admit the head and hands of a man and light was shone into the natural vault encompassed by the slabs. The space was empty: it contained nothing at all, other than a few scraps of builder's rubble.

On 5 September 1820 Pius VII pronounced the relics authentic.[29]

RECONSTRUCTION OF ST FRANCIS' INTERMENT

The discovery of St Francis' remains enables us to reconstruct with greater precision and detail the measures Elias took to house and safeguard the body after St Francis' death, though some uncertainties remain. It was the opinion of Dr Giosafat Rossi and his colleagues, who examined the position and state of the remains in 1819, that the corpse had been laid to rest in the stone coffin in which it was found very shortly after death, probably within the first twenty-four hours, but in any case before corruption set in.[30] Francis' death was not unexpected. It is very likely that decisions were taken and arrangements made before it occurred. It could well be that the stone coffin was already acquired and waiting at San Giorgio ready to receive him. Elias' choice of it reveals something more of their relationship. It was not something that St Francis would have wanted. And yet it would have been generally regarded as a fitting resting place for a holy man. St Dominic, who had died five years earlier than Francis, on 6 August 1221, was first buried in a wooden coffin. In 1233 a plain marble sarcophagus was procured for him as a preliminary to his canonisation.[31] Given Elias' twin preoccupations with fostering the cult and with security, it had a certain suitability. It was not a high-quality product comparable to the carved marble sarcophagus vividly illustrating the story of Jonah in which the Perugians buried brother Giles[32] (Plate 74). Elias chose a cheaper model, a rough specimen of its kind, and the fact that it had been in use as a drinking trough for animals imparted to it a humble, serviceable image. The placing within it of a stone for his head was a gesture Francis would have appreciated. He objected to feather pillows.[33]

What of the iron gratings? When were they fixed around the coffin? Again these could have been ordered and made in advance. What is certain is that they were in place before the coffin was deposited, in May 1230, in the cavity hewn out for it in the rock. The blacksmith who dismantled the cage in 1819 pointed out that the surrounding space was too restricted for the work to have been carried out in situ. The coffin itself measured 2.14 m by 0.77 m and the gratings extended beyond it on all sides, the upper grating being 2.33 m by 0.97 m, while the floor of the vault was only some 2.36 m by 1.13 m. The blacksmith who assisted at the second recognition of the body in 1978 confirmed that it would have been impracticable, after the coffin had been lowered, to thread the horizontal bars that encircled it halfway up its sides through the rings in the ten vertical iron bars, and impossible in 1230, with the technology then available, to weld these vertical bars to the gratings. There was no room in the vault for a forge. Nor could the

---

[28] For what follows, see Gatti 1983, pp. 278–9.   [29] Gatti 1983, pp. 292–300.
[30] Gatti 1983, p. 42 and n.   [31] Vicaire 1964, pp. 375, 380–6.
[32] AF III, 114–15; Gatti 1983, pp. 37–8 n. 184.   [33] See SL no. 94; Gatti 1983, p. 266 and n.

Plate 74 Perugia, Church of San Francesco, ancient sarcophagus reused for the tomb of brother Giles (Photo C. N. L. Brooke).

irons have been heated in a forge in the Lower Church and handed down. They would have cooled too quickly, before they could have been fashioned into the closed rings of the finished work.[34] In all probability the cage was constructed right away, as part of a planned design. The original lid of the coffin had presumably become detached by the time of its change of use to a water trough, and some covering was necessary. An open coffin would invite the pious removal of its contents piece by piece. The cage had the advantage of enabling pilgrims to catch a glimpse of the body without being able to touch it or extract any relics from it; the apertures in the upper grating were so small.[35] They were however large enough for votive offerings to have been posted through them. The presence inside the coffin of the ring and the beads at Francis' feet, and of the coins, is perhaps to be explained in this way. They could have been donated while the body rested in San Giorgio – could the ring have belonged to Lady Jacoba de Settesoli? – or conceivably some or all of them could have been cast in when the coffin was lowered into its permanent home. It seems more likely that members of the public would make such offerings than the friars themselves; and that they found their way in because the public had, during the four years Francis lay in San Giorgio, a limited degree of access. Similar coins, also minted in Lucca, have been found in the tomb of St Mark at Venice.[36] Could they have represented a rite of passage, Charon's obol? Whatever the explanation, they seem peculiarly incongruous here in the vicinity of St Francis.

[34] Gatti 1983, pp. 100–1, 264 and pl. 3.
[35] Gatti 1983, pl. 15; see p. 460 and Plate 73.   [36] Gatti 1983, p. 267 n.

It has been suggested that the stone coffin in its iron cage was further enclosed in a large wooden chest on legs, the lid of which was normally kept locked, but which could be unlocked and opened to enable the body to be viewed on special occasions, such as the canonisation ceremony, or for special visitors. After the canonisation it is further argued that this chest served as an altar until the translation from San Giorgio to the Basilica in 1230.[37] This hypothesis is based upon pictorial evidence provided by Franciscan altar panels. The earliest of these is Bonaventura Berlinghieri's altar panel at Pescia, dated 1235. Another important source is the altar panel now in the Treasury at Assisi, which is attributed to the 1250s[38] (Plate 15; Colour Plate 3). The wooden chest can be most clearly seen in the Assisi panel, bottom left, but the same chest may well be represented in Berlinghieri's earlier rendering of the same miracle scene, also bottom left; it has the same thick legs each made of one solid piece reaching from the top of the body of the chest to the floor without join, and the same conspicuous lock just below the lid. The source for all the miracle scenes on both panels was the collection of posthumous miracles recorded by Celano at the end of his *First Life*; and he explicitly states that these were the miracles publicly read out in the presence of Gregory IX by one of the pope's subdeacons, Octavian, during the canonisation ceremony held at Assisi on 16 July 1228.[39] They therefore occurred while Francis' body was housed in San Giorgio and so the artists could be depicting his tomb as it was there. There is no question that these artists could and did portray actual objects but it does not therefore follow that they portrayed events with historical accuracy. The artist of the Assisi panel used as his model in the exorcism miracle, top right, the altar in the Lower Church of the Basilica, painted from the life, with its arches and its row of lamps hanging inside them[40] (Plate 16; Colour Plates 3, 4). But this altar, though it may have been in existence before its consecration in 1253, was not in existence before the Lower Church was built and was certainly not the altar in San Giorgio. It found more favour with artists on account of its dramatic pictorial potential. In the Assisi panel the wood chest in the scene bottom left and the altar in the two scenes on the right are clearly not intended to represent the same object. But Gatti suggests that in Berlinghieri's panel the altar in the two scenes top and bottom right could be the wooden chest serving as an altar, the altar frontal effectively concealing legs and lock.[41] Close comparison of the three scenes, however, does not confirm this. In both scenes to the right the altar is lower, reaching only to the friars' waists; the wooden chest is represented as unusually high, extending up to their armpits.

The miracle of the healing of the girl with the dislocated neck, in which the wooden chest figures, introduces Celano's collection. He puts it first as it is the only one recorded as having taken place on the very day Francis was buried. The girl is described as placing her head for some time under the box (*sub arca*).[42] It is possible that the wooden chest in the altar panels is a faithful representation of the mortuary chest in which the dead Francis was conveyed from the Portiuncula to San Giorgio. Celano implies that it had a lid, because he states that when it was brought to San Damiano it was opened so

---

[37] Gatti 1983, pp. 44–5 and nn.   [38] See pp. 173–6; it is also pictured in the Bardi panel: see Plate 17.
[39] 1 *Cel.* 127 ff, 125; see pp. 37–8.   [40] See pp. 174–5.   [41] Gatti 1983, p. 45.   [42] 1 *Cel.* 127.

that the Poor Clares could venerate the body.[43] It is possible, but it is not an altogether satisfactory explanation. It seems inherently unlikely that the friars would have chosen a chest on legs constructed in the way illustrated in which to carry the body all the way uphill. A normal box coffin could have been carried much more easily and conveniently. It seems to me more plausible that the wooden chest on legs was devised in an artists' workshop in order to illustrate realistically – for their purpose more important than literal accuracy – Celano's description of the miracle, whereas a box coffin could have been temporarily laid on a bench perhaps or a table, thus enabling the girl to put her head under it. That the stone coffin encased in its iron cage was put into such a wooden box on legs seems an impractical supposition: the coffin was very heavy, 1200 kg, the two iron gratings together weighed 211 kg; and something further would have to be allowed for the iron bars joining them and the body itself. Even a sturdy box might collapse, and in any case would render the iron cage largely redundant.

During the four years that Francis remained at San Giorgio there is no record of any extraordinary precautions being taken. The iron cage, so well adapted for its function, could reasonably be regarded as sufficient protection. A protection of similar type was erected at the end of the century round the body of Santa Margherita of Cortona, who died in 1297[44] (Plate 75). Immediately after her death her body was embalmed and arrayed in purple garments. She seems to have been displayed for several years to encourage pilgrims to come to her in Cortona in the hope of miraculous cures. A watercolour copy of a scene in a lost fresco cycle in the church built in her honour, to which her body was translated, illustrates the approbation of her *Legenda* and miracles by Cardinal Napoleone Orsini during his visit to Cortona as legate in 1308. The fresco was probably painted in the mid-1330s, so was not contemporary, but there will have been a number of local people still alive who could remember the early arrangements, and in 1634 the judges conducting her canonisation process were shown an *arca* in the shape of a gilded iron grille in which, according to ancient tradition, Margherita's body had been kept for some years after her death. The picture is not entirely accurate. She is dressed as a penitent, not in the expensively dyed cloths mentioned in her *Legenda*; and her placement directly in an iron cage of very open construction is unconvincing and probably due to the artist's concern to render her clearly visible. She was probably originally laid in an unlidded wooden coffin (a pine coffin is referred to in 1343) which was then enclosed in an iron cage with apertures small enough to obstruct pilfering fingers – more akin to the cage protecting St Francis. When Gregory IX came to Assisi in the summer of 1228, first to discuss the canonisation and then to perform the ceremony, on both occasions he paid his respects to St Francis in San Giorgio. Since he descended steps, the body was probably housed in the crypt, and he will have been able to discern it, lying in the open stone coffin, as he bent to kiss the close iron lattice-work of its encircling cage, which was probably raised on a wooden trestle.[45]

But shortly before the translation ceremony was due to take place Elias and the civic authorities got wind of some danger: some plot, some threat, we do not know exactly

[43] 1 *Cel.* 116.
[44] Cannon and Vauchez 1999, esp. pp. 54–5 and n. 7, 60–3 and n. 50, 154, and pl. I, XI, figs. 23, 193–4, 203.
[45] 1 *Cel.* 123, 126; and see Plate 73 and Figure 12; Gatti 1983, p. 43 and n. 224.

Plate 75 The Visitation of the body of Santa Margherita of Cortona by Cardinal Napoleone Orsini. Cortona, Biblioteca Comunale e dell'Academia Etrusca, MS 429, watercolour no. xvii. 'In the presence of Margherita's body, protected within the iron arca, witnesses testify on the Bible (held by a bishop) to miracles achieved through Margherita's intervention. Cardinal Napoleone Orsini (on the left of the central section) listens to the evidence, which is recorded by a notary, seated in the left foreground. Behind the notary and beyond Margherita's body stand a group of civic and ecclesiastical dignitaries. In front of the body, to the right, the sick approach in hope of a cure' (Cannon and Vauchez 1999, p. 250). (Photo Joanna Cannon.)

what, though Perugian involvement may be suspected. Whatever it was, they agreed in regarding this danger as so serious that they were prepared to risk offending everyone – the rank and file of the Order who had come from near and far, the citizens of Assisi, not to mention the three cardinals representing the pope – in order to forestall it. Together they succeeded in surreptitiously moving Francis from San Giorgio to the Basilica three days early.[46]

We do not know what Elias' original intention may have been. He may have planned a shrine in the Lower Church where pilgrims could have touched the iron bars and the sides of the stone coffin and glimpsed the body through the tiny apertures of the upper grating. I am inclined to think this very likely. Or he may all along have intended to bury it, in which case the hole in the pavement of the Lower Church would have been made ready as part of the initial building works. If it was decided upon in response to

[46] See p. 55, and Brooke 1959, pp. 138–42.

a sudden emergency, the hole could have been cut into the rock after St Francis had been moved. It was dug in the centre of the crossing, some 3.5 m deep, at the point where the high altar was subsequently raised. Its floor was paved with ten flagstones and the sides, which narrowed towards the bottom, were faced to a height of about 1.5 m with pieces of chiselled stone. The coffin in its iron cage was lowered into its confined resting place, St Francis' head to the south, his feet to the north. It has been argued that the burial could have been left in this state for a time to enable pilgrims to peer down, but as the purpose of the exercise was to make St Francis absolutely safe it is probable that Elias would not have allowed any delay in finishing the work. A single massive stone of travertin, the same width as the upper grating and a fraction longer so that it completely covered it, was lowered into place. When the excavation was carried out in 1818 Zabberoni thought that this stone was fixed to the wall on one side, but it proved to be simply resting on the grating.[47] Above it, three iron bars were fixed into the side walls along its length. A second great stone was lowered to rest on these. This stone was firmly cemented into the walls on all four sides; it was then covered with a layer of cement and a third great stone placed on top and also cemented in. This third stone (the first to be reached during the excavation) seems to have served both as roofing over the coffin and as the floor of a very small chamber. Starting from the surface of the stone and overlapping its edges, so that the work could not have been done before the stone was in place, the upper reaches of the side walls were faced with blocks of dressed stone. Unfortunately the excavation was conducted rather roughly; and in his eagerness and impatience to see more clearly what lay beneath, Zabberoni ordered the two upper stones to be broken up, and no care was taken to preserve the pieces. But the Conventual Stefano Rinaldi, writing in 1826, stated that the masons who uncovered it in 1818 and then smashed it up observed that the surface of the topmost stone was smooth and worn.[48] The signs of wear could have been caused by the feet and knees of pilgrims. It would seem that Elias had constructed a tiny crypt or *confessio*, its maximum measurements at floor level 2.81 m by 1.20 m, on the model of the *confessio* to be found in some early Christian basilicas, built for the martyr underneath the altar.[49] The presumption is strengthened by the fact that St Clare was buried in a very similar manner, below a small vaulted crypt underneath the high altar in Santa Chiara. Francis' *confessio* would likewise have been vaulted.[50] It is not clear whether it would originally have had a door or opening large enough to admit a pilgrim to enter, or whether perhaps it had a window through which a head or arms might be thrust to get as near as possible to the saint buried unseen below.

Although two of the great stones were destroyed, the one immediately above the coffin was preserved, evocative evidence of the original dispositions; in its damaged state it now forms the dossal of the altar in the crypt.[51] Procuring such stones, of exactly the right size, must have presented a problem, especially if the interment was effected under the pressure of external threat. A document drawn up by a notary and dated

[47] Gatti 1983, pp. 102–3 and n.
[48] Gatti 1983, p. 156 and n.; for the date 1826, see ibid. p. 114.   [49] Gatti 1983, p. 105.
[50] Gatti 1983, p. 105, citing L. Di Fonzo, 'Francesco d'Assisi', in *Bibliotheca Sanctorum*, v, col. 1101.
[51] Gatti 1983, pl. 3.

27 May 1239, still preserved in the archives at Assisi, records an undertaking given by Elias, who is referred to as 'lord and custodian of the church', and the procurator of the Sacro Convento Giacomo de Mevania to repair a wall belonging to two Assisan brothers, Sanguonio and Tommaso di Uffreduccio, a wall from which great slabs of travertin had been removed for walls and other building works at the Basilica.[52] It is tempting to wonder whether the wall was robbed precisely because it contained the three great slabs of travertin of which Elias had need in 1230. If so, we can sympathise with the brothers, who had, after a delay of almost a decade, to resort to law in their efforts to get the wall made good.

It could of course be argued, and has been, that the slabs were not fixed in place so early as 1230.[53] Elias could theoretically have been responsible for them at any time up to his deposition in 1239. What is certain is that they were in position before the high altar was raised directly above them. Once the high altar was there it would have been impossible to lower the slabs into their close-fitting cavity without first dismantling the altar completely, and there is no record of that ever having been done.[54] We do not know whether or not Elias was responsible for the altar. It is likely that he would have wished to provide a magnificent altar in keeping with the splendid double church he raised in Francis' honour. That he had the requisite talent to conceive it, drive to realise it, and lack of qualms as to whether it was appropriate, the Basilica itself is sufficient proof. When Innocent IV consecrated the altar on 25 May 1253 he donated relics of St John the Baptist. These were housed in a little column among those surrounding the altar. In style it is distinct from the rest, which suggests that it was a later insertion into a pre-existing altar.[55]

What of the hard cement which filled the little chamber? When was it added? It would seem to be an afterthought. It would have been pointless, a waste of time, to face the walls of the chamber with dressed stones if it was immediately to be filled up with rubble and mortar. It was an obstacle to Tebaldi, who complained of its virtual impenetrability, when he conducted his excavation in 1755–6.[56] There is only one intermediate record of authorised modification of the original arrangements. In November 1442 Assisi, which had been under the control of Francesco Sforza, was taken and sacked by the Perugians, under the rival condottiere Niccolò Piccinino. The Perugians tried to take advantage of their victory and petitioned Eugenius IV, who was then living under the protection of Cosimo de' Medici in Florence, for permission to translate St Francis' body to Perugia 'for its greater safety'. But Eugenius IV, who was soon to feel strong enough to return to Rome, was prepared to exert his authority in the factious and unruly Papal States on this issue. In the bull *Accepimus litteras* of 21 December 1442 he declared that St Francis' body should not be removed, because if it was taken elsewhere that might drive the people of Assisi to despair: they might believe it would lead to their final ruin and the desolation of that venerable church. To prevent any such disastrous consequences he involved the Perugians in the implementation of his verdict; he ordered the archbishop of Naples, who was then governor of Perugia, the Provincial Minister of the Friars

---

[52] Lempp 1901, pp. 173–4, cited and corrected by Gatti 1983, p. 111.   [53] Gatti 1983, pp. 108 ff.
[54] Gatti 1983, pp. 132–8.   [55] See p. 66 and Plate 16; cf. Gatti 1983, p. 108.   [56] See p. 455.

Minor of Umbria, and the condottiere Niccolò Piccinino, acting jointly, to take suitable measures to ensure that the body could come to no harm. Arranging for the small underground chamber to be completely filled with rubble and mortar, which then set hard, was probably the way in which they discharged their responsibility.[57]

Elias did not, after all, hide the body. He put it in an obvious place, directly under the high altar. There was no secret passage, no locked door, no third church, no custodian sworn to divulge its whereabouts only on his deathbed to his successor. When, in 1260, it was desired to enable St Clare to conform closely to St Francis in death as she had so heroically striven to do in life, they knew where to lay her and how to design her tomb. They put her in a stone coffin without inscription, surrounded this with thick bands of iron and buried her in a vaulted chamber, without entrances on any side, under the high altar in her church, which they modelled on the Upper Church of Francis' Basilica. Rather, Elias, with the backing of the civic authorities, made Francis safe from predators, as safe as he knew how. And the civic authorities approved and were satisfied. When nearly forty years later, it came to their attention that some friars in Austria were claiming to have a relic of St Francis, a part of one of his fingers, the podestà of Assisi and his council issued an official document, dated 6 June 1279, affirming that nothing had been taken from the body – the skeleton was indeed found intact in 1818 – and that it was guarded in its integrity by the friars in the Basilica in a place 'most safe and most secure'.[58] In the course of time, because the body and the coffin had been invisible ever since the translation, and, especially after the mid-fifteenth-century infilling, completely inaccessible, legend could flourish.

[57] See Gatti 1983, pp. 114–15, pl. 21; and see Figure 11.
[58] Gatti 1983, pp. 167–8. On the tomb of St Clare, see Gatti 1983, p. 105.

CHAPTER ELEVEN

ANGELA OF FOLIGNO'S IMAGE OF ST FRANCIS

We know little about Angela before her conversion. She was born probably in 1248. Her family was well-to-do and she married a wealthy husband and bore him children. As a young woman she seems to have been attractive, lively, proud, vain, fond of pleasure and admiration – 'all my life I have studied how to make myself adored and honoured'.[1] Her initiation into a more religious way of living was a common and normal spur at that time. She became conscious of her sinfulness, and was overcome by a great fear that she would be damned and go to hell, a prospect which led her to weep bitterly.

Her awareness of St Francis was probably first aroused by contact with the Franciscans of Foligno. She may have attended their sermons. At any rate when she became seriously uneasy about her spiritual state it was to St Francis she turned for guidance in finding a confessor she could trust. She had a hyperactive conscience. She felt ashamed to confess fully all she had done wrong or said or thought, and so very often she received communion only partially confessed, itself a sin as she well knew. So she prayed to St Francis to find her a confessor who had a thorough understanding of sins, to whom she could make a complete confession. That same night an old friar appeared to her and said: 'Sister, if you had asked me sooner I would have done it for you sooner, but what you ask is granted.' At once, in the morning, she went to the church of St Francis but quickly left. On her way home she went on impulse into the cathedral of San Feliciano, and there a Franciscan friar was preaching. To him she had the confidence to make a full confession. He assured her that he was qualified to grant her absolution, though to quiet her scruples he offered to inform the bishop of all her sins if she so wished. He was the bishop's chaplain, and so this encounter between Angela and this friar, traditionally identified with her kinsman brother Arnaldo, who was to become her confessor, spiritual guide and writer of her *Memoriale*, must have taken place after July 1285, as the bishop of Foligno up to July was a Dominican, who would not have

---

[1] Thier and Calufetti 1985, pp. 25–7, 406. There is an English translation of her works in Lachance 1993. I am not convinced by the attempt to cast doubt on the authenticity of the portrayal of Angela and her works in Dalarun 1995: cf. Burr 2001, pp. 335–7; and p. 307 note 85.

chosen a Franciscan chaplain but rather a member of his own Order.[2] It is interesting that Angela visualised St Francis as an old man. She was still a comparatively young woman – she would have been about thirty-seven in 1285 – while Francis was only around forty-four or forty-five when he died, not much older than her.

Angela described her spiritual journey as a series of steps.[3] Each of these steps requires time, some longer than others. She cried out at how sluggish the soul is to advance from one to the next, how fettered are its feet. For her the next steps were devoted to doing penance for her sins, and she lingered painfully on each small step and wept. From the seventh step on she began to look at the cross. Understanding more clearly how Christ had died for our sins, she was moved to grieve exceedingly for her own sins and to feel that she had crucified Him. But she still did not know which was the greater benefit, that he had led her back from sin and from hell and converted her to penitence, or because he was crucified for her. Her increased sensibility set her on fire, so that, standing near the cross, she stripped herself of all her clothes and offered herself totally to him, vowing perpetual chastity in all her limbs and senses. On the ninth step she sought the way of the cross, so that she could stand at the foot of the cross, where all sinners find refuge. She was inspired to understand that if she wanted to go to the cross she must strip herself, so as to be much lighter, and go naked to the cross. She must forgive all those who had offended her, divest herself of all worldly things, of all human ties to friends and family and all other men and women, of her possessions and her very self, and give her heart to Christ, who had bestowed such benefits on her, and travel by the thorny road of tribulation.[4]

It is already clear that she had absorbed a considerable depth of Franciscan spirituality under the guidance of her confessor and other Franciscans at their convent in Foligno.

Her first practical steps were somewhat less ambitious than her resolution suggests. She stopped wearing her best clothes and head-dresses, and gave up eating delicacies. Even that much was difficult, because she made these sacrifices without love. Her mother was very unsympathetic and critical – perhaps Angela's new catering regime affected not just her own but her family's meals. She was still living with her husband, and she found it bitter when he spoke insultingly to her or treated her harshly, though she bore it as patiently as she could. Her husband may well have resented the vow of complete chastity she had made without consulting him. Then her mother died, and then her husband, and in a short time all her children. Because she thought they hindered her spiritual development she had asked God that they might die, and she believed that because her prayer had been heard, her heart would always be in God's heart, and God's heart always in her heart. She was not quite as unfeeling as this sounds; she admitted later that she had felt great sorrow at the deaths of her mother and children. But it is a reminder of how difficult a saint, or a saint in the making, could be to live with, and how devastating it could be for their families.

---

[2] Thier and Calufetti 1985, pp. 132–4 and n. 5, 28–9 and n. 14.
[3] On 'steps' in St Benedict and St Bernard, cf. Southern 1953, pp. 223–34.
[4] Thier and Calufetti 1985, pp. 134–8, 148.

On the tenth step, Christ encouraged her to look at his wounds, saying: 'all these things I have borne for you'. Grief-stricken she finally determined to give up absolutely everything and make herself poor.

On the fourteenth step, as she stood at prayer and wide awake, she became acutely aware of Christ on the cross. He called her and told her to put her mouth into his side wound, and it seemed to her that she saw and drank blood that flowed fresh from his side, and understood that it would cleanse her. She felt great joy, while at the same time consideration of the Passion made her sad. One is reminded that St Francis felt a similar tension of joy and sorrow when he experienced the vision of the crucified seraph on La Verna; and meditation on the side wound was deeply embedded in Franciscan spirituality by this time.[5]

On the seventeenth step she received further grace from the Virgin Mary. Her faith took a qualitative leap, and her grief over Christ's Passion and Mary's sorrow felt more genuine. She began to dispose of her property. First she sold, for the benefit of the poor, her house in the country, which was the best property she owned. It was about this time that her screaming fits began. If she heard anyone talk of God, she screamed.[6]

To assist her vocation, she went on pilgrimage to Rome, to pray at the tomb of St Peter, to ask the apostle to obtain for her from Christ the grace to become truly poor, and also probably for guidance as to her hope of joining the Franciscan Third Order. This was probably either in 1290 or during the first half of 1291. She was received into the Third Order in the summer of 1291.[7]

After her return she continued with the distribution of her goods, but felt God was not with her. So she prayed: 'Lord, what I do, I only do to find you. Will I find you after I have completed this work?' She was answered: 'What do you wish for?' She replied: 'I do not want gold or silver, and if you were to give me the whole world, I would not want anything other than you.' Then it was told her: 'Exert yourself, because when this that you are doing is done, at once the whole Trinity will come to you.'

On the twentieth step, when she went on pilgrimage to the Basilica of St Francis at Assisi, this promise was fulfilled on the way.[8]

Angela regarded St Francis as having set a perfect example, and there were times on her own spiritual journey when she followed his example literally. At the point when she had resolved to give up everything, but was fearful of the dangers and privations she would face as a beggar, she went on pilgrimage to Rome to pray to St Peter for the grace of voluntary poverty. When Francis reached the stage of seriously considering the practical consequences of voluntary poverty, he had gone on pilgrimage to Rome to pray to St Peter and to experience for a few hours the life of a beggar.[9]

After Angela joined the Third Order, when Maundy Thursday came round, she suggested to her companion that they seek to find Christ. She said: 'Let us go to the hospital' – San Feliciano, built next door to the cathedral in 1270 – 'and perhaps we

---

[5] Thier and Calufetti 1985, pp. 138–44; 1 Cel. 94–5.   [6] Thier and Calufetti 1985, pp. 144–52.

[7] Thier and Calufetti 1985, pp. 178 and n. 5, 33–4. The grouping known as the Order of Penitence – the terms *penitenti*, *continenti* and *mantellati* were all current at this time – was officially reconstituted by Nicholas IV in 1289 as the Third Order of St Francis: Cannon 1999, pp. 2–3 and n. 5.

[8] Thier and Calufetti 1985, pp. 154–6 and n. 29. See pp. 305–6.

[9] Thier and Calufetti 1985, pp. 472, 142, 178; 2 Cel. 8.

may find Christ among those poor, tormented and afflicted people'. They took a number of veils with them for the nurse to sell, and all the bread they had been given in alms for their own sustenance. They washed the feet of the women and the hands of the men, especially those of a leper, which were rotting and withered and putrid, and they drank some of the water. It seemed to Angela that she had actually taken communion, because she felt the greatest sweetness, just as if she had taken communion.[10] Francis before his conversion shrank instinctively from lepers in disgust, and it was a major step on his road when he forced himself to treat them as human beings, to kiss them and wash their sores, 'and that which before had seemed to me horrible was transformed into sweetness of mind and body'.[11]

Francis' understanding of his vocation was fundamentally deepened as he knelt in prayer before the painted crucifix at San Damiano, and the image of the crucified Christ spoke to him. Angela's spiritual progress was influenced by visual images even before her pilgrimage to Assisi. When she reached the stage when simply hearing God talked about triggered uncontrollable fits of screaming, she also became sensitive to pictures of his suffering. 'When I saw a painted Passion of Christ I could scarcely bear it, but became ill and feverish, so that my companion concealed pictures of the Passion from me and took care to hide them.'[12] On her first visit to the Basilica, when she stood in the Lower Church, she could have seen the narrative cycle of St Francis' life facing scenes of the Passion; indeed the sight of the Passion sequence may have contributed to the emotional build-up which erupted in the screaming fit later that day.[13]

Her prayers and meditations led to increasing illumination. In discussion with her confessor she told a parable – a sign of how her thought processes were becoming akin to Francis'. A father had some sons who did wrong. He, innocent, was killed for their offence at a place where three roads meet, and blood still stains the ground. Imagine the remorse and grief felt by his guilty sons. They would avoid passing that way, and if they did, even long after the event, their sense of their responsibility for his cruel and shameful death would exacerbate their grief. How much more then, O soul, ought you to grieve over the death of Christ, who is more than an earthly father, and who died for your sins. Lament and suffer, soul, because you ought to pass near to the cross on which Christ died. It is needful for you to place yourself there and rest there, because the cross is your well-being and your bed and ought to be your delight, because your salvation is there. It is astonishing how a man can pass by so quickly and not pause there. If a soul fixes itself there, it will always find blood there that appears fresh.

Angela explained to her confessor that since this parable had been revealed to her, her response to visual images had changed. When she passed near a painted cross or Passion scene it now seemed to her that what was painted bore no comparison to those exceedingly great torments that were inflicted on Him in fact, which had been shown to her and impressed on her heart. So she no longer wished to look at painted

[10] Lachance 1993, pp. 162, 373 n. 54 – this Maundy Thursday was probably 3 April 1292; Thier and Calufetti 1985, pp. 240–2 and n. 14.
[11] Testament, Esser 1976, p. 438; 1 *Cel*. 17; 2 *Cel*. 9.
[12] 2 *Cel*. 10; Thier and Calufetti 1985, p. 152. These will have been small private portable devotional images.
[13] See pp. 288–96 and Plates 27–30.

images, because they seemed to her to convey almost nothing.[14] Some of the pictures she was referring to would have been traditional images of Christ triumphant on the cross, others representations of the suffering Christ, and these aimed at tearing the heart-strings and did not stint the blood.[15] The Passion cycle in the Lower Church can be taken as a good example of the latter, and one that would have become familiar to Angela. The Passion scenes the Master of St Francis painted on the altar panel in Perugia provide us with a clear idea of what they would originally have looked like.[16]

A little later Angela's response to visual images underwent further change. She was attending Vespers and looking at the cross; and while she was looking at the crucifix with her bodily eyes, her soul was suddenly kindled with love, and every part of her body felt it with the greatest joy. She saw and felt that Christ was inside her, embracing her soul with that arm with which he was crucified. In no way now could she feel any sadness over the Passion; it delighted her to see and come to this man. Total joy is now in this suffering God/man. Sometimes it seems to the soul that it enters, with great joy and pleasure, completely into Christ's side – a delightful experience which cannot be put into words. This new and contradictory sensibility affected her reaction to another kind of visual image, this time a dramatic one. She attended a staging of a Passion play in the Piazza of San Domenico in Foligno. It seemed as if there must be wailing – but as for her, quite the reverse. She was miraculously seized and thrilled by such happiness that she was struck speechless.[17]

During Lent in 1294 the eyes of her soul were opened to see love coming plainly towards her; she saw within herself two sides, as if she were divided by a road. On one side she saw total love and all good, which were from God and not from her; on the other she saw herself dried up, and nothing that was good sprang from her. So she understood that it was not she who did the loving, although she was totally in love, but that that love came from God alone. After dwelling in that love, she remains so utterly content and in such an angelic state that she loves toads and snakes and even demons – she was evidently not normally a totally committed animal lover. If a dog were to eat her she would not care, and she did not think she would feel it or suffer. To be in this state is greater, she said, than to stand at the foot of the cross, as St Francis stood. This claim of Angela's is an indication of her ability to enrich her narrative by drawing a comparison between a mystical state and a visual image. It must be based on painted crucifixes she had seen. She may well have seen the large crucifix in Santa Chiara, painted by the Umbrian Master of Santa Chiara c.1260, in which St Francis stands embracing Christ's right foot while the blood flows freely down his habit. There is a related cross in the church of San Francesco at Arezzo[18] (Plate 76). There may well have been a similar cross in San Francesco at Foligno which has not survived.

Angela, like St Francis, had a great devotion to the Virgin Mary. On one occasion, when she was not at prayer but simply resting after a meal, her soul was suddenly and

---

[14] Thier and Calufetti 1985, pp. 236–40. This may have been in 1292, as the very next section probably refers to Easter 1292: ibid. pp. 240–2; Lachance 1993, pp. 161–3 and p. 373 n. 54.
[15] For example, see Plates 3, 76.   [16] See Colour Plate 6 and pp. 300–1.
[17] Thier and Calufetti 1985, pp. 276–9 and nn. 22, 24.
[18] Thier and Calufetti 1985, pp. 298–302 and 298 n. 10; Cook 1999, pp. 63–4, no. 28, and p. 29, no. 5; Martin 1993, fig. 152.

Plate 76 Crucifix by an anonymous Umbrian master in San Francesco, Arezzo
(© www.Assisi.de. Photo Gerhard Ruf).

unexpectedly uplifted, and she saw the Virgin in glory. Her comments have a remarkably
modern ring. She expressed herself as truly delighted when she grasped that a woman
was set in a position of such nobility, glory and dignity, and the Virgin was interceding
for the human race. 'I saw her endued with such truly indescribable humanity and virtues
that I was indescribably entranced.' While she was gazing, Christ suddenly appeared
there, sitting next to the Virgin in his glorified humanity. The inspiration behind this

vision surely lay in a picture, or pictures, of the Enthronement or Coronation of the Virgin.[19]

During Holy Week and Easter Week, Angela, along with other worshippers, will have been encouraged to enter imaginatively into each and every successive unfolding event of the Passion story. Such spiritual exercises were widespread, and in Franciscan circles they had been given a powerful initial impetus by St Francis' re-creation of the physical circumstances of the Nativity at Greccio.[20] On Easter Saturday, 1294, Angela enjoyed a vivid personal experience of a moment not often highlighted. She stood in the sepulchre together with Christ, in an ecstatic state. He was lying with eyes closed, as the dead lie. Christ's breast was kissed first; after that his mouth was kissed. She received a wonderful and indescribably delectable odour from his mouth, which was breathed out from his mouth. Afterwards she laid her cheek on Christ's cheek, and Christ put his hand on her other cheek and pressed her to him, and she heard him say these words to her: 'Before I was laid in the sepulchre I held you thus tightly.'[21]

Her senses played a vital part in Angela's religious experience. She heard the Holy Spirit speaking to her on the road to Assisi in 1291; she heard Christ speak to her in the sepulchre. On her way back to Foligno after that first pilgrimage to Assisi she felt Christ's cross 'corporaliter', 'physically'.[22] She admitted to her confessor that she had seen God. 'I saw a plenitude, a clarity, which I felt so filled me that I do not know how to speak of it, nor how to give any meaningful analogy. I do not know if I can tell you that I saw anything corporeal, but He was as He is in heaven, that is, of such beauty that I do not know what to say to you other than Beauty and All Good. All the saints were standing before His majesty, praising him . . . And I was told to gaze also on the angels who are seen standing above the saints.'[23] She smelt the odour emanating from Christ's mouth when she kissed it as he lay in the sepulchre. She tasted transubstantiation in the host when she communicated: 'she said it did not have the taste of bread, nor of the meat that we know, but it most certainly tasted of meat, but a different, most tasty, taste . . . an unknown taste of meat'.[24]

St Francis in his letter to the faithful stressed the importance of confessing all sins to a priest and receiving from him the body and blood of our Lord Jesus Christ.[25] Angela attended Mass devoutly, and struggled to get to church in the morning even if she had been very ill in the night. She once told her confessor that if it were possible she would wish to communicate every day. For she understood and felt absolutely certain that

[19] Thier and Calufetti 1985, p. 304. On Sunday 31 July 1300 Angela attended Mass celebrated at the high altar of the Upper Church, dedicated to the Virgin, and on the Monday morning, 1 August, Mass at the altar of St Michael, also in the Upper Church, in the left transept (ibid. pp. 486–94, 496–501 and nn. 14, 18). On each of these occasions she may have succeeded in catching a glimpse of Cimabue's frescoes of the Assumption of the Virgin and the Enthronement of the Virgin in the apse. See pp. 358–62 and Plate 52. As she approached Santa Maria degli Angeli (the Portiuncula) in the procession on the Monday afternoon she had a vision of 'The Queen of Mercy herself and the Mother of all grace bending over her sons and daughters . . . in a new and most gracious way reiterating the sweetest blessings over all': Thier and Calufetti 1985, p. 500.

[20] 1 Cel. 84–7; Bonav., x, 7. Cf. also Thier and Calufetti 1985, pp. 392–6: on the feast of Candlemas (2 February), when candles were given out to commemorate Christ's presentation in the temple, she believed the presentation of her soul to God was effected.

[21] Thier and Calufetti 1985, pp. 296–8.   [22] Thier and Calufetti, 1985, pp. 178–84, 296–8, 186.

[23] Thier and Calufetti 1985, pp. 210–12; Cf. ibid. pp. 316–18.

[24] Thier and Calufetti 1985, pp. 296, 308–10.   [25] Esser 1976, p. 209.

communion cleanses, sanctifies, comforts and preserves the soul.[26] On one occasion when she was sick, as she went up to take communion, she heard a voice saying: 'Beloved, the All Good is within you, and you go to receive the All Good.' It seemed to her that she saw God Omnipotent, and she prayed and confessed her sins to God, and asked for mercy and not judgement. Then she began to question within herself: 'If the All Good is within me, why do I go to receive the All Good?' In other words: what is the need to take communion if you are already in a state of union with God? She received an immediate answer: 'The one does not reject the other.'[27] These admissions of Angela's reveal that her devotion to the Eucharist was different from Francis'. St Francis was careful to stress the essential mediation of the priest; only a priest can consecrate the elements. Angela confessed to a priest before communicating, but she also confessed her sins directly to God. As a laywoman, as a recipient who could never be a celebrant, Angela reveals a woman's viewpoint, which helps to explain her highly subjective attitude to the Eucharist as compared to Francis' more clerical one.

St Francis saw the cross as an altar, uniting the crucifixion and the Eucharist.[28] Angela came to see the cross as Christ's deathbed. 'The king of kings, whose whole life was an unspeakable cross on account of the continual and ineffable sorrow he bore, in death, instead of a gilded room with a bed decked in purple [as befits a king], had an abominable cross.'[29] From this, in her mystical states, it was easy to make the transition to the cross as a bed to rest on; probably helped by such passages as this from the Song of Solomon: 'By night on my bed I sought him whom my soul loveth' (3. 1). This inspires her with a desire to sing and to praise, and she breaks into a spontaneous lauda:

> Io te laudo Dio dilecto,
> ne la tua croze . . . zo fato il mio leto;
> per piumazo over cavezale,
> trovai aver la povertade;
> l'altra parte de lo leto,
> a reposare aspeto despeto,
> e dolor trovai.

> I praise thee, beloved God,
> in thy cross I have made my bed.
> For a pillow or feather pillow
> I have found poverty.
> As the other side of the bed
> for resting on
> I have found pain with contempt.

St Francis used to burst into songs of praise in the vernacular. The Franciscans encouraged lay groups of penitents to sing laude, vernacular religious songs; songs commemorating Christ's incarnation, and especially his Passion, songs to the Virgin and the saints. The earliest surviving anthology of laude, a book complete with musical

---

[26] Thier and Calufetti 1985, pp. 306, 372–4.   [27] Thier and Calufetti 1985, pp. 306–8.
[28] Esser 1976, p. 208.   [29] Thier and Calufetti 1985, pp. 480–2.

notation, belonged to a lay group which met to sing praises in the church of San Francesco at Cortona. It contains two of the earliest *laude* to St Francis, heading a group praising saints especially venerated in Franciscan circles – Mary Magdalene, St Michael, John the Baptist and St John the Evangelist. The verses of the two *laude* on St Francis are based on St Bonaventure's *Legenda Maior*. Both emphasise Francis' devotion to the crucified Christ, and the stigmata, and both mention how the birds listened to his preaching. Popular song thus mirrored the favourite iconographic themes of the early panel paintings.[30] And the images conjured up by popular song, in her lifetime marvellously enriched by the *laude* of Jacopone da Todi, will have been another contributing factor in the formation of Angela's piety.

Angela will also have been familiar with religious chants and hymns that formed part of the Franciscan liturgy: for example, St Francis' *Praises to be said at all the Hours*, his *Salutation of the Virgin* and *Salutation of the Virtues*; Julian of Speyer's *Office of St Francis*, which included a hymn and antiphons attributed to Gregory IX; and Thomas of Celano's *Legenda ad usum chori*.[31]

Already there is a rich harvest of instruction absorbed through a variety of visual and oral images, but the chief source of Angela's spiritual understanding was in books. Her ability to read is beyond doubt. The Scriptures were naturally her firm foundation. From quite early in her conversion she possessed a missal. In a vision it was revealed to her that the understanding of the Epistles was a thing so delightful that if someone understood it well they would forget all worldly things. This experience was vouchsafed her, and she was told that understanding the Gospels was so superlatively delightful that one would forget not only all worldly things but oneself as well. Led into this further experience she was in such heavenly joy that she did not want to wake up. Her ability to think for herself, however, is already evident. She comments that nothing is preached about this heavenly joy; preachers are not able to preach on this, and what they do preach about it they do not understand.[32]

It is the Gospels that provide the record of the life of the God/man Jesus Christ, who is the epitome of poverty, pain, humiliation and true obedience. His life is the Book of Life. So she urges any who sought spiritual guidance from her: 'If you wish to be fully enlightened and taught, you may read in this Book of Life; for if you do not race through it or skip through it in reading, you will be illuminated and instructed in all things necessary for yourself and others, whatever your station in life.'[33] The phrase 'whatever your station in life' draws attention to a very important aspect of Angela's understanding of Christ's call, reiterated by St Paul and by St Francis. The Book of Life, as revealed in the Gospels, is accessible to all, whether they can read or not. Passages from the Gospels were read out at services in church; they were quoted and interpreted in sermons, they could be discussed with confessors and spiritual mentors. In the earliest account of Francis' conversion, when the crucial passage from the Gospel was

---

[30] Thier and Calufetti 1985, pp. 480–2, 354–64; cf. Lachance 1993, pp. 205–6, 386 n. 135; Moleta 1983, pp. 33–54, esp. 33–7.

[31] Esser 1976, pp. 319–21, 417–18, 427–8; AF X, 119–26, 375–88.

[32] Thier and Calufetti 1985, pp. 26, 148–50. On the sixteenth step she recited the Lord's Prayer very slowly and consciously, meditating on each single word (ibid. pp. 146–8).

[33] Thier and Calufetti, 1985, p. 462. For the 'Book of Life' see references in n. 46.

read which determined the direction he and his Order were to take, Francis humbly asked the priest after Mass to explain the text more fully.[34] Access to God and spiritual understanding and grace are not just the preserve of the learned and the clergy; they are within the reach – absolutely within the reach – of lay people, and women.

Angela can tell her confessor that one day during Mass she heard God say that the implementers of Scripture were to be commended, not its distinguished readers, or commentators. The whole of Holy Scripture was implemented, put into practice, in the example of Christ's life. Here she is echoing St Francis' teaching. '"The saints wrought works and we wish to receive honour and glory for reciting and preaching about them" – as one should say: "Knowledge puffs up, but love builds."'[35]

As a member of the Third Order Angela will have been familiar with some at least of St Francis' own writings. The first version of his Letter to the faithful is believed to contain his earliest instructions to married and other lay people wishing to do penance and follow a religious way of life in their own homes. Its beginning provides a succinct statement of the guidelines Angela was to follow: 'All those who love the Lord with their whole heart, with their whole soul and mind, with their whole strength, and love their neighbours as themelves, and hate their bodies with their vices and sins, and receive the body and blood of our Lord Jesus Christ, and produce worthy fruits of penitence: Oh how happy and blessed are these men and women when they do these things and persevere in them, since the spirit of the Lord will rest upon them, and He will make his home and dwelling among them. They are the children of the heavenly Father whose works they do, and they are spouses, brothers and mothers of our Lord Jesus Christ.'[36] There are passages in Angela's *Memoriale* and in the *Instructiones* which contain verbal links with early Franciscan sources. There are quotations from 1 *Celano* in Instruction II: 'They should look back to our father bl. Francis, who, although he was the mirror of all holiness and all perfection [1 *Cel.* 90], and the example for all wishing to live spiritually, although he was near his death, in the most excellent of states and united in such ineffable union with God, said: "Brothers, let us begin to do penance because until now we have made little progress"' (1 *Cel.* 103). Her reticence, when she evinced any – 'my secret is mine' – shows the influence of Francis' *Admonition* XXVIII and 1 *Celano* 96; possibly also of 2 *Celano* 135.[37] Angela had followed St Francis' example by going on pilgrimage to Rome in the course of her conversion. The story of Francis' pilgrimage is first told in 2 *Celano* 8; it is also in the *Legend of the Three Companions* c. 10; but as it is also told in Bonaventure's *Legenda Maior* I, 6, it is probable that Angela learnt of it from there. That she had any knowledge of 2 *Celano* therefore cannot be established, though it is possible.

Her account of her visit to the hospital in Foligno shows an interesting possible link with a source one might have thought was not available to her, the *Writings of brothers Leo, Rufino and Angelo*. Angela suggested to her companion that they go to try to find Christ

---

[34] 1 *Cel.* 22; cf. Duffy 1997, pp. 221–2.

[35] 'edificat', clearly meaning 'edifies' as well as 'builds': SL 72 and n. 1; Esser 1976, p. 110; cf. also SL 69–71; Thier and Calufetti 1985, p. 374.

[36] Esser 1976, pp. 176–8, 178–80.

[37] Thier and Calufetti 1985, pp. 424, 496. For 'the joy and sadness she felt when she drank blood from Christ's side-wound', cf. 1 *Cel.* 94.

among the sick and afflicted, who included a leper. We are told, in SL 22, that St Francis called lepers 'Christian brothers'.[38] The phrase 'inwardly and outwardly' occurs in SL 22, one of the usages characteristic of the style of the *Scripta Leonis*. It is a phrase Angela uses too. In her panegyric on St Francis she uses it three times in the course of one paragraph and once in the next.[39] There are other possible verbal links. In SL 22, when describing how Francis ate from the same dish as the leper, two words for 'dish' are used, one of which is *scutella*. Angela told a parable, inspired by Christ's parables in Luke 14. A man who had many friends invited them to a feast. Not all came. All that did, he loved and provided for lavishly, but those he loved more he placed at a special table near to him. Yet with those he loved particularly he ate from one dish, *scutella*, and they drank from one cup (cf. Matt. 20. 20–23).[40] Much earlier, Angela described how she came to have a vision when keeping Lent in a tiny room in her house. The phrase she used, 'dum eram in carcere', when I was in a cell, recalls the use of the same word by St Francis: 'The Lord when he was in the hermit's cave', 'Dominus quando stetit in carcere.' A little later on Angela uses the more normal word for cell, *cella*, and St Francis uses *cella* further on in the same sentence.[41]

How could Angela have possibly had access to the Leonine writings? The Franciscan convent at Foligno at the turn of the thirteenth century had strong sympathies with the Spirituals. Its guardian was brother Francis Damian of Montefalco, brother of St Clare of Montefalco. The friars there are likely to have been in touch with many individual friars living in hermitages throughout Umbria and the Marches who consciously endeavoured to keep alive the memories of the early days of the Order through a network of contacts and transmission which stretches right back to St Francis' companions.[42] It is conceivable that Angela gained privileged access to this material through friends among the Poor Clares, or through Ubertino da Casale. Ubertino met Angela probably in 1298. He had been a friar already for twenty-five years, having joined the Order in 1273 or 1274 at the age of fourteen – but during his years of study in Paris his spiritual life had languished. His meeting with her had a profound effect upon him. To her Christ revealed the defects of his heart, and also secret divine graces, which convinced him that it was indeed Christ speaking through her. Through her all the previous graces which he had lost were restored, and he felt a changed man. He described her as 'the reverend and most saintly mother Angela, a true angel on earth'.[43] Angela uses some language that is Leonine. She may not have seen the written texts, but she can have heard the stories recited by those who knew them by heart. The culture around her was steeped in reverence for what brother Leo stood for and represented.

---

[38] Thier and Calufetti 1985, pp. 240–2. Angela's comment that she felt 'the greatest sweetness' after drinking water in which she had washed a leper's hand can be linked to the Testament (Esser 1976, p. 438) and 2 *Cel.* 9.

[39] SL pp. 24–5; Moorman 1940, pp. 99–101; Thier and Calufetti 1985, p. 474; and see p. 485.

[40] Thier and Calufetti 1985, pp. 230–2, 236: 'scudella' in the vernacular version, p. 233, 237.

[41] Thier and Calufetti, pp. 148, 154 – 'carzere' in the vernacular version, p. 149; SL 13 and Appendix, no. 2, p. 295.

[42] Cf. Stanislao da Campagnola 1999, pp. 177–89. For Francis Damian of Montefalco, see Lachance 1993, p. 45. For the relations of Clare of Montefalco and Angela of Foligno with the Spirituals, see the very judicious comments in Burr 2001, pp. 315–24, 334–44.

[43] Ubertino da Casale 1485, Prologue, c. iii [col. 5], corrected by Thier and Calufetti 1985, pp. 36–7 and n. 46; Lachance 1993, pp. 110–11.

It was also steeped in St Bonaventure's thought and writings. Angela will have studied the *Legenda Maior*, the standard Life of St Francis in her time. At a fundamental level St Bonaventure's spirituality, and his presentation of St Francis, moulded and guided Angela's approach and her own understanding of priorities. To take, as an example, chapter IX, on the fervour of his love, and his desire for martyrdom. 'Francis, the Bridegroom's friend, burned with an ardent love which no one can sufficiently describe . . . As soon as he heard the love of God spoken of he was roused, moved, inflamed, as if the inner chords of his heart had been touched from without by the plectrum of the voice . . . He used to say . . . "His love, who loved us very much, is greatly to be loved." . . . He exulted in all the works of God's hands . . . In beautiful things he beheld Beauty . . . he followed the Beloved everywhere; of all things he made for himself a ladder by which he might ascend to Him who "is altogether lovely" [Song of Solomon 5.16]. Moved by unheard of devotion he tasted that Goodness, the fount for all creatures, as if in brooks [IX, 1]. Christ Jesus crucified dwelt within his soul . . . He always communicated devoutly – that he might render others devout – while he was rapt in the delicious tasting of the Lamb without blemish; rapt also in a deep ecstasy [IX, 2] . . . With the burning fire of love he equalled the triumph of the holy martyrs, in whom the flame of love could not be snuffed out [IX, 5]' Angela echoes all of this.

St Bonaventure elaborated on the theme of the desire for death and martyrdom elsewhere in his writings. The ascetic life inspires the urge to sacrifice one's self for the love of Christ, as Christ gave his own life for mankind. St Francis offers the perfect model – yearning for martyrdom joining wonderfully in union with the Crucified. Bonaventure concludes: 'So to desire death for Christ, to expose oneself to death for Christ and to joy in the agony of death, is an act of perfect love.'[44] When Angela, at prayer, felt filled in every part of her body with the delights of God she wanted to die; just as she had wanted to die in Assisi when the Spirit of love departed from her, and again when she returned home to Foligno. There she felt such a sweet tranquillity that it hurt her to live; to live was more painful to her than the sorrow she had felt over the deaths of her mother and children, more painful than all the sorrow she could imagine. This desire for death, which she continued to experience, was for Angela, as for many Christian mystics, equivalent to the desire for martyrdom.[45]

In her teachings Angela laid great stress on the importance of prayer: 'If you wish to have any virtue, pray. And pray in this wise, that is, by reading in the Book of Life.' The term 'Book of Life', to indicate meditation on and imitation of the life of Christ, is used by St Bonaventure and other Franciscan writers, though it is not new.[46] The list of four benefits she believed to be derived from receiving communion – it 'cleanses, sanctifies, comforts and preserves the soul' – is substantially the same as the five given by St Bonaventure: 'For this sacrament strengthens to action, raises to contemplation,

---

[44] Thier and Calufetti 1985, p. 200 and n. 3, citing Bonaventure, *Apologia Pauperum*, iv. 3 (*Opera Omnia*, VIII, 253).

[45] Thier and Calufetti 1985, pp. 200, 184, 186. For Angela's desire, on the fourteenth step, to shed all her blood for love of Christ and to suffer a particularly protracted and degrading crucifixion, cf. Thier and Calufetti 1985, pp. 142–4. Cf. Brother Leo's *Life of blessed brother Giles*, c. 18, SL, pp. 346–7.

[46] Thier and Calufetti 1985, p. 454 and n. 11; cf. Lachance 1993, pp. 234, 399 n. 35.

disposes to divine revelation, inspires and kindles to contempt of the world and to the longing for the eternal heavenly blessings.'[47]

It was also revealed to Angela that nobody can have an excuse regarding salvation, because it is not necessary to do more than a sick person does who goes to the doctor, which is to show him the infirmity and be prepared to follow his directions. There is no need to do anything more or to dose oneself with other medicines; only show yourself to the doctor and be ready to do everything he says; and take care not to mix in anything contrary. Angela's soul understood that the medicine was His blood and that Christ dispensed the medicine to the sick. If they dispose themselves aright, the doctor will heal their infirmity, in other words their sin, and grant them health, that is, salvation. St Bonaventure wrote a treatise on the theme of Christ the Doctor, who heals mankind through spiritual medicaments, the sacraments.[48]

Finally, she will have been encouraged, and will have been eager, to study tracts of popular devotion. It is likely that she read, for example, James of Milan's *Stimulus amoris*, whose relevance to her particular situation, and to Franciscan spirituality in a wider context, has already been discussed in relation to her reaction to the stained glass window in the Upper Church depicting St Francis' union with Christ[49] (Plate 39).

In her *Instructiones*, aimed at the circle of her friends and admirers, Angela has left us her appreciation of what St Francis meant to her:

'The first man fell by the road of poverty, and by the road of poverty the second man – Christ both God and man – lifted us up again. There is an evil poverty which is lack of understanding. Adam fell by lack of understanding, and all who have fallen or fall or will fall in the future – all fall by the same lack of understanding . . .

'We have an example of true poverty from Jesus Christ, himself both God and man. He lifted us again and redeemed us by poverty. Truly his poverty was ineffable when it concealed such mighty power and total nobility. He allowed himself to be blasphemed, set at nought, cursed, captured, led, scourged and crucified – and he always acted as if he were powerless. This poverty is the model for our life; from this poverty must we draw out its example . . .

'How perfect an example we have from our glorious father Francis! He held the ineffable light of the most true poverty. He was so full of this light – and overflowing with it – that he made and revealed to me the unique road. Nor can I think of any other saint who shows us more clearly the unique road of the book of life – that is, the model of the life of Jesus Christ, God and man; nor do I perceive anyone who embedded himself in Him in such a unique way. He never took the eyes of his mind off Him, as could be plainly seen in his flesh.[50] And because he embedded himself there so very fully, he was filled with the highest wisdom; and from the store of that wisdom he filled and fills the whole world.

'Our glorious father the blessed Francis taught us two things uniquely.

[47] Thier and Calufetti 1985, pp. 372–4 and n. 27; Bonaventure, *Sermo* III, *Opera Omnia*, v, 557.
[48] Thier and Calufetti 1985, pp. 218–20 and n. 24; Bonaventure, *Breviloquium*, c. VI, *De medicina sacramentali* (*Opera Omnia*, v, 265–80).
[49] Poulenc 1983, esp. pp. 705–8; see pp. 326–31.   [50] A clear reference to the stigmata.

'One is to recollect ourselves in God – to set our whole mind in that divine infinity. And because he was full to overflowing with the Holy Spirit . . . the Holy Spirit was with him in all his works and deeds. The Holy Spirit . . . cleansed him in mind and body; it sanctified him within and without;[51] it gave him strength in every way, it directed him most truly, it made him most pure within and without; it made him one with God in a union constant and ineffable . . . This ordering of the Holy Spirit, is supremely wonderful: it has thus marvellously ordered his soul and made it the seat of God; at once and uniquely too it has ordered his body. I see him uniquely poor; I see him as the unique lover and follower of poverty, for he was poor both within and without; and I see him utterly transformed in poverty. He not only prescribed it for himself, he prescribed it for the whole world; and this prescription he drew out of the book of life – that is, from the life of Jesus Christ, God and man. Therefore let us believe in it, since it was not false, nor has he prayed in vain.

'The second lesson the blessed Francis taught us was his teaching on poverty, suffering, humility and true obedience. He was himself that very poverty within and without, and by it he constantly lived. Everything which Jesus, God and man, despised, he most perfectly despised. Everything which Jesus, God and man, loved, he loved supremely too in his bowels: he followed in His footsteps with perfection indescribable, so that he was made conformable to Him in every way that is possible. Because he saw God most perfectly according to the vision ineffable, thus ineffably he loved Him. In accordance with this transformation, he showed it most fully in everything he did. That which we most love we desire most to have . . . and everything which Jesus, God and man, loved, Francis, poorest of the poor, loved too. He was cleansed again and again, and continually cleansed, because of the pure vision which he always held on to. And because God had called him in a unique fashion, he gave him unique gifts for his own and others' use. The uncreated God wished to make manifest to us the true fulfilment which our blessed father Francis had, a fulfilment we cannot comprehend.[52] And he had these unique gifts and this fulfilment by true and constant prayer . . .

'The more perfectly and purely we see, the more perfectly and purely we love . . . The more we see of Jesus Christ, God and man, the more we are transformed into Him by love . . . Just as I said of love . . . so of suffering . . . the more the soul sees of the suffering of Jesus Christ, God and man, the greater is its vision of this ineffable suffering, and it is wholly transformed in this suffering. Thus is the soul transformed in Jesus Christ, God and man, by love – thus is it transformed in Him by suffering . . .

'All these things were perfectly fulfilled in our blessed father Francis, on whom we should fix our eyes that we may follow him.'[53]

Having studied Angela's life and spiritual development in some detail, we should now be able to answer a question fundamental to the subject of this book. To what extent had the Order, in sermon and spiritual instruction, in liturgy, in books, in stained

---

[51] 'interius et exterius' is repeated four times in quick succession.

[52] 'Fulfilment', *impletura* in Latin, is 'dipintura . . . pentura' in the MS of the Italian version, meaning representation – and foreshadowing the modern use of 'image'. See Thier and Calufetti 1985, p. 477 nn. x–y.

[53] Thier and Calufetti 1985, pp. 470–83, much abbreviated: my own translation. Cf. also Lachance 1993, pp. 239–44.

glass, fresco and painted crucifix, succeeded in passing on to a highly sensitive and receptive woman an appreciation of Francis that was true to his spirit and his life's work? Admittedly Angela was a quite exceptional woman, but still, we can deduce from what she singled out as his essential qualities and message, how far his followers were successful, and how far faithful. It is valid evidence of the actual image of St Francis the Order did put across to one individual in the course of the last quarter of the thirteenth century.

Angela herself was in no doubt that St Francis thoroughly approved of her. Once when she was ill Christ came to comfort her and sat by her bed. He brought St Francis with him, saying: 'Here is he who after me you love so much', and Francis also comforted and edified her. He ended by saying: 'You are the only one born of me.'[54] There is even an element of truth in what seems on the face of it an extraordinary assertion. Angela grasped, in these later years of the century, an essential component of the Franciscan message that the Friars Minor had come to neglect in their own ranks. The Order had changed markedly since its early days. Not only had it become institutionalised; its composition had been transformed. Since the early 1240s the recruitment of laymen, with few exceptions, had been discontinued.[55] It was thought more efficient to concentrate on training an educated clerical élite dedicated to the cure of souls. It is true that you had had to qualify to join Francis. But anyone could qualify provided he summoned up the right disposition; provided he was firm in the Catholic faith, willing to follow the Gospel precepts, sell all his possessions and give to the poor, and to live in poverty, humility, chastity and obedience.[56] Francis ate with lepers, as Christ had eaten with publicans and sinners. Already on her first pilgrimage to Assisi Angela was made aware that the invitation was inclusive, not exclusive. The Spirit told her: 'There is not anyone who can claim excuse, because every single person can love him [God], and he does not require anything other than that the soul should love him, because he himself loves the soul, and he himself is the love of the soul.' Another time she was told: '"I have called and invited all to eternal life . . . Behold, the invited are coming and are placed at table," and was given to understand that he [Christ], was the table, and the food which he gave.' There was equal opportunity too, of a kind, to sit at the high table. Consciousness of sin and unworthiness is not a bar. Indeed the Father rejoices over sinners who return to him and gives them special grace and joy, which he does not give to virgins who never strayed – Angela's own personal slant on the parable of

---

54 Thier and Calufetti 1985, p. 598; cf. Lachance 1993, pp. 276–7. Thier and Calufetti believed that the B family of MSS, which omit this and many other sections of the *Instructiones*, represented the original form of the work, to which additions were made after Angela's death in a second edition, represented by family A and the earliest vernacular MS, M (Thier and Calufetti 1985, introduction, esp. pp. 108–15 – the omissions of B are listed in the table on p. 112 and marked in italic in the text). This view – which might undermine the authenticity of the present passage – has been doubted by other scholars (see Lachance 1993, pp. 53–4 and 345 n. 153, citing e.g. E. Menestò) and is now untenable. Langeli (1999) has established the authority of Assisi 342, the earliest MS of family A. He has shown that it was written by a scribe who worked in the scriptorium of the Sacro Convento in Angela's lifetime, shortly before her death – the date of which the MS records in a note added by the original scribe as 4 January 1309 (Langeli 1999, pp. 14–15). I regard the passage as authentic.

55 Leonardi 1984, pp. 24–5; Brooke 1959, pp. 243–5.

56 *Regula bullata*, cc. 1–2, Testament, Esser 1976, pp. 366–7, 438–44.

the lost sheep.[57] A sinner, any sinner, can aspire to the highest places, provided he or she loves – 'the right road to salvation is to love, and to want to suffer for [Christ's] love'. Again, on the road to Assisi, Angela was assured of this: 'I will do for you that that I have done for my servant Francis, and more, if you love me.' The road to Assisi was even her road to Damascus; though her soul was already privileged to hear greater revelations from the Holy Spirit than weaker men – 'I [the Holy Spirit], have spoken less of these things to others, and he to whom I spoke fell down, neither sentient nor seeing.'[58]

Angela was also in her time a leading exponent of the strand of feminine sanctity rooted in Franciscan spirituality which derives from one of Francis' most outstanding early converts and followers, St Clare. St Clare clung tenaciously to the virtue of absolute poverty, and devoted her life to loving contemplation of the poor Christ. St Clare's letters to blessed Agnes, daughter of King Ottokar I of Bohemia, who entered the convent of Poor Clares in Prague, clearly state the basic principles by which women as well as men can live the religious life in accordance with the new emphasis pioneered by Francis. St Clare praised Agnes, who had accepted a more noble spouse than the Emperor who had asked for her hand, the Lord Jesus Christ, and chosen with all her heart and soul most holy poverty and bodily penury (Ep. 1). She exhorted her, 'poor virgin, to embrace the poor Christ. Look on Him who was made contemptible for thy sake, and follow Him, making thyself contemptible for his sake in this world. Thy spouse, "fairer than the children of men" [Ps. 44(45). 3], for thy salvation became of all men the most worthless, despised, struck, his whole body flogged in manifold ways, dying amidst those agonies on the cross; look on Him, most noble queen, consider, contemplate, desiring to imitate Him. If thou suffer with Him, thou wilt reign with Him, grieving with Him thou wilt rejoice, dying with Him on the cross of tribulation thou wilt possess heavenly mansions among the splendours of the saints. And thy name will be written in the Book of Life and will be glorious among men' (Ep. 2).[59]

St Bonaventure has been charged with shifting the focus on St Francis' image by so extolling his sanctity as to diminish perception of his humanity. His St Francis exhibits such heroic virtues and supernatural powers that his followers would regard him with awe and wonder, and be unstintingly proud of him as the founder of their Order, but would tend to be deterred from making any serious attempt to follow his example by the sheer magnitude of the task they would face. If this were true, Bonaventure would have succeeded not only in totally undermining his stated purpose of describing the life of a man most worthy of all imitation, by whose example we are taught to conform our lives to Christ (Prologue, 1), but in totally undermining St Francis' whole teaching strategy, which was to draw everyone to repentance and to Christ, the way, the truth, and the life, by immolating himself as a living example to others. Angela's life may be cited as one small item of proof that Bonaventure's cast of mind and style did not put potential admirers of St Francis off. St Bonaventure was clear – and Angela vividly enforced the message – that it was Jesus, not Francis, that the friars, together with

---

[57] Thier and Calufetti 1985, pp. 214, 230–2, 220–2.
[58] Thier and Calufetti 1985, pp. 208, 180, 182 and n. 13; cf. Acts 9.3–9.
[59] Clare 1985, pp. 82–90 (Ep. 1), 92–8 (Ep. 2).

all men and women who had ears to hear, were called to imitate. St Francis would have been angered and distressed beyond measure by disobedience and misguided adulation.

'For often, when St Francis was honoured and told he was a holy man, he would reply with such words as these . . . "In whatever hour God might wish to take from me his treasure which he has lent me, what else would remain to me but a body and a soul, and these the heathen have also. I ought rather to believe that if God had bestowed as many blessings on a robber or even on a heathen man as he has on me they would become more faithful to God than I." He said: "In pictures of God and the blessed Virgin painted on wood, God and the blessed Virgin are honoured and God and the blessed Virgin are held in mind, yet the wood and the painting ascribe nothing to themselves, because they are just wood and paint; so the servant of God is a kind of painting, that is a creature of God in which God is honoured for the sake of his benefits. But he ought to ascribe nothing to himself, just like the wood or the painting, but should render honour and glory to God alone"' (SL 104).

I would like, in conclusion, to offer another image to add to the tally of mirror of perfection, new evangelist, morning star among the clouds, and liken St Francis to a window, through which one may see Christ, both God and man.

A man that looks on glass
On it may stay his eye:
Or if he pleaseth, through it pass
And then the heaven espy.
George Herbert

BIBLIOGRAPHY

Abate, G., 1966, *La casa natale di S. Francesco e la topografia di Assisi nella prima metà del secolo XIII*, Rome, 1966 (= Bollettino della Deputazione di Storia Patria per l'Umbria 63 (1966), 5–110)

Abbott, E. A., 1898, *St Thomas of Canterbury: His Death and Miracles*, 2 vols., London, 1898

Abulafia, D., 1988, *Frederick II*, London, 1988

Acta Sanctorum: Acta Sanctorum Bollandiana, Brussels, etc., 1643–

AF: *Analecta Franciscana*, Quaracchi, 1885–

AFH: *Archivum Franciscanum Historicum*, Quaracchi and Grottaferrata, 1908–

AFP: *Archivum Fratrum Praedicatorum*, 1931–

Alan 1654: *Alani Magni de Insulis, Opera moralia, paraenetica et polemica*, ed. C. de Visch, Antwerp, 1654

Albanés, J. H., 1879, *La vie de Sainte Douceline*, Marseilles, 1879

Alberzoni, M. P., 1999, 'L'Approbatio: Curia Romana, ordine minoritica e *Libro*', in Barone and Dalarun 1999, pp. 293–318

Alessandri, L., 1915, 'Bullarium Pontificium quod exstat in Archivio Sacri Conventus S. Francisci Assisiensis, I', AFH 8 (1915), 592–617

Alessandri, L., and Pennacchi, F., 1914, 1920, 'I più antichi inventari della Sacristeria del Sacro Convento di Assisi (1338–1473)', AFH 7 (1914), 66–107, 294–340, repr. as *I più antichi inventari della sacristia del Sacro Convento di Assisi (1338–1473)*, Quaracchi, 1920

Alexander of Hales, 1951, 1952, [ed. V. Doucet], *Glossa in quatuor Libros Sententiarum Petri Lombardi*, Bibliotheca Franciscana Scholastica 12–13, Quaracchi, 1951–2

ALKG: *Archiv für Litteratur- und Kirchengeschichte*, ed. H. Denifle and F. Ehrle, 7 vols., Berlin and Freiburg-im-Breisgau, 1885–1900

Andaloro, M., 1984, 'Ancora una volta sull'Ytalia di Cimabue', *Arte medievale* 2 (1984), 143–77; English summary, pp. 178–81

— 1995, 'I mosaici del Sancta Sanctorum', *Sancta Sanctorum* 1995, pp. 126–91

Angela of Foligno, 1993, see Lachance 1993; Thier and Calufetti 1985

Angeli, Padre, 1704, *Collis Paradisi amoenitas seu sacri conventus Assisiensis Historiae Libri II*, Montefalco, 1704

Angiola, E., 1977, 'Nicola Pisano, Federigo Visconti, and the classical style in Pisa', *Art Bulletin* 59 (1977), 1–27

AP: *L'Anonyme de Pérouse*, ed. P.-B. Beguin, Paris, 1979

Armstrong, J., and Brady, I. C., 1982, trans., *Francis and Clare: The Complete Works*, London, 1982

Arturi a Monasterio, ed., 1939, *Martyrologium Franciscanum*, edn of Rome, 1939

Assisi 1974: La 'Questione Francescana' dal Sabatier ad oggi: Atti del I Convegno Internazionale, Assisi, 18–20 ottobre 1973, Società Internazionale di Studi Francescani, Assisi, 1974

Assisi 1978: Assisi al Tempo di San Francesco: Atti del V Convegno Internazionale, Assisi, 13–16 ottobre 1977, Società Internazionale di Studi Francescani, Assisi, 1978

Assisi 1980: Il Tesoro della Basilica di San Francesco ad Assisi, ed. R. B. Fanelli et al., Assisi, 1980

Assisi 1999: The Treasury of St Francis of Assisi, ed. G. Morello and L. B. Kanter, Milan, 1999

Aston, M., 1990, 'Segregation in church', *Studies in Church History* 27 (1990), 237–94

Aubert, A., 1907, *Die malerische Dekoration der San Francesco Kirche in Assisi*, Leipzig, 1907

Auvray, L., ed., 1896, *Registres de Grégoire IX*, I, Paris, 1896

Ayrton, M., 1969, *Giovanni Pisano Sculptor*, London, 1969

Baker, D., ed., 1978, *Medieval Women, Dedicated and Presented to Professor Rosalind M. T. Hill on the Occasion of her Seventieth Birthday, Studies in Church History, Subsidia 1*, Oxford, 1978

Balduinus ab Amsterdam, 1970, 'The commentary on St John's Gospel edited in 1589 under the name of St Bonaventure. An authentic work of John of Wales O. Min.', *Collectanea Franciscana* 40 (1970), 71–96

Barone, G., and Dalarun, J., eds., 1999, *Angèle de Foligno, Le dossier*, Rome, 1999

Basetti-Sani, G., 1972, 'San Francesco è incorso nella scomunica? Una bolla di Onorio III et il supposto pellegrinaggio del Santo a Gerusalemme', *AFH* 65 (1972), 3–19

Beguin 1979: see *AP*

Bellosi, L., 1985, *La pecora di Giotto*, Turin, 1985

    1998, *Cimabue*, trans. A. Bonfante-Warren, F. Dabell and J. Hyams, New York, 1998

Belting, H., 1977, *Die Oberkirche von San Francesco in Assisi*, Berlin, 1977

Benton, J. R., 1993, 'Antique survival and revival in the Middle Ages: architectural framing in late Duecento murals', *Arte Medievale*, 2nd ser., 7.1 (1993), 129–45

Bériou, N., 1994, 'Saint François, premier prophète de son ordre, dans les sermons du XIIIe siècle', in Bériou and d'Avray 1994, pp. 285–308

Bériou, N., and d'Avray, D., 1994, *Modern Questions about Medieval Sermons*, Spoleto, 1994

Bernard of Clairvaux, St, *Opera*, ed. J. Leclercq, C. H. Talbot and H. M. Rochais, 8 vols., Rome, 1957–77

Bibliotheca Sanctorum, ed. F. Caraffa, 12 vols., Rome, 1961–9; *Indici*, 1970; *Prima Appendice*, 1987

Bigaroni, M., ed., 1975, '*Compilatio Assisiensis' dagli Scritti di fr. Leone e Compagne su S. Francesco d'Assisi*, Assisi, 1975

Bihl, M., 1908, 'E sermonibus Friderici de Vicecomitibus, archiepiscopi Pisani, de S. Francisco (1263–67)', *AFH* I (1908), 652–5

    1926, 'De quodam elencho Assisano testium oculatorum S. Francisci stigmatum', *AFH* 19 (1926), 931–6

    1940, 'Bibliographia' [review article on literature and controversies on the Portiuncula Indulgence], *AFH* 33 (1940), 199–210

    1941, 'Statuta Generalia Ordinis, edita in capitulis generalibus celebratis Narbonae an. 1260, Assisii an. 1279, atque Parisiis an. 1292', *AFH* 34 (1941), 13–94, 284–358

    1946–8, 'Contra duas novas hypotheses prolatas a Ioh. R. H. Moorman', *AFH* 39 (1946–8), 3–37

Binski, P., 1986, 'The early portrait: verbal or pictorial?', in *Europäische Kunst um 1300. XXV Internationaler Kongress für Kunstgeschichte Wien 1983* (Vienna, 1986), VI, 211–15

    2002, 'How northern was the Northern Master at Assisi?', *Proceedings of the British Academy* 117 (2002), 73–138

    2004, *Becket's Crown*, New Haven, 2004

Binski, P., and Noel, W., eds., 2001, *New Offerings, Ancient Treasures: Studies in Medieval Art for George Henderson*, Stroud, 2001

Blume, D., 1983, *Wandmalerei als Ordenspropaganda*, Worms, 1983

Blumenfeld-Kosinski, R., and Szell, T., eds., 1991, *Images of Sainthood in Medieval Europe*, Ithaca, 1991

Bologna, F., 1960, 'Ciò che resta di un capolavoro giovanile di Duccio', *Paragone* 125 (1960), 3–31
    1969, 'Povertà e umiltà. Il San Ludovico di Simone Martini', *Studi Storici* 10 (1969), 231–59
    1983, 'The crowning disc of a Duecento crucifixion and other points relevant to Duccio's relationship with Cimabue', *Burlington Magazine* 125 (1983), 330–40

Bolton, B., 1978, '*Vitae Matrum*: a further aspect of the *Frauenfrage*', in Baker 1978, pp. 253–73

Bolvig, A., and Lindley, P., eds., 2003, *History and Images: Towards a New Iconology*, Turnhout, 2003

Bolzoni, L., 2004, *The Web of Images: Vernacular Preaching from Its Origins to St Bernardino of Siena*, Aldershot, 2004

Bonav.: Bonaventure, St, *Legenda Maior S. Francisci*, cc. I–XV, referred to by chapter and paragraph in the Quaracchi edition, AF X, (1926–41), 555–652

Bonav., *Miracula*, referred to by chapter and paragraph from the Quaracchi edition, AF X, 627–52

Bonaventure, *Opera Omnia*, 10 vols., Quaracchi, 1882–1902; and see Bougerol 1993, Delorme 1934, De Vinck 1960

Bonsanti, G., 1997, *La volta della Basilica Superiore di Assisi* (photos by G. Roli), Modena, 1997
    ed., 2002a, *La Basilica di San Francesco ad Assisi*, 4 vols., Modena, 2002
    2002b, 'La pittura del Duecento e del Trecento', in Bonsanti 2002a, III, 113–208

Borst, A., 1953, *Die Katharer*, Schriften der MGH 12, Stuttgart, 1953

Boskovits, M., 2000, 'Giotto a Roma', *Arte Cristana* 88 (2000), 171–80

Bougerol, J. G., 1983, 'Saint François dans les premiers sermons universitaires', in Gieben 1983, I, 173–99
    1984, *Francesco e Bonaventura: La Legenda Major*, Vicenza, 1984
    1988: *Bonaventuriana: Miscellanea in onore di Jacques Guy Bougerol*, ed. A. C. Blanco, 2 vols., Rome, 1988
    ed., 1993, *Saint Bonaventure: Sermons De Diversis*, 2 vols., Paris, 1993

Bourdua, L., 2004, *The Franciscans and Art Patronage in Late Medieval Italy*, Cambridge, 2004

Brady, I., 1976, 'St Bonaventure's sermons on Saint Francis', *Franziskanische Studien* 58 (1976), 129–41

Branca, V., 1949, 'Il Cantico di frate sole: studio delle fonti e testo critico', AFH 41 (1948, publ. 1949), 3–87

Brem, E., 1911, *Papst Gregor IX bis zum Beginn seines Pontifikats*, Heidelberg, 1911

Brett, A., 1997, *Liberty, Right and Nature: Individual Rights in Later Scholastic Thought*, Cambridge, 1997

Brieger, P., 1957, *English Art 1216–1307*, Oxford History of Art 4, Oxford, 1957

Brooke, C. N. L., 1970/1999, 'The missionary at home: the church in the towns, 1000–1250', *Studies in Church History* 6 (1970), 59–83, repr. in Brooke, C., 1999, ch. 4
    1971, *Medieval Church and Society*, London, 1971
    1985, 'The churches of medieval Cambridge', in *History, Society and the Churches: Essays in Honour of Owen Chadwick*, ed. D. Beales and G. Best (Cambridge, 1985), pp. 49–76
    1986, *The Church and the Welsh Border*, ed. D. N. Dumville and C. N. L. Brooke, Woodbridge, 1986
    1989a, *The Medieval Idea of Marriage*, Oxford, 1989
    1989b, 'Priest, deacon and layman, from St Peter Damian to St Francis', *Studies in Church History* 26 (1989), 65–85, repr. in Brooke 1999, ch. 13
    1999, *Churches and Churchmen in Medieval Europe*, London, 1999
    2000, *Europe in the Central Middle Ages*, 3rd edn, Harlow, 2000
    2006, *The Rise and Fall of the Medieval Monastery* (rev. edn of Brooke and Swaan 1974), London, 2006

Brooke, C. N. L., and Swaan, W., 1974, *The Monastic World*, London, 1974

Brooke, R. B., 1949 (R. B. Clark), 'Brother Elias, and the Government of the Franciscan Order 1217–1239', University of Cambridge Ph.D. thesis, 1949

 1959, *Early Franciscan Government: Elias to Bonaventure*, Cambridge Studies in Medieval Life and Thought, 2nd Series, 7, Cambridge, 1959; repr. 2004

 1967, 'The Lives of St Francis of Assisi', in Dorey 1967, pp. 177–98

 ed. and trans., 1970/1990, *Scripta Leonis, Rufini et Angeli sociorum S. Francisci: The Writings of Leo, Rufino and Angelo, Companions of St Francis*, OMT, Oxford, 1970, corr. repr. 1990: SL

 1974, 'St Bonaventure as Minister General', in *S. Bonaventura Francescana. Atti del XIV Convegno di Studi*, Todi, 1974, pp. 77–105

 1975, *The Coming of the Friars*, London, 1975

 1981, 'The "Legenda antiqua S. Francisci"', *Analecta Bollandiana* 99 (1981), 165–8

 1982, 'Recent work on St Francis of Assisi', *Analecta Bollandiana* 100 (1982), 655–76

Brooke, R. and C., 1984, *Popular Religion in the Middle Ages: Western Europe 1000–1300*, London, 1984

 1999, 'St Clare', [originally in Baker 1978, pp. 275–87] in C. Brooke 1999, ch. 15

Brown, P. R. L., 1971, 'The rise and function of the holy man in late antiquity', *Journal of Roman Studies* 61 (1971), 80–101

Brufani, S., ed., 1990, *Sacrum Commercium sancti Francisci cum Domina Paupertate*, Assisi, 1990

Buchthal, H., 1957, *Miniature Painting in the Latin Kingdom of Jerusalem*, Oxford, 1957

Bughetti, B., 1926a, 'Vita e miracoli di S. Francesco nelle tavole istoriate dei secoli XIII e XIV', *AFH* 19 (1926), 636–732

 1926b, 'Di un presunto nuovo ritratto di S. Francesco', *AFH* 19 (1926), 936–9

Burkitt, F. C., 1926, 'The study of the sources for the life of St Francis', in *St Francis of Assisi, 1226–1926: Essays in Commemoration* (London, 1926), pp. 15–61

 1932, 'Fonte Colombo and its traditions', in Burkitt et al., *Franciscan Essays*, British Society of Franciscan Studies, Extra Series, 3 (1932), pp. 41–55

Burr, D., 1989, *Olivi and Franciscan Poverty*, Philadelphia, 1989

 2001, *The Spiritual Franciscans: From Protest to Persecution in the Century after Saint Francis*, Pennsylvania, 2001

Bynum, C., 1982, *Jesus as Mother: Studies in the Spirituality of the High Middle Ages*, Berkeley, 1982

 1995, *The Resurrection of the Body in Western Christianity, 200–1336*, New York, 1995

Cadei, A., 1983, 'Assisi, San Francesco: l'architettura e la prima fase della decorazione', in Romanini 1983, pp. 141–74

Cambell, J., ed., 1966, *I Fiori dei Tre Compagni*, with Italian trans. by F. Vian, Milan, 1966

Campagnola, see Stanislao

Cannon, J., 1982, 'Dating the frescoes by the Maestro di S. Francesco in Assisi', *Burlington Magazine* 124 (1982), 65–9

 1998, 'Dominic *alter Christus*? Representations of the founder in and after the *Arca di San Domenico*', in *Christ among the Medieval Dominicans: Representations of Christ in the Texts and Images of the Order of Preachers*, ed. K. Emery and J. Wawrykow (Notre Dame, Indiana, 1998), pp. 26–48, 555–8 and figs. 1–37

Cannon, J., and Vauchez, A., 1999, *Margherita of Cortona and the Lorenzetti*, University Park, Pennsylvania, 1999

Carlettini, I., 1993, 'L'apocalisse di Cimabue e la meditazione escatologica di S. Bonaventura', *Arte Medievale*, 2nd ser., 7.1 (1993), 105–28

Cat. Générale IV: Catalogue Générale des Manuscrits des Bibliothèques Publiques de Départements, IV, Paris, 1872

Catholic Encyclopaedia, The, 16 vols., New York, 1907–14

Cattaneo, E., 1970, 'Il battistero in Italia dopo il Mille', *Miscellanea Gilles Gerard Meersseman* = *Italia Sacra* 15–16 (1970), I, 171–95

Causse, M., 1987, 'Paul Sabatier et la question franciscaine', *Revue d'Histoire et de Philosophie Religieuses* 67 (1987), 113–35

    1989, 'Question franciscaine (2e article): du *Speculum Perfectionis* aux "Rotuli" de Frère Léon', *Revue d'Histoire et de Philosophie Religieuses* 69 (1989), 285–307

    1993, 'Recherches sur les sources franciscaines à partir des travaux de Paul Sabatier', Thesis for Doctorat en Théologie, Institut Protestant de Théologie, Paris, 1993

    1995, 'Citations des biographes primitives dans les *Annales Minorum* de Lucas Wadding' (unpublished printout, Saintes, 1995)

Caviness, M. H., 1981, *The Windows of Christ Church Cathedral, Canterbury, Corpus Vitrearum Medii Aevi*, Great Britain, II, London, 1981

1, 2, 3 *Cel.*: Thomas of Celano, *Vita Prima, Vita Secunda* and *Tractatus de Miraculis S. Francisci Assisiensis*, referred to by paragraphs in the Quaracchi editions, AF X (1926–41), 1–331

Chadwick, O., 1981, *The Popes and European Revolution*, Oxford, 1981

Cheney, C. R., and Jones, M., 2000, *A Handbook of Dates*, 2nd edn, Cambridge, 2000

Christe, Y., 1970, 'A propos du décor absidale de Saint-Jean du Latran à Rome', *Cahiers Archéologiques* 20 (1970), 197–206

    1980–1, 'L'Apocalypse de Cimabue à Assise', *Cahiers Archéologiques* 29 (1980–1), 157–74

Chron. 24 Gen.: 'Chronicle of the Twenty-Four Generals' in AF III (1897)

Ciardi Dupré dal Poggetto, M. G., 1991, 'La committenza mecenatismo artistico di Niccolò IV', in *Niccolò IV: un pontificato tra Oriente ed Occidente – Atti del Convegno Internazionale di studi in occasione del VII centenario del pontificato di Niccolò IV*, ed. E. Menestò, Ascoli Piceno 14–17 dicembre 1989, Spoleto, 1991, pp. 193–222

Ciatti, M., 2002, 'The restoration and the study of the Crucifix', in Ciatti and Seidel 2002, pp. 25–64

Ciatti, M., and Seidel, M., eds., 2002, *Giotto: The Santa Maria Novella Crucifix*, Florence, 2002

Clare 1985: Claire d'Assise, *Écrits*, ed. M.-F. Becker, J.-F. Godet and T. Matura, Sources Chrétiennes 325, Paris, 1985

Clark, R. B., *see* Brooke, R. B.

Clasen, S., 1961, 1962, 'S. Bonaventura S. Francisci legendae maioris compilator', AFH 54 (1961), 241–72; 55 (1962), 3–58, 289–319

    1967, *Legenda Antiqua S. Francisci*, Leiden, 1967

Cole, B., 1974, 'Giotto's apparition of St Francis at Arles: the case of the missing crucifix', *Simiolus* 7 (1974), 163–5

Collinson, P., Ramsay, N., and Sparks, M., eds., 1995, *A History of Canterbury Cathedral*, Oxford, 1995

Constable, G., 1979, '"Nudus nudum Christum sequi" and parallel formulas in the twelfth century: a supplementary dossier', in *Continuity and Discontinuity in Church History: Essays Presented to George Hunston Williams on the Occasion of His 65th Birthday*, ed. F. F. Church and T. George (Leiden, 1979), pp. 83–91

    1995, *Three Studies in Medieval Religious and Social Thought*, Cambridge, 1995

    1996, *The Reformation of the Twelfth Century*, Cambridge, 1996

Constantine of Orvieto, *Legenda S. Dominici*, ed. H. C. Scheeben, in Walz et al. 1935 = MOPH 16 (1935)

Cook, W. R., 1999, *Images of St Francis of Assisi in Painting, Stone and Glass from the Earliest Images to ca. 1320 in Italy: A Catalogue*, Florence and Perth (Western Australia), 1999

    ed., 2005, *The Art of the Franciscan Order in Italy*, Leiden, 2005

Cooper, D., and Robson, J., 2003, 'Pope Nicholas IV and the Upper Church at Assisi', *Apollo* 157, no. 492 (Feb. 2003), 31–5

Cousins, E., ed. and trans., 1978, *Bonaventure: The Soul's Journey into God, The Tree of Life, The Life of St Francis*, New York, 1978

Cousins, H., 1988, 'The image of St Francis in Bonaventure's *Legenda Maior*', in Bougerol 1988, I, 311–21

Cramer, P., 1993, *Baptism and Change in the Early Middle Ages, c. 200 – c. 1150*, Cambridge, 1993

Creytens, R., 1948, 'Les constitutions des Frères Prêcheurs dans la rédaction de S. Raymond de Peñafort', *AFP* 18 (1948), 5–68

Cristofani, G., 1912, *L'iconographie des vitraux du XIIIe siècle de la basilique d'Assise*, Paris, 1912

Cusato, M. F., 2000, 'Talking about ourselves: the shift in Franciscan writing from hagiography to history (1235–1247)', *Franciscan Studies*, New Series, 58 (2000), 37–75

Cuthbert, Father, 1913, *The Life of St Francis of Assisi*, London, 1913

Dalarun, J., 1985, *L'impossible sainteté: la vie retrouvé de Robert d'Arbrissel*, Paris, 1985

    1994, *Francesco: un passaggio*, Rome, 1994

    1995, 'Angèle de Foligno a-t-elle-existé?', in *Alla Signorina: mélanges offerts à Noëlle de La Blanchardière* (Rome, 1995), pp. 59–97

    And see Barone and Dalarun 1999

Daniel, E. R., 1988, 'Symbol or model? St Bonaventure's use of St Francis', in Bougerol 1988, I, 55–62

Dante, *see* Petrocchi, Sinclair, Singleton

d'Avray, D. L., 1981, 'A Franciscan and history', *AFH* 74 (1981), 456–82

    1985, *The Preaching of the Friars*, Oxford, 1985; and see Bériou and d'Avray 1994

DBI: Dizionario Biografico degli Italiani, Rome, 1960–

Delaruelle, E., 1975, *La piété populaire au moyen âge*, Turin, 1975

Delorme, F.-M., 1910, '"Diffinitiones" capituli generalis O.F.M. Narbonensis (1260)', *AFH* 3 (1910), 491–504

    1922, 'La "Legenda Antiqua S. Francisci" du MS. 1046 de la bibliothèque communale de Pérouse', *AFH* 15 (1922), 23–70, 278–332; rev. edn in *La France Franciscaine* 2 (Paris, 1926)

    ed., 1923, *Dialogus de gestis sanctorum fratrum minorum auctore Thoma de Papia*, Quaracchi, 1923

    ed., 1934, *S. Bonaventurae Collationes in Hexaëmeron et Bonaventuriana quaedam selecta*, Quaracchi, 1934

Demus, O., 1970, *Byzantine Art and the West*, Glückstadt, 1970

Derbes, A., 1996, *Picturing the Passion in Late Medieval Italy*, Cambridge, 1996

Desbonnets, T., 1972, 'La légende des trois compagnons. Nouvelles recherches sur la généalogie des biographies primitives de saint François', *AFH* 65 (1972), 66–106

    1974, '*Legenda Trium Sociorum*: édition critique', *AFH* 67 (1974), 38–144

De Vinck, S., trans., 1960, *The Works of St Bonaventure*, 4 vols., Paterson, NJ, 1960

de Wesselow, T., 2005, 'The date of the St Francis cycle in the Upper Church of S. Francesco at Assisi: the evidence of copies and considerations of method', in Cook 2005, pp. 113–67

Dictionnaire de spiritualité, ascétique et mystique, doctrine et histoire, ed. M. Viller et al., 17 vols., Paris, 1932–94

Di Fonzo, L., 1972, 'L'Anonimo Perugino tra le fonti francescane del sec. XIII: Rapporti letterari e testo critico', *Miscellanea Francescana* 72 (1972), 117–483

Dodd, C. H., 1944, *The Apostolic Preaching and Its Developments*, 2nd edn, London, 1944

    1963, *Historical Tradition in the Fourth Gospel*, Cambridge, 1963

Dodwell, C. R., 1961, ed. and trans., *Theophilus: The Various Arts*, Nelson's Medieval Texts, Edinburgh, 1961 (repr. Oxford Medieval Texts, Oxford, 1986)

Dondaine, A., 1953, 'Saint Pierre Martyr', *AFP* 23 (1953), 66–162

Dorey, T. A., 1967: *Latin Biography*, ed. T. A. Dorey, London, 1967

Doucet, 1951, 1952, see Alexander of Hales

Douie, D. L., 1973, 'St Bonaventura's part in the conflict between seculars and mendicants at Paris', in *S. Bonaventura 1274–1294* (Grottaferrata, 1973), II, 585–612

Doyle, E., 1983, *The Disciple and the Master: St Bonaventure's Sermons on St Francis of Assisi*, Chicago, 1983

Dufeil, M.-M., 1972, *Guillaume de Saint-Amour et la polémique universitaire parisienne 1250–1259*, Paris, 1972

Duffy, E., 1997, 'Finding St Francis: early images, early lives', in *Medieval Theology and the Natural Body*, ed. P. Biller and A. Minnis (York, 1997), pp. 193–236

Dunn, J. D. G., 2003, *Christianity in the Making*, 1: *Jesus Remembered*, Grand Rapids, MI, 2003

Eccleston: *Fratris Thomae vulgo dicti de Eccleston Tractatus de adventu fratrum minorum in Angliam*, ed. A. G. Little, 2nd edn, Manchester, 1951; also cited from the edn of Paris, 1909

Elizondo, F., 1963, 'Bulla "Exiit qui seminat" Nicolai III (14 Augusti 1279)', *Laurentianum* 4 (1963), 59–119

Erlande-Brandenburg, A., 1994, *The Cathedral: The Social and Architectural Dynamics of Construction*, Cambridge, 1994

Esser, K., 1940, 'Zu der "Epistola de tribus quaestionibus" des hl. Bonaventura', *Franziskanische Studien* 27 (1940), 149–59

    1958, 'Franziskus von Assisi und die Katharer seiner Zeit', *AFH* 51 (1958), 225–64

    1973, *Studien zu den Opuscula des hl. Franziskus von Assisi*, ed. E. Kurten and I. da Villapadierna, Rome, 1973

    ed., 1976, *Die Opuscula des Hl. Franziskus von Assisi*, Spicilegium Bonaventurianum 13, Grottaferrata, 1976

Eubel: Eubel, C., ed., 1908, *Bullarii Franciscani Epitome*, Quaracchi, 1908

Eubel, C., 1913, *Hierarchia Catholica Medii Aevi*, I, 2nd edn, Rome, 1913

Farmer, D. H., 1987, *The Oxford Dictionary of Saints*, 2nd edn., Oxford, 1987

Finucane, R. C., 1977, *Miracles and Pilgrims: Popular Beliefs in Medieval England*, London, 1977

Firmamenta: *Firmamenta trium ordinum beatissimi Patris nostri Francisci*, Paris, 1511–12: Hugh of Digne's *Expositio Regulae* and *Disputatio* are in this edition in *quarta pars*, 1511

Fisher, M. R., 1956, 'Assisi, Padua and the boy in the tree', *Art Bulletin* 38 (1956), 47–52

Fleming, J. V., 1982, *From Bonaventure to Bellini: An Essay in Franciscan Exegesis*, Princeton, 1982

Flood, D., 1967, *Die Regula non bullata der Minderbrüder*, Werl in Westfalen, 1967

    ed., 1972, *Peter Olivi's Rule Commentary: Edition and Presentation*, Veröffentlichungen des Instituts für Europäische Geschichte Mainz 67, Wiesbaden, 1972

    ed., 1979, *Hugh of Digne's Rule Commentary*, Spicilegium Bonaventurianum 14, Grottaferrata, 1979

    2002, 'John of Wales' Commentary on the Franciscan Rule', *Franciscan Studies*, New Series 60 (2002), 93–138

Flores d'Arcais, F., 1995, *Giotto*, Milan, 1995

Florovsky, C., 1912, '"De finibus paupertatis", auctore Hugone de Digna, O.F.M.', *AFH* 5 (1912), 277–90

Foot, S., 1999, 'Remembering, forgetting and inventing: attitudes to the past in England at the end of the first Viking age', *Transactions of the Royal Historical Society*, 6th series, 9 (1999), 185–200.

Foreville, R., and Keir, G., ed. and trans., 1987, *The Book of St Gilbert*, OMT, Oxford, 1987

Four Masters, see Oliger 1950

Francesco d'Assisi 1982: *Francesco d'Assisi: Storia e Arte*, Milan, 1982

Friedberg, E., ed. 1879–81, *Corpus Iuris Canonici*, 2nd edn, 2 vols., Leipzig, 1879–81

Frugoni, C., 1993, *Francesco e l'invenzione della stimmate*, Turin, 1993

Fulton, R., 1996, 'Mystic devotion, Marian exegesis, and the historical sense of the Song of Songs', *Viator* 27 (1996), 85–116

1998, '"Quae est ista quae ascendit sicut aurora consurgens?": the Song of Songs as the *Historia* for the office of the Assumption', *Mediaeval Studies* 60 (1998), 55–122

2002, *From Judgment to Passion: Devotion to Christ and the Virgin Mary, 800–1200*, New York, 2002

Füser, T., 1999, 'Vom *exemplum Christi* über das *exemplum sanctorum* zum "Jedermannbeispiel". Überlegungen zur Normalität exemplarischer Verhaltensmuster im institutionellen Gefüge der Bettelorden des 13. Jahrhunderts', in Melville and Oberste 1999, pp. 27–105

Gallia Christiana, 16 vols., Paris, 1715–1865

Gamboso, V., ed., 1981, *Vita prima S. Antonii O Assidua*, Fonti Agiographiche Antoniane 1, Padua, 1981

— ed., 1986, *Vita del 'Dialogus' e 'Benignitas'*, Fonti Agiographiche Antoniane 3, Padua, 1986

Gams, P. B., 1873, *Series Episcoporum Ecclesiae Catholicae*, Ratisbon, 1873

Garay, K., and Jeay, M., 2001, *The Life of Saint Douceline, a Beguine of Provence*, Cambridge, 2001

Gardner, J., 1973, 'Pope Nicholas IV and the decoration of Santa Maria Maggiore', *Zeitschrift für Kunstgeschichte* 36 (1973), 1–50

— 1978/9, Review of Belting 1977, *Kunstchronik* 32 (1978–9), 63–84

— 1981, 'Some Franciscan altars of the thirteenth and fourteenth centuries', in *The Vanishing Past: Studies of Medieval Art, Liturgy and Metrology Presented to Christopher Hohler*, ed. A. Borg and A. Martindale, Oxford, 1981, pp. 29–38 and pls. 3.1–9

— 1982, 'The Louvre stigmatization and the problem of the narrative altarpiece', *Zeitschrift für Kunstgeschichte* 45 (1982), 217–47, repr. in Gardner 1993, ch. VI

— 1984, *Studies in Late Medieval Italian Art*, London, 1984

— 1987, 'Bizuti, Rusuti, Nicolaus and Johannes: some neglected documents concerning Roman artists in France', *Burlington Magazine* 129 (1987), 381–3

— 1992, *The Tomb and the Tiara: Curial Tomb Sculpture in Rome and Avignon in the Later Middle Ages*, Oxford, 1992

— 1993, *Patrons, Painters and Saints: Studies in Medieval Italian Painting*, Variorum Collected Studies Series, CS 414, Aldershot, 1993

— 1995, 'L'architettura del Sancta Sanctorum', in Sancta Sanctorum 1995, pp. 19–37

— 1997, 'The artistic patronage of Pope Nicholas IV', *Annali della Scuola Normale Superiore di Pisa*, 4th series, 2 (1997), 1–8

Garrison, E. B., 1949, *Italian Romanesque Panel Painting: An Illustrated Index*, Florence, 1949

— 1972, 'Note on the survival of thirteenth-century panel paintings in Italy', *Art Bulletin* 54 (1972), 140

Gatti, I., 1983, *La Tomba di S. Francesco nei secoli*, Assisi, 1983

Gattucci, A., 1979, 'Dalla "Legenda antiqua S. Francisci" alla "Compilatio Assisiensis": storia di un testo più prezioso che fortunato', *Studi Medievali*, 3rd series, 20, 2 (1979), 789–870

Gauthier, M.-M., 1987, *Highways of the Faith: Relics and Reliquaries from Jerusalem to Compostela*, trans. J. A. Underwood, London, 1987

Geary, P. J., 1999, 'Land, language and memory in Europe 700–1100', *Transactions of the Royal Historical Society*, 6th series, 9 (1999), 169–84

Ghiberti, L., 1998, *I Commentarii* [c. 1450], ed. L. Bartoli, Florence, 1998

Gibbs and Johnson 1984: Wolfram von Eschenbach, *Willehalm*, trans. M. E. Gibbs and S. M. Johnson, Harmondsworth, 1984

Gieben, S., ed., 1983, *Francesco d'Assisi nella Storia*, 2 vols., Rome, 1983

— 2001, 'Das Tafelkreuz von S. Damiano in der Geschichte. Mit einem ikonographischen Anhang', *Collectanea Franciscana* 71 (2001), 47–63

Gilson, E., 1924, *La philosophie de Saint Bonaventure*, Paris, 1924

Goetz, W., 1904, *Die quellen zur Geschichte des Franziskus von Assisi*, Gotha, 1904

Goffen, R., 1988, *Spirituality in Conflict: Saint Francis and Giotto's Bardi Chapel*, University Park, 1988

Golden Legend, The, see Maggioni 1998; Ryan and Ripperger 1941

Golding, B., 1995, *Gilbert of Sempringham and the Gilbertine Order, c. 1130 – c. 1300*, Oxford, 1995

Golubovich, G., 1906, *Biblioteca bio-bibliografica della Terra Santa e dell'Oriente Francescano*, I, Quaracchi, 1906

    1919, 'Disputatio Latinorum et Graecorum seu Relatio Apocrisariorum Gregorii IX de gestis Nicaeae in Bithynia et Nymphaeae in Lydia, 1234', *AFH* 12 (1919), 418–70

Gordon, Dillian, 1982, 'A Perugian provenance for the Franciscan double-sided altar-piece by the Maestro di S. Francesco', *Burlington Magazine* 124 (1982), 70–7

Gratien, P., 1928, *Histoire de la fondation et de l'évolution de l'Ordre des Frères Mineurs au XIIIe siècle*, Paris and Gembloux, 1928

Greenway, D. E., 1968: John Le Neve, *Fasti Ecclesiae Anglicanae 1066–1300*, I, St Paul's London, compiled by D. E. Greenway, London, 1968

Gregorovius, F., 1906, *History of the City of Rome in the Middle Ages*, trans. A. Hamilton, V, 2nd edn, 2 parts, London, 1906

Grundmann, H., 1961, 'Die Bulle "Quo elongati" Papst Gregors IX', *AFH* 54 (1961), 3–25

    1995, *Religious Movements in the Middle Ages* (English trans. by S. Rowan of *Religiöse Bewegungen im Mittelalter*, 1935), Notre Dame, 1995

Habig, M. A., 1979, *St Francis of Assisi: Writings and Early Biographies*, 2nd edn, London, 1979

Hager, H., 1962, *Die Anfänge des italienischen Altarbilden*, Munich, 1962

Hall, M. B., 1970, 'The tramezzo in Santa Croce, Florence and Domenico Veneziano's fresco', *Burlington Magazine* 112 (1970), 797–9

    1978, 'The Italian rood screen: some implications for liturgy and function', in *Essays Presented to Myron P. Gilmore*, ed. S. Bertelli and G. Ramakus, Florence, 1978, II, pp. 213–18

Harkins, C., 1969, 'The authorship of a commentary on the Franciscan Rule published among the works of St Bonaventure', *Franciscan Studies* 29 (1969), 157–248

Hayes, Z., 1988, 'The theological image of St Francis of Assisi in the sermons of St Bonaventure', in Bougerol 1988, I, pp. 323–45

Hellmann, W., 1988, 'The seraph in the legends of Thomas of Celano and St Bonaventure', in Bougerol 1988, I, pp. 347–56

Henderson, G. D. S., 1981, *Bede and the Visual Arts*, Jarrow Lecture 1980, Jarrow, 1981

Hertlein, E., 1964, *Die Basilika San Francesco in Assisi*, Florence, 1964

Hewlett, H. G., ed., 1886–9, *Rogeri de Wendover liber qui dicitur flores historiarum*, 3 vols., RS, London, 1886–9

Hinnebusch, W. A., 1966, *The History of the Dominican Order*, I, Staten Island, NY, 1966

Holmes, G. A., 1986, *Florence, Rome and the Origins of the Renaissance*, Oxford, 1986

Housley, N., 1982, *The Italian Crusades, 1254–1343*, Oxford, 1982

    1992, *The Later Crusades, 1274–1580*, Oxford, 1992

Howe, W. N., 1912, *Animal Life in Italian Painting*, London, 1912

Hueck, I., 1969, 'Der Maler der Apostelszenen im Atrium von Alt-St Peter', *Mitteilungen des Kunsthistorischer Institutes in Florenz* 14 (1969), 115–44

    1981, 'Cimabue und das Bildprogramm der Oberkirche von San Francesco in Assisi', *Mitteilungen des Kunsthistorischen Institutes in Florenz* 25 (1981), 279–324

    1982, 'L'oreficeria in Umbria dal seconda metà del secolo XII alla fine del XIII', in *Francesco d'Assisi* 1982, pp. 168–87

Hugh of Digne, *De finibus paupertatis*, see Florovsky 1912; *Disputatio de paupertate evangelica*, in *Firmamenta, quarta pars*, fols. 105r–108v; *Expositio Regulae*, see Flood 1979

Hurst, D., ed., 1955, Bede, *Opera homiletica*, Corpus Christianorum 122, Turnhout, 1955

Huygens, R. B. C., ed., 1960, *Lettres de Jacques de Vitry*, Leiden, 1960

James of Milan, 1905, *Stimulus amoris fr. Iacobi Mediolanensis: Cantica pauperis fr. Ioannis Peckam*, Quaracchi, 1905

Joinville, J. de, 1874, *Histoire de Saint Louis*, ed. N. de Wailly, Paris, 1874

Jordan: *Chronica fratris Jordani*, ed. H. Boehmer, Paris, 1908

Jotischky, A., 2002, *The Carmelites and Antiquity*, Oxford, 2002

Julian, Julian of Speyer: Fr. Julianus de Spira, *Vita S. Francisci*, in AF X, 335–71

Kaftal, G., 1950, *St Francis in Italian Painting*, London, 1950

    1952, *Iconography of the Saints in Tuscan Painting*, Florence, 1952

    1965, *Saints in Italian Art, II: Iconography of the Saints in Central and South Italian Schools of Painting*, Florence, 1965

Katzenellenbogen, A. E. M., 1939, *Allegories of the Virtues and Vices in Mediaeval Art*, London, 1939

Kelly, S. N. D., 1986, *The Oxford Dictionary of Popes*, Oxford, 1986

Kessler, H. L., and Zacharias, J., 2000, *Rome 1300: On the Path of the Pilgrim*, New Haven, 2000

Kirschbaum, E., Bondmann, G., Braunfels, W., et al., 1968–76, *Lexikon der christlichen Ikonographie*, 8 vols., Freiburg, 1968–76

Kitzinger, E., 1966/1976, 'The Byzantine contribution to western art in the twelfth and thirteenth centuries', *Dumbarton Oaks Papers* 20 (1966), 25–47, repr. in Kitzinger, *Art of Byzantium and the Medieval West: Selected Studies* (Bloomington, 1976), ch. XIII, pp. 357–88

Kleinberg, A. M., 1992, *Prophets in Their Own Country: Living Saints and the Making of Sainthood in the Later Middle Ages*, Chicago, 1992

Kleinschmidt, B., 1915–28, *Die Basilika San Francesco in Assisi*, 3 vols., Berlin, 1915–28

Klingender, F. D., 1953, 'St Francis and the birds of the Apocalypse', *Journal of the Warburg and Courtauld Institutes* 16 (1953), 13–23

Knowles, D., 1948–59, *The Religious Orders in England*, 3 vols., Cambridge, 1948–59

Knowles, D., and Brooke, C. N. L., eds., 2002, *Lanfranc's Monastic Constitutions*, revised edn, OMT, Oxford, 2002

Knowles, D., Brooke, C. N. L., and London, V. C. M., 1972/2001, *The Heads of Religious Houses, England and Wales, I: 940–1216*, Cambridge, 1972, 2nd edn 2001

Krautheimer, R., 1975, *Early Christian and Byzantine Architecture*, 2nd edn, Harmondsworth, 1975

    ed., 1977, *Corpus Basilicarum Christianarum Romae*, V, Vatican City, 1977

Krüger, K., 1992, *Der frühe Bildkult des Franziskus in Italien*, Berlin, 1992

Krusch, B., and Levison, W., eds., 1951, Gregory of Tours, *Libri X Historiarum*, MGH, Scriptores Rerum Merovingicarum, I, i, 2nd edn, Hanover, 1951

Laberge, D., 1935–6, 'Fr. Petri Ioannis Olivi, O.F.M., tria scripta sui ipsius apologetica annorum 1283 et 1285', AFH 28 (1935), 130–55, 374–407; 29 (1936), 98–141, 365–95

Lachance, P., 1993, trans., Angela of Foligno, *Complete Works*, New York, 1993

Lambert, M., 1961, *Franciscan Poverty*, London, 1961

    1992, *Medieval Heresy*, 2nd edn, Oxford, 1992

    1998, *The Cathars*, Oxford, 1998

Langeli, A. B., 1978, 'La realtà sociale assisana e il patto del 1210', in *Assisi 1978*, pp. 271–336

    1997, ed., with M. I. Bossa and L. Fiumi, *Le carte duecentesche del Sacro Convento di Assisi (Istrumenti, 1168–1300)*, Fonti e Studi Francescani 5, Inventari 4, Padua, 1997

    1999, 'Il codice di Assisi, ovvero il *Liber Sororis Lelle*', in Barone and Dalarun 1999, pp. 7–27

    2000, *Gli autografi di Frate Francesco e di Frate Leone*, Corpus Christianorum, Autographa Medii Aevi 5, Turnhout, 2000

Langlois, E., ed., 1886–1905, *Les Registres de Nicolas IV*, Paris, 1886–1905

Lapsanski, D., 1974, 'The autographs on the "chartula" of St Francis of Assisi', AFH 67 (1974), 18–37

Latham, R. E., ed., 1975, *Dictionary of Medieval Latin from British Sources*, I, London, 1975

Lawrence, C. H., 1960, *St Edmund of Abingdon*, Oxford, 1960

Leclercq, J., and Rochais, H. M., eds., 1963, *Opera Sancti Bernardi*, III, Rome, 1963

Legenda S. Clarae, see Pennacchi

Lempp, E., 1899a, 'David von Augsburg. Eine Studie', *Zeitschrift für Kirchengeschichte* 19 (1899), 15–46

    1899b, 'David von Augsburg. Schriften aus der Handschrift der Münchener Hof- und Staatsbibliothek Cod. lat. 15312 zum erstenmal veröffentlicht', *Zeitschrift für Kirchengeschichte* 19 (1899), 340–60

    1901, *Frère Elie de Cortone*, Paris, 1901

Leonardi, C., 1984, 'Santità femminile, santità ecclesiastica', in *Il movimento religioso femminile in Umbria nei secoli XIII–XIV*, ed. R. Rusconi, Perugia and Florence, 1984, pp. 19–26

Lerner, R. E., 1974, 'A collection of sermons given in Paris *c*. 1267, including a new text by Saint Bonaventura on the life of Saint Francis', *Speculum* 49 (1974), 466–98

Lewis, S., 1987, *The Art of Matthew Paris in the Chronica Maiora*, Aldershot, 1987

    2001, 'Parallel tracks – then and now: the Cambridge Alexander Apocalypse', in Binski and Noel 2001, pp. 367–86

Liber Extra, X: 'Decretalium Gregorii pp. IX compilatio', in *Corpus Iuris Canonici*, ed. E. Friedberg, II, Leipzig, 1881

Little, A. G., 1898, 'Decrees of the General Chapters of the Friars Minor, 1260 to 1282', *English Historical Review* 13 (1898), 703–8

    1914a, 'Brother William of England, companion of St Francis, and some Franciscan drawings in the Matthew Paris Manuscripts', in *Collectanea Franciscana*, I, British Society of Franciscan Studies 5 (Aberdeen, 1914), pp. 1–8

    1914b, 'Definitiones Capitulorum Generalium Ordinis Fratrum Minorum, 1260–1282', *AFH* 7 (1914), 676–82

    1926, 'The first hundred years of the Franciscan school at Oxford', in *St Francis of Assisi: 1226–1926: Essays in Commemoration*, ed. W. Seton (London, 1926), pp. 163–90

    ed., 1937, *Franciscan History and Legend in English Medieval Art*, British Society of Franciscan Studies 19, Manchester, 1937 for 1935–6

    1943, *Franciscan Papers, Lists and Documents*, Manchester, 1943

Little, Lester, 1978, *Religious Poverty and the Profit Economy in Medieval Europe*, London, 1978

Longhi, R., 1948, 'Giudizio sul Duecento', *Proporzioni* 2 (1948), 5–54

Love, R., ed., 1996, *Three Eleventh-Century Anglo-Latin Saints' Lives*, OMT, Oxford, 1996

Luard, H. R., ed., 1872–83, *Matthaei Parisiensis, monachi sancti Albani, Chronica Maiora*, 7 vols., RS, London, 1872–83

    ed., 1890, *Flores Historiarum*, 3 vols., RS, London, 1890

Lunghi, E., 1996, *The Basilica of St Francis at Assisi*, trans. C. Evans, London, 1996

Lusanna, E. N., 2002, 'La scultura in San Francesco', in Bonsanti 2002a, III, 209–30

Luscombe, D. E., 1976, 'The "lex divinitatis" in the bull "Unam sanctam" of Pope Boniface VIII', in *Church and Government in the Middle Ages: Essays Presented to C. R. Cheney on his 70th Birthday*, ed. C. N. L. Brooke, D. E. Luscombe, G. H. Martin and D. Owen (Cambridge, 1976), pp. 205–21

    1985, 'The reception of the writings of Denis the pseudo-Areopagite into England', in *Tradition and Change: Essays in Honour of Marjorie Chibnall*, ed. D. Greenway, C. Holdsworth and J. Sayers (Cambridge, 1985), pp. 115–43

    1988a, 'Thomas Aquinas and conceptions of hierarchy in the thirteenth century', in *Thomas Aquinas*, ed. A. Zimmermann, Miscellanea Mediaevalia 19 (Berlin and New York, 1988), pp. 261–77

    1988b, 'Denis the pseudo-Areopagite in the Middle Ages from Hilduin to Lorenzo Valla', in *Fälschungen im Mittelalter*, Schriften der Monumenta Germaniae Historica 33, I (1988), 133–52

McGinn, B., 1988, 'The influence of St Francis on the theology of the high Middle Ages: the testimony of St Bonaventure', in Bougerol 1988, I, pp. 97–117

Maggiani, V., 1912, 'De relatione scriptorum quorumdam S. Bonaventurae ad Bullam "Exiit" Nicolai III (1279)', AFH 5 (1912), 3–21

Maggioni, G. P., 1998, Iacopo de Varazze: Legenda Aurea, 2 vols., Florence, 1998

Maginnis, H., 1997, Painting in the Age of Giotto, Philadelphia, 1997

Manselli, R., 1980, Nos qui cum eo fuimus: contributo alla questione Francescana, Rome, 1980

Marcellina da Civezza and Domenichelli, T., ed., 1899, Legenda Trium Sociorum, Rome, 1899

Marchini, G., 1973, Le vetrate dell'Umbria, Corpus Vitrearum Medii Aevi, L'Umbria, Italia 1, Rome, 1973

Marinangeli, B., 1911, 'La serie di affreschi giotteschi rappresentanti la vita di S. Francesco nella chiesa superiore di Assisi', Miscellanea Francescana 13 (1911), 97–112

Martin, F., 1993, Die Apsisverglasung der Oberkirche von S. Francesco in Assisi, Worms, 1993
    1996, 'The St Francis Master in the Upper Church of S. Francesco/Assisi: some considerations regarding his origins', Gesta 35, 2 (1996), 177–91

Martin, F., and Ruf, G., 1998, Le vetrate di San Francesco in Assisi, Assisi, 1998

Martinelli, V. V., 1973, 'Un documento per Giotto ad Assisi', Storia dell'Arte 19 (1973), 193–208

Mas Latrie, J. M. L. de, 1889, Trésor de chronologie, Paris, 1889

Meersseman, G. G., 1946, 'L'architecture dominicaine au XIIIe siècle: législation et pratique', AFP 16 (1946), 136–90

Meiss, M., 1967, Giotto and Assisi, 2nd edn, New York, 1967

Melville, G., and Oberste, J., eds., 1999, Die Bettelorden im Aufbau, Münster, 1999

Menestò, E., and Brufani, S., eds., 1995, Fontes Franciscani, Assisi, 1995

MGH: Monumenta Germaniae Historica

Millor, W. J., and Brooke, C. N. L., eds., 1979, The Letters of John of Salisbury, 11, The Later Letters (1163–1180), OMT, Oxford, 1979

Misc. Fr.: Miscellanea Francescana

Mitchell, C., 1971, 'The imagery of the Upper Church at Assisi', in Giotto e il suo tempo (Rome, 1971), pp. 113–34

Moleta, V., 1983, From St Francis to Giotto, Chicago, 1983

Monferini, A., 1966, 'L'Apocalisse di Cimabue', Commentarii 17 (1966), 22–55

Moore, R. I., 1977, The Origins of European Dissent, London, 1977

Moorman, J. R. H., 1940, The Sources for the Life of S. Francis of Assisi, Manchester, 1940
    1943, 'Early Franciscan art and literature', Bulletin of the John Rylands Library 27 (1943), 338–58
    1968, A History of the Franciscan Order, Oxford, 1968

MOPH: Monumenta Ordinis Praedicatorum Historica, see Walz

Morris, C., 1972, The Discovery of the Individual 1050–1200, London, 1972

Murbach, E., and Heman, P., 1967, Zillis: Die romanische Bilderdecke der Kirche St-Martin, Zurich, 1967

Murray, A., 1972, 'Piety and society in thirteenth-century Italy', Studies in Church History 8 (1972), 83–106
    1981, 'Archbishop and Mendicants in thirteenth-century Pisa', in Stellung und Wirksamkeit der Bettelorden in der städtischen Gesellschaft, ed. K. Elm (Berlin, 1981), pp. 19–75

Murray, P., 1953, 'Notes on some early Giotto sources', Journal of the Warburg and Courtauld Institutes 16 (1953), 58–80

Narb.: Narbonne, Constitutions of, see Bihl 1941

Nessi, S., 1982, La Basilica di San Francesco in Assisi e la sua documentazione storica, Assisi, 1982
    1991, Inventario e regesti dell'Archivio del Sacro Convento d'Assisi, Fonti e Studi Francescani 3, Padua, 1991

New Catholic Encyclopaedia, 17 vols., New York, 1967–79

Nicholson, A., 1930, 'The Roman school at Assisi', Art Bulletin 12 (1930), 270–300
    1932, Cimabue, Pinceton, 1932

Nicolini, U., 1978, 'La struttura urbana di Assisi', in Assisi 1978, pp. 247–70

Nold, P., 2003, *Pope John XXII and His Franciscan Cardinal: Bertrand de la Tour and the Apostolic Poverty Controversy*, Oxford, 2003

ODCC: *The Oxford Dictionary of the Christian Church*, 3rd edn, ed. F. L. Cross and E. A. Livingstone, Oxford, 1997

Oertel, R., 1968, *Early Italian Painting to 1400*, trans. L. Cooper, London, 1968

Offner, R., 1939–40, 'Giotto Non-Giotto', *Burlington Magazine* 74 (1939), 259–68; 75 (1940), 96–113

Oliger, L., ed., 1950, *Expositio Quatuor Magistrorum super Regulam Fratrum Minorum (1241–1242)*, Storia e Letteratura 30, Rome, 1950

OMT: Oxford Medieval Texts

Ov, Ordinem vestrum: the bull is cited from Eubel 1908, pp. 238–9

Oxford Classical Dictionary, 2nd edn, ed. N. G. L. Hammond and H. H. Scullard, Oxford, 1970; 3rd edn, ed. S. Hornblower and A. Spawforth, Oxford, 2003

Pace, V., 1983, 'Presenze oltremontane ad Assisi: realtà e mito', in Romanini 1983, pp. 239–46

Paciocco, R., 1990, *Da Francesco ai 'Catalogi Sanctorum'*, Assisi, 1990

Pagnani, G., 1959, 'Frammenti della Cronaca del b. Francesco Venimbene da Fabriano (+1322)', AFH 52 (1959), 153–77

Palumbo, G., 1972, 'Un nuovo gruppo di ceramiche medievale Assisane', in G. Palumbo and H. Blake, *Ceramiche medioevali Assisane, estratti da Atti del IV Convegno Internazionale della Ceramica, Albisola, 1971*, Assisi, 1972, pp. 5–37

Partner, P., 1972, *The Lands of St Peter*, London, 1972

Paul, J., 1975a, 'Le commentaire de Hugues de Digne sur la règle franciscaine', *Revue de l'Histoire de l'Eglise de France* 61 (1975), 231–41

  1975b, 'Hugues de Digne', in *Franciscains d'Oc: les Spirituels ca. 1280–1324*, Cahiers de Fanjeaux 10, Toulouse, 1975, pp. 69–97

  1983, 'L'image de saint François dans le traité "De miraculis" de Thomas de Celano', in Gieben 1983, I, pp. 251–74

Péano, P., 1983, 'Saint François au chapitre d'Arles', in Gieben 1983, I, pp. 239–49

Pecham, *Expositio*: *Expositio Regulae S. Francisci* in Bonaventure, *Opera Omnia*, VIII (1898), pp. 391–437 (on Pecham's authorship, see Harkins 1969)

Pennacchi, F., ed., 1910, *Legenda Sanctae Clarae*, Assisi, 1910

Petrocchi, G., ed., 1994, *La Commedia, Opere di Dante Alighieri*, 7, IV, *Paradiso*, Florence, 1994

Philippart, G., 1974, 'Le Bollandiste François Van Ortroy et la *Legenda Trium Sociorum*', in Assisi 1974, pp. 171–97

Pichery, E., ed., 1955–8, *Jean Cassien, Conférences*, 2 vols., Sources Chrétiennes 42, 54, Paris, 1955–8

Pickering, F. P., 1970, *Literature and Art in the Middle Ages*, English trans., London, 1970

PL: *Patrologiae Cursus Completus, Series Latina*, ed. J. P. Migne, 221 vols., Paris, 1844–64

Poeschke, J., 1985, *Die Kirche San Francesco in Assisi und ihre Wandmalereien*, Munich, 1985

Polo de Beaulieu, M.-A., 1999, 'L'image du père fondateur dans les recueils d'*exempla* franciscains des XIIIe et XIVe siècles', in Melville and Oberste 1999, pp. 215–41

Potestà, G. L., 1980, *Storia ed escatologia in Ubertino da Casale*, Milan, 1980

Potthast: Potthast, A., ed., *Regesta pontificum Romanorum A.D. 1198–1304*, 2 vols., Berlin, 1874–5

Poulenc, J., 1969, 'Hugues de Digne', in *Dictionnaire de Spiritualité*, VII (Paris, 1969), I, pp. 875–9

  1983, 'Saint François dans le "vitrail des anges" de l'église supérieure de la basilique d'Assise', AFH 76 (1983), 701–13

  1988, 'Thèmes bonaventuriens dans les vitraux de la Basilique Supérieure d'Assise', in Bougerol 1988, II, pp. 763–86

Powicke, F. M., and Cheney, C. R., eds., 1964, *Councils and Synods with Other Documents Relating to the English Church*, II, 2 parts, Oxford, 1964

Prinz, O., et al., eds., 1967, *Mittellateinisches Wörterbuch*, I, Munich, 1967

Qe, Quo elongati: see Grundmann 1961

Ratzinger, J., 1971, *The Theology of History in St Bonaventure*, edn of Chicago, 1971

Reeves, M., 1969, *The Influence of Prophecy in the Later Middle Ages: A Study in Joachism*, Oxford, 1969

Ricognozione: Ricognozione del corpo di San Francesco, la 24 gennaio–marzo 1978, Assisi, 1978

Robertson, J. C., and Sheppard, J. B., 1875–85, eds., *Materials for the History of Thomas Becket, Archbishop of Canterbury*, 7 vols., RS, London, 1875–85

Robinson, J. A. T., 1976, *Redating the New Testament*, London, 1976
　1985, *The Priority of John*, London, 1985

Robson, M., 1997, *St Francis of Assisi: the Legend and the Life*, London, 1997
　2006, *The Franciscans in the Middle Ages (1206–1456)*, Woodbridge, 2006

Rocchi Coopmans de Yoldi, G., 2002, 'L'architettura della basilica di San Francesco in Assisi', in Bonsanti 2002a, III, pp. 17–111

Romanini, A. M., ed., 1983, *Roma Anno 1300: Atti della IV Settimana di Studi di Storia dell'Arte Medievale*, Rome, 1980, Rome, 1983
　1990, *Skulptur und Grabmal des Spätmittelalters in Rom und Italien*, Rome, 1990
　1991, ed., *Roma nel Duecento*, Rome, 1991

Romano, S., 1982, 'Le storie parallele di Assisi: il Maestro di S. Francesco', *Storia del Arte* 44 (1982), 63–86
　1984, 'Pittura ad Assisi 1260–1280. Lo stato degli studi', *Arte Medievale* 2 (1984), 109–41
　1995, 'Il Sancta Sanctorum: gli affreschi', in *Sancta Sanctorum* 1995, pp. 38–125
　forthcoming: two studies cited in Binski 2002, p. 75 n. 4: 'I maestri del transetto destro e la pittura romana', in *Il Cantiere pittorico della Basilica Superiore di San Francesco in Assisi*; and *La Basilica di S. Francesco ad Assisi: artisti, botteghe, strategie narrative*, Rome, forthcoming

Rossmann, H., 1976, 'Das Bild des hl. Franz von Assisi in den Franziskuspredigten des Franz von Meyronnes', *Franziskanische Studien* 58 (1976), 142–84

RS: Rolls Series

Rubinstein, N., 1997, 'Le allegorie di Ambrogio Lorenzetti nella Sala della Pace e il pensiero politico del suo tempo', *Rivista Storica Italiana* 109 (1997), 781–802

Rudolph, C., 1999, 'In the beginning: theories and images of creation in Northern Europe in the twelfth century', *Art History* 22, no. 1 (1999), 3–55

Ruf, G., 1974, *Franziskus und Bonaventura. Die heilsgeschichtliche Deutung der Fresken im Langhaus der Oberkirche von San Francesco*, cited from Italian trans. R. Faller-Buser, *S. Francesco e S. Bonaventura*, Assisi, 1974; see also Martin and Ruf 1998

Ruf, G., Diller, S., and Roli, G., 2004, *Die Fresken der Oberkirche San Francesco in Assisi*, Regensburg, 2004

Rule, M., ed., 1884, *Eadmeri Historia Novorum in Anglia*, RS, London, 1884

Runciman, S., 1954, *A History of the Crusades*, III, Cambridge, 1954

Rusconi, R., 'Una donna e un libro tra Lione e Vienne', in Barone and Dalarun 1999, pp. 385–91

Ryan, G., and Ripperger, H., trans., 1941, *The Golden Legend of Jacobus de Voragine*, New York, 1941

Sabatier, P., 1893/4, *Vie de S. François d'Assise*, Paris, 1894 (publ. 1893), usually cited from the English trans. by L. S. Houghton, London, 1894: F = French edn
　1910, 'L'incipit et le premier chapitre du Speculum Perfectionis', in *Opuscules de critique historique*, II, fasc. xii (Paris, 1910), 333–67
　ed., 1912, *Franciscan Essays*, British Society of Franciscan Studies, Extra Series, I, Aberdeen, 1912
　1914–19, 'À propos des fresques de l'église supérieure de la basilique S. François à Assise', in *Opuscules de critique historique*, III, fasc. xviii (1914–19), 105–10

Sabatier, P., and Rawnsley, Canon, 1904, ed. and trans., *Sacrum Commercium: The Converse of Francis and His Sons with Holy Poverty*, London, 1904

Sägmuller, J. B., 1896, *Die Thätigkeit und Stellung der Cardinäle bis Papst Bonifaz VIII*, Freiburg-im-Breisgau, 1896

Salimbene, H. and S.: Salimbene de Adam, *Cronica*, ed. O. Holder-Egger, MGH Scriptores XXXII, 1905–13 (H); ed. G. Scalia, 2 vols., Scrittori d'Italia 232–3, Bari, 1966 (S)

Sancta Sanctorum, 1995, Milan, 1995

Sandron, D., 2004, *Amiens: le cathédrale*, Paris, 2004

Savage, J. J., 1957, 'Virgilian echoes in the "Dies Irae"', *Traditio* 13 (1957), 443–51

Sayers, J. E., ed., 1999, *Original Papal Documents in England and Wales from the Accession of Pope Innocent III to the Death of Pope Benedict XI (1198–1304)*, Oxford, 1999

Sbaralea: Sbaralea, J. H., ed., *Bullarium Franciscanum*, 4 vols., Rome, 1759–68: referred to by p. and no. – G9 = Gregory IX, I4 = Innocent IV, C4 = Clement IV, N3 = Nicholas III, N4 = Nicholas IV, B8 = Boniface VIII; and by no. in Eubel 1908

Scarpellini, P., 1978, 'Assisi e i suoi monumenti nella pittura dei secoli XIII–XIV', in *Assisi 1978*, pp. 71–121

— 1980, 'Le pitture', in *Assisi 1980*, pp. 91–126

— 1982a, *Fra Ludovico da Pietralunga. Descrizione della Basilica di S. Francesco e di altri santuari di Assisi*, Treviso, 1982

— 1982b, 'Iconografia francescana nei secoli XIII e XIV', in *Francesco d'Assisi: storia e arte*, Milan, 1982, pp. 91–126

Scheeben, H. C., ed., 1935, *Libellus de principiis Ordinis Praedicatorum*, in Walz et al. 1935 = MOPH XVI (Rome, 1935)

— ed., 1939, *Die Konstitutionen des Predigerordens unter Jordan von Sachsen*, Quellen und Forschungen zur Geschichte des Dominikanerordens in Deutschland 38, Cologne, 1939

Schenkluhn, W., 1991, *San Francesco in Assisi: Ecclesia Specialis*, Darmstadt, 1991

Schlegel, U., 1969, 'On the picture program of the Arena Chapel', in *Giotto: The Arena Chapel Frescoes*, ed. J. Stubblebine (London, 1969), pp. 182–202 (first publ. as 'Zum Bildprogramm der Arena Kapelle', *Zeitschrift für Kunstgeschichte* 20 (1957), 125–46)

Schmucki, O., 1971, Review of SL, *Collectanea Franciscana* 41 (1971), 141–7

— 1988, 'Literatur zur Stigmatisation des hl. Franciscus von Assisi 1963–1985', in Bougerol 1988, II, pp. 695–728

Seidel, M., 2002, '"Il crocifixo grande che fece Giotto". Questions of style', in Ciatti and Seidel 2002, pp. 65–157

Selge, K.-V., 1967, *Die ersten Waldenser*, 2 vols., Berlin, 1967

Seneca, L. Annaeus, *Ep.*: *Epistolae, Ad Lucilium Epistulae Morales*, ed. L. D. Reynolds, 2 vols., Oxford, 1965

Sevcenko, N. P., 1999, 'The Vita icon and the painter as hagiographer', *Dumbarton Oaks Papers* 53 (1999), 149–65

Silvana di Mattia Spirito, 1988, 'San Bonaventura e la povertà francescana (l' "Apologia Pauperum")', in Bougerol 1988, II, pp. 417–30

Sinclair, J. D., ed., 1958, *The Divine Comedy of Dante Alighieri*, III, Paradiso, London, 1958

Singleton, C. S., ed., 1975, *Dante Alighieri, The Divine Comedy*, III, Paradiso, part 2, Princeton, 1975

Sisto, A., ed., 1971, *Figure del primo Francescanesimo in Provenza: Ugo e Douceline di Digne*, Florence, 1971

Skinner, Q., 1986, 'Ambrogio Lorenzetti: the artist as political philosopher', *Proceedings of the British Academy* 72 (1986), 1–56

SL: *Scripta Leonis, Rufini et Angeli sociorum S. Francisci: The Writings of Leo, Rufino and Angelo, Companions of St Francis*, ed. and trans. R. B. Brooke, OMT, Oxford, 1970, corr. repr. 1990

Smalley, B., 1952, *The Study of the Bible in the Middle Ages*, 2nd edn, Oxford, 1952

1982, 'The use of scripture in St Anthony's "Sermones"', in *Le fonti e la teologia dei Sermoni Antoniani*, Il Santo, 2nd series, 22 (1982), 285–97

Smart, A., 1971, *The Assisi Problem and the Art of Giotto*, Oxford, 1971

1978, *The Dawn of Italian Painting*, Oxford, 1978

Smith, J., 1978, 'Robert of Arbrissel's relations with women', in Baker 1978, pp. 175–84

3 Soc.: *Legenda Trium Sociorum*, ed. T. Desbonnets, AFH 67 (1974), 38–144

Southern, R. W., 1953, *The Making of the Middle Ages*, London, 1953

1958, 'The Canterbury forgeries', *English Historical Review* 73 (1958), 193–226

ed., 1962/1979, *The Life of St Anselm, Archbishop of Canterbury by Eadmer*, Nelson's Medieval Texts, Edinburgh, 1962; repr. OMT, Oxford, 1979

1963, *St Anselm and His Biographer*, Cambridge, 1963

1972, 'Aspects of the European tradition of historical writing: 3. History as prophecy', *Transactions of the Royal Historical Society*, 5th series, 22 (1972), 159–80

1986, *Robert Grosseteste: The Growth of an English Mind in Medieval Europe*, Oxford, 1986

Speculum Minorum, ed. N. Morin, Rouen, 1509; also cited in edn of 1513

Sp S: *Speculum Perfectionis*, ed. P. Sabatier, 2nd edn, 2 vols., British Society of Franciscan Studies 13, 17, Manchester, 1928–31

Stanislao da Campagnola, 1971, *L'angelo del sesto sigillo e l' 'Alter Christus'. Genesi e sviluppo di due termini francescani nei secoli XIII–XIV*, Rome, 1971

1977, *Francesco d'Assisi nei suoi scritti e nelle sue biografie dei secoli XIII–XIV*, Assisi, 1977

1999, *Francesco e francescanesimo nella società dei secoli XIII–XIV*, Assisi, 1999

Stegmüller, F., 1940–80, *Repertorium Biblicum Medii Aevi*, 11 vols., Madrid, 1940–80

Stein, J. E., 1976, 'Dating the Bardi St Francis Master dossal: text and image', *Franciscan Studies* 36 (1976), 271–97

Stott, J., 1999, *The Birds Our Teachers*, Carlisle, 1999

Striker, C. L., 1983, 'Crusader painting in Constantinople: the findings at Kalenderhane Camii', in *Le Proche-Orient et l'Occident dans l'art du XIIIe siècle* (XXIVe Congrès Internationale de l'Histoire de l'Art), 1983, pp. 117–21

Striker, C. L., and Kuban, Y. D., 1997, *Kalenderhane in Istanbul: The Buildings, Their History, Architecture, and Decoration*, Mainz, 1997

Stubblebine, J., 1985, *Assisi and the Rise of Vernacular Art*, New York, 1985

Stüdeli, B. E. J., 1969, *Minoritenniederlassungen und Mittelalterliche Stadt*, Werl and Westfalen, 1969

Supino, I. B., 1924, *La Basilica di San Francesco d'Assisi*, Bologna, 1924

Swaan, W., 1969, *The Gothic Cathedral*, London, 1969

Swanson, J., 1989, *John of Wales: A Study of the Works and Ideas of a Thirteenth-Century Friar*, Cambridge, 1989

Theophilus: see Dodwell

Thier, L., and Calufetti, A., eds., 1985, *Il libro della Beata Angela de Foligno*, 2nd edn, Grottaferrata, 1985

Thode, H., 1885, *Franz von Assisi und die Anfänge der Kunst der Renaissance in Italien*, Berlin, 1885

Thompson, S., 1978, 'The problem of the Cistercian nuns in the twelfth and early thirteenth centuries', in Baker 1978, pp. 227–52

1991, *Women Religious: The Founding of English Nunneries after the Norman Conquest*, Oxford, 1991

Tomei, A., 1990, *Iacobus Torriti pictor: una vicenda figurativa del tardo Duecento romano*, Rome, 1990

1995, 'Un modello di committenza papale: Niccolò III e Roma', in *Sancta Sanctorum* 1995, pp. 192–201

Townend, G. B., 1967, 'Suetonius and his influence', in Dorey 1967, pp. 79–111

Treasury: see *Assisi* 1999

Trexler, R. C., 1989, *Naked before the Father: The Renunciation of Francis of Assisi*, New York, 1989

Tugwell, S., 1982, *Early Dominicans: Selected Writings*, London, 1982

Ubertino da Casale, 1485, *Arbor Vitae Crucifixae Iesu*, Venice, 1485

Underhill, E., 1912, 'A Franciscan mystic of the thirteenth century: the Blessed Angela of Foligno', in Sabatier 1912, pp. 88–107

Van Dijk, S. J. P., 1949, 'The Breviary of St Francis', *Franciscan Studies*, New Series, 9 (1949), 13–40

    1954, 'St Francis' Blessing of Brother Leo', AFH 47 (1954), 199–201

    ed., 1963, *Sources of the Modern Roman Liturgy: The Ordinals of Haymo of Faversham and Related Documents*, 2 vols., Leiden, 1963

Van Dijk, S. J. P., and Walker, J. H., 1960, *The Origins of the Modern Roman Liturgy*, Westminster, MD, 1960

Van Ortroy, E., 1900, 'La légende de S. François d'Assise dite "Legenda Trium Sociorum"', *Analecta Bollandiana* 19 (1900), 119–97

Van Os, H. W., 1974, 'St Francis of Assisi as a second Christ in early Italian painting', *Simiolus* 7 (1974), 115–32

    1983, 'The earliest altarpieces of St Francis', in Gieben 1983, 1, pp. 333–8

Vasari, G., 1550, *Le Vite de più eccellenti architetti, pittori et scultori italiani*, 1st edn, 3 vols., Florence, 1550

    1568, *Le Vite de' più eccellenti pittori, scultori e architettori*, 2nd edn, 3 vols., Florence, 1568

Vauchez, A., 1968, 'Les stigmates de Saint François et leurs détracteurs dans les derniers siècles du moyen âge', *Mélanges d'Archéologie et d'Histoire, École Française de Rome* 80 (1968), 595–625

    1997, *Sainthood in the Later Middle Ages*, English trans., Cambridge, 1997

Vaughan, R., 1958, *Matthew Paris*, Cambridge, 1958

Vicaire, M.-H., 1964, *Saint Dominic and His Times*, trans. K. Pond, London, 1964

Volpe, C., 1969, 'La formazione di Giotto nella cultura di Assisi', in *Giotto e i Giotteschi in Assisi*, ed. C. Palumbo (Rome, 1969), pp. 15–59

Von Matt, L., and Hauser, W., 1956, *St Francis of Assisi: A Pictorial Biography*, London, 1956

Von Matt, L., and Vicaire, M.-H., 1957, *St Dominic: A Pictorial Biography*, London, 1957

Wadding, L., 1731–1933, *Annales Minorum*, 2nd edn, 25 vols., Rome etc., 1731–1933

Waley, D., 1961, *The Papal State in the Thirteenth Century*, London, 1961

    1978, 'Le istituzioni comunali di Assisi nel passagio dal XII al XIII secolo', in Assisi 1978, pp. 53–70

    1982a, 'Colonna, Giacomo', DBI 27 (1982), 311–14

    1982b, 'Colunna, Pietro', DBI 27 (1982), 399–402

Walker, D., ed., 1998, *The Cartulary of St Augustine's Abbey, Bristol*, Bristol and Gloucestershire Archaeological Society, 1998

Walz/ Walz et al., 1935, MOPH xvi, ed. A. Walz et al. (esp. *Legenda S. Dominici* by Constantine of Orvieto, ed. H.-C. Scheeben, pp. 263–352, and *Legenda S. Dominici* by Humbert de Romans, ed. A. Walz, pp. 355–433), Rome, 1935

Wayment, H. G., 1972, *The Windows of King's College Chapel, Cambridge*, Corpus Vitrearum Medii Aevi, Great Britain, Supplementary Volume 1, London, 1972

Weitzmann, K., 1944, 'Constantinopolitan book illumination in the period of the Latin Conquest', *Gazette des Beaux Arts* 86 (1944), 193–214

Wesjohann, A., 1999, 'Simplicitas als franziskanisches Ideal und der Prozess der Institutionalisierung des Minoritenordens', in Melville and Oberste 1999, pp. 107–67

White, J., 1956, 'The date of "The Legend of St Francis" at Assisi', *Burlington Magazine* 98 (1956), 344–51

    1967, *The Birth and Rebirth of Pictorial Space*, 2nd edn, London, 1967

    1979, *Duccio*, London, 1979

    1984, *Studies in Late Medieval Art*, London, 1984

    1987, *Art and Architecture in Italy, 1250 to 1400*, 2nd edn, Harmondsworth, 1987

Whitelock, D., Brett, M., and Brooke, C. N. L., eds., 1981, *Councils and Synods with Other Documents Relating to the English Church*, 1: 871–1204, 2 parts, Oxford, 1981

Wilpert, J., 1916, *Römischen Mosaiken und Malereien*, Freiburg, 1916

Wilson, C., 1990, *The Gothic Cathedral*, London, 1990

Wolff, R. L., 1944, 'The Latin Empire of Constantinople and the Franciscans', *Traditio* 2 (1944), 213–37

Wolfram von Eschenbach, *Willehalm*, ed. K. Lachmann, 6th edn, ed. E. Hartl, Berlin, 1926; and see Gibbs and Johnson 1984

X: see *Liber Extra*

Yapp, B., 1981, *Birds in Medieval Manuscripts*, London, 1981

Zanardi, B., 2002, *Giotto e Pietro Cavallini: la questione di Assisi e il cantiere medievale della pittura a fresco*, Milan, 2002

Zanardi, B., with F. Zeri and C. Frugoni, 1996, *Il cantiere di Giotto: le storie di san Francesco ad Assisi*, Milan, 1996

Zanotti, G., 1990, *Assisi: la Biblioteca del Sacro Convento*, Assisi, 1990

INDEX

Page references in **bold type** denote illustrations or references in captions. Place names outside Italy are identified by country or region or, for England, pre-1947 county.

The following abbreviations are used:

Basilica = The Basilica of St Francis at Assisi; LC = Lower Church, UC = Upper Church; Cycle = St Francis Fresco Cycle in UC

br = brother, member of the Franciscan Order; more recent friars are noted as OFM = Order of Friars Minor; OFM Conv. = Order of Friars Minor, Conventual

OP = Order of Preachers, Dominican friar

For other abbreviations, *see* List of abbreviations